HAVELOCK ELLIS

A BIOGRAPHY

HAVELOCK ELLIS

A BIOGRAPHY

By

PHYLLIS GROSSKURTH

McCLELLAND AND STEWART

ISBN: 0–7710–3641–8

The Canadian Publishers
McClelland and Stewart Limited
25 Hollinger Road,
Toronto M4B 3G2

Published simultaneously
in the United States of America
by Alfred A. Knopf, Inc.

Printed in the United States of America

For Eileen and François Lafitte,

and Marie Jahoda,

with affection and gratitude

CONTENTS

LIST OF ILLUSTRATIONS

All pictures not otherwise credited are from the Lafitte collection.

PREFACE

It may well be that this is one of the last lives that can be depicted and documented through a great mass of personal letters. Born in the middle of the nineteenth century—1859—Havelock Ellis developed a routine of writing letters which he never abandoned even after the unwelcome introduction of a telephone into his home. To his first great love, Olive Schreiner, he wrote almost daily. During his marriage—1891 to 1916—he and his wife lived apart for much of the year, and when separated wrote to each other every day. To his great friend Margaret Sanger he wrote at least twice a week from 1914 until his death in 1939. To Françoise Delisle, his close companion for the last twenty years of his life, he wrote almost daily from 1918 until 1929, when they began to share a household together. After this date they were often living apart in the two households they maintained, and many letters survive from this period. As Ellis grew famous, particularly in America, hundreds of people wrote to him with their problems, and he tried to answer every letter. He also boasted that he never lost a friend; but the consequent sacrifice was to set aside hours of every day for writing letters. What is remarkable about all these letters is that each one conveys a sense of Ellis's highly individual attitude to his correspondent and something of the personality of the person he is addressing.

I cannot establish precisely how many unpublished letters I have examined, but a reasonable estimate would be well over twenty thousand. The correspondence has been widely dispersed, and the preparation of this biography required a great deal of travel—by boat, bus, train, plane, and once by motorcycle. At one point I had so many photostats in my tiny flat that I had to move to larger quarters. This was a houseboat, on which most of the book was written in conditions of idyllic tranquillity, shattered eventually by a series of crises—water in the bilges, fire, flood, broken water mains, frozen sewage pumps—but somehow the manuscript managed to stay intact.

Among the libraries which have provided material for this book are the Library of Congress; University College London; Fales Library, New York University; Public Archives of Canada; Sophia Smith Collection, Smith College; Mugar Library, Boston University; Beinecke Library of Yale University; Mitchell Library, State Library of New South Wales; British Library; Humanities Research Center, University of Texas at Austin; Robarts Library, University of Toronto; Fisher Library, University of Sydney; Sheffield City Libraries; University of Bristol Library; New York Public Library; Morris Library, Southern Illinois University; Houghton Library, Harvard University; Pennsylvania State University Library; Butler Library, Columbia University; Brotherton Library, University of Leeds; Newberry Library, University of Chicago; Lockwood Memorial Library, State University of New York at Buffalo; Dartmouth College; Lilly Library, University of Indiana; University of Iowa; University of Southern Illinois at Carbondale; University of Sydney; Institute for Sex Research, Indiana University; International Institute of Social History, Amsterdam; National Library of Australia; Clarke Library; Huntington Library; University of California at Los Angeles; Berg Collection, New York Public Library; Princeton University Library; British Library of Political and Economic Science; Public Records Office; and the Law Society of Great Britain. I wish I had space to mention by name all the individuals who assisted me in these various libraries. I have also had access to extensive collections held by private individuals—Dr. Joseph Wortis, Mrs. Faith Powys, Dr. Helena Wright, and the late Edmond Kapp.

There are some libraries to which I must draw particular attention: the wide resources of the Library of Congress (whose Margaret Sanger collection was invaluable); the riches of the Humanities Research Center, University of Texas; and the Mugar Library, Boston University, which has over a thousand letters exchanged by Ellis and Françoise Delisle, the largest concentration of Ellis material anywhere. I should also like to add the Sophia Smith Collection at Smith College, whose Margaret Sanger papers provided enrichment and elucidation of other sources.

But all these collections led back to a house in Birmingham, where Professor François Lafitte, Ellis's adoptive son and literary executor, had chests, cupboards, and boxes full of unsorted letters. There was a neat stack of Ellis's pocket diaries which verified events and his whereabouts on specific dates. Among the papers was new evidence about the famous Bedborough trial. While I worked through these dusty piles of papers, Professor and Mrs. Lafitte provided me with kind hospitality, intelligent observations, and warm comradeship. We became a team, our excitement mounting as each new discovery was made. In case after case a corresponding set of letters to collections already located emerged from the Lafitte "archives"; Ellis's letters to Jane Burr were in the Sophia Smith Collection, Smith College, Jane Burr's to Ellis in Birmingham; Ellis's letters to Marguerite Agniel were in the Morris Library, Southern Illinois University, hers in Birmingham; Ellis's letters to Josephine Walther in the Lilly Library, Indiana University, hers in Birmingham; Ellis's letters to Faith Oliver in Folkestone, hers in Birmingham; Ellis's letters to Dr. Joseph Wortis in Brooklyn Heights, Wortis's letters in Birmingham; Ellis's letters to Thomas Davidson in the Yale University Library, Davidson's in Birmingham; and so it went. Other letters, such as those from Hugh de Sélincourt, Margaret Sanger, and Marie Stopes, were scattered among various libraries, the trail leading back ultimately to Birmingham. The intricate and complex strands of Ellis's life were gradually unravelled, and the search became an adventure of the most intensely interesting kind. Through Rache Lovat Dickson I learned of a set of Ellis letters to Radclyffe Hall which he had deposited with the Archives of Canada. The matching set was at the University of Texas. Consequently, I had to rewrite a chapter after I thought the manuscript was completed.

The pursuit was made possible by generous scholarships from the Canada Council, the Killam Foundation, and the John Simon Guggenheim Memorial Foundation. I am grateful to the University of Toronto for granting me an extended leave of absence in which to complete the book. The number of kind friends who have helped me is legion. To Tony Grey I shall always be grateful, for it was he who first suggested that I write this book. Professor Lafitte's intense interest in the project and his deep knowledge of Ellis's life and work were invaluable. Noël Annan has encouraged me in this as in so many other instances in my life. Marie Jahoda, Professor Emeritus of

Psychology at Sussex University, and my daughter and son, Anne and Brian Grosskurth, read the manuscript at every stage, and made many perceptive suggestions. Other biographers have been extraordinarily generous in their help. I wish particularly to mention H. Montgomery Hyde and Michael Holroyd, whose wide experience, good sense, and shrewd advice have been appreciated more than I can ever tell them. Numerous individuals have aided me in all sorts of ways: Mavor Moore; Jacqueline Korn; Claire Smith; Dr. Joseph Wortis; Negley Harte; Ralph Glasser; Dr. Maurice White; Robert Sprich; Dr. Anthony Storr; Dr. and Mrs. Donald MacLeod; Steven Marcus; Dr. Michael Gormley; Lord Amulree; George Sirolli; Kenneth Lohf; Dr. Frank Forster; the late Edmond Kapp; Professor Paul Rosenzweig; Jeffrey Weeks; Dr. Helena Wright; Mrs. Faith Powys; Suzanne Bloch Smith; Anatole James; Timothy d'Arch Smith; Jill and John Conway; B. A. Lopez; Roland Penrose; Michael Levey; Dr. John Tanner; Margaret Branch; Jim Silvester; and Ann Scott. I am indebted to Glenn S. Burne of Harpur College, State University of New York, for his bibliography of Havelock Ellis's works, which, though necessarily incomplete, has provided me with a valuable *vade mecum*. I have made every effort to trace the copyright of letters. I am grateful to Professor François Lafitte for permission to quote from the unpublished correspondence of Havelock Ellis, Edith Ellis, and Françoise Lafitte-Cyon; to Dr. Grant Sanger for allowing me to quote from Margaret Sanger's letters to Havelock Ellis; to Mrs. Helena Wayne-Malinowska for permission to quote from the letters of her father, Bronislaw Malinowski; to P. C. Raine for permission to quote from the unpublished letters of Olive Schreiner; to Dr. Harry Stopes-Roe for permission to quote from Marie Stopes's letters to Ellis; and to Mrs. Ernest Jones for permission to quote from Ernest Jones's letters to Ellis.

I thank my research assistants, David Sorenson and Jean Elliott, for their unfailing good humour, their zest in the search, and their imaginative feel for "leads." Victoria Gallop was a cheerful companion in working through the Lafitte papers. I wish also to express my appreciation to three invaluable ladies: Mrs. Eileen Scott, of Scotts Office Services, Susan Blee, and Jill Mabbitt for her patient and intelligent typing of a much revised manuscript.

Mayflower, Chiswick Mall, 1979   P.G.

INTRODUCTION

HAVELOCK ELLIS WAS A REVOLUTIONARY, ONE OF THE SEMINAL FIGURES responsible for the creation of a modern sensibility, although, like most revolutionaries, he would not have been happy with the world he helped to create. A mild, withdrawn man, he nevertheless realized what he was doing. As a late Victorian, he rebelled against the general conspiracy of silence surrounding sex. As a youth of sixteen, miserable and guilty with strange, incomprehensible forces stirring within him, he made an unusual resolve: he determined to make his life's work the exposure, the explanation, and the understanding of sex in all its manifestations. It never occurred to him that such a task was beyond the capabilities of a single individual; it never occurred to him because he was totally ignorant of the magnitude of his task. When he thought he had completed his *Studies in the Psychology of Sex* in 1910, he felt assured that he had done the work which he had been set in the world to do. He viewed himself—and rightly so—as a pioneer of the highest order, since he was pursuing what he always regarded as "the central problem of life." When he started out he believed, like most Victorians, that any problem could be solved by assiduity and logical thinking. By the time he had finished, his task had chastened him to the realization that the "problem" could only be stated. He was as bewildered as anyone else by Freud's unsettling hypothesis that there were explosive forces within man which could not be resolved by classification and accumulation of data. Ellis's great contribution lay in his assumption that sex was an aspect of man that could be examined with dignified rationality. While this theoretical approach to generalized sex proved a poor defence against the particularized feelings that repeatedly

assailed him, his investigations led him to realize the wide divergences in sexual behaviour, to the point that he was able to accept
aspects of himself that his less enlightened contemporaries might
have considered peculiar.

Ellis regarded himself as both a scientist and an artist; and he
believed that he could and should separate these two aspects of himself. He welcomed recognition from those able to appreciate this
duality, and never disagreed with those who described him as a
genius. One of the rather disturbing features of his life after his name
had become a household word was the cult of hero-worship that
surrounded him, sometimes cloying in its adulation. Among the
twenty people I have spoken to who knew him, some very intimately,
I have been startled by the persistence of this uncritical admiration.
For one thing, he looked the part of an Old Testament prophet
with his arresting height, his strikingly formed cheekbones, and the
flowing beard. He fell easily into the role of the sage who could
solve, if not the riddle of the Sphinx, at least any of the problems
which people brought to him. Women found this combination of
archetypal Father and sensual Faun irresistible. I mentioned this
attraction to one woman who was not overawed by him, and she
asked tartly, "But were they *undeveloped* women?"

In the course of writing this biography I have frequently been
baffled and frustrated by the elusiveness of Ellis, despite the massive
documentation at my disposal. I gave a rough draft of one chapter to
a woman who was extremely close to him at one time. She did not
hide her disappointment. "All this concentration on relationships! I
thought you were going to capture the essential Havelock!" I pointed
out to her that what she wanted was portraiture, a frozen icon; and
that biography was something more, and something less. What I
have tried to do is depict Ellis *in process.* "What is character,"
Henry James asked, "but the determination of incident? What is
incident but the illustration of character?" I have tried to show Ellis
in his approach to his work, his reaction to the world around him,
how and why he loved certain people and why they loved him, and,
most difficult of all, how he viewed himself. My attitude towards
him has changed many times in the course of writing this book. I
hope I have succeeded in being fair.

HAVELOCK ELLIS

A BIOGRAPHY

CHILDHOOD

HAVELOCK ELLIS ONCE REMARKED THAT PEOPLE SELDOM REMEMBER their childhoods. From the account he gives of his own childhood in his autobiography it is difficult to visualize him as a child at all. There were certain images that remained with him—but these had generally been passed down as family lore: a photograph of an un-smiling, stolid infant gazing at the world with mute distress;* a silent toddler standing immobile in the middle of the road, refusing to budge; a submissive boy, meekly allowing himself to be tormented by school bullies. Ellis's memories of himself as a child interested him only to the extent that he could trace a connecting link to the grown man. The emptiness of those unremembered years is dis-quieting.

Stories about his Suffolk ancestors were far more interesting to him than the memory of a small, helpless person with whom he no longer felt any connection. A firm believer in the organic and un-conscious influences of heredity on aptitude and temperament, he later developed something of an obsession with the tracing of his own forebears. To his Suffolk ancestry he attributed what he con-sidered his most outstanding characteristics—individuality, persist-ence, and fidelity to his own ideals.

Early in his autobiography, *My Life*, Ellis gives an account of the momentous events that took place in the year of his birth, 1859: *The*

---

* Unfortunately later lost by Olive Schreiner.

Origin of Species, Mill's *Essay on Liberty,* the founding of the Red
Cross, the unification of Italy,* the commencement of the building
of the Suez Canal, the publication of *Essays and Reviews,* which he
says marked "the spiritual revival of the Anglican Church."† One
might construe that his own birth was not without significance, if
one were looking for signs, from a ferocious storm that shook
the world—well, at least Croydon—the night before he was born.
This piece of family lore Ellis repeated throughout his life. The
propitious day was February 2nd, Candlemass, and each year his
mother celebrated the occasion by ceremoniously lighting candles.
The emphasis on premonitions and omens is related without irony
or humour; it might have been lifted out of the pages of Plutarch
or Cellini, with their superstitious conviction of supernatural forces
involved in an unusual destiny, rather than from the lips of a man
who regarded himself as an objective scientist. Natural forces in the
form of hereditary strains, he was convinced, also played their part
in the pattern of his life. Although he grew up in South London
and never visited Suffolk until he was a grown man, many of the
early pages of *My Life* are devoted to a *résumé* of his Suffolk ancestry
in which he views himself as the inevitable outcome of a race of
sturdy individualists, many of them associated with the sea. His
maternal grandfather was a sea-captain and an uncle disappeared at
sea. His own father spent fifty years at sea as a merchant captain and
all his uncles worked in the East India docks. Ellis never discouraged
those who wished to describe him as a navigator of unknown waters,
and in his posthumously published autobiography he declared that a
full-rigged sailing ship was the most beautiful sight in the world to
him, adding that "It is perhaps fitting that such a sight should be
so moving to one who has been a pioneer of unknown seas of the
spirit, haunted by the longing to search out remote lands that no
keel has yet touched."[1] Nevertheless, despite his family's many associations with the sea, he was christened Henry Havelock after a
distant relative, the distinguished soldier who was the hero of the
Indian Mutiny. He was always called Henry (or Harry) by his family, and the habitual use of the name "Havelock" he cultivated only
after he had begun his literary career.

---

* Italian Unity was not actually achieved until 1861.
† *Essays and Reviews* was published in 1861. He seems to be confusing its significance with that of the Tractarian Movement. Why did he make these unnecessary
errors? Out of a peculiar megalomania?

His parents emerge from his pages as placid, sensible people who were proud of their oldest child and only son without seeming to attach undue importance to him. His father was away for months on end; and his mother, a strong-willed woman, was the predominant influence in the household. Ellis's imagination, however, was always more responsive to the image of his maternal grandmother, who had died many years before his birth, than it was to either of his not particularly interesting parents. He liked hearing stories of this vain, lively girl who had sat up the entire night before her wedding in order not to disarrange her coiffure; a woman of will-power, apparently, for she persuaded her seafaring husband to abandon his trade in order to spend his days with her. Well read and quick-witted, she managed a successful girls' school until her death at the birth of her third child, Susannah Wheatley, who was to become Ellis's mother. Susannah, also by nature a boisterous, active girl, in her teens underwent a change of personality; she seemed to react against the frivolity she had inherited from her mother and was converted to an earnest evangelicalism. Photographs disclose a large, plain face, hair drawn back severely, and a tense, uncompromising mouth. There is nothing here to reveal an irrepressible streak of adventure which took the form of a compulsive need to be constantly changing houses. Her favourite recreation was to prowl the streets of South London looking for a new house, although the facts suggest that she simply moved from one grim little dwelling to another. Captain Edward Ellis, on more than one occasion, is supposed to have had difficulty finding his new home on his return from sea. His parents, Ellis recalled in later life, always behaved like sweethearts and during his father's periodic visits they would generally go off for a little honeymoon together. The household, quite clearly, was both very conventional and rather odd. The ill-assorted pair managed famously so long as they saw each other only occasionally. Henry regarded his father with casual affection. Captain Ellis was very much a visitor in his own home. Ellis never defined any negative feelings towards him beyond a mild contempt for the passive way he accepted his wife's dominance in the household, and it was to his mother that he always looked as the authority figure. There never seems to have been the slightest suggestion that he would follow his father's profession. Even though he took two trips around the world with his father, no intimacy developed between the hearty sailor and the solemn boy, nor did he ever seem to have the faintest dream—even as a child—of becoming a sailor himself. He was his mother's son, serious and literal-minded. His father liked pretty women and music and jolly laughter, propensities which he had to suppress when he was in South London. His visits were an interruption in the harmonious routine of the household. Captain Ellis is rather summarily dismissed from his son's memories, while Havelock always spoke lovingly and reverently of his mother. In 1889 he wrote in his journal:

> It is nearly a year since mother's death, and I have never felt able to write of it. I cannot look at the curves of her cheeks in her photo, or think of her without tears. Her death has always been for me a dreadful possibility; but I never realised how much I loved her, even though I knew that I cared about giving her pain. But I have nothing to be remorseful for; for that I am thankful for always. No one could have had more admiration and reverence for a mother. If I have any good qualities they come from my mother.[2]

Her first child did not appear until she was thirty, and it was to be almost four more years before the first of four daughters was born. In this highly important early period, without any competing attractions, Susannah gave her young son, through her own stolid strength and reliability, an indispensable sense of trust which was to develop into a confidence in himself that never wavered through the rest of his life. As Freud, three years his senior, was to write: "A man who has been the indisputable favourite of his mother keeps for life the feeling of a conqueror, that confidence of success that often induces real success."[3] Ellis frequently surmised that from his mother he also inherited a strong feminine streak which he believed most fully developed men to possess.

When his first sister, Mary, was born, Havelock is supposed to have said, "Take away that piece of dirt and rubbage." His early letters indicate a certain irritation towards her, and throughout his life she is rarely mentioned. Only Louie, the second sister, is mentioned by name in *My Life*, but this is probably not surprising since Ellis was separated from his sisters not only by age difference but by the fact that he went off to live in Australia when he was fifteen. Ellis selectively recorded only those memories which seemed important for his development. He does not record that his father was away at sea when the youngest girl, Edith, was born and that it was he who wrote to tell him of the event, adding that he had chosen the baby's name. It seems possible that he was also present with his mother at her other confinements. It would be interesting to know how he felt about these births, particularly since he never had any children of his own. For the two youngest sisters, Edie and Laura, he felt a distanced affection, but to the second one, Louisa (Louie), he was always deeply attached and in later life described her as "by far the most interesting of my sisters and the one to whom I have always felt the closest."[4] But in the recollections of his childhood his sisters play a shadowy part; he inflicted lessons on them or persuaded them to act as congregation when he played at preacher.

When he was seven, his parents decided that he should accompany his father on a voyage around the world. Ellis suggests that this was probably because of his delicate health; there is the possibility, too, that they felt he needed a change from the exclusively female atmosphere of his home. Whatever the reason, the experience stimulated his curiosity, and his memories are no longer hazy and diffuse but abundant and vivid. The account of the voyage in *My Life* is all too short, and one wishes that he had expanded it at the expense of the long-winded ruminations on his ancestors.

Setting off in a full-rigged ship, the *Empress*, they first stopped at Queenstown, where they picked up a large number of Irish immigrants bound for Australia. There was also a contingent of Catholic priests and nuns; and among the latter he never forgot gentle Sister Agnes, who supervised his lessons. Another person who befriended him was a German steward who lent him beautifully illustrated natural-history books because he felt that the child read too many stories. Both figures awakened his interest in the wider world, incomparable teachers for a latent imagination. For hours he was left alone to explore the ship's library, where he delighted in Hans Christian Andersen and devoured Marryat's *Masterman Ready*.

One letter to his mother survives from this voyage.

Ship Empress
at Sea
June 29th 1867

My dear Mother

We are in hopes of soon getting a fair wind and father says we shall take the first opportunity to send letters on shore as we are sure that you must be getting anxious about us now. I shall be very glad to see you & dear sisters once more. love to Johnnie & all kind friends Kisses many to your dear self Mary & Louisa

Believe me ever
Your Affectionate Son
HH Ellis[5]

On this trip he had his first experience of real playmates. When the ship was berthed in the harbour of Callao, the port of Peru, while loading guano, Havelock and the son of another captain were allowed to take a dinghy and explore among the rocky islands for starfish, and with a little girl he played house very decorously among the folded sails.

At this age, too, he had his first recollected sexual experiences. He emphasizes how little effect they actually had on him, yet of all the experiences during that memorable year he is able to summon up these memories with startling clarity. The first involved his friend in Callao. The boy, he recalled,

confided to me his scatological interest in his own person, but I was but mildly interested—not repelled, merely indifferent; the association of grace and beauty would have been needed to arouse my interest. This same boy confided to me his habit of what I, much later, learned to know was commonly called masturbation, though, as he told me, it was simply a method of promoting the wholesome development of the organs, an object which seemed to me entirely praiseworthy.[6]

Peru held the most enthralling memories of all. Here the child viewed the first mountains of his life. Later he was to dislike mountains, but now he would scrutinize the Andes through a telescope, seeking to identify the moving spots on the slopes. And then there was the excursion to Lima with his father which left him with a life-long romantic attachment to things Spanish. In his travel book, *The Soul of Spain* (1908), he recalled the charm it implanted on his susceptible early responses:

It was the first great foreign city I had seen and the unfamiliar features of its streets, such as elsewhere have become so familiar to me—the huge gateways, the pleasant courtyards one looked into beyond—made an ineffaceable impression on my mind. It has since seemed to me a fact not without significance that this first glimpse of the non-Anglo-Saxon world should have been of a foreign city founded on those

Spanish traditions which have since been so attractive to me, so potent to thrill or to charm.[7]

Three rather strange incidents were never to be forgotten. One involved a young Englishman, taken on board as passenger at Callao. Forty years later Ellis even remembered his name—Whelock. The man, whom he recalled as gentle and well-bred, gave him a copy of Mrs. Craik's moralistic tome *A Noble Life*, but for some reason— "which has always been completely obscure to me"[8]—the child refused obstinately to thank the sweet young donor. Another incident remained even more vividly in his memory.

> There was a large cat on board, a favourite with the sailors, who had fastened various objects round its neck. One day I was watching this cat making his way between the rails at the ship's stern; he was sure-footed, but the position was perilous, a touch would send him into the sea. Moved by a sudden impulse, when the cat was passing to the sea-ward side of the rail, I supplied that touch. I at once went to my father and told him the cat had fallen overboard and a rope was thrown over, but the cat had already disappeared. No one suspected me of any part in the cat's death, and I never revealed to anyone—I believe unto this day—that I was guilty in the matter. I have always, however, regarded it as a criminal act.[9]

An *acte gratuit* or a means of diverting attention from the cat to himself? Or a streak of cruelty that was later repressed, at what cost?

Finally, his first glimpse of a corpse was almost hallucinatory. As the ship glided swiftly through the seas, the child glimpsed the floating body of what appeared to be a Negro in a red shirt. "I alone saw it, and with my characteristic reticence said nothing about it."[10] Only seven years old, already he manifested those traits of self-containment and intractability that were to be characteristic marks of the mature man.

The final memory of the trip was of Antwerp, where he shouted with joy at the spectacle of galloping horsemen in the circus; in Antwerp, too, he immediately recognized Rubens's *Descent from the Cross*, a reproduction of which hung on the wall in his mother's bedroom. He also remembered clearly the return to the house in Addiscombe Terrace in Croydon, but had no recollection of the reunion with his mother. "Affection is undeveloped in early life" is his laconic comment.[11]

Now that he was home again he returned to the small school run by a Mrs. Granville, who was a great admirer of Pestalozzi's methods. Because of his ill-concealed aversion to games, the Headmistress asked his mother if she thought her son was quite right in the head. While his mother reacted indignantly to such a suggestion about her clever boy, Ellis's mild comment from the hindsight of forty years was that "it is possible that this shrewd and intelligent old lady ought to have the credit of first detecting in me whatever strain of mental anomaly I may possess."[12]

By nature a solitary learner, he always found school something of an ordeal to be endured. The books he remembered were chiefly those he discovered pushed to the back of a cupboard; most of them had belonged to his Grandmother Wheatley, to whose memory Ellis became attached as she seemed to be the only bookish person among his near relatives. By the time he was twelve he had absorbed a varied collection of books which undoubtedly influenced his propensities in taste. Among these was *Nature Displayed*, a compendium of the whole realm of nature with excellent illustrations and a book which he remembered as a model of precision and scientific honesty. Rowlandson's *Dr. Syntax in Search of the Picturesque* proved an unceasing source of delight. In the capacious bureau also he found the first French book he ever encountered—Rousseau's *Rêveries d'un promeneur solitaire*, a book which he later recalled as the source of his lifelong fascination with French culture. The subject appealed to innate, undefined instincts, while the actual personality of Rousseau took many years to arouse his interest.

Boys' books of travel and adventure aroused the normal interest in a child his age, but it was the entire canon of Scott's novels which held him enthralled until the age of sixteen. While *Ivanhoe* seemed to him the most perfect of all the books, particular affection was reserved for *The Abbot*, especially for the figure of the ultra-feminine Catherine Seyton, with whom he fell hopelessly in love.

By the age of ten he had begun to keep notebooks filled with commentaries on almost every book he read. The precocious child asked for Macaulay's *Essays* for his birthday and these he meticulously annotated. With time the notebooks became more elaborate and he began to index them and to co-ordinate passages under various headings. Here he was forming a method which was basically one that he always followed in his later work. By the time he was twelve he had prepared a little book called "The Stones of the

Bible," compiled by patiently assembling all the data he could find in his small supply of books. With the encouragement of his sympathetic mother he resolved to publish twelve copies of his treatise, but when it was discovered that the project would cost £12, it was hastily abandoned. Ellis looked back on the experience as an invaluable step towards what he considered his way of working—"the natural history method," although, he added defensively, it was "a method to which some would deny the name of science."[13]

Among the extensive notes on his reading, the entry for July 1874 records his reactions to *Tom Brown's School Days:*

> It is in one sense quite different from what I expected. And my opinion of the author is much elevated. There is something singularly noble and frank and his words in the preface about preaching—with which I most entirely agree. And the book itself is so plainly *vraisemblant*, so thoroughly wholesome and elevated and yet completely a boys' book and withal so pervaded by a true manly religion that I wish there were a hundred Tom Hughes in this world of ours.[14]

Far more space in his autobiography is devoted to the account of his reading than to the recollection of his school days. Big for his age, the quiet, thoughtful boy took no interest in games and never showed any unusual proficiency in his work. At nine he was sent to the French and German College in Merton as a day scholar for three years. His principal memory of the place was his sympathetic feeling for the faded wife of the Headmaster, who, entirely ignorant of his interest, one day reported to her husband that he had passed her on the street without raising his hat. His other memory of the period was his feeling of revulsion at the sight of the sexual organs of the swimming teacher. Both facts are recorded briefly, without comment.

When he was twelve Mrs. Ellis decided that he should go to boarding school, and in her zeal decided impetuously upon The Poplars at Mitcham, which attracted her by its impressive atmosphere, although the fees were higher than she had planned to pay. Harry was enrolled as a weekly boarder, since she wished to continue to exert an influence over his religious education. It was taken for granted that this studious son should have the best possible education, but similar arrangements were never contemplated for any of his sisters.

At Mitcham, Ellis maintained the same friendly but distant

relationship with his schoolfellows, although his nights became ordeals of silent torment. He shared a room with two boys several years older than himself. One of them was an inoffensive lad if left to himself, but pliable to the will of a bully, Willie Orr. The latter was the son of a colonel in the Indian Army and was himself later killed while serving with the Indian Frontier Mounted Police. Fixated on horses, he conceived the diabolical plan of using young Ellis as a mount and constructed spurs to which pins were attached. Night after night Harry submitted to what he tersely described as "the required duties," enduring the misery without a single protest. He gives no indication of how long the silent martyrdom continued, but it would seem to have lasted some months of his first year at Mitcham. At length his mother detected that something untoward was happening, extracted the truth from him, and made a hasty visit to the Headmaster, with the result that Harry was immediately transferred to a room with two more congenial boys.

What was the effect of this traumatic experience; and why did he allow himself to be used in this almost masochistic manner? In *My Life* he says, "I had no instincts of pugnacity, and the idea of attacking or resisting a robust and brutal boy older and bigger than myself never occurred to me."*[15] However, the fact that he had not resisted continued to rankle three years later when he wrote a private essay entitled "Leaving School," dated July 27th, 1874. "To say," he writes,

> that my school-life has been one continuously pleasant road strewn with roses would (despite my sorrow at the completion) be a monstrous falsehood. By the malign influence of one diabolically disposed boy (I would not apply this epithet were there only one to whom it occurred), my character has suffered far more sadly that I could have dreamed it possible. It was no moral influence, more a physical one; but it is sad to think that I have allowed my character to be, in a

---

* Ellis was obviously recalling this incident in a footnote in *Studies in the Psychology of Sex*: "A minor manifestation of this tendency to cruelty, appearing in quite normal and well-conditioned individuals, is the impulse among boys at and under puberty to take pleasure in persecuting and hurting lower animals or their own companions. Some youths display a diabolical enjoyment and ingenuity in torturing sensitive juniors, and even a boy who is otherwise kindly mutilating a frog. In some cases, in boys and youths, who have no true sadistic impulse, and are not usually cruel, this infliction of torture on a lower animal produces an erection, though not necessarily any pleasant sexual sensations" (*Studies in the Psychology of Sex*, New York: Random House, 1936, Vol. I, Part Two, p. 70). Is there some connection here, too, to his cruelty in pushing the cat overboard?

degree, broken without resistance; though I could hardly do otherwise. I have no doubt now that it was not further back though when I look back at the agony real & prospective which my sensitive nature & melancholy temperament underwent I believe that had I foreseen it I would sooner—but hasten from the subject.[16]

It is interesting to compare this passage with Ellis's comments in *My Life*:

I am inclined to think that the suffering I had silently endured was not without evil influence on my nervous system. I was just then at the critical period of puberty. While subjected to this treatment, at about the age of thirteen, copious seminal emissions began to take place during sleep, once or twice a week, always without dreams or any sensations, and continued whenever I was alone, for some thirty years. Doubtless my temperament predisposed me to such manifestations, though my thoughts and my habits were, at this period, alike free from any physically sensual tincture, but I incline to think that the state of nervous excitement in which every night I fell asleep was a factor in causing this lack of nervous stability in the new function then developing. The emissions were themselves a source of nervous apprehension, for I vaguely felt they were something to be ashamed of; I constantly dreaded their occurrence and feared their detection.[17]

When he speaks of the seminal emissions continuing "for some thirty years," he is speaking, presumably, of 1901—the probable date at which he was writing these words. While comments of a later date are often inserted clumsily into the text—though more generally in the form of footnotes—there is no indication that the flow of the narrative has been interrupted or revised at this juncture. Is there, then, a strong possibility that these "copious seminal emissions" which he linked with an exacerbated nervousness continued indefinitely? It is a question that will have to be examined in more detail in a later consideration of Ellis's puzzling sexual aetiology.

Always inclined to be a loner, in 1874, upon leaving school, Ellis reported in his journal that he had not made a single friendship because he could not find a boy who shared his tastes.

This same year he was confirmed, an event that elicited a long comment in his journal. He was particularly conscious of the "white-robed maidens" who

behaved admirably, listening with great attention, never looking about, and quietly kneeling the greater part of the time. The male

part of the candidates hardly behaved so well, though of course I do
not mean to say they behaved badly positively, but only comparatively.
Somehow or other women have a much better idea of propriety than
men have.[18]

More important, he read a book called *Behavior: A Manual of
Manners and Morals* by an American living in London, Dr. T. L.
Nichols. He wrote a letter to the author, who sent him another of
his books, *The Basis of Social and Sanitary Science,* of which he made
a long analysis in his journal. One section deserves quotation:

> Part IV, dealing with Reproduction of the Human Species and the
> organs of generation and sexual relations generally, touches upon deli-
> cate ground of which Dr. Nichols is fully conscious. I was myself not
> altogether convinced of the propriety of this part of the work, but a
> perusal of it has filled me with admiration of the delicacy with which
> he has gone to work leaving nothing uncovered or unexplained but
> without hurting the feelings of the most sensitive reader. To the pure
> all things are pure; in the hands of all indiscriminating people I should
> not care to place this portion of the book, but everyone else, except
> perhaps some few morbid prudes, may and ought to read it. I, for one
> have learnt a great deal from it. It deals with a subject which most
> current books on physiology totally ignore. Dr. Nichols says that to
> read Huxley's work* you would not so much as suspect that there was
> any reproduction of the species. If every married couple in England
> could have it, it would do a vast amount of good.[19]

At intervals, scattered through this early section of *My Life,* Ellis
refers to childhood experiences connected with women and urination. The first of these was of walking with his nursemaid and baby
sister when he became aware of a flow of water at his side. He must
have been about four when this occurred, the period at which he was
disturbed by the obtrusive birth of his first sister. This incident is
inserted without any comment whatsoever. Many pages later he
reflects, in a leisurely ruminative way, on the effect of early experiences on later sexual patterns. His conclusion is that he was singularly
innocent, devoid of "morbid" curiosity. He decided that babies
emerged from their mothers' navels, "but this was to me a purely
scientific question which involved no morbid feelings, nor any undue
attention." "On the physical side," he recalls,

---

* *Elementary Lessons in Physiology* (1866).

There was really nothing to say until I had passed boyhood and reached adolescence. There were no spontaneous sexual manifestations, and no companion, no servant girl, ever sought to arouse such phenomena, or to gratify curiosities that before puberty had not come into being. Indeed, strange as it may appear to some, throughout the whole course of my school-days until they ended at the age of sixteen, I cannot recall that I heard or saw anything that would have shocked an ordinarily modest schoolgirl. The incident there was to tell merely shows my innocence.[20]

What incident? He neglects to mention any. It is a curious oversight.

There are—with one notable exception—no reflections on the nature and effect of his relationship with his mother as an only son and oldest child with a father away almost all the time, although at one point he remarks that a mother is usually half in love with her firstborn and only son. The allusions to his mother are invariably reverent and admiring. Mrs. Ellis was not at all demonstrative; and much later in his autobiography Ellis says of himself that he has never been able to address a woman as "dearest" and could never swear undying love to anyone.* As though it were of no importance whatsoever, he mentions the fact that his mother would sometimes call him into her room to wash her back, adding that she was so aloof that any further putative curiosity about her person would have been summarily checked. He gives no indication of his age at the time these sponge baths occurred. It seems strange that a man who investigated sex so thoroughly should never allude in any way to the role his mother played in his sexual development.

Above all, he stresses his naturalness, his normality, his lack of repression because he has never had anything to hide. "What others have driven out of consciousness or pushed into the background, as being improper or obscene, I have maintained and even held in honour."[21] One is tempted to ask at this point: how can he be so absolutely convinced of his transparency?

Ellis was certain that he felt no hostility to his father and that his feeling for his mother was affection untinged by cravings for more demonstrative expressions of love from her. At the same time he is willing to admit that she "exerted some moulding influence on my later sexual life"—but hastens to add, "This would have been much greater if, as never happened, she had allowed her love for me to

---

* This comment appears many times in letters to women.

become unduly tender but, as it was, her chief influence lay in unconsciously moulding my ideal of womanhood generally."[22] Ellis
seems positively reluctant to establish any linking sexual influence
with his mother. Throughout these pages he several times stresses
both his normality—indeed, more than normality: complete and un-
blemished innocence—and the relative distance between his mother
and himself. But eventually he finds himself in a position where he
must face up to the fact that perhaps there were some manifestations
of sexuality in his childhood:

> I have said that probably in childhood I was sexually normal. But I
> think I can trace a slight fibre of what, if possibly normal in child-
> hood, is commonly held—though this I doubt, since I have found it
> so common—not to be so when it persists or even develops after pu-
> berty. I mean a slight strain of what I may call urolagnia, which never
> developed into a real perversion nor ever became a dominant interest,
> and formed no distinguishable part of the chief love interests of my
> life.[23]

This is a curious passage. What it seems intended to convey is
the following: "I was completely normal but, oh yes—before I
forget—possibly there was some connection between incidents in my
childhood and a later manifestation which is commonly believed to
be a perversion but I have found it to be so widespread that I know
it is commonplace." He then goes on to discuss how in adolescence
he became "scientifically" interested in the subject by noting the
relative distances his schoolfellows could pee, adding casually, "my
own vesical energy being below the average."* The paragraph concludes with the statement that in adult life this preoccupation became integrated with his tender feeling for women but it was "never
to me a vulgar interest, but, rather, an ideal interest, a part of the yet
unrecognised loveliness of the world."[24]

The next paragraph opens ingenuously: "In later years, I would
now further note, it has seemed to me that I may have inherited this
trait from my mother. . . ."[25] He then relates three incidents. When
he was nine or ten his mother suddenly thrust a wet diaper playfully
into his face, and he turned his head away in disgust. Then when he

---

* His continuing interest in the subject was expressed in an article, "The Bladder
as a Dynamometer," in *The American Journal of Dermatology* in May 1902; and in
"The Phenomena of Sexual Periodicity" in Volume I of *Studies in the Psychology of
Sex*: "An annual curve may be found in the expulsive force of the bladder as measured
by the distance to which the urinary stream may be projected."

was twelve, as they were walking in the gardens of the Zoo, she stopped and he heard a stream of water falling to the ground. When he looked back at the puddle, she murmured shyly: "I did not mean you to see that." It would have been perfectly possible, he comments, for her to have gone to the ladies' room. Then, "some time later"— without any shyness this time—she made him privy to her intention and he spontaneously guarded her privacy. In later life he confided these experiences to his sister Louie, who told him that their mother had always been very circumspect with the girls and added, after some reflection, "She was flirting with you."[26]

His childhood contained one love—overwhelming, devastating, never to be forgotten. The daughter of his mother's step-brother was invited to spend a week or two (Ellis didn't remember the precise length of time) with the family during the summer of 1871. Half-child, half-woman, Agnes would alternately romp or walk staidly arm in arm with him. One day they passed Dr. De Chastelain, his Headmaster; and Ellis proudly recalled that he had the courage not to remove his arm but simply courteously lifted his hat. However, a coolness developed between the parents when Agnes's mother discovered that her daughter had been asked to shell peas, a task she considered demeaning. Letters soon ceased; but for the next four years Ellis was haunted by his memory of the girl. Night after night he would lie in bed with streaming eyes, praying that somehow she might eventually become his wife. "I have often felt thankful since that our prayers are not answered," he concluded dryly.[27] Nevertheless, Agnes was one of the most powerful forces in his life, the means of fully arousing the deep emotional springs of his nature.

All through his childhood there was no male authority figure to whom he could look as a model. It is curious that Ellis makes no reference to this, apart from the fact that his appreciation of his mother was probably the cause of the "womanly" strain in his nature, a feature of himself he valued highly. Lacking friends, to him solitude and self-reliance became habitual, traits which were soon to be of inestimable value. Shy and gauche, on Christmas Day 1876 he confided to his journal the wistful longing that he might have been taught some social graces. After he went to boarding school, the first fully satisfying intellectual relationship entered his life. Angus Mac-Kay, a young English master, was the only person to expand his mind to wider possibilities of viewing the world. A poet of sorts, with a firm knowledge of nineteenth-century literature, of radically inclined political views, MacKay enabled him to see beyond his mother's lower-middle-class conservative limitations. MacKay was the liberator of his mind.

One other man made an impression on his expanding sensibility: the Reverend John Erck, Vicar of Merton, who Sunday after Sunday moved the boy with his eloquent preaching. It seemed to be generally agreed that Ellis was to enter the Church and Erck wrote to him, urging him to go into the Church of England because it offered "the liberty of prophesying." There are extant many sermons in childlike hand which Ellis apparently delivered to his sisters, using the end of the sofa as a pulpit. By the time he left school in July 1874 there seemed no prospect open to him except the Church, but in the unpublished notes he wrote for his own benefit at that time he does not seem to show any enthusiasm or dedicated sense of vocation.

> . . . now as I think of studying for the Church, (& this I owe intrinsically in some degree to the suggestion of my fitness made by Mr. MacKay which called my attention to the subject) for which I feel that I am in many ways suited although it involves some sacrifices— a sacrifice of idleness & a sacrifice of wealth in which also are—the former at least—no sacrifices at all. The latter I do not look at so philosophically, chiefly because a curate & very many vicars cannot— I could not, I know with a good conscience—can not marry. I know at all events that I should have too great an affection for the object of my love than to marry her on £120 a year. If I study for the Church, I was about to say I shall have to work especially hard if I go to London University. I intend beginning in a few days. I am not aware that I have anything more to say & so conclude.
>
> Henry H. Ellis
July 27th 1874[28]

This passage was written during a troubled period when Ellis was beginning to have serious anxieties about his future. Some of these spilled over into a novel he started to write entitled *An Earnest Life*, whose young hero is "preparing to take the burden of mankind on his shoulders." This was clearly written under the influence of MacKay, whose wider outlook had begun to make inroads into the narrow piety of Mrs. Ellis's religious faith which the boy had never questioned before. His teacher's influence was both liberating and unsettling. Possessing a very real faith of his own, MacKay at the same time, by his greater tolerance, served to undermine what faith the boy had. (Apparently he did not force on Henry those attentions that later cost him his job.) Ellis bought a copy of Renan's *Life of Jesus* and although the comments he made in the margin were critical, the book undoubtedly contributed to the broader paths he was now approaching. Other influential books of this period were George Drysdale's *Elements of Social Science* and Swinburne's *Songs Before Sunrise*, which had a deep effect on many another youth. Shelley was an object of adoration for the next few years. In 1916 Ellis told Hugh de Sélincourt that

> "the word 'adoration' alone expresses my attitude towards Shelley & towards no other being who ever existed, the kind of feeling which the devout Christian ought to feel, but doesn't, about Jesus. From 16 to 20 I was always re-reading & re-reading & meditating on his poems & life; I never have since, & never feel that I need to, but my attitude remains unchanged. I have never felt able to write about him rationally on this account."[29]

It seems symbolical that the completion of his spiritual apprenticeship should have been on a ship bound for a remote part of the world where he had to forge his ultimate faith in solitude and loneliness.

CHAPTER 2

AUSTRALIA

On APRIL 19TH, 1875, ELLIS LEFT ENGLAND ON HIS FATHER'S SHIP, the *Surrey*, on a second trip around the world. Sensing their son's restlessness and uncertainty about his future, and troubled about his rather uncertain health, his parents decided that a complete change might be in order before he settled upon some fixed course in life.

For some years Captain Ellis had been transporting emigrants to Australia, and it was decided to list Henry as a "captain's clerk" since ordinary passengers could not be booked. There was a good deal of chaffing among the emigration officials about his size and the havoc he would cause among the single girls, and his father later teased him during the voyage about his impassivity in this respect. At Plymouth, where they anchored for a few days to take on 325 emigrants, Captain Ellis took him for his first visit to a theatre, although he never remembered what it was they saw. Far more vivid in his memory was the visit in Devonport to a buxom lady who had two vivacious girls slightly older than himself. He found himself completely at a loss in this unusual situation, and he was told by the lady that he needed some "jolly girl friends." Apparently the Devonport lady was a completely different woman from his mother.

On April 22nd they set sail. After an initial bout of seasickness he settled down contentedly to the pleasant shipboard life. He does not seem to have been assigned any duties and predictably spent his time reading the collection of books he had brought with him—*Faust*, Montaigne, and Spenser chiefly—and writing turgid verse modelled on the excesses of the Spasmodic poets to whom he had been introduced by MacKay. Shortly after leaving England he began to keep a diary with notations on the changing weather and, more important, invaluable descriptions of his mental attitudes during this period. The manner is sententious and humourless, as most such accounts written at that age tend to be:

I am beginning to collect materials for the poem which I have had in my mind for some time. It is to be somewhat like Alex Smith's "Life Drama," only will deal with deeper questions than that poem, like Bailey's "Festus." Blank verse I have chosen as the most suitable medium for what I have to say. One or two short passages have already been written. But the form which it is to take is still somewhat shadowy. One of the questions into which I shall be led is the future of man on earth. Now, of course, I have no sympathy with those who consider that the world may, and probably will, come to an end in a very short time. I hold that that consummation is very far distant. The great discovery of development would lead us to suppose that man may, in the natural course of things, yet reach a higher position morally & physically than he has yet attained. We see that nothing in nature is stationary, not even the universe. Then why should man be so? Moreover we see that all things move by the slow process of development, that nothing goes backwards, progression being the order of nature. And when we see all this I cannot perceive how we can make man an exception to the rule. If indeed it is true, as it probably is, that man has arisen from the simplest organic forms to his present proud station, and when we consider that he is yet far from perfect, why ever should he stand still? But supposing he is progressing, where is he to stop? And can he ever be perfectly happy? Now, with regard to the body. When pain is present perfect happiness cannot be, that may, I think, be taken as granted. Yet, although it has been shown that there is no reason why man should not live for a hundred years on the average, and though by extreme means communicable and hereditary diseases might be crushed out, nobody has ever attempted to prove that the laws of nature may be made perfectly harmless. Now whatever degree of progress the race may attain, if a man let go his hold and fall off a tree he would still break his leg. So that I think we must retain the operation of the laws of nature, when they are baneful as when they are beneficent. And after all the evils which result from the operation of these same laws by which we live are very small when compared with the whole sum of pains and evils which afflict mankind. There are two very important studies, however greatly neglected, but the diligent and scientific pursuit of which will, I believe, lead to the most important results, the one as to our future in the world, the other in a world to come; I allude to the philosophy of history and psychology.[1]

His idealistic fantasies and sexual reveries were expressed in a good deal of ponderously turbulent verse:

> *Lay thy cheek on mine,*
> *And let me breathe its fragrance, feel its softness,*
> *Full on mine own; let thy black flowing hair*
> *Mingle with mine; I love thy laughing tresses;*
> *My eyes have ever gazed with joy, my hands*
> *Wandered among their wilderness of wealth,*
> *Feeling a quiet pleasure. Thy lips, my love,*
> *Thine angel—nay, thy woman's—lips, I scarce*
> *Can think they are from heaven. I hardly dare*
> *To look upon their sweetness,* etc., etc.

The days passed peaceably and as the *Surrey* approached the tropics he noted the appearance of the Southern Cross, the change in the sunsets, and the sight of a sperm whale, a dolphin, and a shark that they caught one day. In the evenings the emigrants gathered in groups on the deck to sing hymns and sentimental ballads. The tranquillity of the passage was broken one July evening by an enormous wave striking the ship and rolling across the decks. The window of the cabin Henry shared with his father was smashed in, and everything drenched, including the harmonium which Captain Ellis had bought especially for the voyage. Henry reacted with his usual imperturbability, asking only "Does this happen often?"—a remark which his father was always to remember laughingly.

On July 25th the ship arrived off Sydney Heads, but was immediately put into quarantine for three weeks as there was chickenpox on board. Henry's most vivid memory of his first days in Sydney was the actress Madame Ristori, whose acting he always considered the finest he had ever seen.* Like a seasoned theatre-goer, he described the Sleep-walking Scene in *Macbeth* and the last act of Carlo Marengo's *Pia de Tolumei*, in which Rinaldo begs forgiveness of his

---

* Ellis's judgement was apparently right. Adelaide Ristori (1822–1906) was an Italian actress who had been a serious rival to Rachel in Paris. Her performance as Lady Macbeth in London was highly praised, Mrs. Kendal acclaiming her as a better actress than Bernhardt.

dying wife: "Totally changed from the Pia of old, she is pale and emaciated, her voice is weak, and her steps tottering. . . . The acting here is painfully realistic, but at the same time I do not think that it is too realistic that it passes the bounds of propriety i.e. that it is revolting."

During the last week in August, events moved very swiftly in Henry's life. The *Surrey* was about to sail for Calcutta when the ship's doctor decided that the Indian climate would not suit the lad's uncertain health. Nearly six feet, he was discovered during the voyage to weigh only 145 pounds, forty pounds less than one of the ship's apprentices of the same age. He had missed a great deal of school through undiagnosed gastric pains, and ever since he could remember his mother had fussed a good deal over his delicate health. Now—on the insistence of the ship's doctor, who was drunk most of the time— his father suddenly decided to leave him behind in Australia for per- haps a couple of years, particularly since the climate there seemed likely to agree with him. Father and son paid a visit to the General Educational Registration Association run by one Alfred Morris, who had been an officer on one of Captain Ellis's ships many years before and had left the ship to settle in Australia. He had little more knowl- edge of educational requirements than did his partner, Frederick Bevill, an enormously fat, good-natured rogue who was supposed to have recently graduated from an unspecified university in Japan. They wrote glowing testimonials to Henry's abilities—although they made no attempt to investigate his qualifications—and assured him that he could easily command £120 as an assistant master at an Aus- tralian school. Henry seems to have accepted the decision in a matter- of-fact way, remarking in his diary the advantage of staying—that he could more easily obtain a degree at the University of Sydney than at London, and that Australia seemed a rather pleasant place to remain for a relatively brief period:

> Australia is advancing without doubt with rapid strides; and Australia has a very fine climate; and the people live very sociably together; and their views are in many respects wider and more liberal than of people at home; but they have not the intellect which we find in England— no literature—no science—no art. We may say that Australia is a young growing tree throwing out strong branches and plenty of healthy leaves—indeed it appears to me both physically & morally a very healthy country—but it has not yet reached the flower nor the fruit. They are yet to come.[2]

He goes on to record matter-of-factly a visit to the Legislative Assembly and to the Museum. Clearly he did not realize that here in Australia, as he recalled many years later, "I was . . . to find my own soul."[3]

And so he was appointed a master in a private school, Fontlands, at Burwood—a pretty spot a few miles from Sydney—by the principal, Mr. Hole. Within a few weeks of his arrival at Burwood, while walking among the trees one evening, he resolved to devote his life chiefly to an investigation of the problem of sex, whose unsatisfied stirrings were causing him considerable anxiety—although these are not recorded in his diary beyond the occasional cryptic comment that he cannot bring himself to record all that lies heaviest on his heart.

Shortly after his arrival he wrote to his father: "I am getting on admirably. Mr Hole I like very much & the work is not very hard. I sleep at a good hotel near; and am altogether very comfortable."[4] Was Mr. Hole letting him off lightly or was he writing too ingenuously to his father when he told him "Mr Hole is satisfied with me in every particular except in Latin in regard to which he is extremely particular, although he acknowledges he is not much of a Latin scholar himself"? It was soon apparent to Mr. Hole that the new master was totally incompetent. He reduced his salary from £100 to £40—a bitter blow to Henry after the sanguine expectations raised by Messrs. Morris and Bevill. Within six weeks it was clear that he had to be dismissed. By the end of the year he was back in Sydney and had placed advertisements offering himself as a private tutor. In his diary, in characteristic fashion, he lists the reasons for this decision:

> (1) I should have more time—in all probability—for my studies, and (2) should be increasing my age & my capacities; while, perhaps my real motive—we generally have a real motive underlying all the rest, unknown almost to ourselves—was my inability of gaining a mastery over the boys so great as was desirable. This, which was also Mr Hole's chief motive for parting with me, has made me rather sick of boys for the present.[5]

For the first time the journal is used as a receptacle into which to pour his troubles. He describes "the agony and suspense" this incident has caused him. His health is not good, he suffers many unlocalized pains. "I can only hope that my present feelings are not the prelude to something worse." In a letter to his mother it is apparent that he was very homesick. The Australians didn't pay much attention to Christmas and mosquitoes were a poor substitute for plum pudding and snow. Then there were the bugs that bred in trees and smelled horribly.

"I have only become acquainted with them at present by means of my olfactory nerves. And then again there is the chance of being killed by the little snake called the slow worm, several of which have been slain lately. And there are the great tarantula spiders whose bite is more poisonous than the slow worms even. These are one or two of the charming features of this glorious country of Australia which poor unsuspecting people are invited to traverse 18,000 miles to share with their brethren on this side of the world."[6]

Poor fond mother!

On Christmas Day he did not attend church service, the first service he had missed in a long time:

. . . for our feelings & habits long survive the extinction of our thoughts and ideas. I felt several mental twinges at what I do really consider no crime or fault in the slightest degree—though hardly care to enter on the subject here. My internal life which is now rendering me miserable, the more truths I seem to find or rather not find, is to me a rather tender and sacred subject; and in all its stages from the earliest I have had a most peculiar dread of referring to or chronicling its progress or feelings; and this feeling, or whatever it is, has always kept at least my tongue inviolably closed—perhaps when it ought to have been otherwise.[7]

This is the first recorded entry of the religious doubts which were to continue to plague him for the next two years. Later he was to recall that these doubts had begun before he left England, and that he substantially lost his faith during the voyage. Still, for many years it had been taken for granted that he would become a clergyman; and now that he found teaching so distasteful, it was impossible to think of any other profession which would accommodate his bookish proclivities. It was a time, too, when he was tormented by sex, but this, more than his religious anxieties, was a subject too private to put down in words. But here in Sydney, homesick, humiliated by his recent experience, uncertain about the future, cast among complete strangers in another continent, he turned to his diary as the only source of solace in which he could confide.

Sunday Evening. Jan 2nd 1876 So we have begun another year with its joys and sorrows and commonplaces, so like yet so unlike to all its predecessors. Speaking for myself, the years are very unlike. I have been accustomed for some years to write down a few of my thoughts at the end of the year. I have not any of these papers in Australia but I know, could I compare them with each other and with my present state, they would exhibit vast, radically fundamental changes. I know I am changing; not in myself, my feelings are the same, my longings for truth and love for man. I always had those feelings, I have them still. Yes, but still how changed! how changed! And this year finds me very differently situated in all respects to what 1875 found me. I did not think then that in a few months I should be engaged in teaching in a school, still less that the school would be in Australia. Little did I think that with friends, tastes, pleasures—all that I live in and from —left 18,000 miles behind my back, I could resolve to stay for an undetermined time in a country which contained for me not a single friend, not even a relative. For I did certainly dream of a voyage, but thought it little more than a dream. And if the external change has been great, the interior has been still greater. All has been changed, and yet not changed. There were great changes twelve months ago; . . . great searchings of heart; and these are there now; and all the thoughts, the longing desires, and the noble aspirations, though modified, running in different channels, some perhaps for a time in no channel at all and in danger of being lost. But still all that is of truth and beauty and nature are there; the feelings, not the opinions. Ah! the opinions have changed. What to? God may know; I know not. A vast chaos of doubts, negations, denials—a seething mass which the deep love of truth can neither direct nor penetrate. . . .[8]

But for the moment he had to take up another teaching post. In answer to his advertisement in the *Herald*, a Mr. Platt of Gongerwarrie, near Carcoar, wrote to say that he wished his eldest boy to be instructed in English, writing, and mathematics. Henry, hardly more than a boy himself, set off in a coach on the long, cold journey of nearly two hundred miles. This was one of the most uncomfortable experiences of his life; gold had been discovered near Carcoar and there was a rush of people to the newly discovered deposits beyond Bathurst. The coach was so jammed that people had to sit on top of each other, and at times the road was so bad that the passengers had to get out and walk. He arrived at Carcoar utterly despondent over the loss of his trunk containing all his precious books.

The next year was quiet and placidly free from external disturbances. To his mother he wrote:

"I pursue the even tenor of my ways, 'The daily round the common task' which as Mr. Erck was very fond of telling us 'should
furnish all we need to ask' (these lines, by the bye, are not Cow-
per's but Keble's). I get up at seven, read till 8, walk till half-past
nine; lessons till half-past twelve; do Latin till dinner at 1—read
a novel or something till 2 lessons again till ½ 3; music till ½ 4,
walk again till ½ 5 accompanied by Shakespeare generally, sometimes Shelley or Wordsworth, tea at six; Children prepare their
lessons while I do German from ¼ to seven till ½. Then I do
half an hour's Greek, read the previous day's newspaper, then
read till 10, at which time Minnie goes to bed, the servants go
to their room & the house gets quiet, & I am always in bed before
11. . . . I live for the most part a very solitary, contemplative
student life."[9]

He concluded with the hope that she was in good health and liked
her new house "wherever it is."

Mr. and Mrs. Platt were kindly people to whom he had little to
say, and the children were blissfully easy to manage. The location
was remote and in a whole year the Platts had only four visitors. It
was here that Ellis first began fully to appreciate Australian scenery,
particularly the brilliant bird life and the variety of exotic trees.

But while the year passed in the main in a state of peaceful tranquillity, his emerging sexuality continued to cause him misery. "I
am too much alone," he confided to his diary,

too much with myself and my books in this quiet place. I want the
world: I want human sympathies; human love; I love and sympathise
too much; I want to be loved and sympathised with. I want to be
shaken up with the rest of mankind; then perhaps I could throw off
my reserve and physical nervousness which are now so hateful to me
because I am so conscious of them.[10]

With a boy's undefined longings, his affections centred themselves on one of his little pupils, Minnie, only ten years old. Small
for her age, stooped, pale, her vulnerable appearance was utterly
endearing to Ellis. In *My Life* he recalls her as intuitively and pro-
vocatively coquettish, but the boy of seventeen who confided in his

diary did not see her in that light. The mature Ellis looked back tenderly at the boy he had been, while the young man was moved by the sweetness of the child, by the strap she wore to correct her round shoulders, by her constant habit of pulling up her stockings. Here for the first time he experienced what he was later to describe as "tumescence" when she snuggled up beside him to do her sums. "I know there is much of sensuousness in her attraction for me," he mused, "but does that sensuousness render my love less pure? That question I will leave unanswered; it is best left alone. I fear I have not yet mastered my tendency to morbid self-analysis."[11]

Early in June he went to Sydney in order to try to pass the matriculation examinations. Mr. Hole and even Morris had advised him against attempting them, particularly as his mathematics was so poor. Not being able to find a copy of the requisite Demosthenes for the Greek test, and pessimistic about his chances of being exempted from the compulsory lectures, he reflected, "Altogether there seems little chance for me; but I shall at all events have gained a little experience." But by the end of the month he found he had passed among those at the top of the list—"Much more than I expected." How well he did is difficult to judge since thirty-five of the thirty-seven candidates passed, but without this qualification he would never have been able to enter medical school after he returned to England.

At this point he was still wavering between teaching and the Church, although neither offered an attractive prospect:

> I certainly shouldn't like to devote my life to teaching. The Church? Well, yes, the Church would suit me in many respects. In her, I believe, I could display what ability I have; there I could do the most good; there, amongst men somewhat inclined to narrow and prejudiced views, my own broad and catholic opinions would attract attention they could excite nowhere else. But my opinions. They have undergone a revolution of the most awful and complete kind. To teach what I don't believe? From Sunday to Sunday? To be a hypocrite—nothing less? Is it to be thought of? Even from the best and highest ends, is it to be thought of?[12]

The quiet, uneventful year came to an end in December 1876. "I shall miss you," Mr. Platt told him, "though we've not had much to say to each other." In his testimonial he wrote that Ellis "gave no trouble in the house." As he left, Ellis confided to his journal that he longed to bend and kiss Minnie. "But this will never do."

He returned to Sydney, resigned to finding another position as assistant master. He had no difficulty finding a teaching post in Grafton on the Clarence River. At the beginning of every year it was his habit to record his intellectual and emotional state, and the opening of 1877—just before his eighteenth birthday—saw him in a fairly sanguine frame of mind:

> My philosophy I imagine is something like that of Matthew Arnold— a belief in the beauty and the use of the things which be; an earnest desire to make them better however, especially everything connected with the physical well-being of man, for on that I consider any future attempt at the regeneration of the world does in great measure rest though I don't believe there will be any such regeneration. Ameliora- tion say . . .[13]

To his father he confided: "I wanted if possible to stay near Sydney and have ended by going twice as far as I did before."[14] The salary was only £60 for the first quarter—"the fact was he couldn't get anybody else to go for that"—and he had considerable difficulty in extracting even his travelling expenses. Before term had started, the Headmaster suddenly died of "brain fever"—brought on, it was believed, by lavish spending—and it was proposed to Ellis that he take over the school. The suggestion that an eighteen-year-old boy should assume such a responsibility was preposterous, but in retro- spect Ellis realized that it would have been an incomparable oppor- tunity if he had had any gift for teaching. But alas, he had not, and the next four months were among the most miserable, and emo- tional, of his life. "I hardly fancy that I shall carry it on after this quarter," he told his father. "It is far too fatiguing and annoying what with boys & parents & accounts I have no time to myself."

His domestic arrangements, however, were entirely pleasant. He boarded with the large family of Mr. F. W. Chapman, the Mayor, and responded happily to the relaxed atmosphere of an easy-going Australian household. The four daughters, he told his father, were "a perpetual source of amusement." On April 22nd he recorded in his diary:

> I know I feel a tenderness for women. I don't mean to say that I have a habit of falling in love. Not at all—I fell in love once—once only—

I mean to say that there is a natural, pure, healthy, yes a *sexual* feeling of affection between man & woman. It is impossible not to feel love when one has lived months in the same house with a fair pleasant face which never wears a frown or looks an unkind thought—which could not do so—and the tall, graceful, well-proportioned form —so sweet and healthy a face and form which make one happy to look at. In truth what are grace and beauty but the manifestations—nay, the incarnation—of *health*. It does not jar on our nerves to know that the same hands which can play among the keys weaving sweet harmony come every morning to empty the slops and make the bed. 'Familiar acts are beautiful through love,' says Shelley (though the quotation is not quite to the point) and that beauty is reflected back on the doer. Miss May Chapman is the young lady I refer to, aged twenty, very tall, most beautifully made—to make one wish to be a painter and have her for a model. She is proud of her height, says so, and looks it too; no womanly nervousness, with all the gracefulness of movement, the restraint and the liberty which must go with perfect womanhood. She is always dressed well. I saw her standing in a careless attitude speaking to her father the other day. I never saw anything more fit to be transferred to canvas; it would have made a splendid portrait; almost a sight to rejoice Titian or Giorgione (rather, perhaps, Gainsborough or Reynolds). And when I saw this grace and pride and sweetness of temper brought to bear on such simple, what we consider mean, domestic duties of daily life, I confess it was a kind of revelation—a subject for thought and perhaps it was a lesson too. One thing I know and feel that we cannot have possibly before our eyes, that which is sweet and pure and noble and womanly, without being ourselves the better for it—the nobler and the purer.[15]

With Bertha, a younger sister, he felt far more at ease. He envied both sisters their breeding and the easy attitudes of their home. In contrast to the persistent ailments of his own sisters, he felt sure that May and Bertha suffered "none of the disorders peculiar to women; I feel confident that they know nothing about amenorrhoea or dysmenorrhea or menorrhagia."* How on earth did he know about these ailments? His observations on Miss Phoebe Chapman, the eldest sister, elicited the following remarks:

I have noticed in the many families with which I am acquainted that those in whose nature the *sensual* element unduly predominates are

---

* Amenorrhoea means absence of menstruation, dysmenorrhea means difficult or painful menstruation, and menorrhagia means excessive menstrual flow (*Gould Medical Dictionary*).

invariably the *eldest* in the family. I never remember to have seen that referred to in any book I have read, but it is a fact undeniably. And the physiological explanation of it seems very simple. The warm love of the parents meeting in the first ardent embrace would, one naturally imagines, impress itself on the offspring. I have an instance before me in the person of Miss Phoebe Chapman. The largely-made fleshy body, the full face, expression of eyes and lips. The hair, and the romping nature with a touch of coarseness and indelicacy—all go to make up the sensual nature, full of animal instincts, and may develop into the licentious. I believe that I am myself an example of the truth of what I am saying—in constitutional temperament, I mean. It is an interesting idea considered physiologically; and morally it has a deep, a sad significance; socially also it suggests the question whether we are not justified in adopting measures by which the sensual element may not unduly predominate in our children.[16]

His feeling for May was the first real love he had experienced since the infatuation he had felt for his cousin seven years before. He worshipped her in silence and she never gave any indication that she observed it, although one of the more perceptive boarders chaffed him about it. But the problems at the school were becoming too much for him and at the end of three months he recorded:

I never had harder work and more vexations and annoyance of all kinds than I have had during these last 3 months, what with the responsibility of being a Head Master, and the fatigue of doing all the work, the fearful annoyance of having extremely troublesome boys over whom you have not sufficient control—and the vexation of dealing with disagreeable & dissatisfied parents. This is my calm and deliberate opinion.[17]

In May he received word that a Scot, Mr. MacIntosh, would relieve him of the school, and the following month he went to Sydney for a mid-year break. Most of his days were spent in the Sydney Public Library, which was the only real university he ever attended. By instinct he was an autodidact; the knowledge he absorbed and treasured was always that which he discovered for himself. Here he came upon Quételet's *Anthropométrie*, the first book to arouse his interest in anthropology, and in a reproduction of Burne-Jones's *Merlin and Vivien* his eyes were opened to a new form of art. He was enraptured by the charm of a never-never world where saints stood stiff and aureoled and angels could walk tip-toe on lily cups.[18]

On the *Surrey*, while reading Montaigne's essays, which he had

purchased prior to leaving England, he happened on a slighting reference to Rabelais. Now on the shelves of the Sydney Public Library
he discovered Rabelais for himself—"in reality a marvellous genius, a
profound thinker, a daring pioneer." For the rest of his life he
adopted the motto of the Abbey of Thelema: *"Fay ce que voudras."*
In Coleridge's *Table Talk*, which he ordered from England, he found
a passage on Rabelais utterly unlike Montaigne's strictures:

> Here was a fellow-adventurer who had discovered the same spiritual
> and enthusiastic recognition of Rabelais' immense genius. Here was
> a fellow-adventurer who discovered the same spiritual content that I
> had discovered! No critical judgement has ever caused me such a leap
> of joy.[19]

Ellis treasured the book for the rest of his life. His only luxury during
these years was books. Some he ordered from England, others he
bought from booksellers in Sydney. From the latter he bought Swinburne's *Poems and Ballads* and a complete set of Heine which he
possessed until his death. By translating many of Heine's *Lieder* he
acquired a knowledge of German which proved of inestimable value
while preparing the *Studies in the Psychology of Sex*.

In addition to Heine's *Lieder* he translated a portion of Goethe's
Dichtung und Wahrheit, Musset's *Rolla*, and Renan's *Song of Songs*.
Inspired by the spirit of Shelley and the technique of Tennyson, he
attempted some rather heavy-handed verse of his own. He wrote out
a long *précis* of *In Memoriam*, diligent and dull. He was never able
to write appreciatively of poetry, and in all his literary criticism there
is very little that touches on it.

In the evenings he was just as solitary as in the library during the
day. Usually he went to the opera, generally sitting close to the front,
where he enjoyed the spectacle while the music and words meant
little to him, although he made notes about the sensual effect of the
music.

He returned to Carcoar by boat. At the entrance to the Clarence
River the boat was grounded for a couple of days. Here he was
thrown into company with a girl about his own age; and as they
paced awkwardly up and down the deck, she broke the silence by
remarking, "Ain't the moon lovely?" Ellis was so filled with revulsion
at her vulgarity that he hurriedly excused himself. This incident, he
recalled, was the closest he ever came to intimacy in all the four years
he spent in Australia.

At the end of nine months it was time to move on again. When MacIntosh arrived to assume command of the school, he refused to pay Ellis more than a small portion of the original sum agreed upon, £50, arguing cannily that the school had deteriorated since Ellis had taken it over, although he knew he would be able to persuade most of the parents to send back the boys who had been withdrawn. Ellis, with his reasonable approach to everything, saw the sense in this, and also passively paid Messrs. Morris and Bevill the commission they charged, although they had done little to earn it. It took many years for him to learn to assert his own rights in money matters, and to the end he handled them with a certain naïveté. On one occasion, on leaving a bank after shyly opening an account, he glimpsed Morris giving the clerk a conspiratorial wink.

It was difficult to part from the Chapmans. He decided not to squeeze May's hand. Although he had rehearsed a little farewell speech, he stumbled over it and could not bring himself to look her in the eyes, an awkwardness that caused him a blush of shame whenever he remembered it. Into Bertha's eyes he looked, however, and was touched to find they were brimming with tears. "It is pleasant to think we occupy even a very small corner in a human breast," the lonely boy wrote. "She shall never know how much pleasure that kind, sympathetic, foolish little mind of hers gave in filling those tender eyes of hers with tears. And she wouldn't understand it, if she did know. Although I never met May's gaze, I do not think there were tears in her eyes."[20]

Another job must be obtained, and if teaching offered the only alternative, he must see to it that he was better qualified. Accordingly he enrolled as a student teacher and during the next three months he boarded in Morris's squalid home. At the end of the three months he seems to have had no difficulty in his test class in reading, and the written examinations were passed satisfactorily. It was time for yet another move, and the New Year, 1878, was again an occasion for summing up his progress:

> I have still no object in life. None whatever. I have not altogether lost my moral earnestness; I long to benefit my fellow-men in so far as I am able to teach them; and I feel, more strongly than ever, that the side on which nearly all the misery of the world ought to be reached is the physical side. I would cry, let me have men's bodies, you may have their souls. Let me free them from disease, and poverty, and you may have the care of their souls. Not that I am inclined to

undervalue the spiritual side of man, but I think that side of his nature is at present quite unlikely to be undervalued, and I also believe
that it is largely under the domination of the physical nature. But I
see no outlet for my earnestness yet, though I suppose it must be
through literature somehow. I recognise as my only aim, at present,
the apparently selfish one of *self-cultivation*. Culture and with all it
means. Perhaps my culture is leading me too much from severe paths;
perhaps it is not sufficiently accurate and exact; but I do not think
anything can be obtained by doing violence to my nature. My faculty
for appreciating science is developing and my reasoning powers have
also become bolder, more self-reliant, more at command. And I am
altogether something more manly grown. On my visit to Sydney in
June, I felt as I was walking along the streets that I had changed
since I had last walked there. I felt more strength, more self-reliance,
more self-possession; though with none of these qualities am I very
highly gifted now or at any other time. I am not only more manly,
but in a manner more youthful than when at Carcoar. There were
many advantages at Carcoar; there were also many disadvantages. Solitude is not fitted to foster the growth of character. And in this respect
I was fortunately situated at Grafton though not so much in the fa-
cilities for study afforded by isolation. I had two most important
advantages which I had never before possessed to any extent; the almost constant society of young men of my own age, though not with
similar tastes; and, not less important, the society of girls of my own
age. I never before knew exactly what I had, or had not in me. To
them, more than to the school—though that undoubtedly had no
small share, am I disposed to attribute the development of character
above referred to.

Physically, also, I think I have improved. During the whole of the
year I have been entirely free from my old attacks, although for nine
months I was in the hot climate of Grafton, and the other three in
Sydney, which I have never considered to agree with me. In nerve also
I think I have improved a little. During the year I became a member
of the N.S.W. Health Society; however, the suggestions offered for
putting a little life into it were considered too advanced for its present infantile state.[21]

In this state of mind he embarked on what was to be the most fateful
year in his development.

CHAPTER 3

SPARKES CREEK

IN FEBRUARY HE WAS INFORMED THAT HE HAD BEEN GIVEN A POST AS teacher at Sparkes Creek, a remote school serving the children of scattered settlers. His salary would be £110 a year. He accepted the news philosophically: "I am not by any means sure that I shall like it. It will exhibit to me a new and fine part of the country; it will help to give me experience; and, altogether I am more reconciled to it than I was a week ago."[1]

His welcome was not particularly warm. At Scone—the nearest town of any size—the local vicar gave him a bed for his first night; he was kindly but seemed reluctant or indifferent about proffering any practical advice. His host introduced Ellis to the town schoolmaster, a highly emotional Welshman, whom Ellis antagonized by his quiet, persistent questions about his avowed atheism. Finally, he met the teacher whom he was replacing at Sparkes Creek, an unprepossessing Australian, who seemed so anxious to be off that he had no time to talk.

The next morning he rode out to Sparkes Creek. Here he met Ashford, the chief settler in the district, who grudgingly allowed him to sleep on a settle for a night or so. However, the next day his host bluntly informed him that he had to leave immediately and must manage as best he could in the school house. Ellis stoically put on his tall silk hat, picked up his bag, and in dignified silence set off for the lonely shack. His resilience during the past three years had been remarkable, but now he had almost reached breaking-point.

In all the time he had been in Australia he had never felt so desolate. He would gladly have gone back to Sydney by the next coach. In *Kanga Creek*, the "Australian Idyll" Ellis wrote between 1884 and 1887, he recalled the bitter emotions of that morning as he brooded on the farmer's petulant outburst:

> It seemed like the climax to the series of petty miseries that had been descending upon him; he felt tired of this new strange life that he could not retreat from, even before it had begun. He walked still faster and as he went down by the gaunt black shea-oaks and stumbled over the smooth grey stones in the creek bed, his eyes were prickly and stinging as though they would burst. He thought it would be sweet to be a child to lie down and cry.[2]

But he did not cry. The school house was perched on a slope about a hundred yards above the creek. Built of large, rough-hewn slabs, the building looked as though it was ready to topple over. Two rooms with peeling walls opened on to a verandah. The one which was used as a school room contained a fireplace and desks, the other had only two pieces of furniture—a stool and a rough hammock of flour sacks which served as a bed. At Scone he had bought an axe, a bucket, a broom, a saucepan, a frying-pan, a plate, a cup, a knife, a fork, and two spoons. Apart from books, these were to be almost his only purchases for the next year. He sat down at a table with his chin in his hand, meditating on his gloomy position, so silent that two mice began to scamper about. Eventually there was a tap at the door and a little girl shyly held out some dishes containing mutton and a peach pie. Such occasional hospitality he was to receive from time to time from his withdrawn neighbours. His meals were frugal—porridge, tinned fish, tea, cocoa, occasionally cheese. His bills with the local Chinese grocer record a considerable amount of flour, so one can assume that he baked bread from time to time. He added a couple of blankets to the meagre furnishings; and the accounts indicate that he bought forty-two pounds of candles and twelve boxes of matches.

The hammock proved not as uncomfortable as it looked, but the first night he had very little sleep because of all the unaccustomed noises. For hours there was scurrying in the chimney and in the morning he discovered that some furry animal had been making a bed in his black silk hat. In *Kanga Creek* he recalled the sensations of that first lonely night:

He was oppressed by a dreary and profound loneliness; all his senses were abnormally awake, the barren and unaccustomed walls seemed to press fiercely towards him through the gloom. At intervals he heard the curlew's melancholy monotonous cry.[3]

But in the morning as he stood on the verandah and felt the warmth of the February sun, his spirits revived. A routine was soon established. In all he had about thirty children in his care and at last he found he had no difficulty in maintaining discipline. He divided his time between this school and one in the next valley at Junction Creek, separated by a low mountain range. At first he found the climb tiring, but soon grew accustomed to it, except for the muddy slope after a torrential rain.

His solitude was almost as complete as if he had been on a desert island. His journal does not indicate that he took any particular interest in his pupils. The settlers seem to have almost completely ignored him, regarding him indifferently as just another fleeting figure who would be gone at the end of the year like the other teachers before him. The others had been driven away by loneliness, but for someone as inner-directed and self-sufficient as Ellis, such an isolated life had much to recommend it. To break the silence he would often read aloud or sing as he climbed the steep path to Junction Creek or shout verses as he paced before his little shack. He did not recall meeting a single person on any of his walks. But there were compensations. His awareness of the natural world around him was heightened. He was fascinated by animals strange to English eyes—huge lizards lying motionless along the branches of the trees, koala bears moving away slowly as he approached, great bounding kangaroos.

He never tired of the walk to Junction Creek. Absorbed as he was in his reflections, he noted the contours of the hills, the hues of the sky, the warmth of the sun on his face. Usually the creek was a series of flat pools, but after a rainfall it could become a churning mass of water impossible for the children to cross. One evening, on his return, he was startled to see roses casting crimson splashes on the rough walls of his hut—"a thrill of rapture went through me, and I saw roses as I had never seen them before, as I shall never see them again."[4]

The simplicity of his daily routine had a tranquillizing effect on a young mind wearied by too much reflection. His face grew ruddy, he put on weight. He found himself freer from religious depression

and emotional cravings. There were no women in his life to arouse
desire, and the memory of May Chapman was fading into an idealized dream. He wrote a poem "To Bertha":

> *You often sang my favourite songs;*
> *I often liked to gaze*
> *Upon your laughing soft brown eyes,*
> *Your little household ways.*
>
> *The months passed on; the time arrived*
> *In warm October days,*
> *To leave the sun-kissed fertile land*
> *Of sugar-canes and maize.*
>
> *And so the evening came whereon*
> *The last farewells we bade;*
> *The best-loved Sonate Pathétique*
> *Once more for me you played.*
>
> *At early morn we met and said*
> *The very last goodbyes;*
> *I looked down to your face and tears*
> *Had leapt into your eyes.*
>
> *All along the grass-grown street*
> *And through the quiet town,*
> *In which my feet no more should tread,*
> *And at the wharf, and down.*
>
> *The broad fair Clarence that I loved,*
> *Your soft eyes still seemed near;*
> *It was a joy to me to think*
> *That I was worth a tear.*

Sparkes Creek Oct. 1878

This was written just a year after I had left. I felt too strongly to be
able to write about her sister, May.[5]

Sometimes he would look into the windowpane which served
him as a mirror and wonder if a woman could ever be attracted to

such an unprepossessing face. For some years he had experienced
nocturnal emissions which he carefully noted in his pocket diary.
But at Sparkes Creek he had for the first time an orgasm when awake
while he lay one day reading Brantôme's *Dames Galantes*—he could
not recall the passage, he claimed in *My Life*. His nocturnal emissions had caused him acute embarrassment because of the stains they
left on the sheets and because of fears he had gained after reading
Drysdale's *Elements of Social Science*, in which the young reader
was warned of the dangers of seminal emissions during sleep, a habit
that could cause eventual impotence—a fear that was to haunt him
for years; but this new sensation struck him as entirely natural and
beautiful. "It was not until after this event," he adds, "that I ever
became definitely conscious of any stirring of physical excitement at
the thought or the proximity of an attractive woman."[6] While Ellis
denies any recollection of the exact passage in Brantôme which excited him so unduly, I feel convinced that it is one which he alludes
to several times in the *Studies*: "The greatest nobles of the Court one
day, not knowing what else to do, went to see the girls make water,
concealed, that is to say, beneath a floor with wide cracks."[7]

In June he went to Sydney for the mid-winter break. He enjoyed
walking among people again, but his isolated life had confirmed his
habit of withdrawal. On July 2nd he wrote to his mother of running
into some French-Canadian acquaintances at the theatre—"or rather
who met me; for I never see anyone, & walk past people I know in
the most astonishing way."[8] *Kanga Creek* records his emotional state
and some of his experiences during this important year. The only
incident in the book which he claimed was entirely imaginary was a
romantic encounter with a girl in his cabin. But there is an account
of a disturbing experience in his boarding-house in Castlereagh Street
which seems to have the stamp of personal knowledge:

> On the last night of his stay in Sydney he went early to his room
> where loud occasional bursts of merriment reached him till long past
> midnight. When he came down in the morning the room was disar-
> ranged, and the air close and heavy, with a vague odour of brandy; a
> woman's chignon of those days lay on the floor.[9]

The incident is not recorded in his journal, but even if the incident
in the boarding-house were not entirely literal—and it was a brothel,
as previous details indicate—it seems evident that he must have had

some experience such as this. Certainly he was exposed in Sydney streets late at night to the squalid scenes common in a raw colonial city.

At Sparkes Creek he had even more time for his wide and varied reading. Here he "rediscovered" the Bible. Since he had begun to feel his faith slipping away from him, he had almost abandoned looking at it at all. Now he turned to it again in a new spirit, and night after night he responded rapturously to its beauties by the light of his candle. His writing at this point began to develop characteristic features. Before he was twelve he was writing a self-conscious, sententious prose; by fifteen he was concentrating on verse; by seventeen he had turned to sonnets, always autobiographical in substance but highly derivative in mood and form. Now at nineteen he began to keep large commonplace books which he filled with observations and comments, generally on his reading. The style is an easy, conversational colloquy with himself, much the same sort of writing that went into his first *Impressions and Comments*. During this period he came, too, under the influence of Newman's graceful cadences, a prose that has proved inspiring but inimitable to many fledgling writers.

Among the religious works regularly read by Ellis after his arrival in Australia were Renan's *Life of Jesus* and Strauss's *Old Faith for New*. Neither of these cool, rational expositions provided any sustenance for a highly emotional and repressed youth. He was suffering from spiritual dryness, acedia, fed by his loneliness; little wonder that the world seemed cold and inhospitable and Henry Havelock an easily dispensable atom. This state of mind was close to that of Teufelsdrock in *Sartor Resartus* or the grieving narrator of *In Memoriam*, both longing for an organic universe in which part was linked to part in luminous beauty. For the mid-nineteenth-century intellectual, Nature no longer provided a stable and comprehensible world. With the impact of those hammers which would never cease tormenting Ruskin, melancholy men stoically faced a Godless, mechanistic world in which Nature appeared not only menacing but, almost worse, stolidly indifferent. Most of late-nineteenth-century poetry became what Lionel Trilling described as "a plangent threnody" for a lost world. Nineteenth-century biographies are filled with spiritual crises; Ellis, temperamentally, was destined to undergo a crisis in any environment, but his isolation rendered the experience all the more intense. At eighteen he was a bewildered child "wandering between two worlds, one dead,/ The other powerless to be born." He grieved for the simple faith of his mother, the certainties of which would never satisfy him again. On the other hand, he tried to persuade himself, his intellect must accept a developmental conception of the universe; and while he could not reject the possibility that the race was moving towards greater and greater potentialities, such rationalized optimism was not sufficient to comfort a yearning young heart.

As a child he had been trained in the unyielding simplicities of an evangelical faith—trained, moreover, by a woman who had been "converted" in her youth. Conversion was a term and an experience which gave spiritual drama to the narrow world of his childhood. Would he, too, be called to the arms of Jesus? His first encounter with anyone who could open wider windows had been with Angus MacKay, the most liberating force in his early life. Now, left alone in Australia for three years, with no supervised religious observances, and in an atmosphere that both geographically and mentally seemed far more tranquil than anything he had ever known, Ellis's spiritual apprenticeship developed in loneliness and freedom, the most suitable milieu possible for a serious and contemplative young man who subjected every book that came his way to rigorous analysis. In 1884 he tried to describe the experience to Olive Schreiner:

> "I said that if you had sometimes been with me at Sparkes Creek I should have been completely happy. I don't know if I ought to have said that. The kind of happiness that I had then was one in which human beings had no part. I loved no one much—not even any of my pupils. I was absorbed in my own thoughts and in nature and in books, I was *delivered* from human beings."[10]

With his romantic longings and unfulfilled religious fervour, he hungered for some message of consolation. This was to come through the silent medium of a book.

His eye, eager always to seize on anything that opened up new aspects of the world, was caught one day by a review either of James Hinton's books or of a recently published biography of Hinton by Ellice Hopkins. At this point he knew nothing of James Hinton (1822–1875). Hinton had lived a tormented existence, and was a strange figure to serve as an emblematic model. As a boy he had worked in a wholesale draper's shop in Whitechapel, where he was shocked by his discovery of the degradation to which women were subjected. He attended medical school, but was deeply interested in philosophic subjects, in which he read widely. He fell in love with a Miss Margaret Haddon, but she rejected him three times because he had lost his religious faith. She finally consented to marry him when he seemed to regain his belief. He built up a large medical practice and became a leading aural surgeon, but his main interests continued to be speculative. In 1859 he published *Man and His Dwelling Place*, an analysis of the relationship between science and religion, followed by *Life in Nature* (1862) and *The Mystery of Pain* (1866). He bought an estate in the Azores and on a voyage there he underwent one of his numerous spiritual crises when he suddenly realized that man is simply a limitation of the divine spirit and can attain true life only through unselfishness. He decided that he must abandon his practice and preach this incomprehensible message to the world, but in order to attain the leisure for his goal, he exhausted himself with work, and on his return to the Azores in 1875 died from what the *Dictionary of National Biography* describes as "acute inflammation of the brain." He was an obscure messiah with a small but fervid following.

What the review contained that aroused Ellis's interest is not known. Without any discriminating supervision of his reading, he tended to read all sorts of unrelated things, the good and the bad undifferentiated. It is a great pity that as a youth he did not have the opportunity to come in contact with any really first-class minds. Hinton was far from being a first-class mind and it is regrettable that he should have gained a permanent influence over Ellis at an impressionable age. Ellis sent off to England for *Life in Nature*, which he duly read with interest but with no particularly intense reaction. He laid it aside for several months, and when he returned to it, it was the one book in the world which could speak directly to him. Ellis was deeply attracted to the mystical vision which Hinton seemed to accommodate to his scientific objectivity. Those who have experienced a spiritual illumination are able to describe it only in the most general terms.* It is easier to trace the "how" than the "what." There is generally a long period of aridity, of isolation, sometimes a sense of unbearable sin. Then there suddenly occurs an illumination, a revelation, a flash of truth conveyed through music, the spoken voice, or the written word. The subsequent period of attained peace, cer-

---

* Ellis's Preface to a 1931 edition of *Life in Nature* leaves Hinton's message as turgid and amorphous as ever.

titude, the possession of an enveloping truth, seems to defy description. "I trod on air; I moved in light," Ellis rapturously recalled many years later.[11] What Hinton seemed to give him was a conviction that all life was one and that he and nature were not separate and apart but flowing each into the other. He suddenly perceived the divine unity in all living things. "I was as far as ever from any faith in Christianity, in God, in immortality; all my definitely formulated convictions on separate points remained unchanged. Yet I was myself the whole universe—that is to say, my attitude towards it—was changed."[12] This same acceptance of the spirituality of the universe, of the Eternal in the Now, he could perhaps have received from Carlyle's *Sartor Resartus*, a book which affected many other youths, although Ellis would not have been impressed by Carlyle's contempt for science. Hinton's message might have been vaporous, but it was readily received by a young man whose senses were acutely tuned to the world of unspoiled nature that lay around him. If he had been living in a city, he might have been unmoved; but in Sparkes Creek it was possible to believe in the divine beauty of the universe.

In later years Ellis wrote about this vital experience in *Impressions and Comments*, in the chapter on "The Art of Religion" in *The Dance of Life*, and in his autobiography. But all these accounts are written in retrospect, with an emphasis on its significance to the mature individual. The record in Ellis's journal of that period gives the full impact of what the experience meant to him.

No "conversion" occurs without fertile minds and ready hands to receive it. A series of messages is imprinted on the receptive sensibility. In the spring he received word of the death of his mother's friend Mrs. Johnson, who had taught him to play the piano and to whom he had been tenderly attached. The entry in his diary is touching in its loving, empathetic understanding:

> She was one of the very few persons who bear me affection; and she was by far my earliest friend, out of my own family. I have always had affection for her; recently it had increased, as my sympathy grasped the fact of one of the unloved,—of whom in our present baneful social state there must needs be many—passing through life with all the great capacities for love undeveloped or wasted on little objects, and finally lost in the grave never having found its fellow. I remember, as a child,—I do not know how young I was—being allowed to look over the treasures in Johnnie's desk. I came upon a little piece of twisted paper; I was about to untwist it, when she prevented me saying that

a young gentleman had been playing with that, when talking to her many years ago. Doubtless she thought I was too young to take any notice of what she said; and it is only of recent years that this little piece of paper has had for me its true significance. I fancy that touching little incident in Wendell Holmes' "Professor" first showed it to me. I think of the whole treasures of affection of a human heart hung on that little scrap of paper twisted by a youth—more loved than loving, probably—kept sacred for fifty years, for a life-time. Probably one or other of Johnnie's treasures may come into my possession as a remembrance; rather than anything I would long to preserve sacredly that scrap of twisted paper.[13]

Then, in May, he heard that the Reverend John Erck, the clergyman whose eloquent preaching had once so moved him, was planning to write to him—"that undoubtedly serves to make visible to myself all the currents of thought with which I have been occupied—for I am always thinking." He found himself rereading Matthew Arnold's essay on Joubert,

> and I was struck, as I had not been before, with that remark of Joubert's: "It is not hard to know God, provided one will not force oneself to define him." I felt that there might be a profound truth in that. I have been going along all the time with the conviction that the intellect only must be appealed to in matters of belief. It never occurred to me that I ought to have proved that first. Notwithstanding the clearness with which I thought I was looking on the subject, here was a most monstrous assumption (whether true or not is another question) with which I set out—the intellect is the only appeal in matters of religion. I begin to see very clearly that there can be no religious belief on *purely* intellectual grounds.[14]

These were the particular events and trains of thought which preoccupied a mind that was congenitally serious and ruthlessly sincere. "The first glimmering of this truth I owe to Hinton, and the results of it on my religious beliefs I am unable to calculate. Already I begin to see a meaning in what had before had for me no meaning."[15]

This was written on May 18th, 1878. The next entry is dated July 21st. The passage deserves to be quoted in full:

> And so I am "converted." The factors in my "conversion" are, 1st hearing that Mr Erck was about to write to me; 2nd reading Hinton's "Life in Nature"; 3rd reading Spencer's "Study of Sociology." But it would be absurd to say that these three things *produced* the spiritual revolution I have undergone. But that I have undergone a spiritual

revolution there can be no question. For the last three years I have known nothing but doubt, and when I felt no doubt I felt misery. I was living in a vacant universe which I felt to be a machine. I was a living thing groping my way amid dead blind relentless laws, ready at every moment to crush me. For the last three years, I said. It was not always so. Four years ago, as a boy, I was religious (for I was always religious), Church of England, and of rather Broad Church tendencies. There came a time when vast questions crowded one after another, threatening to overwhelm me. For I would not shirk them—rather I could not. And so one by one I met them and was conquered, and they left me alone with my sorrow. I always sought for Truth—for Truth, even if it were Truth crucified. And I believe that even then I was following Truth; it was at the command of Truth and not of any phantom that I gave up my beliefs. For I had no right to them. I had found them and adopted them; they were not mine. But if Truth takes away, she poured thousand-fold in my bosom. She took away my beliefs because they were not mine. And thus there is for me no more doubt. I met the waves of the sea of doubt, and battled with them, and never looked back at the lowlands I had left. And I have reached shore now. I have reached a height I had not dreamed of before.[16]

He goes on to discuss the fact that he has acquired no new beliefs, rather "a friendly disposition towards the real order of the universe." By September 1st he was able to record the occurrence of another great mental revolution. By now he had received Ellice Hopkins's *Life and Letters of James Hinton*. He came upon a passage in which Hinton, at the age of nineteen, on the advice of a medical friend, entered St. Bartholomew's Hospital as a student:

When I got so far a flash of thought, as it were, passed through my brain. I laid the book down and jumped up. I may not be fit to be a doctor, but I shall never make anything else. And then I wondered how ever it was that this had never occurred to me before. Since that evening, my opinion has not altered in the least.[17]

Ellis then goes on to list and analyze the advantages for taking such a course:

... for the last four years I have felt a kind of passion of ameliorating in so far as may be, human suffering and ignorance, and to start from the physical side. And I can see now how well it is that my thoughts never turned in that direction till now; that *culture* has been my aim, that I have striven, in so far as may be, to put myself in sympathy with literature, religion, science, art, and thought in their different forms, and that my tastes have never been more for one than for another. For I know, now, that such culture, little though it may have been, was not wasted, and that I can never become a *mere* "medical practitioner."[18]

By November 24th he could write, "The entire settlement of my religious feelings seems accomplished." He admits that after reading Kingsley's *Hypatia* he had experienced "a slight revulsion of feeling." A drawing back, an uneasy reassessment of seemingly momentous decisions, is a frequent reaction, part of the general pattern of conversion. Ellis seems to have rapidly regained his equilibrium and he went on to read another book with great admiration—Herbert Spencer's *First Principles*, intending to follow this with the *System of Philosophy*:

> I was fascinated by that large, calm all-seeing gaze with so profound an insight, with nothing of that one-sidedness of so many clear-seeing minds, was able to assert that all things are "very good." It was not so much his clearness & positiveness; but rather the sense of the vastness & complexity of all things, of a great mystery, too, which surrounds us & which we cannot penetrate—it was this rather that fascinated me.[19]

But emotionally there was something lacking in Spencer, and here James Hinton provided all that he wanted. This was to be the last entry recorded in his journal in Australia. Apparently the School Inspector arrived in October and found everything satisfactory but, with Ellis's eye on the future, the visit did not seem worth recording. At the end of what he called "the most eventful year in my life," he shut the door of the school house for the last time, rode into Scone, paid his bills, and bade farewell to his acquaintances, all of whom commiserated with him for having endured a long year in such total isolation. "How little," he later mused, "they all knew of the gateways to heaven!"[20]

His father had made arrangements for him to return to England on the ship *La Hogue*. Kindly Mr. Chapman, his former employer, came to Sydney to see him off. His main preparation for the voyage, as it had been before he left England, was the accumulation of a store of books. During the whole period he had been in Australia he had kept accounts with two Sydney booksellers, and the records of his extensive purchases are still extant.

On February 26th, 1879, as the ship threaded its way through icebergs near the Falkland Islands, he summarized the year he had passed through:

I have at last found peace—not perfect peace, we never find that, but still, relatively, peace. My doubts are all at rest now. I can look with calmness on the world; not only with calmness, but with joy. I no longer feel myself isolated from things or from men. And I have that for which I aimed so ardently—an aim. I can see now a definite outlet for my energies, a point round which my efforts must centre, instead of as hitherto, being dissipated in all directions. And yet all these energies which seemed dissipated, were not really so. Nothing of that self-culture was wasted. These three years I have spent in Australia seem to me like those three years during which Paul was in Arabia; and, like him too, I also have seen and felt unspeakable things.[21]

THE LONDON IDEALISTS

FIFTY MILES FROM ENGLAND TWO CHAFFINCHES CAME OUT TO MEET
the ship. Ellis felt a thrill of pleasure at coming home. He arrived
on April 22nd, 1879, now twenty years old. He had left almost four
years before to the day; he had led an extraordinary, isolated life, almost symbolic in the initiatory setting it provided for silence, for
reflection, for decision. Few youths are given such an opportunity to
mature *in extremis* without unnecessary distractions. If it were argued
that a laboratory situation, cut off in large measure from other people,
was not a normal atmosphere in which to nurture a developing mind
and body, it could also be plausibly argued that an unusual individual
would have chafed at the restraints of a conventional background.
Given what we know of Ellis's background, and what we are to
learn of his later life, the Australian experience seems a preternaturally appropriate interval in the pattern of his life, and certainly
one that he never regretted. A year later he was to write: "I
sometimes long to be back in Australia. Not since I left Sparkes
Creek have I known anything of the *ecstatic*—I may well call it—joy
of thought. Nor do I now feel anything of that delightful communion with Nature—it was such—that I then often felt."[1] Never
again was he to experience those same rhapsodic vibrations of silent
communion with nature, although he was often to seek them. In an
essay written in 1896, "An Open Letter to Biographers," Ellis advised
a biographer to concentrate upon "the curve of life that has its
summit at puberty and ends with the completion of adolescence:

whatever else there is to make is made then. The machine has been created; during these years it is wound up to perform its work in the world. What follows after counts for something but always for less."[2]

A pause followed his return, a quiescent period, *reculer pour mieux sauter*. He found his family still in South London, settled at 24 Thornsett Road, Anerley, not far from the Crystal Palace, where they were to remain for the next two years. Shortly before his return Louie wrote to ask if he had grown a beard or a moustache: "I like to see men with a bare chin they look so good."[3] (He retained an unshaven face for most of the year following his return.) He and his sister greeted each other with shy curiosity. The two older ones were growing into young women. Edie, the youngest, had been less than a year old when he left. After a long period of emotional aridity, Ellis found it delightful to be in close contact with four lively girls. He was especially attracted to Louie, whom he loved tenderly until her death in December 1928; and we should listen attentively to his brief comments about her in *My Life*:

> The most vivacious and intelligent [of my sisters], Louie, was especially sympathetic to me, and with her I formed an intimate friendship which at first was touched by sexual emotion. This could not have arisen if the long absence during which she grew into womanhood had not destroyed that familiarity which inhibits the development of sexual interest. This little experience was valuable to me, apart from the permanent deeper tenderness which it brought into our relationship. It enabled me to understand from personal knowledge how it is that, as a rule, sexual emotion fails to spring up between close relatives or people living together from before puberty, and under what circumstances—by no means of such rare occurrence as is usually believed—it may spring up. I was thereby enabled in later years to give clear precision to my conception of the psychological foundation of exogamy.[4]

A few years after his return, in 1884, he recalled to Olive Schreiner this "sexual emotion" as "passion." This is all we know of it, but it must be borne in mind when we consider his relationships with other women. Ellis, who always liked to consider himself a daring pioneer in speaking frankly about sex, was usually very reticent about committing his personal problems and experiences to print; he might have admired Rousseau's candour, but he never emulated it. It is significant that he spoke so freely to Olive Schreiner, who came into his life as the ideal confidante at a time when he was

longing to pour out his heart with unrestrained abandon. Only one
reference to Louie appears in the diary in this first year after his
return to England. He had begun to neglect his journal and there are
no entries between one written on board *La Hogue* and January 1st,
1880, when he resumed it once more. He had just returned from
midnight service with Louie and he writes:

> I have thought a good deal lately about my sister Louie and her
> spiritual difficulties. I always have thought of her, but now more than
> ever. I long, also, to gain her entire sympathy, & to give her all the
> help I can, with such poor wisdom as my own experience may teach
> me.[5]

Three days later he wrote her a remarkable letter.

> "I don't want to seem to be advising you, Louie. Because I know
> we always find it so very easy to give advice. I only want to tell
> you what I have found to be so very true myself. And I know that
> you must some day find much of it to be true too. I think a great
> deal about you for I know that you must change a great deal, and
> I want very much that you may change wisely. I know it is not
> probable because we seldom learn to go right except by going
> wrong, and we are often most wrong when we think we are most
> right. But even that perhaps is good. So that, if you care at all for
> what I think, I want you to remember that we must not *distort*
> our nature. Remember that naturalness and spontaneousness of
> character such as you have (it is not naïveté; naïveté is being
> *childlike*, and you are not childlike) are gifts. Even if they had no
> other good they are a means of making people love you and so
> increasing your influence. I know we cannot alter our character
> easily; but by believing our nature to be all wrong we shall help
> to change and distort it. I have noticed in you a kind of sense of
> the impropriety of being natural—as if you didn't like yourself—
> and wanted to be *proper* and affected and at those moments you
> have been least lovable, and therefore least Christ-like. But do
> not suppose I do not sympathise with you. You do it because you
> know, as we all do, that you are not good, that there are all sorts
> of things about you that you would give anything to alter. We
> must *empty by filling*. If we want to get rid of our badness we
> must do it by embracing goodness. Mind, this is not a matter of
> theory."

And so it went on for pages, ending up:

"All that I have been writing comes to this:

"*Be natural*. Be yourself. Do not try to repress your nature, but to develop it, not to make it smaller, but larger. Embrace everything that you can—nothing that you cannot. Throw your arms around the world and kiss it—Christ's world.

"*Be true*. Be quite straightforward and honest in your beliefs. Believe nothing that you cannot with all your soul. Never mind what other people believe, or what other people think you ought to believe. Be true to *yourself*, make all things true to yourself and yourself true to all things. Do not mould yourself to other people's beliefs; that is never right.

"*Educate yourself*—in every way (you know *educate* means lead out). Sympathise with human souls when you are able to do so; go into communion with nature; love all forms of art. In all these ways you will be making your nature richer and deeper and more fitted to do God's work in the world."[6]

The skills and fervour that would have gone into an Evangelical preacher, the firm beliefs he had arrived at in Australia, the impact of James Hinton—all these have coalesced in this extraordinary letter for a young man to write to his sister. He had obviously not yet rejected traditional Christianity, but no reference to it was ever again to appear in his writings.

Although his appearance at church services was becoming increasingly desultory, so long as he lived in his mother's house he continued to kneel through prayers every morning with the rest of the family. He tutored his younger sisters, read, went for walks. Temporarily the question of a career remained in abeyance, but it could not continue to do so indefinitely and in the spring of 1880 he took a teaching post in Smethwick, a suburb of Birmingham. The only entry for this period in his journal is the account of a visit to Stratford. His letters to his mother are concerned exclusively with matters unrelated to his teaching. He despised the Headmaster; and in *My Life* it is significant that the only incident he records is of the Headmaster's tearful wife stumblingly confiding her marital problems to him. He was too inexperienced at this point to know how to handle the situation, and his awkwardness prevented the development of further complications. "She never came again. That was the first time in my life such an incident had happened to me"; and, he added wryly, "it was far from being the last."[7]

He continued to think about James Hinton's teaching, although he was beginning to see that it was Hinton's spirit and method, rather than his opinions, that he admired. He was a little uneasy, too, about the way Hinton couched his message in orthodox Christian terminology. But he still greatly admired Hinton's willingness to question assumptions that were generally taken for granted and to follow his speculations into unknown terrain. Almost immediately after returning to England he decided to write to Ellice Hopkins, the editor of *Life and Letters of James Hinton*, inquiring about unpublished manuscripts to which she had referred in her book.* Ellice Hopkins forwarded his letter to Hinton's widow, who wrote him a warm letter inviting him to visit her and her sister, Caroline Haddon, one of Hinton's most devoted supporters. On January 6th, 1880, he was invited to dine with Mrs. Hinton, her son, Howard, and Miss Haddon at her home in High Barnet. Their mentor seemed to have been forgotten by the world, and it was delightful to have an eager young man come from the other side of the globe to tell them that his life had been changed by James Hinton. Ellis, in turn, was informed that they did not much care for Ellice Hopkins's *Life and Letters*. Miss Haddon stated her conviction that Hinton's spiritual biography had not yet been written, and Mrs. Hinton added that if the complete truth were known about him, it would not be believed. Her husband had told her that when he was dead people would say that he was a good man. "Will you always say that I was not?" he instructed her; "*You* know I am not," to which she replied loyally, "You are a darling."[8]

Ellis then told them about the part Hinton had played in his conversion. He was obviously sincere, a providential gift from heaven, and he was invited to stay with them for three days at the beginning of March. Hinton had died in 1875, and his widow had saved masses of unpublished papers; the group began to make eager plans for making these presentable to the world. Ellis's first suggestion was to compile a volume that would be called "Thoughts on Genius and Art." Young Hinton thought that the two men could

---

* He also wrote to Herbert Spencer, but received a form letter announcing that Mr. Spencer's diminished energies made it impossible for him to reply personally to inquiries.

collaborate on this venture and suggested that perhaps Ellis should receive a share of the profits. Later, in his room, Ellis jotted down his impressions of the conversation. He was clearly troubled by Hinton's views on women which were beginning to emerge in the family discussion, views that had not been expounded in *Life in Nature*. It seemed "inadvisable," he believed,

> to show his MSS to people except to a small circle of intimate admirers. It is easy to imagine the nature of the solution he proposes; and from some of the MSS Mrs. Hinton has lent me I see it distinctly expressed from this principle; put *others* first and all pleasure will be right. Pleasure thus rests on self sacrifice.[9]

Mrs. Hinton assured him that Hinton's belief in the necessity of *serving* women had been misinterpreted by some of his followers; and in the coming weeks he was to meet some of these devotees, most of whom proved to be elderly women. A Miss Agnes Jones was particularly anxious to discuss Hinton, whom she obviously venerated, although she was still somewhat aggrieved that Hinton had shown to someone else a "Confessional" that she had written for his eyes alone. She compared him to Shelley, and, as an example of his impulsiveness, described how he once went barefoot down Fleet Street to understand a beggar's feelings. Again, at a dinner party, while discussing the poor, Hinton flourished the carving knife at a terrified lady, shouting, "We want blood, Mrs. Chambers, we want blood!" On another occasion he got drunk in order to see whether he would attack his wife. "The results," Ellis noted in his humourless way, "I believe, were not remarkable." He began to hear even more disturbing anecdotes about Hinton. Some people considered him "serpentine and insincere"; there were odd stories about the nature of his dedicated service to women; some people said he was distinctly mad before he died, and there was an ugly rumour that he had died of syphilis. Another rumour had it that he committed suicide in the Azores. It was all very confusing, and not at all what one would expect of a spiritual mentor; but, after all, Ellis reasoned, did it really matter? What was important was the *spirit* of Hinton's work. Hinton had been responsible for his own conversion; now Ellis could repay the debt by helping to introduce him to a wider public. He was more than willing to do most of the work in pursuit of this noble task, and the startled Hintons were immensely grateful to this youth who promised to raise Hinton from his undeserved obscurity.

Working from the unpublished manuscripts, Ellis completed a *précis* of what seemed to him the major aspects of Hinton's meandering thought. This was accepted by a liberal religious magazine, *The Modern Review*, and published in October 1881, under the title "James Hinton as Religious Thinker." In this article and in "Hinton's Later Thought" (*Mind*, July 1884) he carefully avoided any discussion of Hinton's views on women. He also spent many hours with Miss Haddon helping her to edit a full volume of extracts from Hinton's work, and went on to collaborate with Mrs. Hinton on another collection, *The Lawbreaker*, published in 1884 under Mrs. Hinton's name although it was the dedicated young disciple who had actually done all the work.

Naturally he told the Hinton circle about his dream of becoming a doctor and the financial problems standing in his way since his father had a large family to support. James Hinton had already been a powerful spiritual force in his life; now he was to prove the practical means of advancing his career. Caroline Haddon, who ran a girls' boarding school in Dover, offered to lend him £200 to add to the £100 which his mother had inherited from his old friend Miss Johnson. As Ellis was often to say, his life was full of miracles. Ellis does not seem to have had many qualms about accepting the money, although he consulted his old teacher Angus MacKay, who urged him to accept the offer. The money was to be regarded as a loan, but Miss Haddon died before it could be repaid. Understandably, Ellis always felt a great sense of obligation both to her and to the Hintons. Almost in a gesture of repayment, in 1918 he published his wife Edith's book *James Hinton: A Sketch*, to which he contributed a preface; and as late as 1931 he brought out a new edition of *Life in Nature* (with another vague preface), a book which predictably had no sale. With time, Ellis's views became more realistic and sophisticated, but he always retained this childlike loyalty to a man who he believed had changed his life. As far as the immediate events in his life were concerned, his gratitude explains his loyalty to Caroline Haddon—and, indirectly, to Hinton—when this loyalty was to be severely tested two or three years later.

By living at home, where he would not have to pay board, he now found it possible to attend medical school. Once the resolve had been taken in Australia, there never seems to have been any deviation in his mind, although there was no sense of enthusiasm or dedication about his chosen vocation. It was simply something that must be done. The question of which medical school he was to attend was settled by the man who had delivered him, Dr. Alfred Carpenter, who by now had a reputation as the foremost private practitioner in England. It was his mother's decision that they should consult him; and it was immediately resolved—in late 1880— that he should attend Dr. Carpenter's own hospital, St. Thomas's.

During the seven long years that Ellis attended St. Thomas's— and in the hindsight of later years—he maintained a curiously detached and compartmentalized view of his medical training. Ellis took seven rather than the usual five years to obtain his degree because of his ineptitude at examinations and because his real interests lay elsewhere. In order to qualify to enter St. Thomas's he tried the University of London examinations and failed, but was able to fall back on his Sydney University matriculation, which surprisingly was recognized by St. Thomas's (perhaps with some encouragement from Dr. Carpenter, who was on the staff). That he had built up his health in the invigorating outdoor life he had led in Australia must have stood him in good stead during the drudgery—for so he viewed it—of those long years. Two hours of each day were spent in travelling between home and hospital. Many of his courses demanded tedious memorization, and in later years, when analyzing the difficulties he had encountered in medical school, he concluded that he had a congenital problem in absorbing and storing facts. He developed a positive antipathy towards anatomy and pharmacology. Examinations were a torment to him and many of Olive Schreiner's letters to him contain pleas that he should study for them. Certainly he must have seemed something of an odd character among the students as he lingered on year after year. Following the pattern of his school days, he made no friends with the other students—with one exception. This was a man ten years older than himself, John Barker Smith, a chemist who entered medical school at the same time. Smith was a high-strung, volatile man who suffered a nervous breakdown while still at St. Thomas's, but among the other raw students he stood out as a figure of mature and varied interests. He and Ellis became close companions in exploring London's museums and attending meetings and lectures of scientific societies. Even as a very young man Ellis made much of his Suffolk ancestry, and Smith, who had been born in Sudbury, stimulated his interest in investigating old Suffolk cemeteries. Ellis often attributed some of his close friendships to the fact that the person he was fond of turned out to

share his East Anglian background. Because of this mutual enthusiasm, Smith remained Ellis's closest friend over the years, and
they keenly enjoyed numerous expeditions into Suffolk until Smith's
death in 1928. During the course of his life Ellis often said that he
never lost a friend. His emotions were deep, his sense of loyalty was
profound and undeviating, and the mutual attachment between the
two men was one of the more important relationships in his life.
While he was never easily sociable, Ellis's capacity for steadfast
friendship is one of the major aspects of his character which begins
to emerge during this period.

After the years in Australia, where he had had no opportunity to
develop friendships, it is understandable that he was ready for
shared intellectual interests and his starved emotions were eager
to form a close attachment. The experience at St. Thomas's might
have drained him entirely were it not for the fact that the excite-
ments and challenges of London acted as a constant stimulus to his
curiosity. It says much for his innate stability that he was able to
cram so much into this first decade after his return to England.
Inevitably there were to be physical disorders as a result of over-
straining his system. He began to suffer from nervous excitability,
especially insomnia, as his mind was racing with ideas by the end of
the day. The nervous agitation was controlled by a prescription for
nux vomica; and he learned to regulate the sleeplessness by avoiding
stimulating books before retiring. Thus he set up a pattern of early-
morning work which he was to follow for the rest of his life. Incidentally, during this period he went to a phrenologist, who told him
that his sense of caution was almost too highly developed—"to the
injury of my resolution, but determination well marked, powers of
language, speech, bad; organ of human nature extremely large—
should always be able to know whom I could trust."

He was brimming with energy, and every subject in the world
(except perhaps pharmacology) seemed interesting. He was longing
to write; and with extraordinary confidence, almost as soon as he was
back in England, he began to send off reviews and articles to various
publications. There is no evidence that any of these was rejected;
and as early as August 1880 a review of a book on Rubens appeared
in *The Pen*. It has the sententiously hectoring tone of a youthful
critic lecturing an author on his defects. Although he could not
have seen more than half a dozen of Rubens's paintings in his life,
this did not deter him from discussing the subject with total con-

fidence. The author, he declared, "falls into several small errors which are at once patent to the student of Rubens." Ellis was soon to abandon this supercilious tone in his writing, but the review nevertheless indicates a remarkable appreciation of Rubens for someone who had recently emerged from the Australian bush.

This lack of hesitation about expressing his views on almost any subject led to a wide variety of articles on the "woman question," socialism, contemporary fiction and poetry, and theology. One of the earliest—and most interesting so far as his development is concerned—is an article, "What Is Pureness?", which appeared in *Modern Thought* in April 1881. When in the previous September an article, "The Sanction of Pureness," had caught his eye with its air of tight-lipped Victorian primness, he decided, by attacking it indirectly, to advance the Hintonian point of view. The major point he attempted to make was that the whole question of "pureness" needed to be re-examined and that, contrary to general opinion, pureness did not necessarily mean sexual continence. Hinton had had privately printed a small pamphlet entitled *Others' Needs*, and Ellis's heavily scored copy bears a close resemblance to the burden of his article. It was not surprising that Hinton's seeming defence of a form of hedonism might have been open to misinterpretation. "When the regard is to others," Hinton had written,

> a man's goodness has no relation to any abstaining from pleasure. In truth, so far from this, a goodness which consists in a wish to serve others must prompt a desire, rather, that the actions by which that service can be rendered should be pleasurable ones. For the desire will be the most efficient service, that is, for the most perfect performance of the pleasurable deed. And deeds are most perfectly performed when they are pleasurable.[10]

It is not difficult to see the close connection that could be drawn between the Epicureanism of the Abbey of Thelema—*Fay ce que voudras*—and Hinton's seductive argument for doing as one likes as long as one persuades oneself that the main object is to please others. But at this point Ellis was still too naïve to understand exactly what Hinton had in mind. All he could see was that Hinton had the courage to point out the destructiveness of conventional restraints. Ellis began his article by stating that Christ had come into a society which regarded pureness as outward action; and although He gave primacy to pureness of heart, this aspect of His teaching had not been accepted. "Charity has nearly lost its connection with love, and pureness has become synonymous with the chastity of the body." Ellis goes on to argue that the highest truth lies in the reconciliation of opposites:

> Let us place the test of pureness in the heart; and not in the outward action, and all is well. The opposites are reconciled. And not until pureness ceases to mean absolute negation of sexual relations, save within certain prescribed and inviolable bonds, shall it have received its sanction.[11]

And what would this mean in practice? The answer, to say the least, was puzzling:

> Let the thought be wholly on human needs or "service" as it has been called; let the mere desire for indulgence apart from the thought of others be thrown aside; let, in short, the self be cast out; and all the conditions are fulfilled. Then it is that all things become ours.[12]

These ideas he had discovered in "one of the original thinkers of our time, to whose unpublished writings on this subject I am indebted, that in what we call sins are the confused expressions of Nature's claims for a higher order. It is towards that higher order that we must look."*[13] The language might have been allusive but the point was abundantly clear, and it was not surprising that his piece elicited some indignant rejoinders. Ellis took the experience to heart. He decided that he had been misunderstood because he had been expressing himself in too indirect, too self-conscious a literary style. The misunderstanding might quite possibly have arisen because of the ambiguity of Hinton's position and by Ellis—inexperienced as he was in the whole matter—not quite knowing what to make of Hinton. At any rate, he decided that in future he would write in a more vigorous, straightforward way.

Far more gratifying was the response to his first fully appreciative

---

* In *My Life* he writes: "I had already taken a tiny step on the path along which my life-work was to lie and I expounded the same conception of 'pureness' more clearly and elaborately in my *Little Essays of Love and Virtue* forty years later." What Ellis neglects to point out is an important difference between the two essays. In the earlier one he makes the operative principle of sexual morality to be "others' needs"— and it seems questionable whether he had any idea what he or Hinton meant by this. In any case he was to stumble awkwardly over the question two or three years later. There is no talk of "others' needs" in the later essay. It is simply an exposition of the dangers of abstaining from natural and necessary sexual expression, and the fatuity of linking sexual behaviour with morality.

essay, "The Novels of Thomas Hardy," which appeared in *The Westminster Review* in April 1883. It is the questioning rebel in Hardy which he admires above all else, precisely the quality that most readers were beginning to feel uneasy about. Ellis examines all the novels that Hardy had written to date and concludes that for Hardy love is essentially "the one business of life."[14] The women are depicted with remarkable delicacy, "Undines of the earth," driven always by native instinct. Interested primarily in the psychology of the novels, Ellis points out that all the women in the novels are weak, even when weakness is an aspect of their strength. While he concluded by stating that "The time has not yet come for forming a final estimate of Mr. Hardy's work," his prognostication that Hardy would continue in the vein of delicate comedy displayed in *The Hand of Ethelberta* was to prove completely wrong; rather, it was to be "the peculiar power" of *Far from the Madding Crowd* that would produce the profound and deeply disturbing books of Hardy's great last period—*Tess* and *Jude*—for which he will be remembered. While Ellis might have been wrong about Hardy's final contribution to the novel, for John Bayley his article is "the most searching and sensitive essay ever written on Hardy, the more so because it neither praises the novels in the conventional way, nor makes what had come to be the equally conventional attack on their vices."[15]

Hardy was delighted with the article and in a letter dated April 28th wrote to say:

> "I consider the essay a remarkable paper in many ways, and can truly say that the writing itself, with its charm of style, and variety of allusion, occupied my mind when first reading it far more than the fact that my own unmethodical books were its subject-matter."[16]

He concluded gracefully that he hoped to read more of Ellis's writings in future, "and I believe I shall discover them without a mark." Ellis was greatly pleased by this recognition, particularly as he had put enormous time and care into the preparation of the essay. He believed that its success indicated that he had now passed beyond his period of literary apprenticeship.

It was important, too, that it had been accepted by the most prestigious of all nineteenth-century periodicals. Soon after the article appeared, the editor, the renowned Dr. John Chapman, expressed a desire to meet him. A meeting was arranged at which Dr.

Chapman encouraged him to contribute more articles to *The West-minster*. Later, in 1886, he again got in touch with Ellis, this time suggesting that he take over as theology editor, which the young man was only too happy to do since a small salary was attached. During the next year and a half he reviewed fifty-three books on religion, a curious undertaking for one who had presumably lost his faith. *The Westminster* was falling on hard times and Chapman was desperately trying to recapture its lost glory by casting it in more modern form. He was so hard-pressed that sometimes Ellis wasn't paid unless he made repeated and embarrassing requests. Chapman told him that if his plans succeeded, he had it in mind to make him a sub-editor, but he fell to his death under a cab in Paris in 1894. Ellis often reflected that a career as a literary editor might have suited him admirably.

More interesting still than *The Westminster* were the contacts he formed through *To-Day* and *Modern Thought*, edited by the able John C. Foulger. *Modern Thought* was a very advanced review which introduced Ibsen to the British public through Frances Lord's translations; it was the first to publish Bernard Shaw's fiction, and it provided a forum for future socialists. In 1884 it was succeeded by *To-Day* under the editorship of H. H. Champion, a pioneer of socialist propaganda who later became a Labour leader in Australia. Foulger's cramped offices in Paternoster Row were the haunt of young radicals who frequently repaired to a nearby tea-shop, the Cyprus. Here Ellis met H. M. Hyndman, founder of the Social Democratic Federation, John Burns,* and other radicals of the day. There was a good deal of heady talk about land nationalization, the "New Woman," and various progressive reforms. Ellis began to be invited to Foulger's Maida Vale home for dinner on Sundays, and on one of these evenings in 1881 Foulger suggested that they form a "Progressive Association" to promote "intellectual and social well being" at regular Sunday-evening meetings with instructive lectures as entertainment; practical political action would be worked out as they went along. This was only one of dozens of such organizations that were springing up around London, and it took them well over a year of talk before they actually had their first formal meeting. Ellis explained the purpose of the society in a letter to his father:

---

* Both arrested as leaders of the Trafalgar Square riots in February 1886. William Morris went bail for them.

"We are just starting the Progressive Association, prospectus of which you have seen. We are going to hold Sunday Evening Meetings for the people, short addresses with readings & music, instructive & attractive. Something of this kind has long been needed. It is time that 'the people' (to whom only we go) should have something else to go to on Sundays but dreary churches and public houses [written in margin: Mother does not agree to that]—of course I don't mean to say that churches are 'dreary' to superior sort of people as we see by their never going to church."[17]

The ardent little group took a hall at Islington Green (a hall, they later learned, shared by the Parnellite members of Parliament, who held secret conclaves there), and every Sunday evening—despite the fact that he was now working late at night as a surgical dresser—Ellis made the long trek between Anerley and Islington. At first the Association was composed of veteran radicals, but it soon came into touch with active participants in the new movements. It is difficult to establish precisely what Ellis's views were, particularly as he took almost no interest in politics in later life. He always described himself as a socialist, but there is no evidence of his practical advocacy of any single measure. In July 1886 his closest friend, Barker Smith, wrote to him: "Passed through the city—astonished to see the crowds in Fleet Street interest on the latest election telegrams. Are you a unionist or non-unionist?* I have not the foggiest notion . . . have never heard you express an opinion on the political situation, perhaps you do not know there is one."[18] In April 1882 he published an article in *Modern Thought* entitled "The Two Worlds," which is so abstract as to be almost vapid. "There are two worlds," he states, "one or other or both of which are always present to our consciousness. These are the ideal world and the real world. But the impressions the one produces are not in harmony with those the other produces. And always these discords are paining us."[19] What discords? Poverty? Inequality? Injustice? He described himself as "the youngest and probably the most enthusiastic [sic] member" of the group, and consequently fell into the position of secretary, but it is more likely he was assigned the position because

---

* There were two elections in 1886. Gladstone was elected in February. He went to the country over the Irish Home Rule issue, and lost his majority. In August a government of Conservative and Liberal Unionists was formed under Lord Salisbury.

he was so shy that he never opened his mouth at meetings. He wrote letters to prominent people asking them to address the meetings, and was responsible for bringing in William Morris, Sidney Webb, and John Stuart Mill's step-daughter, Helen Taylor. Before meetings he distributed handbills in the neighbouring streets and developed a chronic sore throat from sitting in draughts near the door, where he was stationed to sell subscriptions and hand out literature. His most enduring contribution to the Association was the compilation of a book of secular Hymns of Progress—in which the word "God" never appeared once; this included a hymn of his own, "Onward, Brothers, March Still Onward," which was later reproduced in a number of socialist song-books.*

After the Association started, it attracted another young zealot, Percival Chubb, a clerk in the local Government Board Department. He and Ellis got into the habit of meeting near St. Thomas's and sharing an indigestible meal at a nearby pastry-cook's. During these meetings Chubb spoke enthusiastically of a man called Thomas Davidson, whose brother, a journalist, Morrison Davidson, Ellis had already met at Foulger's office. Davidson was a Scot in his mid-forties, a wandering scholar of some reputation. Ellis appeared slightly sceptical of Chubb's eloquent description, but the facts were true enough, and the man was undoubtedly remarkable. After reading classics at Aberdeen, Davidson had travelled through the United States and Canada. Through Longfellow's influence he had been appointed to an examinership at Harvard. He spent a year in Greece, where he struck up an acquaintance with Heinrich Schliemann, who gave him a piece of pottery found in Agamemnon's tomb in Mycenae. In Rome he had an audience with the Pope in the garden of the Vatican. He had already written books on Longfellow and the Parthenon frieze, and had spent the past year in a remote village in the Piedmontese Alps, where he was translating the philosophical system of Antonio Rosmini-Serbati (1795–1855), the founder of an Institute of the Brethren of Charity, designed to adapt monasticism to the conditions of the modern world. Now it appeared that Davidson was coming to London for a brief visit in the autumn of 1883 and, as he loved to gather interested and interesting young men around him, Chubb urged Ellis to come to his rooms on the Embankment to meet the sage.

---

* See Appendix A.

Everyone who ever met Davidson fell at least for a time under the spell of his magnetism. Stout, with glowing cheeks and blazing eyes—"ruddy and radiant" was Henry James's description of him—Davidson dominated a room with his animated response to ideas, particularly if they accorded with his own. He seems to have combined moral fervour with impressive erudition. Ellis came away from this first meeting convinced that "this was the most remarkable man, the most intensely alive man, I had ever met."[20] When he left, he and William Clarke, a prominent liberal journalist, walked along the Embankment, talking animatedly about subjects raised during the evening.

Ellis was to meet Davidson on a number of occasions in the following weeks. Davidson had taken rooms in Chelsea and groups of young people began to meet there regularly to listen to Davidson expound the ideal of a Vita Nuova, a Fellowship of the New Life inspired by the Brethren of Charity. Such was the enthusiasm generated by Davidson that the group decided there was no time to lose and that some practical steps must be taken before he left England. They were particularly inspired by Davidson's paper, "The New Life," in which he described the ultramontane community founded by Rosmini-Serbati, the basic aim of which was moral perfection. Davidson thought he saw in the eager Ellis a probable disciple after the latter confessed to him that, quite independently, he had been envisaging a new social community. But cracks in the putative friendship began to appear within days. The course of attraction and eventual disenchantment was remarkably similar to that between Carlyle and John Stuart Mill. On the evening of October 2nd a meeting was held in Chelsea and Davidson was deeply disturbed by the tone of the discussion. Fully expecting Ellis to agree with him, he wrote to tell him that he thought they

> "had better take the bull by the horns, and boldly say we accept the metaphysical basis [for an ideal society]. We gain nothing by compromise in this matter. . . . You are entirely right in saying that any attempt to build a system without new forces, that is, *new metaphysical entities*, is like building a house out of nothing."[21]

Ellis was quick to disabuse him of the idea that he agreed with him; indeed, he could not have disagreed more profoundly about his metaphysics. On October 4th, after another meeting, each felt im-

pelled to write to the other. "I am anxious to see you," Davidson
wrote, "and to bind again the broken threads of our progress. I
hope you will keep Dr Barker Smith up to the mark and that we
shall be able to 'convert' Miss Jones."[22] Ellis, for his part, wrote on
the same day:

> "I am afraid that sympathy of mine which you refer to some-
> times serves to conceal real differences. I have always a tendency
> to agree with people. But I certainly believe that it would be
> desirable for a community to be founded where life would be
> arranged on a truer basis than at present. I would gladly see it
> done even although personally I could not accept all its prin-
> ciples."[23]

Ellis went on to say that he distrusted Davidson's insistence on the
necessity of a metaphysical basis for an ideal society. "The only true
basis for society," he argued,

> "seems to be a moral basis and that to me seems the only thing
> worth fighting for. I wish to live peacefully with all men whatever
> their metaphysical opinions may be. You and I are not aiming
> at the same things. You want to change people's metaphysical
> opinions. I want to make people's relations to each other true.
> And I say (with Hinton) that this may be done only by the
> acceptance of a true moral law and the falling off of traditional
> and rigid laws."[24]

For everyone in a community to share the same metaphysical views
"would seem to me most disastrous. It would mean spiritual and
intellectual death (Hasn't it always done so? Why should it be
different in the future?)." What Ellis was talking about was ethics,
not metaphysics. The letter, which continues for several more pages,
is an invaluable source for understanding Ellis's views at a very important moment in his development. The following passage is
particularly relevant:

> ". . . if I am to follow the true law of life (the law of response to
> facts, I should say) I must give up following the numberless rigid
> and arbitrary laws of men. By [taking on?] the hard task of doing
> this latter I shall have gained a vast new force to follow the
> simple and natural law of response to claims. And that is why I
> am prepared to accept Hinton's position in regard to sexual

questions, (though I know how easily one may be misunderstood in speaking about these things so that I don't often venture to do so)."

Again and again he hammered home his rejection of any acceptance of metaphysics. Religion, he declared, is "a psychological process; it is the harmonising of emotion with intellect. It is freedom, & the only perfect freedom—the way we escape from our own individuality." Davidson had urged him to devote the next two years to studying the thought of Rosmini; Ellis, in turn, had thrust on him some of Hinton's manuscripts, as well as an article he had written which was to be published in *Mind* in July 1884 as "Hinton's Later Thought" (after first being rejected by *The Westminster* as "too metaphysical" [!]). Ellis's admiration of Hinton must have been galling to a man who was compelled to have disciples.

> "Hinton was *always* changing and developing [he remarked pointedly]; but that seems to me the only way to see any truth at all. There is no break in his development. His metaphysics is very attractive for some people; it is grand & rather vague. I prefer him as a moralist. He is indeed the only man of ethical genius that I at present know of."[25]

On October 17th Ellis wrote him another long letter, and it was clear that his initial optimism about the formation of a new society was beginning to flag. He mentioned the practical difficulties that stood in the way of his joining such a community.

> "In regard to myself it does not seem very possible, although I should doubtless like it. It is probable that I shall have to go away. I don't know where yet—& begin professional work before long. Also I am poor; at present I live at home & even with pecuniary sacrifice I could not manage to meet the expenses which would be inevitable in forming such a scheme."[26]

By now it seems that there was almost nothing in Davidson's position with which he could agree. Ellis was even blunter than in the previous letter:

> "I have always felt that you are neither altogether on the side of the 'New Life,' nor altogether on the side of the old, but midway between each."[27]

Reverting once more to the thorny question of metaphysics, he made it clear that he strongly objected to a metaphysic which was synonymous with immortality of the soul, knowing full well how passionately Davidson believed this.

> "I question whether any notion of man's has done so much not only to crush and stifle life, but to extinguish the fundamental conceptions of spiritual life. The sanest men, as the sanest nations, have ever been, as Emerson says, 'incurious of immortality.' In an artificial state of society like ours we have a prejudice in favour of immortality. But this is where religion comes in. Religion to me is the spiritual process whereby we are liberated, not from this prejudice only, but from every form of selfishness. The region of religion is the region of joy & freedom."[28]

Davidson was agitated by this spirit of defiance and wrote off immediately:

> "I think I have left you under two misapprehensions, both of which may be disagreeable. I have rather 'chaffed' you. I felt I cared for you enough to make it harmless. Confessions of strong personal regard are not common in England; but I have ceased to be an Englishman & so I will speak out *once for all*, my deep regard and strong admiring affection for you. You have been a great deal to me & I leave you with much regret. My consolation is that distance does not diminish spiritual sympathy or affection."[29]

He begged him to write often to him in Italy "and, as your strength lies in writing, we may be able, in course of time, to come to a clear agreement." Ellis was mollified by his tone, and although emphasizing that he should not be counted on as a bulwark in the proposed community—"I am not at all a suitable person for taking the initiative in anything practical"—assured him that he looked forward to meeting him again "some day."[30]

Ellis had brought the Hintonians—Mrs. Hinton, Miss Haddon, and Agnes Jones—into the group, which met several times during October. Chubb, the organizing spirit behind Davidson's visit, had a wide circle of acquaintances; some of these were far more eager to participate actively than Ellis was. On October 24th a meeting was held at 17 Osnaburgh Street in the rooms of Edward Pease, later secretary of the Fabian Society, with the aim of setting up an actual framework for the Fellowship of the New Life. Ellis was present, but there is no record that he contributed anything to the discussion. This was the first of a series of fortnightly meetings which were to continue for many years. Davidson again read his paper, "The New Life." Chubb read the draft of a constitution that he had drawn up. There followed a general discussion of what form the new communal society should take. There had been some rather wild talk of emigrating to South America, but this plan was hastily rejected, and it was also deemed impractical to consider an independent community, even in England; but it was quite possible for a group of people to unite on a communal basis, pursuing their separate activities in the world while at the same time seeking to make the inner community as far as possible self-contained and self-supporting.

Between this and the second general meeting on December 7th, Davidson returned to Italy. There had been thirty-one people present at the first meeting, but only fifteen turned up on the second occasion. Undeterred, Dr. Burns-Gibson introduced a specific plan for the Fellowship of the New Life which had been drawn up by Chubb and Ellis.

> Object—The cultivation of a perfect character for each and all.
> Principle—The subordination of material things to spiritual.
> Fellowship—The sole and essential condition of fellowship shall be a single-minded, sincere, and strenuous devotion to the object and principle.

In the subsequent discussion it was decided that a community was to be founded, the spirit of competition to be abolished, and among the positive values to be stressed were adequate education, simple living, and the importance of manual labour and religious "communion" (whatever that meant). This manifesto was signed by nine people, including Havelock Ellis, Percival Chubb, and William Clarke. It was announced that this statement of principle would form the basis for the Fellowship, whether or not the propositions were accepted or rejected by the majority.

Meanwhile Ellis and Davidson were continuing their argument about metaphysics. At the outset of their acquaintance, Davidson, out of deference for Ellis's admiration for Hinton, treated Hinton with distanced respect. Now he lashed out from Rome:

> "Mr. Hinton was so innocent of philosophical training that he could not distinguish the actual from the real, the eternal from

the continuous. It is mere waste of precious time to take such a man seriously. To say that 'everything of real spiritual value may be attained in this world' is to use words without meaning."[31]

Davidson had also been receiving letters from Chubb about wrangles that were developing among the idealistic brethren. It was very difficult to control such an intractable group from so great a distance:

"I must confess to being a little sorry that certain persons having no motives higher than those of economic utility have been taking a prominent part in our little movement, and I have no hesitation in saying that, if their voices prevail, those of us who desire something higher, ought to secede and begin all over again for themselves."[32]

It is difficult to determine who seceded from whom. The fact that the second meeting in Pease's rooms was attended by only half as many people as the first is evidence of an ideological split that was present from the outset. At a further meeting on January 4th, 1884, the Fabian Society was formally launched. The resolutions which Ellis had drawn up and signed at the previous meeting were repudiated, and in their place a series of propositions calling for practical involvement in society was substituted. George Bernard Shaw (who, with Sidney Webb, was to join the Fabians later) commented dryly that "Certain members of that circle, modestly feeling that revolution would have to wait an unreasonably long time if postponed until they personally attained perfection," decided to form a more active society.[33]* The names most prominent at this crucial meeting were Hubert Bland, Frederick Keddell, and Frank Podmore. Havelock Ellis was not present, but, curiously enough, both Mrs. Hinton and Miss Haddon were there; and indeed, in a paper by Caroline Haddon, "The Two Socialisms," delivered at a meeting on March 21st, 1884, the word "socialism," first appears in the records of the Fabian Society.

Havelock Ellis always found it ironic that the Fabian Society emerged from such an unlikely source as the extremely conservative Thomas Davidson. He himself might be in profound disagreement

---

* An interesting difference between the two men was that Shaw, after his meagre years in Dublin, was converted to socialism by a lecture of Henry George on poverty. Ellis, after his Australian solitude, seemed absolutely indifferent to the poverty of the masses.

with Davidson over the latter's basically orthodox religious views, but they shared a conviction that an ideal society could be produced only by "superior" people. Ellis had no taste or temperament for politics; he decided to stay with the Fellowship of the New Life because it accorded more with his own beliefs, but in time he grew bored with its limited possibilities. Nevertheless, as late as October 17th, 1884, he was writing to Olive Schreiner about a scheme Chubb and some others had for a communal farm:

> "It would be nice to have a place of this kind founded by people in sympathy with each other and where you and I and other members of the New Life would have a right to go and stay when we liked, combining manual and intellectual work. I have for a long time thought that we need something corresponding to the old monastery—of course on a perfectly modern basis. However much we might object to socialism in the world at large we might still recognise it in an establishment of this kind—a socialism like that of Rabelais's beautiful dream in the Abbey of Thelema."[34]*

He continued to maintain friendly contacts with people such as Henry Salt (who was both a member of the Fellowship and a founder of the Humanitarian League); and it was at one of the meetings that he first met Edward Carpenter, whose friendship would later mean much both to him and to his future wife, Edith Lees, whom he was also to meet through Percival Chubb. The Fellowship bought some property at Merstham, where the members went for hikes and picnics, and for a time there was talk of setting up some sort of communal centre there for "a single-minded, sincere and strenuous devotion to the object and principle." In 1891 Edith Lees became secretary of a house bought by the Fellowship at 49 Doughty Street, Bloomsbury, as a co-operative venture. Here she was joined by Ramsay MacDonald, the future Prime Minister, in running the house, but she resigned in 1892 shortly after her marriage to Ellis. Recalling the various disputes that she had to cope with, she later declared, "Fellowship is hell."

But to return to Thomas Davidson. Long, argumentative letters continued to flow between Rome and South Penge Park (the Ellis

---

* This letter is particularly interesting for its revelation of Ellis's limited and élitist form of socialism.

family had moved again). The two final letters deserve to be quoted almost in full. On January 4th, 1884, Davidson wrote:

"Your letter, which reached me on New Year's Eve, has pained me more than I could tell you, by reason of its unfairness, its unkindly tone and its overbearing manner. I have already written four answers to it; but I find that they are all useless. Why, indeed, should I reply to one who has no 'position,' who calmly tells me that my most solemn statements 'upon analysis, mean nothing,' and treats me throughout as if I were a mere novice in thinking, not capable of making any distinction between religion and metaphysics.

"I have not the smallest desire to force my convictions on you. I have never at any time tried to do so. I did not ask you to join the little band whom I helped to collect with a view to a new spiritual life; and even now, if you do not like the spiritual convictions which we have in common, you are in no way bound to us. We have a very distinct position. I think, and, though the expression of it may 'mean nothing' to you, you might at least leave us to it. Negation never does very much good, and I am told that you 'do nothing but object and bring forward crotchets' —a fact which your letter painfully brings out."[35]

Ellis now fired off a final salvo:

"I cannot rest while this note remains unanswered—in which you have so strangely tried to prevent and misconstrue what I have said. That you have really scarcely read my letter appears from your assertion that I claim to have 'no position'! To say that I treat you as 'a mere novice' is absolutely monstrous in face of the reiterated assertions that I have no claim to be called a metaphysician myself at all. (But surely even the most humble individual may try to think for himself.) I was induced by the way in which you spoke to me to speak to you in the same frank and direct manner in which I speak to old & dear friends. I should certainly not have done so had I imagined that I was earning for myself a storm of unconsidered abuse.

"You have attacked my beliefs (as you have yourself said) 'fiercely,' and I have borne it quite patiently. But when I venture to criticise your own statements of belief—statements in which, as I believe and as I implied, you do injustice to yourself—I am treated to this outburst.

"But when you confuse my criticism of your own individual metaphysical statements into an attack on a non-metaphysical Fellowship of which I am myself one of the oldest members—it is really too much. Whichever way I look at it I can only with difficulty acquit you of unfairness.

"In regard to the Fellowship I am not careful to defend myself. My feeling towards it is known to most of the members, and not misunderstood. I have always wished to keep as much as possible in the background. In the future I intend if possible to do so even more. As to 'bringing forward crotchets,' if any charge is made against me it is that I do not bring forward suggestions enough.

"I do not regard you, however, with any unkindness. I have defended you in the past when I thought you unjustly accused & shall probably do so in the future. And if, as you formerly led me to suppose, you are glad to write to me, it will give me pleasure to continue our correspondence."[36]

This was too much for Davidson, and the correspondence came to an abrupt end.

Davidson eventually emigrated to the United States, where he again attempted in a newer society to inculcate his ideas at the Glenmore School of the Culture-Sciences in the Adirondacks and later at a New York settlement for Russian Jews, the "Breadwinners' College." On July 25th, 1888, after four years, Ellis suddenly wrote to him again. He was organizing the Contemporary Science Series and wanted Davidson's advice about American contributors. Almost casually, towards the end of the letter, he remarked, "Possibly you would care to take part in the Series."[37] Davidson replied in a friendly way, suggesting a number of names, including William James for a book on psychology, and expressed a willingness to write a couple of books for the Series. There is no evidence that Ellis ever wrote to him again.

OLIVE SCHREINER

In January 1884, while turning the pages of *The Fortnightly Review*, Ellis paused at an article on contemporary novels in which the reviewer, Henry Norman, spoke glowingly of a new novel, *The Story of an African Farm*, by an unknown writer, Ralph Iron. Ellis was intrigued by the description of the book and went to a library, where he borrowed a copy. He found himself delighted with its freshness, its simplicity, and above all by its setting in the solitude of a remote southern land. Impulsively he wrote to the author in care of the publishers, Chapman & Hall: "I have recently been reading 'The African Farm' and I have found so much in it of interest to me that I cannot resist giving myself the pleasure of telling the author so." There was much about it that reminded him of Hardy—a high compliment from Ellis—and he continued: "To me personally I daresay that 'The Story' is especially fascinating because I have myself been in a similar world and passed through similar mental experiences as are described in your first volume. Even in matters of detail, it deals with things that I know."[1]

Not long afterwards Ellis received a gracious reply from St. Leonards, dated February 25th, 1884. In a beautifully flowing hand, the author told him, "The book was written in an upcountry farm in the Karoo and it gives me much pleasure to think that other hearts find it real. I have been now almost three years in England but I long always for the old life."[2] "Ralph Iron," it now appeared, was actually a woman, Olive Schreiner, at twenty-eight only four years older than Ellis. The daughter of a German missionary, Olive had been a governess in South Africa before coming to England on March 30th, 1881, with the manuscript of *The Story of an African Farm* under her arm. One publisher after another had rejected it until George Meredith, as reader for Chapman & Hall, gave it his enthusiastic recommendation, and it was published late in 1883. It was an immediate success and a second edition was printed before the year was out. Olive was torn between writing and a medical career. Soon after coming to England she had to abandon the idea of becoming a doctor because she suffered acutely from asthma; and at this point she was spending the winter on the south coast in St. Leonards, one of a long series of places to which she fled in her hopeless quest for health.

Ellis immediately replied to her letter, and during the next three months they built up an epistolary friendship in which they discussed many of their mutual interests. They confessed their longing for the wider spaces of South Africa and Australia. "Yes," Olive wrote, "our African sky gives one the same sense of perfect freedom and wild exhilaration, sometimes one feels as though, for no reason that could be given, one were almost in an ecstasy of happiness when one goes out alone. Here one never is alone."[3] She touched a deeply sympathetic nerve when she asked him, "Do you not miss the starlight nights when one can be out all night? I miss them so. It is so hard to *think* shut up in a room."[4] For some months Ellis had been vaguely contemplating returning to Australia, but in response to her comment about longing for Africa, he replied: "I sympathise with your desire to return to the old life. Still I have thought for myself, that it is impossible for any part of one's life to be lived over again. New elements have entered into it and make it a different thing. And the difference would be a torment."[5] Olive agreed entirely: "Yes, it would be impossible to return to the old life: the outward circumstances might be recalled, but the hope that made it beautiful would never come back when once the unknown world had been known, and found empty."[6]

Ellis sent her some of his sonnets and his article on Hardy, and in her letter of March 28th she makes some interesting comments:

"I think your criticism very adequate and just. I shall read 'Far from the Madding Crowd' and then I shall better be able to make up my mind whether I like Hardy much or not. Now I hardly know—there seems to me a certain shallowness and un-realness about his work—no, that's putting it too strongly; it seems to me as though he was only fingering his characters with his hands, not pressing them up against him till he felt their hearts beat."[7]

She, too, felt that her whole life had been changed by a single book—in her case, Spencer's *First Principles*. Then, for the first time, she mentioned Ibsen, a name which was to occur frequently in their correspondence:

"Have you read a little play called 'Nora' by Ibsen, translated from the Swedish [sic] by Frances Lord? It is a most wonderful little work. I would like it to be reviewed by some able reviewer that it might be more widely read, but perhaps you would not like it. It shows some sides of a woman's nature that are not often spoken of and that some people do not believe exist—but they do, I think."[8]

They discussed writers whom they both admired, including Heine and Shelley. Ellis told her about the founding of the Progressive Association and the Fellowship of the New Life. They discussed socialism and the "Woman Question," agreeing that a freer conception of marriage lay ahead. The relation between the sexes came up repeatedly. One night in a mood of great sadness Olive wrote:

"I want to tell you what my feeling is about woman, but I can't tonight, because I would have too much to say. I have just got a letter I should like to show you. It is from a woman whose heart is being broken; and the man who is doing it doesn't *realise* what he is doing. Why can't we men and women come near each other, and help each other's lives?"*[9]

"There is no need why it should not be so," Ellis replied.

"Those mistakes and misunderstandings between men and women are so terribly sad and so frequent. Men often so totally misunderstand women (far more, I think, than women misunderstand men, though women often feel their own ignorance in an exaggerated way) and make their misunderstanding into ideals and cling to them. And we can help a little to make it different, —I think we have much to say about all this bye and bye."[10]

---

* It seems probable that she was referring to Eleanor Marx and Edward Aveling.

Naturally he spoke to her about Hinton and sent her some of Hinton's manuscripts to read. At first she was impressed by Hinton's attitude to women. "James Hinton's life has been a help to me. Sometimes I get an almost despairing feeling, that woman will have to save woman alone—*and yet I feel that to be impossible.*"[11] They evidently had so much to say to each other that they both found themselves yearning for Olive's return to London in May.

Olive was constantly having trouble with her landladies and upon her arrival at a lodging-house in Harrington Gardens where she had taken rooms sight unseen, the drunken landlady would not let her remove her luggage until she had paid thirty shillings. On May 12th she wrote to Ellis in great agitation, fearing that his letters had been torn up and possibly some of Hinton's manuscripts destroyed. Within the next week she settled at 7 Pelham Street, where Ellis called for her on May 19th to escort her to a meeting of the Progressive Association. There seems little doubt that she had been falling in love with her sympathetic epistolary friend, and was bitterly disappointed to find that the reality did not correspond with her image. Tall, grave, with curiously shifting eyes and a high, squeaky voice, he clearly was not the figure of her imagination. Some time later she confessed to Ellis that when she had gone into her room to get her hat, she had burst into tears. Ellis didn't know what to think of her because he had never met anyone remotely like her before. His first impression was of her restless vitality: "I still recall the first vision of her in that little sitting-room of the South Kensington lodging-house: the short sturdy vigorous body in loose shapeless clothes, sitting on the couch, with hands spread on thighs, and, above, the beautiful head with the large dark eyes, at once so expressive and so observant."[12]

Before the end of the month she settled in more permanent quarters in Fitzroy Square to be near her friend, Karl Marx's daughter, Eleanor, who had recently begun living with Dr. Edward Aveling in the same area. (Ellis had already met Eleanor Marx at a meeting of the Progressive Association.) The momentary disappointment Olive had felt about Ellis vanished—at the meeting he had seemed like "a tall angel"—and they were soon seeing or corresponding with each other daily. They discovered that they had been attending the same concerts at the Crystal Palace the year before. "What a wonderful change it would have made in my life if I could have known you then," Ellis sighed.[13] In what was apparently one of the first notes written after their initial meeting, he told her: "I shall always like to see you. We have so many experiences in common, so many thoughts and feelings that I feel as if you were somehow my sister. I really do not know anyone with whom I feel that I have so much in common, though I am happy in having many friends whom I sympathise with and love, and who are worthy of being loved."[14] "I wish I was really your sister," Olive replied; "it would be very nice."[15] There has been a great deal of speculation about the precise nature of their relationship. There are four sources one can collate to establish something like the truth: Ellis's recollections in *My Life*; the private journal he kept when he visited Olive in Derbyshire the summer of 1884, into which Olive wrote some comments; Olive's letters to him; and his to her. In 1917 Olive pleaded tearfully with him to destroy her letters—and this he finally reluctantly agreed to do. While he must have destroyed many of them, fortunately many survive.* It is an inestimable blessing to the biographer that most of Ellis's early letters can still be read. Nevertheless, since almost all of them are undated it has often been necessary to attempt to establish an approximate date by internal evidence.

Only days after Olive arrived in London she began to hear disturbing stories about Hinton's relationships with women. By June 3rd she was warning Ellis not to let Hinton submerge him—"you mustn't. It's not good for you."[16] Ellis replied: "It is true that Hinton says many exaggerated and absurd things. But I have not yet got over my pleasure at finding someone who rebels as I rebel and can say so, clearly and strongly. I long to find someone who rebels more strongly and severely but as yet I have not."[17] She continued to argue with him: "Don't think too much of Hinton. Your nobler, stronger, many-sided self must not be crushed by him, or rather I should say warped, for it will *not* be crushed."[18] He was eager for Olive to meet the Hinton circle as quickly as possible. He arranged for Miss Jones to call on her and during this month he took her to meet Caroline Haddon and Mrs. Hinton. She liked Mrs. Hinton immensely, but she continued to press him not to be completely influenced by Hinton. "It's just because I know and feel you are so unlike Hinton in many ways that I don't want you to be drawn out of your natural line of growth by him. Can you understand what

* Ellis told Hugh de Sélincourt that he had received nearly two thousand letters from Olive in the course of her life (Nov. 1923, Library of Congress).

I mean?"[19] She heard a story that when Hinton was dying he cried out that "it was all a mistake, all wrong, wrong, wrong," and that everything he had written in the past seven years must be burnt and thrown away.

Ellis also took her to meet his mother and sisters. Louie took an instant liking to her—although she disapproved of her referring to her brother as "Ellis"—and as a dressmaker advised her against wearing such frumpy clothes and to choose a loose gown to disguise her heavy body. By now Ellis and Olive were completely devoted to each other. They went to meetings and lectures together; they wandered through art galleries; late at night after the theatre they would stroll along the street, the tall, lean youth and the short, squat girl holding hands and chattering endlessly in a carefree way Ellis had never experienced before. Olive had endured more disturbing emotional experiences than he had ever known—a disastrous affair in South Africa and another, apparently somewhat masochistic relationship with a school teacher on the Isle of Wight during her first winter in England. Ellis was completely fascinated by her and kept long notes about her background and her health. Referring to their feelings for each other, Ellis quoted from Emerson's "Spiritual Laws":

> Then, when all is done, a person of related mind, a brother or sister by nature, comes to us so softly and easily, so nearly and intimately, as if it were the blood in our proper veins, that we feel as if someone was gone, instead of another having come; we are utterly relieved and refreshed; it is a sort of joyful solitude.

Many people wanted to meet the successful author of *The Story of an African Farm*, but during this period everyone took second place to Ellis. If a day passed in which they didn't meet, they would write to each other. She was the first person to whom he could entirely open his heart:

> "You know that the last six or seven years—ever since I came back to England I have always felt as if I had ceased growing, as if I were only living on my past experiences. Now I no longer feel that at all, I feel just as alive, in numbers of ways just the same as I used to in Australia—I can't tell quite what is different; I haven't got any new ideas or new plans but something is different. And I am certain that *that is all* owing to having been near you. Nothing else new has come into my life except you. It's a

very subtle kind of thing—emotional more than anything else—
I haven't got any new ideas from you—but it is a very great deal
more than ideas. I have so little to give you in return."[20]

"I have often thought," he told her,

"comparing myself to men generally—that what seemed to distinguish me was that while they seem to find it so easy to take
things as a matter of course or treat them indifferently, to me
things always seemed fresh and curious and unfamiliar. That has
always given me the feeling of being a kind of stranger in the
world. At one time it used to make me very miserable. Now I
realise the delight of it more."[21]

Both found excitement in new books, especially books that were
condemned as immoral; the conventional was anathema to them.
After reading Vernon Lee's *Euphorion*, he said, "I was rather predisposed in her favour but the book made me hate her. She is
thoroughly disgusting, narrow, conventional, superficial, sickly."[22]

Their relationship was stimulating, gentle, and loving; and soon
they kissed and embraced. Olive felt completely at ease with him and
on one occasion she was so absorbed in a conversation she was con-
ducting with him from another room that she rushed in to make a
point, oblivious of the fact that she was stark naked. While writing
My Life many years later, he recalled: "She was in some respects the
most wonderful woman of her time, as well as its chief woman-artist
in language, and that such a woman should be the first woman in
the world I was to know by intimate revelation was an overwhelming
fact. It might well have disturbed my mental balance, and for a
while I was almost intoxicated by the experience."[23]

Frequently Olive expressed concern that Ellis loved her too
much. "You mustn't trouble yourself about my loving you too
much," he assured her,

"especially as it is scarcely in your power to regulate it. . . . When
one is beautifully adapted for torture, especially self-torture, as
I have always been, it doesn't matter so much what one is
tortured about. If it wasn't the thing it is it might be something
worse. I find that consoling sometimes. I have all my life been on
the look out for the consolation in things. So long as one's
sensitiveness is to run from the rough impact of life it is not

strenuousness nor austerity that one needs but only consolation—the feeling of a child whose mother tucks it up in bed and kisses it and leaves it, and its body is thrilling all over with the warm bath it has just had, and the shadows from the fire are playing about on the wall, and it goes to sleep.—It is curious but that has always been the simile that connects itself with this idea. That is the very ideal embodiment of what I mean by consolation—I never knew any sweeter sensation."[24]

This was his first fully reciprocal love and he was never to love in the same way again. Ellis's letters do indeed seem to have been written in a state of intoxication. They are filled with compassionate concern about her health, her work, her lodgings; and they always contain many loving endearments. Olive's letters are more restrained, but they express a deep yearning for his loving support. "You are the first human being who has been perfect rest to me," she told him gratefully. Occasionally Ellis asked for the expression of more tenderness. "Please say a little loving word to me now and then, when you feel it." And on a cold, solitary evening he cries: "Oh, if I could only put my arms around you and feel you close close to me for a little while!" Olive, lonely, constantly ill, restless, had found the perfect "better self," as she sometimes called him, upon whom to lean. Ellis was by nature what Erik Erikson has called a "motherer," one with a deep need to comfort and cherish. "What could I do without my little mother and sister and baby and everything—my own self—that will do all the things in the world I have dreamed of doing." Olive agreed that they were "a little like children together." "I like that," Ellis told her, "I have always been so little of a child." Frequently he would ask questions such as "You haven't felt faint again, have you? Do you feel cold still? Your lips are so cold. It makes me want to kiss you and make you warm, to think of it."[25]

As their relationship deepened, Ellis became increasingly aware that Olive was not the competent, self-assured lady of her first letter. She was essentially a waif, and her handwriting degenerates as she pours out complaints about her head, her asthma, her moods of depression. He is always solicitous, always there when she needs him. By the middle of June she felt that the air in London was aggravating her asthma and on the 25th she moved into rooms at Woburn, Bedfordshire, where she felt she could work without the distractions of the city. Within two days she had decided that the place didn't suit her at all and that she would leave for Derbyshire, where the air was better. Would Ellis come and visit her there? "Why we thought so strongly and brightly in the far away countries had to do with other things except solitude." No wonder Ellis was alarmed when she exclaimed at the end of this letter, "I wish I was dead."[26] Two days later she told him, "Henry, you are spoiling me by being so good to me. . . . When I say 'good' I mean good to me. And by 'good' generally I mean 'unselfish.' I don't know if I care for you much (no I won't say that) I care so much about, ach, I won't say anything of that."[27] He never failed to pour out sympathy to her:

"Ah, my Olive, life has been cruel to you. You pay that price for the good things that you have. They are strictly related. But it is cruel and whenever I think of it my heart gets cruel and firm. I grinded my teeth but that doesn't do any good. Ah Olive, what is the good of all my wanting to help you—But I shall feel glad if I am even so little good for you."[28]

In one of her moods of self-hatred she told him that she had been striving for nearly three years to crush the sensual part of her nature and went on to describe men who think that it is only a woman's body which they think they touch, but in reality it is her brain and her creative power. Apparently she often suspected that her inability to concentrate and to finish the novel she was working on was due to the guilt and shame she felt over the two affairs in her past. She tormented herself with the thought that she had been "bad" and would walk the floor for hours in a state of sexual frustration. Ellis was constantly trying to persuade her to cut down on the large doses of potassium bromide which she told him that she had been taking for two years as an expectorant. She now confessed to him that she was actually taking it to diminish her sexual drive. There has been much speculation about the nature of Olive's illness and the cause of her perpetual restlessness. My own belief is that she was suffering from "bromidism." Bromide is no longer prescribed, and Olive's symptoms suggest why it has been discontinued. It is a drug that is not easily eliminated from the body and its effects are cumulative: skin rashes, mental confusion, depression, and ultimately there is produced what could be described as a psychiatric syndrome.[29] Ellis's pleas with her to reduce the bromide suggest that he realized the deleterious effect the drug was having.

"It is because you are ill & weak that you think these things; you don't think them when you are well. You must have plenty of nice things to eat; take a little Guinness every day. Oh, how I wish I could come and stay with you and make you strong and careless. Please go away from there as soon as you can. I long so to come and love my own Olive a little who is so sad and lonely and needs so to be loved—love her so that she'll be ashamed to get hard and careless and forget all about her poor boy, who won't mind, if she is happy. . . .

"My Olive, my Olive, how can I make my Olive feel that I love her. Words are not any good. But I am her own boy that nothing can take from her; I am her other self; I am like the blood that runs in her veins. I know my Olive nothing in the world could make me despise her, even in the most secret corner of my heart."[30]

And again: "If only I had plenty of money and could come and take care of you."

By July 7th she was packing and happy to be leaving for Derbyshire, where Ellis had promised to visit her. "Yes, I have the feeling as if we were so young together. The dream, the faith, that I should find someone just like myself was with me all through my childhood."[31] But as soon as she reached Derbyshire she began to worry lest it might be as bad as Woburn, and London, which she had viewed as the source of all her sufferings, was now referred to as "dear old London." However, within hours of settling into her new rooms in Bole Hill* she could say that she felt near God there. Henry would soon join her and they planned to read French together. They were by now entirely open with each other. Ellis sent her his private Australian journal to read and she confessed to him how strong her sexual feelings were during menstruation, and with this Eleanor Marx agreed.† Already he was making tentative steps in his sexual investigations: "It's very difficult to ask people about such things as sexual feeling. I was wondering whom I could ask. I really don't know more than one or two men whom I would much care about asking. I am so glad that you don't mind telling me about these things. It makes me feel so much closer to you."[32] Ellis had told

---

* Near Wirksworth, the setting of *Adam Bede*.
† He later incorporated this material into "The Phenomena of Sexual Periodicity" in Vol. I of the *Studies*.

her that he found it difficult to look anyone in the eyes and she told him that on the rare occasions when he actually turned his eyes on her they were "godlike."

Her work continued to oppress her and on July 12th she cut up and rearranged the novel she was writing—*From Man to Man*—and it now seemed impossible to reorganise it. On the 24th she had a visit from Eleanor Marx and Edward Aveling, who had taken rooms nearby. "Dr. Aveling and Miss Marx have just come to see me," Olive wrote. "She is now to be called Mrs. Aveling. I was glad to see her face. I love her. But she looks so miserable."[33] At this point Olive and Ellis did not seem to be aware that Aveling was already married. With their emancipated views, they regarded a union based on principle with admiration—but with a man like Aveling it was a different matter. On August 2nd Olive wrote again:

> "I am beginning to have such a horror of Dr. A., other-self. To say I dislike him doesn't express it at all. I have a fear and horror of him when I am near. Every time I see him this shrinking grows stronger. . . . I love her, but *he* makes me so unhappy. He is so selfish but that doesn't account for the feeling of dread. Mrs. Walters* has just the same feeling. I had it when I first saw him. I fought it down for Eleanor's sake, but here it is, stronger than ever."[34]

Ellis also found him despicable, one of the very few people he ever spoke about in such strong terms.

Early in July she received the Australian journal which he had promised to send to her. At the end he appended a note especially for her eyes:

6 July /84

> "*Olive*—I have been looking into this book, here and there, before sending it to you. it *does* contain something of what I was from the age of 16 to 24. But I wish it were a more simple, transparent and complete record of what I was. I see that I am even more willing to be more sincere to you now than I was then even to myself. I find that I haven't said many bad things about myself, though there are plenty of silly and stupid things of which I am ashamed still. Generally I only wrote when I had

---

* Mrs. Walters, a friend of Olive's, was active in women's suffrage; she translated Letourneau's books on marriage and property for Ellis's Contemporary Science Series.

a strong impulse to say something—anything—which would give the relief of expression; mostly it was written very hurriedly, often at midnight—and written so abominably that I am afraid you won't be able to read it all. But if you can it will give you some idea of what my life was like. There are lots of things I haven't written—including things that I might have found hard to write—which I can tell you some day when you care to hear.

"I am very much struck now by the curious and disagreeable air of self-consciousness which is so often obtrusive in this book. I am also impressed by the little traces of what *seems* to be like orthodoxy here and there as regards religious feeling. I was inclined at first to think that I really might have had at one time a revulsion of feeling towards orthodoxy (I think it was during the voyage out that I lost my early religious beliefs finally). But on consideration I think not. It was rather that, believing that *all* religious forms have a core of emotional reality, I was willing to some extent to use the forms for the sake of the reality. This seems to me now rather a dangerous thing to do.

"The self that I am now and the self that is contained here do not seem to me quite the same; nor does this book even, quite adequately, represent the self that I was. But it *does*, I suppose, so far as it goes; and my other self may think just what she likes of it, and I won't mind."[35]

On August 11th he arrived in Wirksworth for the long-awaited holiday with Olive. He was very tired after completing some medical examinations (which he had passed although fully expecting to fail) and was wearied by the long, hot journey. The period together which they had looked forward to so eagerly had its train of mishaps. First of all, there were the Avelings. They went on many walks together, excursions which were marred by a feeling of constraint. On one occasion when Olive put her arm around Ellis affectionately, Aveling turned around and gave them a sharp look. Aveling would high-handedly ignore "No Trespassing" signs and pull the reluctant, law-abiding Ellis through woods and fields. Eleanor would return from these excursions glowing—and "it is perhaps a bodily trait of her powerful personality that I have never known a woman who on a long summer's day ramble diffused so potent an axillary fragrance."[36] Sometimes in the evenings Aveling read to them, and on one occasion he invested some of Ellis's youthful sonnets with such passionate fervour that Ellis was quite astounded. But the journal is concerned not with the Avelings but with the interlude of Ellis and Olive. They shared it to the extent that Ellis showed her everything he had written in it and she added an occasional comment.*

> One day we took Olive's rug and some ham sandwiches and a bottle of milk and Rousseau's *Confessions* and Olive's diary and went to Bawl Edge and found a nice place tolerably sheltered from the sun to lie down together and talk and read and . . .
>
> There was not enough milk, and we didn't like the sandwiches. There was a slope down in front and some trees. Nobody came near, but some children once peeped over the rocks above our heads. Then we went back to Mrs. Walker's and had dinner. Mrs. Walker gives us very weak tea.
>
> The first night I stayed at Mrs. Flint's at the other end of Bole Hill. We both felt a little sad that night. For the next six nights I had the room next to Olive's at Mrs. Walker's. That was better.
>
> We have been reading French together—Rousseau and Madame Roland's *Mémoires*. I have been trying to get ready an article for "Today" on Socialism and Woman. Olive has not been working at her book yet, but I think she is going to now. Harry has not been working much at his article.
>
> The Avelings have been at Middleton close by, till yesterday when they went to London. I have an "intuition" that they are in trouble.
>
> On Sunday Olive felt better, not so tired; she took two pills. I felt better and better every day, stronger and more appetite. It was partly the fresh air and rest, partly being near Olive. I felt so restless for a few days before I came.
>
> On Monday Mrs. Walker said that it was too much trouble, etc, for me to stay there. Then we put our things for the night in my bag and walked to Matlock and took the train to Miller's Dale; there we found Blackwell Farm; we went to the Railway Inn and had some eggs and bread & butter and shandy gaff as soon as we got there and had some more shandy gaff before we left. We took the train to Monsal Dale and walked along a little stream there; we wanted to go and wash there and take off our boots. We saw the men and girls come out of the factory, and then go up a winding path that led through the wood to the village and disappear. Then at about 7 o'clock we went to Mary Massey's Cottage near the station and had some eggs and tea; then walked up and down the platform; then we went to Bakewell. As we

---

* Olive's passages are underlined.

were going up the steps at the station a man said "Are you strange?", and was going to help us. And I only said "Thank you." We walked to the town in the dusk. At the old bridge just before you enter the town we stopped; we did not know what would be best to do. He nearly broke that man's heart.

At last we went to the Castle Commercial just at the right of the bridge and asked if they had two rooms; but they were full, and we went to the Wheatsheaf and the Peacock and they were full too. Then we went to the Red Lion, and drank shandy gaff.

We had some shandy gaff but nothing to eat except two or three plums and a little piece of chocolate; and it was very close and we both felt weak and faint and could not sleep. Olive had benaauwdheit [indigestion: Dutch word]. I hate Bakewell. [But she wrote a few days after: Harry, I don't hate Bakewell.]

Next morning (Tuesday) we went to Rowsley; we tried to find rooms; every place was full; it was rather, *very* miserable; we did not know what to do. We went to the Peacock to have some lunch but there were people in the room there and we went away, and as there was no other place to go we waited till we got to Matlock; then we walked to Cromford and at last took these rooms for a week—Mrs. Thomas Holmes, 2 Alma Terrace, just opposite the Bell. Last night we were both sad and cried. Olive felt as if it was wrong to be near me. She said that she thought that 'some day you will *really* care for some one, and then you will think this impure.' I think that that chiefly made me feel so miserable because it was not understanding. But that was the only time. She feels sometimes that she is not unselfish, but she is—very. I think that sometimes she distrusts herself a little somehow. That is not quite good. She has a desire—which seems a little morbid—to see everything from the standpoint of Providence, to be abnormally selfless. I think that it may be a reaction from an opposite state of mind. No, it is a development.

This morning I was near to her and I feel happier and I know she feels near to me. It was morbid to be like that last night. We are going to work today. That will be better. Olive has not been well the last two days.

We are going to Matlock to get some provisions and we want to go to a farm to see about getting cream etc. Olive is sitting at a little table very close to me, writing letters. It is a beautiful day and not too hot. Olive is certainly much better: she was very [word blacked out] *good* this afternoon, because she was writing letters all the morning. I hope she will work now.

Friday. We went to Bole Hill this morning. Went to get our letters from Mrs. Walker's. Went to the little Railway Inn and drank shandy gaff (Our shandy gaff is all ginger beer) and then sat on the stone wall and read Louie's letter. I slept nearly all the afternoon. This evening we worked a little.

Sunday. At seven o'clock yesterday we went to look for Hawley's farm to get some cream. We couldn't find it, but went for a long walk. Olive said I was the most quietly obstinate person she had ever known. The purple heather was very beautiful. Got back soon after 9; had breakfast and wrote during morning. Olive sits down in the corner to write, in her thin dressing gown which she does not like but which she looks best in. After writing at her MS for a few minutes, she walks up and down two sides of the room for half an hour [words crossed out] thinking [one word crossed out] about her new dress and looking [one word crossed out] in the glass to see how it will go; then she sits down and writes at the MS for a few more minutes; then walks for another half hour, then ejaculates 'Poor Mrs. Smith!', then sits down again and writes to her Dadda. We resolved, when we are together again, to work in the morning, read in the afternoon and talk in the evening. In the evening walked to Matlock, bought a cucumber, plums, tinned herring, and ink.

Monday Morning. We went and got some cream yesterday morning and 10 eggs for 1/–. We read French in the afternoon. We were going to Miller's Dale today, but it looks like rain, and we are going to Via Gellia this afternoon.

Tuesday Morning. Ellis is leaving for London in an hour or two. We are just putting our papers etc together. He has been a great deal of help to me. I have got on much with my French. He and I are going I think to buy some cream for him to take home.

Wednesday. Olive was ill and very sick; I think partly from eating too much cream; so I did not come home till today. I kissed away her tears and left her in bed in that front bedroom at Mrs. Walker's at Bole Hill. She came to the window and we sent kisses to each other as long as I could see her as I walked away. That indistinct white-clad figure at the window is the vision that remains in my mind. It is like the last vision before she left London—the white figure in the dark leaning over the foot of the bed with oustretched arms—only this time there was less passion, more tenderness on Olive's part; I had not so much to *tear* myself away. It is not quite so sad as the parting in the back room in Fitzroy Street. I have been *very* happy. I am quite satisfied. It is strange that such little things can sometimes make us feel so satisfied and happy.[37]

I think these entries establish the nature of their relationship. There were certainly intimacies, but it seems highly doubtful that actual intercourse ever took place. In *My Life* Ellis has this to say about it:

> It is necessary to be precise. She possessed a powerfully and physically passionate temperament which craved an answering impulse and might even under other circumstances—for of this I could have no personal experience—be capable of carrying her beyond the creed of right and wrong which she herself fiercely held and preached; while, as she once remarked, if I were ever to do a bad action it would be really bad because it would be deliberate. For a brief period at this early stage of our relationship there passed before her the possibility of a relationship with me such as her own temperament demanded. But she swiftly realised that I was not fitted to play the part in such a relationship which her elementary primitive nature craved. I on my side recognised that she realised this and knew that the thought of marriage between us, which for one brief instant floated before my eyes, must be put aside. I have had no reason to regret that inevitable conclusion. We were not what can be technically, or even ordinarily, called lovers. But the relationship of affectionate friendship which was really established meant more for both of us, and was really even more intimate, than is often the relationship between those who technically and ordinarily are lovers. It is not surprising that some among our friends assumed that we were engaged.[38]

A little earlier in his autobiography he describes an encounter he once had with a prostitute who accosted him in the street and put her hand on his penis in a provocative way. In a footnote he says: "Not so very much later a woman I loved once touched me, as we were walking along a country lane together, in what was, physically, exactly the same way. I often thought afterwards how well this illustrated the fact that two things may seem the same thing, and yet be a whole universe apart."[39] There seems little doubt that the woman was Olive.

After he left on the 29th of August Olive wasn't able to work, particularly after looking out the window and seeing on the Wirksworth road a man in a black hat and carrying a bag—"it made it seem somehow as if you *ought* to be arriving." The next day she assured him that she had been working for hours—"I *have* to keep on working or I would miss you."[40] In Ellis's first letter to her after his return to London he wrote that

> "there is an extreme nervous irritability at present at leaving you, which will be better soon. But I am quite happy. Do not be

unhappy, dear, at all. And do not distrust yourself or anything. I feel as you do about a physical feeling towards each other. At least I think so. I should have felt more as you do, if you had felt less. I don't like any constraint in our relation. If I don't always show quite what I feel you mustn't misunderstand. I am afraid you do a little sometimes. When I seem not to care is often when I care most. I know this isn't right; it is part of my old self."

The following day he wrote again:

"I have been wondering if you are better, if you are able at all to work yet. I went to the Health Exhibition today because Louie wanted to go. Ever since I left you I have had a dull aching sensation in my heart. I don't know how it is; I hope it will go soon. I don't feel sad, I'm not unhappy. Oh, Olive, Olive, Olive.

"I have such an intense thirst for music. It seems to be telling me about you. It doesn't excite me at all. Any kind of music almost I like. I enjoyed that Albert Hall organ this afternoon. I wish you could have heard all the things I was thinking of you then.

"When you went away from London I felt that I *must* come near to and know you, but I didn't *want* you, didn't want *you*. Now I feel that I know you so well; I don't think I could know you better or be nearer to you. But I don't think I can be happy or I shouldn't feel this sensation at my heart. I want to feel you somewhere near me.

"Goodnight, sweet, goodnight."[41]

Olive later told him that the period following this visit was the time she felt most passionately about him, but she had to keep a bridle on her emotions. "You are dearer to me than you have ever been." Their loving concern for each other seems to have become even more intensified. Olive was happy to have seen him looking less skinny: "I should like to make you quite fat with happiness and sleep." She had warned him about the possibility of his reading and thinking too much in one line, to which he replied:

"You would be very puzzled indeed if you had to discover what the 'one line' of my reading is. And as to thinking I am only able to define, even to myself, in the very vaguest way as yet the end, half ethical, half artistic, that is before me and I am certain that even you couldn't do it at all. The only part of me which is tolerably clear to me yet is my critical method and that is the least important part of me, though I am not able to use it properly yet."[42]

Again he complained of "that dull ache at my heart. My heart wants you. It feels dead when it isn't near you." A few days later, while continuing to analyze his feelings for her, he decided that it was "tenderness" rather than "passion" that he felt. He had put only one mark (indicating masturbation) in his pocket-book since his return, he announced with satisfaction.

By September Olive was frantic to get back to London and Ellis began house-hunting for her. In the meantime she took a room at a farm near Bakewell. The landlady was horrible and demanded more than the sum originally agreed upon. Olive was overcome by uncontrollable fits of weeping. She was in despair, longing for a haven in which to rest her head. Again she wrote to Ellis begging him to find her a lodging, perhaps in Hampstead, but then it would be only temporary as she planned to move on to St. Leonards. Would he also find Eleanor Marx and give her a letter? Whatever she demanded, Ellis carried out with uncomplaining patience. "I kiss you all over," he ended one letter after spending an unsuccessful day looking for rooms, especially discouraging as she didn't want to pay more than £1 a week. Often she would apologize for interrupting his life with her demands for books from the London Library, for medicine, for news of the Avelings. But, as he told her again and again, he only wanted to be of help to her. She told him once more that she wished she really were his little sister, because for her he was always her "pure, beautiful, unselfish brother," the kind of brother she had always wanted, a sad commentary on her yearning for her own brother who was living in England but who paid her little heed.

Ensconced in a room in St. John's Wood by mid-September, she assured him that she was once more perfectly well and working hard. But by October she was back in St. Leonards. Wherever she was, the seriousness of their shared intellectual interests continued. She sent him a copy of Nora.* The "Woman Question" was a constant source of discussion with them as he worked on his article "Women and Socialism," based on Bebel's Die Frau:

---

* The first title of A Doll's House.

> "I was wondering the other day [Ellis mused] how it is that I am so different (I think talking with you made me realise the difference more—though I've always known it) from other people —women as well as men—in my feeling about men and women. I mean, that I should have had ever since I can remember such a deep feeling of the equality of men and women in every respect —that I should have had it not merely intellectually but emotionally, *instinctively*—I had it before I knew in the least what women were like. It has occurred to me that I owe it to my mother. Although she is so orthodox in most things she is very unorthodox in this. It is part of her nature almost and I don't know that she even fully realises it. She didn't *teach* me that, but I've left the things she did teach me and kept that."[43]

He went on to tell her that women should strike out on their own, that they shouldn't be guided by men. He admitted that he felt uneasy that she had felt impelled to use the pseudonym Ralph Iron for *The Story of an African Farm*. "It seems like betraying a cause. . . . You don't mind my saying this, sweet?" But had he offended her? If he had been disagreeable, it was because "my mind isn't healthy. I've wondered once or twice whether this mental irritability has some connection with the sexual side of my nature, the physical side, seeming to have been dead during the last few weeks. I think it has." Then a few lines further on:

> "I was struck this morning by a passage in that book on neuralgia, taken, of course, in connection with what you have told me. He refers to young people who lead, for the most part, a solitary and unsocial life; they acquire an exalted and unhealthy ambition, they acquire the habit of masturbation; they produce premature work in literature or art. He says that physically this results most commonly in asthma or neuralgia. I had never put all those things together before. He says they are 'comparatively frequent.' "[44]

They were both entirely open with each other about their habit of masturbating. In reply to Olive's question if he had made any more marks in his pocket-book, he replied on October 27th:

> "For the last ten days I have been taking bromide of potassium as an experiment, to see whether it affects the number of marks in my pocket book—as it is said to. I think it does decidedly, taken twice a day in rather large doses. Only it has a depressing

effect on the brain just as much as on the spinal cord. That may have helped to make me feel miserable. But I don't today nearly so much; I think that is owing to your letters. Do you know that since I knew you I am distinctly better physically than during the last 2 or 3 years. I mean as regards my nervous system; I haven't had to take strychnine. I don't mean to say that you are necessarily the cause of that, but I don't know anyone else that is; I haven't had less nervous excitement; *decidedly* more on some days."[45]

During these months they were intensely, passionately close. Ellis constantly questioned her about her life at the Cape, about the exact dates of certain occasions. It was as though by knowing everything about her he could merge himself into her.

"It is curious that I care so *very* much more for the smallest details of your life before I knew you than for anything you have said or done to me. These are sweet to think of, but the others— all sorts of things you have told me, sometimes quite small even —stir me much more intensely and passionately and I think of them far oftener. It is funny: perhaps it is because they *were* much more real for you than anything that I have a part in—but that doesn't account for it altogether, because it is quite little things that make me feel so. I like feeling you older than I am; it seems to make me feel even tenderer to you; nearly all the people I have cared for much have been older than I."[46]

Talking about their past made him consider the idea of writing something about his Australian experiences—

"it would be a picture almost more than a story, though I would introduce something that didn't happen—almost in the style of Flaubert. . . . I fancy there is something a little peculiar and piquant in a shy dreaming boy being thrown suddenly among those out of the world Australian hills and the strange things and rough people and having to look after himself and go on dreaming at the same time."[47]

Meanwhile Olive's sufferings were a constant source of anxiety: pains in her chest, perspiration, palpitation, a feeling of suffocation— these were her perpetual complaints. No detail in her life was without interest for him. He was in torment about the competence of her doctor, whether she was lonely, whether her room was comfortable. Agnes Jones, the Hintonian, was also in St. Leonards and was constantly pursuing her with questions about Ellis. Olive believed that she was in love with him and asked him if he had ever done anything to encourage her, to which he replied: "Miss Jones is terrible. I shall come and kill her," and added that he was not aware of any effect he had produced on her.*

In November he managed to get down to St. Leonards to visit her. He recorded his impressions in his journal.

Wednesday Night. Nov. 12th.

This evening I came home from St Leonards. I went on Monday morning; Olive met me at Warrior Street Station. I had the room behind hers. Yesterday evening we read together some of her old journals etc. I was very happy. I had never felt so near her. She had never felt so near me. Both nights she had asthma very badly after I left her. Just before leaving this afternoon I made her feel very sweet— it was a sudden impulse which I had never felt towards anyone before. Ever since she left London a month ago I have felt more or less sad in many ways just as I used to before 1879 in Australia. It has given me pain to think much of Olive. It would be good for me to see her oftener; that helps somehow to produce—not less love—but a kind of more healthy indifference. I mean an absence of morbid hypersensitiveness. I shall not forget yesterday evening; it was sweet and quiet; and was good for me both mentally and physically. When she woke this morning, even in spite of the asthma, she still had a sweet sensation.[48]

He had brought down a microscope, as she was curious to use it, and in *My Life* he records: "She wished to observe living spermatozoa, which there was no trouble in obtaining."[49] That is all. Such cryptic comments, which appear throughout *My Life*, are very disturbing, and may account to some degree for the hostile reception it received. They give an impression of deliberate evasiveness and, sometimes, as in this case, of something worse—archness. But many years intervened between the experience and the recollection of it in his autobiography.

---

* He later realized that she had become infatuated with him.

THE HINTON IMBROGLIO

On JANUARY 1ST, 1885, ELLIS RECORDED IN HIS DIARY: "AT THE END of every year in Australia I used to review the past year, to see where I had moved to. There is only one thing to say about last year, but that is a great thing. I have learnt to know Olive. Last January I read the *African Farm.*"[1]

1885 was to be a very difficult year both for Ellis and for Olive Schreiner; a great many of the letters covering this period have been destroyed or mutilated so that it is extremely difficult to reconstruct the sequence of events.

It is impossible to pin-point the moment when a love relationship begins its downward path. Generally the decline begins when it appears to be in its most rapturous phase. In the case of Olive and Ellis that moment was in Derbyshire, although at the time they felt that they could never be closer. Here they came as close physically and emotionally as they were ever to come, yet the strain of their sexual incompatibility was already apparent. Olive was a sensual, full-blooded woman who felt guilty about her sexuality. Ellis was undoubtedly erotic, but he was not passionate. This relationship is complicated, and while one must be careful about reaching definitive conclusions, certain elements ought to be considered. First, it should be remembered that Ellis admitted that he had felt sexually drawn to his sister Louie after his return from Australia in 1879. How long this feeling lasted we do not know; but we do know that the first woman with whom he had a real love relationship was Olive, whom he ad-

dressed frequently as his "little sister," and that he repeatedly told her
that he wished she were really his sister. Did Ellis confuse his feeling
for Olive with his feeling for Louie? Did he want to do things with
Olive that were forbidden with Louie? Did the fact that he identified
Olive as a "sister" shield him from asserting a sexuality which he
feared he did not possess? Did Olive frighten him with her greater
sexual experience? I do not think that any of these questions can be
dismissed; nor can the fact that they openly discussed masturbation
be under-estimated. Through the practice and the discussion of it,
they were enjoying vicarious and exhibitionistic sex. For Ellis this
was adequate; for Olive it was frustrating and guilt-laden. In a letter
written in 1906 to S. C. Cronwright-Schreiner (whom she married in
1892) Olive told him that there was "a strong element of abnormality" in Ellis: "I felt it from the first day I met him; he never denies
it; and we have often discussed it. He is only interested in the abnormal—not the exceptional, but the diseased. . . . To a certain extent
Ellis is a true decadent."[2] When, in Derbyshire, they approached
something like a sexual union, it appears that Ellis proved incapable
of full erection. From this Olive deduced that he did not feel sufficiently passionate towards her and that what they were doing, according to her principles, was then wrong. "Sex intercourse is the great
sacrament of life," she declared; "he that eateth and drinketh un-
worthily eateth and drinketh his own damnation."[3] Nothing was
explicitly said until after Ellis's visit to St. Leonards; but in retrospect
he could see that Olive's attitude had changed after Derbyshire. The
letters in the first part of 1885 undergo a dramatic difference in tone.
There are no longer the same spontaneous effusions but rather a
worried note, an insistent demand for clarification, and passages
from their letters indicate a groping for definition. "Oh, Harry,"
Olive cries, "I want to be good, I want to be good, not good in the
ordinary sense, good to my idea."[4] Sensing that they are drifting
apart, she writes:

> "Keep me close to you. I have of late such a *dead* feeling emo-
> tionally. I think it is the result of my physical illness. Do not
> you? I have been in a nightmare all these months and it is not
> gone. Somehow my life is ebbing away from me. I don't fear
> death. What I fear is a long life of dying. To live month after
> month, and year after year, and watch yourself ebb and ebb. To
> be at your own funeral."[5]

She feared that he believed she had been playing with him; to which he replied:

> "You must not think that I have ever in any way distrusted you. I know that your feeling for me is quite real. You know I have said and felt for some years that passion cannot form a real and lasting bond of union between people. And I think, too, that very few people feel a real and *deep* passion more than once. And I don't know that there is much passion in my feeling about you. (Yes, I do—one reason at least. If I want to be near you what does it matter to *me* what you feel, if I can't.) But my feeling isn't by any means a restful one and it seems not very consoling to me."[6]

And in another letter:

> "if I could be clearly convinced of what is wrong for you I think I might not mind so much, but now I feel as if I could scarcely bear to see you if we are to draw rigid lines of what may or may not be and so kill the simplicity and sweetness of intimacy.
>
> "My Olive, I am not feeling the least unloving. I am not saying you are wrong in any way. I only want us to be quite simple and childlike with each other; that we should know what we are doing. We have no code of morals which forces us to be hypocrites. We may look everything in the face."[7]

During the previous year Henry had been all-in-all to Olive. Now the intrusion of other people and other interests emphasized the dissatisfaction she had been feeling about the incomplete nature of their relationship. In the same month in which he paid her a visit at St. Leonards—November 1884—she met an extremely intelligent woman, Mrs. Elizabeth Cobb. Some pamphlets which Mrs. Cobb showed her on socialism and the "Woman Question" written by a young professor of mathematics at London University greatly impressed her;* and she was to meet Karl Pearson† himself through Mrs. Cobb on June 25th. She found herself strongly attracted to this intense man, an attraction which in time was to develop into passion,

---

* Ellis was actually the first person to show her one of Pearson's papers, which struck her so forcefully that she felt she might have written it herself.

† Goldsmid Professor of Applied Mathematics and Mechanics at University College, 1884–1911; Galton Professor of Eugenics at University College, 1914–1933; founder-editor of *Biometrika*.

but even the first attraction was enough to undermine her uneasy relationship with Ellis. Compared to Ellis's "Women and Socialism" (September 1884), with its vague views on the future of women and his uncertainty about what socialism was all about, Pearson's essays displayed vigour, forthrightness, and a committed ideology. In contrast to 1884, there are few surviving letters of 1885, and those from Ellis reveal the anguish he felt at other people coming between them. On a Sunday when the family was at church he was so agitated that he couldn't work, but sat down at the piano, which he scarcely touched nowadays, and restlessly played passages from Beethoven sonatas. "Half-loving and half not loving will always be a torture to me. I'd like to come to you when you are ill and tired and lonely; then perhaps the other people wouldn't care for you so much."

Although Olive's physical complaints continued, she seems to have spent a good part of 1885 in London, where she moved in an increasingly wide circle of acquaintances, and was particularly attracted to groups working for the advancement of women. When Ellis in May 1884 had tried to persuade her to join the Progressive Association and the Fellowship of the New Life, she had replied:

> "I think I should like to join that Society though, like you, I have not much faith in societies. An old woman sitting in her bedroom alone, reading her Bible alone, is sincere, but six old women at a 'class meeting' make humbugs—very often. Ideally, nothing can be more perfect than the aims of that Progressive Association. I like the *New Life*, especially the clause on the necessity of combining physical with mental labour. My feeling about Socialism is exactly yours."[8]

Olive finally joined the Fellowship in March 1885, and later tried unsuccessfully to persuade Pearson to come to some of the meetings. She also tried to arrange a meeting between Ellis and Pearson:

> "I would like so much that you and Henry Ellis should know each other, but he is so silent and has such a thick shell and so many prickles, and you have such a thick skull and so many prickles that if you did meet you mightn't know each other any better than before. I think the best thing in life is to find the people who belong to us, and when I see people who seem to belong to each other I feel such an irresistible wish to bring them together. But it doesn't succeed sometimes."[9]

The great difference between the two men is expressed in a letter to
Ellis from Olive dated January 25th, 1888, from Alassio. She tells
him that when she wants to go to Trafalgar Square to fight the ene-
mies of freedom, he tells her that she is a fool.

> "You of *all* people I ever met (infinitely more than Karl) *are* a
> man of the study and nothing else. You are perfectly dead on the
> other side, *that* is your weakness and your strength. That is why
> you will do great and useful work in the world. The world is
> crashing about you—and you sit grubbing out whether an old
> English dramatist put two dots over his i. Your dearest friends
> are being dragged to prison and theories you have been interested
> in are being practically tested, cruel and wicked wrong is being
> done to innocent little children—you look with astonishment
> and disapproval on another when you come to see them and they
> are not untouched by it! . . . Your very medical work you only
> undertake under compulsion and necessity; give you £200 a year
> and you would curl yourself up in abstract study and thought. In
> time of revolution you will never be in the market place. . . .
> You stay by quietly and felt nothing and did nothing. . . . I
> don't think you have ever realised your own character or your
> aims. K.P. has about a thousand times as much enthusiasm of
> the market place as you have."[10]

She is referring specifically to the two mass meetings held between
the middle of July and the middle of August 1885, at which W. T.
Stead was the principal speaker at the time the Criminal Law
Amendment Act for the protection of young girls from prostitution
was before Parliament. Ellis wrote a paper on the meetings, entitled
"The Red Spectre in England," in which he, as narrator and observer,
stands aside and records what he sees—completely uninvolved in any
sense. He submitted it to the editor of the *Temple Bar*, but it was
rejected. The pseudonym he chose for himself was Karl Richardson!*

How right Olive was! Pearson felt an immediate distrust of any
suitor of Olive's who presumed to write on the same subjects as he
did; and he felt condescension towards any society to which Ellis
might belong. Consequently, he and some of his own friends—Mrs.
Cobb, H. B. Donkin, Ralph Thicknesse—formed a club of their

---

* The original is now at the Humanities Research Center, University of Texas at
Austin.

own: the Men and Women's Club. Olive subsequently joined this
as well and brought along the Hintonians, Agnes Jones, and Caroline
Haddon. It was reported to Karl Pearson that Miss Haddon had un-
wisely said that the Club was infused with Hintonian ideas. Pearson
was a young man of immense, humourless, self-important rectitude.
He loathed everything Hinton stood for and he was so enraged by
Miss Haddon's rash remarks that he set about unmasking Hinton for
the charlatan he believed him to be. To force Miss Haddon's hand,
he suggested that she write a paper on "Hinton: Treatment of the
Sexual Relations," which she nervously declined, asserting that Hinton's papers on women must someday be given to the world, but for
the present she wished to be judged by her book on Hinton's ethics,
The Larger Life, which was just about to appear. Olive's doubts
about Hinton had never been put to rest. "Did he," she asked Ellis,
"apply the same measures to man and to woman? Would he have
been satisfied if his wife had had six 'spiritual husbands'?"[11] In the
meantime a Miss Emma Brooke wrote Pearson a long letter telling
him how Hinton had made advances to her at a house-party and how
he had set about trying to convert her to polygamy. Many sordid
stories about Hinton began to circulate and Pearson avidly seized on
all of them, many of them repeated to him by Olive, who had long
been trying to break his influence over Ellis. She told him that Hinton's sister-in-law, Miss Haddon, who had originally professed to have
known nothing about Hinton's sexual views, had finally confessed to
her that he had indulged in extreme intimacies with her. "My loathing for Hinton grows so strong that it is painful to mention him, but
I want to be just to him," she told Pearson. Apparently all sorts of
women were involved with Hinton and his justification for his behaviour was that he was "serving" them as an artist in love. The
rumours about his madness and his suicide were becoming more
widely voiced. Pearson was infuriated by the hypocrisy that surrounded Hinton, to such a degree that Olive warned him: "I must
have a talk with you about Hinton. You are going too far on one
side."[12] Pearson, in his mania, became suspicious about the New
Lifers and the Fabians, but was assured that any Hintonian elements
among the New Lifers had disappeared and that the Fabians were
totally uninterested in the whole subject.

Caroline Haddon was subjected to the greatest pressure of all.
On December 23rd, 1885, she wrote to Pearson: "Mr. Ellis told me
it was a pity I had spoken of the Men & Women's Club as 'Hin-

tonian' in its principles."[13] She then went on to say that she had only meant its candour in discussing sexual subjects. But gradually she began to reveal that she knew more than she had at first admitted. In a letter of January 3rd, 1886, she told Pearson about the disturbed sexual state Hinton was in shortly before his death: "What upset his morals was not his own morbid sexual desire, but the conviction that was forced upon him of the needs of women. . . . The very fact that his attention was concentrated upon sexual matters stimulated his passion to an unusual extent and these in their turn influenced his theories."[14] Emma Brooke told Pearson that Miss Haddon's admissions about her brother-in-law really corroborated the stories about Hinton. "You will find, I believe," she wrote,

> "that want of straight-forwardness, that sophisticated twisting of words, in all followers of Hinton: their method is to sanctify impure actions by the use of lofty language. You will not be able to get any hold of Miss Haddon's mind: by this time it is slippery. The ruining of the sense of truth in his followers is the least ghastly part of Hinton's influence."[15]

Caroline Haddon grew ill under the strain of Pearson's unremitting onslaught, and Ellis—knowing how much Pearson distrusted him because of his connection with the Hintons—felt impelled to write to him. Significantly, he had never been invited to join the Men and Women's Club, and there is evidence that Pearson was determined to keep him out of it. His letter to Pearson indicates not only his concern for Miss Haddon but the humourless morality that characterized all these young people.

> In regard to "Hintonianism" and my supposed connection with it, I have long been aware that one or two persons have gone about asserting, for reasons best known to themselves, that I advocate—possibly that I practise!—"Hintonism"—even that I am "the sole cause of Hintonism." I have taken no notice of these reports because I find that one will always be misunderstood and that the best plan is just quietly to go straight on one's own way and pay no attention to what people say. Few people are capable of clear thinking; they seem to imagine that one cannot be interested in, say, syphilis, without being oneself infected. . . .
> Still, I feel so much sympathy with your aims that I do not like that you should be left with this impression, so let me say,

once for all, I have never had anything to do with what is called "Hintonianism"; at one time I was inclined to attach greater importance to Hinton, *taken altogether*, than I am now, but I am constitutionally incapable of being attracted by Hinton's "Hintonianism." What you say under this head, I might have written in substance. When I was investigating it, I saw a good deal of some of the people who came under his influence and hence gained gradually an insight into his methods and their results so that I am able to speak with some decision in the matter. At the same time I am bound to confess that I cannot altogether sympathise with your (may I say?) rather fanatical anti-Hintonianism. Hinton seems to me very interesting and many-sided. Also, I think that everyone ought to be not only allowed but encouraged to express his own convictions, however much they may be opposed to some. I should like to see all that Hinton wrote published tomorrow; I am sure that it would aid discussion and help forward the whole sex question. A few foolish persons would undoubtedly with some show of reason, attribute their ruin to him—just as temperance lecturers solemnly tell of drunkards who ascribe their fate to one particular glass of wine.

This is a longer letter than I meant to bother you with; I really have no time to write at all.

Yours sincerely,
H Ellis[16]

Ellis was not being entirely truthful. Caroline Haddon—before the storm broke—had shown him a paper she had written in which she advocated polygamy. Olive had wanted her to omit this section and Ellis had agreed with her. But Miss Haddon had, after all, been responsible for his being able to go to medical school and he always remained fiercely loyal to her and to Hinton. He later encouraged his wife, Edith, to write two books on Hinton to which he contributed prefaces, and he never in print said anything against Hinton except that he took exception to his using the terminology of orthodox Christianity. Indeed, Hinton is praised frequently throughout the *Studies in the Psychology of Sex*, and at one point he is held up as the man who made a clear possibility of "a positive morality on the basis of nakedness, beauty, and sexual influence."[17] Hinton represented for Ellis the epitome of anti-Victorianism. Ellis always admired Hinton's championship of women and his indignation about the fetters that marriage frequently placed on them. Undoubtedly Hinton was the major influence in his life, both in Ellis's attitude to sex and in his own relations with women. But in *My Life* there is absolutely no discussion of the Hinton controversy of 1885. This omission and the fact that he never discusses the coldness that developed between him and Olive Schreiner during 1885 are further indications of the lack of candour in his autobiography.

Olive's erratic peregrinations never ceased. January 1885 found her in Shanklin, where her brother kept a boys' school. By the middle of February she had moved on to Bournemouth, where she wrote longingly: "Havelock, it was so strange when I got here last night, I had such a longing for you, almost like a child wanting its mother or a mother longing for her child. I felt as if I *must* see you."[18] But at the same time she wrote to Pearson that she was planning to return to South Africa; and added that she had received a letter from Miss Haddon but did not intend to answer it: "I can't waste more time over Hinton."[19] Then Ellis announced in a mood of desperation that he thought he would return to Australia and Olive decided that she would accompany him as far as the Cape. Dr. Donkin, Karl Marx's doctor, who had been introduced to her by Eleanor, was proposing to her repeatedly and his entreaties added to her distress. "I would like so much to have a child, but I couldn't *bear* to be married," she told Ellis,[20] and in April she moved into a convent at Harrow "where I can have kindly human beings near me. You don't know what it is to have a mother like yours that looks after you."[21] She began to sign her letters "The Wandering Jew." By the end of April she was declaring to him from her retreat: "I'm going to stick up for Miss Haddon like old boots. Compared to those white-washed sepulchres, the Hintonians are simply saints."[22] Between Donkin, Pearson, Ellis, and the Hintonians she felt as though she were being driven out of her mind. Ellis was miserable because he couldn't seem to reach her any longer. He implored: "Send me a little letter now and then if you can. Don't forsake me more than you can help, leave me a little bit of your heart." Knowing that she sided with Pearson in his views on Hinton, he wrote: "I wonder if you are working or just waiting for Karl Pearson to come this evening. You are sweet to me & I am very nasty. I can't help wishing often that you hated me in a genuine thorough way. Then perhaps I shouldn't feel such self-contempt."[23]

The Hinton imbroglio was far from over. In October Hinton's son, Howard, was arrested for bigamy. He had been apprehended in a King's Cross hotel with a woman, Mrs. Weldon,* who had borne him twins. Karl Pearson felt the wrath of an Old Testament prophet, for here was the most dramatic proof of Hintonian immorality! "Will this not give the desired publicity to the Hintonian dogma and stop the secret teaching?" was Olive's grim question to Pearson.[24] Mrs. Hinton was in hysterics, walking up and down, wringing her hands.

Only a few letters from Olive survive from this period, and none from Ellis to her. It is as though they had been scrupulously removed or destroyed, and this hiatus cannot be accidental in view of the plethora of letters before this date. In the surviving notes from Olive she tells him that Mrs. Weldon (whom she had met through Ellis) is distraught and begs her to stay with her. Apparently Olive remained with her until the trial, which took place in October. Olive pleaded with Ellis to come and see her at Bow Street and begged him to visit Hinton in prison. "What a terrible deadly theory that Hinton theory is, like a upas tree blighting all it comes in contact with because it is false to human nature."[25] Whether Ellis went to see Hinton in prison, why he had once attended Mrs. Weldon, what his reaction to the unfortunate business was, is impossible to know. Olive's growing contempt for him would suggest that he lay low. On Wednesday the 27th of October Howard Hinton was put on trial, charged with having committed bigamy with Maude Florence Weldon. The prisoner pleaded guilty and through his counsel expressed regret at his behaviour. A letter of high commendation of his character from Benjamin Jowett, Master of Balliol, was read out in court. Hinton was sentenced to three days in prison and then released.†

Subsequent events are very confusing. Howard Hinton tried unsuccessfully to find work lecturing on four-dimensional space, about which he seemed, like his father in his way, to be an obsessional. He eventually emigrated to America. Olive was completely exhausted. On November 2nd Mrs. Cobb (who had originally introduced her to Pearson) told Pearson that Olive "seems almost to have taken the guardianship of this unhappy Mrs. Weldon upon herself. She had been to see her, through Mr. Ellis who as a doctor attended her, sometime ago before she ever knew she [Mrs. Weldon] had anything

---

* Whom apparently Ellis had treated in a medical capacity. Did he deliver her children?
† See *Daily Telegraph* and *Daily Chronicle*, 15 and 16 Oct. 1885.

to do with Howard Hinton."[26] On December 13th Olive's rejected suitor, H. B. Donkin, wrote to Karl Pearson: "I found her this morning in a state of complete temporary madness—and being without her normal control, I gathered from her words for the first time what I have known myself for long, that she loves you."[27] The same day Pearson received a telegram: "I leave England tomorrow evening am better good bye thank you Olive."[28] The relationship between Olive and Karl Pearson is a matter for Olive Schreiner's biographer. Clearly she was hopelessly in love with him, but his feelings for her are ambiguous. On the day she was supposed to leave England she went to Gower Street and waited fruitlessly in the rain outside University College for a glimpse of him. There was an air of hysteria and confusion and misinterpreted motives about her departure. On the day of her planned departure, Pearson received another telegram: "Should be able to see you after 3 doctors will not let me leave till tomorrow."[29] She then wrote to him that she realized that he had never loved her as a woman but her feeling for him was "deeper than the feeling I have had for any human being—but it is not *sex* love." She then went on: "If ever you thought you saw an element of sex creeping into my thought or feeling for you why didn't you tell me of it, and crush it."[30] On December 17th she left for Switzerland and for the next three years she moved restlessly from place to place, driven by her private demons.

What is one to make of these complex relationships? Ellis was clearly deeply in love with her. She loved him tenderly, but her expectations of him died when he disappointed her sexually. With Karl Pearson she fell desperately in love, although always protesting that it was a "pure" feeling because she believed him too idealistic for anything as earthy as sex; and one can only speculate about his feelings since all his letters to Olive were probably destroyed.* He replaced Ellis as her ideal figure, especially after he confided to her that he was dying of some unspecified disease.† Certainly by 1885 he had taken over the role of confidant which Ellis had occupied exclusively the previous year. He was concerned enough about her interests that he intervened with Chapman & Hall to obtain better royalties for her. He lent her money. After leaving England Olive told Ellis on

---

* Certainly her husband, S. C. Cronwright-Schreiner, included none of the Pearson letters in *The Letters of Olive Schreiner* (1924).

† Pearson somehow managed to hold on until 1936.

several occasions that she had received anguished letters from
Pearson. It must have been bitter to Ellis to hear Olive now proclaim Pearson as a "genius," a term which she had formerly applied
to him; and that she ". . . loved Karl better than anyone else in the
world."[31] In the Hinton controversy she undoubtedly sided with
Pearson and repeated to him all the scandalous stories she heard
about Hinton. She turned bitterly against Mrs. Cobb, whom she saw
as possessively trying to drive a wedge between herself and Pearson.
This was not entirely paranoid, as Mrs. Cobb's letters to Pearson
speak of Olive in a very condescending way.* Olive furiously berated
Ellis when he suggested that there might have been a sexual relationship between Pearson and Mrs. Cobb. "You don't know Pearson," she fumed. "The kind of love he makes women feel for him
is like that of Dante for Beatrice. You can't understand Pearson."[32]

During these years Olive wrote regularly to Edward Carpenter.
Three comments she made about Ellis are worth quoting. From
Clarens on January 13th, 1887, she writes: "Yes, Ellis has a strange
reserved spirit. The tragedy of his life is that the outer man gives no
expression to the wonderful beautiful soul in him, which now and
then flashes out on you when you come near him. In some ways he
has the noblest nature of any human being I know."[33] Again, from
Alassio, on April 16th, 1888: "I don't know if Ellis will come out at
all. The mother is dangerously ill, 'sinking' he writes me. I am in
painful doubt as to whether Ellis ought to come at all. Whether it
will be happiest for him. When two people are friends and the one
loves the other with a love that the other cannot return, is it not
better for them never to meet? Yet I, if I loved a person would much
rather see them than not see them."[34] And finally, on February 5th,
1889, from Menton: "You must always stick up for Ellis if ever you
hear anyone talk against him; he's one of the quite purest noblest
souls, and people don't understand him."[35]

These "emancipated" late-Victorian young people were constantly discussing the relations between the sexes. The fascination
of the Hinton doctrine to its followers was that it seemed to advocate sex without prudery or hypocrisy. But for someone as essentially
puritanical as Pearson, these doctrines appeared prurient, licentious,
and even more hypocritical than the codes they attempted to replace.

---

* Karl Pearson married Mrs. Cobb's sister, Maria Sharpe, on June 30th, 1890.

And idealistic, ardent Olive—filled with guilt because of her previous affairs—talked nobly of relationships which would transcend sex (although she told Ellis that she would be willing to give herself to Pearson if he needed her). Ellis was so absorbed in his own troubled sexuality that he kept a complete record of his sexual dreams between 1876 and 1888. A month before he joined Olive in Derbyshire he wrote to her that his poems were full of allusions to people who tried to crush their sexual nature—"the physical being taken, of course, as a symbol of the spiritual. I cannot feel anything at all about physical sexual feeling except as a 'sacrament'—the outward and visible sign of an inward and spiritual grace. I'm glad you feel that so too."[36] No wonder they were to worry so much about their mutual intimacies and those accusatory "dots."* Ellis, inexperienced, naïve, and troubled about his own sexual potency, saw Hinton as a transitional figure ushering in a new age of clarity and emancipation.

But they still had to live in a world in which Victorian attitudes prevailed. In March 1889 Olive wrote Ellis an anguished letter from Menton. A group of guests, South Africans who knew about her relationship with Julius Gau, her first lover, jeered and taunted her— or she thought they did. She begged Ellis to meet her in Paris at the Oxford and Cambridge Hotel, which, faithful to the end, he did. She sent him a telegram with one word: "Paris." Nothing is known of the week they spent together in Paris.

His feeling for her seems to have continued unabated. In January 1887 he went to Lancashire for a spell as an assistant to a doctor. Before leaving, he wrote in his journal:

> I should not like going so far if Olive was in London. . . . My sweet Olive is at Clarens; she says she is well and jolly. I believe she really thinks she is—she does not understand herself so well as I once thought she did—but I know that her love for K.P. has possession of her whole being and renders her an abnormal person; and, say what she will, she is always betraying herself. Divine Child! She wants me to go to Florence and Rome with her. I must get money.[37]

On October 9th, 1889, he finally saw her off to South Africa. In her last note, begging him to meet her at the East India Dock Basin, she cries: "I must see your face. . . . Harry, I'm so dead, dear."[38] He described their parting in his journal:

---

* The marks in his diaries signifying masturbation.

A long kiss—the sweetest except the first—softly, slowly receding from the wharf, and the familiar little figure in the blue cloak and light hat, resting on the bulwarks, close against the iron stanchion. Sometimes a sweet tender half-smile rests on the pale little face and the large eyes; sometimes it grows indifferent; once—but only for a moment—it turned red and then came that pathetic despairing face of the child who is going to cry, that I have seen there before and that goes so to my heart. Then the face grows dim and distant, and the white flutter of a handkerchief is gradually lost. Since then I keep seeing against the stanchion the little figure that holds so much that is loveliest to me in the world, and my heart is heavy.[39]

CHAPTER 7

EARLY PROFESSIONAL YEARS

THE TURBULENT RELATIONSHIP WITH OLIVE SCHREINER MIGHT SEEM to suggest that it involved almost all Ellis's working hours. Certainly it consumed his emotional energies, but he did put in seven years at St. Thomas's Hospital during the eighties; in addition, during this decade he established his future literary and scientific reputation in a number of directions. Considering the time needed to travel between these various activities, his stamina must have been truly astounding.

These years, too, were filled with many diverse personalities. Two of the most notable friendships which he and Olive shared were those with Edward Carpenter and Eleanor Marx. Carpenter had recently (1881) published his Whitmanesque prose-poem, *Towards Democracy*, when Ellis first met him at a meeting of the New Fellowship. His attention was drawn to a figure in sandals—then a novelty—sitting near the door. He was utterly silent, but his gleaming eyes were evidence that he was absorbing everything around him. Carpenter, now in his forties, had left the Church and had set up a communal farm with friends at Milthorpe near Sheffield, where he was also involved in various workers' organizations. At one of the first meetings of the New Fellowship someone had shown Ellis a copy of *Towards Democracy*. He glanced rapidly through it and handed it back with a curt dismissive comment, "Whitman and water." Later he chanced upon a copy in a bookstall, bought it, and soon recognized that here was "a genuinely original book full of inspiring and beautiful and consoling things."[1] On March 12th, 1885, he wrote to Carpenter, enclosing a copy of Caroline Haddon's pamphlet *The Future of Marriage* (it would be interesting to know what Carpenter made of *that!*). Ellis expressed delight with *Towards Democracy*— "It is a source of strength to know that even one man is fighting so well on the right side."[2] He next sent Carpenter a copy of *The Story of an African Farm*. Carpenter admired its "poetic power" and made a point of meeting Olive the next time he was in London. Ellis wrote to him again about *Towards Democracy*, this time to contrast it with *Leaves of Grass*: "I think that T.D. compared to L. of G. is (in no bad sense) *feminine*. W. is so strenuously masculine."[3] It is doubtful if Ellis knew at this time that Carpenter was homosexual. Ellis also told him that he had no objection to his views on vegetarianism—he himself had lived almost exclusively on a vegetarian diet for the year at Sparkes Creek—but felt that he was stating the case too categorically. To Carpenter's expressed concern about Olive's restless peregrinations around Europe in 1887, Ellis, with his knowledge of the past two years, replied:

> "It is true that she is alone, but that is really the best thing for her; she gets more harm than good from being with people (of course I don't include harmless individuals as ourselves!) She knows this, but (as Schopenhauer says) even when we take that course of action that is most suited to us, those faculties which would have been exercised in an opposite course, are still within us, crying out for satisfaction."[4]

Carpenter was not greatly impressed by Ellis's preoccupation with "the Woman Question." "Woman at present," he commented dryly, "except as a mother (when she is divine) is a very unsatisfactory creature."[5]

The other notable friendship formed during this year was with Eleanor Marx. Olive had met her in the spring of 1882 and the two emotional young women soon became close friends. Olive became particularly protective of her after the death of her father, Karl Marx, in March 1883. Shortly after meeting Ellis, Olive took him to call on Eleanor, who was living close to her in Fitzroy Street. In an essay he wrote on Eleanor Marx in 1935, Ellis could not be absolutely sure of the exact date he had previously met her at the Progressive Association, but it would seem to have been earlier that same year, 1884. He could not recall what they said, but had a vivid memory of her radiant face and plump body perched on the edge of his desk.* Now Eleanor, Olive, and Ellis had an excited conversation about their mutual love of Heine. In the course of the discussion Eleanor produced an album full of letters from the poet to her father. On June 16th, in a long letter to Olive, Eleanor wrote:

"When can we have that day you rashly suggested we should have with Henry Ellis? It is too delicious a thought to be given up, and my only dread is that H.E. with his unselfishness pretends to like me for your sake. There is so little in me to like or interest people. I *can't* believe such a man as he could care for me, except just to please you."[6]

Later that month she invited him to a theatre party, but he was unable to attend. At Bole Hill he had his best opportunity of getting to know her, but the companionship was marred by the malign influence of Aveling, who was obviously making her very unhappy.

Olive was constantly worried about the debts under which the Avelings laboured. The following spring Olive, still at Hastings, received a note from Eleanor, pouring out her anxiety over Aveling's illness. Olive immediately wrote to Ellis: "Please go and see them and tell me just how Aveling is. If he gets dangerously ill, I must go. If the Avelings are very hard up I must try to send them something."[7] Ellis then called at their rooms at 55 Great Russell Street, opposite the British Museum, where the situation did not seem as serious as he had been led to believe. Aveling was suffering from an attack of gall-stones. William Morris was "sitting in a friendly fashion by the fire; I have little doubt that at this period he was proving financially helpful."[8]

It was through Olive's and Eleanor's enthusiasm for *Nora* that Ellis first became interested in Ibsen. On the 15th of January 1885 Eleanor held a gathering in their rooms in Great Russell Street to hear a reading of *Nora*. Eleanor read the part of Nora, Aveling that of Helmer, and Bernard Shaw took the part of Krogstad. It was intended that Olive should make a few introductory remarks, but she

---

* Yvonne Kapp, Eleanor Marx's biographer, has been very critical of Ellis for two articles he wrote on Eleanor Marx for *The Adelphi* in September and October 1935. Here he said that she was "not yet" absorbed in socialist activities in 1888 when he helped to find her literary work. I have attempted to adhere strictly to the correspondence of the period rather than to the recollections of an old man whose lively account does not seem to justify Yvonne Kapp's indignant and rather possessive attitude towards Eleanor Marx.

was too ill to travel up from Hastings and asked Ellis to take her place. Eleanor also wrote to him, adding her pleas to Olive's:

> "I *do* hope you will. I have just written to Olive. I *would* rather she could have done it, but if the right woman can't then we must have the right man. I *know* you will say just what one wants said. We *must* make people know them [Ibsen's plays]. It is, it seems to me, a real duty to spread such grand teaching as his, and my little effort tomorrow is just a poor beginning."[9]

"I hope you will not mind my asking you to do this," she added charmingly. "You see tho' I have met you so little I seem to know you very well. There are some people one gets to know *at once*—I mean to know in all essentials—and others that one is a stranger to after a lifetime passed together." "It is certain, however," Ellis recalled, "that I was not present at the reading, and in any case, I should not, then or later, have agreed to speak or read in public. On what ground, reasonable or unreasonable, I was absent, I cannot recall."[10]

They all became wildly excited over *Ghosts*, but Ellis failed to persuade Foulger to publish the play in *To-Day*. "In 'Ghosts,' it seems to me, Ibsen reached the highest point of his art," Ellis was to write in *The New Spirit*. He himself wrote a preface to *The Pillars of Society and Other Plays*,* published in the Camelot series in 1888. Eleanor wrote to tell him that she liked his introduction. "It is simple and to the point. But I am sorry Nora is not included in the volume. It sh^d have been, I think, in any *first* vol. of Ibsen."[11] Nevertheless, the collection, the first cheap edition of Ibsen, was highly successful and sold fourteen thousand copies within the next four years.

Ellis's connection with the Camelot series began indirectly through his gregarious friend Percival Chubb, who introduced him to Ernest Rhys, who had become editor of the Camelot series issued by the Walter Scott Publishing Company (and later was editor of the Everyman series). Walter Scott had a remarkable flair for business and had chosen as his manager a man called Gordon—who was known as a "Napoleon of business"—and was rapidly expanding the fortunes of the firm with cheap reprints of the classics. The first

---

* William Archer translated *The Pillars of Society* and *Ghosts;* Eleanor translated *An Enemy of the People.*

volume Ellis edited for the series was Landor's *Imaginary Conversa-tions* (1886), which had been a joyful experience at seventeen in the Sydney Public Library. While Ellis sometimes used literature as a vehicle to encourage greater tolerance in moral standards, his attitude towards Landor is an indication of the way in which he never lost sight of aesthetic criteria. Landor always remained for him the great-est of English stylists; and Landor's majestic serenity despite personal afflictions and the anxieties of his age were ideals Ellis set for himself. This was followed the next year by Heine's *Prose Writings,* of which Ellis had already translated *Florentine Nights* at Grafton when he was teaching himself German. The Heine was done at the suggestion of Olive Schreiner, who loved the poet passionately. "Years ago in Australia," Ellis told her, "I used to want so much to 'do' something for Heine and this will be one little way."[12] He showed Olive all his work and valued her comments. She made many suggestions for an article he wrote on contemporary criticism which he submitted to Escott, the editor of *The Fortnightly,* who, after a good deal of hesi-tation, decided to reject it—a great disappointment to them as Ellis had hoped to use the money to visit Olive in St. Leonards in the autumn of 1884. It was eventually accepted by a small magazine, *Time* (December 1885), which paid him £5 for it. In this essay—which he sent to John Addington Symonds—he elevated Symonds to the rank of doyen of English critics, whose approach indicated "the most marked catholicity" in contrast to that of a critic like Pater, who had "the advantage or disadvantage of a definite method." Ellis did, however, conclude with the statement: "It is doubtful whether Mr. Symonds possesses the dangerous gift of a keen intuition."[13] "What you say gratifies me," Symonds wrote in reply.

> "It is the first word spoken clearly, which shows that anybody has taken my drift and criticism, and understood what I have been always aiming at. You could hardly have stated my inten-tion better, or have more kindly pointed out the impediments in the way of manner or descriptive tendency which I long used to carry about me. . . ."[14]

Years later Ellis was to say that he had been so impressed by *Renais-sance in Italy,* which he was then reading, that he had over-estimated Symonds while under-valuing Pater, "who was perhaps not ethical enough for my frame of mind at that time."[15] He might have added that he was also influenced by Olive, who was a great admirer of Symonds. The essay is interesting for a manner he began to cultivate of saying and un-saying the same thing, so that no clearly defined position was ever formulated.

Ellis was determined not only to establish his name in the literary world but to earn some money from his writing, since he had no other source of income. In 1874 he had developed a love of the Eliza-bethan playwrights through reading Philip Massinger's *A New Way to Pay Old Debts*; and it now occurred to him that there was a real need for a series of unexpurgated texts of the Elizabethan dramatists. He wrote to Henry Vizetelly, the *avant-garde* publisher who had issued a number of Zola's novels as well as Eleanor Marx's translation of *Madame Bovary*. Vizetelly was immediately enthusiastic about the idea and suggested that Ellis take over the editorship, on condi-tion that he first secure one or two distinguished names for the pre-liminary announcement of the series. Vizetelly would handle details of the production, while Ellis was to select the dramatists and choose the editors. The words "Unexpurgated Edition" were to appear con-spicuously on each volume. Ellis was to be paid three guineas per volume, while the editors were to receive £5.6s. Ellis went about the job in a business-like way, persuading well-known people like Sy-monds, Swinburne, and Gosse (who characteristically complained that Symonds had chosen all the best playwrights for himself, leaving only Shirley to him). To Eleanor Marx, Ellis gave the task of editing *A Warning to Fair Women* (of unknown authorship). He could not give her a more important play, as these were reserved for authors of established reputation. Eleanor was immensely grateful: "I should be glad to get *any* work I am capable of doing. I need much work, and find it very difficult to get. 'Respectable' people won't employ me."[16] Eleanor asked if she might do some more editions for him because she found them interesting as "documents"—"they are, for the most, so poor as plays."[17] Ellis was young but not brash enough to pass himself off as a literary scholar. He did not attempt any elaborate reconstruction of texts, but relied on the work of such established scholars as A. H. Bullen and Alexander Dyce. Ellis him-self edited Marlowe, Middleton, Ford, and Porter. Just how closely he was involved in the textual editing is difficult to estimate. There is extant the correspondence between him and W. M. Mackenzie (a friend of Olive's) over an edition of Rowley in which Ellis evinces a close and well-informed control over the work. The Marlowe is more difficult to pin-point. Symonds wrote the general Introduction; Ellis is named as editor, but he used A. H. Bullen's edition of *Tamburlaine*. Bullen—as well as Symonds and Swinburne—was horrified when Ellis, true to his original intention, printed in the appendix for the first time the charges of blasphemy brought by an informer, Richard Brome, against Marlowe just before his death. The usually courageous Vizetelly quickly took alarm and withdrew the offending volumes, so that the only books with the offensive statement that survive are those which Ellis himself sent to people as complimentary copies. Even the *enfant terrible* Swinburne told him how pleased he was that Vizetelly had decided to suppress "the horrible and disquieting passage in your appendix, and I greatly regretted to find these monstrous abominations made public."[18]

Suddenly—in 1888—Ellis's involvement in the series came to an abrupt end. Vizetelly was charged with publishing an obscene libel in Zola's *La Terre*, fined £100, and placed on a year's probation. The following year he was again charged at the Old Bailey after issuing works by Flaubert, Bourget, and Maupassant. He went to prison for three months and was finally released through a petition signed by Symonds, Ellis, Leslie Stephen, Thomas Hardy, Olive Schreiner, and others, but he was sixty-nine and the prison experience undoubtedly broke his health and hastened his death in 1894. Fisher Unwin thereupon took over the series, dropped Ellis unceremoniously as editor, and a number of editions which he had commissioned (including Eleanor Marx's) were never published. This is another incident in life where he never raised his voice in protest.

But there were benefits that he had gained from the series; it had provided, for example, the opportunity of meeting someone who was to become a lifelong friend. Arthur Symons, six years younger than Ellis, at the time was living with his family in Coventry. Ellis's attention was first drawn to him by an article on the Provençal poet Frédéric Mistral in the *National Review*. He was impressed and made some inquiries about him, learning that he was editing some volumes of the *Shakespere Quarto Facsimiles* for F. J. Furnivall. Ellis then wrote and asked him if he would be interested in editing Massinger for the Mermaid series. Symons suggested that the next time he came to London they should meet at the National Gallery. They liked each other immediately, and within a few years they were to share quarters in the Adelphi and to go off on many trips together.

Undeterred by the setback over the Mermaid series, Ellis already had another scheme in mind. With his growing interest in science, it occurred to him that there was a real need for a series of up-to-date books on the latest developments in science. He suggested this to D. Gordon, manager of the Walter Scott company, and this time he had no compunctions about suggesting himself as editor. Gordon agreed and, since he was completely ignorant of science, virtually left all the arrangements in Ellis's hands. At first he planned to bring out a new volume every month, but soon found his writers so recalcitrant to this pressure that a more leisurely pace was adopted. The authors were generally paid between £40 and £50 (depending on their status); the volumes ranged between three and four hundred pages in length and sold for a shilling. Scribner's distributed them in the United States. The initial agreement which Gordon insisted on was a test run of twelve volumes; and if these proved successful, the series would be continued. Ellis received an advance of £50, and eventually made something over £250 a year from the job. When his father expressed some scepticism over the scheme, Ellis was able in December 1889 to tell him that "the Science Series is not by any means a myth; have sent you a volume in proof of this, 'Electricity in Modern Life,' in which you may be interested."[19] The books proved in effect so successful that nearly fifty titles were printed and the series continued until wartime conditions caused their discontinuation in 1915; during these years they provided Ellis with his main source of income. They were intended principally for the intelligent layman, and Ellis stipulated that the style should be as simple and straightforward as possible. The correspondence entailed by the series was staggering. Ellis wrote to a number of people, including Sidney Webb and Thomas Davidson, asking them to suggest appropriate contributors. Webb himself wanted to write a book on the history and theory of interest, but nothing came of the idea. Ellis seemed to have a fairly clear idea of what fields he wanted covered. It was a rather audacious idea to introduce the series with a work by two distinguished Scottish academics, Patrick Geddes and J. A. Thomson—*The Evolution of Sex*—but its sober tone forestalled any objections. Ellis was disappointed to be turned down by Sir James Frazer, who wrote a gracious letter wishing the series well but regretting that he was already too deeply involved in his own monumental work on anthropology. William James agreed to write a preface to Edwin D. Starbuck's *The Psychology of Religion*. Ellis wrote to

Bernard Shaw—who had recently (1887) published *An Unsocial Socialist*—asking him to write on some economic subject and suggesting a payment of between £35 and £40. Shaw was interested in writing on production and exchange; but he wanted to be paid on a royalty basis rather than a flat fee. His book was intended to be the third volume in the series. "Of course he [Gordon] will accept a reasonable arrangement," Shaw wrote, "but I want to make an unreasonable one."[20] Shaw raised so many objections to any alternative offers proposed by the publishers that Ellis finally wrote acidly to him, "I see that I ought to have asked you to do the book for nothing"[21]—and Shaw's involvement in the scheme came to nothing. Ellis found Shaw's acquisitive attitude extremely distasteful and in *My Life* he explained that he had never gone out of his way to obtain good terms for himself, for "I would rather receive little than haggle to obtain much."[22]

Karl Pearson was persuaded to contribute *The Grammar of Science* (which he later withdrew from the series, a subject which will be discussed in another chapter). Ellis's view of science was "organized order"—a view that laid greater stress on methodology than on subject, and as a result the series was catholic in its intention and scope: *Electricity in Modern Life; The Science of Fairy Tales; Manual Training; Bacteria and Their Products; Property: Its Origin and Development.* Ellis believed that the great and growing sciences of his day were anthropology, sociology, psychology, and political economy, and this preoccupation is reflected in the choice of a large number of titles: Dr. Isaac Tayler's *The Origin of the Aryans*, G. L. Gomme's *The Village Community*, Elie Reclus's *Primitive Folk*, and C. Lloyd Morgan's *An Introduction to Comparative Psychology.* The outstanding success of the series was Albert Moll's book on hypnotism, which was reprinted many times.

Ellis himself translated Cesare Lombroso's *The Man of Genius* and contributed two books to the series, *The Criminal* (1890) and *Man and Woman* (1894). *The Criminal* was a book in which he never took particular pride. One day in 1888 by chance he drew from a bookstall Tarde's *La Criminalité comparée.** He had never taken the slightest interest in criminals, but his eye was drawn to that magic word, criminal "anthropology." If he knew nothing about the

---

* Gabriel Tarde (1843–1904), head of the Bureau of Statistics in the French Department of Justice, in *La Criminalité comparée* (1886) set forth the theory that crime was essentially a social phenomenon. He was highly critical of Lombroso's theories.

subject, the chances were that no one else did either, and, with uncharacteristic impulsiveness, he resolved to write a book on the subject. Certainly one of the outstanding characteristics of his mind was
his tendency to look for fields in which there had been little investigation. He was a born pioneer. During the next year he sent out
questionnaires to officials in a number of British and American
prisons and, not to his surprise, found that British attitudes were
hidebound and years behind the Americans and the Europeans. For
all its weaknesses, the book undoubtedly broke new ground in England. It has often been said that his views were highly derivative from
those of Lombroso, the cultural anthropologist; in actual fact, all
through *The Criminal* he seems to go out of his way to take Lombroso to task for his indiscriminate procedures in collecting data, but
Lombroso is quoted more often than any other authority, so it is
probably fair to say that Lombroso was the main inspiration for the
book. To John Addington Symonds Ellis wrote in 1892: "Nothing
too severe can be said of Lombroso's lack of critical judgment and
historical insight and accuracy; one forgives it all because he has
opened up so many new lines of investigation and set so many good
men to work."[23] He was to go on to translate Lombroso's *The Man
of Genius* (1891) and from this book he came to the unshakeable
belief that the criminal and the genius were complementary forms
of degeneration (one can see how he was moving towards the estab-
lishment of a criterion for the norm). His book is propagandistic to
the extent that he argues for a more rational "scientific" view of
crime, he is opposed to fixed sentences, hanging, flogging, and
he advocates the necessity of weighing medical evidence. His
over-simple commitment to the notion of indeterminate sentenc-
ing of offenders remains still a controversial point among penol-
ogists. The book simply must be viewed in the context of the
time. While he asserts that the criminal is often the product of his
society, it is none the less clear that he is primarily interested in the
congenital "criminal type." Pages are devoted to discussions of phys-
iognomy, to such questions as hairiness, motor activity, etc. "The
criminal," he says, "is simply a person who is, by his organisation,
directly anti-social." Among geniuses he describes Verlaine as "distinctly criminal." Other notable figures whom he selects are François Villon, whose "crimes never degrade his art"; Cellini, who
"bears more distinct marks than Verlaine of instinctive criminality";
and Casanova, whom he describes as "a man of various and extraor-

dinary abilities, who has in his Memoirs . . . produced . . . a most complete and complaisant history of his own criminal offences. It is difficult to say whether in him the criminal or the man of genius is most prominent."[24] It is easy to smile indulgently at such seeming simplicities, but Ellis was trying conscientiously to make a contribution to what he called "criminal anthropology" by the assemblage of sedulously collected data. Influences are extremely hazardous to assign, but this book was undoubtedly epoch-making in its own field. Interestingly enough, on the 4th of June 1893 he wrote to the scientist F. H. Perry-Coste: "Many thanks for your notes on *The Criminal*. The book was written four years ago, and I should now be more cautious concerning some of the points you mention—especially the question of inheritance of acquired characters."[25] *Man and Woman*, constructed from a similarly typological point of view, will be discussed in a later chapter.

When Houston Peterson was working on his book on Ellis in 1928, the latter told him that he was astounded to remember how much he had crowded into the decade between 1879 and 1889. Young and unknown when he arrived back from Australia, with all London and its attractions beckoning to him, he plunged into a life of multifarious activities, a complete and dramatic contrast from Sparkes Creek; yet it had been the solitude and leisure of Sparkes Creek that enabled him to absorb the vast amount of reading which gave him the background necessary for the varied subjects on which he now wrote. To recapitulate: His association with the Hintons runs like an uneasy thread through the whole period. Then there was his involvement with radical politics and utopian idealistic groups such as the Progressive Association and the Fellowship of the New Life. He met a wide assortment of intellectuals, chief of whom was Olive Schreiner, with whom he maintained the most important emotional relationship of these years. He wrote for most of the leading journals. He contributed to the Camelot series; initiated and edited both the Mermaid and the Contemporary Science series, as well as attempting to found a journal of anthropology. Beginning in 1881 he also made numerous trips to Belgium and France. And by 1890—by then thirty-one—had published his first two books. Little wonder that it took him so long to get through medical school!

For someone who laid so much emphasis on the importance of science, the only aspect of medicine in which he achieved any distinction was midwifery. He chose the summer as his period of duty

and on many hot July nights he would hurry through the dark streets
near St. Thomas's to deliver a child. He was proud of the fact that a
death never occurred during all his deliveries. He found this part of
his work more rewarding than any other, a satisfaction probably related to his innate understanding of women. In later years he often
recalled that in all the time he spent at St. Thomas's the only reference to contraception he ever heard was a passing but very grave
warning by the obstetrical lecturer on its extreme harmfulness.

In many ways his life consisted of a series of unrelated contrasts.
During these years he made only sporadic entries in his diary; the one
dated January 10th, 1886, is interesting:

> About a year or more ago I thought that when I was about 10 years
> older I would write a series of scenes—*Dichtung und Wahrheit*—
> from my own life in the Whitman style, which would allow me more
> freedom and realism. (I don't think I could have done it well; I am
> analytic rather than synthetic). This evening I resolved instead, if I
> live to be 40, to write then a slight but truthful sketch of my own
> life and development. However much work one may do after 40, one
> does not develop much. There are not very many people who can
> analyse themselves; still fewer who are willing to put down the results
> of their analysis. And if I should ever become of sufficient interest to
> be written about, I have not much faith in biographers. But, above
> all, I do earnestly wish to help some few who will live after I am dead.
> I have not been very happy. I do not think now that I ever shall be,
> but I have learnt a little, and I do not think one can help others in
> any way more effectively than by lifting up the veil that hides per-
> sonality, by showing them what one really is, and where one has failed.
> Other hearts may answer and grow wiser too.[26]

By the winter of 1886–7 he had finished his course work at St.
Thomas's but still had a number of examinations to pass. At that
time it was customary for a young unqualified doctor to take on a
post as assistant to a doctor, and shortly before Christmas of 1886 he
secured such a position in the northern part of Lancashire, further
north than he had ever been before. It was a period of withdrawal for
him. Olive, whom he still loved, had abandoned him physically and
emotionally. He was still directing the Mermaids by post but had
left most of the work in the hands of an assistant. His idealistic
friends in the Fellowship of the New Life seemed to be on a different planet. He got along well enough with Dr. Gray, but Gray was a

man who had little real interest in his work, and his patients were inclined to be taciturn and dour. Ellis took to spending lonely hours at the ruined Abbey of Furness. The Australian years had left him with an invaluable solace for the future, a tranquil acceptance of total solitude.

Despite the confidence with which he entered into so many activities, Ellis was still somewhat vague about his future plans, as is indicated by this entry of July 17th, 1887:

> I want to take up anthropology—or some branches of it. That is really the science in which I have always been most interested, though I have never quite realised till now how very much it bears upon the social problems in which I am interested. Must join Anthropological Institute. Get medical qualification first. Curious that I found myself vaguely tending towards anthropology ten years ago.[27]

Later in life Ellis often claimed that in Australia he became determined to apply himself to a rigorous lifetime investigation of "the problem of sex," but none of his early letters or entries in his journal indicate this resolution.

The following winter he accepted another post in Lancashire, this time in Blackburn with a Dr. Aitchison. Here he found himself in a much more agreeable atmosphere, almost a jolly household, consisting of the doctor, his father—an amusing old character—and his two sisters, who were about Ellis's age. Ellis captured the flavour of the household in a letter to his favourite sister, Louie:

> "Dr. Aitchison is fond of sermons, makes the two girls go to church twice on Sunday, and, it is said, sometimes reads them a third sermon in the evening. Polly rebels at that and sometimes laughs, which her brother thinks very wicked, so the sermon ends up in a free fight. Isabel, the eldest sister is about 26, is domesticated and rather intellectual—has all the culture of the family, but wants developing a little. Polly is younger and prettier and more frivolous—likes dancing and music and theatres (but goes *very* little to them)—she doesn't *look* more than 18 but must be about 22. They are both very simple, genuine, unaffected girls."[28]

He found himself fascinated by the life in a factory town and the people were far more agreeable than those in Dalton. To Edward Carpenter he wrote:

"I am in love with the Blackburn folk, they are so easy to get on with—that no wonder they are conservatives! Evidently there is nothing like wellbeing."[29]

It was a pleasant interlude in his life, highlighted by a visit to Manchester, where he saw a fine collection of his favourite Pre-Raphaelite painters and heard a Hallé concert. By March it was time to leave. A few days before his departure a man came into the surgery complaining of a sore throat. He examined him, not aware at the time that the patient was developing scarlet fever. On the morning he was due to leave Ellis was feeling decidedly unwell and the Aitchisons urged him to delay his departure, but Ellis, believing that he probably had nothing worse than a cold, decided to leave for London since he was extremely eager to see the Annual Winter Exhibition of Old Masters at Burlington House, which he had never missed since his return to England. By the time he arrived home in Earlswood it was obvious that he was very ill. His mother called for the doctor, who diagnosed scarlet fever. The girls were put into isolation and Mrs. Ellis assumed that she would nurse him, but within a few days she had caught the infection and a nurse was sent for. As Ellis stood above her—by this time able to move about in his dressing-gown— she remarked calmly, "I shall not get over it." When the nurse rested or went for a walk, Ellis would sit by her bedside, bent over his Mermaid editorial work. On the morning of April 13th the nurse went for a walk and his sisters were out of the house. His mother seemed a little better and asked for some bread and butter. With his aid she even got out of bed for a few minutes. After he had tucked her back into bed he returned to his chair by the fire to a German translation of *Peer Gynt*, which he was reading for the first time, quite unaware of the course of the poem. At the moment when he was totally absorbed in the experience of Peer Gynt at the death-bed of Mother Aase—what he was to recall as "perhaps the most wonderful death scene of a mother in the whole of literature"—he was suddenly startled by the sound of heavy breathing. He hurried over to apply the brush to her throat, then poured a little champagne into her mouth. Seconds later a slight convulsion passed over her features and then she was gone. The first death he had ever witnessed was that of the person closest to him in the world.

Stunned, Ellis sat by her side for a little time. Then he went and

lay on his bed, waiting for the nurse to return. The next day he broke
the news to an old rag-and-bone man, who started to weep: "She
was like a sister to me." For some inexplicable reason Ellis did not
attend the funeral. Perhaps he felt Edward Carpenter was one of
the people who would understand his feelings. Carpenter always
seemed to know the right things to say: "A mother's death must alter
all one's life," he wrote in consolation. "Perhaps you will still however feel her very near you."[30] From warm, loving Eleanor Marx
came a note:

> "I have only just heard through Olive of your great loss. I know
> there is nothing to be said—but I know, too, from sad experience
> that there is some sort of comfort in feeling others sympathise
> with you. I myself have lost so many dear ones that I *know* what
> it is. If there is any way in which I can be of use to you, any
> merely mechanical work that I can take off your hands, will you
> tell me? I should be so glad if I could be of *any* service to you in
> *any* way. Let me help you if I can."[31]

It was a whole year before he could speak about her death in his
journal:

> For the manner of her death I shall never cease to be thankful. She
> could never have chosen a happier way of death, or one she could have
> liked better—to die 'in harness,' as she wished, nursing her own child,
> after a few days' illness, with scarcely any pain. How she would have
> hated to die by inches! She was so full of energy and love. Ah! dear
> mother, I never told you enough how I loved you.
>
> So curious that before she was ill she said, 'If I am, I shall never
> get over it.' And then the weaker she became the better she thought
> she was getting. Not one word of religion! only thought for her chil-
> dren and husband, even when she was unconscious. (I suppose it is
> not the really religious people who are so mawkishly pious when they
> die. When she thought she might die from the operation the year
> before she never talked about religion.) I was the only person with
> her when she died, and this is a sweet privilege to me.
>
> One strange thing I have realised. People tell of the death of
> loved ones making one long for immortality and it has seemed to me
> that this was quite natural. But what my mother's death has made me
> realise (and Louie too, I find) is the absolute hollowness and unreality
> of the notion of immortality. What would it be to me to see her in
> some far away orb, in some radiant form—or even here, under strange

and remote conditions. It is here and now as she lived and moved—
to see her come into the room as she used to come here when I lay
ill—it is this that one longs for. Nothing else.[32]

During that year he was able to write nothing except an essay
on Diderot which was published in *The Westminster Review* in
September 1889. But there was much to do. Shortly after his
mother was buried, he and his sisters went for a brief period of recu-
peration to Babbacombe near Torquay. The home had to be broken
up and the girls settled. He wrote frequently to his father—as usual,
away at sea—discussing plans for the future of his sisters. Edie found
a job as a nannie. The others settled together in Tunbridge Wells,
where they were provided for by their father. In September, Ellis himself moved in with Louie to 9 St. Mary's Terrace, Paddington, where
she was setting up as a court dressmaker.* He had two rooms on the
first floor, the first rooms of his own he had ever possessed.

Only a month before his mother's death, he finally obtained a
Licentiate in Medicine, Surgery, and Midwifery from the Society
of Apothecaries, a somewhat inferior degree which always rather
embarrassed him, although he strenuously defended its validity.
Probably more important to him was the achievement of becoming a
Fellow of the Anthropological Institute that year. In May he obtained
a three-month post as medical superintendent of a hydropathic es-
tablishment at Harrogate. "An inexpensive holiday," he described it
to his father, although he received no salary. All he needed to do was
advise the patients on the waters and to preside at table. Most of the
time he had to himself, and this precious period he used to complete
The New Spirit and *The Criminal*. He was still uncertain about a
fixed course for his future life, as this passage in a letter to his father
of June 11th indicates:

"I am not in a hurry to begin active medical work, and I am
working at two books nearly finished. I think of going to France
in autumn to get M.D. if possible. Next year, if it proves at all
feasible and I am able to afford it, I have an idea of going across
America to 'Frisco and on to some of the Pacific Islands and
trying to work up my scientific reputation. I shall at all events,
I think, go over to America, which is now a very simple affair,

---

* A woman who made gowns for ladies who were to be presented at court.

and it will enable me to work up some of my scientific Series arrangements."[33]

In September he went with Arthur Symons for a week to the Paris Exhibition. Symons, who was later to write the definitive book on French Symbolism, had never visited Paris—indeed, had never been out of England before—and Ellis introduced him to the dangerous delights of wine and cigarettes. Ellis had visited Paris with his former schoolmaster Angus MacKay in 1883. It was to be the first of many trips Ellis and Symons were to make together. For Ellis it was the culmination of his apprenticeship. The final entry in his journal is dated "Sunday Night 16 March 1890" and reads:

> Tomorrow with Arthur Symons to Paris—medicine, anthropology, etc. It seems the right step to take. I am in a receptive mood after doing two books. *The New Spirit* ("ambitious not to say pretentious" as a reviewer remarks) is the programme of all my life's work; it contains the germs of all I shall ever do. *The Criminal* (to be published next month) is the first application of *The New Spirit*.[34]

CHAPTER 8

THE YOUNG HERETIC

In March 1890 Ellis published his first book, *The New Spirit*. The previous December he had written to his father about his collection of essays: "These ought to establish my reputation. I don't know if the profits will be much but the publisher believes in the book and has taken all the risks."[1] Of the five essays—Diderot, Heine, Whitman, Ibsen, and Tolstoi—only the essay on Tolstoi, the Introduction, and the Conclusion had not appeared before. I agree with Arthur Calder-Marshall that the thread "running through the whole is the sensibility of the author"; but I do not at all agree with him that "for Diderot we could as well choose Rousseau, for Whitman Herman Melville, for Ibsen Strindberg, for Tolstoi Dostoievski, for Huysmans the brothers Goncourt,* and clamped between the introduction and conclusion, almost unchanged, they could have been presented to the public as *The New Spirit* without the general message being changed."[2] The figures Calder-Marshall has paired together represent very different types of people, while those writers whom Ellis has selected are a reflection of his own tastes and enthusiasms and are used as media for expressing ideas of his own. In the Preface to the Third Edition (1892) he refers to the fact that there

---

* There is no essay on Huysmans in *The New Spirit*. Calder-Marshall is most likely confusing it with *Affirmations* (1898), which does contain an essay on Huysmans.

had been some speculation as to why he had omitted representative figures such as Goethe, Kant, Hegel, Comte, Mill, and Herbert Spencer. The answer was simple: "I cannot remember even proposing to include these names." The only possible alternatives he had considered were Rodin, Wagner, and Burne-Jones, whose *Merlin and Vivien* he had loved so much when as a youth he had pored over a book of reproductions in the Sydney Public Library.

Looking back many years later, in the Fourth Edition (1926) he wrote a new Preface to explain what he had been trying to do:

> One might best indicate the nature of that spirit, I thought, by carefully selecting certain significant personalities and studying them in the light of one's own personal temperament, that is to say, not as objects of abstract literary criticism, but, as it is now sometimes phrased, tendentiously. According to the motto I had carefully chosen for the title page, it is by carrying to the highest point his most intimate feelings that one becomes the first in file of a great number of others; to acquire a typical value it is necessary to be as individual as possible. In order to present the "new spirit" I had, therefore, selected men who seemed in an eminent degree to have fulfilled this function. But, in the back of my mind, I was also aware that I had selected special aspects of these selected men, so that it was my own most intimate feelings that I was really setting forth.

The New Spirit is worth some examination, both as a reflection of Ellis's attitudes at that time and as a representative work of its period. If there was one obvious influence, it was Pater, whose name appears several times in its pages. The structure of the book is clearly modelled on *The Renaissance* (1873)* and the melodic cadences of the prose are sometimes almost comic parodies of Pater's style:

> A strange and troublous art, it seems sometimes,—like the sinuous melodies of Renan, which seem to belong to some far-haunted past, and yet contain the intimate secrets of our own hearts,—but it fascinates and holds us as though music became visible before our eyes.

Above everything else, his central idea that the *Zeitgeist* is in a constant state of fermentation is a direct borrowing from Pater's thesis that the Renaissance cannot possibly be encapsulated within a time-

---

* The controversial "Conclusion," which was dropped from the 1877 edition, was replaced in the third edition (1888), the one with which Ellis would have been familiar. Among his contemporaries he was thought to share Pater's "Epicureanism."

frame. Ellis sent a copy of his book to many distinguished people,
and from Pater's retreat in Brasenose he received a gracious reply:

> "It is a book to return to. You have raised in me a lively desire
> to become acquainted with Ibsen's work. The matter of your
> book is interesting; the manner elegant: its tone fresh and
> original."[3]

In the Introduction Ellis had his one real opportunity to speak
with his own voice. He alluded to his own development by way of
literature to an awareness of wider social issues such as the relationship between men and women. His own education had not been
channelled into the narrow grooves of orthodoxy, and his exposure
to a wider environment might be regarded as a new concept in education and himself the product of this "new spirit." He then goes on
to discuss the manifestations of the new spirit abroad in the world:
the growing sciences of anthropology, sociology, and political science; the increasing importance of women; the disappearance of war;
the substitution of art for religion as a social and emotional outlet.
He shared his contemporaries' naïve optimism that war would disappear as a result of the inevitable collapse of unrestricted competition. His attitude toward women was not as emancipated as one
might expect after all those discussions with Olive Schreiner. Ellis
commented, for example, that "It might probably [sic] be maintained that the average level of women's intelligence is fully equal
to that of men's." Although this sounds rather condescending, he
did maintain that women's role is in some undefined way to take
part in new social organizations and that they must be given the
widest possible educational opportunities. Otherwise "their vast
power of interference in social organization might have disastrous as
well as happy results."* The nervousness of the phrasing is a reflection of his conventional attitude towards the role of women. He was
to continue to argue for their finding fulfillment within their traditional sphere, and he viewed with distaste the strident militancy of
the Suffragettes.

The Introduction provided Ellis with a forum, but it had little

---

* In Ellis's own copy of *The New Spirit* there are a number of pencilled alterations. On p. 10 opposite "The rise of women . . . to supreme power in the near
future is certain" he wrote "to their fair share of power," an emendation which appears
in all subsequent editions.

connection with the individual essays, which were, after all, written separately at different dates. Diderot is admired for his ability to follow ideas through to their conclusion; and Ellis's view of the encyclopaedist is remarkably like the view he developed of himself—an encyclopaedist of the human spirit. The essay on Heine is a celebration of the poet who, by his acknowledgement of his own irreconcilable conflicts, had meant so much to him in the Australian bush. Whitman was a product of the best possible education, taught by the wide world itself. Ibsen is the Hinton of the stage with his disturbingly emancipated views, particularly on marriage. Tolstoi is praised as a psychologist whose realism is the sincere expression of his own experience. The figures Ellis had chosen to celebrate might not have been conventional ones, but his attitude exhibits all the veneration of Victorian hero-worship. It is a reflection, also, of accepted Victorian aesthetic criteria in which the value of a work could be estimated by its "sincerity," its expression of actual experience above imaginative creation.

The Conclusion had been written shortly after his return to England as an introduction to a book on religion he was planning to write. Some of the ideas are advanced for their time—namely, that religious emotions derive from physiological stimuli, and that these emotions can be described as an expression of the interaction between the organism and its environment. The argument looks forward to the theories of twentieth-century behaviourism, and it is understandable that the bewildered reviewer in *The Spectator* exclaimed indignantly, "Anything more confused, chaotic, and unintelligible than the last chapter, headed 'Conclusion' which professes to sum up the drift of the five essays . . . we have never read."[4]

Those to whom he sent the book were of course more complimentary. Edward Carpenter told him that "It is like the Lord on his throne, surveying the generations of men, *all very good*," but reserved most of his comments of approval for the fact that the book contained so much about Morris—"quite the finest figure in England today."[5] John Addington Symonds was delighted that he had the audacity to group Whitman, Millet, and Tolstoi together, an indication of "a deep critical sympathy between us." At this point Symonds was still trying to persuade Whitman to commit himself about the homosexual meaning of *Calamus*, and he tried to sound out Ellis on this as well: "I have ventured to touch on this point to you because I see, from the note to p: 108 [within Ellis's text], that you have already considered it—and, as it seems to me, have both arrived at the conclusion that Whitman *is* hinting at Greek feeling, and also that his encouragement of 'manly love' would necessarily and scientifically imply a corresponding separation of women."*6 Ellis replied guardedly that in his view Whitman did not exclude sexual intimacy from male friendships, although he later admitted that he had had no idea what he was talking about at the time.

It so happened that Ellis's development ran very much in tandem with the spirit of the time and his book touched on a current nerve-centre. Although he had little to say that was radically new, his book appeared up-to-date because it discussed figures who happened to be fashionable, and in a tone bordering on arrogant confidence which some readers read as conceit. It was preferable, if one were embarking on a career, to espouse the newest of the new rather than the oldest of the old. His title was one of the first to contain the recurrent word "new," an attitude which seemed the only possible stand to take as one was about to enter a new century. It became the catchword of the decade—the New Woman, the New Drama, the New Realism, the New Hedonism, etc. Why, then, choose Diderot? The only significant discussion of him in English before Ellis's essay had been Carlyle's attack in *The Edinburgh Review* in 1832, in which he was described as "utterly unclean, scandalous, shameless, sanscullotissamoeudic." A reappraisal of Diderot seemed to be the order of the day; and John Morley's thoughtful two-volume study appeared the year after the publication of *The New Spirit.* Shaw's *The Quintessence of Ibsenism,* which also appeared the following year, brought the Ibsen controversy to a climax. "Ibsen's solution of the matter in 'The Wild Duck,' " said Ellis, "seems to be that there can be no true marriage without mutual knowledge and mutual confession." (These words were to prove prophetic in his own emotional life before the year was over.) This theme was to be taken up in Hardy's *Tess of the d'Urbervilles* (1891), Arthur Wing Pinero's *The Second Mrs. Tanqueray* (1893), and Grant Allen's *The Woman*

---

* In a footnote Ellis had spoken of "the vigorous manner in which an element of 'Manly love' flourishes in 'Calamus' and elsewhere. Whitman is hardy enough to assert that he expects it will to a large extent take the place of love between the sexes." Ellis was later to say that he knew very little about homosexuality when he wrote this.

Who Did (1892). Ibsen, rather than James Hinton, spearheaded a period of intense reaction against the insincerity and double standards of the Victorians.

When one considers, then, how closely Ellis's views coincided with the intellectual currents of his time, it is startling that the critical reception of his book should have been so violent, but the criticism seems to have been directed more at the tone of the book than its content. *The Spectator* devoted a particularly vitriolic three-page review to the book, which concluded, "We cannot imagine anything of which it could be more necessary for human nature . . . to purge itself, than the 'New Spirit' of Havelock Ellis."[7] The *Athenaeum* commented acidly, "Mr Ellis must be very 'inquiring' for we have seldom met with one who knows so many things that other people do not know."[8] One of the few critics who had anything good to say about the book was Oliver Elton in *The Academy*, who declared that "the last word upon so suggestive and finished a piece of work ought to be one of ungrudging praise."[9]

The critic in *The Echo* was under the impression that Ellis was Hinton's nephew. He has given us an interesting description of Ellis's appearance at that time:

> He is probably some thirty-six years of age, is tall, and has the face of an idealist. Plentiful and somewhat untidy hair, a broad expanse of forehead, eyes wide apart, and occasionally a very engaging smile on a face which is habitually grave, and even sad. He is a most modest and retiring man—shy even to nervousness when in society, where he rarely speaks, unless directly appealed to, though he gives evidence of having heard every word that has been said.

He goes on to describe him as a "neo-Pagan":

> His reading has been rather too exclusively among the rebels and heretics of literature; and he would be well advised if he were to restore the balance by devoting more attention to the older, more conservative, more historic writers, whose influence, we may depend upon it, will survive the fame of several of the new men for whom our present-day critics are erecting very lofty pedestals. Mr. Ellis is thoroughly modern, his ideas of the latest mould and fashion—Socialism, freer sexual relations, defiance of authority, revolutionary conceptions generally possess his mind in a degree unusual among English authors.[10]

Well, this piece might at least have scotched the rumour that the author of *The New Spirit* was a woman! Certainly he was being talked about, and the book sold well.*

In *Everyman Remembers* Ernest Rhys recalled Ellis at this period as preternaturally grave for his age, speaking little, but kindling to utopian ideas. Rhys constructed a very funny imaginary conversation around his frustrated attempts one afternoon in his Chelsea rooms to force Ellis into defining his view of religion, of which this section forms a part:

RHYS: Where does that religion come in; how does it begin?

ELLIS: Who knows?

RHYS: But what is your constructive idea?

ELLIS: Every man who has reached the stage in which he can truly feel the joy of philosophic emotion must build his own hall of philosophy. A philosophy is a House of the Mind, with open doors, walls, and windows.

RHYS: And shutters?

ELLIS: No shutters! Jules de Gaultier says: "Philosophy is the recital of personal adventure, the world seen through a temperament,"† . . . through windows. But the human mind is not a clear mirror, not transparent as windows are.

RHYS: A painted window? Is all religion a painted window?

ELLIS: (raising his voice) Whenever a joyous expansion or aspiration of the mind comes . . . there is religion. It is the infinite we hunger for, and we ride gladly on every little wave of light that can bear us toward it.

RHYS: We ride, but we question as we ride the finite to the infinite.

ELLIS: The great facts of the world are not questionable—hunger, sex, the propagation of one's kind, religion too. Our best thoughts should be spent in settling the questionable things, so as to enlarge the sphere of the unquestionable . . . the sphere of real life . . . It is a waste of life to use literature for proving again the unquestionable.

RHYS: But literature must restate the old terms.

ELLIS: I was thinking of the literature which is not all art, the Literature of Life. Like Walt Whitman who was groping after a poetry, an expression of life for life's sake, a protest against art for art's sake.

RHYS: I see, and I don't see.[11]

---

* It went through three editions by 1892.
† Rhys is making fun of Ellis's tendency to lard his writing with quotations.

Rhys has beautifully captured the exalted mood of *The New Spirit*, the youthful intensity that pervaded all Ellis's writings of this period. As I have said, its pages are perfumed by the fragrance of Pater, the figure who, more than anyone else, affected and inspired Arthur Symons. But there was another important, if later to be discarded, figure hovering over *The New Spirit*: Paul Bourget.*12 On the title page appeared an epigraph:

> En portant à leur plus haut degré ses sentiments les plus intimes, on devient le chef de file d'un grand nombre d'autres hommes. Pour acquérir une valeur typique, il faut être le plus individuel qu'il est possible.

Ellis, with a curious caution which was part of his nature, omitted the name of the author of this passage. Or was it a bit of knowing show-off? The author, Paul Bourget, at the time seemed to represent all that was *outré* in French letters. In the early eighties Ellis had been enchanted by Bourget's analytic studies of the psychology of love and in 1885 devoured the two volumes of the *Essais de psychologie contemporaine*. It is my belief that these essays on Baudelaire, Stendhal, Flaubert, the Goncourts, and Turgenev were the model on which Ellis constructed *The New Spirit*. Ellis was particularly attracted to Bourget's book as an innovative force, speaking in a language the younger generation understood and ultimately affecting their later lives. This was very much Ellis's own attitude to literature and one which he associated with France—a country which always held both glamorous and cultural connotations for him.

His friend Arthur Symons (who published *The Symbolist Movement in Literature* in 1899) had first encountered France when urged to visit the Paris Exhibition of 1889 with Ellis.† The young men were so enthusiastic about this brief foray that they talked repeatedly of returning together for a longer visit. In 1889 Symons's first volume of poetry, *Days and Nights* (dedicated to Pater), appeared; Ellis had finally obtained his medical degree, and by the summer of 1890 had made his mark in literary and scientific circles with the almost simultaneous publication of *The New Spirit* and *The Criminal*. It seemed

---

* Paul Bourget (1852–1935), author of a number of psychological novels, and essays on psychological novelists: *Essais de psychologie contemporaine* (1883–5).

† Ellis always seemed rather piqued that his role in introducing Symons to his land of heart's desire was omitted from *Mes Souvenirs*.

the moment for taking an extended holiday. The arrangements were divided according to their respective temperaments: the meticulous Ellis saw to practical details like bookings and time-tables; Symons, who had a remarkable knack for making literary acquaintances, gathered together a dossier of letters of introduction to figures prominent in letters and art. Professor Patrick Geddes recommended the historic Hôtel Corneille opposite the Odéon, where they settled down for three months of happy occupancy (at forty-five francs a month), joined by Louie for the first fortnight (which some of their French acquaintances found very unconventional behaviour in a young lady).

Confident in their view of themselves as advanced young authors, they were determined to meet only the prominent leaders of the younger generation. When they had first talked of going to Paris, Ellis had justified it to himself—and to his father—as an opportunity to promote his medical studies. In the city irradiated by the spirit of Bourget it was soon apparent how shallow Ellis's commitment to medicine really was. He attended one—and only one— of Charcot's famous demonstrations at the Salpêtrière.* (Charcot made a powerful but unpleasant impression on him as a large-scale Napoleon.) He followed up his anthropological interests by attending a meeting of the Anthropological Society and by making the acquaintance of a number of anthropologists, including Charles Letourneau,† who was remembered chiefly for taking him to meet Madame Lafargue, Eleanor Marx's sister, with whom Olive Schreiner had stayed the previous year.

They eschewed the haunts of young sports—the Opéra and the Folies-Bergères—but attended a performance of *Ghosts*, which no English producer had yet dared to stage.‡ They were invited to some fashionable salons, but were very *gauche* when it actually came to approaching the *haut monde*. Invited to a *soirée* by Madame Darmesteter (A. Mary F. Robinson), for fear of arriving too early they arrived too late, only to pass the great Taine as he was leaving. Elie

---

* Freud had studied under Charcot and his interest in hysteria was aroused during a visit of some months in Paris five years previously.

† Author of *La Biologie* (1876) and *L'Evolution du mariage et de la famille* (1885).

‡ *A Doll's House* had been the first of Ibsen's plays to be produced in England on June 7th, 1889; the first performance of *Ghosts* in England was on March 13th, 1891, at the Royalty Theatre.

Reclus,* the gentle anarchist, was extremely kind to Ellis and invited him to dinner to meet some interesting men, but Ellis, even more taciturn than usual because of his embarrassment about speaking French, maintained a stolid silence. The evening was not a success.

The more voluble Symons brought them into contact with some of the exciting figures whom they really wanted to meet. They shared the expense of inviting the critic Charles Morice to their favourite restaurant, the Boulant in the Boul' Mich. Their major object in cultivating Morice was to meet Verlaine,† about whom Morice had recently written a monograph in *Littérature tout à l'heure*. Verlaine in turn invited them to his sordid hotel, where he produced a coin and announced in English, "*I have money*; I—will have—*pleasure!*" Someone was sent out to buy a small bottle of rum, Ellis produced his cigarette case, and an incandescent evening of talk about the French classics ensued.

Another evening of wonderful discussion took place in Mallarmé's minute dining-room. One of the guests was Huysmans, whom Ellis recalled in the manner in which people were later to remember Ellis himself after he had developed the reputation of a sage: capable of quietly devastating remarks, yet gentle and never bitter. But the one real friendship that was formed during their sojourn was with Rémy de Gourmont,‡ who had already written a favourable review of *The New Spirit* in the *Mercure de France*. Gourmont was to remain interested in all Ellis's subsequent work and was responsible for making arrangements for the translation of much of it into French. This was the beginning of Ellis's literary reputation in France, where it always stood higher than anywhere else. Henri Béranger—the future Ambassador to the United States—for example, was to translate his essay on Whitman for *L'Ermitage* in 1892.

Ellis sent Olive Schreiner a journal of his activities and she wrote wistfully from South Africa: "How long are you going to stay in

---

* Elie Reclus (1827–1906). He and his brother Elisée were close associates of Bakunin, and in the Paris Commune of 1871 he was appointed Director of the Bibliothèque Nationale. He had to flee to England until the amnesty, when he returned to Paris and devoted himself to a study of anthropology. After the Vaillant bomb incident of 1893 he moved permanently to Brussels. Ellis wrote on him in *Week's Survey*, 21 May 1904.

† Whom Ellis had described as a criminal type in *The Criminal*!

‡ Rémy de Gourmont (1858–1915). A Symbolist poet, he wrote a few insignificant novels and many literary essays.

Paris, *for good?*"[13] After a decade of astonishingly hard work, it was a holiday savoured joyfully and always remembered affectionately. In 1932, in a nostalgic article, "Early Impressions of Paris," he spoke of "that long and fruitful summer."[14] Since he arrived in Paris in April, it is significant that an old man's memory should linger on a time that seemed eternal summer.

CHAPTER 9

MARRIAGE

After the Fabians broke away from the Fellowship of the New Life in 1884 Ellis's attendance at meetings was irregular, but he continued to join them on their occasional outdoor expeditions. He also sometimes strolled along Whitehall with Percival Chubb, who began to speak enthusiastically about a young woman by the name of Edith Lees who was proving a great help in the secretarial work of the Fellowship. Chubb had met her at the home of the outspoken cleric Stopford Brooke, whose daughters had befriended her when she was alone and in great trouble.

On one of the Fellowship's outings in 1887 Chubb invited Edith Lees to join the group. Her attention was drawn to a tall, bearded young man. She asked Chubb who he was and he replied ("impressively," according to Ellis), "*That* is Havelock Ellis." However, she was not impressed by his badly fitting clothes and his awkward manner; but after being introduced they walked along together for some minutes, talking of indifferent subjects. Nor was Ellis particularly attracted to her. She was tiny—scarcely five feet—and although the three women with whom he was most closely involved during his life were extremely short, he was aesthetically far more attracted to tall women. Moreover, her protuberant blue eyes rather repelled him, although he later loved her expressive lower lip, her compact hands and feet, and proud, curly head, and, above all, her deep voice (his own, it will be remembered, was unusually high). Edith's first impression of Ellis was not enhanced by his heavy playfulness in tolling a bell in a deserted chapel.

In *My Life* Ellis does not mention whether Olive Schreiner was present on this occasion, but there is some reason to believe she was there, particularly as she often attended such gatherings of the Fellowship. Certainly it is clear from a letter to Ellis that she had seen Edith some time before her departure for South Africa in 1889. In his recollections Ernest Rhys may be telescoping a number of occasions, or possibly his memory was correct in his recollection of a picnic attended by Ellis, Edith, Olive, and Louie. "That holiday excursion," he commented many years later, "left me thinking of an imminent new race of women whom I, as a decadent Victorian male, might well have reasons to fear."[1]

Apparently Ellis caught glimpses of Edith from time to time, but they were not to meet decisively until August 13th, 1890. Ellis devotes almost one-half of *My Life* to Edith and to what many have considered their peculiar marriage. Seldom has a husband spoken so freely and candidly about his wife; yet at the same time there are aspects of their relationship that are evaded. They spent twenty-five years together; and since these were the most important and productive years of his life, no account can surpass his own recollections of his marriage. One must consider attentively both what he has to say about it and what he has omitted to say.

Edith was born in 1861 in Cheshire. Her family background was deeply disturbed. The Lees family were "thoroughly Lancashire" in type and character, whereas her mother's family, the Bancrofts, had a Celtic strain which Ellis believed accounted for Edith's vivacity. "The ancestral traits which the child of these stocks inherited were her destiny," Ellis comments.[2] Her mother was sweet and generally loved—or so Edith mythologized her. Edith was born two months prematurely and Ellis always believed that this accounted for her childlike qualities and for the fact that her physical powers of resistance were so low. She never knew the mother who died shortly after her birth, but she worshipped her image and always kept a large photograph of her on her desk.

Edith's feelings towards her father were very akin to hate. Her grandfather, a collier, would chase his wife around the room with a carving knife when in a drunken rage. A self-made man, he acquired a great deal of money, much of which he left to Edith's father, who squandered it in disastrous schemes. Samuel Lees was choleric, unpredictable, cruel, and he vented his nervous irritability upon his child, leaving her with not only a deep resentment against him but a suspicion of all men. After her mother's death, her father married a woman who had no capacity to love or comfort the lonely child.

When she was about twelve she was put into a convent at Manchester, where, responding to the kindness of the nuns, she announced that she wanted to become a Catholic. Her enraged father immediately moved her to a school near London kept by a German lady of free-thinking opinions. Here she received a perfunctory sort of education, and it is clear that Ellis did not consider her well educated.

For a time Edith ran some sort of girls' school in Sydenham, but she found herself totally incapable of coping with its financial problems and she broke down completely. Almost desperate, she was rescued by Honor Brooke, the older daughter of the Rev. Stopford Brooke, who took her back to their comfortable home in Manchester Square, and here her kind guardian angel gradually nursed her back to health. The Brookes introduced her into cheerful and cultivated society, and it was in their drawing-room that she first met Percival Chubb. They also introduced her to a kindly Harley Street physician, Dr. Birch, but her progress was slow, and night after night, she suffered tortures of loneliness in a little garret room off Manchester Square where she had moved after leaving the Brookes.

At the time of Ellis's fateful meeting with her in August 1890 she seemed the embodiment of the confident New Woman, and her air of competence gave no indication of her basic fragility. Her tiny figure in its crisp shirtwaist was brisk, efficient, and direct. By now she had become secretary of the Fellowship of the New Life, she was giving feminist lectures and contributing to a journal founded by the New Lifers, *Seed-Time*. The following spring she and Ramsay MacDonald (who was already talking of being Prime Minister some day) were to become joint secretaries of a Fellowship House at 29 Doughty Street, Bloomsbury. She found MacDonald high-handed even then, and he never bothered to contact her again, even when she wrote him a letter of condolence after his wife's death. She described her experiences at Fellowship House in her novel *Attainment* (1909), in which she depicted Fellowship as hell on earth.

In August of 1890 she was on a walking tour through Cornwall with her servant, Ellen Taylor; and she planned to drop in at Lamorna to see Agnes Jones, Ellis's Hintonian friend, to speak to her about some matters concerning the Fellowship. Miss Jones prevailed upon her to spend the night, later casually mentioning that Havelock Ellis was due to arrive for a visit of ten days. Edith returned to her room and told Ellen that a man she didn't like was expected, and should they press on? Ellen protested that her feet were so swollen that she couldn't walk another step. Ellis would later say that his fate was determined by a servant's sore feet.

It is a little puzzling why Edith reacted as strongly as she did. At the Fellowship picnic in 1887 she had been repelled by Ellis's lanky figure in ill-fitting clothes; but in the spring of 1890 she read *The New Spirit* and was enormously impressed by it. Indeed, many years later she often gave a lecture which began: "When many years ago, about twenty-eight, I first read *The New Spirit*, I knew I loved the man who wrote it."[3] Her feelings that afternoon must have been in a state of ambivalence, susceptible to liking or disliking intensely the man whom she later watched from her window as he slowly climbed the path in his torn mackintosh and dusty hat, carrying a medical bag.

It proved to be an unexpectedly pleasant evening, and Ellis responded to her earnest sincerity. They quickly fell into harmonious rapport. The following day he and Miss Jones accompanied the two women along the coast-guards' path as it wound through the little bays towards Land's End. Finally he stood watching with friendly approval as the small figure with heavy knapsack and sturdy stick receded into the distance.

Ellis had been spending a week in Probus, near Truro, as *locum tenens* for a doctor, and his visit to Miss Jones was his first holiday in Cornwall. He was immediately enraptured by the landscape to which he was to return time after time in the ensuing years. He would lie on the cliffs delighting in the ever-changing sea and occasionally he caught glimpses of young foxes frolicking among the dunes. At night, from the loft where he slept he could see the light of Eddystone. One day—following some obscure instinct—he made a trip across the Cornish peninsula to St. Ives. It so happened that Edith also reached St. Ives that day, and Ellis could never remember whether it was by chance or by prearrangement. At any rate, Edith was standing in a cobbler's shop having her boots repaired when she caught sight of Ellis striding past. She rushed out in her stocking feet and pulled him back into the shop with her. When the boots were ready he accompanied her along the Carbis Bay and Lelant coast as far as the Hayle ferry, which she was boarding for Gwithian, where she planned to look for lodgings. With Ellen bringing up the rear, Edith and Ellis trudged along, talking animatedly about their views on many subjects, particularly marriage, which both disapproved of in its conventional form. So close had he begun to feel towards her that as he stood forlornly watching the Hayle ferry slip away, he realized he must see her again as soon as possible.

Within two or three days he received from Condoldon a little note addressed to "Dear Mr. Ellis" and signed "Yours in haste"; it told him of her whereabouts, adding: "Make your way here if you can, as it is cheap and comfortable and ye fashionable corners are stocked."[4] Ellis carefully put away this brief epistle, and after Edith's death he found what might well have been his first letter to her. It was dated October 15th, addressed to "Dear Edith Lees," and asked her, when she returned to town, to visit him and Louie: "Will you not come some day, before long—when Satan can find no worse mischief for your energetic feet to do—and narrate what women can do at Tintagel and the rest?"[5] ("What Woman Can Do" was the title of a lecture she was giving at the time.)

The previous month he and Louie had taken a house in St. Mary's Terrace, Paddington. It was the first time he had lived in Central London and he enjoyed his bachelor rooms, which he had decorated in shades of straw and gold. Here he was more independent than he had ever been while living at home and he could continue to pursue his active and varied life even more energetically. Edith, too, was busy; but she took to dropping in to see him, generally staying longer than she at first intended. A sense of close comradeship was growing between them; there was no talk of love and no overtures towards intimacy. Ellis was still writing to Olive Schreiner, but by now he had accepted the hopelessness of his love for her, even though Karl Pearson had married the year before. He must have told Olive about Edith shortly after meeting her because on September 10th she wrote to him: "Everything Alice [Corthorn] has told me of Edith Lees makes me feel she must be exceptionally fine and noble, singularly sincere and straightforward. I read a very nice article of hers somewhere some time ago."[6] Again, on November 22nd, Olive wrote: "Don't let anything I said of Edith Lees prejudice you against her; I saw her once a long way off, and liked her very much; felt she was true." Then, immediately following this, as though she instinctively knew what lay ahead: "Dear, if I could be jealous of *anyone*, it would be of you. You seem so much mine, how could you love anyone else, and yet I want you to marry; no one would be so glad as I, dear, if anybody beautiful came to you. If ever you have a little child you must get your wife to call her after me!"*[7]

What was it Olive had said to him about Edith? Perhaps there was an intervening letter which was destroyed. Had Ellis told her of his developing feelings for Edith? Was he in fact contemplating marriage as early as this; or had Olive instinctively sensed where this friendship was leading?

A year elapsed before the wedding took place. It is important to know something of what they talked about, what the nature of their developing relationship was, and what, indeed, they knew about each other before their marriage. Since Ellis had no intimate women friends now that Olive had gone and Edith had no close men friends, it was natural for them to spend more and more time together, interrupted for a month in the spring when Ellis and Arthur Symons went on their first visit to Spain together. On his return he and Edith resumed their excursions to music-halls, concerts, and to Ibsen's plays, which were now beginning to be performed in London, but not to art galleries, as Edith was not particularly interested in painting, and certainly she did not accompany him to scientific lectures, as she always retained an irrational hostility towards anything that seemed connected with science. Above all, they talked for hours upon end, although Ellis never showed her his journal or questioned her obsessively about her early life, as he had done with Olive.

To criticize conventional marriage—that rock upon which the whole edifice of Victorian life rested—was to indulge in an activity that seemed to their generation stimulating, provocative, and responsible. Edith and Havelock began by discussing it theoretically; soon they were intent upon how they could apply abstract principles to their own situation. Within a very short time it was apparent that they both wanted a permanent relationsip—but what kind? The young woman who first signed her notes "Your little comrade Edith" was soon torn between conflicting moods of a need for secure emotional dependence, and a terror that her freedom might be curtailed in some way. There was never any question of passion on either side.

---

* Her husband, S. C. Cronwright-Schreiner, omitted this last sentence from her collected *Letters* in 1924. Both Ellis and Cronwright-Schreiner omitted the first reference to Edith. The original is in the Humanities Research Center, University of Texas.

From the outset it was what Ellis described as "a union of affectionate comradeship, in which the specific emotions of sex had the smallest part, yet a union, as I was later to learn by experience, able to
attain even on that basis a passionate intensity of love."[8]

By June Edith experienced some sort of crisis in her wavering
attitudes towards the future, and on the 13th Ellis wrote her a letter
which deserves to be quoted at length:

> "We have never needed any explanations before, and that has
> always seemed so beautiful to me, and we seemed to understand
> instinctively. And that is why I've never explained things that
> perhaps needed explaining. This is specially so about Olive. I
> have never known anyone who was so beautiful and wonderful,
> or with whom I could be so much myself, and it is true enough
> that for years to be married to her seemed to me the one thing
> in the world that I longed for, but that is years ago. We are
> sweet friends now and always will be; but to speak in the way
> you do of a 'vital relationship' to her sounds to me very cruel.
> Because one has loved somebody who did not love one enough
> to make the deepest human relationship possible, is that a reason
> why one must always be left alone?* I only explain this to show
> that I am really free in every sense—perhaps freer than you—
> and that I haven't been so unfair to you as you seem to think.
> The thing I wanted to tell you about that has been bothering
> me was this: I had to decide whether it was possible for me to
> return the passionate love of someone whom I felt a good deal
> of sympathy with, and even a little passionate towards. She
> would have left me absolutely free, and it hurt me to have to
> torture her. But I had no difficulty in deciding; the real, deep
> and mutual understanding, which to me is more than passion,
> wasn't there, and the thought I had constantly in my mind was
> that my feeling towards you, although I do not feel passionate
> towards you (as I thought you understood), was one that made
> any other relationship impossible. I wonder if you will under-
> stand that.
>
> "Now I've got to explain what I feel about our relationship
> to each other—and that will be all. Perhaps the only thing that
> needs explaining is about the absence of passionate feeling. I

---

* This muddled explanation of his relationship with Olive indicates that he was
still smarting from hurt pride.

have always told you that I felt so restful and content with you, that the restless, tormenting, passionate feeling wasn't there; and I have seen that you didn't feel passionate towards me, but have said over and over again that you didn't believe in passion. So we are quite equal, and why should we quarrel about it? Let us just be natural with each other—leaving the other feeling to grow up or not, as it will. It is possible to me to come near you and to show you my heart, and it is possible to you to come near me; and (to me at least) that is something so deep and so rare that it makes personal tenderness natural and inevitable, or at all events right.

"In reference to marriage: I said (or meant) that I did not think either you or I were the kind of people who could safely tie ourselves legally to anyone; true marriage, as I understand it, is a union of soul and body so close and so firmly established that one feels it will last as long as life lasts. For people to whom that has come to exist as an everyday fact of their lives, then the legal tie may safely follow; but it cannot come beforehand. I have seen so much of unhappy marriages—which all started happily—and I do not think anything on earth could induce me to tie myself legally to anyone with whom I had not—perhaps for years—been so united in body and soul that separation would be intolerable. Surely, Edith, you, too, understand that you *can't* promise to give away your soul for life, that you can't promise to love for ever *beforehand*. Haven't you learnt this from your own experience?

"I don't think I've anything more to explain. Now it's your turn, and then we'll have a rest from explaining. I've told you simply and honestly how I stand towards you. I took it for granted before that everything I have said was what you could have said too. Tell me where you don't feel with me, and tell me quite honestly, as I have told you, how you feel towards me. We aren't so young that we need fear to face the naked facts of life simply and frankly. You know how much you are to me—exactly how much. Putting aside Olive, I have never loved anyone so deeply and truly, and with the kind of love that seemed to make everything possible and pure, and even my relationship to Olive has not seemed so beautiful and unalloyed as my relationship to you. It has seemed to me that we might perhaps go on becoming nearer and nearer, and dearer and dearer, to each other as time went on. My nature isn't of the passionately impetuous kind (though it's very sensuous) and my affections grow slowly, and die hard, if at all. Even as it is, we shall be dear comrades as long as we live. You have hurt me rather, but I don't mind because there mustn't be anything false, and our relationship is strong enough to bear a good deal of tugging. Havelock."[9]

Undoubtedly some of Edith's unease stemmed from jealousy of Olive, a feeling that had been pricked by what Ellis described as "absurd rumours" repeated to her by a man whom she greatly respected. By mid-summer Edith had managed to put her doubts and fears to rest, and on July 7th she wrote this characteristically impulsive letter:

"Dear Olive Schreiner, I wish you were here—I want to take your hands and I should like you to kiss me. I have grown to love you, though, long ago, this would have made me smile to think of. I feel you are very beautiful and true and that is why I am writing to you. It is strange, and yet natural too, that you should even care a little for me. I looked up at you once at Chenies Street Chambers and you looked down upon me—do you remember it? We both smiled and went away. I wish you were here. Yours in sincerity. E.M.O.L."[10]

As for any relationships that Edith had experienced in the past, these too must be revealed and analyzed. One day she burst into Ellis's study eager to confide in him that she had been in love with "one of the leading spirits of the New Fellowship, a friend of my own, who had, however, shown no recognition of this attraction, or experienced any corresponding attraction, and had now passed out of her life, having left England altogether."[11] This could mean no one else but Percival Chubb, who had emigrated to the United States, following the lead of his mentor, Thomas Davidson. Chubb was very kind to her at the time of her breakdown, and that is probably why she responded as ardently as she did. Two men had, however, been very much attracted to her. One was the leading journalist William Clarke, whom Ellis had originally met at his first meeting with Davidson. Clarke had always taken a friendly interest in his work, but when Edith broke the news of her impending marriage to

him, he went into a state of shock and avoided Ellis from that moment. The other man was Algernon West, who was secretary of the
library at the Crystal Palace (where Edith had worked for a time)
and who remained doggedly loyal until the end. Neither man ever
married.

There has been much speculation as to whether Ellis was aware
that Edith was a lesbian at the time of their marriage. Percival
Chubb, he tells us in *My Life,* was the only man Edith ever felt
attracted to, adding, "Whatever passionate attractions she had experienced were for women."[12] Some pages further on, he says of their
marriage: "It was certainly not a union of unrestrainable passion; I,
though I failed yet clearly to realise why, was conscious of no inevitably passionate sexual attraction to her, and she, also without yet
clearly realising why, had never felt genuinely passionate sexual attraction for any man."[13] Before her marriage Dr. Birch advised her
against getting married, and strongly insisted that she have no children. At the same time he told her that he believed she would never
find her way into a lunatic asylum, but if she were ever to enter one
she would never come out again, a curious form of reassurance. As
for Ellis, he had no particular desire to have children, he couldn't
support them, and he feared the result of the union of Edith's unstable stock and his own nervous disposition. A number of people
warned them against marrying. Ellis does not say what objections
were raised against him, but a rather eerie forewarning occurred in
connection with Edith. James Hinton's daughter, Margaret, sometimes went to Bethlehem Hospital to play the piano for the inmates.
When asked what the patients were like, she replied that some of
them were "like that Miss Lees." Thirty years later Ellis was to find
himself tortured as to whether he should have Edith committed to
Bethlehem.

In July 1892 Edith published an article in *Seed-Time* called "Sincerity in Marriage"—the first time under the name Edith Lees Ellis.

Driblets of enforced confession after marriage are sorry makeshifts
for complete mutual revelations before marriage. The conventional
folk tell us that the "engagement" period is the happiest time in the
love cycle. To a really conscientious man or woman this can scarcely
be possible. In a true marriage it surely ought to be the time when
one's cupboards are thrown wide open for the family and individual
"ghosts" to come forth. That can never be a covert peaceful time if
absolute sincerity be the leading motive.[14]

Ellis must have told her of the intimacies in his relationship with Olive; and she in turn told him about the women in her past. "I knew," he later wrote in *My Life*, "that when a schoolgirl . . . friendships had sometimes possessed a slight but definite sensuous character, though it had not found that experience in later adult friendships with women. I knew that such feelings were common in young girls. But at that time I had no real practical knowledge of inborn sexual inversion of character."[15] (If we are to believe the graphic details in what appears to be her case-history in *Sexual Inversion*, the relationships after she passed girlhood were far more erotic than this passage would suggest.) He clearly entered the marriage with his eyes open, but naïve enough to believe that her love for him would rule out female rivals. He simply did not know what he was talking about when he elevated affectionate comradeship above passion in their theoretical discussions. He is extremely careful not to spell out to what degree sex was to enter this companionate marriage. They decided on a legal marriage because they both wanted a permanent union, and the tragic case of Eleanor Marx and Edward Aveling was enough to frighten them away from a totally free arrangement. It was possible, too, to be *almost* economically independent of each other.* When she was twenty Edith had inherited a small income of between £150 and £200 a year. With Ellis's income from the Contemporary Science Series, in addition to the flow of articles, reviews, and introductions he was writing, money seemed no immediate problem. Finally, although they planned to spend much time together, they would continue to maintain separate establishments. In May Edith wrote: "I believe in folk separating at intervals, don't you? Yes, I know you do. How I should loathe a creature I was *always* near!"[16] Karl Pearson wrote to congratulate Ellis on his forthcoming marriage, adding that he himself was not "a strong advocate for matrimony," and asked if he knew the lady in question. Ellis replied the next day.

---

* In a pamphlet written a year after their marriage, *A Noviciate for Marriage*, Edith wrote: "The very root of the whole sex question is the absolute economic and social independence of woman, so that love may be freed from commercialism and able to clearly face its own needs. In order to attain this we shall inevitably have to try experiments which will bring social ostracism on those who have the honesty to put their principles into action." While Edith could be a careful housekeeper, she rashly ordered a thousand of these pamphlets to be printed; and after her death in 1916 most of them were still lying about in great piles, a rueful reminder to Ellis when he was saddled with the enormous debts she had accumulated at the end of her life.

"I am in the position of an advocate for marriage who is a decided opponent of legal marriage (of the present sort). But to act consistently with that position means expending a great deal of energy which I think I can apply better in other ways. I am marrying in such a way as will make it fairly easy for both parties to retire into single life if—as I by no means expect—that seems desirable; and I am marrying someone (Edith Lees—you may possibly know her name) who is most heartily in agreement with me about these things. It is not quite satisfactory to give up one's principle in practice, but I shall at least be helped to work out some sexual problems which I have much at heart."[17]

In July he and Edith resolved to have their first holiday together. While Miss Jones was away for several weeks Ellis took her cottage at Lamorna—almost a year since they had met here—while Edith was to come and spend a week with him and then go on to a cottage she had taken at Carbis. Ellis wrote to her before her arrival:

"It's very lovely here—so delicious to lie in the sun and hear nothing except an occasional insect or bird, and to know that our dear brother men are at a safe distance. Burton the fisherman and his wife have pleasant recollections of the clever little female who spent a day here with her lady's maid, and they were glad to hear that she is coming again. (That's the result of kissing the dirty babies!) But they won't be so glad as I will.—I've taken a little house (rent free) made of granite and bracken and honeysuckle. It's a lovely little house, hidden away from the world; the pillars of it are two huge foxglove stems which tower up above you against the sky when you lie down in it. I've got room in my house for a little wife—but she must be small—I've also got a nest in the rock right over the sea—and a very, very tiny sweet bird might nestle in close beside me there,—I've also got an ordinary rock, the same I had last year, where I lie and bask in the sun and read and dream."[18]

Edith arrived on July 8th at Penzance Station, where Ellis met her, and they walked over to Lamorna. This period at Lamorna they always regarded as their true honeymoon. They spent whole days wandering along the cliffs, lying together on fragrant mounds of thyme and heather, constantly talking about their plans for the future.

Some form of close sexual intimacy certainly seems to have occurred, judging from a letter written by Edith the following summer:

"My love, do you know that by the day of the week this is the day a year ago when you and I went to our little house with the foxglove towers and gave ourselves to ourselves? I look back and it seems years and years ago. I was shy and frightened, and cried over my wee babe that was never to be, and you!—you made me think of how beautiful men could be."[19]

In November 1891 Edith gave a lecture, "The Masses and the Classes: A Plea," to the Ancoats Brotherhood in Manchester. This was the first of her lectures to be printed, and on the evening before the wedding they corrected the proofs together. They had gone halves on the purchase of a wedding ring bought in Hatton Garden. On Saturday the 19th of December Ellis woke early, put on his velvet jacket, and Louie adjusted his cravat. They sat before the fire, where the composed bridegroom read an article in *Nature*. Louie complained that her hands were cold and Ellis took them in his and rubbed them affectionately. Presently they set off through the slush to the Paddington Registry Office. The bride could be seen in the distance in an ulster, waving her umbrella. She was accompanied by the two Brooke sisters, who were to act as witnesses. They were ushered into a small office, where they had to wait a rather a long time for the clerk. Edith was very nervous, but Havelock sat bolt upright, talking steadily in an even voice about what he had been reading that morning; and during the ceremony he responded in a firm, decisive tone, while Edith was barely audible. Louie, Edith, and Ellis then walked back arm in arm to St. Mary's Terrace for a bowl of porridge. Not long afterwards Edith returned by underground to Fellowship House to prepare for a reception which she was having for her friends during the afternoon. Ellis slipped in briefly at the end. They then parted until the next morning, when they left for Paris.

Ellis had decided against the Corneille in favor of the more conventionally British Hôtel d'Oxford et de Cambridge in the Rue d'Alger. It was his bride's first visit to Paris, and Ellis sometimes rather wished that she would be a little more restrained in her ebullient outbursts of pleasure. She, in turn, was roused to quick resentment when he tried to quiet her shouts at the sight of the cabmen's white hats, but she later had her revenge when a street photographer asked to take "the leetle miss's" photograph, teasing her husband that she had been taken for his grand-daughter.

On the 28th Ellis wrote to his father in Melbourne.

My dear Father,

You have no doubt heard that we were safely married on the 19th inst. at the Paddington Registry Office, with the assistance of two genial Registrars—and two witnesses—according to the Act. It only takes a few minutes. We came here the following day, and have been having a very happy time. We return in three or four days. Edith has never been to Paris before and enjoys it immensely. We have had bright sunny weather while in London they had been in thick darkness.

Edith has had heaps of wedding presents—over 50—and more to come: yours is not yet bought. I have only had a few including a picture from Miss Haddon.

Your affectionate son
HHE

Edith enclosed a note:

My dear Pater

We are very happy together in this world of gaiety and luxury. I hear I have to thank you for a kind gift to me. I'll kiss you for it when I see you. H. looks happy, though married—strange, is it not?

Yours lovingly,
EMO Ellis[20]

The happiest moment of all occurred when listening together to Beethoven's Ninth Symphony at the Châtelet Theatre. The experience should be told in Ellis's own words:

In the exaltation of that solemn hymn to Joy my own new personal life seemed to blend harmoniously with the vision of my mission of work in the world. This realisation shone radiantly out of my eyes, and in much later days Edith would still sometimes describe my face as she saw it then. I have heard the Ninth Symphony since, but I never again re-captured the rapture of that moment.[21]

MARRIED LIFE

THEY RETURNED TO LONDON EARLY IN JANUARY. ELLIS WENT BACK to his bachelor rooms in Paddington, and Edith returned to the Fellowship House. Before her marriage she had sent in her resignation as secretary, but the actual date of parting took place some weeks later when the members of the Fellowship had a little party for her and on their behalf Edward Carpenter presented her with a complete set of Emerson's works.

In these first months a pattern of shared living had to be worked out. The most basic priority was where they were going to live, separately and together. The summer before their marriage Edith had secured a tiny cottage at Carbis. Now she found a bungalow—High Stoatley Cottage—at Haslemere in grounds belonging to the Hon. Rollo Russell (son of the former Prime Minister, Lord John Russell). They furnished the bungalow with things Edith had brought from the Fellowship House, the only major new acquisition being a large double bed which they sold when they left Haslemere a few years later, to be replaced by single beds in their little Cornish cottage. Eventually they were to have separate rooms. They soon fell into an established routine: the winters were always spent together in Cornwall, the summers usually at Haslemere. During 1892 they spent more than half the year under the same roof, although the separations became more frequent with the passing of time; for example, Edith acquired a number of cottages around Carbis which she fitted

up to let—Ellis greatly admired her artistic ability in this direction—
and this activity entailed her staying in Cornwall for longer periods.

The first months of their marriage were tranquil, probably the
most restful and contented of Edith's life. In June Ellis wrote to her
from Paddington:

> "Louie and Symons came to the conclusion the other day that
> I had not been at all spoilt by marriage; you'd hardly know, Sy-
> mons said to her, that I was married. Rhys, on the other hand,
> they decided, had been spoilt. Although better groomed than
> formerly (or perhaps because!) he looks pale and depressed and
> has no spirit for anything; always has to be with his wife. . . ."[1]

Haslemere could have been an ideal place to work, completely
cut off from the world, but the gregarious Edith loved to invite troops
of friends to visit her. Ellis, shy, awkward, anxious to get on with his
work, found these visits very trying. He was moved to protest, and
the over-sensitive Edith reacted with some "stupid naughty words."
On the 12th of August she wrote Ellis in a state of disenchantment
about their marriage, but the following day she had contrite second
thoughts:

> "My husband, After a night's sleep and with your patient letters
> in my hands I'm utterly ashamed of my wild stormy nature, and
> its moods, and yet—it is me, too. Love me for my faults, and not
> my virtues, Dear, and then I shall never disappoint you! Poor
> sweet old love, I wish I had your dear head here now, and I'd
> bury it in my wee breast and kiss the poor brain where I have
> kicked. Poor dear Havelock—yet, paradoxical as it seems, if I did
> not love you I could not kick you. However, I can only promise
> to try. Love can do much, and to know you really love me will
> probably work miracles. You see why I have to be quiet and not
> over-work or worry; it is an inheritance, and I fear will for ever
> make your *utter* reverence for me impossible. I seem to want you
> very badly. I think I can pour in the oil and wine now, if you'll
> let me."[2]

Peace was temporarily restored; but these explosions—usually due to
nervous exhaustion—continued for the rest of their married life, although towards the end they were no longer followed by bouts of
remorse and scenes of tender reconciliation.

There was little rest or peace with Edith, who alternated between joyous laughter and profound depression. She submitted so deeply to every mood that exhaustion was the inevitable outcome. She carried around a tiny pillow and could fall asleep on it in a minute. Her friends adored her—but in small, exhilarating draughts; Havelock—who found scarcely anyone congenial for any length of time—loved and understood her, but felt an increasing need for gentleness, solitude, and silence.

Work provided this, and it was silent, solitary work above all that he craved. He went twice again to Probus as *locum tenens* for Dr. Bonar—in July 1892 for several weeks and finally in January 1893, the last practical medical work he was ever to do. In 1892 he brought out a small but rather important book, *The Nationalization of Health.** In the Introduction to *The New Spirit* he had argued for the identification of the self with the state, and here he was to advocate the duty of the individual to support a scheme whereby the state was to be responsible for the physical well-being of the individual, a revolutionary suggestion in its time. Against an historical background of the development of health movements, he discusses the role of the private practitioner, the existing hospital system, the hospital of the future, and the necessity for a Ministry of Health. These ideas were to be amplified later in *The Task of Social Hygiene* (1912). In *The Nationalization of Health* a national health scheme is, as far as I know, advocated for the first time; certainly most of his recommendations have been adopted by the British Health Service. This book was the most overtly political act of Ellis's life. He always described himself as a socialist, but even the Fabians seemed too active for him. It is impossible to know whether the message of this book fell on deaf ears, whether it was premature or perhaps had a quiet, long-term influence. By 1934 Ellis told a friend who had come across a copy: "I never see it. But it was reviewed with unqualified praise on its appearance, and later the publisher wanted to bring out a new edition. But it seemed to me it would need far too much revision. The changes now taking place slowly in England are much on the lines I advocated. But I would now avoid using the word 'nationalization.' "[3]

In 1893 he attempted to interest Walter Scott in a new illus-

---

* To Isaac Goldberg, his first biographer, he wrote in 1926: "It was an unimportant book from my standpoint, & though its points were freshly felt & freshly put, they are not at all new or original" (Manuscripts and Archives Division, New York Public Library, Astor, Lenox and Tilden Foundations).

trated monthly journal to be called *Man: A Journal of Psychology and Anthropology*. He envisaged a format like the current *Folk-lore*, of about sixty-four pages, to sell for a shilling an issue. In the prospectus he drew up, he described the purpose of the journal:

> To deal with psychology and anthropology in the widest sense—including also Sociology, Ethnography, Demography, Hypnotism, the study of genius, and, of course, criminal anthropology, with those branches of medical research which border on anthropology and psychology and are of general interest. Archaeology of the old-fashioned type would be ignored.
>
> It would not be a journal for specialists in any one branch but would bring together the groups of specialists interested in man, on a common ground, and would especially seek the "cross-fertilisation" of anthropology and psychology, which in the future is bound to be very productive, and has already been in America.[4]

When there was a topic of wide public interest—such as a criminal trial—instead of the issues being distorted as they inevitably were in the press, *Man* would attempt to present a balanced and well-informed view. Ellis wished to make it international in tone, with a large number of foreign contributors. It was an idea that appealed immensely to him and he was greatly disappointed when he found it impossible to launch, because he always believed that he would have made an able editor of an advanced journal. The idea held fire for some time until June 1897, when he reported regretfully to F. H. Perry-Coste: "Flinders Petrie and others have robbed me of my title *Man* for a periodical—mainly archaeological—which they propose to issue in the autumn."*[5]

The work to which he devoted most of his attention during the early period of his marriage was *Man and Woman*, a study of secondary sexual characteristics. This was almost completely written at Haslemere, and the slow, laborious task of collating all the data he had been collecting for a number of years was possibly the most congenial task to engage his energies at a time when he needed a good deal of self-discipline to control unexpected emotional pressures. This book will be discussed in some detail in a later chapter, but suffice it to say at this point that there are many passages in which Ellis could not fail to be thinking of Edith. One such passage in the Conclusion strikes an ironical note:

---

* This scheme never seems to have materialized.

The female retains her youthfulness for the sake of possible offspring; we all exist for the sake of our possible offspring, but this final end of the individual is more obviously woven into the structure of women. The interests of women may therefore be said to be more closely identified with Nature's interests. Nature has made women more like children in order that they may better understand and care for children, and in the gift of children Nature has given to women a massive and sustained physiological joy to which there is nothing in men's lives to correspond.[6]

All through his career Ellis continued to write rapturously about the joys of motherhood, which he viewed as the chief fulfilling purpose for women on this earth. His attitude to the New Woman seems somewhat ambivalent. In the Introduction to *The New Spirit* he seems rather uneasy about what part woman should play in the social organization of the future. Olive Schreiner he always described as the only woman of genius he had ever known. He was somewhat patronizing about Edith's mind, although he loyally supported her rather effusive lectures and he genuinely seemed to admire her mediocre fiction, which he was always pressing on friends; and after her death he made strenuous efforts to get some of her books reissued. Was this a gesture of propitiation towards her frustrated motherhood? When he married her there was a very clear understanding that there were to be no children, but from time to time Edith manifested a thwarted maternal instinct. Their tenderness towards each other was usually expressed as parent and child, and, depending upon the emotional situation, they could exchange roles at will. Ellis always regarded her as a perpetual child, with a child's charm and aggravations. Did he, one might speculate, ever view her lesbianism as arrested development; did he see her as an incomplete woman unable to take on what he considered the normal functions of a woman? Some comments by Bernard De Voto in his review of *My Life* should be pondered:

> They could meet, of course, only as children. On page after page of the letters which make up a large part of the book, each repeatedly calls the other "baby." Each is forever repeating his desire to be the other's child. Their love-making is the play of children, their tenderness is the mutual gratitude of children for help in remaining Peter Pan, the highest maturity that either could attain (Edith shows it oftener than Ellis) is the phantasy that he is the other's mother. Each was the other's ally against the terrifying necessity of growing

up in a world of adults, and neither could tolerate sex except as it evaded its own necessities and provided a childish escape from the obligation of adult heterosexuality. There are words for it in "Studies in the Psychology of Sex." There are more accurate words for it in Freud.[7]

Ellis entered marriage believing that all it needed was tenderness, intelligence, and emancipated understanding. He was soon to discover that it held terrifying complexities and in later life he frequently described marriage as a "tragedy," the only true way of experiencing the tragic vision of life. Not many months after his marriage he began to lose his innocence. At the end of their first summer Ellis returned to London to work, and Edith went down to stay in her cottage at Carbis with an old friend whom Ellis calls "Claire" in *My Life*. They were both exceedingly happy, congratulating each other on the modern independence they were achieving in their extremely advanced modern marriage. "You are, *really*, my sweetheart, are you not?" Ellis asked her. "I can't bear to think that you are ever such a tiny bit like those wives who hang round their husbands' necks like millstones."[8] But there was a worm at the heart of their happiness. "And in the climax of her felicity," Ellis recalled, "my felicity received a jar which affected, directly and indirectly, the whole course of our subsequent relations."[9]

Out of the blue Ellis suddenly received a letter from Edith telling him that she had developed a passionate attachment for Claire. He generally kept all her letters, but this one disappeared; its loss, of course, was the expression of his desire to rid himself of its painful contents. In *My Life*, therefore, he could rely only on his memory of what he believed she had said.

> She wrote to tell me of it with all her native trustful confidence, simple, direct and spontaneous. If I remember right, she wrote with a misgiving hesitation at first. There was, as I now look back, a pathetic wonder and beauty in that appeal to my comprehending love, as though addressed to a divine being superior to the weaknesses of a human heart.[10]

Ellis had never regarded himself as a divine being, but he had not regarded himself as an ordinary husband either. Never at any time did he feel for her what is generally meant by passion, but he felt a deep and growing tenderness for her, a feeling that was to grow into an undeniably conjugal love. What Edith's letter brought him was suffering of a most intense kind. Theoretically he might speak against the exclusivity of relationships, but at the same time he believed that what existed between him and Edith was profound and unique, and so he felt a vague but nevertheless real hurt that she had in some way betrayed him. He also experienced an acute shock because, in his naïveté about inversion, this new situation was totally unexpected. Ellis never completely overcame certain rigid stereotypes regarding inversion; and particularly at this early date he was totally bewildered because Edith seemed lacking in those masculine traits which he associated with lesbianism. Of those male characteristics he was later to write: "Most people, I believe, failed to see them, and I cannot too often repeat that she was not really man at all in any degree, but always woman, boy, and child, and these three, it seemed, in almost equal measure."[11]

Despite his hurt and his shock, he wrote tenderly to her; and Edith's replies indicated that she fully expected such understanding from him. Ellis's emotions worked slowly and during that bleak winter he had time enough to brood over the course events had taken. He would pace up and down his study in Paddington, aching over a letter such as one dated February 14th: "I told Claire you would be trusted with all and she smiled 'You *are* two odd people!' It is her purity and sweetness which have made me love her; she is so child-like and unprudish, and gives me like a child a love which has rested and comforted and strengthened me in a way that amazes me."[12] Yet Ellis had the magnanimity to write the following on March 8th: "My own Wifie, my letter was very lovely this morning; I read it over ever so many times. Yes, nothing in the world or out of it will tear you away from my breastbone—unless you want to go. I am perfectly happy that you should be so close to Claire. I feel very tender to her. Give her my sweetest love."[13] And Edith replied: "It is so wonderful to have married a man who leaves a woman her soul. I'm utterly satisfied in you, Havelock. It passes all my comprehension, though, why you love me."[14]

Nevertheless, Ellis continued to be tortured by the suspicion that in Edith's obsession for Claire her love for him was inevitably diminished. He always claimed that he never felt jealousy towards Claire, but in Edith's letters he suspected he detected a growing detachment from him, which he described as "philosophic" in tone, and his unhappiness began to seep into his letters. A crisis was reached in March of 1893 when Edith, accompanied by Claire, went to Man-

chester to lecture to the Ancoats for the first time since their marriage. Apparently she was so distressed by the misery throbbing
through a letter she received from him on the day of the lecture—a
misery prompted by Ellis's knowledge that Edith was there giving
her love exclusively and joyfully to Claire—that she almost collapsed
and could no more than stumble through her lecture. The contrite
letter which Havelock wrote on hearing of her state should be quoted
and pondered for its expression of how much he really cared for her.

"My Sweet Heart, I am so pained at your letter, that I have hurt
you so—and when it was only out of my love. It makes me hate
myself. But you say *exactly* the things that I have been feeling.
Only your letter isn't like a 'philosophic' lover's, you know. And
in that, although it pains me you are hurt, it takes a great load off
me somehow. You know I have all these weeks been loving you
so much, and seeming never to be able to think of anything else
but you and I was so glad about Claire—and I think I got into
a morbidly sensitive state and that is why your philosophy hurt
me so. I feel so angry and ashamed with myself I let you see it;
I tried not to. And yet I can't love and *not* tell you what I feel.
. . . That letter needn't have pained you so. It only showed that
I loved you a great deal more than is wise. It is funny that only a
little while ago I was writing to Olive such an enthusiastic letter
about how I love you, and about how at last I had got to that
exalted state in which mere loving itself is sufficient and one
doesn't crave so much about the amount of the return—and it
isn't true at all! (I mean about the return). I do wish it wasn't
my nature to love so intensely. All my life long I have been trying
to be philosophical, but I haven't succeeded. And now I know
I shall never succeed. You see if I could love you quite moderately
and peacefully you would be quite happy and undisturbed!
Please do not imagine that I felt miserable before a week ago and
was hiding it, or that it was because of your love to Claire—but
I know you won't suspect me about that. Love is funny and I am
funny. It needs its wifie's little breasties every two hours like a
baby and if they seem far off—it do shriek! (But you know, my
Love, when the mother hears her baby, and knows she has that
within her to soothe it, she doesn't feel that she must yell too!)
Your own troublesome and unphilosophic but absurdly loving
Husband."

In a postscript he added: "I seem to be a mother, and you my fretful babe that I fold and smother in my breast."[15]

The crisis passed. Edith was to have a succession of passionate relationships, although—and Ellis regarded this as an extenuation— only one intense friend at a time. He learned to accept the succession of "dear friends"; he never quarrelled with any of them and the only test he applied to them was whether they were good for Edith or not. It is difficult to know how secretly these relationships were guarded or whether they were common knowledge among their friends. Certainly Edward Carpenter knew the truth. Edith became very close to him and stayed at Milthorpe a number of times, completely at ease in a homosexual household, sitting by the fire mending socks or talking livestock in the pub with the men. Edward Carpenter recounts in his autobiography that one of the farmers asked, "When is that little lady coming again with that curly hair, like a lad's, and them blue eyes, what talked about pigs and cows. I shall never forget her."[16] Edith always asked to be remembered to "the boys."

Ellis's emotional mettle had been tried in his long and difficult love for Olive Schreiner, torturing himself at the spectacle of her obsession for Karl Pearson. After Olive, Edith had seemed more predictable, the lifelong comrade he was seeking. Despite Hinton's doctrines, Ellis cherished a conception of mutual devotion in marriage, and here was a tempestuous partner kicking over all his intellectual theorizing. And surely Edith's behaviour was not out of line with Hinton's plea for a completely emancipated marriage? But on a deep emotional level a flaw had entered their marriage and no amount of baby-talk would mend it. From one point of view, Ellis's sense of justice could not tolerate a situation in which only one partner had sexual liberty. Furthermore, he began to see Edith more realistically. He continued to love her deeply; but he realized that the homosexual qualities which made her a splendid comrade were "inimical to the purely feminine qualities of sweetness and repose which a man seeks in a woman, and therefore opposed in our case to a strict conjugal fidelity. And so it proved."[17]

By the spring of 1893 a *modus vivendi* seemed to have established itself. Late in March Edith was writing with tenderness and a profound appreciation of this singular husband of hers:

"Your letters make me glow that you love me so. You know, in your ear this is how I wanted you to love me—with passion and

force—and I know now you were not *quite* in love with me when
we went to the registrar's. I am not 'far away' but in your very
bowels and heart. I believe I have an exceptional power of loving.
What has hurt you? I don't think you can ever guess what this
deep great love of you is to me, and your love—and Claire's too.
I live and I bathe in love, and you must not grudge it me. *Nothing* can make me 'far off' for you—it is impossible."[18]

Towards the end of May Edith found herself in the bungalow at
Haslemere with no servant sleeping in and Havelock in London most
of the time. She was always terrified of being alone at night, and since
none of her own friends was available, Ellis suggested that the daughter of his old friend Barker Smith might keep her company. Mneme
(whom he disguises as "Amy" in *My Life*) was twenty-four, gentle,
extremely feminine. Ellis had known her for about ten years—since
he and Barker Smith were at St. Thomas's together—and he had always more or less taken her for granted.* Now, within the confines
of the small bungalow, he became keenly aware of the contrast between the soft, pliable girl and Edith's volatile moodiness. He
became aware, too, of Mneme's infatuation for him. One afternoon
when they were out for a walk he kissed her; and when they returned
to the cottage, true to their mutual principle of sincerity—of which
Edith boasted to all and sundry—he confessed what had happened.
Edith exploded and there followed one humiliating scene after another. Havelock felt indignation at the one-sided justice of the situation. He was later to rationalize that if Edith had behaved a little
more sensibly his attraction to Mneme might have faded away; as
it was, the seed became rooted more firmly. It took some years to
mature and when it did—although Ellis is very furtive about the
relationship in *My Life*—for some years he was sexually obsessed
with her.

Nevertheless, there was still a very firm basis to the marriage. In
September 1893 from Manchester, where she had returned to lecture,
Edith wrote:

"I don't know what on earth is the matter with me, but I feel a
nearness and sweetness, strength and depth, about you that is
like the rush of the sea or a mountain ridge. I seem to have lived

---

* The first reference I can find to her in his correspondence is a letter to Olive
Schreiner on November 17th, 1884, when he tells her that he had been visited by
Barker Smith and his daughter, "a very pretty girl" (University of Texas).

years and years; and that tiny misery and problem about Mneme has helped me so in helping others. . . . I shall always tell you everything, and lie on your heart. I am surged with love of you and nothing in the world could make me not bear what you may bring to me, for men and women *seemingly* must hurt those they love. . . . Think of me and know that in your arms and on your breast is my one complete home."[19]

Many, many years later Ellis advised a young man that what he wanted in a wife were "constitutional ideals." "In my wife, for instance," he recalled, "I always knew that (though highly sensitive and nervous) she would be brave, I always knew she would seek to conquer any impulse that might work for disharmony, and all this not because she merely felt she 'ought' to, but because it was *her* nature."[20] And such qualities were very much to the fore during these years of comparative peace. Despite the emotional upsurges, most of their early life together was passed in a quiet, steady routine. The Cot, Edith's cottage at Carbis Bay, was completely unsuitable for Ellis to work in, and Edith found him an ideal little building at Hawkes Point, a fifteen-minute walk away. It had been a mining shed at the head of a now disused shaft. From there he could look down on the Lelant Sands, and in the distance see St. Ives to the left and to the right the deserted dunes stretching towards Godrevy lighthouse.* At that time there was not a house in sight and Edward Carpenter, on one of his visits, assured him that it was the finest prospect in England. Setting off after breakfast, Ellis would write all day in the shelter of an overturned boat. It was here that he developed what was to be a lifetime habit of doing all his writing in the open air. Always he wanted sun and the prospect of land and sea, and he liked to think that these elements swept through his writing.

In the evenings husband and wife frequently worked together. During 1894 he made a complete, unexpurgated translation of Zola's *Germinal* for the Lutetian Society† (printed privately in order to avoid Vizetelly's fate; and reissued by Knopf in 1925). Ellis dictated the translation and Edith wrote it out, occasionally offering a sugges-

---

* The model for the lighthouse in Virginia Woolf's *To the Lighthouse*.

† The Lutetian Society was founded to translate works that would not generally be acceptable to Victorian readers. The naïve idea was that if they were expensive enough they would not be thought to contaminate the masses. The result was that they soon went out of business. Several of Zola's novels were translated, including *L'Assommoir* by Arthur Symons.

tion for the improvement of an idiom. Ellis received £50 for it, half of which he gave to Edith. This was a particularly quiet period in Edith's life, the lull before her later frenetic activities, and she was also able to help him with some of the translations for the Contemporary Science Series.

At Haslemere their days were more varied. Edith could run up to town to see her innumerable friends whenever she pleased, and Ellis generally spent two or three days a week in the Reading Room of the British Museum, and in the evenings attended concerts and scientific lectures. Years before—at Burwood, in Australia—during an evening stroll he had decided that his major life-work would be to devote himself to unravelling the "problem" of sex. Now, on a similar evening walk in Haslemere, strolling back and forth in the twilight, he thought out the General Preface to his sex *Studies*. Slowly, slowly, the general outline of the work was forming itself in his mind.

Such quiet, scholarly pursuits might be exactly what Havelock needed, but the highly strung Edith was bound to explode unless she could inject more excitement into their life. One day, when they were staying at Carbis, she rushed in to announce in her breathless, impulsive way that she had bought the Count House. This was an old building, constructed forty years before as the official business headquarters of the mine, and boarded up when the mine was abandoned. Superficially, as a home it presented no attractions at all, but it had a beautiful view over moor and sea, and with her artistic sense Edith was able to make it a charming enough house to live in for the next ten years. Bernard Leach, the distinguished potter, moved into it later, and discovered a prehistoric hut-dwelling just below the garden wall—a discovery Ellis was sorry not to have made for himself.

The move to a larger house, Edith explained, was absolutely necessary because they had scarcely room to breathe in the Cot. What she really meant was that she needed to push back the walls. The next sign that she was entering a period of intense activity was her dramatic announcement that she was taking up farming. There were several fields attached to the Count House and here she gradually collected a menagerie of cows, donkeys, pigs, fowls, and ducks. She knew nothing of farming, but, undeterred, she plunged into it with all her native enthusiasm. "The sex question is for ever with me on my farm," she told Carpenter. "I've come to the conclusion that if some of these spiritual dames and man hating shrews would only farm they'd know more in a year than all their lecturers and big books can teach them."[21] It was taken for granted that the bewildered Havelock need take no part in these activities beyond being asked occasionally to kill a fowl.

But it was necessary for Ellis to spend a good deal of time in London, particularly in connection with the Contemporary Science Series, which continued to provide his chief source of income. Early in 1894 Louie gave up the house in St. Mary's Terrace, and in the autumn of the same year Ellis and Edith decided that the bungalow at Haslemere no longer suited their purposes, so it was necessary for Ellis to find a *pied-à-terre* in London; and he eagerly accepted Arthur Symons's offer to rent him two small rooms in his chambers at Fountain Court in the Temple. Symons retained two rooms at the top of the building, overlooking the court, and Ellis took the two below overlooking Essex Street. These he retained until Symons's marriage in 1901. There were two separate doors on the landing, so that they could remain in close touch if they wished, or could entertain their own visitors in complete privacy.

It was now that the relationship with Mneme was enabled to develop into deep intimacy. She lived in Dulwich and could get up frequently to London to visit Ellis. Less is known about this friendship than about any of his other close relationships with women; Ellis tends to be very circumspect about it in *My Life*, as Mneme and her husband were still alive, and he left instructions that his autobiography was to be published as soon as possible after his death. Moreover, Mneme—who was one of his literary executors— after the funeral descended on the house he had shared with Françoise Lafitte and destroyed all her letters.

However, there are certain details that can be pieced together. Mneme gave him the feminine gentleness which was quite impossible to find with Edith. She did not share any of his intellectual interests, so we can assume that this was primarily a sexual relationship. Ellis told her that he could not bind her to him permanently nor could he promise that his affection would last. Nothing was concealed from Edith, he says; and despite her protestations two years previously, and despite the fact that she was exercising exactly the same liberty, she again began to create hysterical scenes. Ellis found himself torn between Mneme's sweetness, which he craved, and his reluctance to cause Edith distress. In June 1898 Edith went up to London to stay with a friend, leaving Ellis alone at Carbis. Mneme at the time was staying with her father at Probus, where Barker Smith had succeeded Ellis as *locum tenens* to Dr. Bonar. According to Ellis, she suggested that she come over for a few hours to visit him in his studio. Ellis, in his open way, wrote to Edith to tell her that she was coming, and that he was glad to have his loneliness relieved. Edith's rejoinder was predictable: "Do cheer up, sweetheart, and if you *must* spoil Carbis Bay for me, why do, for after all she can never rob me of all the best and sweetest memories of my life which laugh in the blue sea and will never be stolen by a mere player at life's realities."[22] Ellis felt that Edith's attitude was totally unreasonable; he had no intention of spoiling Carbis Bay for her and would not dream of taking Mneme inside the Count House. Besides, he reasoned, Mneme's presence would be like a benediction which would linger long after her departure. Within a few days Edith's mood had changed again:

> "The demand that when we love that love should be true to *us* and to our share in it is all anyone who lives and thinks can ask: to *demand* more is to court deception, estrangement, and misery. I've arrived at this conclusion after *intense* suffering about Mneme, but I shall never suffer again. Do what you will—be what you will and don't feel you must ever *make* me understand. I shall ask no questions; but we will be both free in the real sense of the word—free to respect and love the love of others, free to *trust* our own love in the face of everything. . . . This is the best of me, so I give it to you as a gift from the woman who loves you."[23]

This was Edith's image of her best self, yet, unfortunately, she was never able to give the freedom which here she proffers so magnanimously. Ellis in time was able to do this—but only at the cost of further suffering.

In two different passages in *My Life* Ellis describes the situation as reaching the "intolerable" stage, and it is not at all clear whether he is referring to a single culminating crisis or to a series of periods of stress. In one section he is discussing his loyalty to Edith in never mentioning her to Mneme:

> That would to me have been an impossible disloyalty, and "Amy" instinctively respected my feelings. Edith sometimes found this a little difficult to believe; but it was true. She had a horror of being 'talked over.' it was also a torture to her to think that anyone would feel

'sorry' for her. That remained a trouble when all other troubles in the matter had passed. She was reconciled to the facts, but when she knew or suspected that they might be a subject of scandal among people who would be 'sorry for her,' she felt the situation intolerable.[24]

In another, earlier passage Ellis writes:

> At one time I felt that the situation was intolerable. I resolved to terminate the relationship and to cease seeing or corresponding with "Amy," while she on her side, willing to second what seemed to me best, took a situation on the Continent and remained there for several years.[25]

And what of her father, Ellis's good friend Barker Smith? Since Ellis is careful to conceal Mneme's identity in *My Life*, there is no mention of Barker Smith in connection with Mneme; but these were middle-class people who did not move in bohemian circles, and it scarcely seems probable that Mneme's parents (her mother was an invalid) would see the situation as Ellis did. Françoise Lafitte recalled that Ellis told her many years later that Barker Smith, fearing a scandal, had secured a nursing post for his daughter in Belgium. This puts a different light on Ellis's explanation that he had voluntarily sent her into exile and that she had meekly acquiesced.

In any event, Ellis was utterly miserable without her and soon began writing to her and arranging trysts with her whenever possible. His private travel notes on journeys to Belgium, Holland, and France during these years are the only remaining evidence of their relationship during this period. Mneme was away for three years and the affair was resumed on her return.

At some point Edith raised the question of having a child. Ellis made no reply, and the matter was dropped. One can only speculate as to how earnestly she wanted a child. It seems curious that Ellis cannot remember the date. If we knew the date, it might be possible to reconstruct the situation differently.* At any rate she had to be content with fondling her husband thus (August 1898): "My own sweet baby, eh' man! thee ought not to go far from your mammy's apron strings for thee wants thy bottle badly!"[26] It was also decided

---

* She wrote a curious letter to Edward Carpenter in 1909: "A new and beautiful person has come like a bolt from the blue, into my life and is as a son to me. A starving artist of 21 . . . He is mine now" (Sheffield Public Libraries). Ellis does not mention this relationship in *My Life*, although he refers to another young man to whom Edith became attached in 1916.

on Edith's initiative—and here again, significantly, Ellis's memory fails him as to the date—that sexual relations between them should come to a complete end.

> On her side, in addition to any feeling she had regarding my relationship with Amy, she had experienced from the outset a dislike to the mechanical contraceptive preliminaries of intercourse. On my side I felt that in this respect we were relatively unsuited to each other, that relations were incomplete and unsatisfactory, too liable to jar on one or other of the partners.[27]

Ellis goes on to say that, rather than diminishing, their love grew into a passion. "Only one thing was left out, a real and definite thing, yet so small in comparison to all that was left that we scarcely missed it." Love such as theirs, he believed, would last forever. Most probably so; but in view of subsequent events, their experiment in marriage was to prove a tragic failure.

CHAPTER 11

CONTROVERSIAL MATTER

THE NINETIES WERE A PERIOD OF INTENSE AND VARIED ACTIVITY, IN every way as rich in event as the previous decade. Life with Edith was enough to keep any man occupied, but Ellis had a livelihood to earn and a life of his own to lead.

This was the period in which he did his most intensive travelling. In April of 1891 he and Symons made their first trip to Spain, and until Symons's marriage in 1901 they went abroad together for six weeks of almost every year. Symons was the best of companions, sensitive to all forms of art, introducing Ellis to company with whom he would have been extremely shy had he been alone. Symons during this period was music critic on the *Star* and he took his friend on many excursions to the music-halls (described in Symons's *London Nights*). In the evenings they would often wander down the Embankment, and to Ellis the stretch of river and cityscape between Blackfriars and Westminster bridges was the most beautiful urban scene in the world. He was very much on the fringe of Symons's artistic circles, but occasionally Symons took him to meetings of the Rhymers Club, where he sat quietly in the background.

But it was Ellis who introduced Symons and Yeats (and possibly Yeats's friend, the poet-playwright Edward Martyn, who had rooms in the Temple)[1] to mescal (Anhalonium Lewinii) in Symons's rooms on at least one occasion. Ellis's attention was drawn to the drug in 1896 by an article by an American psychologist, Dr. Weir Mitchell,

who had experimented on himself in the United States. Early in
1897 Ellis obtained a fairly large supply of mescal buttons from
Potter & Clarke at 60 Artillery Lane East. He tried the experiment
on Good Friday when he was entirely alone in the Temple, the
quietest place in central London. He made an infusion of three
buttons and drank this in three doses, at intervals of an hour, beginning at 2:30 after a light lunch. He did not touch tobacco or
alcohol during the day. His detailed account of the changes that
took place in him with the passing hours makes fascinating reading.
Just before he went to bed, shortly after nine, he recorded:

> I had to break off as I cannot write for long at a time. The visions
> continue as brilliantly as ever: I think I see them better in a room
> lighted by fire than in a dark room. I have seen thick glorious fields
> of jewels which spring into forms like flowers beneath my view and
> then seem to turn into gorgeous butterfly-like forms. When I speak
> my voice seems strange to me and certainly sounds hoarse.
>
> As I write (by electric light) vague thin colour washes seem to
> lie on the paper, especially a golden yellow, and even the pencil seems
> to make somewhat gold-tinged marks. My hands seen in indirect
> vision seem strange, bronzed, scaled, flushed with red. Except for
> slight nausea I am feeling well, though when watching the visions I
> once noticed slight right frontal pain. The chief inconvenience is de-
> cidedly the motor incoordination. It involves inability to fix attention
> long; but otherwise attention is perfectly clear.[2]

No wonder Symons was eager to participate in an experience
which involved jewelled visions and fragrant perfumes! Ellis seems
to have been the first Englishman to experiment with the drug and
certainly the first European to write about it. By 1899, when he had
experimented on about half a dozen people, in response to an inquiry
by Francis Galton, he sent him three buttons and advised:

> "There is no ground at present to believe that any serious or
> permanent harm has been done by mescal. I consider, however,
> that though it may not be dangerous it is certainly most un-
> desirable to experiment with mescal if not in good health. It is
> specially important that heart & lungs should be sound, &
> nervous system; no severe after effects of influenza, etc. Mescal
> has physically (though not mentally) a decidedly depressing
> action, especially on the respiration, so that it does not seem de-

sirable to experiment with it unless one has some slight amount of reserve force to meet the occasion."[3]

Such caution was typical of Ellis, and once he had made the experiment, he never had any temptation to repeat or increase the dosage. "What an excellent use for a medical congress," Galton remarked waggishly, "to put one half under mescal, and to make the other half observe them."[4]

Ellis was in no sense a bohemian, but his interests and associations might have led people to consider him an *enfant terrible*—that is, unless they met him. For example, after Symons and Aubrey Beardsley founded *The Savoy* in 1896 he contributed to six of its eight numbers, essays which were later to be collected in *Affirmations* (1898).* In *The Savoy* Ellis was in the company of the most advanced writers of the day, and while all his attitudes were basically *épater les bourgeois*, he is seldom associated with the *Yellow Book* set, possibly because literary historians have regarded him as something of an anomaly. Yet the publication of "Concerning Jude the Obscure" in the pages of *The Savoy* marked him as an advanced radical. The novel, as Ellis remarked in his essay, had caused "a great stampede." Many of Hardy's former supporters deserted him because of the book's explicit sexuality, and Hardy was never to write another novel. Ellis seized upon the scandal not only to defend the book but to spell out his own views on the relationship between art and morality. Flinging down the gauntlet, he declared, "In all the great qualities of literature *Jude the Obscure* seems to me the greatest novel written in English for many years." The artist has not only the right but the duty to deal with subjects considered "immoral" by general opinion. In words which anticipate the aesthetic expressed in Joyce's *Portrait of the Artist as a Young Man*, for Ellis "the artist is god in his own world." "To outrage morality" is the inevitable consequence of speaking boldly. Victorian critics had frequently used as moral criterion of a book the Young Person for whose eyes it must be suitable; for Ellis "if the Young Person should care to read *Jude the Obscure* we ought for her own sake, at all events, to be thankful," since the book gives an "artistic picture of a dilemma such as the Young Person, in some form or another, may one day have to face. . . .

---

* As well as a translation of Lombroso's *A Mad Saint* (April 1896).

A book which pictures such things with fine perception and sympathy should be singularly fit reading."[5] It was sheer iconoclasm, and once more Hardy had reason to be grateful to Ellis as one of his very few defenders.

In the spring of 1894 Symons was making a prolonged visit to Venice and Ellis went off alone to the International Medical Congress in Rome. This trip he regarded as the most glorious holiday of his life, a period of unalloyed delight. Rome had always been the city of his dreams—just as it was to Freud—and he spent ecstatic hours exploring its beauties.

While not by any means completely absorbed in the Congress, he did make some important contacts with people like Dr. Hans Kurella, who was later to translate his sex *Studies* into German. By now Ellis had some scientific standing as editor of the Contemporary Science Series, and as author of *The Criminal* and the recently published *Man and Woman*. On the strength of these contributions he was visited in his hotel room by the distinguished Cesare Lombroso,* who appointed him secretary of the Psychiatric Section, a post which, to Ellis's relief, was almost purely honorary.

At this point a word or two might be said about Lombroso's influence on Ellis. In *The Criminal* Ellis seemed to go out of his way to emphasize where he disagreed with Lombroso, but in actual fact he followed basically the same tradition. Ellis regarded the founding by Paul Broca of the Société d'Anthropologie de Paris as one of the great events of the *annus mirabile*, 1859. The outstanding racial anthropologists of the latter part of the nineteenth century—Broca, Virchow, and Lombroso—believed that the psychology of a race or ethnic group could be understood, provided results were evaluated on the evidence of measurement of skulls, brain capacities, and social behaviour. Hence *The Criminal* and *Man and Woman* are replete with anatomical charts, graphs of measurements, and diagrams of various sorts purporting to show the relationship between height or spinal curvature and certain emotional characteristics. To Ellis such compilation of data seemed highly advanced and "scientific" during the nineties, and it was an approach which he never abandoned. It permeates "The Genius of Russia," an essay written

---

* Cesare Lombroso (1836–1909), Italian criminologist. His most famous works were *L'Uomo delinquente* (1889) and *L'Uomo di genio* (1888). He held that the criminal is a special type, standing midway between the lunatic and the savage.

after his 1897 visit to Russia, and *The Soul of Spain* (1908); and with him it became an almost obsessional belief in the influence of his own Suffolk ancestry (even though he was born in Croydon). Times without number he would seize delightedly on the discovery of a person's Suffolk ancestry; and if, after the event, he learned that someone to whom he had been attracted came of Suffolk stock, he would proclaim triumphantly that this was undoubtedly the reason for the affinity between them.

But to return to the pleasures of the Italian journey. When the Congress was over he travelled south to Naples, where he revelled in the treasures of the museum and the ruins of Pompeii. At Capri he found the Blue Grotto disappointing. On his return journey he joined Symons for a few days in Venice, where he stayed with Horatio Brown, the British historian of Venice. Brown, in typically theatrical manner, met him at the railway station in a gondola, by which he conveyed him to his home on the Zattere. Ellis was already collecting case-histories for his Sex *Studies* which he discussed with Brown, who was an overt homosexual. At this point neither of them could foresee the difficulties they would share within a very few years.

In August 1897 he went to the next International Medical Congress, this time held in Moscow. Arthur Symons accompanied him and the Congress seems to have been the excuse for an extended jaunt around Europe. A *frisson* of adventure added flavour to the trip with Edward Carpenter's request that he smuggle a copy of *L'Amour homogénique et sa place dans une société libre* (which Carpenter had arranged to have published in Paris the previous year) into Russia for Tolstoi. Ellis agreed, adding semi-facetiously: "*Any* book, you know, may be confiscated on the frontier (who knows what dangerous meanings may not be hidden under the simplest language?) and the experienced officials would certainly smell dynamite in your book in a twinkling, burn it, and perhaps 'intern' me!"[6] Ellis cut a hole in the lining of his jacket, where he stowed the book away, but at the frontier no one paid any attention to the delegates to the Congress. Tolstoi invited him and Symons to Yasnaya Polyana, but an hour or so before they were to leave for the visit, much to their disappointment, Ellis received a note from the novelist that his daughter was dangerously ill and that everyone in the household was occupied in looking after her. Ellis had no alternative but to leave Carpenter's book at Tolstoi's town house, where the servant could speak only Russian but seemed more reliable than the Russian post.

Ellis was delighted with the whole experience in Russia, although they had experienced an abominable heat wave in Moscow; and he told Carpenter:

> "Altogether Russia is quite the *freest* country I have ever been, and the people are the kindest people, and the most genuinely polite. Everything was very different from what I expected, and one was able to get into proper perspective the reports one hears from one's Russian friends in London. We saw the Tsar at Warsaw; he goes about almost unguarded."[7]

Before leaving Russia they also visited St. Petersburg and thence on to Munich, Bayreuth (where to Ellis's great delight they heard *Parsifal*), Prague, Budapest, Vienna, and the Rhine. He arrived back in London late in September to find many serious considerations awaiting him.

Ever since Ellis's return to England from Australia he had slowly been working towards an objective "scientific" study of sexuality, a subject that troubled and intrigued him. The only woman with whom he had been able to discuss frankly such subjects as masturbation and menstruation was Olive Schreiner; and in turn he had helped her to gather material on prostitution for her novel *From Man to Man*. Also, until his marriage to Edith, Olive seems to have been the only woman with whom he indulged in sexual intimacies, however unsatisfactory they may have been. In other words, the man who wrote *Man and Woman* (1894) was almost totally inexperienced, and when he departs from physiological description he sounds remarkably naïve. He wrote it primarily for his own instruction—or "edification," as he called it—a prolegomenon to his more extensive investigations, although from the outset he had formulated no clear-cut plan as to what pattern these would take. Yet while *Man and Woman* might have been intended as a semi-private proem, he was nonetheless disappointed that it received so little critical attention at the time of its publication, although it subsequently went through four more editions.

This book led to the only public controversy Ellis ever engaged in during his life. Karl Pearson, now professor of biometrics at University College, was becoming notorious for his pugnacious encounters, usually with theologians. He had never forgotten or forgiven Ellis for his espousal of Hinton. In "Variations in Men and Women" in a collection of essays, *The Chances of Death* (1897), he attacked Ellis's proposition that there existed greater possibility of variations of physical characteristics in males than in females, an argument based primarily on the fact that the larger male head has greater difficulty coming through the birth canal and hence can be moulded to widely differing shapes. Pearson described this as a "pseudo-scientific superstition" to which he was going to "lay the axe." Behind his attack was also the tacit assumption that somehow Ellis's theory cast a slur upon women. Pearson's attack was brought to Ellis's attention immediately after his return from Russia and he at once sat down and wrote Pearson a long letter of self-defence. The tone at the outset was placatory. "I am very glad that my book has in part led to such a laborious investigation. I was supported in my mere pioneering & necessarily unsatisfactory work, in what was then only a howling wilderness of facts which could often only by courtesy be called 'facts'—by the thought that I should at least have prepared the way for better work." He had to admit that "it is now impossible to go over the ground I went over without using more accurate methods." Again he repeated the heart of his argument: "The problem before me was the organic tendency of males and females to vary, & I clearly pointed out at the outset that so far as bulk is concerned I—rightly or wrongly—regarded the pelvis as an important disturbing factor. Males are larger than females, but both must creep into the world through the same small hole. Naturally— before birth, at birth, & for some weeks after—it is the males who suffer, & the statement that males are more variable in size, both in the whole & in parts, means, if correct, as much as the statement that the rats entering a rat-hole have a greater range of variation in size than the ferrets who enter it & would tell us nothing regarding the comparative organic tendency to variation in ferrets and rats." Finally, he expressed his gratitude to Pearson, since his criticism would now enable Ellis "to present the matter more clearly & precisely than before."[8] There is no indication that Pearson ever replied to this letter; but to show his contempt for Ellis as a scientist, he withdrew his *Grammar of Science* from the Contemporary Science Series. It was undoubtedly a humiliation for Ellis, and for the sake of his own reputation he had to respond publicly. He worked laboriously on the reply, perhaps because he was a little nervous about the validity of his argument. He did not complete it until 1901, and did not submit it for publication for another year, so that it appeared as an article in *Popular Science Monthly* only in

January 1903; he also printed the reply as an appendix to the fifth edition of *Man and Woman* (1914). "I still maintain my general objection to controversy," he told Perry-Coste, "but I don't think any rule should be quite rigid, and this seemed a suitable occasion for breaking the rule."[9] Ellis, in heavily ironical language, suggested that Pearson might know a lot about crabs, but the human organism was much more complex and depended on many more considerations than size, which was the only criterion which Pearson would admit as being measurable (but, after all, Ellis himself had been arguing from *bulk*). To Professor J. M. Cattell, the editor of *Popular Science Monthly*, he wrote: "It seemed difficult altogether to avoid this controversial element in view of the aggressive character of Pearson's paper, but I have tried to avoid everything that is *merely* controversial, and to make the article a connected statement, complete in itself, of an argument for which there still seems much to be said."[10] Pearson remained a sore spot with him and he often discussed him in letters with Perry-Coste, who came in contact with Pearson through their mutual admiration of Francis Galton and their interest in eugenics. To Perry-Coste Ellis wrote, after the appearance of his reply:

"I have always admired Pearson's work. Personally I have experienced both his pleasant and unpleasant sides. I was introduced to him in ways quite apart from science, through friends, and he was always extremely nice and courteous to me, until I published *Man and Woman* [had he forgotten the Hinton affair?]. That seems to have been an unpardonable offence; his attack on me in *Chances of Death* was absurdly obvious—as, even if wrong (which I dispute) I was wrong with Hunter and Darwin—and he withdrew his *Grammar of Science* from my series, without a word to me. I know other cases in which he had behaved the same way, only much more brutally. There must be an element of morbidity in it. . . ."[11]

The scientific truth of the argument has never been settled; but certainly neither Ellis nor Pearson had sufficient evidence for taking a strong position, although evidently they viewed themselves as working in the great nineteenth-century Darwinian tradition. Hereafter Ellis always referred to Pearson as "my enemy" and was very patronizing about the famous journal *Biometrika*, which Pearson founded in 1901.

Ellis makes no reference to the controversy in *My Life*. As for *Man and Woman*, "That task being completed,"* he writes, "I turned to the *Studies* themselves. The volume I resolved to put into shape was 'Sexual Inversion.' "[12] Ellis's memory is flagging at this point. *Man and Woman* was not published until 1894, but there is abundant evidence that Ellis was seriously contemplating a book on inversion by the summer of 1892—exactly the time when he learned the horrifying truth about Edith's relationship with Claire.

Ellis goes on to say that his decision to initiate a series of investigative studies of sexuality with a book on homosexuality was "a mistake."

> It was indeed a kind of accident. Homosexuality was an aspect of sex which up to a few years before had interested me less than any, and I had known very little about it. But during those few years I had become interested in it. Partly I had found that some of my most highly esteemed friends were more or less homosexual (like Edward Carpenter, not to mention Edith), and partly I had come into touch through correspondence with John Addington Symonds, for whose work I had once had an admiration which somewhat decreased with years.†[13]

At the time, then, when Symonds first contacted him about the possibility of a book on sexual inversion, Ellis—by chance—was still reeling from the shock over Edith and was obsessed with a desire to understand her behaviour. Symonds, too, had strong personal reasons for wishing to see the appearance of such a book. At this point he was regarded as one of the leading English men of letters, the author of the seven-volume *Renaissance in Italy*. Irritable and tubercular, he had in 1877 settled permanently in Davos Platz for his health. Here and on visits to Venice, where he stayed with his friend Horatio Brown, he was able to freely indulge his homosexual proclivities, whose suppression in England had brought him time and time again to a state of nervous collapse. Because of the anguish he had suffered he was almost obsessional about British hypocrisy, and he was particularly embittered by the Criminal Law

---

* *Man and Woman* "was deliberately planned (at least as early as 1880 or 1881) as an Introduction to the future Sex Studies proper, clearing the ground by disposing of all sex differences that are not in the narrow sense 'sexual' " (Letter to Isaac Goldberg, 8 Nov. 1925, Manuscripts and Archives Division, New York Public Library, Astor, Lenox and Tilden Foundations).

† He first expressed his admiration of Symonds in 1885 in "The Present Position of English Criticism" for his "marked catholicity" of taste and his "calm breadth and sanity"—qualities which Ellis consciously cultivated in himself.

Amendment Act of 1885. This law was the outcome of investigations by the reforming editor of the *Pall Mall Gazette*, W. T. Stead, into the current traffic in adolescent girls. In order to reveal to the public how easy it was to procure a young girl, Stead himself obtained one, but neglected to get her father's permission in addition to her mother's, and, by an ironic twist of fate, was imprisoned for three months for abduction. But his zeal bore fruit in the passing of the law raising the age of consent from twelve to sixteen. However, with the memory of the Cleveland Street Scandal and its revelations of male prostitution* still lurid in the minds of the shocked, an extra clause, known as the Labouchere Amendment, was slipped in, by which any act of "gross indecency" between males, in private or in public, was a misdemeanour punishable with two years of hard labour; and connection, *per anum*, was a felony punishable with penal servitude for life. The Labouchere Amendment stood out conspicuously as one of the most stringent laws for a sexual offence in Europe. In 1889 an act was passed in Italy abolishing punishment for sexual relations between men as long as they were not accompanied by violence, infringement of the rights of minors, or outrages to public decency. In France the Code Napoléon protected minors, but no legal measures were taken against adult homosexuals, although strong social feeling was organized against them; nevertheless, of all European countries it was probably the most tolerant towards aberrant sexual behaviour. In Germany and Austria the laws were severe, but the practice was widespread and regarded far more tolerantly than in England.

Symonds had privately published two pamphlets, one on Greek "homogenic" love and the other on the predicament of the invert in modern society. Naturally these had to be circulated surreptitiously; and Symonds was anxious to reach a wider public in order to create an understanding of the prevalence and "normality" of homosexuality and thus ultimately to engender a climate of opinion in which it would be possible to abolish the iniquitous law.

In the summer of 1892 Symonds, instead of writing directly to Ellis, asked Arthur Symons if he would approach him about considering commissioning Symonds to write a book on sexual inversion for the Contemporary Science Series. Symons brought up the subject

---

* In 1889. See H. Montgomery Hyde, *The Cleveland Street Scandal* (New York: Coward, McCann & Geoghegan, 1976; London: W. H. Allen, 1976).

at the Empire music-hall, where they had gone to watch a troupe of acrobats. Ellis replied the next day: "It is curious that only a day or two ago I had some idea of writing to you about this subject. My attention has been frequently drawn to it of late, partly through often finding how it exists to a greater or less extent in many persons whom I know, or know of, and whom I much love and respect." But as for a full-scale book, "the difficulties are certainly serious."[14] He rejected the possibility of the inclusion of such a volume in the Contemporary Science Series; he knew that the Walter Scott people would be horrified at such an idea: "Several of the volumes approach various forbidden topics as nearly as it is desirable, and I am inclined to agree with the publisher that there is too much at stake to involve the Series in any really risky pioneering experiment."[15] He also felt reluctant about the unscientific value of entrusting what would be a case of special pleading to a committed advocate. While it was not widely known that Symonds was a homosexual, Ellis was aware of it,* although in the extensive correspondence that ensued Symonds never once admitted his bias and perpetually maintained the fiction that case-histories involving himself and his lovers had been brought to his attention by other people. Aware that Ellis had recently married—and knowing nothing about Edith's problem—he clearly felt that Ellis was the first member of the public whom he had to win over completely to his own point of view. He pointed out to Ellis that with the present state of public opinion, "an impartial and really scientific survey of the matter" could probably best be accomplished if the two of them worked together. "I feel that, in a matter of this sort, two names, and two men of different sorts, would be stronger as affecting public opinion than any one alone of any sort, and also would be more likely to get a wide and serious attention."[16] For Symonds, collaboration with Ellis was imperative. As he told Edward Carpenter, "Alone, I could make but little effect—the effect of an eccentric."[17]

Ellis saw the advantages of such a collaboration. There was much that Symonds could contribute on the scholarly and historical

---

* Ellis did not know this from the outset. In the letter to Arthur Symons in which Symonds proposed that he sound Ellis out on the project, he said, "I hope I shall see you when I am in England. You are so good to me, and so understanding of the real man who has 'never spoken out' yet, that I should like to tell you some things about myself wh cannot well be written" (*The Letters of John Addington Symonds*, Vol. III, eds. Herbert M. Schueller and Robert L. Peters, Detroit: Wayne State University, 1969, p. 691).

side, as well as being in a position to gather a number of case-histories, while Ellis could concentrate on current medical theories. Accordingly, he suggested that they meet during the summer when Symonds was to visit England; but, curiously enough, although Symonds was in England for nine weeks of busy social engagements, he made no attempt to contact Ellis and on September 21st wrote to him that he was leaving England the following day as he was afraid of "having some kind of breakdown in health if I continue this sort of life."[18] It appears that Symonds had got it into his head that Ellis was not sympathetic enough, particularly when Ellis had added, after suggesting that they meet to talk over the matter, "I am not sure that I should altogether agree with you." To this Symonds took alarm: "Writing perhaps would be difficult to you"—but was obviously reassured by Ellis's next letter sent to Davos and the collaboration by post resumed in earnest.

"Collaboration is difficult," Ellis admitted candidly, "but in this case the advantages to be gained seem quite enough to make it worth while to smooth out the difficulties."[19] Despite the inherent difficulties of the project, compounded by their different experiences and temperaments, both men emerge from the correspondence as remarkably moderate, considerate of each other's opinions, and deeply earnest that the truth should be presented in as impartial a way as possible. Symonds told Carpenter that he found Ellis "full, eager, open-minded, scientifically conscientious: the sort of man, I think, to lead to our joint inquiry."[20]

Ellis made it clear from the beginning that he feared Symonds might be carried away by a wave of emotion, and that he would not want to see the pamphlet *A Problem in Modern Ethics* serve as a model for the projected book: "It seems to me . . . that we should adopt a rather austere style in this book avoiding so far as possible a literary or artistic attitude towards the question—appealing to the reason rather than to the emotions. (For this reason some passages in your modern *Problem* ought, I think," he added tactfully, "to be omitted.)"[21] Symonds raised no objection to this: "I never regarded myself as really competent to deal with the psychology of the matter, and my sense of a great injustice having been done by law and social opinion has made me less judicial than the treatment requires."[22]

They read and discussed together the current writers on the subject—Lombroso, Schrenck-Notzing, Moll, Krafft-Ebing, Tarnowsky, Tardieu. Symonds tended to reject all psychiatric theorizing on the subject because its exponents viewed homosexuality as a morbid deviation from the norm. Ellis naturally attached far more credence to medical opinion: "I do not wish to put myself in opposition to the medical psychologists, the people who have most carefully studied the question; to do so in any case would be bad policy: I simply wish to carry their investigations a step further."[23] But Symonds, as a homosexual, was extremely worried by Ellis's apparent willingness to accept the widespread "morbidity" hypothesis, and in letter after letter he distinguished between two types of invert—congenital and acquired—and, while agreeing that neurosis might be a frequent accompaniment of inversion, insisted that it was certainly not a cause and, indeed, homosexuality was generally a matter of sexual-aesthetic preference as normal in its way as heterosexuality. Ellis, able to judge only from Edith's unstable background, clung to the conviction that it was an hereditary "anomaly." If there was an element of "morbidity," Symonds suggested, it was only to the degree that, say, colour-blindness was; Ellis felt a more accurate analogy could be found in colour-hearing. However, in the final analysis, they reached full accord on the subject of their study: it should be, in Ellis's words, "primarily a study of a psychological anomaly."*

Among the people they both called on for help in providing case-histories was Edward Carpenter. Ellis's letter to him displays the consummate tact and gentle flattery which characterized his handling of many delicate situations throughout his life.

> "Symonds has given much study to this subject, both in old Greek and in modern times (has previously printed pamphlets about the matter), and feels very strongly about it, partly through realising, also, how outrageously severe the law is in this country (compared with others), and how easily the law can touch a perfectly beautiful form of inversion. We want to obtain sympathetic recognition for sexual inversion as a psychic ab-

---

* In this view Ellis was greatly influenced by the German pathologist Rudolf Virchow (1821–1902), who drew a sharp distinction between disease and abnormality. In the Appendix to the fourth edition of *Man and Woman* (1904) Ellis described Virchow as "the greatest of pathologists." Karl Pearson, incidentally, was highly critical of Virchow's theory of the pathological accident or anomaly. Virchow was the leader of the German opposition to Darwinism, and Pearson, an avowed Darwinist, had been a student in Germany during the bitter Darwin controversy.

normality which may be regarded as the highest ideal, and to clear away many vulgar errors—preparing the way, if possible, for a change in the law. I feel sure that we shall have your sympathy in this work; if you are able to supply any notes or suggestions that may help to throw light it will be doing a good deed. Nothing of the kind has yet been published, at least in England, and I cannot help feeling that the book will do much good.—We are both resolved to put our names to it, but of course every care will be taken with regard to those who help us with this material."[24]

Within the next few years Carpenter and Edith were to grow very close, but from the tone of this letter it does not appear that Carpenter was intimate enough with Ellis to discuss Edith's lesbianism. In any case, it was a subject Ellis was always very circumspect about in letters.

Ellis asked Symonds if he could contribute any case-histories of lesbianism. Symonds admitted that this was an aspect of the phenomenon to which he had given little attention; he had been puzzled, he mused, as to why it played so large a part in current French fiction. It was left, then, to Ellis to collect these from the story of his own wife and her friends. Arthur Calder-Marshall has asserted that Edith resented being "used" in this fashion, but I can find no documentary evidence to support this contention. Indeed, in a letter of July 1st, 1892, Ellis says to Symonds: "Many thanks for congratulations on my marriage. My wife—I may say—is most anxious I should collaborate and can supply cases of inversion in women from among her own friends."[25]

When Symonds tried to draw sweeping racial conclusions from his own experience of Swiss peasants and Venetian gondoliers, Ellis warned him against this dangerous tendency. Eschewing wide generalizations in a book that had to be scrupulously documented, the case-histories, as Ellis always insistently emphasized, must serve as the empirical foundation of the book. "I only recognise two classes," Ellis told Carpenter, "—complete inversion and psychosexual hermaphroditism—I call them both 'abnormal' (in the sense in which genius and criminality are also abnormal)* which does not involve

---

* Both Hinton and Lombroso had argued that genius was an abnormality. In *The Law-Breaker* Hinton described genius as "the point of least resistance through which nature passes into life."

morbidity though it permits of more or less morbidity in any particular case."[26] This was the final principle on which the book was organized, but in all fairness it must be emphasized that the great majority of the case-histories had been collected by Symonds, to whom Ellis confessed, "It seems to me that my contribution of fresh material to the book will be a very humble one compared to yours." Symonds insisted that they should not fall into the trap of a "fixed style" of confession, but allow the speakers the spontaneity of their own voices. However, they carefully "doctored" the cases to protect anonymity, particularly in Edith's case (History XXXVI),* where Ellis omitted such important details as her mother's early death and her father's cruelty. However much he insisted on scientific accuracy, he was the victim of the atmosphere of his times.

In April 1893, while the book was still far from complete, Symonds died suddenly in Rome of lung congestion during an influenza epidemic. Ellis was relieved to see the end of the collaboration because he had felt uneasy about how their different styles could be fused and he was also nervous about how seriously the book would be taken once it became generally known that Symonds was an invert himself. He allowed work on the study to languish for the next year while he completed *Man and Woman*. By 1895 it was finally complete—including the extracts from Symonds's pamphlets which Ellis felt "loyally" bound to use. Never was Ellis to be involved in a book that was to cause him so many problems.

Dr. Hans Kurella—whom he had met at the International Medical Congress in Rome in 1894—had already translated *Man and Woman (Mann und Weib)* and *The Criminal (Verbrecher und Verbrechen)* for Wigand of Leipzig. Both he and the publisher were willing to issue *Sexual Inversion* as part of a current series on social subjects. "I am not anxious to publish it in Germany—where it isn't required," Ellis told Carpenter, "but that may pave the way for English publication."[27] Accordingly it appeared in Germany in 1896 as Volume VII of the Bibliothek für Sozialwissenschaft—*Das Konträre Geschlechtsgefühl (Contrary Sexual Feeling*—a title Ellis didn't particularly like), with both Ellis's and Symonds's names on the title page. It was reviewed respectfully, but caused no particular stir.

---

* Calder-Marshall seems convinced of this identity, although he gives no documentation. I have no documentation, but the accumulation of detail has persuaded me beyond a doubt.

In England Ellis submitted the manuscript to a small house, Williams and Norgate, who seemed suitable as they had a firm reputation for issuing solid scientific works. *Sexual Inversion* was rejected on the advice of their reader, who by chance happened to be Dr. Hack Tuke,* the editor of the *Journal of Mental Science*, which had published a number of Ellis's articles. Tuke, who had also been a close friend of Symonds's physician father, had always refused to discuss the subject with Symonds. He was on a friendly footing with Ellis and told him candidly why he had rejected it: he feared that it could not be confined to specialists and might contaminate the wider public. "There are always," he said solemnly, "the compositors!" Ellis did not feel the slightest rancour towards him, knowing that he was a Quaker of an older generation. He might have added another, more personal reason—his son, the well-known painter Henry Scott Tuke, was homosexual; and in the atmosphere that prevailed after the Wilde trial (1895) Tuke's attitude was probably very realistic.

Another publisher had to be found. F. H. Perry-Coste, a scientifically trained friend for whom Ellis had great respect, suggested that he contact a man of some wealth who was about to set up a small printing and publishing house for scholarly works with no wide general appeal, as well as a magazine devoted to scholarly articles. This man's name was G. Astor Singer and his agent in London was his brother-in-law, Dr. Roland de Villiers. A meeting was arranged with Dr. de Villiers. Mr. Singer, it appeared, travelled extensively on the Continent and left the business negotiations in the hands of de Villiers, a large, fleshy man with a stealthy tread like a cat's, who aroused a vague sense of misgiving in Ellis. But the books he proposed to publish seemed eminently respectable (particularly those of the highly regarded free-thinker J. M. Robertson), and, most important of all, he agreed to publish Edith's first novel, *Seaweed* (later called *Kit's Woman*). For Ellis this novel was

> a real work of art, well planned and well balanced, original and daring, the genuinely personal outcome of its author, alike in its humour and its firm, deep grip of the great sexual problems it is concerned with, centring around the relations of a wife to a husband who by accident

---

* Tuke was renowned for his books on insanity. Indeed, Ellis had contributed an article, "The Influence of Sex on Insanity," to Tuke's *Dictionary of Pathological Medicine* (1892), II, 1152–6.

has become impotent. I say it was "genuinely personal," but it is not, I now add, till long after I wrote those words that it has seemed to me that the story was consciously or unconsciously inspired by her own relations with me and of course completely transformed by the artist's hand into a new shape.[28]

The book, in actual fact, is almost unreadable, partly because of Edith's attempt to cast the dialogue into Cornish dialect, and for its childish psychology. It is astounding that Ellis should have thought so highly of it. Perhaps no other publisher would touch it for artistic rather than moral reasons.

But everything connected with this publishing enterprise seemed questionable. From the outset Ellis suspected that "Mr. Singer" was the creation of de Villiers's brain, for some unfathomable reason of his own. "Have you ever yet seen anyone who ever saw 'G. Astor Singer'?" Ellis asked Perry-Coste. "As you introduced me to him or his shadow, I hold you responsible for his production, or, if necessary, creation! I am distinctly inclined to believe that the signatures to letters from 'G. Astor Singer' are in the same hand as those from 'R de Villiers.' (But this statement is confidential!)"[29] Then there was "Mrs. Singer," who shared Dr. de Villiers's house—ostensibly his sister-in-law, but Ellis suspected a rather closer relationship. All the financial transactions were done in her name.

Complications began to come thick and fast. At first Symonds's literary executor, Horatio Brown, from Venice gave every encouragement possible. On August 8th, 1895, he wrote, after reading the manuscript: "I think that it is admirable in its calmness, its judicial unbiased tone. And if anything can persuade people to look the question in the face this should."[30] But Mrs. Symonds—who apparently never saw the manuscript—felt nervous and wanted her husband's old friend, the philosopher Henry Sidgwick, to look it over carefully. Sidgwick insisted on some omissions, and Brown, now in London, was obviously beginning to waver and told Ellis that he fully agreed with Sidgwick. Suddenly, in July 1897, Ellis received word from Brown that he had consulted both Herbert Asquith* and a Professor George Poore (an authority on sanitation), who advised that the publication "will do more harm to Symonds's

---

* Asquith had been secretary of state for home affairs in the last Gladstone cabinet, which fell in 1895. He was probably consulted because of Symonds's close friendship with Margot Tennant, whom Asquith married in 1894.

name than good to the cause." The matter, he believed, should be left entirely to medical men. As for Asquith, he believed the treatment was far too "literary."[31] Pressure was being put on Brown from all sides, and while he personally might have liked to have seen the publication of the book as it was (as well as the publication of Symonds's autobiography), he felt obliged to ask Ellis to remove Symonds's name from the title page as well as all material attributed to Symonds. He would not allow further distribution of the book and, after buying up the entire edition from de Villiers, had it destroyed. When Carpenter wrote to ask him what had happened, Ellis replied, "I thought I had told you the issue of the latest difficulty with the book. Brown (turning round on himself & J.A.S.) insisted that the book would be injurious to ["Himself" crossed out] J.A.S.'s reputation & friends, & bought up the first edition."[32] Carpenter then wrote to protest to Brown, who replied:

"I should like to say a word on the charge of acting unfairly to J.A.S. The question was, for me, one of great difficulty; I should like to point out that as far as J.A.S.'s place in the history of the controversy is concerned that is secured by the German book which contains all he has to say, and more than Mr. Ellis was prepared to publish in English. J.A.S. had all this matter by him for years, most of it, in print; the problem in Greek Ethics was finished & published more than ten years before his death and yet he never published it; never even put his name to the few copies he printed—this proves to me that he had at least grave doubts about publishing—of course in view of his wife and family —he never came a quarter as near publication as I did, and I dont feel sure that he would have faced the inevitable anxiety and possible pain to his family. You probably do not know that the very last words he wrote, when he was past speech, and within a few hours of death, were a strong injunction to me to regard his family in all matters of publication. An appeal from one of his family; the strongly expressed opinion of his oldest and most intimate friends when I got to London; the best legal & medical opinion I could obtain, all combined to take the step I did: and though I may not have done quite what he would have liked (but did not do), I think I have done what he would have done in the circumstances."[33]

Ellis philosophically set to work preparing a new edition. "The new edition will not contain J.A.S.'s name," he told Carpenter, "and the Greek essay with various minor passages will be omitted. In some ways the change will be an improvement, and it certainly renders it safe from attacks of all kinds (Asquith, consulted by Brown, thought the literary element would be against the book). I have not yet had proofs of new version but trust everything will now go right."[34] After looking through the manuscript and making a few notes, Carpenter commented: "I think it all promises *well*—and will be a first rate book altogether—tho' I doubt whether you *quite* appreciate the 'true inwardness' of this kind of love which appears to me to need no mark of authenticity which the other love can show, except that question of race-propagation—which yet has a quality of its own."[35]

Ellis worked rapidly and the new edition appeared by November 1897. Advance copies were sent to the medical reviews. Its quiet appearance had all the sobriety Ellis could have wished. It was the lull before the storm. Meanwhile de Villiers and the Singers continued their mysterious comings and goings. "I have lately heard from 'Dr de Villiers of the Chinese Puzzle Co. (Unlimited),'" Perry-Coste was told, "that Mrs. Singer is removing to Paris, and he has been going backwards and forward to superintend the arrangement. And where, oh where, is dear 'George Astor' meanwhile?"[36]

CHAPTER 12

SEXUAL INVERSION

ELLIS ALWAYS REGRETTED THE DECISION TO PUBLISH *Sexual Inversion* as the first of the *Studies in the Psychology of Sex.** It was an error of judgement to launch on the British public, however quietly, a book which was in effect an apologia for homosexuality at a time when Oscar Wilde had only just been released from prison (March 1897) to wander, as Sebastian Melmoth, an exile and an outcast from respectable society. It seemed an act of quiet courage on Ellis's part; but the consequences were so disturbing that he never again allowed himself to become in any way embroiled in a public controversy.

In order to discuss *Sexual Inversion* adequately, it is necessary to anticipate the later editions, the second (1901) and the third (1915), which were published in the United States. Indeed, this book became as much an exile from its homeland as Wilde was. In 1901 Ellis renumbered it as Volume II in order to deflect undue attention from its uneasy existence, and *The Evolution of Modesty* (!) became Volume I. The *Studies* have never been published in England to this day. Since only a few copies of the 1897 edition were circulated, it seems appropriate to treat the final edition as the definitive

---

* To Isaac Goldberg, his first biographer, he confessed: "Of all the volumes of the 'Studies' it is that which interests me least" (9 Aug. 1928, Manuscripts and Archives Division, New York Public Library, Astor, Lenox and Tilden Foundations).

one—the only changes were the addition of extra case-histories, a discussion of Walt Whitman (whose homosexuality Ellis was the first to spell out elaborately), and the consideration of the attitudes of other authorities, notably Magnus Hirschfeld and Sigmund Freud. The emphasis, the tone, and the recommendations in all editions remained the same.

Sexual Inversion was an unprecedented book. Never before had homosexuality been treated so soberly, so comprehensively, so sympathetically. To read it today is to read the voice of common sense and compassion; to read it then was, for the great majority, to be affronted by a deliberate incitement to vice of the most degrading kind.

Ellis's aim was to dispel myth, to puncture prejudice, and to present as factual a report of the real situation as possible. The first sentence of the book marks his consistent view of the subject: "Sexual inversion, as here understood, means sexual instinct turned by inborn constitutional abnormality towards persons of the same sex." Ellis was not the first to proclaim the organic nature of inversion, but he was the first person to write a book in English which treated homosexuality as neither a disease nor a crime. That such sexual proclivity is not determined by suggestion, accident, or historical conditioning is apparent, he argues, from the fact that it is widespread among animals and that there is abundant evidence of its prevalence among various nations at all periods of history. The incidence of relatives sharing the same propensities, Ellis also sees as firm evidence of the inherited character of inversion. Ellis rejects Ulrichs's theory of an invert as a man in whom a female soul is imprisoned; but he does take pains to emphasize the artistic inclinations of a large proportion of his subjects and their tendency to "Neurasthenia"—that vague nineteenth-century word covering a wide spectrum of nervous ailments. Most people regarded homosexuality (a word rejected by Ellis because it could cover experiences arising out of temporary circumstances) as manifestations of the criminal or the insane, but Ellis stresses that none of his cases has been charged with a misdemeanour (although many had contemplated suicide) nor are they degenerates, but are frequently found among the most cultivated members of the community. Famous inverts include Erasmus, Leonardo, Michelangelo, Cellini, Sappho—most of them non-English, it is true. He decided to omit Shakespeare's name, as this might prove too outrageous for English readers to swallow.

The persuasiveness of his argument is based on his thirty-three case-histories. Credibility is created by the first-person narratives, but it would be simplistic to conclude—as Ellis does—that these people are emotionally healthy simply because of their own avowals. Unfortunately, no copy of the questionnaire he used has come to light, but as most of the histories cover certain aspects of temperament and experience, it is reasonable to make a fair guess as to what information was asked for: data about parents, siblings, and education; relatives who had been inverts; first sexual experience; masturbation; erotic dreams; preferred form of sexual activity; responses to opposite sex; avocations; favourite colour; ability to whistle; and attitude towards their anomaly. Some few of the subjects were known to Ellis personally, but most of them had been supplied by Symonds, Carpenter, and—the American cases—Dr. J. G. Kiernan of Chicago.* There was no attempt to do a sampling on a representative cross-section of different levels of society—most of them seemed to be members of the upper middle class—and Ellis appeared unaware of the limitations of his restricted selection. His theoretical assumption seemed to be that if a sufficient number of cases was amassed, the evidence would speak for itself. Nor is there any adequate statistical basis for his surmise that the incidence of homosexuality among the general population was between two and five per cent. The enigmatic "A correspondent" who is frequently cited is to be distrusted as an elliptical mode of persuasion. It was a hit-or-miss method, but it is questionable whether a more sophisticated mode of sampling such as Kinsey's (and even his far more ambitious method came under criticism for some of these same reasons) could have yielded the evidence Ellis was seeking—because he was seeking support for something he already believed: namely, the congenital nature of inversion and the fact that the invert was leading a furtive, often tragic existence because of the guilt imposed upon him by collective prejudice. Ellis's book, then, was fundamentally a polemic, a plea for greater tolerance, and the forces of current morality were quite right in recognizing the revolutionary nature of its proposals, all the more dangerous because they were couched in straightforward, simple

---

* Secretary of the Chicago Academy of Medicine.

language appropriate to the natural acceptance of what was currently regarded as a highly unnatural phenomenon. Edward Carpenter might complain that "I doubt whether you quite appreciate the 'true inwardness' of this kind of love,"[1] yet Ellis's relative detachment did far more for the invert than the *parti pris* of a Symonds.

It is not happy reading. Dean Inge threw his volume into the fire. Marie Stopes described it as "like breathing a bag of soot; it made me feel choked and dirty for three months."[2] Even Margaret Sanger was later to read these accounts and recoil in disgust from the long sequence of abnormal behaviour, but it is difficult to understand the lack of sympathetic understanding for those whose lives were crippled by remorse and undefined longing. Towards these unfortunate people Ellis's attitude strikes a reasonable balance: he describes, he explains, but he never launches into impassioned rhetoric or sentimentality. A note of romanticism does unfortunately creep in when he quotes from "Z" (Symonds) with his high-flown talk about altruistic "comradeship." I have a suspicion that the form which the sexuality of the cases assumes is perhaps manipulated slightly to give the impression of harmless and innocent caresses. Also, a reader could not fail to take note of the fact that many of these inverts did not practise masturbation, that nineteenth-century bugbear to which was attributed all manner of dire results.

Ellis was more indebted to the method and attitude of Krafft-Ebing's *Psychopathia Sexualis* than he acknowledged. He, too, addressed his book exclusively to doctors and lawyers. The information he required from his case-histories was much the same. Like Krafft-Ebing, Ellis was convinced of the hereditary basis of inversion; one's parents were one's fate, experience was simply a confirmation rather than an education of sexual patterning. The fundamental difference between them lay in Krafft-Ebing's rather inconsistent view that inversion could and should be cured by hypnotism or suggestion. Above all, they differed on their attitude towards inverts. For Krafft-Ebing they were virtually pariahs, "step-children of nature," whereas Ellis was the first heterosexual investigator to grant them dignity as complete human beings.

His treatment of lesbianism is a good deal more uncertain, its tentative tone the inevitable result of insufficient evidence. He ventured the speculation that female inversion was probably far more common than in males but was not regarded as a social evil because men tended to view it with amused condescension. He presents only six case-histories; one of them—History XXXVI— obviously represents Edith, who has found that "repression leads to morbidity and hysteria. She has suffered much from neurasthenia at various periods, but under appropriate treatment it has slowly diminished. The inverted instinct is too deeply rooted to eradicate, but it is well under control."[3] He finds significant differences between the male and the female invert. The male is depicted as resisting stereotypes, with a tendency perhaps to mild neurosis, yet by and large appearing and acting like most "normal" males; but the female emerges as someone distinctly nervy, boyish in appearance, with a deep voice, able to whistle, capable of deep-enduring attachments— someone, in fact, rather like Edith.

In the final edition of *Sexual Inversion* (1915) Ellis had to take into account later theories and investigations subsequent to the first edition. Magnus Hirschfeld's massively documented *Die Homosexualität* (1914) he acknowledges as the authority in its field. Hirschfeld, as a practising homosexual, was only too happy to find his cases supporting the invert's usual self-defence; and Ellis was grateful to have Hirschfeld's evidence to buttress his own case. Freud and the Freudians, however, presented an unwelcome and divisive strand in the movement towards a general acceptance by medical authorities of the congenital nature of inversion. In *Three Essays on the Theory of Sexuality* (1905) Freud enunciated his theory, subject to later refinements, of homosexuality as a manifestation of diverted sexual development.* According to Freud, inverts have never recovered from an initial intense love for their mothers; and unable to move on to a re-directed love for the opposite sex, in a narcissistic turn-about seek another male to love as their mothers loved them. Ellis totally rejected the theory of the Oedipus complex. In his literal way, he took the nomenclature in an absolutely descriptive sense.† He found it ludicrous to assign in-

---

* In his monograph on Leonardo da Vinci (1910), Freud applied his theory to an actual historical figure. See also "Psycho-analytic Notes on an Autobiographical Account of a Case of Paranoia (Dementia Paranoidas)," 1911, in the *Standard Edition*, Vol. XII, 60–1.

† His literal-mindedness was allied to his lack of humour. He chided H. L. Mencken for describing prostitutes as "charity girls"—"quite wrongly, as they are not moved by charity" (20th Sept. 1923, H. L. Mencken Papers, New York Public Library, Astor, Lenox and Tilden Foundations).

cestuous interpretations to the vague, unlocalized feelings of small children. While Ellis admits that inverts often have a rather over-developed attachment to their mothers, this he attributes to a shared community of tastes involving the sort of trust they cannot find in the outside world. While he will grant that the psychic mechanism may in some cases correspond to the process described by Freud, Ellis asserts categorically: "any theory of the etiology of homo-sexuality which leaves out of account the hereditary factor in inversion cannot be admitted."[4] Ellis is particularly disturbed by the assumption held by some of Freud's followers that psychoanalysis could "cure" the invert; while he will concede that morbid fears, suspicions, and irritabilities might be modified (actually Freud's own position), he rejects utterly the attempt to re-direct an organic inborn temperament. A further exploration of Ellis's reactions to Freud's theories will be attempted in its appropriate context, but in extenuation of Freud's views it must be said that the validity of data on inversion among ancestors is highly questionable. More important, Ellis ignores entirely the different evidence on which he and Freud based their conclusions. Ellis liked to think he was investigating the healthy, while Freud was confining himself to the pathological. But Ellis had no way of knowing the relative emotional health of his subjects. There was a large element of the naïve in his outlook, and he tended to accept the obvious, practical, British commonsensical appearance of things. A dream could be explained, for instance, by what one ate before retiring or the way one was lying; he never questioned the "why" of the particular content of a dream. Freud's theories were derived from intensive contact with the psyches of his patients, Ellis's from devised questionnaires.

Freud was later to object that Ellis avoided "decisions"—that is, committing himself to certain positions (perhaps the Freudian!) about the dynamics of the psyche. But in this book he spoke out more clearly, more directly, more responsibly than he was ever to do again. "When I review the cases I have brought forward," he concluded, "and the mental history of inverts I have known, I am inclined to say that if we can enable an invert to be healthy, self-restrained and self-respecting, we have often done better than to convert him into the mere feeble simulacrum of a normal man."[5] From his pages the invert emerges as a mutation, an anomaly, a "sport," to be compared perhaps with those who possess colour-hearing, which, after all, may be regarded as a sort of talent, so that it is possible to assume that the invert is not only an acceptable member of society but a talented one. But if Ellis presumed to make such "decisions," it was to be expected that the forces of outraged convention would combine to enforce their demolition.

THE BEDBOROUGH TRIAL

THERE WAS AT THAT TIME IN LONDON A VIGOROUS LITTLE SOCIETY known as the Legitimation League, whose main object was the legalizing of illegitimate children. Its honorary president was Lillian Harman, daughter of the famous American radical Moses Harman. Miss Harman was considered something of a martyr because she had been imprisoned in Chicago for living openly with the father of her illegitimate child. The English branch of the Legitimation League had originally been founded in Leeds in 1895 by Oswald Dawson, an odd man who had the time and money to dabble in fringe groups such as the League, which was soon embroiled in deep trouble. A Miss Edith Lanchester was confined to an asylum by her family because of her support of the League; and she was eventually released through the agitation of some of the members, among them a young man by the name of George Bedborough. A few months later the League removed its headquarters to London; Dawson resigned as secretary and was succeeded by Bedborough.

George Bedborough (whose real name was Higgs) was the son of a clergyman, twenty-seven years old, affable, attractive, and deeply committed to such advanced causes of the day as free love and divorce by mutual consent. These he advocated in the League's publication, *The Adult*, which he edited and for which he wrote numerous articles under assorted pseudonyms. This passage from the issue of July 1898 is typical:

And what after all are the vaunted verities which the state professes itself so anxious to uphold? And these vices it is so anxious to suppress? What virtues do our present marriage laws preserve? Patience, self-control, prudence, constancy—Yes; and what compensating vices do they encourage and engender? Sordidness, life-long prostitution, deception, and secret faithlessness. To what else is due that cesspool of abominations, the marriage-market?

Many years after these events—in 1922—Bedborough provided Ellis with his own case-history, in which he described himself and his wife as freethinkers, communists, feminists, neo-Malthusians, vegetarians, and abstainers. He and his wife had a harmonious marriage: they maintained separate bedrooms where they entertained their respective lovers.[1]

The Legitimation League was the object of great interest to the police, not only because free love seemed a threat to the *status quo*, but because meetings of the League attracted large numbers of anarchists, whom the police viewed as the most dangerous of subversives.

In 1905 John Sweeney, the policeman who had been in charge of the Bedborough case, published a book, *At Scotland Yard*, in which he gave a colourful account of his dealings with the Legitimation League. When the League held its weekly meetings in the Holborn Restaurant or St. James's Hall, Sweeney mingled in the audience, carefully noting the names of the other guests. He became very friendly with Bedborough, whom he found an extremely agreeable fellow, and even convinced him that he was interested in the same causes. Sweeney has left an amusing description of one of the League's meetings in April 1898:

> It is not every day in the week that the Holborn Restaurant has a private dinner-party whose photographs reveal the presence of two detectives (on duty), a dozen dangerous Anarchists, a "woman who did" (and suffered imprisonment for doing), a miscellaneous bunch of free-lovers, two lady officials of the Rational Dress Society (clad in low-necked "rational costume"), two editors, two poets, a novelist of world-wide reputation, and a baby aged eighteen months.[2]

George Bedborough also had a connection with the peculiar Singer-de Villiers combine, since their firm, the Watford University Press, published *The Adult*. (Although Singer-de Villiers were later to deny any connection with the Legitimation League, Detective

Sweeney claimed that de Villiers was in the chair at least once at their meetings and that he was due to appear on several occasions until he learned that Sweeney was present.) In any event, Bedborough used the front room of his home in John Street (which Singer-de Villiers had previously used as business premises) to sell *The Adult* and several other publications, including a few copies of *Sexual Inversion* by Havelock Ellis.

It so happened that a copy was sent to a young man in Liverpool and on discovering it his horrified parents made a protest to the police. This was just the sort of opportunity Detective Sweeney was waiting for. On May 27th, 1898, he entered Bedborough's office, paid him ten shillings* for a copy of *Sexual Inversion,* and subsequently applied for a police warrant for Bedborough's arrest, "convinced that we should at one blow kill a growing evil in the shape of a vigorous campaign of free love and Anarchism, and at the same time discover the means by which the country was being flooded with books of the 'Psychology' type."[3]

On May 31st Bedborough, on leaving his house with Lillian Harman, who was visiting Britain, sighted Sweeney and stepped forward pleasantly to shake hands with him. When informed that he was being arrested, Bedborough's *sang-froid* did not desert him as he went off in a cab with Sweeney, chatting affably all the way to Bow Street. Lillian Harman in the meantime rushed to the nearest post office to wire the news to Ellis at Carbis Bay; this blow was followed by de Villiers's dramatic report that he had heard privately that Ellis was to be arrested also. De Villiers, alas, found himself called away on urgent business to Cologne, but instructed Ellis to obtain counsel with the assurance that the firm would pay all expenses—which it accordingly did.

For some reason Ellis did not leave for London until June 6th, when he went to stay with Arthur Symons. Through W. M. Mackenzie (later Lord Amulree), a friend of Olive Schreiner (and the man to whom Ellis had given the Rowley plays to edit for the Mermaid series), Ellis secured the solicitors, Messrs C. O. Humphreys & Sons, who had represented Wilde. At the time Edith was staying at Claire's home in the north of England. On hearing the news, she wrote immediately:

---

* Ellis received two pence in the shilling for each copy. This was in fact the third copy sold!

"My love, I'm just starting off on my way to you, you poor old Love. Never mind, I'll stick to you and help you, and I'm at last *glad* to come home to you and cheer you and love you and comfort you. We'll live in England and spit at them, and two together can pull a boat that would else sink. If I get a wire to-night I shall be off tomorrow to you as fast as civilisation can bring me. Claire sends love and hopes all will be well. Your own Wifie. Here is a cheque for £2."[4]

Stick to him she did; and she also suffered from the police's ham-handedness, for in their indiscriminate raid they carried off *Seaweed* as well,* and it was not reissued until 1907 under a different title, *Kit's Woman*, by a little-known publisher, Alston Rivers. Ellis always seemed to feel that the lack of success of this strange, badly written novel about a man who accidentally becomes impotent was due solely to bad luck.

From the outset Ellis and his supporters tended to see the case as police persecution of a noble individual, and *Sexual Inversion* as a test case in the right to freedom of speech. The police undoubtedly wanted to suppress *Sexual Inversion*, but even more they wanted to smash the Legitimation League, particularly as a way of striking terror into the hearts of the anarchists. If they could manage to secure a conviction against Bedborough, all these goals would be accomplished at one blow.

At first Bedborough was denied bail, but after three days in the cells he was released on a surety of £1,000, an unusually large sum. On June 13th the preliminary hearing was resumed at Bow Street. In *Regina v. Bedborough* the central count read against Bedborough was that he had "sold and uttered a certain lewd wicked bawdy scandalous and obscene libel in the form of a book entitled *Studies in the Psychology of Sex: Sexual Inversion*."† There were then read out certain passages from the case-histories. Following this, passages from *The Adult* were cited as constituting an obscenity. The case was then adjourned for the prosecution to prepare for the trial.

Meanwhile an anarchist friend of Bedborough's, Henry Seymour, began to organize a Free Press Defence Committee. He also took over the editorship of *The Adult* from Bedborough. Ellis described

---

* Other books and periodicals seized were *The Free Review*, ed. G. Astor Singer; *The University Magazine*, ed. R. de Villiers; *The Saxon and the Celt* by J. M. Robertson; *The Blight of Respectability* by Geoffrey Mortimer.

† He was indicted on two other counts as well: for selling *The Outcome of Legitimation* by Oswald Dawson, and for various issues of *The Adult*.

him as "this admirable little man who took the leading part in the defence, as staunch as Edith, and even more unwearied and selfless, for he had no personal concern in the matter and yet was willing to sacrifice his own time and labour and business interests in this impersonal cause."[5] Whether Seymour was as admirable and disinterested as Ellis thought might be questioned from later evidence, but then Ellis's attitude throughout was extraordinarily ingenuous. In any event, an impressive group of people joined the committee, including George Bernard Shaw, Frank Harris, George Moore, and H. M. Hyndman (curiously, Arthur Symons's name was absent). Shaw's letter of acceptance is particularly interesting.

Dear Mr. Seymour

The prosecution of Mr. Bedborough for selling Mr. Havelock Ellis's book is a masterpiece of police stupidity and magisterial ignorance. . . .

My own attention was called to the subject many years ago by the passing of a sentence of twenty years' penal servitude on a harmless elderly gentleman who had been ill-advised enough to plead guilty to a piece of folly which involved no danger whatever to society. At that time I was as ignorant as most people are on the subject; but the sentence so shocked my common humanity that I made an attempt to get the press to protest. I then discovered that the fear of becoming suspected of personal reasons for desiring a change in the law in this matter, makes every Englishman an abject coward, truckling to the vilest vulgar superstitions, and professing in public and in print views which have not the slightest resemblance to those which he expresses in private conversation with educated and thoughtful men. This hypocrisy is much more degrading to the public than the subject of Mr. Havelock Ellis's book can possibly be, because it is universal instead of being accidental and peculiar. In Germany and France the free circulation of such works as the one of Mr. Havelock Ellis's now in question has done a good deal to make the public in those countries understand that decency and sympathy are as necessary in dealing with sexual as with any other subjects. In England we still repudiate decency and sympathy and make virtues of blackguards and ferocity.

. . . It is fortunate that the police have been silly enough to select for their attack a writer whose character stands so high as that of Mr. Havelock Ellis; and I have no doubt that if we do our duty in the matter, the prosecution, by ignominiously failing, will end by doing more good than harm.

Yours faithfully,
G. Bernard Shaw[6]

There is no evidence that Shaw attended a single meeting of the committee; but in any case the committee could never muster more than four members on any one occasion.

Ellis received a large number of testimonials from doctors and scientific workers. His German translator, Dr. Hans Kurella, wrote:

"Honoured Colleague . . . For us on the Continent such a proceeding i.e. the prosecution is altogether incomprehensible. What would become of science and of its practical applications if the pathology of the sexual life were put on the index? It is as if Sir Spencer Wells* were to be classed with Jack the Ripper.

"No doubt the judge (unless suffering from senile dementia) will accord you brilliant satisfaction. But in any case the whole of scientific psychology and medicine on the Continent is on your side."[7]

Possibly so; but Ellis began to feel very embittered when not a single British physician could be persuaded to join the Free Press Defence Committee or to speak in defence of the book in court.

The long summer dragged on. Lillian Harman had secured for Bedborough one of the most brilliant counsel of the day, Mr. Horace (later Justice) Avory. On August 9th Avory, in an effort to secure judgement on the scientific value of *Sexual Inversion*, attempted to have the case removed from the Central Criminal Court to the High Court of Justice on the ground that the book charged as obscene was a scientific work and entitled to consideration by superior judge and jury.† The plea was rejected.

Something else happened that summer. On July 28th Ellis was required to give a sworn affidavit. In this he begins by listing his credentials as Editor of the Contemporary Science Series and also as honorary member of the Chicago Academy of Medicine, a member

---

* Physician to the Queen.
† De Villiers, it was said, had cabled his "brother-in-law"—who now apparently was in New York—for further funds if the case was taken to High Court.

of the Medico-Legal Society of New York, one of the Secretaries of
the International Medical Congress of Rome, and Vice President of
the International Medical and Legal Congress of New York in 1895.
The book in question was published by the University Press of
Watford, "a firm of respectability and repute." The body of his
statement deserves the greatest attention:

> The said book was written by me as the result of many years scientific
> study, investigation and observation and was written purely in the
> interests of science and scientific investigation and to the best of my
> ability in a scientific spirit. The said work is the first volume of a series
> of works which I am engaged in writing being studies in the psychol-
> ogy of sex. It deals with the subject of sexual abnormalities and in
> order to properly treat of these matters from a Scientific point of view
> and to arrive at a conclusion with regard to the remedies for the prac-
> tises dealt with (which frequently lead to crime disease and insanity)
> it has been necessary to instance cases which have actually occurred.
> The matter has been treated to the best of my ability in the least pos-
> sible objectionable manner and with the sole object of elucidating the
> truth and arriving at a satisfactory conclusion as to remedial treat-
> ment. The general scope and objects of the book appears from the
> prefaces and also from the concluding chapter and I crave to refer to
> those portions of the book on those points.

There are two issues raised here that are so remarkable that they
contradict the whole purpose of his book. The first is that inversion
"frequently leads to crime disease and insanity"; yet in *Sexual Inversion* he had argued from the precisely contrary point of view—
that, indeed, many of the finest figures in a community were congenital inverts. Secondly, not a word about the congenital and
unalterable nature of inversion. He here would have it that his purpose was to find a remedy or cure, that he was in fact performing a
social service for the conventional elements of society. It is all so
astounding that one can only assume that Ellis was a very frightened
man indeed.

During these weeks of interminable waiting, Ellis occupied himself in working on the phenomenon of sexual periodicity in males for
his second volume, exchanging data with F. H. Perry-Coste, who
worked out elaborate graphs for him; to Perry-Coste he wrote on
one occasion, "It *may* be true that women only require a sexual
explosion once a month (though I remember a lady—unmarried, it

is true—shyly confiding to me that she thought once a *day* would not be excessive in her case)."[8] This extraordinary statement was made after Ellis had been married seven years and had been having an "affair" with Mneme for four years. Perry-Coste, it will be remembered, had recommended de Villiers to Ellis; and the two men also continued to exchange amused remarks about the bizarre Dr. de Villiers. De Villiers's address was now " 'on board steam yacht, Albatross'—but who knows across what far oceans the 'Albatross' may be ploughing its way?"[9] But he promised to return in time for the trial. "I hear from de Villiers," Ellis commented just before the trial, "of the yacht's visit to the mountain forests of the Tyrol; the post-mark, however, suggested a less remote forest—St. John's Wood. I do not think de Villiers really proposes to give up the business; but is only 'lying low' in an ostentatious manner, until this fury be over."[10]

During the summer Ellis also wrote and "privately" printed—by de Villiers's press—a pamphlet entitled *A Note on the Bedborough Trial*. Now, in *My Life* Ellis says that he completed the pamphlet "directly after the trial." However, evidence indicates that there was one pamphlet published before and another, amended one* published afterwards at the beginning of November. Bedborough knew about it before the trial, and its critical attitude towards him, as well as its announcement that Ellis was going to do nothing to defend his book, contributed to the bitter feeling that Bedborough began to develop towards Ellis, for in his nervous, agitated state his *sang-froid* had long since deserted him. Certainly "advance" copies were sent out *before* the trial. Perry-Coste was sent one on October 25th—"for which a few friends are subscribing a small sum for gratuitous distribution."[11] Ellis later described his method as: "without directly defending my book or answering any criticism, I calmly set forth my position and stated my resolve to continue my own work in my own way but no more to publish it in England."[12] Affixed to the pamphlet were testimonials from an impressive list of physicians

---

* Which reflected Ellis's changed and now derogatory view of Bedborough. It, too, was published by the Watford University Press, and that Ellis was later embarrassed by this connection is apparent in a letter to his first biographer, Isaac Goldberg: "Better to refer to it as a privately printed pamphlet without mentioning the 'University Press,' as the printer's name is unimportant" (Corrections to ms., Goldberg Collection, New York Public Library, Astor, Lenox and Tilden Foundations).

and scientists who had written privately to him. Before the trial, too, he made arrangements with the elusive de Villiers to publish the second volume of the *Studies*! De Villiers promised Ellis that it would bear the imprint of Leipzig by "The University Press"— although it was actually printed in Watford as before. In *My Life* Ellis claims that, apart from de Villiers's mysterious behaviour, he felt "honour bound" to give the book to de Villiers—and that he did not learn about the Watford connection until later. His ingenuousness in this matter is almost beyond belief.

Before the trial—by the 11th of October—Ellis had become thoroughly disenchanted with Bedborough and his friends. To Perry-Coste (who was in Cornwall) he wrote: "Seymour, who is an extremely decent fellow, is greatly disgusted with all their crew, and probably will not keep on the *Adult*. (Don't mention this, however.) The less one has to do with 'reformers' the better—with *other* reformers, of course!"[13] Despite conflicting accounts of motives and events, at least a week before the trial—which took place on October 31st—Ellis and the committee knew that Bedborough had made some sort of deal with the prosecution. Two hundred pounds had been raised in Bedborough's defence* to pay for counsel and solicitor (chosen by "a prominent member of the League"†), by name Wyatt Digby. In *My Life* Ellis described the latter in unusually strong language:

> How anyone could have chosen a solicitor who bore his character so clearly marked on his limp, shady, and shabby figure, it is not easy to understand. He was unsatisfactory from the first, inattentive to the case, not to be found when wanted and scarcely helpful when found.[14]

All was confusion before the trial commenced. At this point we shall try to confine ourselves to events—as far as possible—as Ellis saw them at the time. A key letter is one sent to Perry-Coste on October 25th in which Ellis answers Perry-Coste's expostulations about a blanket condemnation of "reformers":

> "I need not say I quite accept the distinction between reformers. Bedborough has proved of the frothy order and has sold us all; to the indignation of my solicitor and the fury of the Committee—those of

---

* This is Ellis's figure, but the sum varies according to different accounts.
† Osward Dawson.

them who know, for the matter is private at present. It appears that the prosecution has made overtures to defence, and Bedborough and Digby have agreed to plead guilty to my book, whereupon charges against *Adult* is [sic] to be withdrawn. B. is quite right to make the best terms for himself, but of course he should not have let the matter be put upon grounds of principle, nor have accepted money—which I and the others have had the unpleasant task of scraping together—on, as it now appears, false pretences. *Morally,* every penny of that money ought to be refunded."[15]

What he means by "grounds of principle" is puzzling. In his affidavit Bedborough simply said that he had sold *Sexual Inversion* in all innocence. And there did not seem any reason why he should go to jail for a book with which he had no connection. De Villiers provided most of the money, so Ellis is exaggerating when he speaks of his own efforts at "scraping together" the funds.

On the morning of the trial there was chaos in the halls of the Old Bailey, with people giving instructions, others countermanding them. The committee instructed Digby to defend Bedborough on the original charge—a gross imposition, surely, since Bedborough was under no obligation to serve as a martyr for the committee's sense of drama. The committee refused to pay Digby unless Bedborough pleaded "Not guilty." Throughout the proceedings Seymour and members of the committee treated Bedborough with the utmost contempt, as reports in *The Adult* (now edited by Seymour) testify. Bedborough instructed Digby to carry out the compromise he had arranged with the prosecution, but since Digby knew he would not be paid, in the end Bedborough had to appear alone in court. He had sworn to sever all connections with *The Adult* and the Legitimation League. The Prosecution, therefore, recommended that sentence should be deferred and that he should be released on his own recognizances.

Ellis was not mentioned by name. Bedborough placed all blame on de Villiers as the controller of the Watford University Press and the recipient of the profit from the sale of the books. "That that is the fact there can be no question at all," said the Prosecution. "My lord, Dr. de Villiers has absconded. Against Dr. de Villiers a warrant has been applied for and granted, and if Dr. de Villiers, who I am told is abroad at the moment, shall venture to return to this country, he may be quite certain that that warrant will be followed by immediate execution."

The Recorder of London, Sir Charles Hall, then addressed the defendant:

> I am willing to believe that in acting as you did, you might at the first outset perhaps have been gulled into the belief that somebody might say that this was a scientific work. But it is impossible for anybody with a head on his shoulders to open the book without seeing that it is a pretence and a sham, and that it is merely entered into for the purpose of selling this obscene publication.

In delivering judgement the Recorder lectured Bedborough: "So long as you do not touch this filthy work again with your hands and so long as you lead a respectable life, you will hear no more of this. But if you choose to go back to your evil ways, you will be brought up before me, and it will be my duty to send you to prison for a very long time." The chastened Bedborough was released on his own recognizances for the sum of £100.

During the trial Edith, Ellis, and Humphreys sat in an anteroom awaiting the outcome. There was no question of Ellis's counsel speaking because no charge had been made against Ellis. Ellis complained that none of his medico-psychological friends were prepared to go into the witness box; but, on the other hand, he wasn't prepared to do so himself. His solicitors felt that it was important that he should testify to the veracity of his case-histories; but this he could not do because these cases had been collected haphazardly, Ellis fully trusting Symonds's and Carpenter's assurances that they could vouch for them. Equally important in Ellis's reluctance to appear as a witness was his extreme nervousness about speaking in public, for he feared he would present a very unimpressive spectacle.

The strain on Edith was cruel. She felt, as it were, that she was in the dock herself and that she had been found guilty of pretending to be a respectable member of society. She always shuddered when she remembered the Bedborough trial, and in the future many of her vagaries of behaviour, particularly her alternating bouts of extreme dependence on Havelock followed by a recoil from such dependence, might be traced to this traumatic event.

As for Ellis, he tried to block out all memory of the awful experience, although its bizarre and melodramatic aspects continued to plague him for years. From time to time information about the various participants would come to his ears, but he immediately put it out of his mind or modified events in his memory so that they always appeared in his mind as remote from any connection with himself.*

The lawyer, Wyatt Digby, was struck off the rolls without any opportunity to appeal; and there is evidence that this might have been a miscarriage of justice. As for the composite publisher, de Villiers-Singer, at the time of the trial Ellis did not have positive proof that he was a crook, yet there was abundant evidence that he was a very shady character and one would have thought that Ellis, under the circumstances, would have felt it incumbent to appear as spotless as Caesar's wife. Nevertheless, he allowed the University Press to handle the second volume of the *Studies*, which de Villiers-Singer assured him would be published in Leipzig, although it was actually published in Watford as the first one had been. Ellis omits all mention of this incident from *My Life*, where he asserts that he had by this time transferred publication of the series to the F. A. Davis Company of Philadelphia.

The following year he finally learned the real name of his publisher, who turned out to be a single fantastic individual—by actual name, George Ferdinand Springmühl von Weissenfeld, son of a distinguished German judge. This peculiar individual had been educated at Giessen, where he won high honours and married a lady of good family. He had to flee Germany because of cheques he had forged, and he settled in England in 1880. Here he was imprisoned for twelve months for forgery. Once released, he again proceeded to involve himself in a staggering number of dubious enterprises, including a Brandy Distillery Company, which consisted only of himself, but distributed prospectuses of photographs of vineyards so convincing that he secured capital of £60,000. He had various aliases—for which he kept specimen signatures—and thirty different bank accounts. His servants entered into the masquerade by wearing different costumes as the occasion warranted. The police finally closed in on him in January 1902. By then he was living in a grand house in Cambridge under the name of Dr. Sinclair Roland. The house contained an elaborate series of secret doors and passages, and here the police finally found him cowering with a revolver pressed to his

---

* He learned in 1920, for instance, from the American radical lawyer, Theodore Schroeder, that Scotland Yard threatened to reveal embarrassing details about Bedborough's family unless he agreed to plead guilty (Special Collections, Morris Library, Southern Illinois University).

head. When handcuffed, he called for a glass of water, took a few drops, and dropped dead. According to Sweeney, he was wearing a magic ring containing poison which he had boasted would leave no trace behind. "I never regarded him as a criminal," Ellis mused in retrospect, "even now it seems to me that he was essentially a man afflicted by a peculiar mental trait which it would have been psychologically interesting to investigate."[16]

And what of George Bedborough, the genial bookseller, who was the real victim of the trial? At no time did Ellis make any attempt to contact him, to reassure or commiserate with him. When he tried to state his case to the committee, the members angrily demanded that he leave the hall. After the trial he had to change his name and for several years he lived in exile in Germany. Then out of the blue, in 1917, Ellis received the following letter from him:

Dear Dr. Havelock Ellis

We are both twenty years older than when we for a moment came into each other's personal life. Will you think me ultra-sentimental if I ask you for some small sign (a post card will do) that you feel no animus now, if you ever did, against the young man I was in 1898.

Although our personal contact was so slight, and so unfortunate, I knew you through your literary work, (particularly the Mermaid plays and the Science series). Since then I believe I have never missed one of your books Sex, Science or Sociology. Few writers write so intimately, so individually as you, and I have *loved* your work. Consequently there is a big and increasing debt on my side which I want to acknowledge.

I have had a wonderfully happy life, but I should be happier still if I knew that you felt no personal bitterness when you remember 1898.

Yours sincerely
George Bedborough[17]

Undoubtedly Ellis answered kindly, for a few days later Bedborough wrote again:

"I cannot tell you how very sincerely I appreciate your generous view of the past. I remember quite well that you said something very similar (about my being dragged needlessly into a question which did not ultimately concern me) quite early in the proceedings. I am and always will be sorry that events probably outside my control made things happen as they did.

You are right in saying that the world has moved since then. It would be difficult to find a jury today quite so prejudiced as then. Certainly judges and educated men and women are more commonly enlightened. The common newspapers too are more tolerant. Novelists are more frank. I am quite certain that your own work has been a great factor in this enlightenment of the educated. Educated men were often very narrow in 1897. I rejoice sincerely in the success of your work. I believe that when you and I are gone, you will have successors, and more widespread investigation will follow. . . . I am doing seventy hours a week war-work. . . .[18]

Apparently Bedborough practised one of the aphorisms of a small book he published that year, *Sayings of George Bedborough*: "Happy is the man who forgets all that he has suffered and remembers all that he has enjoyed."[19]

Nevertheless, in a letter of November 1930 to the American anarchist printer Joseph Ishill, Ellis could still say, "Bedborough's attitude at the trial was not heroic."[20] Neither, for that matter, was Ellis's.

NORMAL LIFE AGAIN

ELLIS REGARDED THE BEDBOROUGH TRIAL AS THE TURNING POINT IN his life. He was in the midst of the most sustained productive period of his career—his best books were still ahead of him—but he began to feel a diminution of the remarkable energy that had carried him through the exertions of the previous twenty years. His hair was rapidly turning grey and he now needed glasses for reading. Money worries began to vex him and, most disturbing of all, his deep anxiety about Edith was never to be absent from his consciousness.

Immediately after the trial husband and wife returned to Carbis, where some of their neighbours seemed under the impression that he had been imprisoned. Curiously, it never seemed to enter his head during his whole career that any of his more conventional neighbours regarded him with abhorrence as the writer of "dirty" books; if such were the case, Ellis was too self-contained to take notice; by inclination and temperament he was a recluse.

He and Edith were both exhausted from the long months of interminable anxiety over the case, and well before the trial was over they decided that they must get away from England for a spell. Tangier seemed the most exotic contrast they could think of after the atmosphere of puritanical rigidity in which they had been suffocating. At the end of November they embarked at Plymouth on an Orient liner, travelling second class, for Gibraltar, where they spent one night ("more than enough" was Edith's reaction in a letter to Carpenter) before crossing to Tangier. Both found themselves enthralled by its Eastern flavour, and for Ellis it was the most powerful visual experience of his life. Edith's delight in the variegated scene and her pleasure in meeting new people seemed to revive her psychic energy, but within a few weeks it was apparent that the climate was enervating to her and the recurrence of an old cardiac condition convinced Ellis that he should never again take her anywhere outside the range of conventional resorts. A pleasant stranger with whom they had struck up an acquaintance provided the answer to the immediate dilemma. This gentleman was an orange-grower from California who was about to sail for Malaga on business, and the idea of accompanying him appealed to them. Edith visibly improved during the voyage, and the sojourn in Malaga in early spring was one of the most delightful episodes they ever shared. Here they were joined by Arthur Symons, who had been spending the winter in Seville. They would sit together lunching under a lemon tree in the garden, and many evenings were spent at a tavern where a talented dancer, Dolores, would perform for them on a table while her fiancé smouldered in the background. Edith, in her characteristic way, persuaded an elderly chamber-maid to come back to Cornwall as their servant until Ellis convinced her of the dangers of uprooting a Spanish woman from her Andalusian home.

The whole experience was so enthralling to Edith that she was never to abandon the dream of some day settling in another country. Nevertheless, she was glad to get home. From Gibraltar she wrote to Carpenter: "We've been away since November 26th and I'm now deadly homesick. We sail for Plymouth on Tuesday and I'm a good deal better for it all but to 'travel is to die continually' and no mistake. . . . When are you coming to us again? You always soothe my nervous system in a mysterious way and I'll mend your socks if you come."[1]

On March 26th they arrived back in England. Settled once again in Cornwall, the tribulations of the previous year faded into the past as they resumed a routine of life which made the next few years the most tranquil period of their marriage. Before their departure Ellis had worked until the last minute to complete his studies on sexual periodicity which had to be sent off to America, and now he immediately set to work on a study of a dystopia, prompted both by his own recent experience and by the flood of eulogies pouring forth at the close of the nineteenth century. *The Nineteenth Century: A*

Dialogue in Utopia is a heavy-handed little book, but it served as a means of venting his suppressed anger over the reaction to *Sexual Inversion*.

The summer of 1899, working in his hut at Hawkes Point, he vented his scorn of Merrie England in this diatribe. Perhaps he found the release of his indignation in some degree purgative, but no one paid much attention to it. It was unfortunate that it was cast into dialogue because he lacked an ear for the flavour of speech. His other attempt, in *Kanga Creek*, is embarrassing, although Arthur Symons loyally told him that it was in the tradition of the French *conte*. Ellis's symbol for the vulgarity of the nineteenth century is a beer bottle; his obsession with excrement is tasteless; and his attempts at Wildean epigram lamentable: "Literature is generally the resort of a period devoid of other consolations." He philosophically accepted the poor sale of the book, and returned to more congenial work.

A far more interesting book is a collection of essays, *Affirmations*, which appeared just before the eruption of the Bedborough case. Its immediate occasion was also prompted by Ellis's hostility to the self-congratulatory optimism of the end of the century. In reaction against the general complacency, he set out to "affirm the existence of those simple eternal facts of life which are wrought into our very structure everywhere and always, and in the face of which the paltry triumphs of an era fall back into insignificance." His own affirmation was made through the study of a series of individualists, writers who had defiantly formulated their own values, often in the face of conventional opinion. *Epater les bourgeois* seems to have been a motivating force behind most of his books. "I do not like drinking at those pools which are turpid from the hooves of my fellow creatures; when I cannot get there before the others I like to wait until a considerable time after they have left," he declared in the Introduction to *Affirmations*. It was also significant that none of the figures he chose as culture-heroes happened to be English, and in his perverse way he praised Nietzsche, Casanova, Zola, Huysmans, and St. Francis for precisely the qualities he realized would disturb the Victorians.

In its way *Affirmations* was a far more reasoned and coherent expression of Ellis's thought than *The New Spirit* had been. Its message, which infused all Ellis's writings, was the need for an enlargement of the spirit, a more expansive acceptance of life's possibilities. "In this book I deal with questions of life as they are expressed in literature, or as they are suggested by literature. Through-out I am discussing morality as revealed or disguised by literature." The particular figures chosen here "affirm" through their work or their personalities some aspect of reality and are in effect creating a more wholesome society; by accepting a reality based on a biological structure, these prophets of the future widen the "sphere of life." While Ellis's aesthetic is expressed in an informing attitude rather than a defined formula, he is in the tradition of Arnold's Hellenism and Pater's Epicureanism,* attitudes which were in part aesthetic reactions against the narrow confines of a philistine culture. If one sought to apply a motto to Ellis's aesthetic, it might be "Only enlarge." At the same time there is a curiously traditionalist attitude towards art as catharsis or sublimation, both for the creator and for the perceiver, a belief in the psychological effect and the therapeutic value of the aesthetic experience. Nietzsche, for example, he praises for his ability to channel his turbulent emotions into the creation of a philosophy entirely at variance with his own nature. Here Ellis is anticipating Yeats's more elaborate theory of the mask.

His treatment of Huysmans deserves attention. Huysmans was the darling of the nineties, the prophet of *The Savoy*, praised above all by Symons; and the exoticism of À *Rebours* had perfumed *The Portrait of Dorian Gray*. Heady stuff indeed, but Ellis, in his in-dependent way, finds Huysmans fascinating not as the purveyor of exotic sins but as a distinctly moral writer. The source of his genius must be traced to physiological disorders, and in disciplined creation he expresses "the sane equipoise of an imaginative temperament." Zola, too, is up-ended. Defenders of Zola had praised his naturalism, but for Ellis he is to be cherished for introducing hitherto forbidden subjects, particularly in his acceptance of the sexual and digestive functions. "If you think of it these two functions are precisely the central functions of life, the two poles of hunger and love around which the world revolves."

Casanova and St. Francis might seem somewhat incongruous figures to group with this collection of "affirmers." Harking back to his usual obsession with heredity, Ellis sees Casanova as a typical Venetian—"the racial soil was favourable to such a personality"—and the qualities produced by such an environment are a genius for

---

* "To produce a Pater is the one exquisite function of a spiritually barren and exhausted age," he says in the essay on Casanova.

sensuous enjoyment, tolerant humanity, and unashamed earthiness. Ellis clearly admires Casanova's power and will to live fully; and one detects that he is speaking out of his own experience when he says that Casanova's life provides the reader with a fantasy world in which he can vicariously indulge himself. Anticipating something he was to write upon a great deal in future years, he praises Casanova for his imaginative attentiveness to the psychical and bodily states of the woman (another Hinton?), a lover who "could have given a lesson to many virtuous husbands of our own highly moral century." After reading the book, William James told him, "I think you too indulgent to that monster of meanness, Casanova, but there are splendid pages in your chapter on St. Francis."[2]

Ellis was perhaps the first person to treat St. Francis as a purely secular figure. He is interested in him not as the saint whom Matthew Arnold described as representing "the mediaeval Christian sentiment in its extreme"*[3] but as an interesting psychological study of a man who balanced conflicting aspects of his personality. The weakness of this whole approach is that Ellis selects only those aspects of the man which he finds interesting. The essay on St. Francis is daring and unconventional, but it ignores his spirituality; just as there is a serious deficiency in the essay on Nietszche, for it leaves out of consideration all Nietszche's later and greater work. Actually, Ellis never appreciated Nietszche's work after 1883. *The Will to Power*, or *Thus Spoke Zarathustra*, or *Ecce Homo* had nothing to say to him; in an article on the philosopher written in 1919 for the *Encyclopaedia of Religion and Ethics* he dismissed them: "All these later writings after *Zarathustra* show a frequent tendency to self-assertion, unrestraint, over-emphasis, and extravagance—all of which are absent from the earlier writing—and they are chiefly responsible for the various misunderstandings of Nietszche's attitude and opinions."[4]

The essays in *Affirmations* are impressionistic, not as elegantly self-conscious as Pater's *Appreciations*, but they are very much the product of their time, just as the mingling of art and life is com-

---

* Here Ellis seems to be telescoping two memories. In *Essays in Criticism* (Macmillan, 1865) on p. 211 Arnold says that St. Francis brought religion to the people. "He founded the most popular body of ministers of religion that has ever existed in the Church." *But* on p. 214 he goes on to say: "No man has approached the Monte Alverno extreme in sentiment, the Christian extreme, the heart and imagination, subjugating the senses and understanding more bitterly than Heine. . . ."

pletely in the tradition of Pater. "To live remains an art, an art which everyone must learn and which no one can teach" indicates that he had totally absorbed the famous Conclusion to *The Renaissance*. A typical reaction was that of *The Academy*, which priggishly observed, "For ourselves, we prefer our criticism to be less closely allied with physiological science, with the sexual and digestive functions"[5] (February 26th, 1898). But it is understandable that Arthur Symons regarded this as the best of Ellis's books.

In *My Life* Ellis recalled the next decade as a period in which he and Edith established a serene working relationship, the memory of which he was to treat as sacred for the rest of his life. The harmony was achieved by compromise, acceptance, and profound mutual love. It was an unusual marriage which for some years worked relatively well because they were unusual people. It worked, above all, perhaps because through the *Studies* Ellis had learned much about the wide divergences among people and their relationships; if he were truly objective about his material, then he must accept his own marriage for what it was. "What it was"—how one is to convey the quality of feeling between two people—is another matter. As Edith's health deteriorated, and as she relied increasingly on Havelock, so his attitude of father-brother-comrade reached a level where his need for her became absorbing because only through Edith could so many springs of his emotional life be touched.

The reality of this tenderness was particularly poignant in later years when he remembered the events of 1902. During the winter Edith's heart was more troublesome than ever, and she was in such misery from shooting pains in her knee that there were days when she was unable to get out of bed. Money had become a real worry, but it was evident that they must get away. Ellis's doctor recommended Aix-les-Bains and it was decided that they should go in October, when the prices were lower and Edith's cottage-letting season was over.* It proved to be a period of unalloyed pleasure. Savoie's delights to the eye were gentle after the dazzling colour of Tangier. They enjoyed the passing spectacle of international visitors, and only three days after their arrival Edith felt so invigorated that she awoke early in the morning and wrote her first short story, which convinced the doting Havelock that she was an "artist." They made several excursions, the most memorable to Les Charmettes, once the

---

* Also, as the wife of a doctor, Edith did not have to pay any medical fees.

home of Madame de Warens and the young Rousseau. The old stone house with its terraced hillside garden was so much as Ellis had imagined it from the description in the *Confessions* that he experienced an uncanny sense of being in close contact with its famous occupants. Rousseau's *Rêveries*, a book which had belonged to his cultured Grandmother Wheatley, was the first French book he had ever read, and Rousseau as a fascinating psychological case appears frequently in the pages of the *Studies*.

Their stay in Aix was so pleasant that they always talked of returning there some day, but one thing or another, particularly lack of money, prevented the realization of this dream. Edith and Havelock had never been closer, perhaps because they were sharing a precious experience, each aware of and tolerating the fact that the other was finding emotional completion elsewhere. Ellis had left ten days earlier than Edith in order to see Mneme, who was still in Belgium, and he returned via Belgium in order to see her again. Edith in turn had fallen rapturously in love with another woman.

While they were in Tangier it was apparent to Ellis that her feeling for Claire had cooled to a comradely friendship, but with her ardent nature it was impossible for her to be long without some love object on which to bestow her adulation. This she found in Lily, an artist in St. Ives, who was made to be worshipped, idealized, and pampered. Delicate, fragile, indulged, Lily became Edith's holy star. Havelock was no longer addressed as "sweetheart" but became "boy," "child," "the one person in the world who understands me." He claims in *My Life* that he did not feel jealous of Lily; he believed Claire had absorbed all his capacity for jealousy. He could appreciate Lily's charm, but it is apparent that he did not like her from his dry comment that "she was dreadfully afraid of being bored."[6] He totally accepted the situation, and even surrendered his Hawkes Point studio for intimate picnics; above all, he listened understandingly to Edith's raptures and eventually comforted her in her grief over Lily's sudden death from Bright's disease in June 1903. Edith was devastated by the loss, particularly as Lily's family would not let her see her darling during her last days and someone told her that Lily had made fun of her behind her back. She treasured every sacred keepsake associated with her friend, particularly her brooch, which Ellis was careful to see that she wore when she was cremated. She became addicted to spiritualism, convinced that Lily would communicate with her from the other world. For all his scientific detachment, Ellis sympathized

with her obsession and helped her with a selection of love poems for
an anthology, *The Lover's Calendar*, published in 1912. It was really
a monument to Lily, "an exquisite shrine at which she could carry on
a kind of worship of Lily."[7] "I might say," Ellis adds, "that unlike
as many of the circumstances were, Lily came to occupy in Edith's
mind and heart much the same place as, with better reason no
doubt, Edith came to occupy in mine."[8]

No one ever took Lily's place, but she was to be followed by a
series of other ardent friendships, the hazards of which were sup-
portable so long as Havelock's loving understanding could be called
upon when needed. And during all these years Mneme was always
in the background and was accepted by Edith so long as she did not
impinge on their special relationship. "My love to Mneme" appears
as the conclusion of many a letter. Ellis's relationship with Mneme
remained intimate for fifteen years, and close even after she married,
yet what was the nature of the intimacy? In *My Life* Ellis set out
to emulate the candour of Rousseau's *Confessions*, but in some
respects he is bafflingly reticent. He always speaks of her as sweet,
gentle, and pliable. Edith regarded her as too superficial to form a
close part of the texture of their lives; and later Françoise Lafitte
found her hard and possessive. Probably they were all correct in their
respective estimates; but she was undoubtedly devoted to Havelock
and offered him a feather bed which seemed necessary during the
trying years with Edith.

But the relationship precipitated at least one crisis during the
period of "acceptance." An admirer of Mneme's, distraught by
jealousy of Ellis, sent Edith a letter containing the story of Havelock's
relationship with Mneme, but "the sting of the attack lay in its
vulgarity and in the diabolical ingenuity with which plausible suggestions and perversions of truth were woven with real facts, in the
manner most likely to make me appear ridiculous and to wound a
wife of Edith's proud spirit."[9] On reading it, Edith was so overcome
by shock that she sank to the floor. She seemed to pull herself together in a dignified way, but for a long time afterwards she referred
bitterly to "that manuscript." Mneme's admirer even hired a private
detective to trail Ellis, an experience that gave the latter a good deal
of amusement since the man chose a day when Ellis took their maid
on a sightseeing tour of London. Ellis's final word on the incident is
not distress that Edith was caused so much pain, but satisfaction
that Mneme dropped her suitor.

It was Edith's perpetually uncertain health that caused real anxiety during these years. After a long bout of pneumonia in 1895 she wrote to Carpenter: "Havelock looks very well and handsome at least all the women artists here tell me so—but I've been an awful incubus on him for months but he's pulled me out of the jaws of death I verily believe."[10] She seemed more vigorous during the strenuous outdoors life she lived while she kept the farm at the Count House, but after they gave it up in 1906 her health deteriorated again. At this period they moved to two near-by adjoining cottages—the Moor cottages. They wished to join these by knocking a door between the two houses, but the landlord wouldn't allow this, and at nights they would communicate by banging on the wall to each other.

By now Edith fancied herself as a fully professional writer. She read aloud everything she wrote to Ellis, usually after lunch or before dinner. Ellis's critical judgement seems to have been suspended when it came to Edith. The short story begun at Aix grew into *My Cornish Neighbours*, which appeared in 1906 and was dedicated "To Havelock." The following year, *Seaweed*, considerably rewritten, was published as *Kit's Woman: A Cornish Idyll,* and in 1909 *Attainment,* which interested Ellis more than any of her other works although he considered it the most artistically unsatisfactory of her books. Based on her experiences at Fellowship House, the heroine was a vague representation of herself, and the hero a compendium of Ellis and a couple of other people, while various characters were suggested by William Morris and Thomas Davidson. Ellis was in London when it came out, but Edith sent him a copy immediately: "My Boy, here is your *Attainment* with my best and truest love. But for you it would never have been written, and but for you probably never given to the world in this very nice way: I wish you were here to let me hug you and then tell you you had ashes on your waistcoat! I feel very near to you and I *do* love you. Your own Wifie."[11]

When not overcome by nervous fatigue, pain, or depression, Edith felt that she was on the verge of a new career, something she could achieve quite independently of Havelock, although she never used any name except Mrs. Havelock Ellis. During one of her confinements to bed she spent two or three mornings dramatizing one of the stories in *My Cornish Neighbours,* "The Subjection of Kezia." Despite Ellis's prudent caution, she sent it off to Otho Stuart at the Court Theatre. It was accepted immediately and for some weeks it was played as a curtain-raiser at a number of London theatres. Edith was overjoyed and from this moment entered into a phase of frenetic optimism and dizzying activity, a pace that was to exhaust Ellis and ultimately to kill Edith. It was difficult for Ellis not to be apprehensive about her nervous energy, particularly after Symons collapsed in Italy with a severe breakdown in the summer of 1909. Only a year before this disaster, Ellis's book about the country he and Symons had travelled to so often together—*The Soul of Spain*—had appeared. At one point they had thought of collaborating on it, but now Symons's creative powers were never to reach the same level again.

It seemed a time of general change and uprooting. Since Symons's marriage in 1901 Ellis had rented a small flat in Rectory Chambers, Church Street, near the old Chelsea Church. He needed a larger place and found what he wanted in Brixton, in Canterbury Road— 14 Carlyle Mansions—opposite the Police Station. The building was thirty years old, solid and substantial, and had seemed an innovative piece of architecture when it was built. On September 7th, 1909, Edith wrote from Carbis:

> "My darling Boy, I think that the flat sounds splendid. Offer them £46 at first and let me one room for £10. Be in it before I come up and I will bring a bed and a few things with me. I would not disturb you a bit as I can always—as I do at the Club [the Lyceum in Piccadilly] cook my own breakfast, etc., and I should be *so* glad to have one room I could lock up and go whenever I wanted. . . . Don't say you would not like me to have a room in your flat—I wouldn't disturb you. I'm used to seeing to myself lately."[12]

Of course Havelock brought her breakfast, as he always had; but in time she found the long journey down to Brixton after her literary evenings exhausting and in 1912 took a flat in a doctor's house in Harley Street.

By the end of the decade Edith felt that she was entering into an exciting new career with renewed energy, but Ellis had reached the end of the great project which had been in his mind for thirty years. At times he had been gripped by fear that he might die before he finished his task. The last and final volume of the *Studies* was brought to completion in the summer house at Carbis, and in his pocket-diary, which usually contained only bald entries, for the

7th of August 1909 he pencilled the words of George Chapman: "The work that I was born to do is done."*

He recalled Gibbon's words as he reached the last sentence of *The Decline and Fall* in his summer house at Lausanne. Ellis, too, was flooded by a deep sense of calm joy. "I had done mankind a service which mankind needed, and which, it seemed, I alone was fitted to do. I had helped to make the world, and to make the world in the only way it can be made, the interior way, by liberating the human spirit."[13]

---

* Opening line of the Postscript to his translation of the Hymns of Homer.

CHAPTER 15

STUDIES IN THE
PSYCHOLOGY OF SEX

"You can do great things for truth and for man," André Raffalovich* wrote to Ellis after reading the first two volumes of the *Studies*.[1] The following decade was to be an interval of massive reading, of careful collation, of quiet reflection. These years in which he built up the superstructure of the *Studies* were undoubtedly the most fulfilling period of his life. Ellis genuinely viewed himself as a liberator of mankind. Why, then, have the *Studies* been allowed to go out of print? Why is it that modern psychologists know little about him? Why was it that Freud, not Ellis, has been accepted as the *conquistador*, the great pioneer of the modern spirit?

It was deeply disturbing to Ellis to witness the rapidity with which Freud, whom he viewed as the historian of the pathological, gained pre-eminent pride of place, while Ellis, who wished men to accept and understand their sexuality, did not receive the recognition to which he felt entitled. One answer may be that while Ellis described, enumerated, and recorded the manifestations of the erotic impulse, he lacked the ultimate courage to look into his own soul, to make the kind of discoveries or "decisions" that are only possible to a man who combines deep insight with extraordinary fearlessness. Ellis was

---

* Marc-André Raffalovich (1864–1934). Born in Paris, settled in London in 1884, where he tried to establish a literary salon, without much success. In 1895 he published in Paris *L'Affaire Oscar Wilde*, in which he discusses his recollections of Wilde. The following year he published in Paris *Uranisme et unisexualité*, a study of homosexuality.

a man of integrity, but he lacked the creative genius necessary for discoveries that touched a disturbing universal emotional pulse. No school of disciples grew around him to perpetuate his ideas because there was no coherent body of doctrine to which to subscribe. Again, it is possible that he had problems so deep-rooted that it was difficult for him to talk about normal male sex. Further, while his writing is graceful and polished, it is not compelling or transfixing and is easily forgotten. The terminology he used to describe erection and climax— "Tumescence" and "detumescence"—is ponderous. The *Studies* are dull reading. How they could have been judged as "dirty" books is hard to imagine.* The discussions are drained of all emotional overtones; that he truly believed that sex is "the deepest and most volcanic of human impulses" is hard to credit from reading the *Studies*. Ellis seems at his happiest when he is able to draw from a wide range of authorities; much of the *Studies* is an elaboration of an extended footnote, and as exciting to read. A great bulk of the text is in small print for no discernible reason, since comment and documentary blend into each other;† this idiosyncratic typography tends to look impressive, but it is daunting to read. Ellis clearly could not bear to waste a single item of laborious research, and the *Studies* are weighed down by the sheer accumulation of supporting evidence. Ellis worked in breadth, not depth, and the only way he could survey human sexuality from his solitary hut in Carbis Bay was to amass the impressive weight of all the authorities who had written *books* on the subject. Ellis was the supreme type of Victorian amateur polymath trying to follow in the tradition of Darwin, Spencer, and Frazer, who confidently assumed that they could take all knowledge as their domain. In most respects, Ellis was a *naïf* as far as sexual experience was concerned; his credulity probably contributed to the tolerance which is the key-note of the *Studies*. He was a late developer emotionally, and at the time he wrote the *Studies* was relatively uncontaminated by experience. The only personal preparation he had for the writing of *Sexual Inversion* was his knowl-

---

* In May 1926 he told his first biographer, Isaac Goldberg, "I have never referred in my writings to Frank Harris. . . . I read the first volume of his autobiography, & found it unsatisfactory, even tedious. How unlike Casanova! All books in which there is too much insistence on sex are tedious" (Manuscripts and Archives Division, New York Public Library, Astor, Lenox and Tilden Foundations).

† In *A Study of British Genius* (1904) the small type is clearly demarcated as reserved for the results of previous investigators (Manuscripts and Archives Division, New York Public Library, Astor, Lenox and Tilden Foundations).

edge of Edith, and a single encounter during his medical-school days when he was once confronted on the street by the question commonly employed at that time: "Were you in the park last night?" I have talked at length with a homosexual, Mr. Anatole James of Cheltenham, who first went to see Ellis in 1913 after reading *Sexual Inversion*. In 1917 he was confined to prison for nine months for congress with a minor, and when he was released he discussed his situation on a number of occasions with Ellis, whom he found "very helpful and very understanding." I mentioned to Mr. James that a number of people had thought that Ellis was a crypto-homosexual. "Heavens, no!" he exclaimed. "He had none of the attributes of a homosexual. I thought he was asexual, a complete virgin. He understood all about sex, but I don't think he knew how to do it. In fact, I was sure he had never done it."

During the years Ellis was working on the *Studies* he made numerous trips to Spain, which was still regarded as an exotic *terra incognita* by the average British traveller.[2] This is as close as he ever approached the South Sea islands he had wanted to visit and record as a young man. *The Soul of Spain* was published two years before the sixth and concluding* volume of the *Studies*, and there is an appositeness in comparing the methodology used in both works. His travel book is in effect a book of essays on Spain in which various aspects of the country are selected as subjects to be discussed and analyzed from a distanced, literary point of view. There is no sense of Gerald Brenan's felt experience, or of Lawrence Durrell's swooning surrender to the genius of place. Far more interesting are Ellis's unpublished travel notes, many of which seem to have been written on café tables by a withdrawn stranger recording the passing scene, a Malinowski observing the strange rites of the natives. Ellis travelled the length and breadth of Spain in jolting buses and odoriferous trains, but the experience of smell, of constriction, of heat, is totally lacking from his observations. He was above all a recorder, the man who was always taking notes on bits of paper and stuffing them into envelopes. One can picture him so absorbed in his own thoughts that the native gives him barely a passing glance. His notes reveal a man who was highly susceptible to the charms of Spanish women—"the Sp.w's hand is, as it were made for caressing—it always seems to be feeling for something to clasp tenderly, and when this is not possible,

---

* He published an additional volume in 1928.

a Spanish woman always tends to clasp or press her own hands, or thighs."[3] He was fascinated by uninhibited Spanish dancing witnessed by an all-male audience, but none of this is recorded in his book. There is no reference to food or drink or conversation. He always seems to be looking—even in his notes—for *types*. Barcelona was his favourite city—"the gayest city in the world"—but it is impossible to conceive of this solemn, studious Englishman joining in the gaiety. I have not been able to establish how much Spanish he spoke, but I suspect as little as possible. In his five extensive journeys through Spain there is no evidence that he made friends with a single Spaniard.

The *Studies* were organized into the same compartmentalized sections as the essays in *The Soul of Spain*. One of the major difficulties with the *Studies* is the lack of conceptual unity, of an organized epistemological framework with logical connectives. Working in such a piecemeal way, how then could he believe that he had covered the entire spectrum of sexuality? In Volume I, for example, what connection is there between the three sections, "The Evolution of Modesty," "The Phenomena of Sexual Periodicity," and "Auto-Erotism"—apart from the fact that it is a rather shrewd grouping of the unspeakable with a scientific study and a thoroughly Victorian treatment of female sexuality? The highly eccentric nature of the organization of the *Studies* is a reflection of its amateur basis and of a descriptive empirical approach to the subject. Furthermore, if he had applied himself to an investigation of "normal" sexuality, as he claimed, it is puzzling why he devoted long sections to aberrations like "cross-dressing" (VII), which he termed "Eonism" after the eighteenth-century transvestite. Such an idiosyncratic hit-or-miss method is misleadingly described as "scientific," and his citation of vague authorities—"a friend," "a correspondent," "a woman who enjoys the confidence of many women"—is ridiculous. Even Krafft-Ebing was far more sceptical of the reliability of the accounts in his case-histories, and Kinsey, who was to owe much to Ellis, devised methods of circumventing lies or exaggerations.

When all is said and done, while I would not go nearly so far as Paul Robinson's claim in *The Modernization of Sex* that Havelock Ellis "stands in the same relation to modern sexual theory as Max Weber to modern sociology, or Albert Einstein to modern physics,"[4] he undoubtedly stands as the major transitional figure in establishing the preoccupations and methodology of later sexual investigation.

Robinson describes him as a modernist in his "enthusiasm" for sex, but his enthusiasm is qualified, for he consistently described sex as "a problem." It was a "problem" to the degree that most people were deeply troubled by this powerful drive that frequently had to be restrained. As Ellis said himself, when he set out to write the *Studies* he thought he could provide answers; at the end he could only pose questions. But the message of all his books was that sex was a mysterious gift to mankind which should be embraced with ardour and attention. For a vast number of people he brought the glad tidings that they were not abnormal in their behaviour, and that their drives were shared universally. "Other Victorians," it appeared, included just about everybody. In 1916 Bertrand Russell wrote to Ottoline Morrell:

> "I have read a good deal of Havelock Ellis on sex. It is full of things that everyone ought to know, very scientific and objective, most valuable and interesting. What a folly it is the way people are kept in ignorance on sexual matters, even when they think they know everything. I think almost all civilized people are in some way what would be thought abnormal, and they suffer because they don't know that really ever so many people are just like them."[5]

Later in life Ellis was to become an enthusiastic exponent of nakedness and sunbathing in the nude, but at the turn of the century the first essay in his *Studies* was to promulgate the thesis that woman's sexual attractiveness to man lay in her subtle guardianship of her delicious secrets. This, surely, is a relatively historical phenomenon; and Ellis was writing at a time when even women's ankles were sheathed in boots. But he is able to summon up historical and ethnic precedents, even drawing from his own experience in delivering babies in the London slums.

The discussion of menstruation in "The Phenomena of Sexual Periodicity" was extremely important—and, regrettably, intended to be read only by physicians and lawyers. Who, before Ellis, had pointed out that sexual desire is often at its highest during menstruation (first suggested to him by Olive Schreiner) and that, despite all the taboos about coitus during menstruation, it frequently takes place, and without harmful effects? Calling on his own experience, as he seldom did in the later volumes, he comments: "When still a student I was struck by the occurrence of cases in which a seduction took place during the menstrual flow, though at that time they seemed to me inexplicable, except as evidencing brutality on the part of the seducer."[6] Turning to men, and basing his conclusions largely on nocturnal emissions experienced by himself* and F. H. Perry-Coste, he argues for a lunar phase for men as well as women, pointing out that most conceptions occur during the spring and autumn. This questionable view has never been established.

Ellis rigorously set himself to puncture the prejudices and misconceptions of the Victorians' view of sex. His most iconoclastic stance was his commonsensical acceptance of inversion. The next was his calm, measured discussion of one of the Victorian bogeys, masturbation. This was subsumed under the more innocuous term "Auto-Erotism," which was defined as "the phenomena of spontaneous sexual emotion generated in the absence of an external stimulus proceeding, directly or indirectly, from another person."[7] Victorian youths had been warned that indulgence in this vicious practice would lead to blindness, impotence, or other ravages of sin. Ellis's mode of procedure was to ignore such extravagant fears and to proceed calmly to an investigation of the phenomenon. Animals, the final arbitrators of human behaviour, practised it—ergo, it must be natural. All the evidence suggested overwhelmingly that almost everybody did it, even respectable middle-aged ladies, and that it frequently acted as a beneficial form of relaxation from tension. Just as sexual inversion had been rendered harmless by comparing it to colour-hearing, so masturbation was allied to emissions that take place during sleep or to daytime fantasies. The argument is somewhat specious, since masturbation cannot be described as altogether involuntary. Not that Ellis turned his back entirely on Victorian beliefs, although these were now couched in more sophisticated form. In a footnote he cites—without comment—one authority who "considers that masturbation plays a large part in producing the morbid fear of the eyes of others"[8]—and here I believe he is thinking of himself, as also possibly in his admission that excessive masturbation not only accounts for many nervous disorders but creates a division between the physical and psychological expressions of sexual feeling.† *The Lancet* found that "this delicate subject is

---

* He appears as W.K.

† Freud, too, pointed out that masturbation creates guilt and he had seen patients damaged by the habit by becoming fixated on infantile sexual fantasies (*Standard Edition*, XII, 239).

treated by Mr. Havelock Ellis with thoroughness and decency."[9] But it was generally apprehensive about the undertaking as a whole.

> His book must not be sold to the public, for the reading and discussion of such topics are dangerous. The young and the weak would not be fortified in their purity by the knowledge that they would gain from these studies, while they certainly might be more open to temptation after the perusal of more than one of the chapters.[10]

The Lancet did not deign to take notice of any of the intervening volumes until the last (presumably) in 1910.

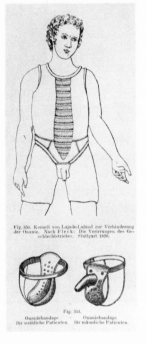

Fig. 350. Korsett von Lajade-Lafond zur Verhinderung der Onanie. Nach Fleck: Die Verirrungen des Geschlechtstriebes. Stuttgart 1830.

Fig. 351.
Onaniebandage   Onaniebandage
für weibliche Patienten. für männliche Patienten.

Top: Lajade-Lafond's *Korsett* for the prevention of masturbation (*Onanie*). From Fleck: *Die Verirrungen des Geschlechtstriebes* ("Sexual Aberrations"), Stuttgart, 1830.

Bottom: *Onaniebandagen* for female (left) and male patients.

Handbuch der Sexualwissenschaften by Dr. Albert Moll, Institute for Sex Research, Indiana University, Bloomington, Indiana.

But: did Ellis contradict himself on masturbation as he did on homosexuality? Steven Marcus has pointed out that as late as 1921 in the second edition of *Handbuch der Sexualwissenschaften* Ellis was recommending "*Onaniebandagen*" or "*Korsette*"—little suits of armour fitted over the genitals and attached to a locked belt—as prophylaxis for masturbation.[11] And at the University of Texas there is a typed and corrected (but apparently unpublished) undated essay he wrote on masturbation which contains some startling observations. If masturbation occurs before puberty, he says, it should understandably arouse anxiety in the parents "as to the complete nervous soundness of the child and the stock he belongs to." If the child is not the victim of a "defective nervous development or bad heredity," there is no reason to worry that he may be introduced to the habit by "a vicious companion." But if the habit is formed, it is very difficult to eradicate. Mechanical devices are seldom successful for a child, but it is desirable to ensure that his hands are kept outside the covers. "If he wakes at an inconveniently early hour, he should have some objects to investigate and play with, such, for instance, as the smooth Eastern images with no dangerous angularities." While masturbation does not always produce evil results, Ellis's conclusions are not very far removed from Victorian horror:

> Even when producing no gross evil results such as impotence, it may still be productive of minor physical evils and of subtle loss of refinement on the psychical side. Moreover, the risk is run, through an early acquired habit of masturbation by an individual with normal moral feelings, of an unnatural divorce between the higher and the lower feelings; the physical feelings associated with masturbation are regarded as low, while the higher sexual feelings tend to a sterile ideality. The most serious results of masturbation, as we now realise, are not usually due to the act itself but to the psychic reaction it excites: apprehension of the results, shame, remorse. Under such conditions any act is injurious.

Nevertheless, occasional masturbation—particularly among women (men more easily find other modes of relief)—is not necessarily injurious. The points to be observed, then, are that Ellis attributes the habit to a nervous constitution or an unsound heredity; and that he sees its habitual practice as capable of producing impotence or guilt. The only conclusion I can draw is that he is speaking from personal experience.

In Volume III (1903) Ellis turns to the psychological process of courtship, and here he expresses some of his most interesting ideas on sex. In the first section, "The Analysis of the Sexual Impulse," he discusses the remarkable physiological changes that take place during arousal and orgasm (or "tumescence" and "detumescence" as he would primly have it). That the instinct is not specifically linked to the organs of sex is proved by the fact that castrated males and females lacking uterus and ovaries continue to feel desire. Ellis foresees that this is a fertile field for future investigation, but is not ready to say that final answers will be provided for what will always remain fundamentally a mystery.

He points out that the most common analogy to intercourse is evacuation, but it is no true comparison. There is one puzzling passage to which attention should be drawn:

> The sexual act presents many characters which are absent in an ordinary act of evacuation, and, on the other hand, it lacks the special characteristic of the evacuation proper, the elimination of waste material; the seminal fluid is not a waste material, and its retention is, to some extent perhaps, rather an advantage than a disadvantage to the orgasm.[12]

Ellis does not explain what he means by this. It was a common nineteenth-century belief that the emission of seminal fluid was the "spending" of vital energy; and it is possible that Ellis had this libidinal economy in mind. Possibly he is thinking of the Karezza method whereby the male never reaches orgasm, a method practised at the Oneida community,* which Ellis was greatly interested in.† The "advantage" of the method was that it enabled the woman to have multiple orgasms without becoming pregnant, but Ellis was too prudish to put this in print. But what about the effect on the male partner?

Ellis was always insistent in his belief that the male and female

---

* Founded at Putney, Vermont, in 1842 by John Humphrey Noyes as a commune in which the property was pooled and conventional marriage dispensed with. The community voluntarily dissolved in 1880.

† In a letter written to Karl Pearson (undated, but probably 1892) Ellis writes: "Yes, I too investigated the Oneida community many years ago and came to much the same conclusions. Only I couldn't make out the precise sexual practice which I learnt from Miller [Noyes Miller, a member of the community] of intercourse prolonged even for an hour, without emission, or any desire for it, but allowing of orgasm in the female. So far as I can make out, this practice (which is quite unlike 'withdrawal') is very far indeed from general. It is interesting that such a practice could be carried on pretty consistently for 30 years in a large community—probably only through training their subjects at an early age—& also interesting that to medical & general observation no evil results were perceptible. The children born under these conditions are turning out well, according to Miller. The low intellectual level is, I think, a characteristic of all communities—not peculiar to Oneida. (They get rich—a convincing proof of low intellectual development!) It does not seem a very desirable or even possible pattern of sexual life but a curious example of human adaptability (Miller admits he does not find it so easy in his own married life)" (Pearson Papers, University College). Ellis evidently regarded the practice with more favour when he came to write Sex in Relation to Society (1910), in which he devotes a lengthy section to it. See Studies, IV (Random House, 1936), 553–4.

were separate and distinct in role and function, and that fulfilling sex could be achieved only by gratifying instinctual courtship patterns. The possession of the female by the male is an exercise of power, a form of mock combat, a semblance of conflict in which the skill of the male is demonstrated in his prowess in subduing the female to his will. Evidence of this is manifested in the mutual satisfaction that each derives from the infliction of pain, but it is satisfaction only as long as it is maintained at the level of play and with the promise of eventual pleasure. Why pain should play such a vital part is "one of the great mysteries of love."

A sensitive lover, Ellis emphasizes, realizes the complex and contradictory nature of a woman's emotions: that she both craves the expression of her maternal feelings towards her lover while at the same time she delights in being shocked into doing something she resists. Normal behaviour is only a modified form of some of the most terrible and repugnant of perversions, and de Sade and Sacher-Masoch the extreme exemplars of general instincts. "It is enough here to emphasize the fact that there is no solution of continuity in the links that bind the absolutely normal manifestations of sex with the most extreme violations of all human law."[13]

He has some perceptive things to say about the relationship between sadism and masochism. "The masochist desires to experience pain, but he generally desires that it should be inflicted in love; the sadist desires to inflict pain, but in some cases, if not most, he desires that it should be felt as love."[14] Frequently the sadist is a disguised masochist who enjoys his victim's pain because he identifies with that pain. Ellis wished, then, to break down the distinctions between the two as they were in fact complementary emotional states.

In "The Sexual Impulse in Woman" Ellis cites the leading nineteenth-century sexologists—Acton, Ferrero, Lombroso, Krafft-Ebing, Moll—all of whom believed that women's sexual appetite was far less than that of men. Not so at all, Ellis asserts; if a woman appears frigid or unresponsive, it is because her lover lacks the understanding and knowledge to arouse her. After thirty years of profound investigation, Freud confessed that he was still bewildered as to what women really wanted. Ellis would have been ready with an answer: a more fulfilled sensual life. This, above all, he had learned from Hinton—an awareness of women's needs; and this awareness has been the greatest factor in the sexual revolution of the twentieth century. But there is no corresponding discussion about the psychodynamics of male arousal and orgasm except in the most technical terms. The great deficiency in the *Studies* is the failure to come to terms with what men—most normal men—want.*

Between Volumes III and IV Ellis produced a rather curious book, *A Study of British Genius* (1904). Inspired by Francis Galton's *Hereditary Genius* (1892), Ellis attempted to take up where Galton had left off. The sixty-six volumes of the *Dictionary of National Biography* had recently been issued and Ellis spent hours poring over them, enumerating and collating data, his favourite activity. His method of exclusion was to ignore those men who had less than three pages devoted to them, royal personages, and women who did not exhibit a high degree of intellectual attainment—which seems to be what he meant by genius. The results were not particularly startling, but there were some data he must have found flattering: a high proportion came from East Anglian stock; in adolescence many of them had spent more than a year out of the country, and they were often the first-born. Incidentally, "The tendency to very high-pitched voice which is so remarkably common in men of intellectual ability [Is it? He doesn't give any statistics] may possibly be due to a slight paralysis of the vocal cords. . . ."† The book is now completely dated because it presupposes a static England where men could be identified by their birth-place, and fails to recognize the greater mobility already in process as a result of the Industrial Revolution and the increased opportunity for passing class barriers with the growing importance of the middle class.‡

In Volume VI (1906) he turned to extensive discussions of elements affected in sexual selection—touch, smell, hearing, and sight. All that he says is fairly self-evident, and this is probably the dullest of the volumes in the series. The factors of age, income, and sheer chance are utterly neglected. But there is a long discussion of incest; his views on the subject, he states in *My Life*, developed from his feelings for his sister Louie on his return from Australia. The absence of attraction between brothers and sisters, as he was often

---

* This is not to suggest that he regarded the woman as complete without the man. See Appendix C for a letter he wrote to the American author V. F. Calverton, who planned to write a history of women.

† Was this the cause to which he attributed his own high voice?

‡ The most rigorous critic of Ellis's simplistic approach has been Jacques Barzun in *Race: A Study in Modern Superstition* (London: Methuen, 1938). In case after case he demolishes Ellis's "bald assertions"; genius, he says, "is *not* a substance like tin or lead" (p. 131).

to insist, requires no special explanation—familiarity discourages desire. But

> Passion between brother and sister is, indeed, by no means as rare as is sometimes supposed, and it may be very strong, but it is usually aroused by the aid of those conditions which are normally required for the appearance of passion, more especially by the unfamiliarity caused by a long separation.[15]

Finally, he proved a poor prophet when he remarked that distinction of dress was necessary for the respective roles of the sexes.

> One of the greatest of sex allurements would be lost, and the extreme importance of clothes would disappear at once if the two sexes were to dress alike; such identity of dress has, however, never come about among any people.*[16]

Ellis never deviated from his emphatic insistence that the supreme and proper end of sex is reproduction. But, with the passing of time, he began to view sex also as the expression of love between two people, and felt that it did not necessarily require any other transcendent end. Even when writing the *Studies* he had to consider the fact that a great many people in the world did not indulge in "normal" sex. This was the accepted premise behind *Sexual Inversion*. Now in Volume V (1906) in "Erotic Symbolism" he is not speaking primarily about "normal" erotic symbolism, but about cases where an object has parasitically absorbed the normal sexual energy which, in Ellis's conventional view, should have for its final end the procreation of the species—in, for example, foot fetishism. While he can find prototypes of most sexual practices in the behaviour of animals, fetishism is, in fact, restricted to the domain of the human. Nevertheless, as in other sexual patterns, the aberrant is only the extreme of the normal. The fixation is a re-emergence, by a pseudo-atavism or arrested development, of an impulse probably experienced by our forefathers, and still often traceable in young children. Ellis then goes on to discuss foot fetishism as an expression of masochism, of emotional submission, substantiating this by several case-histories. He then embarks on a discussion of his own "germ of perversion," urolagnia; despite the horrific case-histories of Krafft-Ebing and Neri, he argues,

---

* He must have been relieved when Olive Schreiner abandoned her determination to wear knickerbockers!

There is ample evidence to show that, either as a habitual or more usually an occasional act, the impulse to bestow a symbolic value on the act of urination in a beloved person, is not extremely uncommon; it has been noted of men of high intellectual distinction; it occurs in women as well as men; when existing in only a slight degree, it must be regarded as within the normal limits of variation of sexual emotion.[17]

One wishes that he would give some examples of the "ample evidence." He also links vesical power with sexual power, and describes the failure to project the urinary stream in a normal manner as an "accepted sign" of impotence. These two preoccupations—which seem to be linked spontaneously in his mind—occur a number of times throughout the *Studies*. The section on "Erotic Symbolism" ends on an extraordinary note:

Yet, regarded as a whole, and notwithstanding the frequency with which they witness to congenital morbidity, the phenomena of erotic symbolism can scarcely fail to be profoundly impressive to the patient and impartial student of the human soul. They often seem absurd, sometimes disgusting, occasionally criminal; they are always, when carried to an extreme degree, abnormal. But of all the manifestations of sexual psychology, normal and abnormal, they are the most specifically human. More than any others they involve the potently plastic force of the imagination. They bring before us the individual man, not only apart from his fellows, but in opposition, himself creating his own paradise. They constitute the supreme triumph of human idealism.[18]

Is this indeed what it appears to be: a paean of praise to aberrant behaviour?

Turning from the abnormal to the normal, in the remaining sections of Volume V Ellis examines the sexual organs involved and the physiological dynamics of copulation in "The Mechanism of Detumescence" in the most objective, toneless manner possible; but he indulges in an ardent celebration of motherhood in "The Psychic State in Pregnancy." Tucked away in the back of the volume are a number of case-histories of sexual development which provided almost the only piquant titillation to early readers of the *Studies*. As usual, Ellis judiciously balances the mixture of the outrageous with the distanced objective eye.

Ellis regarded the final volume (VI, 1910), *Sex in Relation to Society*, as the most important of the series. In the Introduction he states that in the previous volumes he had sought to be as objective as possible, but now "I have here to set down not only what people actually feel and do but what I think they are tending to feel and do"[19]—a rather puzzling distinction. It is a gallimaufry of offerings: the mother's relationship to the child, sexual education, prostitution, venereal disease, the art of love—and more. The authorities most often cited are Iwan Bloch, Sigmund Freud, Magnus Hirschfeld, and James Hinton. The volume contains some advanced ideas for its time, such as the opinion that wives in comparison with prostitutes were vastly under-paid for services rendered. Marriage he describes as a more fashionable form of prostitution, and in many similar declarations throughout the book he expresses his scorn for current morality (many of these ideas harked back to his discussions with Olive Schreiner). As far as sexual morality is concerned, there is in fact no such thing, since there is a wide disparity between what people do and what they think other people ought to do. A case in point was the current divorce law. An adulterous wife could be sued for divorce, but not an unfaithful husband.* The wife's offence, after all, was very serious—it was an offence against property. This leads Ellis to turn to Christianity, which he sees as largely responsible for the obscurantist attitudes towards sex prevailing in the Western world. By de-sexualizing the idea of man and over-sexualizing the idea of woman, Christianity degraded the position of women and the role of motherhood. But, in his strong feeling that he is part of a moral revolution, Ellis argues for economic independence and moral responsibility for the woman; and emphasizes that the state has no right to interfere in the conduct of her personal life until a child is involved. As far as his own views are concerned, unions that are more or less permanent are desirable from the point of view of both the individual and the state. Ellis always saw his point of view as that of reconciling opposites, and this was never more clearly exemplified than in the following passage:

> There are two currents in the stream of our civilization: one that moves towards an ever greater social order and cohesion, the other that moves towards an ever greater individual freedom. There is real harmony underlying the apparent opposition of these two tendencies,

---

* The Matrimonial Causes Act in 1857 introduced civil divorce for adultery. Wives were not allowed to divorce husbands until 1923. In 1937 three additional grounds for divorce were introduced: desertion, cruelty, and insanity.

and each is indeed the indispensable complement of the other. There can be no real freedom for the individual in the things that concern that individual alone unless there is a coherent order in the things that concern him as a social unit.[20]

Ellis, in this final volume, set down his *Weltanschauung*—a view reflective, tolerant, and responsible. Here, at length, he spoke throughout a whole long volume in his own voice—a role which his admirers were constantly urging him to assume. It is probably the best and most sustained of all his work.

Ernest Jones (then teaching at the University of Toronto*), later to be Freud's most ardent disciple in Britain, wrote: "Will you allow a fellow-countryman and fellow-worker in the sphere of sexology, to send you a word of warm congratulation on your latest volume, 'Sex in Relation to Society'? I know that in your relatively lonely path you have steeled yourself to dispense with such expressions, and it may perhaps seem presumptuous as coming from a younger man, but I cannot refrain from saying how keenly I enjoyed reading your sane and yet fearless exposition of the subject" (Lafitte Collection).

The Lancet liked the "broad quiet" historical survey of the early part of the book, but took alarm at the section on "The Art of Love."

> For the husbands of highly sensitive brides some teaching in skill and tact may certainly be useful, but it is doubtful if the refinements in the *ars amandi* detailed in this chapter are desirable for general adoption. If dyspareunia† occurs occasionally as it does, on sentimental grounds, the trouble is limited to a few persons; and a widespread contemplation of methods which we find in the pages of Martial or a re-issue of the eighteenth century editions of the "De Variis Veneris Schematibus" (with cuts) is not to be tolerated; they must inevitably have engendered an undesirable degree of concupiscence in those who came under the influence of such instruction.[21]

Nevertheless, Havelock Ellis had become "a scholar in his peculiar field, and has given the dignity of scholarship to a very delicate and difficult subject, and this is the proper method of treatment."

The two areas, then, that marked Ellis as a modernist in the great divide at the turn of the century were his acceptance of abnormal behaviour and his recognition of a woman's right to a fulfilled sexual life. Dr. William Acton, whose *Functions and Disorders*

---

* Professor of Psychiatry, and Director of the Ontario Clinic for Nervous Diseases.
† Difficult or painful coitus in women.

of the Reproductive Organs (1857) was the authoritative text supporting most Victorian sexual superstition, regarded it as an insult to woman to consider her capable of sexual responses.* The Victorian wife did her duty by submitting to sex; she felt "good" because she did not enjoy it. But for Ellis, woman emerges as a creature of diffused sexuality whose numerous erogenous zones needed to be coaxed or courted into arousal. The woman was an instrument from which the man evoked music.† She was the passive receptacle of the thrusting penis which was "the point at which, in the male body, all voluptuous sensation is concentrated, the only normal masculine centre of sex."[22] Woman is a complex creature, made up, on the one hand, of pity, tenderness, and compassion, and, on the other, of a longing for roughness and pain to be inflicted by her lover. One side of her nature should be channelled into motherhood, which remains for Ellis the supreme function of women; while the development of her erotic temperament is largely the creation of a skilful and understanding lover. Ellis believed that a woman should be given full opportunity to develop her potentiality, but he always insisted that she was different in kind and function from man. "They have the laws of their own nature; their development must be along their own lines, and not along masculine lines." In a phrase which would arouse the anger of all feminists, he declared, "In a certain sense their brains are in their wombs."[23] It is a romantic, idealized conception of woman—"old-fashioned" at any period of history—and one which diminishes his right to be described as a modernist despite the fact that he opens a far greater arena of experience to women.

While Ellis claimed that the main object of sex was reproduction, he never took into consideration the family or the relationship of sex to actual children. Lewis Mumford has praised him because "he peered where no one had dared to look"; nevertheless,

> Ellis's description of the sexual act becomes a study of the "mechanism of detumescence"; and in all his studies, although he wrote on marriage, he never follows the sexual embrace as far as the child or

---

* F. H. Perry-Coste had also taken this point of view in his correspondence with Ellis. In the *Studies*, Vol. I, Part Two, p. 196, Ellis cites Adler's view in 1904 that the sexual needs of women are less than those of men.

† Margaret Mead later remarked acidly that this concept omitted "The idea that women must be very good musical instruments in order to please the men who played on them" (*Blackberry Winter*, New York: William Morrow, 1972, p. 117).

allies his fresh insights on sex to the nature of the family and psychological reconditioning of sex that springs out of permanent parental
relations. This prophet of sex celebrated the flower and forgot the
seed. This self-absorbed bachelor, whose marriage was a denial of marriage, whose own low-keyed sexual life was as slow as Napoleon's
pulse, alas! exemplified the sterility and the impotence that the civi-
lised—as Fourier called the type—carried along with his mechanical
advances.[24]

Moreover, it is never entirely clear what Ellis meant by "the
psychology of sex." He might have been more accurate to describe
himself as an anthropologist of sex. The main thrust of his "psychology" is behaviour and response in courtship, and the categoriza-
tion of types and responses (through the case-history) embraces both
emotion and activity. The demarcation line between the two disci-
plines was still somewhat blurred,* and the only distinction Ellis ever
draws between them is that one is concerned with man's outer behaviour, the other with the inner workings of his mind. In 1889 he
joined the Anthropological Institute of London. In 1890 he read the
first chapters of William James's *Principles of Psychology* in *Mind*,
and there seems little doubt that he was greatly influenced by James,
especially in his underlying assumption that emotional and bodily
changes are one and the same. With Ellis, psychology is still very
much in the realm of the amateur, and his observations are not
very different in approach from Kinsey with the gall-wasp or Karl
Pearson with the crab: if one observes an impressive number of
specimens, one is bound to arrive at truth. On a more complex level,
what goes on in people's minds breaks through into the case-histories,
but Ellis never questions the sequence of cause and effect. The great
weakness of his method is that there is no way of dealing with what
people fail to say. The case-history for Ellis is a window, an un-
clouded transparency. The case-history by the end of the nineteenth
century had become a widespread empirical mode of investigation,
the paradigm of which, according to Michel Foucault, was Jeremy
Bentham's panopticon, the model prison in which the prisoner
could be under constant observation.[25] In Ellis's hands the case-

---

* See "Psychology in Relation to Sociology and Anthropology," pp. 333–42, in
J. C. Flügel, A *Hundred Years of Psychology* (London: Duckworth, 1933). Also
essential is Michel Foucault's *The History of Sexuality* (London: Allen Lane, 1979),
in which Foucault gives a brilliant exposition of the validity of lived experience as
"scientific" evidence.

history is the sum-total of the individual who stands as it were exposed in the centre of a symbolical panopticon, but in Ellis he has a trusting, credulous, innocent observer. Historically speaking, Ellis appears at an important point in the development of what Foucault calls "a confessional science." With Alfred Kinsey the case-history developed into the interview, but Kinsey, far more sceptical than Ellis, devised methods to penetrate concealment. Kinsey, it must be remembered, was a post-Freudian, one who had been trained to believe that things are seldom what people tell you they are. Freud, who drew his theorizing from his experience of his own patients, was interested not in transparency but in opacity, the elements of texture, his ear cocked to detect nuance and contradiction.

Freud develops as a menacing *dramatis persona* in the accumulating pages of the *Studies* during the decade of their inception. In the beginning, his is just one name among many others. The first sign of any disagreement occurs in "Auto-Erotism," where Ellis remarks in a footnote:

> Professor Freud, while welcoming the introduction of the term "auto-erotism," remarks that it should not be made to include the whole of hysteria. This I fully admit, and have never questioned. Hysteria is far too large and complex a phenomenon to be classed as entirely a manifestation of auto-erotism, but certainly aspects of it are admirable illustrations of auto-erotic transformation.[26]

Ellis praises Freud for drawing attention to the effect of the sexual life on the nervous system but feels that Freud's method of interpreting dreams, based on "subtle and slender clues," is far too subjective. Frequently Ellis refers to Freudian theories without comment, as in the case of taboos. The first reference to "the Freudians" in his writings seems to have appeared in the third edition of *Sexual Inversion* (1915), in which at some length Ellis describes Freud's theory of the process leading to inversion, all of which Ellis rejects, but in fairness adds: "Freud himself, however, is careful to state that this process only represents one type of stunted sexual activity, and that the problem of inversion is complex and diversified."[27] But while it is Freud's followers who have seized on the possibility of "cure," Ellis held Freud himself responsible for what Ellis regards as the pernicious doctrine of the Oedipus Complex. In "The Doctrine of Erogenic Zones," while Ellis repeatedly draws attention to the fact that he himself coined the phrase, "erogenic zones," he admits that Freud has gone into the question more searchingly and penetratingly than anyone before him. He was obviously inspired by Freud in his history of Florrie,* the girl who had a penchant for being whipped: "Freud more than anyone has shown us, the minute and prolonged study of an individual can rarely fail to be profitable";[28] but Ellis's account of Florrie is flat-footed beside Freud's narratives of Dora or Little Hans. Actually, two years before Ellis wrote the Florrie paper, Freud had published "A Child Is Being Beaten," and in a footnote Ellis hastens to add that the two essays are not in conflict. "Freud's deals with flagellation mainly as a phantasy throughout, not, as I have, putting forward a case in which early whipping was an experienced fact and the demonstrable foundation for phantasy."[29] Praising his own sympathetic attention to Florrie's story, he compares it favourably with the method of "transference," commenting ironically,

> One is tempted, indeed, to ask whether an investigator who encounters "negative" transference might not be well advised to retire from the world for a time and to practise a little auto-psychoanalysis. The investigator, instinctively and unconsciously, however good his intentions may be, often forgets that it is his part to educate and develop; he falls into the attitude of combat; he unconsciously adopts the gesture of tilting against a foe, and so inevitably he arouses the corresponding impulse of hostility and resistance on the opposing side. It is a plausible fallacy to fall into.[30]

Ellis completely misses the point that transference is a necessary means of effecting a psychoanalytic cure. Again, in Volume III Ellis gets into a debate over dreams. In "The Synthesis of Dreams"† Ellis was to categorize one hundred of Françoise Lafitte's dreams. The essay was meant as a retort to Freud's *Die Traumdeutung*; he compares Freud's method to that of a geologist, his to that of a geographer. While dream analysis by then was so well established that "It has long ceased to have any pioneering interest, or to offer any scope for scientific adventure"[31]—a barb at Freud!—Ellis sees himself as offering something entirely new: "I venture to think that I have been able to carry the method a step forward. That is all I

---

* "The Mechanism of Sexual Deviation," *The Psychoanalytic Review*, VI (May 1919), 229–67; VI (June 1919), 391–423 (reprinted in Vol. VII of the *Studies* as "The History of Florrie").

† *The Psychoanalytic Review*, XII (July 1925), 251–94; XII (Oct. 1925), 425–69; XII (Jan. 1926), 38–63.

claim." Alas, his project fell on deaf ears—what could accumulation of data offer in the way of intellectual excitement? He could never agree with Freud that dreams of flying were erotic, or dreams of undress exhibitionistic. Freud simply seemed to him slightly whimsical in these interpretations as in so many other instances.

Long after the *Studies* had been completed, Ellis continued to refer to Freud in almost every one of his books. He was finding it difficult to be both Jack the Giant Killer and Father Christmas.

COMPLICATED RELATIONSHIPS

As ELLIS BEGAN TO BECOME SOMETHING OF A FAMOUS FIGURE, EDITH made it abundantly clear that she wasn't going to let it go to his head. When other people were around she took to making derogatory comments—often a jeering reference to the "scientific" value of the *Studies*—which she knew he found painfully embarrassing. When friends protested, she would snap, "It's good for him."

It was more than mere coincidence that Edith's confidence in her new career developed after the completion of Ellis's *magnum opus*. She was always high-strung and "difficult," but in retrospect it was clear that the real beginning of her personality disintegration, of behaviour that exceeded the usual volatile bouts of depression—which Ellis loyally ascribed to physiological causes—dated from this period. The excitement of her own success was more than she could handle. She was convinced that there were no heights which she could not scale. Had not an admirer told her that she was "the light and hope of our future civilisation"?

Now that Edith seemed embarked on a public career as a playwright and lecturer it was necessary, she claimed, to be closer to London than Cornwall. She became friendly with all the members of the cast of *Kezia* (the dramatized version of *Kit's Woman*), particularly with the actress Beryl Faber, who invited her to her home at West Drayton, thirteen miles from London. Edith was immediately attracted to the charming place, and when she heard that a neighbouring cottage was available, she rushed off to inspect it, and saw in an instant that Woodpecker Farm was just the haven she and Havelock had often talked about for their old age. When the news was broken to Havelock, he found it difficult to share her exalted enthusiasm, but there was no use protesting that they needed a little time to think it over because Edith had already signed the lease. His heart sank as Edith led him around the property pointing out all its possibilities, and his doubts increased when he caught a smirk on the builder's face as Edith proclaimed that the whole place could be made into a dream for £50.

Her first great disappointment was Beryl Faber's announcement that she would not be Edith's neighbour after all; the ostensible reason was that she had had a row with her landlord, but Havelock suspected that she was alarmed by the prospect of having Edith in such close proximity. Edith didn't have time to brood over the rebuff (as she generally would have done), because she was so completely absorbed in banishing dry-rot and making innumerable improvements which they could ill afford.

They moved into Woodpecker Farm in August 1912. In the summer it was rather pretty, Ellis reflected philosophically as he sat under a lovely walnut tree in the garden. But as the weather became colder and their finances more meagre, it became necessary to take in paying guests, a situation which the withdrawn Ellis found intolerable. To his horror, Edith installed a telephone, a delightful new toy to her, but to Ellis a hated intrusion on his privacy. Edith also began to row with servants, and they now often found themselves without help. Edith's first enchantment with the house began to sour as its endless demands increasingly interfered with her literary work. The perfect marriage, too, was beginning to show signs of strain, and it was the last attempt they ever made to share a household. When a wealthy American lady turned up and made an offer on the house, Edith was only too happy to rid herself of it.

During these years Edith continued to write short stories, which were collected under the title *The Imperishable Wing*. Most of these were concerned with death, and Ellis suggested the title after Rossetti's line "The wind of Death's imperishable wing."* One of these, "The Idealist," deals in an oblique way with inversion. Edith often talked of writing a novel based on her painful situation, and Ellis believed she would have done so had she lived longer. In 1911

---

* In Rossetti's sonnet "Lovesight."

she delivered a paper to the Eugenics Society in which she spoke out publicly for the first and last time about inversion. "Some of the best men and women I have known," she told the members, "belong to the 'peculiar people,' and to know their intimate struggles and victories and even apparent failures is a strange *Pilgrim's Progress* story which would astound many who think they alone are the Pure in Heart."[1] It was meant as a statement of the possibilities that lay open for the invert to lead a noble life despite his disability, but it was too much even for the emancipated members of the Eugenics Society and they never invited her to speak again.

Nevertheless, there were other requests for her lectures. As a personality she was impressive on the platform. The intense earnestness of her youth had grown into a seriousness shot through with humour. She took great pains with her lectures and felt it important always to be immaculately groomed when speaking in public. With growing experience she learned to speak without notes. She loved performing and she basked in the flattering admiration of her listeners. Havelock was always regaled with every little bit of praise she had received about her lovely blue eyes, her curls, her youthfulness, her beautiful deep voice. She was like a small child with her insatiable craving to be pampered and praised.

As their life became more centred on London, they took to meeting at the British Museum, at concerts, at tube stations. One of the most moving passages in *My Life* is Ellis's recollection of these rendezvous:

> It sometimes seems to me that at every step of my feet and at every movement of my thought I see before me something which speaks of her, and my heart grows suddenly tender and my lips murmur involuntarily: "My darling!" The streets of London, even when I walk them carelessly beside some unheeding friend, have a new poignancy for me, sometimes "Stations of the Cross" on the way to Calvary, sometimes the starry arch of a Milky Way.[2]

These lines were written shortly after her death when life seemed to have ended for him.

Once timid about travelling, Edith's sense of adventure increased as she grew older. She began to go off on a series of excursions to the Continent with the dear friend of the moment. While staying with one of them, she wrote: "Oh! Havelock, don't feel you don't want me. I let myself drift into thinking you only want

Captain Edward Ellis,
Havelock Ellis's father, in 1868.

Susannah Wheatley Ellis,
Havelock Ellis's mother, in 1868.

Henry Havelock Ellis, aged eight.
Taken in Sydney, Australia, on
his trip around the world with his
father in 1868.

James Hinton, *c.* 1874.

Havelock Ellis as a medical student
at St Thomas's Hospital in 1883.

John Barker Smith,
in 1883, while a student at
St Thomas's Hospital.

Thomas Davidson, 1883.

Olive Schreiner, 1883,
at the time of the
publication of *The Story
of an African Farm.*

Karl Pearson, 1885.

Edward Carpenter, 1897.
Inscribed "to E. Ellis in hearty
friendship."

Edith and Havelock Ellis in 1896, in the Count House, Carbis Bay, Cornwall. This was Ellis's favourite picture of Edith.

Mneme Barker Smith, 1897.

Lily, 1902.

Edith Ellis. Given to Margaret
Sanger in 1915, and inscribed
"From your loyal friend Edith Ellis."

Margaret Sanger in 1914, when
Havelock Ellis first met her.

Havelock Ellis in 1893, when he first began working on the *Studies in the Psychology of Sex.*

The hut at Hawkes Point in Cornwall, where Ellis wrote the first six volumes of *Studies in the Psychology of Sex* between 1894 and 1910.

George Bedborough, 1898.

Françoise Lafitte-Cyon shortly
after Ellis first met her in 1918.

Hugh de Sélincourt about the
time Françoise first met him
in 1920.

"HD" (Hilda Doolittle
Aldington) in 1919, when Ellis
first met her.

Jane Burr on the roof of the
Savoy in 1922. Ellis called her
"the knickerbocker lady" because
of her enthusiasm for
unconventional dress.

Faith Oliver, 1926. This
photograph was taken at Ellis's
request soon after he met her.

Margaret Sanger in 1922, when she was the acknowledged leader of the world birth control movement. It is signed "To Havelock—devotedly—Margaret Sanger."

24 Holmdene Avenue, Herne Hill —"Fairy Tale House"—which Margaret Sanger's generosity made it possible to buy in 1929.

Havelock Ellis in 1923.

Louie Ellis, 1925.

Winifred de Kok, 1925.

Marie Stopes in her garden at Leatherhead. This was sent as a
Christmas card to Ellis in 1921.

"Little Frieth," the cottage in Buckinghamshire which Ellis rented during the summers of 1925–28.

Hildegart Rodriguez, 1933.

Dr Joseph Wortis in Vienna
in 1934.

Sigmund Freud, 1932. It is signed
"von Ihrem herzlich ergebenen
Sigmund Freud—1932."

Dr Norman Haire, 1934
(from the portrait by
P. Tennyson Cole).

The American dancer Marguerite Agniel dancing to the music of the gramophone in the garden of "Haslemere," Wivelsfield Green, Sussex, in the summer of 1929. Ellis has written on the back: "for Agniel the spirit of the dance hovers over the Philosopher of Love! H. Ellis."

Havelock Ellis sun-bathing in the garden of "Little Frieth," 1927.

Françoise in 1932.

At Haslemere, *c.* 1934.

Havelock and Françoise caught by a street photographer on the Brighton front, 1936.

Mneme and not me and my poor brain is tired and suffering and worrying over money."[3] She might flaunt her independence, but Havelock always had to be there, waiting tenderly for her return. For all the difficulties of her temperament—perhaps *because* of them— she gave him the life he was too timid to experience for himself. And she needed him now more than ever. One autumn evening in 1913 they met as they often did at the Down Street tube station. Edith had been trying to raise a loan by taking out an insurance policy, but the medical examiner had turned her down. As they paced slowly up and down the street, Edith broke the news to him that she had diabetes; in those days insulin had not yet been discovered, so they were faced with a very grave situation. Nevertheless, she did nothing to modify her over-energetic way of life; in fact, her activities during the next months might almost suggest that she was bent on self-destruction. What is inexplicable is why she was in such a frantic state over money. There never seems to have been any question about Ellis helping her; he certainly did not have much,* but at least he had enough to go on trips with Olive Schreiner and Mneme Barker Smith. Perhaps they were adhering rigidly to their pact of economic independence as a matter of principle.

In March 1914 another semi-invalid—Olive Schreiner—was back in England but, restless as ever, soon left for Florence, where she wanted Ellis to join her. Anxious about Edith's health, he was re-luctant to leave her, but she generously urged him to go; Olive was also trying to be self-sacrificing: "Dear Havelock Boy, don't come for my sake. I'm so sick and faint all the time it will be no pleasure to you. Unless, indeed, the joy of seeing you makes me better."[4] So he went for ten days in March, but the years had passed, and after the closeness of their earlier relationship it was difficult to find a new basis for friendship. Olive had become obese and was still in a con-stant state of despair about her work and her health, and hoped she wouldn't live long. She had left her husband behind in South Africa and was living on what her brother lent her. Ellis found that she was becoming intractable in her ideas as she grew older; certainly she no longer regarded him with unqualified admiration. The trip was not a success. After ten days in a large, dull, cosmopolitan hotel he went off on his own to Ravenna and Bologna. On his return

---

* In 1914 the Contemporary Science Series, his main source of income, came to an end.

journey he visited Rheims Cathedral, and later was to be thankful that he had been among the last people to see it intact.

He was back in Brixton for only a week before Edith set off for America with vague promises of a lecture tour ringing in her ears and £10 in her pocket. She was desperate for money and was going in the wild hope of making a fortune. From The Beyond, Lily, her dearest of friends, whose memory was still sacred to her, had advised her that this was the answer to all her troubles. Knowing the condition of her health, it is surprising that Ellis did not do more to convince her of the foolhardiness of such an exhausting venture, but perhaps he realized that she had reached the point where she no longer listened to reason. Before her departure she left six letters with the porter of the Lyceum Club with instructions to post them on subsequent days to Ellis. "Do, do take care. You are more to me than you have ever known; it is a strange world and grows stranger day by day. I wish you were here. I see you now with your dear eyes all gone in, getting our breakfast, but you are not alone. I am there every inch of the way."[5]

Other letters allude to some difficulties in his relationship with Mneme, and the hope that they will be closer than ever before. Her prediction proved correct, for as soon as she left he and Mneme went off to East Anglia, where they had a blissful reconciliation. Mneme was now a middle-aged woman, and they stayed in separate rooms in hotels and went about on excursions in a spirit of defiant independence which they had never experienced before. As for Edith, on her arrival in New York she found that the lesbian friend who was to launch her had left for Europe, but Edith's ready charm, as always, attracted new friends. She loved everything about America— the countryside, the warm people, and, above all, the self-importance of being interviewed by newspaper reporters. She didn't realize that she shouldn't speak frankly and spontaneously to the press about her companionate marriage, and Ellis wrote, begging her to be more discreet because it was reported to him that many people were amused or shocked by her outspoken remarks.

In July she was back, feeling thoroughly invigorated by the ocean voyage. No signs of diabetes were evident yet. They had taken a little cottage at Stanwell, where they spent two happy months in that beautiful, never-to-be-forgotten summer just before war broke out— what Ellis called "the peaceful sunset of the long working-day of my life." He seemed, as always, utterly oblivious of the momentous political events that were taking place. In August they moved to an even more delightful spot at Speen in the Chiltern hills. Here they talked often about her projected longer trip to the United States, and she constantly tried to persuade him to accompany her this time. Her obtuseness in thinking that he would consider such a scheme is amazing, but Ellis felt grateful that she wanted to spend the last hours before her departure with him rather than with her friend Yvonne Orchardson. In late October they travelled together to Tilbury, where she was to embark on the *Minnetonka*. She was anxious for him to come on board, but wartime regulations were now in force and Ellis had to stand miserably on the dock, staring at her as though he would never see her again. Finally he turned and walked disconsolately away. Did he remember that other poignant parting from Olive so many years before? The day before she left he had posted ahead a letter which would be waiting for her in New York:

> "This is a line to meet you, I hope, when you arrive, and to tell you how I am with you in the spirit all the time and thinking of you and loving you and praying that all goes well with you—as I still have faith that it will. I am always looking forward to your safe return (with or without money!) and to the prospect of our settling down peacefully for a time in Speen or Carbis, if possible without any worries. In the meantime I shall be shut up in my flat, safe no doubt though rather dreary, and trying to work hard. I shall be writing to you twice a week at least—though you mustn't be worried at delays for the mails seem so uncertain in length of passage—and, anyhow, alive or dead, I shall always be loving you."[6]

The voyage was dreadful and she was sick all the way across the Atlantic. However, in the exhilarating pace of New York her gloom quickly faded away. She was treated like a celebrity and Ellis seemed to take an extraordinary vicarious satisfaction in her success and the important people she was meeting. But it was all too exciting for her over-wrought nervous system and she began to complain about disturbing symptoms. She was treated with ice-packs and massage, and time after time she barely struggled to the podium. The letters to Ellis were cries for help, but while he worried about her, he had excuse enough for the moment not to go over and look after her; he was over-whelmed with the details to be attended to following his

father's death in Folkestone at the age of eighty-seven. "Dear old
Pater! how sweet he is," Edith wrote when it was apparent he was
dying. "I wish I could see him once more before he boards the
greater Winifred [the last ship Captain Ellis commanded]."[7] The
cheerful old man had said that he was content to go because he
had had "a good innings." "In spite of his tradition, no humble
reliance on the blood of the Saviour!" Ellis approvingly commented
to his rationalist friend Perry-Coste.[8]

It was a period of great loneliness for Ellis. Day after day in his
Brixton flat he worked away at the revisions to the third edition of
Sexual Inversion and various pieces which were later to appear in
collections of his essays. He could no longer count on Mneme to
run in and out as she had always done because she was nursing a
dying mother and also—a sad blow—seeing another man. At this
point a woman—and a friendship—entered Ellis's life, an event that
was to precipitate Edith's tragedy. Early in December Ellis received
a letter from a stranger, an Irish-American woman, Margaret Sanger,
who, though just over thirty, had been involved in a life of spectacu-
lar excitement. Her driving demon was an evangelist's passion for
enlightening the world about birth control. Her own mother had
died from bearing too many children and it had fallen on her to
bring up her sisters and brothers. In New York City she had been
indicted under the Comstock Law for using the mails to disseminate
birth-control literature. There were nine counts against her, and she
could be imprisoned for forty-five years. Her lawyer had advised her
to plead guilty because he hoped to get her off with nine months'
imprisonment or perhaps a fine, but, feeling so passionately righteous
about her cause, she made the agonizing decision to desert her
children (she was already separated from her husband) and flee to
Canada; she had no passport, but she managed, by quick wit and
charm, eventually to reach London under the name Bertha Watson.
On the advice of Dr. and Mrs. C. V. Drysdale,* the moving spirits
in the Malthusian League, she wrote to Ellis recounting her history.
She had read the *Studies* and had been appalled by the relentless
cataloguing of perversions and abnormalities, but Ellis was someone,
she realized, whom she should meet. He sent a kind reply to her

---

* Also on the advice of Stella Browne, a socialist feminist, who was a friend of
Ellis's. Ellis had refused Dr. Drysdale's invitation to become vice president of the
Malthusian League.

letter: "The ferocious antagonism to anything so simple, humane and necessary as the regulation of conception is a perpetual puzzle to me."[9] He invited her to tea the following week and was startled to find her so pretty and so comparatively young. At first she was overwhelmed by his patriarchal beauty and his refusal to make small talk. She was also surprised—as many others were on first meeting him—by his thin, high voice, so unexpected in a man of his size. As they sat facing each other over tea, her shyness evaporated and, as she recalled in her autobiography, "I was at peace, and content as I had never been before."[10] Encouraged by his interest in her difficulties, she told him that her plan was to study the literature and practice of birth control in Britain and on the Continent and, armed with this knowledge, to return to the United States to fight her case. With factual information about the situation in Europe, she believed she could bring to the public the realization of how antediluvian the Comstock Law was. Unlike the Drysdales, Ellis did not share her attitude to flouting the law; he cautioned her to use moderation in her campaign. "I was not excited as I went back through the heavy fog to my own dull little room," she recalled. "My emotion was too deep for that. I felt as though I had been exalted into a hitherto undreamed-of world."[11]

Ellis had assured her that he would do everything possible to help her. They must meet often—at home for discussions, and at the British Museum, where he would advise her on her reading. A friendship was developing with sudden alacrity, but he did not yet feel that he knew her well enough to invite her to spend Christmas with him. On Boxing Day he wrote:

> "I was wondering if you had many friends here but in any case it is lonely to be in a strange city so far away from all those you care for most; and especially at Christmas—always a hateful time, I think. I am more alone—though not without friends—than I have ever been at this season for a great many years. So I fell back on my Christmas habit when in Australia long ago and went to High Mass at the Catholic Cathedral!"[12]

Margaret had given him copies of her magazine The Woman Rebel, a name which Ellis playfully began to apply to her. He in turn presented her with his recently issued Impressions and Comments: "It is such a personal sort of book that I am never sure whether people will like it or dislike—though I certainly think that if they don't violently dislike it they ought violently to like it!"[13] By New Year's Eve they knew each other well enough to spend it together. In the second collection of *Impressions and Comments* (published in 1921) appears this entry under January 1st, 1915: "I cannot tell in what lurid gloom mixed with what radiant halo this year will stand out from all the years in the eyes of men alive on the earth after us. Yet we, too, are still living, and for all living things hope springs afresh from every fresh despair. So it is that I have begun this new year at the stroke of midnight with a new kiss."[14]

From Havelock's next letter it appears that Margaret had tried that night to push the relationship beyond a New Year's kiss and cautious Havelock was beginning to feel alarmed:

> "What I felt, and feel, is that by just being your natural spontaneous self you are giving me so much more than I can hope to give you. You see, I am an extremely odd, reserved, slow undemonstrative person, whom it takes years & years to know. I have two or three very dear friends who date from 20 or 25 years back (& they like me better now than they did at first) & none of recent date. I'm not the least good for gobbling up rapidly— really don't repay the trouble! AND I don't feel a bit anxious to be gobbled up, while the gobbler is already unwinding her scarf to wave to someone else!
>
> "I fear this sounds very rude & horrid & not at all as it is meant."[15]

A few days later he attempted to make his position even more clear to her:

> "I think we should agree, Dear Twin, on the subject of love. I think that *passion* is mostly a disastrous thing, & certainly ruinous to work for it makes all work seem of less than no account. And then, too, it's always felt for the wrong person. Indeed its very intensity seems due to a sort of vague realisation of the fact that *there's nothing there!* But I cannot say that I think that *love* is anything but good, & good for everything, including work. I mean by 'love' something that is based on a true relationship & that has succeeded in avoiding the blind volcano of passion (or has contrived to pass safely through that stage). To secure the peaceful joyous & consoling & inspiring elements of love—& to escape the others—seems to me a very desirable & precious thing.

Do we agree? As you say, the average man & woman usually only knows passion—& not or very often even that!"[16]

But by the end of the month it was apparent that in his vulnerable state his emotions had been stirred and that he was throwing scruples to the winds. Margaret sent him a rose for his birthday, and the tone of his reply is ecstatic:

"Oh, you Darling Woman—
how wicked of you to send me that lovely present—the most beautiful present I have ever received, & the precious rose, which is now before me in a little vase & has almost as delicious a fragrance as the woman it comes from, & which I mean to preserve *for always*, & the dear message—oh you darling woman."[17]

The relationship developed more quickly than he had experienced with any other woman. In *My Life* he refers to her only as "M" and describes their relationship as "calm friendship" in which there was "a sweet touch of intimacy about it," adding, "There was no trace of guilty consciousness to spoil its delight."[18] He is describing what the relationship was to *become*, not what the evidence suggests it was at the time. Margaret was remarkably beautiful, feminine, and vivacious. She did nothing to hide her adoration of Ellis, welcome solace to a lonely man. Also she needed his help, his advice, and his wisdom, allowing him to play his favourite role of mentor. Soon they were seeing each other almost daily, dining in Soho, attending concerts, meeting at the British Museum; most often Margaret would go to his flat. It is significant that it was some weeks before he told Edith of his new friendship. The reason for the delay he gives in *My Life*:

I wished to feel sure about my new friendship. To form a friendship so quickly was such a novel experience in my life, to form any new friendship had indeed so rarely, if at all, happened during the previous twenty years of steady emotional equilibrium, that I needed to know first exactly where I stood.[19]

Perhaps, too, he realized that Edith would sense the emotional quality of the friendship.

At last he began to mention Margaret, and every letter was filled with references to her; but it took three weeks for a reply to reach him, and he had no idea what a devastating effect these letters were having on Edith. The first of his letters referring to Margaret arrived on the eve of her most important lecture, which she was to read on February 4th—the day of his ecstatic letter to Margaret—at Orchestra Hall in Chicago; it was a paper on "Masculinism and Feminism" which Ellis had been persuaded to write for her. Early on the day of this lecture she wrote a long letter:

"My Darling Boy, Here on the great day of my public life I awake at five and write my English letters, for never am I alone now. I got all three of your letters and read them when resting after my Turkish bath. Of course I got a fearful jump when I realised there is another ——. If it makes you happy I am glad, but somehow it is a kind of strange realisation which makes it still easier for me to die. I *want* to die, and yet I am at my zenith, and if I can only live two more months I shall not die in debt. Everything is opening, as Lily said—everything, but oh! the reporters and the chatter is so very trying. Yesterday I spoke at a banquet of 600 men—such fine men—at the Chamber of Commerce. It was a unique experience. It is curious how I have felt a strange feeling about you for some time—a realisation how it is a law of life that a vacuum fills. Thank God someone has put life and joy into your sad face. . . . Be careful for I realise here how hero-worshipping is like drug-taking. I've had to cope with it, and even sometimes had to be brutal, in a way, as it is mawkish. A curious aloofness from the world makes me feel sure that at last I am nearer leaving it than I thought. Houghton Mifflin will soon publish my plays. They are sweetly acted at the Little Theatre and *The Pixy* is fine. Of course I'm pretty tired. I've never worked so unrelentingly night and day as now. I've never time even to put a button on or to think, but it is telling at last. I lectured on Olive at the smartest Club here on Tuesday and they went crazy over me; they have given me the run of their beautiful Club; it is close by here and a great rest. . . . I am terrified of to-night. It is a huge hall, but my voice carries, even in a whisper, almost all over it. They are all crazy over my voice. Isn't it dear of these medical women? . . . I wonder how you spent your birthday, Dear One? Which of the —— came, or did they come in relays? Now I must have my bath and my breakfast, go through my lecture, and then dictate to my typist. After lunch I mean to cut off the telephone and sleep. People say I look splendid. Wish my dearest love and all tender hope for your happiness. Your Wifie. P.S.—I drank to you and your new —— in a cocktail last night."[20]

In quoting this letter in *My Life* Ellis left blanks for certain words; it is not difficult to imagine what they were. Ellis's description of this letter is that it was "a little excessive in its references to a desire for death, but it was always natural to her to be a little excessive, and for the rest it was simply sincere, affectionate, natural, with a touch of mischievousness, altogether characteristic of her normal level."[21] How could he have been so obtuse?

Apparently this occasion was one of Edith's outstanding successes. She was carried off to a champagne supper, and the guests signed a sheet with warm greetings to Ellis; Edith wrote a few words to her "sweetheart boy" and for the first time since her marriage signed herself "E. M. O. Lees." This is very curious, for while she liked to think of her tour as a personal triumph, she was listened to as the wife of Havelock Ellis, and the lectures she delivered were on James Hinton, Olive Schreiner, Edward Carpenter, and her own husband.

From now on, her letters vary between great need and affection and paranoia that Havelock was confiding her secrets to Margaret. Margaret was not a nonentity like Mneme. She was young, she was plucky, she had reached fame—or notoriety—on her own initiative. No wonder Edith was terrified. Understandably, her letters are appeals for applause for *her* bravery, admiration for *her* success, and reassurance of Havelock's complete devotion. While his letters are filled with love, he perhaps did not realize how desperately necessary it was for her to have greater expressions of concern. He saw himself as a stabilizing force in her life and did not want to say anything to feed her anxieties. On the other hand, it is clear that he simply did not see that she was headed for an inevitable breakdown. It seems likely that he convinced himself of her marvellous recuperative powers so that he could push her problems to one corner of his mind in order to bask in the pleasure of his new-found friend; and each day he was with Margaret had to be treasured because she would be leaving soon for the Continent.

In the middle of February she sailed for Holland to meet people in her field, to some of whom Ellis had given her letters of introduction; and almost on the day she left, Havelock began to receive letters from Edith, who was now acutely aware of Margaret's existence. Both women returned to England in May, within a week of each other; so it is interesting to compare the sort of letters Ellis was writing to each of them. On February 12th he wrote to Margaret in Amsterdam: "You said in your last letter, before leaving, that I was to *miss* you. But I had begun to miss you even before you had left. . . ."[22] He had wandered down to Victoria Station, hoping to catch a glimpse of her, but did not know what train she was leaving by, "so I just had to wander sadly back again." When he did get a letter from her, he was greatly relieved because he had worried about her crossing the Channel in wartime conditions. On the 18th he tells her that "the sacred J.A.R. longs to be filled with sacramental wine"[23]—a reference that occurs a number of times in his letters, and one can only assume that this is a coy allusion to his urolagnia, in which she apparently participated.

Edith's letters during this period are filled with consuming worry—"I mean to die in peace over debts."[24] Her delusions about her great financial coup are a little pathetic when a lecture she considered a great success netted only £51—"You see the Hall & advertisements & things cost just on a hundred, but it was a fine advertisement & has led to many other lectures."[25] A few days later she wrote: "I do hope M. is out of trouble. People say she is deep & sweet & good, & that is beautiful. Tell her from me to take care of you always, and Mneme too. . . ."[26] Ellis passed this on to Margaret: "Edith hears very nice things about you in America—that you are 'sweet and deep and good,' which is beautiful. (A few say you are fanatical & unbalanced.) I am sure you must have many friends."[27] (Ellis omitted the passage about Margaret being "fanatical and unbalanced" when he quoted Edith's letter in *My Life*.)

In his letter of March 18th it is clear how deeply disappointed he is that Margaret's plans for a longer Continental trip would cut down the time she would have on her return to England. "I feel like threatening to come along with you! And it is sad to realise that you may scarcely be in England at all any more, when there are so many millions of things we have to say & do together which require years & years."[28] It was particularly hard to think of her in Barcelona without him. "Oh, you bad wicked woman to go to Barcelona without me! I quite ache to think of it." What Ellis did not know was that she was enjoying Barcelona with a Spanish anarchist, Lorenzo Portet, who had become her lover before she left England.

In the States gossip was circulating, and Edith sent a newspaper cutting which made Ellis realize that Margaret—as well as Edith—must be more prudent. The story said that Margaret Sanger was in London "working with Havelock Ellis." "I trust, Dear," he chided gently, "you will agree with me that it is better *not* to mention me in your letters home, as everything you may chance to say becomes public property at once, and makes mischief & sets inquisitive people on the prowl. Do you agree?"[29] When Margaret expressed her regret about embarrassing him, Ellis was quick to reassure her: "Do not think I was troubled about the points I mentioned. . . . It is only that when statements are transformed into that positive shape and published they are liable to prove embarrassing & lead to questions being asked. I do not myself mind at all";[30] but Edith minded, very much. She was particularly distressed by a rumour that she and Ellis were not actually married. "I wish I'd brought those 'Marriage lines' to upset them! Oh! I'm *so* tired & feel, once I get somewhere beautiful & quiet, I'll die as a sheer luxury."[31] But her ardent spirit returned and she decided to fight back. In the last lecture she delivered in America, which she entitled "Semi-Detached Marriage," she started off by commenting on the fact that sea-captains and their wives—and she clearly had Havelock's parents in mind—maintain the romance in their marriages because they are not constantly living in each other's pockets. She then went on to describe an experiment in marriage, and there could be no doubt to anyone in the audience who the partners were:

Perhaps a reliable illustration as to an instance of a sane experiment may be given here, as theories count for less than actual facts. Twenty-five years ago two writers of unusually sensitive temperaments, when entering the bond of matrimony, which so often ends in disaster, decided like Godwin and Mary Wollstonecraft that they would not always dwell in the same house, in order to escape the usual fate of boredom or indifference observed among so many of their friends. In fact, they resolved to ignore tradition and make only one vow on their wedding day, the vow of the lovers of tomorrow. They simply promised never to deceive one another. The man and woman are economically independent of one another, and in all external matters have behaved as true comrades or business partners would do. In their approaching old age they contemplate living side by side as a natural outcome of their experiment. The gossips, of course, have been busy, and the experimentalists have had their personal difficulties. No artist in any path of life can arrange his pictures, his music, or his books without smudges, discords, obliterations, and additions. It is only the amateur who is content with a rough draft. If in the end, however, some slight blow is given to the slavery of women and the traditionalism of men, any struggle or suffering in experiments is not in vain.[32]

Havelock was longing to be in Barcelona eating wild strawberries with Margaret, and Edith was in Buffalo telling him, "I love you always—deeply and more than you can ever have realised, but more and more I see how I ought never to have been allowed to be born or to grow up. I'm a waif and an alien."[33] On the other side of the water Margaret was just as much a waif and an alien, but she had youth and health on her side.

As Edith grew weaker, her pleas to Havelock to join her became more plaintive, but in his letters there is no suggestion that he ever considered the possibility. In New York at the beginning of April it was clear that she was seriously ill with a throat ulceration. She had to be operated on without anaesthetic, and the rest of her lecture tour was cancelled. On April 20th—for the first time—Ellis mentioned Edith's illness to Margaret. The same day he wrote to Edith:

"My own darling Wifie, your three letters of the 5th, 8th and 9th have arrived during two days, and tell me how bad you have been with that awful throat and that you now seem to be recovering. Of course I still feel very anxious and long to get later news. I do trust you will be able to convalesce nicely, and wish you were leaving earlier as the rest and peace of the voyage at this lovely time of the year may do much good. And I trust too, you will have no worries, financial or other. You speak of fearing complications over here, but do not say what they are, not serious, I hope. That blizzard you mention seems to have been a bad one. . . . We have been having the most lovely spring days lately, but the spring is late. . . . I go on quietly as usual, as when you left, except that now I have the joy of looking forward to you and the spring. I take out your new photos sometimes to look at, but they make me long too much to see and hug you. There is no news at all here. I have not heard from M. for nearly a fortnight, nor seen her for nearly two months, but suppose she will be back to London soon for a little while."[34]

The following day he wrote to Margaret again:

> "Your beautiful letter came this morning, Darling Woman, and is a joy to me, but I am horrified to hear you are still in Barcelona, and that you are now even talking of not reaching London until 1st May! It is all very well to send me your thoughts to eat in the meanwhile, & I'm glad to have them, but when you *do* arrive I shall be eating *you* up, if you aren't careful, I shall be so hungry. And what millions of things there will be to talk about!"[35]

Margaret was still worried about the newspaper gossip, and again he reassured her: "You must on no account worry yourself or anyone else about the little remark as to 'working with H.E.' It may be left to die out, and was of course meant quite innocently. Various people came to Edith about it, but she said she just told them that she was very glad."[36] The next day—the 22nd—he sent yet another note to Paris in the hope that she would have arrived there by then.

Margaret reached London on May 7th and immediately rushed down to Brixton to see Havelock. The following morning he sent off a note to her: "Lovely to see you again though you were so shy!—and I was awake for hours thinking of you & of little fascinating details. I look forward to seeing you tomorrow, darling woman."[37]

Meanwhile Edith wrote on April 15th, obviously worried about Havelock's worry over her: "Try not to worry. I've done my best and any way I feel you are safe. My Dear—I fear I've hurt you and yet I've suffered so and my heart seems broken."[38] Dates are very important at this point. There is an extremely puzzling aspect to all this that appears in Margaret Sanger's autobiography. She says that Edith was going to bring her daughter, Peggy, over to England to join her, but received a slip warning her at the last minute to transfer from the *Lusitania* to another ship and, in view of the danger of the situation, decided to leave Peggy behind. This seems preposterous. I have not been able to find a shred of evidence that Edith ever intended to sail on the *Lusitania*, and that she would bring Margaret Sanger's child seems incredible in view of the tense emotional situation. My own guess is that Margaret fabricated the story in order to lay at rest her own uneasy conscience, both over Ellis and over leaving her child, who was to die before the year was out. On the other hand, Ellis read her *Autobiography* (1938) and made no comment about the incident when he wrote to thank her for the beautiful things she had said about him. According to Margaret's biographer, Madeline Gray, when she rejoined her lover, Portet, in Paris late in August and hesitated about staying on with him indefinitely, she had a series of guilty dreams about Peggy.

On May 7th—the day of Margaret's return to London—the *Lusitania* was torpedoed with the loss of 1,193 lives. The following day Ellis wrote to Edith that it had been a great shock to him, and added:

> "It is of course quite ridiculous to refer to me as 'merged in someone else'; I can't think what I can have said to put so silly an idea in your head. M. is quite nice and a very pleasant companion, but she has no power to help or comfort me; I should never dream of telling her I *needed* help or comfort. It makes no difference at all to me when she goes away. It takes me years to get really attached to a person. Mneme means much more to me. And you know, or you never will know, that only *one* person has really hold of my heart strings, for good or evil."[*39]

In *My Life* he quotes this letter as an indication of how much he cared for Edith. He then adds a rather garbled comment: "If there is some modification as regards M. and if I should now speak of her with a greater degree of affection that is simply in accordance with what I have said in this letter: 'It takes me years to get really attached to a person.'" This does not accord with his earlier statement, "I had rarely known a more congenial companion and I had never found one so swiftly."[†40] Nor does it accord with the tone of his letters to Margaret, none of which he quotes in *My Life*. This section of the autobiography was written shortly after Edith's death the following year, and it is apparent that he wants to remember— and to have it recorded—that all his thoughts and anxieties were concentrated on Edith. This recalls the tone of remorse one finds in Carlyle's reminiscences of Jane, particularly of the torment he caused her over Lady Ashburton. Ellis blamed himself for not going to Edith when she needed him. If the situation had been

---

* Ellis included this letter in *My Life*, which was published in 1940, a year after his death; it caused great pain to Margaret Sanger.

† When he says, "I should *now* speak of her with a greater degree of affection," he means that he is inserting a passage years after the original autobiography had been written. The numerous insertions which appear throughout *My Life* are erratic and distracting.

reversed, she would have rushed to him; but he rationalizes (and the tone is disturbingly complacent), "But I know, and she knew, that my nature and my devotion were not of that impulsive kind."[41] Is it cruel to suggest that if he had gone to America he would have missed Margaret's return to England?

All the evidence suggests that Edith had been booked on an American liner, the *Philadelphia*, which left the day after the sinking of the *Lusitania*. Frantic passengers transferred from other ships, as the *Philadelphia* seemed the safest, but now this old ship, over-run with vermin at the best of times, could barely hold its surging passengers, and the whole atmosphere was one of anxiety and dread. Edith arrived in Liverpool more dead than alive.

EDITH'S DEATH

"ARE YOU ALONE?" WAS THE FIRST QUESTION THE HAGGARD WOMAN asked after she and Havelock were reunited on the Liverpool quay. He took her immediately to a comfortable hotel in which he had reserved a room where she could rest before pushing on to London. For the first time in years they occupied the same bed that night. The following morning she did not want to get up; she complained of being exhausted, and longed to spend the day in bed. Ellis argued about this: Liverpool was an ugly city; it seemed crazy to spend the day in a hotel room; she would be freer in the flat in Brixton. In retrospect he realized that he had made a mistake in not complying with her wishes, but he believed at the time that he was acting only with her welfare in mind. Was he not perhaps hankering to get back to London—and Margaret? Edith, with uncharacteristic docility, allowed herself to be argued into leaving, but long before they reached London she became so querulous that Ellis realized she should have been allowed to rest.

In the flat she could not drag herself out of bed. A day or so after she returned, Mneme dropped in—rather tactless, under the circumstances—and assured her that she knew she would soon get well under Havelock's tender care. Her possessive, rather smug manner was more than Edith could take. In the few minutes she was alone while Havelock was seeing Mneme to the door, she quickly swallowed a quantity of morphia tablets. As soon as he returned to the room, she confessed what she had done, and he rushed to prepare an emetic. It was the act of a lost child crying out for reassurances of love.

Within a week they moved out to Speen, to the cottage they had occupied before Edith left for America; here they hoped to recapture something of the tranquil happiness of the previous summer. Ellis's account of this period bears a very close reading:

> We had, I know, many calm and happy moments together, and the letters I received during the occasional days when I was away in London bear witness to her affection. But, somehow, it is the more poignant and anguished moments which have cut deepest into my memory, and I know that even the more peaceful hours of my life there that summer had beneath them a perpetual undercurrent of apprehensive solicitude. Certainly, if ever I was at fault before, I know I cannot reproach myself with coming short in love and tenderness at that time.[1]

Margaret Sanger's name disappears completely from the pages of his autobiography, but in actual fact he was in a state of acute conflict during the weeks following Edith's return. He speaks of "the occasional days when I was in London." But—as his letters to Margaret Sanger testify—he was in London day after day engaged in a desperate search for her in her habitual haunts. In the period immediately following Edith's return he had lost touch with Margaret, and could only address agitated notes to her c/o American Express in the Haymarket.* On May 27th he wrote: "Dear Woman, what has become of you? In accordance with my note of yesterday, I went to the Museum this morning & when you never came, I got desperate & had the impertinence to call at your private residence where, of course, I merely heard that you were out." On June 1st: "Yesterday & again today I journeyed to the Museum expressly in the hope of seeing you, as opportunities now will be very few."[2] Again on June 3rd: "*Every* day this week, including today, I have gone to the Museum about 12 in the hope of seeing you & carrying you off for lunch. What has become of you & how are you?"[3]

His emotions and relationships were in the most confused state of his entire life. He finally had a loving reunion with Margaret, who was by now planning to return to the States. It was apparent that with Edith's return this relationship must be accepted as an

---

* Years later Margaret Sanger wrote an explanatory note on one of these letters: "I often went for mail late in the afternoon & not every day."

affectionate friendship and no more. Margaret was run down with tonsilitis and suddenly—as was characteristic of her—left for Switzerland to recuperate. She saw Havelock the night before her departure and afterwards he sent off a brief note: "My sweet Margaret Woman, Just a good night kiss. You are & always will be very lovely to me— HE."[4] He tried to persuade her to meet him in Paris in mid-August, but by then she had returned to London prior to her final departure on August 28th; the times they were to see each other again were very few, since she was anxious to re-join Portet in Paris. Before she sailed from Bordeaux in September, Havelock wrote sadly: "As you know, I am likely to go on feeling nearer & nearer to you, in absence or in presence, and I trust you will always understand that. I am sad we have seen each other so little & it is hard to feel that my twin will be so far away. I shall always now expect to see you in the Reading Room, & I shall not feel able to go to our little coffee room till your return, & of course I shall think of you at Oxford Circus & along by Victoria Station. You are a perfect comrade, and everything you have said & done is lovely."[5] His one consoling thought was that he had spent his first winter in London in twenty years, for otherwise he might have missed meeting her altogether.

In the brief period before Margaret's departure he was able to spend more time in London, as Edith's friend Yvonne Orchardson went to stay at Speen to look after her. Edith's letters of this period are unusually loving: "My darling Boy, I do pray you are all right. You looked so sweet when you went away and I loved you more than you can ever tell. Y. is utterly dear. If you care to go with Mneme for your week in Somerset *now*, do, or I can arrange for Y. to return later. . . . When you come back we can easily have M. [Margaret] here one day. I hope and feel when you see me next I may have turned the corner. I think of you with M. tomorrow: say I hope she will come here before she sails. *I mean this.* I've waged it out at last. I miss you and long to hear you are rested. No more as it makes my head ache."[6] I cannot establish precisely the date when the meeting between Margaret and Edith took place, but it was probably late July. There was certainly one occasion Margaret recalled in later years when they met at a rather plebeian restaurant. Edith was carrying a bag of cherries which she was taking as a gift to Havelock. She thrust her hand into the bag and offered a handful to their waitress. Before the meal was over she had given away all the cherries to the other waitresses as well. Apparently she later returned to the restaurant to ask the waitress to visit her at Speen, but Margaret did not know the sequence of the incident. She was very shocked at the derogatory way Edith spoke to her about Havelock, telling her things which she regarded as an unforgiveable breach of confidence. At a luncheon they shared with Olive Schreiner (possibly this one), Edith persisted in insisting that Havelock should return with her on yet another journey she was planning to make to America. "But what does Havelock want to do?" Olive asked. Edith had to admit that he didn't want to go. "Then he should be allowed to make up his own mind," Olive asserted firmly. Margaret's final impression of Edith was of an extremely selfish and demanding woman.

But Edith was ill, and in the midst of hysteria and suicide attempts Havelock suddenly went off on a holiday to Somerset with Mneme! It seemed vitally important to him because it was the last holiday they were to spend together, as Mneme had decided to marry the solid Scottish widower of whom Ellis had been so jealous. He was trying to accept the situation philosophically, but he could not help feeling somewhat aggrieved that she was going to desert him after so many years. "The other M.S.," he told Margaret Sanger, "(after 23 years) is seriously thinking of marrying & settling down in a home of her own. She is rather worried over it; I do not try to influence her as I want her to do what she thinks best. It looks as though there would be only one M.S. soon!"[7] In another letter he said, "I seem to be taking it calmly, though of course I shall be more lonely, & only trust she will be happy."[8] But *My Life* suggests that his only concern during this period was for Edith.

The long section devoted to Edith in *My Life*—written immediately after her death—and the strong under-current of guilt indicates that this was an act of atonement on Ellis's part, that he never ceased to blame himself for wrong decisions and for a failure to give her the quality of love she needed. On the other hand, perhaps her demands could never be met. She dearly longed to return to Aix, where she had recovered her health in 1902, but Ellis could not be reproached if he did not have the money to send her there. Nor could he be blamed for not falling in with her wild plan to return yet again to America to ease their financial worries. She asked various friends such as Edward Carpenter and Olive Schreiner to support her in urging him to accompany her, but Olive had told her bluntly that he shouldn't be forced to do something he didn't want to do. Again and again Ellis returned to decisions which must have been wrong, with always the presumed question: What alternative had I?

During the preoccupations of this troubled year Ellis wrote relatively little in comparison with his usual prodigious output. Some of his articles appeared in *The Birth Control Review*, which on her return to America Margaret Sanger founded to succeed *The Woman Rebel*. Birth control was not a subject to which he devoted any attention in the *Studies*; but most of the reasons why he would support it were predictable: that to base marriage solely on procreation was to ignore the spiritual element in a relationship, and he viewed the sexual act as the most intimate and the most spiritual that could take place between two beings;* that to regard woman only as a child-bearing creature is to degrade her; and, most interesting from his own preoccupation with eugenics, birth control provided not only a safeguard against over-population, but also a means of propagating a more wholesome race. As a mitigating factor in German militancy, he mentions their problem of over-population. While Ellis often pooh-poohed the notion of progress, his adherence to eugenics was in the tradition of nineteenth-century meliorism. He by no means saw birth control as a panacea—"no royal road to the millennium"—and through the years he often tried to persuade Margaret Sanger to channel her energies into other interests. He continued to write articles on the subject out of his affection for her and to lend prestige to her journal, but he frequently asserted that he had said all he wanted to say on the subject—indeed, he seemed to find it rather distasteful.

Some of these essays are included in *Essays in War-Time* (1917) —a curious selection, considering what the title might seem to offer.† This volume deserves some discussion as his letters contain so few references to the war; in fact, one feels that he had insulated himself from its horrors. In *Impressions and Comments* under the entry (October 1914), he wrote: "By day and by night I think of the Great War. But I never have any wish to write about it. If I

---

* Although to Margaret Sanger herself he said (29 May 1917, Library of Congress), "I wanted to add that I do not regard the act of intercourse as the *only* sign of spiritual union . . . but I thought it would be best not to complicate the statement."

† On June 16th, 1914, he told Hugh de Sélincourt: "I am just now finally revising a little volume of 'Essays in War-Time' to send to Constables, mostly printed already in American & English papers, but it does not interest me much" (Library of Congress).

could I would forget it."[9] One of the very few times he mentions
the war in a letter is a description of a zeppelin raid in October—
"the biggest we have had yet. It was really quite exhilarating!
Seemed to make people laugh and cry."[10] Ellis had shared the general late-nineteenth-century belief that with extended communications war would gradually disappear among so-called civilized nations.
War, he always argued, appeared as a relatively late manifestation
of man's pugnacious spirit, and, as a transitory phenomenon, it was
bound to pass away. As late as 1913 he wrote a pamphlet for the
World Peace Foundation on *The Forces Warring Against War* in
the calm assurance that there would not be a war. The outbreak of
war, then, was something of a shock to him; just as he had seen an
era of peaceful progress expanding before Russia when he wrote his
article on "The Genius of Russia" for the *Contemporary Review* in
September 1901, so he was forced to rewrite it completely in 1917
after the Kerensky revolution; and in *The Soul of Spain* (1908) he
spoke of the innate good sense and moderation of the Spaniards in
political matters, but again had to add a new preface on the Spanish
Civil War in 1937. He had no understanding or even interest in
Realpolitik. His description of himself in *The Labour Manual of
1895* gives the impression that he was more politically involved than
he actually was:

> One of the founders [sic] of the Fabian Society and New Fellowship;
> believes in the socialisation of all material necessaries of life as the
> only means of obtaining freedom for individual development; regards
> democracy, the influence of women, and science as the chief new
> forces which will mould the social order of the future; considers the
> sex problem next to be faced, and before dogmatising believes in
> getting facts.*

Some of his friends have asserted that he never voted in his life, although in one letter he says that he always seemed to vote for the
losing candidate. In 1906 he wrote to Perry-Coste: "I do not take
any part in politics. Both parties are the same sort of things. But I
quite agree that I am not a model for imitation."[11] He was absolutely
indifferent to the practicalities of politics; many of his views represent that state interference was repugnant to him, some even suggest
the anarchism and mutual aid advocated by Kropotkin, yet an essay

---

* David Marquand is mistaken in suggesting that Ellis contributed to the
Progressive Review (*Ramsay MacDonald*, London: Jonathan Cape, 1977, p. 57).

on Kropotkin (1923) shows a disappointing grasp of Kropotkin's ideas. But there were areas where he regarded state interference as essential, particularly in the field of medicine, although later he was to object violently to legislation to sterilize the unfit (because he was afraid that voluntary sterilization would then be made illegal). Fundamentally, he made an obstinate effort to avoid becoming implicated in any social or political movement; in scientific societies, for instance, he would agree to act in an honorary capacity so long as he did not have to put in an appearance or take any active part.* He wanted, above all, to pursue his own interests in solitude and withdrawal. In the first year of the war he brought out *Impressions and Comments*, a quasi-diary, recording passing vignettes and random thoughts. Ernest Jones wrote appreciatively: "What a treat to turn from war's alarms to the sweetness, culture (not Kultur) and charm of such a delightful book, full of suggestions and original thoughts. How I wish I could write *one tenth* part as well . . ." (Lafitte Collection).

In *Essays in War-Time* he stresses that it cannot be argued that warfare provides a necessary outlet for the aggressive instincts since there are now innumerable other activities that can claim men's energies. War is a lamentable anachronism; and as preventive measures Ellis argues for international law courts and an international organization of police strong enough to carry out their decisions. Finally, he sees war as a devastating tragedy for the human race since it tends to wipe out the class which the eugenist would like to see preserved. He wrote three articles on war for *The Nation* which are perplexing in their absolute detachment from what was taking place on the other side of the Channel. "On a Certain Kind of War" (January 5th, 1918) argues that the English are really fighting a civil war because the Germans and the British belong to the same ethnic stock (he even goes into a long digression on his East Anglian forebears). "Europe" (November 3rd, 1917) is a graceful essay on the civilized charm of Europe—without even mentioning the war! Finally, in "The Origin of War" (January 18th, 1919) he makes some astounding predictions for the future:

> We can see the line along which war must eventually disappear, even without any active human interference. Its two causes are already

---

* "I hate conferences & wish them all to the bottom of the sea" (25 Aug. 1930, Margaret Sanger Papers, Library of Congress).

decaying. The excessive birthrate is falling, and necessarily falls with every rise in culture. Excessive industrialism has likewise passed its climax; there is no more world left to fight for; and with the regularisation of industrial and commercial activities, of the whole material side of life, the economic cause of war falls away, and the energy thus released is free for sublimation into other & possibly more exalted forms of human activity.

Cornwall seemed far removed from the war. Ellis wanted to spend the winter there, but Edith demurred. However, she could think of no alternative, and in early November she and Yvonne went down to prepare the cottage for Ellis's arrival, but he refused to be committed to a firm date. Why he left her to cope with the confusion is puzzling since she was in no fit state to manage things, and one minor disaster after another contributed to her frazzled nerves. All was chaos. Yvonne sprained her ankle and had to stay in bed. Workmen were constantly running in and out of the cottage. A typist was clattering away in the background. A gale smashed the shed in which they worked. Edith pleaded with Havelock to join her: "I am so weak I don't know what to do. I want you so I feel I'll just be meek & sweet for ever and ever! Come directly moment you can. The mere sight of you will revive me. I love you & long for you & belong to you. My pride is all broken."[12] There was nothing pressing to keep him in London and at this same period (November 5th) he wrote to Margaret Sanger: "I am going rather often to Museum just now, and always look carefully at L [the row in which she always sat]. I suppose I still have a sort of lingering hope that a dear vision of a little figure in familiar dress & hat might suddenly appear. It would be so lovely if she did!"[13] Despite Edith's reiterated promises that Yvonne would vanish the moment he agreed to join her, he remained obdurate. "Just to hold your hand & hold it," Edith begged, "just to know you forgive me the pain I've given you, though I never meant it. We'll talk and plan a sweet old age together. . . ."[14] Nevertheless, he postponed joining her until the end of the month. Clearly he was not eager to discuss the plans for a shared "sweet old age."

On November 6th Margaret's daughter, Peggy, died. As soon as she heard the news Edith sent warm and genuinely affectionate words of sympathy from Carbis Bay: "Margaret—Margaret! I *felt* it even before the news came. It is impossible to say a word except that we love you. Thank heaven you had had her first but oh! the ache and the pain and the loneliness. Havelock & I are both not up to much—hand in hand we are trying to struggle back to rest & health. This is only a line to put my arms round you & to try & bring you some ray of hope in the darkness. Let me have a line when you can. Take all we can give you of love & understanding sympathy. Yours ever Lady Tobias."*[15]

Ellis's letter was brief: "Margaret Dear, I am so grieved at the sad news in your letter today, for I can understand all that it means to you. And then you have so often talked to me about Peggy that I feel that I know & love her too. I am only thankful that you were with her and not away in Europe at the time.

"I came down here to join Edith at the cottage two days ago. We are neither of us in specially brilliant health, but improving, I think.

"I hope you will write when you can, Dear. I am always thinking of you lovingly, as you know. H."[16]

On Christmas Day it was warm enough to sit outside and he wrote to her again: "I am anxious to know how your health is, & I cannot help hoping also that you are promising to be 'good' & that there will be no trial yet awhile.†

"There is no news here. We are getting along fairly well, & I am feeling much better. It is pleasant to feel out of the world here, & to know very little about Christmas which is a sad time."[17] Not a word about Edith, yet there were ominous signs of how serious things were with her. A friend always sent her a traditional Christmas tree festooned with little candles, and on this occasion Edith seemed to cherish it more than ever, bringing it to the table at dinner and slowly lighting its candles, and with unusual patience steadying its precarious balance. All these little traditions she carried out like a docile automaton. Gone were her gaiety, her impatience, her surging changes of mood—for a very brief time. Shortly after New Year's Day, things began to go from bad to worse. She quarrelled with the new maid, Millie—as she had done with so many servants—and as Millie slammed out of the house she called some sympathetic words to Ellis, who replied with a brusque mutter. Millie had to stay in the cottage next door as she could find no other work, and Edith

---

* Tobias Trewidden is the hero of her novel *Love-Acre: An Idyll in Two Worlds* (London: Grant Richards, 1915).

† Margaret Sanger was arrested in November 1916 for operating a birth-control clinic. She was tried in January 1917 and sent to the workhouse for thirty days.

rightly suspected that she was spreading stories among the neighbours about her erratic behaviour and the fact that she was drinking too much. Edith had always been much loved and welcomed in St. Ives, and now she began to have the terrifying impression that people were avoiding her, and as she walked around the town she would glimpse furtive faces hastily withdrawn from behind curtains. She clung to Ellis like a frightened child. He would prepare her breakfast and take it to her in her little upstairs sitting-room. Then he would leave her to take her bath. After pacing up and down in the garden for a half-hour or so, he would climb the stairs to see how she was making out, only to find her usually standing forlornly beside the bath. She had enormous difficulty in deciding what to wear: things seemed to be either too old or too good. She would descend the stairs, only to sit down suddenly and refuse to go any further. She barely touched the meals which he prepared with great care. For one whose usual gait was a stride, she could now drag herself only a few feet without collapsing. During the day she was listless; at night she was tormented by the shapes of terrors which could only be assuaged by Havelock's comforting arms.

He had never been one to confide his problems to anyone, but in the increasing strain he began to drop revealing comments in his letters to Margaret Sanger, and finally to speak very openly of Edith. By the 21st of January he told her that he was "a little worried one way & another" and that Edith was "not at all well just now, & much weakness."[18]

Events now moved swiftly. Early in March their local physician, Dr. Hamilton, strongly recommended that she enter a local convent nursing home at Hayle. There could no longer be any doubt that she was suffering from a severe nervous breakdown. The idea of going into hospital at first terrified her, but in the end she capitulated quietly. She was forbidden letters or visitors. Ellis took rooms close by in case he should be needed. The moment she entered the doors of the nursing home their marriage effectively ended. On March 24th Edward Carpenter, realizing how tight things were, in his characteristically generous way, sent Ellis £5. "I am sending you, dear Havelock, a little cheque—as I am sure you must be rather put to it just now—& I am doing *well* with my books (*mirabile dictu*). It would be a real pleasure to help—so please accept!"[19] Ellis accepted gratefully: "Your letter is comforting, and I am badly in need of comfort just now, and it is most sweet & good of you to send the cheque which under present & probable future circumstances I feel I can only accept thankfully, for Edith, with the best intentions, has never had the art of economy & is always too lavish and generous beyond our means."[20]

Ellis's good intentions were to go astray. He wrote to Yvonne, suggesting that she send Edith some fruit or flowers without attaching her name. When Edith received the parcel, she knew instinctively who had sent it. With the paranoia characteristic of her condition, her immediate response was: "So she has found me, has she?" A few minutes later she slipped away into the lavatory and flung herself out of the window. She fell from the fourth floor, and although barely conscious, it was miraculous that she was still alive. Ellis could not fathom her motives; in bewilderment, he wrote to Carpenter: "Quite what she was feeling & thinking these last few days I do not know. It was some kind of despair. She has been despondent & self-reproachful as not having lived up to her ideals for some time past, and has lost her faith in things & in her spirit. But there are no *real* serious anxieties of an acute kind—less than sometimes in the past. The condition has been fundamentally neurasthenia, with mental symptoms—distressing loss of will power and helplessness, vague delusions, etc—lately super-added."[21] Shortly after this, in commiserating with Margaret over the death of her daughter, Ellis seemed to sense what the future would be like: "I can understand how restless the thought of Peggy makes you. But I feel that she was too lovely to live. As time goes on you will not try to escape from the beautiful thought of her, but rather to cherish it, and find joy and comfort in doing so.

"I have a sort of feeling as though Edith were my child, and being face to face with the thought of losing her—it is not yet clear what will happen—I can enter into your feelings."[22]

For a short time Ellis was allowed to speak to her through the window. Edith seemed subdued and concerned over the motives for her suicide attempt, which her rational mind could not comprehend. Ironically enough, on November 1st of the previous year—1915—Ellis had recorded the attempted suicide of a friend in *Impressions and Comments*, where he spoke of "the youthfulness of such a proceeding." Emile Durkheim had based his great study of 1897 on the premise that the act of suicide reflects the destructive pressures at work within any given society. Ellis sees it in far more individual terms. "The search for death," he wrote, "after all, is an index of vitality, of a vigour that has too impatiently sought to conquer the world's problems and when, for a moment, these seem too hard, rushes impulsively at Death because it knows in its heart that it is itself far too alive ever to be sought by Death."*[23]

In the interval Dr. Hamilton had died; the new doctor and the Mother Superior insisted that Edith be moved to a nursing home better suited to handle such serious cases. One was found in Sydenham, and Edith agreed willingly enough to be moved. Havelock was able to visit her nearly every day and for a time things were ominously peaceful. Then an American friend dropped in to see her and stayed too long; Edith imperiously demanded a bed for her, was curtly refused, and the worried visitor felt it expedient to send a telegram to Ellis. He hurried over in the morning and found Edith packed and ready to leave. For the next few weeks she moved restlessly from friend to friend. Wild gossip circulated. "She is still far from herself," the usually reticent Ellis told Margaret Sanger, "and talks wildly and most mischievously to people about me, doing the greatest mischief (without, I am sure, at all meaning to) to the distress of her and my friends. But we are all helpless to stop it.—I have suffered so much over the various phases of her illness that I now seem unable to feel more."[24] Margaret suggested that they discontinue writing if it could in any way prevent the gossip, but Ellis assured her that it wouldn't make any difference, and besides, "I need your letters now more than ever."[25]

Edith now claimed that she wanted to return to Cornwall. Ellis never knew what she would do next. "I am very low and restless and I feel altogether as though I were living in an earthquake."[26] Mneme was married on June 1st; and Olive Schreiner suggested that he go off to Spain for six months, but a few days in Saffron Walden was all he could manage. To be away from Edith for a brief period did him some good, but she was seldom out of his thoughts. As an accompaniment to his gloomy reflections he could hear(!) "the thud of the guns in Flanders—several to the minute—quite distinctly though some 150 miles away."[27] To Margaret he sent the usual news: "I have not seen or heard from Edith just lately and am feeling very sad over her. She is rather better but still far from being herself. It is the result of the disease, but it is so sad that disease

---

* Ellis reviewed *Le Suicide* in *Mind*, VII, N.S. (1898), 249–55. Characteristically, he simply describes the contents of the book, without making any evaluation or judgements.

should take a form which distresses & alienates many of her best & oldest friends."[28]

While he was away Edith set off for Cornwall with a young man she had picked up, an unemployed actor of sorts. Expecting her friends to greet her with delight when they saw how she had recovered, she was cut to the quick by the cold reception she received and immediately returned to London, where she assured the sceptical youth that Havelock would receive them with open arms. Havelock, however, was in Norfolk. Somehow the young man was eventually mislaid in the clutter of their lives.

Once again Havelock seemed to have deserted her. There was only one way she could retaliate—by decisively showing him that she didn't need him. One morning there was a solicitor's letter in the post: Edith wanted a legal separation. Ellis would at this point submit to anything, however nonsensical. It was nonsensical to the extent that such a deed simply described what their marriage had always been—namely, that Edith could in future "live separate and apart as if she were sole and unmarried." Edith also insisted, however, that a clause should be added whereby he would not be responsible for her debts, an ironical measure in view of the burden he was to carry after her death. The final clause expressed her continuing pathetic dependence on him: "It is expressly agreed and declared that in case the said parties hereto shall at any time temporarily live together as man and wife the same shall not put an end to or render void the separation or any of the covenants herein contained."

The signing of the agreement carried the same air of seemingly cool impersonality as their wedding twenty-five years before. One morning in early June they met in the rooms of the Law Society in Fetter Lane and in the presence of two lawyers signed the document. Afterwards they went off—Edith still wearing her wedding ring— and had lunch together. The subject of the separation was never broached again. Edith, however, made a point of telling Margaret Sanger about it; indeed, not until after Havelock's death did Margaret reveal that Edith had threatened to name her as co-respondent in a divorce. Ellis was forced to give his views on the matter in an unusually detailed account: "As to the Separation Deed, it was an absurd idea, but we thought it might ease her mind to agree to it, as she imagined I was 'dangerous' & might want to put her in an asylum. It really of course introduces no change into our relationship. I think she is much better, & she is always sensible & affectionate when we meet or in her letters,—but one can never be quite certain. That is why it has been such an anxious time. I say as little as possible about it all, but you ask me to tell you how she is, & I can best explain by just telling an incident that happened only ten days ago and which I heard of immediately after. She was giving a lecture on Carpenter, very nicely, when in the middle she could not find in 'Towards Democracy' a poem she wanted to read. After a time she appealed to the audience if anyone knew where it occurred, and a woman in the audience who knew, and who is a friend of mine, though I do not see her often, came forward. Tobias, who had met her and had tea with her a year ago and had then liked her, stared at her, evidently with dim & confused recollection, & then said, 'I have never seen you before, but I am a "psychic," and I know that you are in love with my husband, and he is in love with you,' then gave her a sort of familiar little slap on the cheek & began asking her questions. She is a sensitive & nervous person, not in good health, and of course was very upset and indignant, but realises that Tobias is not quite responsible at present, and so kept her temper, only telling her that she had no right to make such statements, & sat out the rest of the lecture. But before she had time to get out at the end, Tobias came up to her, held out her hand with a sort of magnanimous air of forgiveness and invited her to come & see her!—You can imagine that so long as her thoughts are fixed on such ideas, and she expresses them so publicly and outrageously, I think it best to see her as little as possible, and not to accept her constant invitations to stay at the flat and that altogether it is very trying."[29]

Edith was growing more and more self-absorbed, more and more convinced that she was involved in earth-shaking projects. She took a flat in Maida Vale, more lavish than anything she and Havelock had ever occupied; it had an extra bedroom which was reserved for the husband who never came, but was frequently occupied by one of her friends who stayed with her to relieve the terrors of the night. She began repeating her American lectures, for which she booked expensive halls, but these were cancelled by the managers when audiences failed to turn up. So compelling was her need to speak that she even turned the sitting-room of the Maida Vale flat into a simulated lecture-hall. The tempo of her life at that time is described in a letter of June 23rd, 1916, to Ellis from Daphne Bax, wife of an old acquaintance, the playwright Clifford Bax. Daphne had been a loyal friend to her and the summer after her return from America had typed a large section of her book on James Hinton from Edith's dictation; the essay was such a mess that Ellis had almost completely to rewrite it after her death. Daphne Bax's letter gives some indication of the kind of strain to which Edith was subjecting her friends:

"Johannes* came to supper at the Three Arts Club last week and immediately accused me of holding private correspondence about her writ with you and tried to extract from me all you had said. I told her that you had said she had had a nervous breakdown; no more; also that I had not answered your letter but fully intended to do so. She was more excitable than ever and informed everyone including the maid of her views on most things, of her newly adopted boy and his circumstances, of her recent concussion of the brain as result of a fall from a fourth story window (news to me) and, this last intended for me but spoken so that everyone heard, of her separation from you so as to put it out of your power, ever, to put her in an asylum. It is all deeply distressing and the only line I could adopt, with a very sore heart, was one of badinage. She is so overfull of vitality and of *self* that I feel sure she will break down again. Clifford has twice taken the chair at her lectures and said it was pathetic that she should be calling the colloquial chat to about eight decrepit females a 'lecture.' He is seeing a good deal of her and thinks the boy an absolute ne'er-do-well. I wish I could write more cheerfully but as a matter of fact I was on tenterhooks the whole time she was with me as to what she would say. She alienates people right and left by her extravagant mode of expression. I love her dearly but there is no helping her, but if you are not for her, you are in her opinion, leagued against her. She is a dangerous friend. I cannot help feeling that the diabetes is responsible for all the years of trouble. She professes undying love and admiration for you, but is firmly convinced that you mean to 'shut her up.' I do most fully realize the dreadful time you had at Speen, and appreciate the interference with your work which seems to me of world importance and beauty."[30]

---

* Daphne Bax called her Johannes "because you are the voice of one crying in the wilderness" (Mrs. Havelock Ellis, *The Mine of Dreams*, London: A. & C. Black, 1925, p. ix).

Edith repeatedly begged Ellis to come and "take the chair" at one of these awkward meetings, something she must have known he would never agree to. She desperately wanted him to be there to show the world that they were not "really" separated, and later he was to add this to the long list of ways in which he had failed her and for which he was always to reproach himself. All this was sad and pitiful, but her frenzied energy began to take on megalomaniacal proportions. From her flat she started a publishing business, the Shamrock Press, whose first assignment was to print a collection of her short stories, *My Cornish Neighbours*. After her death Ellis found bales of these sheets in her flat and, in the desperation of having to attend to so many bizarre details, simply left them behind, hoping that someone would destroy them. So magnetic was Edith's personality that she persuaded Marie Corelli to publish a pamphlet with the Shamrock Press—permission that was hurriedly withdrawn as soon as the magnetic personality had disappeared from view. In order to visit Marie Corelli in her home at Oxford she hired a car, by which she made a number of other long journeys, none of which she paid for but which Ellis gradually paid off after her death. She became enamoured of a Sufi group led by Inayat Khan, whom Ellis suspected of being a charlatan,* especially as Edith was going hungry while she donated her meagre funds to him. Craziest of all was a scheme for a film company, for which she hired actors, secretaries, and for which she tried to write scenarios. With some difficulty Ellis persuaded her that the British Museum would not provide her with a private room in which to carry out these vital activities. Her erratic behaviour he always ascribed to the ravages of diabetes, but during these frantic months he would tell friends that Edith seemed greatly improved and that her health was better than it had been in some time. But it was all too much for him. In early September he and Barker Smith planned to go off for a few days to Suffolk in pursuit of his favourite hobby, genealogy-hunting. Just before his departure there was a period of several days of extraordinary silence, days that seemed all the more silent after the almost daily explosions of incredible events that had become more habitual than the usual quiet tenor of his days. On Sunday morning—the 10th—he made his way across London to Maida Vale

---

* Inayat Khan (1882–1926) arrived in London from India in 1910. He lectured on Sufi philosophy and his message stressed the spiritual and the beautiful in life: "Why was I born, O God, if not to find Thee?"

to learn precisely what the situation was before he and Barker Smith made their quiet pilgrimage to the cemeteries near Clare.

Edith was in bed with a nurse by her side. She had been suffering from an attack of pleurisy; she had caught a chill a fortnight before during a zeppelin raid when, in a characteristic gesture, she had taken off her coat and put it around the shoulders of a shivering bystander. But Ellis was assured that she was well on the way to recovery—as he told Margaret Sanger in a letter he wrote to her that same day after his return to Brixton. Edith was affectionate and vivacious and talked about plans for making another triumphant tour of America. There seemed no reason to defer his excursion. She would not let him kiss her for fear of infection, so he pressed her hand to his lips, the last kiss he was ever to give her. He left, feeling more at peace than he had been for months.

On Monday morning just before he left for Suffolk, he received a message from Edith's attendant: "Mrs. Ellis is improving hour by hour and the fever is diminishing. Instead of being as at the beginning 103° it is now only 100°. And all is sure to be well in a few days. She sends her love, and hopes you will have a good time while away."[31] On Tuesday morning at his breakfast plate at the Bell Hotel in Clare there was the last message he was ever to receive from her: "Your wife has just got your kind letter and wishes me to say that she is going on well, has no fever now, and the doctor says she is a miracle as usual. She has a mountain of grapes by her bedside! Mrs. Ellis has written to Mrs. Schreiner to ask her to stay here for a few days and sleep in her lecture room. She hopes you will have a lovely time, and says she and Yvonne thought it the loveliest place they had ever been in."[32] The time in Suffolk passed as if in a dream, and all the while he moved about among the grave-stones with a feeling of vague unease. On Wednesday morning when he arrived back at Dover Mansions there was a telegram lying on the mat. It had been there for forty-eight hours. The words were those he had intuitively been waiting for: "Mrs. Ellis dying. Come at once."

This time he took a taxi, and when he reached the flat she was in a diabetic coma. Shortly before becoming unconscious she had pointed feebly to his picture, but apparently her last cry was for Lily. Eight hours of life remained for this too, too vivid spirit—her breathing quiet and regular as though she were finally at peace. Exhausted, Ellis finally went to lie down in the room that had always been kept in readiness for him. After a few minutes the nurse came

to tell him that she thought the end was near. The first time he had
been present at a death was his mother's; the second—and last—was
Edith's: the two women who meant most to him in the world. "It
was a gentler & happier end than I have always ventured to hope
for," he told Margaret Sanger.[33]

How strange, how unbelievable it all seemed. As he wandered
around her flat, he found a sheet of paper headed "Readings from
Havelock Ellis"—probably the last words she ever wrote: "When
many years ago—about twenty-eight—I first read *The New Spirit* I
knew I loved the man who wrote it. Today, in reading *Impressions
and Comments*, I realise that the man who had written both books
is worthy of love, forgiveness, and eternal comradeship, as a fine
spirit forges into beauty, however long it takes, and that not one of
us but many write not with ink but blood." Ellis cherished this
writing-pad until his death, when it was burned with many of his
treasured possessions. He could not bear to reveal in *My Life* that
Edith's last cry had been for Lily.

Carpenter, whom she had venerated, wrote immediately: "Well!
what a stormy life passage she has had—on which I fancy she looks
back now from some calmer zone—not without a humorous enjoyment."[34] Within the next week he again wrote: "You must be feeling
rather lonely after so many years of companionship with Edith; and
her astounding vigour served to impress her personality so strongly
on oneself & all with whom she came in contact. Only it has seemed
a pity for the last year or two that her entire absorption in her own
affairs has parted her somewhat from her friends. I felt that myself.

"However Death washes all our little differences & apartnesses
away & makes us sensible of our union with the whole."[35] And again,
a few days later: "One finds it difficult—and you must find it very
difficult—to think of her as gone, for her intensity & vitality were so
abounding towards life. Have you had any dreams or other intima-
tions of her continual presence? The people round here are quite
grieved to hear of her departure."[36] Shortly after Lily's death Edith
had bought a plot beside hers, but in recent years had expressed a
strong desire to be cremated. She had always hoped that Carpenter
would read her funeral address, but he declined, giving as an excuse
that he had committed himself to talking on socialism to some
children—which, he assured Ellis, was an immensely important undertaking. Ellis never seemed to hold any rancour towards him for
evading a task he obviously didn't want to take on, and explained to

everybody that he was in frail health. The service at Golders Green was completely simple apart from the playing of Handel's Largo, which Edith had always loved. No formal notice of the service was given, but a considerable number of people turned up, including the ailing Olive Schreiner, who felt that Edith would have wanted her to be there. As the coffin slid into the furnace, Ellis stepped forward. He would have preferred to be alone, but Algernon West, the man who had been in love with Edith for years, asked if he could accompany him, and, to his dismay, Inayat Khan also took his place possessively at his side. The young actor whom she had befriended was nowhere to be seen. Three days later—on September 18th—the ashes were scattered through the garden at Golders Green, which looked particularly beautiful at that time of year.

Margaret Sanger and Edward Carpenter were the two people to whom Ellis could unburden himself. "She was always a child," he told Margaret, "and through everything, a very lovable child, to the last. Even friends whom she only made during the last few weeks are inconsolable at her loss. I have the same sort of aching tenderness in my heart that I expect you feel about Peggy, and everything else seems indifferent."[37]

It was a strange, inexplicable, complex relationship, and for a man who avoided immersing himself in what Conrad called "the destructive element" of life with all its terrors, the highly charged vitality of Edith had been the very embodiment of the life-force. There seemed nothing left to live for.

RENEWAL

THE MONTHS FOLLOWING EDITH'S DEATH WERE A PERIOD OF WRETCH-
edness and gnawing worry. Edith's wild enterprises had left a burden
of debt which Ellis felt obliged to honour even though he was not
technically responsible since they had been legally separated.* It was
impossible for the time being to do any work of his own. Edith had
left her manuscript on Hinton in a disorganized state and he occupied much of his time in trying to put it into some kind of order.
The only consolation he could find was an occasional Sunday-
afternoon concert at the Albert Hall. There seemed no relief for the
loss of Edith. To Margaret Sanger he wrote: "In spite of all recent
anxieties and misconceptions, due to her illness & the progress of
the disease, I miss her acutely all the time."[1] He was pleased that
some of her friends—even someone in Chicago—proposed to establish an Edith Ellis Fellowship Society to "keep alive her ideals,"
but after a couple of meetings the brave idea evaporated. Except for
Christmas two years before when Edith was in America, this was the
first time Ellis had spent Christmas in London—and alone—for
twenty-five years. He reminded Margaret of this, and added: "I am
trying to forget it is Christmas, for I always find it a sad & lonely
time, & this time it is sadder and lonelier than ever."[2] Her concern

---

* His sisters were to become an increasingly heavy burden on him. Louie's court-
dressmaking business was ruined by the war, and she was gradually so crippled by
arthritis that she had to live permanently in a nursing home.

was very precious to him and he carefully kept and reread her letters many times.

For her journal *The Birth Control Review* he wrote the only essays produced during the months following Edith's death. The first one, "Birth Control in Relation to Morality" (February 1917),* emphasizes that morality has changed with the changing status of women. While women were under the subjection of men, they had no right to freedom, to responsibility, or to knowledge.

> Our ideal woman to-day is not she who is deprived of freedom and her knowledge in the cloister, even though only the cloister of her home, but the woman who, being instructed from early life in the facts of sexual physiology and sexual hygiene, is also trained in the exercise of freedom and self-responsibility and able to choose and follow the path which seems to her right.[3]

In a much longer essay, "The Objects of Marriage" (for which Margaret Sanger paid him $200, an unusually large fee), he contends that sexual pleasure wisely used may prove the stimulus and liberator of our finest and most exalted activities. Moreover, "apart from any sexual craving, the complete spiritual contact of two persons who love each other can only be attained through some act of rare intimacy. No act can be quite so intimate as the sexual embrace."[4] He admits the unaesthetic nature of contraceptives (Edith's objection to them), but regards them as mechanisms like spectacles to mend the deficiencies of nature, a curious way of putting it. Finally, he looked to birth control as the chief key to the eugenic improvement of the race, the only aspect of birth control that would continue to hold his interest.† Such stress on the sexual aspects of marriage is curious as his only public utterance immediately after the death of the wife with whom he had had a non-sexual union.

But he had taken up the writing of his autobiography again. When Edith died he had recorded his life only up to the age of sixteen, although he had been working on it for twenty years. But now he spent hours writing feverishly to bring it up to date, recording and analyzing every facet of those final difficult years of his marriage, so that ultimately they would seem to dominate his life more than any

---

* Actually first published in *Physical Culture* in November 1915.

† "Somebody says in this week's 'Nation,'" he told Margaret Sanger on September 1st, 1921, "that I regard B.C. as the guardian of civilisation. But I don't think so. It is only an important condition of progress" (Library of Congress).

other aspect of it. The manuscript was used as a means of clarifying for himself and for posterity exactly what this relationship had meant to him. It was more than this—it was his apologia, and he always regarded it as his most important work. It ended with the death of Edith because he saw this as the symbolic end of his life. In the ensuing years—particularly shortly before his death in 1939—he inserted passages written from the vantage point of the particular date at which he was writing. This is highly regrettable, because the chronology of *My Life* inevitably became extremely erratic.

The letters written to Margaret Sanger during 1917 reveal the slow but unmistakable ascent from the dark winter of despair to a sense of gradually revived pleasure in life, although he did not regain the weight he had lost during the strain of the previous two years. In April he went to a concert with Arthur Symons, the first time he had been out in the evening in six months; and a few days later travelled down to Tunbridge Wells to visit his sisters Laura and Mary, the first time he had been out of London since Edith's death. Here he planted potatoes and sat in the garden basking in the sunshine. To Margaret he reported: "Everyone says how well I am looking. We are having perfect weather now, warm & bright, the kind that exactly suits me, & I long to be in the country & lie out of doors all day. Of course with a dear and darling companion."[5] Late in May he made an excursion to his beloved Kew Gardens: "It is just now the most perfect moment of the year—sad that it lasts so short a time— hot and yet not too hot, and everything looking bright & fresh & delicious."[6] In the course of the summer he made two genealogical forays into Suffolk with Barker Smith and talked of taking a cottage in Essex with his sisters, but abandoned the idea when he discovered that all available accommodation was occupied by munition workers. In October he signed over the lease of the Carbis Bay cottage: "So Cornwall is now over, I no longer have any ties there & don't know whether to be sad or glad."[7] By November he could write: "I am feeling in wonderfully good health and spirits."[8]

As the end of the war began to be in sight, the first piece of serious writing he undertook was the revision of an article he had written on Russia in 1901.* In his essay on Tolstoi in *The New*

---

* *Contemporary Review*, LXXX (Sept. 1901), 416–33; the revised essay on Russia appeared posthumously in *The Genius of Europe* (London: Williams and Norgate, 1950; New York: Rinehart, 1951).

Spirit he had predicted that Russia, with its intermingling of Eastern and Western cultures, would be the locale of the next great flowering of the *Zeitgeist*. He felt that his essay on Russia written shortly after visiting the country in 1897 had to be rewritten to take into consideration the Kerensky revolution, but he never fully realized the implications of the Communist revolution, as a comment to Margaret Sanger in a letter dated April 6th, 1918, indicates: "The Social Revolutionaries, *not* the Bolsheviks, seem to represent the bulk of the Russian people. I quite admire the *international* attitude of the Bolsheviks, though it was from the first impossible but at home they have shown themselves far more cruel & autocratic than the Tsardom. It is always the scum of the frothy violence that first comes to the top in every revolutionary pot."[9] In 1912 in *The Task of Social Hygiene* he had already dismissed Marx and his theories as "a dream" and a fading influence.

Edith had left Algernon West in charge of her financial affairs, to Yvonne Orchardson she had left the copyright of her plays, and to Havelock her novels—and the task of informing all her widely scattered friends of her death. Among the numerous unknown names was that of a Madame Françoise Cyon, whom Edith had engaged not long before her death to translate *Three Modern Seers* into French. Plucky and passionate, this woman, in her early thirties, had a stormy background behind her. She had originally come to England to escape her artistic but stultifying family. At first she taught school in Eastbourne, but moved to London, where she did a little journalism and met some people who shared her zeal for socialism and pacifism. She had two small sons, one by an American syndicalist, and the other by an exiled Russian journalist, Serge Cyon, whom she had married and from whom she was now separated. Every attempt she made to support herself and her children seemed doomed to failure. She tried dressmaking, French lessons, even invested in lessons in film acting. Finally, in June 1916, she met Edith Ellis, then at the height of the raging megalomania which characterized the tragic months preceding her death. With her quick spontaneity, Edith took an immediate interest in the little Frenchwoman's predicament and, in her eagerness to help, suggested that she translate *Three Modern Seers* (1910). When Françoise protested that she didn't think a book on Hinton, Carpenter, and Nietzsche would have a wide sale in France, Edith airily brushed aside all her objections. Her first impression of Edith was of a wrinkled, fat, ugly woman, but, like so many others before her, she soon fell under the spell of her vivacious enthusiasm and spent evenings excitedly discussing the book with her. On several occasions Edith, who was terrified of the long nights alone, persuaded her to sleep in her flat, and the naïve Françoise never realized until long after her death that the older woman was a lesbian. On August 25th, 1916, Edith sent her the following note: "Dear Lady Translator, could you possibly sleep here on Tuesday? I will then pay you seven pounds ten shillings and the balance when the book is finished. I am sorry I could not pay it before, but many who have owed me have not paid up. If you can sleep here, we shall have two hours alone for reading."[10] With her last pennies Françoise made her way across London, from Crouch End, only to find that Edith was not there. She borrowed the bus fare from the lift-boy and, on her return home, wrote to ask Edith if anything was wrong. On September 3rd Edith sent a distressed reply: "My dear—I was horrified when I came home to find that you had been and gone. I thought we had decided you were not to come on Tuesday because there was so little done, and I had gone at 6.30 to a friend to stay the night as I was alone."[11] The misunderstanding was a measure of Edith's confused state of mind. On September 14th she died; and the first news Françoise had of her death was on September 22nd when Ellis wrote to tell her what had happened as one of the many obligations that were left to him to fulfill. Until that date Françoise had never heard of Havelock Ellis.

By now she was in urgent financial need and she wrote to Ellis asking if he could let her have £5 for the work she had done, adding that she was not requesting the full £15 as she doubted whether the book could find a publisher in France, but she wanted permission to do what she liked with the translation. She also sent him an essay, "The Mental Havoc Wrought by the War," which she had written after a visit with her parents the previous year. Ellis explained to her that he himself was poor and plagued with obligations incurred through Edith's recklessness. He hoped that she would consider finishing the translation some time, but agreed with her that it would be difficult to get it placed. "I should also like to send you a little money. I cannot easily do so at once, but will, if possible, in a week or two. If before then you *badly* need money, please tell me, & I will send what little I can at once. A little later we may have a chance to meet & talk over things."[12] As for her essay, he had read it "with much interest and sympathy" but didn't know where it could be placed except in America. Later he was to suggest that she send it to Margaret Sanger.

The following months were the most difficult in Françoise's life. From time to time she wrote Ellis begging for help, pleas to which he would respond by sending a pound at a time. When he sent the third instalment in January 1917, he expressed regret that she still found herself "in difficulties." Françoise's "difficulties" were not only financial. She had left her husband because they were completely incompatible, and he had done nothing to help her with money. Now, however, he was exerting pressure on her to return with him as he was planning to go back to Russia, and had suggested that a decision could be reached if an arbitration group composed of their friends discussed the matter. Not surprisingly, she felt distrustful of such a bizarre suggestion, but was uncertain whether she was doing the right thing in depriving her children of even a moderately decent home. She had no idea to whom to turn; and then remembered that Ellis had suggested that they might arrange a meeting some day. In late April 1917 she wrote him asking if it were possible for them to meet since she sorely needed advice. He suggested the afternoon of May 8th.

Françoise had absolutely no preconceptions about him as a person. He must be old because he had been married to Edith. If they had lived apart, the marriage must have gone awry and she felt slightly uncomfortable about the prospect of mentioning Edith. She was completely ignorant of the fact that he was a writer of some distinction. She had made the suggestion that they meet, yet once it was decided she was in a state of panic. What on earth should she wear? Anything decent she owned had been pawned long ago. With bits and pieces of other people's wardrobes, tottering on borrowed shoes which pinched terribly, the waif shyly rang the bell of the Brixton flat. Her first reaction to Ellis was bewilderment. She had not been at all prepared for this tall, grave, astonishingly handsome man who looked more like a patriarch than anything else. And he appeared as shy as she was. He liked her pert, square face with the thick eyebrows, and her heavy French accent was immediately attractive to him.

It might have been an awkward situation, but it was Edith, to Françoise's initial surprise, who provided a sympathetic chord between them. Ellis responded eagerly to Françoise's expression of admiration for Edith's book and encouraged her to speak of her

memories of his wife. She told him of an evening when she had heard
Edith give readings from Oscar Wilde, and of the times they had
spent discussing the book. Ellis told her that he was working on
Edith's book on Hinton, which had been such a chore for her at the
end of her life, and he was trying to make it suitable for publication.
(It was published in 1918.) The visit was devoted almost entirely to
a discussion of Edith, and Françoise felt reassured that Ellis did not
seem to notice her shabby clothes. But, as it later proved, he was
keenly aware of her great distress and the following week invited her
to lunch. In the meantime Serge's arbitration council was actually
held; but instead of the calm atmosphere of friends giving their
advice objectively, it turned into an emotional outpouring from
Serge, who hurled himself on his knees before Françoise and begged
her to give him the chance to be as good a father as she was a mother.
Françoise found herself extremely moved by this lavish praise of
her as a mother and began to falter in her resolve. The time for
Serge's departure was approaching and she had to come to some firm
decision one way or another.

On her second visit to the Brixton flat she intuitively knew that
she had come to a "healer." After lunch Ellis made her lie on the
sofa and tell him frankly about the problems that were troubling her.
He listened attentively, his eyes habitually averted, a characteristic
she had noticed on her first visit. This was the first time she learned
that he was a doctor and the author of some books on sex. He told
her that marriage was difficult at best and urged her to consider a
reconciliation, since a woman on her own with two small children
was bound to have a difficult time; but he approved of her decision
not to rejoin Serge for at least six months, which would give him time
to prepare a home for them in Russia. Serge agreed to these terms
and consented to send regular sums of money, a move that was to
initiate a period of relative respite for Françoise.

During the following months Françoise continued to visit Brixton regularly. Frequently she lapsed into depressions, particularly in
September after learning from an acquaintance that Serge had probably never been divorced from a first wife whose existence she had
never heard of before. A still-grieving Ellis and a bewildered Françoise began to find solace in each other. She was moved by the simple
way in which he opened his heart to her. "I hope you are feeling
better," he told her. "You must not become depressed and cry. But
save your tears & come & cry them here! I too have been feeling sad

& depressed of late."[13] But Stella Browne was able to tell Margaret Sanger that "Ellis is looking better than I've seen him for some time: he seems slowly recovering from all he had to go through last year."[14]

And so the months passed, with the friendship growing steadily deeper. In March of 1918 Françoise was terrified by the news that Serge might return soon because of the success of the Bolsheviks. Overcome with emotion, she wrote immediately to Ellis, the tone so heightened that one suspects—what one often suspects with Françoise—that she is wallowing in emotions for their own sake: "I hate life, & hate it. And, despite what you say, I hope I will grow old quick & end it all. I love life, & love it & love it so don't you see, that it has come to intense hatred at times. Can you understand such a paradox? But it is so, I cannot explain any better. It is all illogical, tragic & terrible—it burns to the quick & yet one goes on loving & loving the emptiness & silliness of it all, for just the few divine glimpses one gets at times."[15] Havelock was able to offer the comfort she needed:

> "Dear Little Friend,
>
> "I am sorry you are feeling sad and hopeless. The hate of life is part of the love of it, and I feel quite sure you will find the love of it come back, if you are patient for a few years, or even perhaps a few months. . . . Tomorrow come here for a rest, and a cry if you want it."[16]

There was some slight improvement in her situation, for that very month she found a means to support herself when she was given a post of French teacher in West Ham at £160 a year.

They began to discuss the significance of dreams and Françoise offered to record her dreams for him. Ellis urged her not to be shy in telling him their contents, but she was sometimes slightly embarrassed to confess their predominantly sexual nature. Waking after one about herself and a man in a bath, she admitted that she had blushed, and asked plaintively: "But what is one to do Havelock? It is to dream or not to dream or rather to tell Havelock or not to tell him and I like to tell him all as he knows no shame & is so pure. Havelock you are a dream."[17] On the night of April 2nd, 1918, he appeared in one of her dreams for the first time. The following day she wrote him a long letter in which she gave full vent to her feelings. "Dear Friend," she wrote,

"I am going to write to you a very difficult letter yet it must be written if I want to find peace of mind.

"The truth Havelock Ellis is that I love you and that I must say so.

"I shall try to set down facts as I have done for the dreams; it will be clearer to you and the most easy way for me."

She then went on to confess that she wanted to be his wife and that after a dream in which he embraced her she had never felt so happy in her life. "So friend," she concluded, "let me hear your advice. The thing I want above all is to retain your friendship at whatever cost, even if this means never seeing you again. If you think this the best course I shall do as you wish me to, but I must know before facing you again."[18] Ellis's reply deserves to be quoted in full:

Dear, I had your letter this morning. It is very, very beautiful, & I am glad you wrote it, because it will help us to understand things & to have everything clear & right. I wanted to put my arms around you when you lay on the sofa half asleep, but I did not want to do anything you might misunderstand, & I should be sorry for you to do anything that you might feel afterwards was not right & that might make you unhappy. I would like to soothe you & comfort you & help you, & it is very good for me, too, to be near you, & I felt much better for your visit. I am sure we could be loving friends, real affectionate & intimate friends. But I wouldn't be any good as a passionate lover or husband. You must remember I am much older than you, & in some ways older than my years, as I have had a great deal to suffer & go through. I am not a bit like the virile robust men of the people in your dreams! I have several dear loving women friends, married & un-married, (most of them just now scattered in various parts of the world, so that I cannot see them), & with some of them I am very close & intimate friends, so that we can be perfectly free & natural & like children together. But there is not one to whom I am a real lover. I don't ever want to be, & if they had a proper lover I should not feel that I had any right to be jealous. That is how I would like to be with you. I feel sure that I am good for you, & I am sure that you suit me. But as lover or a husband you would find me very disappointing. When you know me more you will feel that as an affectionate friend, as close as you like, someone whom you can be perfectly natural & yourself with, you will have all the best that I can give. It may be all the better for beginning just as it has begun, for that has happened with one or two friends who are very dear.

But there is nothing in all this to prevent you from being a good & faithful wife. I should be very sorry to do anything that was not fair to your husband, & I should be very sorry for you to have any sort of guilty thoughts. I would like you to feel that the love you have for me is not a love that you feel the least bit ashamed of, or that you have any need to be ashamed of. If you feel that this kind of affectionate friendship is *not* possible, then it would be best for us not to meet. But I think it *is* possible, & that you will find it quite easy & beautiful & natural & helpful. It would be all that to me too. I am, in some ways, understanding, as you say, but I am also like a child, & it is lovely to me to be able to be like a child.

Write very soon & tell me what you feel about it.

That was a lovely dream you had and I am glad you felt quiet and happy after it; that is how I would like to make you feel. "Impressions and Comments" is my favourite among my books because there is most of me in it. If you like the book, then you like the real me!

Ever affectionately yours,
H.E.

You had better destroy this letter, for it would be misunderstood if anyone saw it.[19]

Ellis's reply indicates the same sort of alarm he had experienced when he was compelled to restrain Margaret Sanger's feelings which appeared to be getting out of hand shortly after their meeting. However, Françoise's reply reassured him. She was, she told him, as proud and happy about their friendship as of "any beautiful thing that has been given me; my children, the love of the forests & the waters, the affection of two of my brothers & all the sunshine that has come into my life.

"Neither do I want you to be a lover or husband. I will have nothing that might spoil the beauty that I have just found. . . . As to you being my lover it would make me long to be beautiful & to have you younger. And even then might not passion kill friendship? I will have nothing but what you offer, it is the very flower of love."

She then went on to describe exactly why he had such a wonderful effect on her: "You are the first man who has *ever* made me feel *ever* so small. That is why I love you. I have been small in front of the woods, the sea, the moors & the plains, but seldom in front of a man. Men have sometimes been my equals, often I have felt them smaller. But you, you are like in my dream; you stand by me & dominate me, the pathetic little figure in green. Yet you have love & tenderness to give me & I love you."[20]

Great relief surges through Ellis's reply: "It was a joy to have your letter this morning, Dear Friend, and to be able to feel quite assured that we understand each other, & on the day after you were here (before I received your beautiful letter which I am so thankful you wrote, & I just worship your lovely courage in doing it, & doing it so well) I felt very happy & was able to work much better than usual. But you must not be *too* enthusiastic about me before you know me well. It is better to begin with a small love that grows big than with a big love—that grows small!—A propos of being small, there is no need for you to *feel* small, but I am glad you *are* small in size, for it is a funny thing that though I *admire* large women (& when I was quite young have fallen in love with them—at a distance) I have never been able to feel close and intimate friends except with small women. So that if you were a large woman I should have to say: 'I am very sorry; I like & admire you very much, but I know we shall never be very dear friends—because you are so big!' I don't know why it is, because—in the abstract—I quite like big women ever so much better!"[21]

Ellis always believed in experiencing rather than naming a relationship. "Am I really your comrade & pal Havelock?" Françoise asked some months later. "I feel so sure about it at times & always that it quite frightens me in case I should wake up one day to find it a dream. But you *are*, you are my comrade & pal, my wise man, my friend & my man."[22] To which Ellis replied, perhaps a little tartly: "I won't call you comrade & pal; it doesn't somehow express my feelings & also I never care to label feelings too precisely. You are a dear & loving person whom it is always beautiful to think of."[23]

After the exchange of the letters in April initiated by Françoise's declaration of love, their relationship was now to be indisputably an erotic one. The precise nature of what it was to become has been a matter of conjecture. Françoise's account in *Friendship's Odyssey* of what happened the first time they met after the series of letters clarifying the situation is evasive. On this first occasion they apparently lay in each other's arms fully clothed, "his lips lightly kissing me, one hand caressing my face, the arms of a man becoming an entrancing home. This I had never known before; nor what treasures of affection dwell in the human hand. He could have done with me as he liked."[24] When it was time for her to go, for the first time he followed her into the bedroom:

> He had recently declared that he would "have to look after you better in the future." So he followed me to minister himself to my needs . . . and did this in so unexpected a fashion as to reduce me to utter bashfulness, but delicious bashfulness, wistful and alluring if puzzled, as I stood in front of him, and he, on his knees, let me caress the glorious head fully accessible to my hand. The caress saved me words. Was he not there in full reverence? What best could match this adoration but my hand all over his head? Henceforth we were more than friends, notwithstanding the bashfulness. I became "a dear little woman" and he truly *mon sage de Brixton.* Of the full meaning of his delicate attention I was then ignorant. Nor did he say anything which could enlighten me. Least of all did I know the name given to it in his sexological books. If urolagnia became clearer to me in time, suffice it here to say that, on this our first day of closer friendship, it proved mysteriously soothing to my soul, and thereby restored peace to my body so long bewildered.
>
> *Honi soit qui mal y pense.* Love's strange ways of expression are far too precious and intimate for me to attempt to convey in words what Havelock's harmless anomaly meant to me in the course of time. This book will nowhere dwell upon it in direct fashion. Simply because I dare not risk soiling what was beautiful by his side that I never consider it abnormal. It was part of our normality.[25]

When *My Life* was published posthumously in 1940, many of Ellis's admirers were shocked and repelled by the disclosures about his urolagnia; and after reading *Friendship's Odyssey* Margaret Sanger felt impelled to tell Françoise how disgusting a friend found what she regarded as a perversion. Françoise wrote a passionate defence in reply: "I longed to pour my heart out to you on this matter, so dear to me. But it is my experience that no one I have met, except Havelock can touch on this subject without soiling it for me. I do not believe this would have happened with you—none the less I am shy on a matter which played a beautiful part in my intimate life. Believe me, Margaret, it taught me incidentally, the way Havelock displayed this anomaly, more about cleanliness, & hygiene, sanitation & health than I ever acquired from books or otherwise, & the teacher made the acquirement a deed of beauty. I was so tempted to dwell on it in my *Odyssey*, but bearing in mind people's clumsiness on such matters I drew the line, limiting myself, indeed, to hints or oblique treatment, a great pity. For what it amounts to, after all, is that there is not one sexual anomaly which cannot be transformed into beauty when there is love and art in both lovers."[26]

On their next meeting they undressed fully. Françoise's account of what happened on this occasion is also ambiguous:

> I foolishly expected the marital act I had so far known, but now with a man I truly loved. There was, therefore, a slight dread when this did not happen. A sudden pang of horror went through me. In one swift irrational moment I felt that I was in for another agonising experience, since he did not seem normal. But instantly came the astounding assurance—as a stroke of lightning before he touched me—that where true love abides everything is perfect. This "travail" of my soul proved the birth of my new being: woman at last, woman in soul. On that bed, in broad daylight, his hands and his kisses, never jerking me with fear, tenderly brought me to this delight.[27]

From a careful reading of the passage and from references in their letters, the probability seems to be that they practised mutual masturbation. Ellis had told Margaret Sanger that his problem was premature ejaculation. Françoise repeats a number of times in her book that his "problem" had been insufficient development. She believed Olive Schreiner rejected him because she did not find him sufficiently virile and that his sexuality was repressed during his marriage because of Edith's abhorrence of sex. She dismisses Mneme as being of little consequence since she simply provided him with gentle solace (Françoise and Mneme were always hostile, so it is probable that she underrated the sexual element of the relationship). The conclusion, then, that Françoise draws is that it took her to awaken the true lover in him. Whether they actually had intercourse she never specifies. In that same letter to Margaret Sanger (written on July 21st, 1947) she says: "He could love his sweetheart more thrillingly by contemplating a rose at her side than many a man does through coitus."[28] Whether a man thirty years older than herself, a man fifty-eight years old, could achieve a sustained erection for the first time is something that I, particularly after examining all the available

evidence, very much doubt. Ellis could persuade Françoise of anything, and it seems probable that he convinced her that true love-
making does not necessarily mean penetration.* The subject of penetration and male orgasm is strangely absent from the sex books, and
while Ellis sympathized with Margaret Sanger's endeavours, his interest in birth control was largely as an aspect of eugenics, and it is
apparent that at times the subject actually bored or displeased him.
Françoise, too, was indifferent to birth control.† Such indifference
may be the natural reaction of people for whom birth control was of
no practical concern. Neither Ellis nor Françoise could entertain the
thought that his urolagnia might be the fetishism of arrested development or of a castration complex, preventing him from developing
a more normal and complete sexuality.‡ However, as he once explained to Margaret Sanger, "*Everything* is good and beautiful sometimes, when it happens naturally & in the right spirit, and is the
symbol of love."[29] The letters he and Françoise exchanged over the
course of the years show clearly that urolagnia formed an intrinsic
part of their love-making. "Naiad"—the water nymph—told an
American friend that Ellis found intense pleasure in having her uri-
nate if they were walking down a street in the rain, and he once had
the supreme satisfaction of persuading her to do it among the bustling

---

* In an essay published after his death, "The Problem of Sexual Potency" (*Sex
and Marriage*, New York: Random House, 1952), Ellis suggests that coitus isn't
particularly important; that, indeed, a woman "may find complete erotic satisfaction
from a partner, who, though inadequately potent, is yet a skilful enough artist in
love to be able to discover a divine hand to satisfy his wife's erotic needs" (p. 179).
    † In response to this comment of mine, Professor François Lafitte writes:
    "(i) I have a vivid memory when a child of finding a box of strange objects
in one of her bedroom drawers. The label on the box said they were 'soluble
pessaries' with coconut (or cocoa) fat. I asked her what they were and she told
me they were for birth control and was rather embarrassed. (In fact such vaginal
pessaries were a standard birth control method of the twenties, used either on
their own + post-coital douching, or together with a 'Dutch cap' or one of
Marie Stopes's cervical caps.) Unfortunately I cannot pinpoint the year when
this happened. So I cannot say whether Ma was using birth control in her relations with HE or with Sélincourt.
    "(ii) Ma made sure in my upbringing (and my brother Paul's) that I knew
all about birth control and repeatedly impressed on us the sinfulness of getting a
woman unwantedly pregnant and the supreme importance of men behaving
responsibly in this matter. We had at Holmdene Avenue virtually all the
popular and learned books on sex and birth control published in the 1920s and
1930s (their authors sent most of them to HE) and we grew up thoroughly
familiar with all this literature."
    ‡ A distinguished psychiatrist has suggested to me that perhaps Ellis did not
develop adequately at puberty. He was particularly interested in the significance of
Ellis's high voice.

crowd at Oxford Circus. Certainly what Françoise calls his "harmless anomaly" was common knowledge among his women friends.

They both found a kind of glory in their relationship. Ellis insisted that as a married woman she must wear a wedding ring at her new school, and he suggested that she buy one (Serge had never given her one) and send the bill to him. On February 2nd, 1919, he wrote after one of her visits: "You were most fascinating, and you are always making new & delightful discoveries in the art of love."[30] Françoise was in a delirium of joy. Her constant expressions of worship become a little cloying to anyone reading them now, but it is difficult for an outsider to share the emotions of someone else's love affair. They began to devise all sorts of pet names for each other. Françoise became Framboise, La Douce, Little Woman, and for Françoise he was *"mon sage,"* Mr. Man, and eventually Faun to her Naiad, his favourite name for her. As for Ellis, he felt as though life had been restored to him. He felt immensely proud in the belief that he had awakened her to satisfied sexuality, and in the spring of 1918 he wrote "The Love Rights of Women," to be followed three years later by "The Play Function of Sex," both inspired by Françoise.*

Margaret Sanger got wind of the fact that the "little friend" whom he had at first mentioned very casually was beginning to occupy a central place in Ellis's life and wrote that she was furious that a French woman was driving an Irish woman out of his heart. Ellis replied placatingly:

> "You must not grudge my dear little French woman any help and consolation she is able to extract from me. The credit for it all is due to her, not to me, & it is just miraculous how far little things will sometimes go. She certainly needs all the joy & consolation she can find, for she has had far more than her share of the griefs, losses, & anxieties of the war. She was becoming very depressed & on the verge of a nervous breakdown, but she is now strong & happy & radiant—a proof that love is so much more a psychic than a physical thing—& is much more attached to her husband!
> —who may arrive any day & absorb her entirely, as the manner of husbands is. Like Jehovah, they say 'Thou shalt have none other

---

* "The Love Rights of Women," *The Birth Control Review*, June 1918; "The Play Function of Sex," *Medical Review of Reviews*, March 1921.

Gods but ME'; but, like Jehovah, they find it very difficult to get that law obeyed.

"It is very sweet that you should be 'furious,' but there is no need. You know quite well what a faithful person I am. There is no danger of that Irish woman you speak of being driven out of my heart by any French woman, & much as I like to be reminded of her, there is no *need* to be reminded of her, for I always love to think of her, & it always thrills me to think, as I often do, of her first kiss."[31]

There was another woman on the scene who was not so easily appeased. Although Mneme had been married for two years, she was still devoted to Ellis. Françoise had by now the run of the flat, but it was firmly conveyed to her that Mneme had certain jurisdictional monopolies such as forwarding his mail to him when he was away. The first meeting between the two women was cool, and the oh-so-sweet Mneme, as she was leaving, managed to whisper, "You think you'll keep him, but you won't!" Françoise had told Ellis that jealousy was not part of her nature, but she was upset by Mneme as she was to be by a number of other women, including even the dead Edith. Ellis had made it plain to her that he had many women friends, some of whom he would not be able to see until the end of the war, and with a number he was on terms of affectionate intimacy. Rabelais's *"Fay ce que voudras,"* she agreed, was a very beautiful motto, but there were times when she struggled with her jealousy. Beside some of his older friends such as the American expatriate journalist Marguerite Tracy, she felt gauche and inconsequential, and Ellis, in his sensitive awareness of her insecurity, was constantly praising her to build up her confidence.

In September 1918, Françoise took her older boy, François, for a holiday at Westcliff-on-Sea. Ellis, who was always extremely shy with children, joined them there. The spectacle of Françoise's radiant motherhood enchanted him. "All day long I have been lying on the cliff or the sands at work," he wrote in *Impressions and Comments*, "while from time to time my eyes rested on the friendly vision of a dear woman, not too far away, playing with her child. The sun and the air, mixed with that radiant vision, enter into my blood, pouring a new vigor into my veins and a new inspiration into my thoughts."[32] It was the mother who enchanted him. After reading *Impressions and Comments* (Second Series, 1921) Marguerite Tracy wrote to him: "It suddenly strikes me that neither in this second volume of *Impressions* nor in the first do children or your reactions to them figure at all. It is as if they had not existed for you, & yet you must have been aware of them exquisitely, always."[33] There is no indication that he had ever been aware of them.

The war ended. On November 11th Ellis went to visit someone in Bloomsbury Square. "When I went in the streets were as usual," he related to Margaret Sanger; "when I came out an hour later, they were transformed, flags flying everywhere, shouting & gesticulating crowds, & vehicles of all kinds, laden with youths & girls, dashing along to nowhere in particular. I felt sad, for Peace does not bring back what War took away, & the ending of the War only makes the difference clearer."[34]

Nevertheless, if the past could not be revived, the future held for him a more vibrant and satisfying emotional life than he had ever known.

THE POST-WAR WORLD

IN FEBRUARY 1919 MARGARET SANGER DEVOTED THE ISSUE OF *The Birth Control Review* to a celebration of Havelock Ellis. Ellis's reputation had somewhat declined, so the tributes were very touching to him. "It is a most beautiful birthday present," he told Margaret Sanger, "& very sweet of you to prepare it for that occasion. It is charming & delightful & sympathetically appreciative—no doubt too much so, though that is for others to decide."[1] These birthday tributes were to continue for a number of years. Margaret Sanger's adulation of Ellis played a large part in introducing him to a wider American public and in building up a group of enthusiastic admirers within the fields of birth control and sexology. Dr. Helena Wright told me in private conversation that she thought that this veneration stimulated by Margaret Sanger "rather went to his head." Nevertheless in America he received an appreciation lacking in his own country, and from a practical point of view—often through the instigation of Margaret Sanger—he received innumerable offers for magazine articles which in many cases were not good for his professional reputation. *Cosmopolitan* and *Physical Culture* were hardly the sort of magazine for which Freud would have written; and perhaps Ellis's reputation has been ephemeral because he adopted the role of popularizer; slight articles on how to tell your children the facts of life were not likely to enhance his prestige with professionals whom he would have liked to regard as his peers. Just as, many years before, he had written for de Villiers's *University Magazine* even after he realized that there was something shady about the editor-publisher, so now he lacked all discrimination about what paper or journal he wrote for. It was all very well to have far-ranging interests, but if he wrote glancingly on too many subjects, the inevitable result was that he developed a reputation for superficiality. Graham Greene made a cruel allusion to his "fake prophet's air" and dismissed him as "rather like a Santa Claus at Selfridge's."[2]

In 1919 he brought out *The Philosophy of Conflict*, which was the second series of *Essays in War-Time* (1917). Ellis had not written a book with a unified theme since *The World of Dreams* (1911). Apart from the random reflections of *Impressions and Comments*, his books now tended to be collections of essays previously published in papers or journals. In many ways careful about money, ever since he published his first book, *The New Spirit*, Ellis saw the pecuniary value of selling a piece twice. However, whereas *The New Spirit* and *Affirmations* were devoted to critical examinations of certain writers, since the nineties Ellis's interests had extended to so many different fields that his collections of essays had become a gallimaufry including "Luther," "Herbert Spencer," "Eugenics in Relation to the War," and "Psycho-Analysis in Relation to Sex."

He had lost touch with Freud during the war, but this latter essay was a means of reviving communication between them. Ellis had been one of the first people in England to write at length about Freud;* and throughout the *Studies* Freud's name was evoked, generally as an authority who, when he needed him, Ellis used for the citation of a case-history. Freud was always treated with respect, and with acknowledgement of the depth of his investigations. Ellis disagreed with his view that the causes of inversion were not congenital, and he thought the theory of the Oedipus Complex absurd; they fell into confusion about the meanings they assigned to auto-erotism, narcissism, and sublimation; Ellis was sceptical about precise analysis of dream-material, which, he always claimed, had only symbolic value (exactly Freud's point); but they were in total agreement about the generally sexual basis of hysteria. Freud's first reaction to Ellis's comments on him was approval; indeed, as his letter to William Fliess on January 3rd, 1899, indicates, he was almost regarding Ellis as a possible disciple:

---

* In *The Alienist and Neurologist*, October 1898. The first article on Freud in England was J. Mitchell Clarke's long review of *Studien über Hysteria* in *Brain*, XIX (1896), 401–14.

". . . a pleasing thing which I meant to write to you about yesterday is something from Gibraltar, from Mr. Havelock Ellis, an author who concerns himself with the subject of sex and is obviously a highly intelligent man, as is shown by his paper in the *Alienist and Neurologist* (October, 1898), which deals with the connection between hysteria and sexual life, beginning with Plato and ending with Freud. He gives a good deal of credit to the latter, and writes a very intelligent appreciation of *Studies in Hysteria* and later publications. . . ."[3]

"Psycho-Analysis in Relation to Sex" is a moderate, fairly reasoned exposition of Freud's views. Nevertheless, the essay contained statements which understandably annoyed Freud. In the *Studies,* Ellis claimed, Freud had found "helpful suggestions" in developing ideas* which "I had not myself been inclined to carry to an extreme or dogmatic form,"[4] and Freud had borrowed Ellis's terms "auto-erotism" and "narcissism"; but the Freudians, he argued, had totally misunderstood what he meant by auto-erotism. They had taken it to mean self-directed sexual feeling, whereas Ellis had meant spontaneous sexuality without external source of arousal. But what particularly annoyed Freud was Ellis's description of him as an artist, not a scientist, "for his activities are individualised, intuitive, and conceptual to a degree which removes them from the impersonal and objectively verifiable basis of science."[5] He was "an artist who arose in science," but his theories, Ellis went on, have been treated as objectively verifiable by his pupils, so that inevitably they have been thrown into consternation and one by one they have fallen away from him. Most of these former adherents were personally known to Ellis, except for Jung, whom he regarded at that time as obscure and totally confused. (In later years when a friend once asked him what he thought of Jung, he replied impassively, "I am my own Jung.")

Freud did not like to be reminded of the defection of his followers, and to be called an artist rather than a scientist implied that he had produced nothing beyond beautiful creations of the imagination. Freud regarded Ellis's attitude as "a highly sublimated form of

---

* In 1919 Freud had in fact added a footnote to his 1910 monograph on Leonardo da Vinci concerning a suggestion by Ellis—in the latter's review of the work that same year, in the *Journal of Mental Science*—that the bird alighting on the young Leonardo's lips might have been an actual event, not a fantasy. Freud argued that such a possibility would not disprove his general theory. (See K. R. Eissler, *Leonardo da Vinci,* New York: International Universities Press, 1961, p. 16.)

resistance," and to Ernest Jones he described Ellis's essay as "the most refined and amiable form of resistance, calling me a great artist in order to injure the validity of our scientific claims."[6] Ellis was a man of peace and he claimed that he spoke sincerely, but he was ingenuous if he honestly believed that Freud would not be annoyed. After the years of silence Freud wrote to say that he had occasionally thought of writing a novel—so to that extent he might be classified an artist—but (ironically enough!) science kept breaking through. Ellis's answer was admirably forthright. He launched into the subject of Freud's most fanatical disciples: "So many of them are mere unintelligent followers of a routine and make psychoanalysis seem ridiculous to their patients. That of course, is not your fault. It is what always happens in the world.—As to me, I am not a disciple, not being young enough to be moulded. But I do not regard myself as an *opponent*, nor am I so regarded here. I have from the first always found your work full of illumination and help. It has greatly affected my own work, & I find that many English people after reading my books are prepared to receive your doctrines, whereas if they had gone directly to your books, they would have failed to understand them and been repelled."[7] "And as to being an artist, I can only say that to be an artist seems to me to be about the greatest thing that it is possible to be."[8] Blunt enough, but, had he actually been affected by Freud in his own work, he might have extended his graciousness to remark on this in his essay, whereas all he there found room to say was that Freud had borrowed from him. At this point Ellis still admired Freud but never failed to register his scepticism of the objective value of psychoanalysis. As Freud grew older and his mood darker, Ellis grew increasingly antagonistic towards his theories—especially as he had reason to believe that Ernest Jones poured his distrust of Ellis into the ears of the Master—and in private comments he often expressed his scepticism, if not overt antagonism.

The end of the war saw the revival of many old friendships. When Françoise first made her avowal of love to Havelock, he had in effect "warned" her that he had many friends overseas from whom he had been cut off by the war. She began to feel a little uneasy that she could not completely fill his heart, particularly as he had a disconcerting habit of withdrawing into himself from time to time. He was still obviously devoted to the wondrous Margaret Sanger, who was planning to return to England as soon as it was practicable, and who pressed Ellis for a promise to visit Ireland with her. When she had first returned to America he had shared her enthusiasm for the scheme, but now, with his usual reluctance to commit himself to other people's plans, he reminded her that he could be very stubborn. Marguerite Tracy, who was to become one of the dearest of his older women friends, had visited Havelock and Edith in Cornwall in 1916* and her last memory of them was of a devoted couple with arms linked as they watched her recede into the distance. This was shortly after Edith's return from America and they talked enthusiastically of the possibility of Edith going to France to lecture. In August 1917, unaware of Edith's death, Miss Tracy wrote from St. Cloud: "Mrs. Ellis had not come to inhabit this little place as I offered—perhaps she did not come to France to lecture as she meant to—Perhaps she overdid so much that she broke down completely. God knows I hope both she & you have been spared that."[9] In the summer of 1919, when she returned to England for an extended visit, she saw a great deal of Ellis. Always delightfully flattering, she told him that he gave her poise and that he was the principal reason why she did not return to America.

The eternal wanderer, Olive Schreiner, was back in England. She had become grotesquely fat, was obviously seriously ill, and was convinced that she did not have long to live. Perhaps if the baby born to her early in her marriage had not died, she might have overcome her nervous restlessness. Havelock of course told Olive of the little French woman who was gladdening his days. Olive expressed a desire to meet her and an afternoon was arranged. Ellis warned Françoise to be careful, if they spoke about Edith, not to mention her novels, since Olive disliked them intensely but valued Edith "as a personality." The two women got along splendidly and Françoise reported to Ellis: "She is wonderfully alive. We however dissected life to some sad effect for myself as it reduced me to tears at the end."[10]

Two other women came into Ellis's life in 1919—the American poet Hilda Doolittle (H.D.) and Winifred Ellerman, whose first autobiographical novel, *Development*, was to be published the following year. At first she adopted the pen-name Bryher, later again Bryer. These women came to Ellis initially for help. H.D. was once described by Amy Lowell as having "a strange, faun-like, dryad-like

---

* She had written first to him in 1913 asking if he needed a secretary.

quality, she seemed always as though just startled from a brake of fern. . . ."[11] The war years had been difficult for her. She had taken over the duties of assistant editor of *Egoist* from her husband, Richard Aldington, who was at the front. She had suffered a miscarriage, her favourite brother was killed in action, her father died, and she and Aldington separated at a time when she found herself pregnant again. To add to all this, she and Bryher had fallen in love. Close to a breakdown, she found solace in Ellis's quiet understanding. Françoise fought down jealous feelings when Ellis informed her that "Hilda, too, has occasional Naiad dreams and told me she had dreamt of lying down in bed on her back while a mighty stream ascended towards the ceiling."[12] Bryher's father was an immensely rich shipping magnate, Sir John Ellerman. Françoise, tired by teaching and fighting fleas in her wretched little East End house, was not particularly happy to hear that the two women had carried Ellis off to tea in "Dada's" sumptuous car. When she heard that Marguerite Tracy and Hilda had been looking after him when he came down with the flu, she could not refrain from snapping, "People like Marguerite Tracy and Hilda who have far more leisure than I *ought* to look after you, and I am delighted to hear that they have done so."[13]

Jane Burr* was another unlikely new friend, an unconventional American in knickerbockers, who first met Ellis in 1921 just after she had published a best-seller, *The Passionate Spectator*. She was on an assignment for an American newspaper chain and was anxious to meet Ellis because of her interest in women's rights, companionate marriage, birth control, and easier divorce laws. At times he found her strident "Jewishness" a little hard to take (with his rigid ideas on race, he always attributed certain characteristics to the Jews); but, true to his tenet that he never lost a friend, he saw her whenever she was in London and they corresponded for the rest of his life; in their letters she became "Rosalind" and he "Prospero."† For a time she seems to have been a little in love with him. After his death she recorded: "I have never been able to decide what Havelock's mental disturbances were. I think he was not a homosexual. I think he was just nothing sexually but adored women as friends."[14] Ellis had warned her: "Although I appreciate affection I do not want anyone

---

* A pseudonym for Rosalind (Rose) Guggenheim Winslow, 1882–1958.

† *The Tempest* was his favourite Shakespearean play; and he explained that many of his friends thought of him as a sorcerer.

to care for me too much."[15] Someone had told her that he was "susceptible," which he denied, asserting that if this were so he wouldn't have had so few intimate relationships.

Ellis saw all these women during the weeks when Françoise was occupied with her teaching. She was often frustrated by the chains of her poverty and her responsibilities. When Ellis suggested that they go to Deal together, the excursion had to be postponed because it would conflict with the children's holidays. Her frustration breaks through when she writes: "I am so longing to kiss you, that it is agony & I am wild with my dreaming brain as it does not even give you a thought at night. I miss you . . . things are not their regular selves, as I like them to be when you are these 'things.' "[16]

It was even worse during the following years, which developed into an unusually active period for Ellis, who, paradoxically, had begun to regard himself as an old man before Françoise's appearance in his life. She had to muster forbearance when he informed her in October that a grateful Bryher had persuaded "Dada" to allow one of his lifelong dreams to come true: he was to travel to Greece by sea, accompanied by his two new friends. Until his departure his talk was full of visas, itineraries, etc. He regarded this as his last great adventure. After travelling through Spain many times in acute discomfort, this time he was to voyage in comparative luxury in a small ship, the *Borodino*. The three set out on February 7th after Marguerite Tracy had arrived on board with a farewell gift of a cake.

The voyage was a delight to Ellis, who posted long rapturous letters to Françoise from Gibraltar and Malta. It felt wonderful to be back on the real sea again, to breathe deeply its exhilarating air, to smell the tar of the ship, to pace the decks, to glimpse falling stars— all these experiences brought back his youth. The weather was sunny and fine and Ellis sat happily in his deck chair and was rather proud to be the only passenger who was not seasick. He was disappointed to find that they had passed Algiers while he was sleeping, but he was able to revisit Algeciras when they put into port at Gibraltar. It held many memories for him, as it was here he had stayed with Edith twenty years before. The old hotels were still there, although they had changed their names. On board one night the passengers had an entertainment, and someone who read Ellis's palm told him that he was "fortunate in love and was loved . . . I expect it's all true."[17]

Malta was fascinating, and, above all, he was intrigued in the museum by a little Neolithic figure of a woman with delicate head and hands and expressive body who gracefully inclined on an elbow. Later he was to write in *Impressions and Comments*:

> The whole of a great period of the world's history, some ten thousand years, perhaps the most significant in the evolution of human civilisation, is summed up by that little figurine in a language we shall never decipher completely.[18]

On March 1st he was up on deck in the cold morning air to watch the approaching outlines of the distant, misty land he had always wanted to see—"all things, it seems, come at last, even without any effort on one's own part—though they usually come too late" —but apparently not in this case. March was spent in Athens. Ellis stayed in a modest pension, but the women were comfortably ensconced in the most luxurious hotel in the city. He did not do as much exploring as one might have thought, but seemed to spend most of his time reading on the side of Lycabettos, at that time of year covered with anemones. The friendship had begun to sour a bit. Hilda and Bryher left him too much on his own. "They are both very peculiar," he decided, especially Hilda, who, in spite of some good points, was "selfish, weak, and excitable."[19] Cyprus, which he had particularly wanted to visit, was now ruled out, as well as Asia Minor, because of post-war difficulties. He decided to set off on his own for England, especially as the two friends couldn't make up their minds when they were going to leave. Later he was relieved that he had decided to journey back alone, for apparently Hilda went *"right out of her mind"*[20] at Corfu and Bryher had to bring her back overland. This was the occasion on which H.D. is supposed to have had a terrifying vision of Helios, the sun-god, and Nike, the goddess of victory, who seemed to walk across the walls of her room and engulf her in the past.

For a man who habitually refused invitations because of his diminishing energies, Ellis exhibited remarkable verve and initiative. From Patras he sailed to Trieste, where he boarded the Orient Express for Paris. Never before had he flitted so fast across Europe, and memories of the past filled his mind as he reflected that he was probably being vouchsafed one last swallow's glimpse over a world that he was leaving forever. But Paris, after an absence of ten years, had never seemed so enchanting, never before had he felt so appreciatively near its people. Every yard of the Latin Quarter was familiar to him and he knew immediately any slight change in its appearance. With his thoughts dwelling both on the past and on advancing age, he reflected that with the passing years he had become even more sensitive to the contemplation of beauty. Françoise received an ecstatic hug from him on her first visit to Brixton in early April, only a few days before the arrival of Margaret Sanger.

Naturally Ellis arranged a meeting with his two women friends alone—as he was to do so often in future years—and Margaret professed herself delighted with Françoise. Margaret's tenacity proved too much for Ellis, who finally agreed to accompany her to Ireland early in August. It was considered a very dangerous time to go to Ireland, but Ellis entered fully into Margaret's spirit of adventure. At Killarney they actually went riding, an horrendous experience when Margaret's horse bolted as soon as she had mounted. It boggles the imagination to visualize them bumping along by jaunting car from Glengariff to Killarney. At Killarney they spent several happy hours rowing about the lake. Most beautiful of all was a Sunday spent on the deserted terraces of a mansion burned out just before the war, with its exquisite view of the lakes and hills beyond. They had to return to England earlier than they had planned because one of Margaret's incapacitating menstrual periods came on. When she apologized for being "nervous and impatient and horrid," Ellis assured her that she wasn't, and even if she had been, "I should understand, & only feel the more tenderly loving."[21] The memory of their wild rush through Ireland would always be a delicious memory to them. When she returned to America in October, he wrote to her: "There were indeed awful changes between your first visit six years ago and the last—both for oneself and for the world—and I, at all events, shall never be the same again. But there will be no such changes between this last visit and your next." "Goodbye, Darling Woman," he concluded, "it is lovely to think you will take care of Margaret for me, as I will of Havelock for you, and that we will take care of both of them for the world."[22]

Since Edith's death he had not been able to return to Cornwall. However, his renewed vigour and his loathing of London during the winter decided him to try a spot he had never stayed in before, the little fishing village of Cadgwith, which Edith had visited briefly during her last sojourn in Cornwall. Here in November he took rooms in the home of local people and shared the expenses of £1 weekly board with the painter Henry Bishop, with whom he ate dinner every evening after a long day's peaceful work, a routine that seemed to suit him admirably. The serenity of this quiet existence was shattered by the news of the death of Olive Schreiner, who had returned to South Africa in August. He had just received a card from her, and a letter of his never reached her before the end. After regarding her as part of his life for so long, it was rather a shock. To Françoise, who had sent him the notice from *The Times*, he commented, "I have for a very long time been reconciled to the idea of her death for I knew for many years her health had been undermined and how much she suffered. I am sure she was quite reconciled herself, though still so full of vivid interest in life, that she went back to Africa to die. . . . It is the end of a long chapter in my life & your Faun will soon be left alone by all the people who knew him early in life."[23]

He had intended to stay on in Cornwall for most of the winter, but was brought back to London by the unexpected arrival at Christmas of Olive's husband, S. C. Cronwright-Schreiner, who took rooms in Brixton so that Ellis could help him with the collection of Olive's letters which he was planning to edit. It was typical of Cronwright-Schreiner, a domineering man, to assume that Ellis would be ready to co-operate at a moment's notice. It was typical of Ellis, under the circumstances, to be prepared to do so. During January and most of February Cronwright-Schreiner came to Dover Mansions every day to "concoct" the biography which Ellis declined to write.* No one could tell him so much about Olive as Ellis, who still possessed many of her letters. Cronwright-Schreiner stayed in England only long enough to select the letters he would use in his collection. Since he acted on Ellis's advice, Ellis in large measure must be held responsible for this collection, which gives such a distorted picture of Olive's life, omitting, for instance, all letters written to Karl Pearson. More will be said about the biography which Cronwright-Schreiner returned to England to work on in 1923.

Ellis managed to get back to Cornwall by February 1921 and by the time he left at the end of the month he had enjoyed two months in all and felt greatly refreshed. In March the *Medical Review of Reviews* published his essay "The Play Function of Sex"—directly in-

---

* Ellis had been her literary executor until she changed her will after her marriage to Cronwright-Schreiner.

spired by Françoise—which it advertised as "the greatest article we have ever published," much to Ellis's amusement. It is not a very long essay, but here Ellis distils his attitude towards sex and also reveals himself as lover, particularly in his relationship with Françoise. He starts out by stating the two main functions of a sexual relationship: the primary physiological function of reproduction and the secondary spiritual function of "furthering the higher mental and emotional processes." Never tendentious, Ellis nevertheless succeeds in showing that our culture is tragically wrong in its priorities. His basic premise is that play is the most important of human activities. There is play that can be regarded as an educative training for life; in this sense the Duke of Wellington was right in saying that the Battle of Waterloo was won on the playing-fields of Eton. Then there is the conception of play as the utilization in art of superfluous energies, which can lead to the grandest of human creations. Finally, there is sex as play, a means of stimulating the complex and inter-related systems of the organism. The desired end is the creation of the "erotic personality," a figure rare among men and far rarer among women. Men generally regard the act of love as an exercise in virility and a means of relieving tension. This attitude is basically selfish and hence so many women are left unsatisfied. And here he reiterates the basic position he learned from James Hinton: love should not be self-regarding; the act of intercourse, however essential to propagation, is only an incident, not essential in love. The fact that so many husbands leave their wives unawakened has caused countless misery because often another man can awaken a woman's repressed sexuality. With Françoise specifically in mind, Ellis continues:

> A woman may have been married once, she may have been married twice, she may have had children by both husbands, and yet it may not be until she is past the age of thirty and is united to a third man that she attains the development of erotic personality and all that it involves in the full flowering of her whole nature.[24]

Remembering that Françoise had told him how her colleagues at the school had remarked on the radiance she had acquired, he continues:

> She feels more mentally alert, and she finds that she is more alive than before to the influences of nature and of art. Moreover, as others observe, however they may explain it, a new beauty has come into her face, a new radiancy into her expression, a new force into all her activities.[25]

Ellis sees lovers at their play as engaging in the most profound activity-sharing, the greatest joy men and women can know.

He included this essay in a collection which also contained "Objects of Marriage" and "The Love Rights of Women" (suggested originally by Margaret Sanger), as well as "The Meaning of Purity," a subject that had interested him ever since he had first undertaken his investigations into sex. The collection was published the following year under the title *Little Essays of Love and Virtue*. He was working on these in Tunbridge Wells, where he was staying with his sisters, when on the day he was to return to London he was prostrated by a violent duodenal-ulcer attack, touched "by a feather of death's wing." He recorded this event in *Impressions and Comments*, March 12th, 1921:

> Last week, when I was feeling, as ever since I left Cornwall I have felt, singularly firm against assault, Death, in his casual tentative indifferent way, just gave me a torturing prick with his scythe as he passed by, leaving me alive but bleeding. Ever since I lie on my back invalid, for the first time in my active life, and whether he is likely to come again soon there is none to tell me.[26]

Françoise's immediate reaction was that she wanted to go to Tunbridge Wells to nurse him, but he insisted that he never wanted to see anyone when he was ill. Laura, however, became incapacitated with lumbago and Mary, the consumptive sister, was too frail to look after anyone, so Françoise triumphantly moved in for a fortnight. Not exactly "triumphantly"—she was filled with apprehension that she would not be equal to the job. But after conquering her initial nerves she ran the house admirably; and on the day of her departure led Havelock out for his first outing to sit on a garden bench in the spring sunshine. Since Ellis was a doctor, he must have gauged pretty accurately the seriousness of his illness. He never had another attack, but after this he watched his diet very carefully. He had suffered from gastric trouble for years and one reason he consistently refused dinner invitations was that he suffered miserably from indigestion. One could speculate on the relevance of this to his probable impotence. (Carlyle, it must be remembered, was both dyspeptic and impotent.)

Mneme, who had moved to Margate with her husband, invited him to stay with them to recuperate. He had always rather despised Margate, but now, feeling strength flowing back into his body, he wandered joyfully among its shallow pools and inhaled the ancient fragrance of seaweed. "I am in another world. I am in a world of Nature which has no name, I am in the world of dreams which has no shore."[27] This was the ecstatic experience of union with nature which had been the essence of his conversion in the Australian bush. Even Ramsgate is celebrated in the third series of *Impressions and Comments* (1920–3), which appeared in 1924. These essays are infused with rejoicing, especially over the beauties of nature, whereas the earlier series had covered a random range of subjects. When the second series had appeared in 1921, Ellis warned Françoise: "It must be remembered that the 'Impressions' are *only* impressions. They must not be regarded as a final, rounded, mature, balanced statement of the *whole* truth."[28] He was referring primarily to the opinions and reactions expressed in the first two volumes, and it was a statement that he was to make to many people. The three volumes of *Impressions and Comments* always remained his favourites among his books. The reason doubtless was that they were written in the open air in scenes which he loved. Also they were written in a completely relaxed way, totally unlike the methodical marshalling of facts in the *Studies* and some of his earlier books. He sent a copy to Carpenter, who replied: "Indeed I am grateful, not only for the concrete book itself, but for the way in which you have revealed your inner self in it—that self which has been so long (too long!) contained away from mortal eyes. . . . I have found it a great help to have you using the word 'I' so frequently, and so to jump to your own inner attitude towards the world—which so often seems to agree with mine. You are a poet in feeling but in so much of your work you are (necessarily) on the scientific plane."[29] Always reluctant to commit himself unequivocally—a trait which irritated Freud—here he could indulge in rumination and leisurely speculation.

He was in Ramsgate when Margaret Sanger arrived in England for one of her whirlwind tours. She was unable to get down to Ramsgate, and her visit was so rushed that there were few occasions for them to see each other, apart from Ellis journeying down to Plymouth to see her off on her return voyage on September 8th. Her conversation during this visit was mainly concerned with her forthcoming lecture tour in Japan, which worried Ellis a good deal. She was constitutionally frail and was constantly collapsing throughout her career; in letter after letter Ellis warned her about over-taxing her strength.

For the time being Ellis seemed to have forgotten his age. Sixty-two was not old, but his long white beard made him look much older than his years, and until the recent resurgence of energy, the difficult years with Edith had made him feel like an old man. He and Françoise had long been planning to make a trip to France together; in order to avoid the fatiguing journey by rail and boat to Paris, Ellis decided to fly over—an adventurous enough undertaking in those days. On their previous excursions they had shared expenses, but this time Ellis insisted on paying for Françoise: "You need not thank me for the flight across," he assured her. "I have just sold the German rights to Edith's 'New Horizons' to a lady in Vienna for £6 (17,000 crowns!!) I always think Edith sent you to console me, and just at the right moment she has sent £6 to pay your fare across."[30] They set off on July 28th and at first all went well, but after they passed Boulogne they ran into heavy turbulence and as the little craft plunged about, almost all the twelve passengers were violently ill—except Ellis, who was too old a sailor to feel anything but a bit dizzy. Finally, after four hours, the petrol was exhausted, and they had to land in a field near Poix. Hailing a passing car, all the passengers except Ellis, Françoise, and three young Americans abandoned ship; but the survivors were bequeathed a picnic basket by some passers-by which was greatly appreciated in the long hours they had to wait until help arrived. Scarcely the worse for wear, that evening they arrived at Blois, where Françoise's brother had reserved rooms for them. After a good night's sleep Ellis was as spry and eager as Françoise to explore the châteaux of the Loire, which neither of them had visited before. They spent ten exquisite days in excursions, the high points of which were Chenonceaux and Azay-le-Rideau. After this they parted company when Ellis went off to St. Cloud to visit Marguerite Tracy and Françoise travelled to Maubeuge to stay with her family, to whom she had not yet dared confess her relationship with Ellis.

After so many eventful months Ellis was anxious to get down to some sustained work. Again Cornwall beckoned with its invigoration and its peace. In November, this time accompanied by Arthur Symons, he returned to Cadgwith. But first they met at Plymouth, where they went to a musical comedy at the Royal Theatre, the first theatre he had ever attended forty-five years before with his father, just before setting out for Australia. Symons had never recovered completely from his severe nervous breakdown many years before and his doctor had advised this change. While Ellis found him nervous, he was still amusing company and they knew each other's habits so well that neither distracted the other from his work. It was at Cadgwith during this extended visit of 1921–2 that Ellis wrote his most outstanding book, *The Dance of Life.*

SOLEIL DE JOIE

ONE OF ELLIS'S GREATEST ADMIRERS WAS A STRIKINGLY HANDSOME writer twenty years younger than himself, Hugh de Sélincourt. He had written a number of undistinguished novels, such as *Realms of Day*, published in 1915, the year Ellis met him. The friendship was initiated by Sélincourt, who was a disciple of Hinton and assumed that Ellis was as well. Ellis had to correct him: "I was never actually a disciple; his sparks of genius & audacity are accompanied by very disconcerting limitations."[1] Ellis added that he had never republished the essay on Hinton which he had written twenty-five years before because he considered it "a little too enthusiastic." He invited Sélincourt to call on him, they began to lunch together occasionally, and to write frequently. These letters were mainly an exchange of opinions on literature, and Ellis's are among the most interesting he ever wrote. The reason so many letters were exchanged was that Ellis would not be tempted to visit Sélincourt and his wife, Janet, in their St. John's Wood home: "I very seldom go out anywhere, so much of a recluse, that any visit proves very disturbing, however much I may enjoy it."[2] In response to another invitation, he replied: "Please believe that I *really* hope that I may some day find myself at your home,"[3] an assurance that was to find ironical fulfilment some years later.

Ellis appears to have been flattered by Sélincourt's adulation, but from the first he had reservations about his extravagant exuberance. He was also quick to put his finger on a quality in Sélincourt's writing which was very much a reflection of Sélincourt's temperament. After reading A *Daughter of the Morning*, a novel Sélincourt had published in 1912, Ellis remarked: "It's 'immorality' is so gracious & artistic. You may object to my labelling your book *First Lessons in Immorality or a Child's Guide to Vice*, but I have really much enjoyed it & think it ought to exert a wholesome influence."[4] (The ambivalence of the remark reflects Ellis's typical reluctance to offend.) In other letters he agreed with Sélincourt about loving and hating Rousseau at the same time: "One can scarcely find any other person so detestable whom one sympathises with so much! That is at once his attraction & his significance."[5] We learn that he detested Robert Louis Stevenson, and that he viewed *Don Quixote* as the world's greatest novel, representing "a man who was at once a ridiculous lunatic & a very noble gentleman & a great idealist, the highest symbol of anything one likes. This synthesis of the serious & the amusing seems to me essential in a great novel & inevitable whenever the novelist is a great creative artist."[6] On another occasion he wrote: "I was sure you must adore Shelley, & you really have a certain kind of affinity with him, I scarcely think I have—I am always more inclined to grab at the roots of the Tree of Life than to fix my gaze on the 'intense inane' above it. But the word 'adoration' does express my attitude towards Shelley & towards no other being who ever existed, the kind of feeling which the devout Christian ought to feel, but doesn't about Jesus. From 16 to 20 I was always re-reading & re-reading & meditating on his poems & life. I never have since, & never felt that I need to, but my attitude remains unchanged. I have never felt able to write about him rationally on this account."[7]

Sélincourt suggested that they meet regularly at his favourite restaurant, the Monico at Piccadilly Circus. Predictably, Ellis resisted being tied down to a fixed habit: "I much appreciate regular & precise habits in purely material matters, whereas in those to which a spiritual element enters,—I think that nothing of the nature of habit, good or bad, should inhere, only at the most, a natural rhythm, like that of the tides, never two days alike."[8] Nevertheless, he seemed interested in Sélincourt's career, made careful comments on where he thought weaknesses lay in his writing, and tried to interest reluctant publishers in his books. He gave Sélincourt his fictionalized account of the year at Sparkes Creek, *Kanga Creek*, to read and was so encouraged by his ecstatic reaction that he decided, after all these

years, to publish it.* He also suggested that Sélincourt meet Margaret
Sanger during her 1920 visit and a luncheon was arranged for May
27th at the Monico. Perhaps he did not expect his two friends to
react *quite* so enthusiastically to each other. Sélincourt found Margaret "entirely free from that tiresome self-importance which women
often acquire as a result of a little notoriety."[9] When Margaret later
described Sélincourt as an "overwhelming personality," Ellis rather
testily disagreed; an "overwhelming personality," as far as he was
concerned, was someone like Olive Schreiner. In any event, an immediate friendship was established, Sélincourt began to pursue Margaret
with flattering letters, and Ellis sometimes found himself in the
rather awkward position of having to ask her whereabouts of her new
admirer. Indeed, it did not take Sélincourt long to invite her to his
lovely new Sussex home, Sand Pit, where she was charmed by his
bohemian household of music and laughter—by his little daughter,
Bridget; his wife, Janet, a talented musician; her lover, critic Harold
Child; and the painter Frank Carter. True to his Hintonian (and
what he considered Ellisian) principles, Sélincourt treated his wife's
liaison as beautifully natural—and Child in turn wrote prefaces for
his books and flattering reviews in *The Times*. According to Margaret
Sanger's biographer, Madeline Gray, Margaret and Sélincourt became lovers in the summer of 1921, and the liaison continued for
years.

Sélincourt was also eager to meet Françoise. As early as 1918 Ellis
referred to her in a letter as "a young French Pacifist friend" and
later told him that "my dear little French friend" admired his books.
No wonder Sélincourt's curiosity was whetted and for some months
he urged Ellis to arrange a meeting,† which eventually took place at
the Monico late in August 1920. Before this meeting, Ellis warned
Sélincourt that she was "rather shy at first meeting people because,
she says, they are always so unlike the picture she has formed of
them."[10] Sélincourt found her "a bundle of delight." "I've been teasing her about it ever since," Ellis chortled to Margaret Sanger.[11] Her
name disappears from their letters until March 14th, 1922, when, in

---

* He offered it to the Golden Cockerel Press, as he did "not care to publish in
the ordinary way" (Hugh de Sélincourt, 3 April 1921, Library of Congress). It was
published in 1922 in a limited edition.
† On July 14th, 1920, Ellis told Françoise that "He has acquired a high opinion
of you through me, and you must meet him some day" (Mugar Library).

response to some comment about her by Sélincourt, Ellis remarks: "Françoise Cyon is shy, awkward with strangers, so arouses a corresponding attitude in other people. Only, of course, at first. Then she is charming and very transparent, more charming than transparent people are wont to be, and with a richly iridescent emotional nature." [12]

Ellis stayed on in Cornwall later than usual the winter of 1921–2 in order to work at his book. On May 7th he wrote to Françoise: "This morning, in bed, I thought of the title of my next book—*The Dance of Life*. Do you like it? Symons thinks it is a beautiful title. I had meant to call it 'The Art of Life,' but that is too hackneyed & feeble."[13] Later in the month he sent her a ticket to hear Sélincourt lecture on him to the British Society for the Study of Sex Psychology at Claxton Hall on May 24th. Françoise reported: "La conférence de Sélincourt fut des plus charmantes . . . tout le 'monde' entendait sans cesse votre nom et Sélincourt parlait de façon si charmante, si aimante, que je l'aurais bien embrassé. Je l'ai félicité après la cérémonie, mais une grosse dame est venue nous interrompre, et il faisait si chaud, et il était si tard, que je suis partie."[14]

Ellis returned to London late in the month and for the first time met both Françoise's small sons on an excursion to Kew. Paul, the younger one, murmured later that he liked him very much, and when Ellis heard this he replied: "I also much enjoyed my afternoon at Kew & am glad to hear what you tell me of Paul. You know I am always very alarmed by children & never know what to say to them."[15]

In July Margaret Sanger arrived for a brief visit prior to going on to a birth-control conference she had organized in Switzerland. She was so rushed that Havelock had to travel around with her in taxis in order to see her, and he asked Françoise to defer some of her visits as he wanted to be with Margaret as much as possible. Françoise could not have been hurt because she was anticipating sixteen marvellous days in the Pyrenees with him. Early in August she left the children with her family in Maubeuge and joined Ellis in Paris, where they visited Sylvia Beach in her famous bookshop, Shakespeare & Co. (Miss Beach was the Paris agent for the *Studies*.) She later told Ellis that she was charmed by his young friend. Unfortunately the weather in the Pyrenees was terrible and Ellis caught a chill, so they had to return to London sooner than they had planned. During this trip he wrote to Sélincourt several times, and Margaret Sanger, who was now back in England, reported that Sélincourt carried his Pyrenees post-cards about with him everywhere and read them over from time to time.

On their return Françoise sent Havelock an ecstatic love letter: "By Jove, Faun, I shall die of pure excess of love for you. . . . I felt yesterday that I could never be too eager to pour myself into that well, to get at all the treasures it hides. I felt also—& is not this the very essence of love—that you were pouring yourself into me as I did into you. I was hungry & thirsty & how well you satisfied me out of your very self!"[16] "Glad to hear of your vigour, dear Naiad," he replied; "and that your visit did not completely exhaust it. But remember Ruth St. Denis's mother also built a well round the fountain & bottled it & sold it, for fear it should all be wasted."[17] In retrospect this warning would seem premonitory.

In October Françoise received a note from Sélincourt asking if he might call on her. In consternation she wrote to Ellis that she could not possibly receive him in her "affreuse petite boîte." Ellis wrote to both of them encouraging the visit, which was eventually set for November 3rd. In the meantime Sélincourt returned Joyce's *Ulysses*, which he had borrowed from Ellis (who had recently bought it from Sylvia Beach).* He pronounced it ugly. When Ellis mentioned this to Françoise, her response was that it was easy for him to see things as beautiful in his environment, but under other circumstances he would have recognized ugliness as well. Ellis also defended *Ulysses*: "Joyce really does bring us up to things that are passed; he enlarges the frontiers of experience, an incalculable service."[18] During these years he read each volume of Proust's *A la recherche du temps perdu* as they were issued, and found them enthralling.

At this period Ellis was seeing a lot of Jane Burr—with whom he found himself "charmed"—and Françoise, in an attempt to suppress her jealousy of the American women, diverted it to Edith. Ellis replied: "I am glad you told me of your jealous feeling about Edith. But there was no need for it. She was a wonderful person & I loved her dearly as she did me. But living with her was full of anxieties, & we were not altogether suited to each other in outer things, though

---

* In 1922 Ferris Greenslet, senior editor of Houghton Mifflin, at Ellis's suggestion, secured from Sylvia Beach a proof copy of *Ulysses* which he took back to the United States.

we were in spiritual things. It was often much more like you & Serge than like you & me."*[19]

On November 9th Ellis told Sélincourt that Françoise had informed him that the visit to Forest Gate was a great success. The letter was written hurriedly because he was preoccupied with innumerable details before leaving on the 21st for Cornwall, where he was going to spend the winter. He was working on the revisions of *The Dance of Life,* as well as seeing through the press Olive Schreiner's *Dreams, Stories and Allegories,* and helping Cronwright-Schreiner by post with his biography of Olive by making extracts from those letters he hadn't already destroyed.

Yes, the visit to Forest Gate was an immense success. Hugh delighted Françoise's sons with his wonderful stories and gave them a copy of *At the Back of the North Wind;* and he delighted their mother with his adulation of Havelock. "If you could hear the way he speaks of you!" Françoise raved to Ellis. "He knows all the wonder of you with such reality that his words thrilled me almost as much as your presence."[20] "Did I tell you," Ellis asked Margaret Sanger, "that Françoise and Hugh de Sélincourt have become quite attached to each other? She says they spend most of their time talking about me —which will grow tedious."[21] Following the visit, they felt impelled to write to each other immediately about the beauty that was Havelock, and they both wept over the beauty of their own emotions. The sentimentality of the whole thing could have been lifted out of *La Nouvelle Héloïse*—or one of Sélincourt's novels. In the midst of all this wallowing emotionalism, Margaret announced that she was going to marry a rich American, Noah Slee. On hearing the news, Françoise exclaimed: "Heureuse Margaret! Heureuse Margaret! comme elle a raison, monsieur mon Faune, de se lancer à nouveau dans cette grande aventure du mariage si l'homme est riche. J'en suis, moi, toujours à rechercher l'homme riche qui consentera à m'épouser, et me laissera libre de conserver le Faune dans ma vie."[22]

Ellis was disturbed to hear that she was sleeping badly. "It seemed to me so nice that Sélincourt and Naiad should be friends but I shall be sorry if he excites her mind too much. The Faun's opium is better."[23] To Sélincourt he expressed himself somewhat differently. He told him that he was delighted that Françoise was enjoy-

---

* By now Françoise was permanently estranged from her husband, with whom she lost all contact.

ing his visits, "for her vigorous vitality is under such crushing weight of work that she had no energy left to seek out of herself the outlet into a larger atmosphere you give her."[24] The next he heard was that Françoise and Hugh were planning jointly to write a book on what women owed to Havelock Ellis. His response was tart: "I trust he won't soon have any bad effect in disturbing your equilibrium too much. It seems so good that you should be friends. But it's all very fine to go and make a baby-book with him—and then pretend I'm the father!"[25] He did not hesitate to tell her that Jane Burr thought she was in love with him—not a piece of news that would pacify Françoise. On hearing that Sélincourt had taken her to lunch at the Monico and to a Casals concert, his disquiet increased: "Of course I am shocked at the exuberant rapidity (so unlike the slow Faun!) with which Sélincourt and Naiad have become such close friends! But though he is exuberant . . . an emotional nature . . . he is a beautiful nature, as you say, & I am delighted (though of course not a bit surprised) that he appreciates you so much & that you find him so good & helpful for you. I think, of course, that it is always best to go slowly, but it is not likely I shall think anything that Naiad does is wrong, & it is a joy to me that anything new & beautiful should come into her life, for she deserves everything."[26] By now the exalted pair had become "Bear" and "Soleil de Joie" to each other.

With her daily letters both to Havelock and to Hugh, it is little wonder that Ellis was concerned that it might all be too much for her. A typical passage in one of her letters to Sélincourt reads: "I am day by day listening to all the confessions, confidences, & deliciously extravagant talk of my big brother. I am so pleased he finds me so helpful, although I fear *it won't last,* one day will come when he won't any longer believe that I am a fairy tale &, as he is so fond of such tales, he will give Françoise up!"[27] At first she made a great point of sending all his letters on to Ellis as soon as she had read them. After a time he began to have qualms about reading them. On December 17th he wrote: "The Naiad *is* getting spoiled nowadays! Though not a bit more than she deserves. I enjoy his letters, but I think, like you, that it would be best *not* to show them to me often, as he might not quite like it, if he knew, & intimate letters are only meant for one person (though there is nothing exactly private in his letter.)" As for "Soleil de Joie," she told Ellis, "je l'aime, mais je voudrais vraiment qu'il m'aimait sans m'adorer. Et quand je pense que *vous,* cher Faune . . . vous m'aimez!"[28] And again, just before leaving for Cornwall to spend ten days with him at Chrsitmas, she wrote: "At present I have your arms often around me, your lovely hands caressing me, all kinds of tender & delicious & playful thoughts about you. . . ."[29] But the date of her arrival was constantly postponed because she had such a multitude of things to attend to. Just before Christmas, at Margaret Sanger's behest, Sélincourt sent Ellis a huge basket of roses. It was all too beautiful. On New Year's Eve Ellis wrote to Margaret: "Probably I told you that Sélincourt and Françoise seem quite in love with each other. By a morning post I have a rapturous letter from Françoise about Sélincourt, & in the evening a rapturous letter from Sélincourt about Françoise. She is just coming down for a few days & wants to tell me all about it."[30] His mood was waggish. Sélincourt's letters were having such an effect, he teased Françoise, that "I feel myself falling in love with her afresh!—if it is possible to fall still further!"[31]

Christmas of 1922 at Cadgwith was the first time that the pair had ever been away in complete solitude together. Just after her return to London he told her, "I have always had an affection for this place because Edith spent a week here & now your week here will add to the place's charm."[32] In actual fact the reason that it is possible to follow this relationship so closely is because they saw each other comparatively seldom. Françoise could get away from home only every other week-end; they christened these assignations "Barnet week-ends" because Françoise pretended that she went off to visit very respectable relatives in Barnet. This fiction was maintained even with her trusted servant, Bessie, because she was so apprehensive about losing her job that the relationship had to be kept entirely secret.

During this Cadgwith visit they seemed as loving as ever. Ellis was nervous, as he often was in a strange house, that they might be observed by their landlady; but, as he later maintained, that was a situation Françoise should be accustomed to, and he was as attentive as ever. On her return to London, Françoise wrote him unusually loving letters. Later, in retrospect, he was to see how far from normal this period really was.

The emotions of the trio follow a complicated course in the following months. A strong vein of irony begins to permeate Ellis's attitude towards the triangle. This is apparent in a letter he wrote to Margaret Sanger just after Françoise's visit: "Sélincourt and Françoise are more drawn to each other than ever. It is no doubt quite the right thing that your adorer & mine should fall into each other's arms!"[33] At times it appeared that Ellis was almost conspiring to throw them into each other's arms. He sent two tickets to Ford's *'Tis Pity She's a Whore* to Françoise, suggesting that she take Sélincourt to see the play: "I don't know who else you could take, as it would not be desirable to take one of your teachers who might be shocked."[34]

Françoise cannot have been entirely ingenuous about the dangerous situation she was allowing to develop. Why did she write that she hoped she would never see any "nuage de souffrance" on her Faun's face? He reassured her that she wouldn't: "That is the advantage of having a Faun who has been so well trained by the discipline of life! Years ago, there probably *would* have been a 'nuage.' But even then, I know, & am quite sure, that the 'nuage' would soon have melted away. As it is, I feel only joy in the happiness of my Fontaine de Vie even when I am not myself the source of that happiness."[35] But did he actually feel so secure? On March 14th he dreamt that he found himself in a magnificent theatre packed with people, and as he groped his way through the crowd and craned his neck, he was disconsolate because he could not find his Naiad.

It is difficult at this point to separate real feelings from feelings they believed they were experiencing. All three held it as sacred dogma that they were incapable of jealousy. Sélincourt, as an avowed Hintonian and Shelleyite, believed in loving—"and then all things are possible"; accordingly, his wife's lover was welcomed affectionately at Sand Pit. But the self-deception of the man—not to speak of hypocrisy—is patent. After Françoise had spent a week-end at his home in St. John's Wood, he wrote to Ellis that the "enchanting" and "adorable" Françoise had won all hearts, especially his wife's. After her first visit in May to Sand Pit with its pool and its flowers and its lovely walks, Sélincourt wrote to her: "You heavenly little sister mine, I can't tell you how I enjoyed your coming: in a beautiful new way I seemed to get to know whole heaps more of you—all so dear & deep & lovely. . . . What a proud proud proud big brother I am to have such an enchanting little exquisite sister. Bless you, bless you, bless you. Hugh."[36] Meanwhile, the adulatory letters to Ellis also continued. Sélincourt had never admired Edith's work, but now that he read *The Imperishable Wing* at Françoise's suggestion, he found himself enraptured by its beauty.

Ellis was slightly troubled by Françoise's vagueness about what had actually taken place on this first visit to Sand Pit—"so frank about vague emotions & at the same time so reserved about important facts."[37] As he told her later, it was all wrapped in mist, "but I expected it would be cleared up satisfactorily some day."[38] He still believed that it could be an affectionate friendship such as he had with Margaret because he had managed to keep her "effervescent affection within the bounds of moderation."[39] But he was beginning to be irritated by the emotional bath. One of Françoise's letters "is full of Naiad's usual wisdom—though," he added drily, "It is true she is so full also of Soleil de Joie she never has time to send me the 'New Leader' or to think of the 'Nouvelles Littéraires.' "[40] One detects, too, a note of disenchantment in his view of Sélincourt, who had written a gushy piece on Ellis for the birthday number of *The Birth Control Review*. He showed it to his sister Louie, who shrewdly observed that Sélincourt was trying to make a picture of Ellis to accord with his own image—"venerable long-bearded sort of working-man, living in a slum, and delighted to have a bottle of wine."[41]

The Dance of Life was finally finished and Ellis returned from Cornwall on February 21st. During March Sélincourt paid him an unusual number of visits. Early in April Françoise collapsed with double pneumonia, and few days later Sélincourt was confined to bed with the same ailment. Late in April Ellis took her to Saffron Walden, one of his favourite towns, to recuperate for a week. Margaret Sanger wrote: "Glad Françoise is better. You are a better tonic for her than Hugh."[42] Ellis repeated the remark to Françoise, adding wryly, "I shall have to tell her that Naiad does not think so."[43]

Cronwright-Schreiner was returning to England to resume work on the biography of his wife. In April, in preparation for his arrival, Ellis destroyed most of Olive's letters of 1886. This was the period of her tormented relationship with Karl Pearson and the Hinton imbroglio. Did Ellis destroy these letters for his own sake or for her husband's? Or Olive's? Cronwright-Schreiner expressed to Ellis his profound disillusionment in reading through the letters at finding that his wife was a liar, and that there was a great disparity between her ideals and her actions. In 1929 Ellis described Cronwright-Schreiner to the American anarchist printer Joseph Ishill as "an excellent man when you know him, though of an ultra virile type, apt to be self-willed and aggressive";[44] but he respected Ellis and they got along very well together. He adopted two of Françoise's suggestions in the biography: the stressing of Olive's retention of youthful ideals, and her proposal that he omit a description of Olive as "a moral genius." The reminders of Olive forced Ellis into a final reassessment of what she was. "I do not think Olive really *developed* in all the forty years I knew her, & I had no influence on her (though she used to call me her 'other self') & at the beginning was too young & uninformed to be able to have any influence. . . . Edith was in many ways superior, both in capacity for development & in her struggle with the special difficulties of her temperament as well as in the greater harmony of her intellect. Edith was always developing: up to 1914, when she first began to be undermined by disease, and her essay on 'The Philosophy of Happiness' represents a much more harmonious & balanced conception of life than Olive had at any time— Edith's intellect was even more emotionally based than Olive's, & they were both too idealistic & too sanguine."[45] But Ellis was delighted with Cronwright-Schreiner's biography. He declared it to be *"quite wonderfully* improved by my hacking at it. Makes a most fine & interesting book—probably the best account of a woman of genius ever written."[46] It is nothing of the sort. It is a truncated, expurgated version of her life, omitting important relationships such as those with Julius Gau and Karl Pearson, and making no attempt at psychological truth, by which Ellis had always set such store; nor, for that matter, unvarnished truth, which he had praised in Casanova's autobiography. It is understandable that he believed that certain things could not be discussed because of the existence of living people. Certainly he himself would not want to be reminded of them. But, under the circumstances, it is puzzling that his critical judgement was suspended.

The American edition of *The Dance of Life* came out in the spring of 1923, the English edition on August 16th, when Françoise and Ellis were holidaying in France. Françoise had left Paul and François at Sand Pit under Hugh's ebullient supervision. To Margaret Sanger Sélincourt wrote: "Françoise becomes more adorable as I know her better. The little boys enjoyed themselves here. I was horribly severe and stern with them. Oh but *odious!*"[47] It was quite the nicest holiday Françoise and Havelock had ever had. Ellis had always resisted the Riviera, but he loved the sun and the sea and they bathed every day. Nevertheless, there was an undercurrent of tension. Ellis seemed listless and distant. Françoise exploded one day when he refused to visit her brother's studio: "I want to die. You have gone from me spiritually." Ellis did not reply, but told her later that he thought she was suffering from the excessive heat and that she was still weak from her illness. Besides, he admitted, there was an element of "a mischievous spirit of cussedness"[48] in his obstinacy. At the end of three weeks Françoise visited her father in Maubeuge and then returned to Sand Pit for another week, while Ellis returned to Brixton to read the glowing reviews of the most important book he had written in years.

The Dance of Life was by far Ellis's most popular book. The American edition went through seven impressions in the first six months and continued to sell steadily for years. Material drawn from numerous articles—mostly in *The Atlantic Monthly*—was incorporated into various sections: "The Art of Dancing," "The Art of Thinking," "The Art of Writing," "The Art of Religion," "The Art of Morals."* Ellis lavished particular attention on this book, revising it many times, as though determined that his last book should be the crystallization of his vast reading, his perception of the inter-relatedness of all life, and the wisdom he had garnered from experience and reflection. *The Dance of Life* was both structurally and thematically modelled on his first book, *The New Spirit*. He maintains time and again that life must be process and development and that only the man who is constantly changing can be viewed as thoroughly mature; and while the tone and style of the later book have a controlled elegance lacking in *The New Spirit*, both books were written as affirmations of certain values, dedications to cherished individuals who had provided inspiration and solace, and were, finally, attempts to synthesize currents of vitality. In the Preface Ellis says that in a sense he was convinced that this book had been born with him. Believing fervently as he did in congenital inheritance, it seemed to him that the serenity, the flexibility, and the open-mindedness which he liked to think pervaded his work were instinctive. Life is always changing, men are constantly in the process of making new worlds, but, like the dance, which can admit of improvisation and variation, the individual has an instinctive silent knowledge of himself, and in the pattern he weaves the parts are subordinate to the whole. Ellis might have quoted Yeats: "How can we know the dancer from the dance?"

Ellis had for many years loved the dance as an art form, particularly Spanish dances with their disciplined intensity. He often dis-

---

* He would have liked to have included the arts of building, travel, and cooking. Why not the art of love?

cussed the philosophic implications of the dance with two of his admirers, the American dancers Ted Shawn and Ruth St. Denis. The art of dancing he saw as the source of all the arts that express themselves primarily through the individual. Dancing is the primitive form of expression in religion and in love; it is the dance that has socialized man. Moving through history from primitive tribes to mediaeval masses to Diaghilev's Russian ballet, he traces the basic need to express the deepest feelings through the rhythmic movement of the body. It is not only the dancer but the spectator who participates in the art, since through *Einfühlung*, or "empathy," we can feel ourselves in the dancer, "who is manifesting the latent impulses of our own being."[49]

In "The Art of Thinking" Ellis adopts a rather unusual approach. All thinking—speculative or synoptic—when it is concerned with *making*, approaches art. Socrates and possibly Jesus were creations of men's imaginations. Let us make a man and a situation as if they actually existed. Ellis finds the most compelling expression of this theory in the contemporary German philosopher Hans Vaihinger's "Philosophie des Als Ob," of which Ellis had written the first English account.* The problem that preoccupied Vaihinger was how it is that from consciously false premises we can reach conclusions that strike us as true and in accord with nature. Because, he concluded, we work in symbols or fictions, and it is the business of thinking to constantly readjust those symbols to approximate as closely as possible to our sense of the truth. "We make our own world; when we have made it awry, we can remake it, approximately truer, though it cannot be absolutely true to the facts."

Ellis then turns to the paradox that great art can grow out of what is commonly regarded as the lowest instinct—sex. Bypassing Freud, Ellis recalls that the historian Ferrero suggested some thirty years before that the art instinct is transformed sexual instinct. Ellis himself, twenty-five years previously, in his discussion of auto-erotic activities, stated that "it is impossible to say what finest elements in art, in morals, in civilisation generally, may not really be rooted in an auto-erotic impulse."†[50]

Finally, he turns to scientific thinking, for he had always con-

---

* "The World as Fiction," *Nation*, XXVIII (Nov. 1920), 282–4.
† He had first enunciated his theory of sublimation in the essay on Casanova in *Affirmations* (1898).

tended that science is an art. He discusses the approach and conclusions of various scientists, and selects Darwin as a model, a man who was both great scientist and great artist, who played with the world, creating a theory of sexual selection—"which made the whole becoming of life art and the secret of it poetry."[51] All speculative thinkers create a fiction, an "as if" world through their imagination, a maligned faculty which Ellis believed should be acknowledged for its dynamic function.

"The Art of Morals" is perhaps the most interesting section of the book in that here Ellis speaks expressly with his own voice. He sets out to demolish the prejudice that a morality treated as art lacks seriousness. Many people tend to regard this attitude as dilettantish and self-indulgent. The reverse, Ellis contends, is nearer the truth. The artist leads a life of discipline, and no discipline can be lacking in pain. Dancing, for instance, is the most austere form of discipline, and for the great dancer it is frequently a form of heroism. A dancer may seem a thing of joy, but when the dance is ended, her slippers are filled with blood. Dancing, he affirms, is the supreme symbol of the art of living. Pain is inseparable from pleasure. Pain must be viewed as necessary, biologically, morally, and aesthetically. Here again he invokes the authoritative figure of James Hinton, who appears in every one of his books in this role. Ellis concludes that pain must be resisted, endured, and overcome—but also welcomed. In what was probably the most personal utterance in the book, Ellis writes: "Life must always be a great adventure, with risks on every hand; a clear-sighted eye, a many-sighted sympathy, a fine daring, an endless patience, are for ever necessary to all good living."[52]

Ellis has often been criticized for quoting too many authorities, for constructing an argument by stringing together the views of many others whose conclusions were based on inductive work of their own. Many readers (including Carpenter and Sélincourt) were continually frustrated because he seemed to mask himself behind other writers: it was a justifiable complaint. (But Sélincourt's judgement is not to be trusted when he inveighs to Margaret Sanger about Ellis's persistence in praising Joyce: "Damn the old King! Damn him! obstinate old devil!").[53] As for Ellis's method in general, he could claim that his eclecticism, his catholicity in casting a wide net, was the proper method of synthesis. But—to what end? In "The Synthesis of Dreams" his descriptive method often points to the self-evident; as a piece of diligent research it may be impressive, but it has no value as theory or as a tool for self-understanding. Before Freud there may have been people who offered hints or glimmerings of the non-rational psyche, but it was Freud alone who grasped that dreams were "the royal road to the unconscious." In this field, for example, Ellis contributed nothing original of any significance.

In the Preface to *The Dance of Life*, Ellis declares: "We verge on philosophy. The whole of this book is on the threshold of philosophy."[54] Unfortunately, there is no clear line of argument; it is difficult to find the linking transitions between discussions. The general conception of the dance as the unifying symbol for life treated as art is a splendid insight, but he gets carried away too easily by preoccupations such as his interest in a semi-martyr, the Australian Chidley, who went around the streets of Sydney half-clad, preaching his doctrine of naturalness. *The Times Literary Supplement* found the conception that all art is a dance interesting but far from clear; hence, it is "difficult to reproduce Mr. Ellis's position." *The Spectator* objected that he pushed the dance symbolism to tiresome lengths. The writing is elegant, the whole performance dazzling, but its sparkle is soon extinguished. What the book was to do was to provide him with an indispensable *vade mecum* in the most crucial emotional crisis of his life.

In a way the book belongs in the category of "mid-cult," and I would suggest that its great popularity, especially in the United States, was due to the fact that readers liked to be soothed by a pleasurable cultural bath without any rigorous intellectual effort being required of them. The American reviews tended to be much more favourable than the British, but to Françoise Ellis wrote: "Like you, I feel I don't like the American reviews, even when favourable. I regret the good old days when people either ignored me or spoke evil of me."[55]

From America also came a visit from his old friend Percival Chubb, whom he hadn't seen for thirty years. (Chubb had telephoned Edith when she was in America, an incident that unsettled her equilibrium because at one time before her marriage she had believed herself in love with him.) He had long been the leader of the Ethical Church in St. Louis, Missouri, and was one of the few people left from the friendships formed in the eighties, and he and Ellis had a pleasant conversation recalling the idealistic days of the New Fellowship.

It was a period of false calm. On September 14th Françoise was at Dover Mansions on one of her "Barnet week-ends." It was Ellis this time who felt that a distance had come between them. As they lay on the bed together, Françoise finally confessed that she was having a relationship with someone else, but refused to give his name. Naturally, Ellis knew at once; and grasped for the first time that Sélincourt was actually her lover. He was devastated because, unbelievable as it might seem, he had blinded himself to the possibility that there must be a physical relationship between them. Françoise knew that he would be hurt if she kept the truth from him, although she expressed astonishment that he was upset because she was involved in a sexual relationship with another man. She tried to justify herself by claiming that she felt he was growing distant from her because he had fallen in love with the American journalist Jane Burr. Ellis was sceptical of this: "I never had the faintest idea that such a process was going on inside you—so stupid am I—but to the psychoanalyst it would be clear. He would say that your *unconscious* self was saying, 'Yes, it's quite true that I have a new lover, but then, you see, the old one is growing so indifferent; he is tired of my caresses, he doesn't give me the caresses he used to, & he is becoming attached to another woman.' It is all so full of interest & some day perhaps we shall be able to see it all clearly & be amused."[56]

Ellis, on his part, accused her of having been deliberately vague about what had happened on her visits to Sand Pit. A tense, tortured scene followed, and the next day they began an endless series of long, analytic letters. For months they were completely obsessed by the situation, although Ellis was too proud even to confide in Margaret Sanger. He was tormented by the realization that Françoise had been unfaithful: "If you had said to me beforehand: 'I am in love with Hugh and I intend to form a relationship of some kind with him but do not intend to tell you about it,' I should have felt sad, but I should have said: 'Then we will say goodbye. You are perfectly free. And I think you are perfectly right. I know what a poor sort of lover I am, & I want you to have everything you need. I shall soon be able to rejoice over it, & anyhow, I shall never cease to feel, as long as I live, what wonderfully lovely years we have had together.' "[57]

Was he testing her? Ellis must have known that she had no intention of leaving Sélincourt, but she had no intention of giving up Havelock either. When she told him this, he was appalled and there was another painful scene. He asked her not to come again for a while because he wanted time to think things out clearly. "You imagine that it is just a little jealousy and that when I have conquered that (like you did your feeling about Hilda, etc), all will be well. But it is much more complicated than that. I learned all that there is to know about jealousy long before I knew you. It always arises sooner or later, & I have always met it with loving sympathy & conquered the jealousy—always it has been I who have retained the love & the other person who has been forgotten. But the difficulty now is more than that—it concerns my deepest instincts, my principles, ideals, things that are nearer to me than you are, because they are myself."[58] He was right that the situation was more complex than jealousy, though jealousy is never simple. What troubled him was that Françoise had been changed by Hugh, and that she had learned to subscribe to views and values which Ellis declared were anathema to him. It now appeared that Françoise had been misinterpreting Hinton's—and Rabelais's—"Love—and do what you like." Ellis asserted emphatically that he believed in fidelity and in not making love to anyone with whom one was not in love—hardly Hintonian—whereas Sélincourt believed that any two people drawn together should feel free to indulge their desires—and in this he was the new Hintonian. As for Ellis, "It has too often been supposed that my own views of love are loose and easy, but it's a damnable lie."[59] He had loved his *pétroleuse* for her fiery independence, but now she seemed supinely to have absorbed all Sélincourt's ideas. He had been a champion of women, Ellis admonished her, because to him it seemed the right of a woman to be a *personality*, and not a part of another person, her husband or anybody else.

Françoise found herself in misery at the suffering she was causing him. She threatened to go to a hotel in Southend for the week-end and tramp the streets. But Ellis summoned her to him by telegram: "Come soon be peaceful and comforted."[60] On October 8th he received a letter from Houghton Mifflin that they expected *The Dance of Life* to pass ten thousand copies before Christmas. "Lucky," he reflected, "that *The Dance* was finished in a state of blissful stupidity."[61] Was the miracle at an end? "I had thought that life was over when you came to me & brought me more joy—more *unalloyed* joy —than I had ever had in my life. I see now, of course, that I must have taken the precious gift too easily, & that I failed to guard against all the risks that surround every precious thing."[62] He advised her to read the chapter on "The Art of Morality" to understand what he really meant. But the question was: Could *he* really *live* what he believed? It was the supreme irony of his life that he was faced with his greatest crisis just after he had published *The Dance of Life*. In what was perhaps the most important letter he ever wrote, he mused: "When I was young I thought it would be possible to settle the problems of love, I thought that we only had to *understand* them,—& all the pains and difficulties of the world of love would melt away. I felt like the youthful Shelley (though I *never*, even when I worshipped him most, adopted his 'free love' notions) that we only had to overthrow ignorance & convention. (That was what inspired me to devote my life to the Sex Studies.) But I know now that what we can do merely touches the surface of things, that the great deep essential facts of life remain exactly the same as they always were, & that even people who really have possessed such large souls & fine intelligences as Olive and Edith and you are just as helpless in the face of insoluble problems as Lucretius and Catullus were two thousand years ago."[63] And himself? In his early naïveté he had confused sex with love. In his relationship with Edith he had learned that they can exist independently of each other; with Françoise he now understood that they were inextricably combined.

All through this period Ellis tried to understand what mistakes he had made and why the relationship had fallen short of perfection. Constantly he compared himself to Hugh. Hugh would have had no scruples about revealing the confidential secrets of others. Was he suggesting, perhaps, that Hugh was lacking in loyalty? Or that it was wrong of Ellis himself not to confide in the person whom he loved most in the world? "I have never told *anyone* (not even, except vaguely, when I *ought* to have done so) about my life with Edith— just as there are things about Olive (before I knew her) I have never, & never shall, tell to any one. Perhaps it is too late now, but I could not give a greater proof of love than to say I feel now I could tell you of the things I have never told anyone."[64]

But the principal difficulty was in coming to terms with the fact that he had to share her with another man. "I have just come across a remark of Olive's in a letter: 'I can *believe*, but I cannot *understand* that a man should be willing to share the woman he loves with another man.' Now *I* can *understand* & can even understand that it is very, very difficult to get the right conditioning for attaining it, while you think it can be attained carelessly, in a moment, under any conditions, & you grow angry when the difficulties are felt & you talk in a lofty way about 'vulgarity.' This attitude is surely not quite kind?"[65]

When Françoise remarked flippantly that the physical was not important, Ellis replied that this was "the very reverse of the truth. In some departments of life, the principle may be unimportant but *not in sex things*. It would be more true to say that the *spiritual* is unimportant. Do you imagine that coitus is unimportant? Olive said to me once that when a man puts his penis into a woman's vagina it is as if (assuming of course that she responds) he put his finger into her brain, stirred it round & round. Her whole nature is affected. Is it unimportant for a woman's whole nature to be affected?"[66] It must have been particularly galling to him to know that Hugh was renowned as a lover in the Karezza method of prolonged intercourse which Ellis had speculated on theoretically in the *Studies*. In *My Life* he allowed his bitterness to spill over into a remark on "sexual athletes" who steal other men's sweethearts.

Never did Ellis have to think more carefully, more realistically, more magnanimously. It was the test of a lifetime's experience and theorizing—and he emerged magnificently from the ordeal. It would have been easy to castigate Sélincourt, and time and time again his thoughts reverted to the extravagant letters Sélincourt had written to him. On the very day of the revelation—September 14th—Sélincourt was writing: "[The Bear's] visit was a delight to all of us from the moment of her arrival, especially of course to me. I firmly 'bagged' the privilege of her company. . . . O King, O King! my love to you Havelock, ears back you know, tail lowered and wagging, in helpless hopeless speechless gratitude—Hugh."[67] These effusive letters, it now appeared to him, really meant, "The angel who was sent from Heaven for your joy and consolation is now my pet monkey, with lots of funny tricks."[68] He tried to reason with Françoise: "One hardly expects a man to show his love and admiration for a writer by going to bed with that writer's sweetheart!"[69] But he was to undergo many conflicts of feeling toward Sélincourt in the course of time, and for the present it was impossible to continue the correspondence with him. Sélincourt was like "a Shelley or a Hinton, who also had beautiful visions of life, but when they tried to carry them out made a terrible muddle of their lives & spread misery round them. These ideas, as you know, have always seemed fascinating to me, but *they*

are not my ideas. They are almost the opposite of them (And when
you spoke of S. d J. carrying out *my* ideas with you, it made me feel
sick)."*[70] He was very sorry that Françoise had told Sélincourt that
he knew about their affair because he realized that there was absolutely nothing that Sélincourt could do at this point to alter the
situation.

These were days of black despair. Early in October he confessed
to her that "Before your letter came this morning, my darling one,
I was almost beginning to wonder whether I could go on living."[71]
Constantly he tried to comfort Françoise, who complained that the
future would only consist of perpetual worry and pain. He assured
her that she was not to blame, that it was life that had done this to
him, and that they were going through "a phase of reassessment"
and when it was accomplished they would be at peace again. He
never realized that his doctrine of change which he had emphasized
in *The Dance of Life* would be put to so severe a test in his own life.
"Love is a *living* thing," he had always told her, "and needs constant
care & nourishment, & like all living things is always changing."[72] He
could not bear to think that his own unhappiness might spoil the
process of radiant development which he had watched so proudly in
Françoise since he had first known her. "I know how unreasonable &
horrid I am. I know that Soleil de Joie, or anyone who knew anything
at all about it, would say about me: *What then could he expect?* He
was considerably older, and an unsatisfactory lover, and in six years
the novelty has worn off & a new exuberant passionate lover was
bound to conquer in a moment. I know all that, & I know it was all
reasonable, & natural, & beautiful. Only *reason* has so little to do
with *miracles!* I was living in a miracle & was completely spoilt by
unreasonably lovely things. Soon, however, I shall be quite reasonable, & I am already learning to laugh at myself."[73] On October 24th
he told her that on her next visit he wanted to buy her new slippers:
"When you come on Saturday, I hope it will be quite *soon* after 12,

---

    * Yet on September 20th, 1923, he wrote to H. L. Mencken, who was asking
him for articles for the newly founded *American Mercury*: "Unless prostitutes are to
be regarded as honourable members of society, it seems to me desirable that
prostitutes should be so far as possible diminished, & there can scarcely be any other
method of achieving that end except by securing, and reciprocating as 'moral,' a
greater degree of sexual freedom among the general population. That seems to me
fairly obvious" (H. L. Mencken Papers, Manuscripts and Archives Division, New
York Public Library, Astor, Lenox and Tilden Foundations).

for I want to take you out to buy new slippers for use here. (You see I am reckoning on our *not* separating!) The old ones are getting very worn; I took them out to look at (& kiss) this afternoon. This seems the right moment, when we are starting a new path of life, to put on new slippers to walk in it, & we shall have to have *better* ones! The old ones I will keep, as a sweet memory of my lovely Naiad, among other sacred treasures which will be destroyed when I die." The only possible solution, he concluded wryly at one point, was to find a Soleil de Joie of his own, but he didn't really want further complications in his life. And he was not "a pale departing ghost, but quite human, capable of suffering acutely, & as deeply & horribly in love as I have *ever* been."[74]

Since he was returning to Cornwall for the winter months, it was necessary to come to some sort of understanding before his departure. He took out all Françoise's letters written during the past year, divided them up into twelve bundles, and read right through them with new insight. What emerged above all else was Françoise's deliberate deception. She would say, Oh, I must tell you about my last meeting with Sélincourt in my next letter, and then deliberately forget ever to mention it again. But Ellis realized that she would never have fallen so rapturously in love with Sélincourt—as he was now certain she had done the first time Sélincourt visited her—if he himself had not failed her in some way. Of course there was the obvious reason that Sélincourt was so much younger and more virile, but Ellis was not going to let himself fall into the trap of self-pity and believe that this could be the only reason. Certainly he asked himself: Where was I to blame? He drew on his own memories of Olive, Edith, and Margaret for comparison. Olive had once told him that sometimes a situation can arise in love when one makes a little ball of snow on the mountainside, it slides from one's hand, rolls down the mountainside, gets bigger and bigger—until it is an avalanche that no one can stop. "That did not happen to her and me. But that is what is happening now. And I can do nothing to help. And you can do nothing to help. We can only look on and watch. No doubt I shall get hardened in time. But even that is not an altogether desirable result. And it has never hitherto been my aim in life to become callous."[75]

He tried honestly to confront his own "infidelities," and the friendships which might have hurt Françoise. Margaret had appealed to him, he begged Françoise to believe, not sexually, but for her femininity. After Françoise had come into his life, Margaret was too close for him to push her away. But if he had known of Françoise's jealousy, "it would have prevented me from allowing friendship to slip once or twice (very seldom) into little acts of physical intimacy which gave me no pleasure even at the moment & made me feel rather ashamed (& which *now*, when I know how you felt, seem a *horror* to me)." Desire was completely lacking in the friendship. "She has never done anything to cause me suffering, & she has never given me joy & inspiration. It is a most beautiful & happy relation-ship—always calm & *level*. But—love—there are glorious heights & awful abysses." Margaret was not the only woman with whom these intimacies occurred, but "The difference between us has been that my 'infidelities' (I never so regarded them) were *sins*, but very small; yours were *not* a sin, but very big."[76]

By late November, when he left for Cornwall, he had faced the fact that they had to live with an entirely new situation and that they would have to maintain a more candid relationship in the future. But the active acceptance of this realization was a matter of arduous effort. One thing was certain: the inequality of the old relationship was at an end. "I realise that we cannot travel backwards but want to go forward & I am attaining courage & peace, while you cannot yet abandon the hope of going back to a stage that is passed."[77] He be-lieved that they could be even closer, "though not perhaps happier, and I shall say all sorts of horrid things to you, about myself, & about third persons." No longer would Françoise be humble before her great and venerated Faun. They had caused each other suffering, the most basic of egalitarian experiences. "You have been much too respectful to me," he told her, "treating me as if I were as old as I seem, & possessing a wisdom which I haven't a trace of."[78] H. L. Mencken had described Ellis as "the most civilized man in England"; and Vita Sackville-West in *The Nation*, referring to Mencken's as-sessment, said that "this little tribute to Havelock Ellis is so gratify-ing to admirers of that splendid intellect." Ellis's reaction was rueful: "Silly intellect *I* call it!" He also thought sadly of all the people who came to him in quest of help while he was unable to help himself.

In Cornwall, completely by himself, he struggled through to a form of peace, although there were days when he didn't seem to make any headway at all. "It is hard to believe that I am the same person who came here a year ago & was eagerly working at *The Dance of Life* and joyfully awaiting the coming of the Naiad. Now my mind is a blank. I want nothing, I have energy for nothing; a moderate walk exhausts me, for when the soul has lost its wings the body too grows weary."[79] On December 2nd the weather turned mild, the sort of gentle Cornish day Ellis usually loved so much: "But somehow it was one of my worst & lowest days—I felt I could not go on any longer. If only I could have died a year ago! Everything then would have been perfect & I might have left a sweet memory behind instead of a hateful one." He was not working absorbedly at a book as he had done the previous year and now there was time for long walks and brooding reflections. Françoise's inability to grasp how fundamentally everything had changed troubled him so much that he found himself telling her, "I often think that the kindest thing we could do for each other would be to separate *completely*. You no longer *really* need me, & I have no peace when I think of you. Only it is not my nature to forget, & I don't know how I can begin now."[80] But he still desperately wanted her to be with him during the Christmas break. "How long do you propose to stay? And when does the Sand Pit come in? Can you stay longer this time? . . . I have a sort of intuition that we may not be together again, so it is well that we should have a nice long time."[81] When she worried about how much this would cost, he assured her: "As to the cost of your Christmas holiday, loving Naiad, don't think of it! The House of Love is not a counting house. Money is *very important* when one hasn't got any; but when one has a little, as I have now for the first time in my life, it has no value for me."[82] Françoise had begun to tease him about his misery and told him that she laughed at his ponderous pessimism. "I laugh at myself," he replied. "Life *is* ridiculous. I always think of the story someone told Edith of the Indian Mahatma, who, when he was told that his great friend, another Mahatma, had been eaten by a tiger, burst out laughing, & exclaimed: 'What a lark!' I am sure that is the right spirit. . . ."[83]

It was a rare moment of humour. Basically, Ellis lacked humour, and the perpetual probings and re-examinations and analyses of nuances of feeling at times seem almost verging on the absurd. But unhappy lovers who often seem comical to other people never seem so to themselves. And for a man who had spent a large part of his life in what he described as "silent suffering," it was therapeutic for him finally to articulate his hurt. On the other hand, he didn't regret the reserve that had always been habitual to him. "It has provided the inner spiritual foundation which is the secret of what you call 'genius' in me. In another way, it has been the main reason why love for me has never *in the end* been a failure, & why I have never had a *broken* relationship with anyone."[84]

The extreme oscillations of mood continued. When, some months before, Françoise had described herself and Hugh as Havelock's "spiritual children," he had reacted with indignation. The recollection of this sentimental notion was even more irritating now to his frayed nerves. "With regard to my 'spiritual children,' it was not that I minded you specially associating yourself with Hugh, in opposition to me, as two children together; it would have been the same if *anyone* else. I don't *want* children. I never did. I hate children. I am a child myself & know too much about them."[85] But the greatest pain of all was his conviction that she no longer looked to him alone for new experiences. In the past it had always been he who introduced her to new books, new places, new music. When he thought suddenly that she must see the Van Gogh exhibition at the Leicester Gallery, his instant reaction now was, " 'Why trouble about it? Her interests are in another person's hands now.' And the same on the physical as the spiritual side. It used to be & still is, delicious to me to think of all the little personal things & beautiful love ways of you. But now, instantly, I am torn away from that thought by the corresponding thought: 'Yes, but that is given to someone else now.' And there is not left one single thing—of which I think peacefully & happily & say: 'Well, anyhow, *that* is left me still.' Of course I know it is natural and inevitable that I should thus be left torn & desolate. In time, no doubt, I shall feel it does not matter."[86]

Ellis "detested" D. H. Lawrence, but he took *Kangaroo** with him to Cadgwith and the novel again and again seemed to speak his very thoughts, particularly of a love relationship being a "kind of magnet or electrical current, always, *even unconsciously*, at work, so long as it remains unbroken, to uphold and inspire."[87] He now realized that he had been unfair to Lawrence without knowing much about him. "I see that there are real streaks of genius & insight in the man."[88]

Shortly before Christmas a note of genuine confidence enters his letters. Françoise had written that the message of *The Dance of Life*

---

* Published earlier that year.

presented the solution to their difficulties. He agreed, but insisted that he had never said that solutions are easy or quick. "I *do* say that life is a dance and that there is in it an infinite flexibility, but I also say that it is infinitely difficult & that the dancer may always expect to find his slippers full of blood. There has usually been blood in my slippers. That is why these wonderful years with you were a miracle— a miracle that can never be repeated in my short life."[89]

CHAPTER 21

HEALING

THE HEALING PROCESS WAS SLOW. HOW COULD IT BE ANYTHING ELSE? When progress was made, it was unconscious; when a measure of peace seemed to be attained, tormenting thoughts would assail him. The three months in Cornwall were peaceful, too peaceful, because he had no serious work to occupy his mind. The F. A. Davis Company—the publishers of the Sex *Studies*—wanted him to add a seventh volume to the series, but while he agreed to the project, he could not get down to making a beginning. He had brought with him the early poems he had written in Australia—these were always of great sentimental value to him—and now he reworked them in the light of real experience.

He knew, what few others realized, that he was basically deeply emotional. His emotions had been completely concentrated on Françoise during the past six years, and it was a shock to him to discover that, for all her quick emotionalism, there was in her something essentially different in kind where her feelings were concerned. Sélincourt was obsessed with a temporary infatuation until he moved on to another woman; Françoise was obsessed with Sélincourt; and Ellis was obsessed with the total situation. The fortnight they spent together after Christmas 1923 did not seem to create greater understanding between them. Shortly after she left, Ellis wrote to her: "You always seem to think that I do not understand your feeling towards S. de J. (as you understand it), or your feeling towards me but I understand them both, & have all along. The difficulty is that *you* never seem to understand how the *character* of your love has changed, & how *you* have changed, & how the whole *situation* has changed, & that those changes have made everything different."[1]

On February 13th he experienced a shock of a different kind. While he was defecating in an enclosed hollow in the cliffs the ground gave way beneath him and he rolled hundreds of feet down the cliff, narrowly escaping death. Miraculously, apart from a sore shoulder, he had no injuries. The mishap did nothing to jolt him out of his obsessionalism. He was rereading all Françoise's dreams from 1918, hoping that somehow these would give him insight into their predicament. Triumphantly he came upon an early one which seemed to show that at the beginning of their relationship, before being contaminated by Sélincourt's views, she believed as fervently as he did in sexual fidelity, what Ellis called "one of the fundamental facts of life." "The most intimate things of all," he tried to explain, "seem to me to have their sacred & sacramental & inspiring character by being reserved; as soon as they are given to another they are no longer precious; they have lost their sacredness; they can no longer touch the *deepest* parts of my nature. The kind of love that is left—cumulative love, courtesan love, as you call it—is very nice, but it is not sacred or inspiring, not, at all events, to anyone who has known the higher kind."[2]

The third series of *Impressions and Comments* (1920–3) was to come out later that year. In the spring of 1921, when Ellis was in Tunbridge Wells recuperating from his duodenal attack, he had written what he considered his finest piece of prose, "A Revelation," and he now wished to include it in the new collection. The opening sets the tone of the over-elaborated style:

> From time to time, at long intervals, she would drift into my room, like a large white bird hovering tremulously over the edge of a cliff, a shy and sinuous figure, so slender and so tall that she seemed frail, yet lithe, one divined, of firm and solid texture.[3]

This divine shape one day suddenly, unexpectedly, miraculously divests itself of its garments and sheds kisses on him. Most wonderful of all, on another occasion, at twilight,

> The tall form languidly arose and stood erect, taut and massive it seemed now with the length of those straight adolescent legs still

more ravishing in their unyielding pride, and the form before me
seemed to become some adorable Olympian vase, and a large stream
gushed afar in the glistering liquid arch, endlessly, it seemed to my
wondering eyes, as I contemplated with enthralled gaze this proto-
typal statue of the Fountain of Life, carved by the hands of some
daring and divine architect, out of marble like flesh, that marble which
has in its texture the mingled warm and matt tones of human flesh,
mortal and immortal at once, motionless and passive, yet of wondrous
energy, the image of creative arrogance; while on the firm austere lines
of the face one read, not pride, but a shy and diffident smile, the fear
lest to the merely human spectator that which is transcendent should
be mistaken for what is gross.[4]

No wonder Hugh de Sélincourt was entranced by it!—"the most
beautiful thing in my opinion he has ever written," he told Margaret
Sanger.[5] The self-conscious artifice indicates that, for Ellis, Pater
was still the supreme stylist. Since the divine form was a real
"Person," Ellis felt it courteous to show it to her before publication. The lady was Hilda Doolittle, now living with her friend
Bryher in Switzerland; and the incident had taken place in 1919
before they left on the voyage to Greece. H.D. was horrified. "Think
of the cheek of that Hilda!" Ellis complained to Françoise. "She
wants me to leave out of the Impression the whole account of the
rainbow stream. I am going to tell her that no one will recognise
that!"[6] H.D. was unconvinced. She wanted both the first paragraph
and "the rainbow stream" passage omitted, as well as minor descriptive details. "I want to make it clear that if the 'stream' portion
remains as you say you wish it, then I think it only fair to the
Person to make some very drastic alterations."[7] Numerous letters
were exchanged, and H.D. eventually surrendered graciously: "It is
certainly quite, quite too beautiful for the 'Person.' I must just
believe it was meant for someone else and so admire it (or try to)
impersonally."[8]

On April 2nd, 1924, Ellis was startled to receive the following
telegram: "If you should have a smile anywhere within reach please
do send it to me Hugh Sélincourt."[9] His first impulse was not to
reply, and in a state of indecision he finally sent the following:
"Good wishes always."[10] Margaret Sanger, who was writing regularly
both to Ellis and to Sélincourt, sensed that something was wrong
between them. An offer was made to Ellis, through Margaret, to go

to America to advise on social hygiene for three months, for which he was to be paid between £5,000 and £10,000—which of course he refused immediately. "As for money," he playfully informed Françoise, "the only golden streams that Fauns value are, as you know, those of Naiad source."[11] Sélincourt commiserated with Margaret's disappointment, adding that he wished also that Ellis could be induced to visit Sand Pit. His obtuse insensitivity is staggering. "And that wish I keep on wishing, as though wishing it strongly actually put powers at work which bring the wish to fulfilment . . . in spite of the fact that its fulfilment seems more remote than ever, as Havelock isn't pleased with me at the moment."[12] When Margaret pressed him for details, he replied that he couldn't possibly answer her: *Don't know anything about it. Never make the least reference to it, as you love me! Time will make all things right. Of that I am confident.*"[13] But Margaret was persistent, and tried another tack. To her inquiries about Françoise, Ellis replied: "Poor darling Françoise is dear & sweet. The only thing wrong with her is that she is too lovable & too loving, & this leads to complications & troubles to herself & to her devoted friends."[14] To "Beloved Bear," Sélincourt wrote on October 1st: "All Margaret *knows* (or rather all I have told Margaret: her intuition is amazing and may have told her more) is that Havelock is displeased with me: but I have complete faith in her; she is really loving and constructive—creative—all she touches: and *she'll only help.* But it makes one's heart ache—these stupid misunderstandings: when it might and should be, the whole thing, one great cumulative source of joy and creative power."[15] It might have been a "great cumulative source of joy," but Hugh was careful not to reveal his affair with Margaret to Françoise, Margaret never told Françoise of her infatuation for Hugh, and no one told anything to Havelock. Of course Margaret wormed the whole story out of Françoise when she arrived in the autumn, and on December 14th wrote to her:

> "They *must* be friends! I did so little yet the situation was too delicate to do more. If only Havelock would talk about it—but he would not. At times I was near being hurt, when I gave every opportunity—made every approach—hoping that the love and confidence I had packed burden like upon his shoulders for these past years would get a 'come back' and consequently a loving

friendly confiding. But it did not happen. So my hands were tied, I felt that friendship can be a useless thing and perhaps a nuisance to one who wishes to be let alone.

"In your poem—lovely, exquisite, delicate—you say almost that—*

"Does our love trouble him?

"Not yours of course—But the rest of us who toss our affection & adoration at his feet for him to try and stumble over."[16]

To add to the complications, Margaret Sanger was now having an affair with Janet de Sélincourt's lover, Harold Child.

In May, Arthur Symons proposed that he and Ellis should go to Paris the following month and recapture the wonder of their marvellous excursion in 1890. They were old, Symons was nervous and cantankerous, Ellis was nervous and heart-broken, but the idea seemed a good one. On this occasion they stayed at a far more elegant hotel, chosen this time by Symons, the Hôtel Régina in the Place Rivoli. The unfamiliar social whirl into which Symons plunged them anaesthetized memory for an interval. "Quite wonderful how sociable I become in France!" Ellis exclaimed to Margaret.[17] He encountered a world he had never known before—the world of Nancy Cunard† and late-night parties. He was bemused by the whole experience; it was interesting meeting people like Nancy Cunard, "but of course they belong to a world that is remote from me, & is not mine," he told Françoise. "But as to that I also feel now that S. de J. and you belong to another world that is not mine, & as you so truly said he had impregnated you with his ideas, so that you can (you say) no longer agree with the simple things I said in my letter of February 16. I realise that I must be content now with my own world and my own lovely memories."[18]

One morning they called at Sylvia Beach's book shop and she rang up James Joyce, who came over immediately, as he remembered an article Symons had written praising *Chamber Music*.‡ They liked him much better than his picture would have led them to expect. "He is very fair (the portraits make him dark) and he has the charm-

---

* "Le Maître," published in the Havelock Ellis birthday issue of *The Birth Control Review*, February 1926. See Appendix A.

† Nancy Cunard (1896–1965) was a leader of intellectual café society in the twenties. She became an active supporter of the Republicans in the Spanish Civil War.

‡ In *The Nation* (London) LXXIII, 15 Oct. 1907.

ing reckless genial Irish way about him. Is still suffering from his eyes (syphilis they say)."[19] Miss Beach, in turn, was observing Ellis and Symons:

> They were a strangely assorted pair of travelling companions: Symons, a pale fragile sort of poet, with a complexion that looked made up, and Havelock Ellis, with his Apostle's head, out of which had come all those volumes on sex to enlighten a whole generation puzzled over their problems.[20]

On another occasion they came to take her out to lunch:

> Sitting at a table between these two winged creatures was an experience as curious as it could be. Their menus were characteristic. Symons, an epicure, conferred with the waiter and the sommelier and won the respect of both by his choice of "cuisinés" dishes and the right wines. Dr. Ellis said he would like vegetables, and no wine, thank you, just water. The waiter was a long time procuring these two articles. My own menu was something between the two extremes.[21]

The conversation doesn't sound very intoxicating. It was confined to Ellis's and Symons's loss of two pairs of shoes in the course of their journey.

On his return Ellis told people that he feared France no longer agreed with him. He had a bad cold and felt "generally fatigued and useless."[22] Françoise suggested that they go away together to Cornwall, which usually did wonders in restoring his sense of well-being. They found a bungalow on a deserted bay on the north coast, but were kept indoors most of the time by persistent rain—an opportunity to revive the past in all its painful detail. His sense of defeat informs a letter he wrote to Françoise shortly after their return: "I woke up lonely & melancholy & had the most desolate day I have had this year—not at all 'resigned' which you find so deplorable. Instead of resignation I just had the abject sense of failure, & that you had no power to understand or comfort me, & that I could not any longer help or comfort you."[23]

The unexpected arrival of Margaret Sanger in England in October failed to shake his nagging preoccupation with Sélincourt. "There is no escaping from the nightmare of his iron heel!" he wailed.[24] His self-pity wasn't relieved by Margaret's ecstatic description of life at Sand Pit. "I was full of pain to think that the only reason why dear Naiad does not go there oftener is all that horrible Faun. She says

Sélincourt is much improved, 'clarified' she called it, & developed. It was as though he had lately gone through some experience—she does not know what, perhaps something to do with Janet—which has developed him. She says that (as you know) he is much absorbed in Blake now. He told her he was much puzzled over a saying he found in Blake: 'One may forgive an enemy, but it is impossible to forgive a friend.' Margaret explained to him that it was quite true. There does not seem to have been much mention of me or you. Margaret asked if I had seen Sélincourt lately, & I replied that I had not seen him just lately."[25]

However, only a week later he was to run into him unexpectedly at Margaret's hotel. On hearing Ellis's name announced, Sélincourt turned white and exclaimed: "Why didn't you tell me he was coming?" Margaret was puzzled, but put it down to his "emotional temperament."[26] (Margaret, at this point, had not yet heard the complete story.) They stayed for four uncomfortable hours and were extremely polite to each other.

But Sélincourt continued to haunt him. Because of the misery his rival had caused him the previous winter, he realized that he could not face Cadgwith again, and decided on trying somewhere completely different, Guernsey. He found the scenery monotonous, the walks exhaustible, and it was difficult to find suitable rooms. Nevertheless, the climate was pleasant and on December 10th he reported: "*Glorious* day today, cloudless sky, & you know that I can never be *quite* unhappy when the sun shines. I should like to die in sunshine."[27] Thoughts of death and the iron heel of Sélincourt still oppressed him: "When Soleil de Joie arrived I went & there is nothing much of me left. . . . But if nothing can kill my love, I am not so sure about killing *me!* In old days when I was stronger & my work in the world not done, I used to feel that nothing could kill me, & nothing did, though one way or another I had awful things to contend with. But now it is different. I am at the end of things. I try to be as cheerful as I can & I am in excellent looking health but I no longer have heart for anything. I am constantly having work offered me, & I refuse it all, saying I am 'too busy' but I am doing nothing, as you know. . . . It is most fortunate that I got the 'Dance of Life' finished when I did, for otherwise I should be earning nothing now."[28] Yet the third volume of *Impressions and Comments*, which he always regarded tenderly as the most personal of his books, had come out in November, and on December 14th he said, "I see that my future work will lie in arranging & finishing off all the things that have been left over, & there is so much that it will take years."[29]

The persistent spirit of life was reasserting itself whether he realized it or not. Françoise arrived just after Christmas in the worst storm in years, but her visit left him with beautiful and peaceful thoughts. After her departure he still felt her presence in the next room "even though I hear no cascades."[30] Françoise, too, continued to have many periods of despair and on February 5th, 1925, he wrote her a long, encouraging letter in which he admitted that, like most restless and anxious people, he often took pleasure in thoughts of rest and death—but usually on damp, sunless days or sleepless nights. However, if he followed his father's example, at sixty-six he would still have twenty-one years of life and health ahead of him. In that case, he and Françoise could grow old together, or, like Goethe at eighty, find "inspiration" elsewhere. "But even if I don't follow my father's example, & die tomorrow, it is still quite right & natural that I should feel content & satisfied at the thought that my work in the world is done & that I have achieved all—indeed far more than all— that as a youth I set out to attempt."[31] But for Françoise, at thirty-nine, to long for death was absurd. She had escaped what he considered the real martyrdom which most women endure in a life of *ennui.* Everyone has moods of despair, he encouraged her, but they mustn't be taken too seriously. "Real life is made up of joy & suffering—I think you have always been really alive—& that is a thing to rejoice over—even suffering is a thing to rejoice over. Nothing in the world more terrible than the people who haven't suffered & can't suffer!"[32]

The moods continued to oscillate, but one can gradually trace the slow climb out of the abyss. On December 16th, 1924, he tells her, "As you see, dear, I no longer have any strength or spirit left. The world (or, if you like, Soleil de Joie) has been too much for me. Ten or twenty years ago it would have been different. Now there is nothing I want or care about. I am sorry I should be a drag on your beautiful energy."[33] By March 19th, 1925, he was able to write: "I am pleased you have heard from S. de J. He exists for me now in, & through you. So if you say you want anything [nothing?] more to do with him I shall be quite content to say the same. And if you keep in touch with him & tell me how fascinating he is, there is always a chance that I may some day say: 'Dear me! I should like to see him.' The misfortune has been that I knew him before he knew you, & that he knew you through me. That is very difficult indeed to get over."[34] But a letter written the previous month reveals a magnanimity and a wisdom that could have been reached only through intense suffering: "I am not a God, but only a very human creature, full of defects & always failing, & with limitations & peculiarities & shyness & reserves—a creature that has always been liable to be wounded at a touch. I cannot alter my nature & I do not think anything is gained by hiding things & pretending, but that it is best in love to be open. . . . I think you made mistakes & I made mistakes. But your mistakes were due to nobility of spirit & mine to reserve & stupidity."[35]

In September 1924 he turned down an offer by Curtis Brown for an American lecture tour which would have netted him $6,000. But attention from America continued to pursue him. An academic, Isaac Goldberg, wrote that he wished to write a biography of him. Ellis agreed, but warned him that it would not be a real biography: "It is impossible to write anything like a *real* biography of a living person, nor is it easy of a person you do not personally know."[36] In the days before the annual migration of trans-Atlantic scholars, Goldberg intended to write the book without even visiting Ellis, but—although Françoise did not like the "smell" of Goldberg—Ellis agreed to supply him with all the information he needed, something he was able to do because he was not occupied with other work. Beginning in February 1924, they corresponded for a year and a half; and Ellis's letters are extremely interesting as revelations of the way he viewed himself, although the book itself must be regarded as suspect since Goldberg did no original work for himself but simply accepted Ellis's views as gospel. Ellis advised him not to ask any of his friends for letters and he especially did not want Hugh de Sélincourt to be troubled. "If you have any questions to ask," Ellis encouraged him, "do not fear that I may be offended! I am quite able to look at myself with scientific detachment. It is satisfactory to me that you propose to put my sex work in a secondary position. The fact that my sex studies have been the chief work of my life has often misled people into thinking that I am concerned with sex to an exaggerated extent. (And the volume of 'Sexual Inversion' led many would-be clever people to conclude—altogether wrongly—that I am homosexual.)"[37] In answer to a query of Goldberg's, he described himself as "firm, inflexible, but quietly, not in an aggressive or combative way."[38] Finally, he told him unequivocally that he was opposed to the publication of intimate facts while he was still alive. "Moreover, though I do not feel that I have any cause to be ashamed, I do not accept conventional standards & do not wish to be judged by them. So I must ask you, please, to avoid suggesting that I can be put forward as a model of conventional goodness. There is no need to raise the question, though, personally, I think it quite right to raise it in a real biography of a person no longer living."[39] People were beginning to write about him as a personality. Jane Burr—who repelled him by her excessive "Jewishness" and fascinated him by her vitality—had returned to the States, and he was alarmed to hear that she had written an "intimate" profile of him; but was greatly relieved to see its innocuous character when it appeared in *The Birth Control Review*. They continued a lively correspondence for the rest of his life.

During 1924, too, he was in constant correspondence with Joseph Ishill, an anarchist, who operated a hand press in his home in New Jersey. Ishill suggested that he print two volumes of Edith's essays and stories in fine limited editions, a proposal that delighted Ellis, who always felt that Edith had not been sufficiently appreciated; and he busied himself with collecting the material for Ishill as well as producing testimonials from Stella Browne, Daphne Bax, and Edward Carpenter.

Another anarchist, Emma Goldman, arrived from America and paid him two visits in 1925. She told him that he had been a great inspiration in her life. She had assumed—as many people did—that he would have extremely radical political views, but was disappointed to find how basically cautious he was. She had been in England in 1898 and had managed to get hold of several copies of *Sexual Inversion*; and later in correspondence she and Ellis agreed on the absurdity of many homosexuals attributing homosexuality to others on the flimsiest grounds. As for political books, particularly on Russia, which she proposed to send him, he replied: "I am not interested in the details of these political questions. I am in general sympathy with what you say of the Russian situation but I do not feel anxious to see the Bolshevik regime violently overthrown to give place to something worse. It may develop into something better if allowed to grow."[40] For a woman of her ardent spirit, his attitude seemed weary

and distressingly pessimistic, the voice of a recluse who had withdrawn from the stress of practical politics. Yet later (1928), when
she looked back on this visit to England during a period when she was
near despair, the only individuals, she said, who gave her any help
were Rebecca West, Edward Carpenter, and—Havelock Ellis. It is
difficult to see what encouragement Ellis could possibly have given
her.

Another American visitor was the dancer Ted Shawn, for whom
Ellis had been an inspirational force, the "Sage of Canterbury Road."
He and his wife, Ruth St. Denis, came to Ellis because they were
having a basic disagreement on what marriage should be. Shawn
believed in sexual fidelity and Ruth wanted a freer arrangement.
After talking to Ellis, Ruth agreed to sexual fidelity for the sake of
their dance school, Denishawn. Shawn wrote gratefully to him: "I
think that yours is the magic touch—that you possess a profound
knowledge of the alchemy of hearts—for we have progressed into a
state of harmony and real love greater than anything we have known
before. I am very grateful."[41] Shawn persuaded Ellis to write the
preface to *The American Ballet* (1926); and whenever they were in
England they made a point of visiting him.

His American contacts were not altogether pleasant. In 1925
he was reminded of his ordeal of 1898. An American woman,
Gertrude Beasley, took him a manuscript of the story of her youth
in Texas—*My First Thirty Years*. He was much impressed by the
frank account and, realizing that it would have difficulty finding a
publisher in England, wrote to Bryher's American husband, Robert
McAlmon, whose firm, Contact Press, was publishing advanced
authors like Gertrude Stein and Hemingway in Paris. The memoir
was published in the summer of 1925 and when it was shipped to
Britain, customs officials—probably alerted—seized the proofs on
entry.* Ellis did what he could to secure her a good lawyer. "The
attack on Gertrude Beasley is a great shock to me," he told Françoise;
"I can think of nothing else. The world is such an evil place that I
have only one wish now & that is to get out of it as quickly as possible."[42] The public prosecutor, Sir Archibald Bodkin, was something of a zealot in ferreting out pornographic literature. The
charge laid against Miss Beasley was that she had neglected to

---

* They were also seized by American customs the following year.

register as an alien. Bertrand Russell offered to pay all her expenses and she was let off with a £5 fine. Ellis arranged for a copy of her book to be sent to Margaret Sanger from Paris. "It is a *remarkable* book though one cannot exactly *like* it, & one feels that G.B. is too much obsessed by her family. She needs a lover to make her forget her family."[43]

Through all these contacts with the world, life was reasserting itself, and in his correspondence of 1925 a new note of cheerfulness appears. It is true that he had reached a stage of acceptance of Françoise's liaison with Sélincourt, but the principal reason for his renewed interest in life was the move to a cottage in the Chilterns in the summer of 1925. He had desired a place of this sort for some years and in February he and the faithful Mneme found exactly what he wanted, Little Frieth, near Henley-on-Thames. It was rather primitive and not as pretty as the ill-fated Woodpecker at West Drayton, the last home he had shared with Edith, but the extensive grounds had fruit trees and the whole atmosphere of the place suggested peace, while London was only thirty miles away if he wanted to get into town. He moved in by the middle of April on a six months' lease, and from this date his letters are filled with details of his daily routine, choosing curtains, planting seeds, an acute awareness of changing weather. He also for the first time bought a gramophone and took great delight in choosing records. When he was alone he would put on Brahms's Violin Concerto and dance around the room. It must have been a splendid sight! Here, too, he could invite friends to stay in complete privacy—provided one maintained a certain prudence. He suggested to Françoise that she bring François for the first part of her visit—"As to gossip, it mayn't much matter, but when new people come in a village, everyone *at first* stares & talks, & it is better that Madame Cyon should *begin* by rubbing in the impression that she is a matronly lady with a son,— as the first impression lasts."[44] Sunbaths in the nude were also initiated after the model of Sand Pit, although greater precautions had to be taken.* With his renewed pleasure in life, he could not refuse Arthur Symons, who wrote asking for a loan of £30. "You know when you stayed with me at Fountain Court, you paid me

---

* His interest in sunbathing was very much stimulated by the enthusiastic accounts of the German *Nacktkultur* Societies by an American acquaintance, Professor Maurice Parmelee. Ellis caught a bad cold from stalking around the house naked.

whenever you liked to do so. My position,—for the present, has changed for the worse. . . . You and you only have always helped me in any emergency—and this is one—And—need I add?—you are my oldest and my best friend."[45]

Most remarkable of all the visitors was Hugh de Sélincourt. For some months Françoise had been working persistently towards a reconciliation between the two men. When she reminded Ellis that he had once loved Hugh, he replied that this was sheer nonsense, that his interest in him was literary rather than personal. "I admired and enjoyed his novels, & I appreciated his admiration for my work, & it gave me pleasure both to give him pleasure & to have the benefit of his literary taste by showing him some of the 'Impressions.' But I did not feel drawn to him personally & the meetings were at *his* suggestion"[46]—a not altogether accurate statement. A long, rapturous piece on Ellis by Sélincourt appeared in the February *Birth Control Review*. "I don't exactly feel that I should have been made the subject of it," Ellis complained to Margaret Sanger, "& there isn't much about friendship in my books as distinct from love."[47]

In any event, by temperament Ellis disliked being on bad terms with anyone and the hurt by now was sufficiently muffled that he could agree to see him. Early in May he sent him a copy of his early sonnets which the Golden Cockerel Press had brought out in a limited edition. Margaret Sanger, who was now privy to the whole situation, was kept informed of every move. Sélincourt wrote: "Oh Margaret—you darling—Havelock sent me his book—'Folk Songs and Sonnets'—with To Hugh de Sélincourt from H E written in it. No letter, no suggestion of seeing him yet, but the old rock is melting, bless him, to me again; I know he must, & I can wait— meanwhile the loveliness of that book!! You can think how happy I am."[48]

The turning-point for Ellis seems to have been reached by May 26th, when he wrote freely to Françoise: ". . . when you are able to write that you accept me & my feelings from the bottom of your heart, as I accept you & your feelings from the bottom of my heart— having faced everything as bravely as I am able to do & rebelling at nothing—then we shall be very, very close. That is the only thing that I want you to write. It is feelings only that matter, & we cannot control them, we can only accept them."[49] The invitation to Little Frieth came accordingly—written rather archly—suggesting that

Sélincourt come on May 29th and stay the night. Sélincourt was in a delirium of expectation. On the appointed day he hired a car and drove up from Sussex and had tea at the next village in order to time his arrival precisely. Ellis and Françoise came down the lane to meet him and, despite a good deal of tension in the air, Sélincourt sat glowing and watching "The Old Wonder." In the earth closet he found a characteristic Havelock touch—the flower of a white weed put carefully in the pail. For dinner there was Spanish wine and fresh asparagus. They laughed over Hugh's limericks, which Ellis seemed to find amusing. "The loveliest thing of all" to Sélincourt "was when Françoise said goodnight to me. She had her back to him, & as her lips touched my cheek, I looked at Havelock & his face was covered with a look of tenderness for me, full of colour, full of kindness. It was a millionth moment of a second—my look—a chance look—but what I saw remains a picture in my heart forever— cut in marble. You can understand. I've never seen such an expression on his face before—except in my happiest dreams."[50] It is doubtful —considering Ellis's outspoken views to Françoise—that he was as benign as he appeared to Sélincourt. As a youth he had practised cultivating an expression of serenity in front of a mirror. Sélincourt left at nine the following morning; Ellis immediately went to bed with a case of severe lumbago which disabled him for several days, and Françoise developed laryngitis. To Margaret, Sélincourt cried, "You can imagine my woe & feelings of frightful selfishness";[51] but to Françoise he wrote, "I'm afraid I ought really not to have come. It was only a strain on me."[52] But within a month he was suggesting that he should become Ellis's secretary, a proposal that made Ellis shudder. This was to be the beginning of long years of tension between Françoise and Hugh, in which Ellis found himself in the unwilling role of arbitrator and comforter.

There was a far more relaxing visit later in the summer from Winifred de Kok, a tall, beautiful South African, who was training to be a doctor. They had become friends the previous year, when he soon christened her "Dryad" and he had become "O Great God Pan." Ellis had a most remarkable effect on women, whose company he preferred to that of men. He once told Françoise: "With my nature, it is not possible to be at all intimate except with a woman. Being shy & reserved, I can only come emotionally near when I am physically near, & I haven't the least wish to be physically near a man.

I can get along all right with a man friend (like Symons) so long as
the relations are superficial. If it threatens to become deeper than
superficial, I am very careful to keep away."[53] He had a facility for
making women feel his intense interest in them, and numerous
women have said that he gave them the confidence to feel that they
could do anything. Almost all these friendships were close and tinged
with the erotic. It is worth quoting in full the letter Winifred de
Kok wrote to him after spending a few days at Little Frieth in July:

> Havelock Havelock How am I to write to you I want to say so
> many things but I don't know even how to begin You are almost
> too lovely to bear, darling, of course you have been wonderful to
> me & I value that tremendously but it is you you that are so
> wonderful. It is as if you have shown me how beautiful life really
> is, as if you *are* all the beauty of life & of everything. You make
> me want to embrace life & kiss it. And that has made me think
> am I like those women who want to die when Havelock dies?
> And for a moment I thought "Yes," but then I knew "no" All
> you stand for can't die. I'd want to die perhaps selfishly but be-
> cause of you I couldn't die but would want to go on still em-
> bracing the beauty of life, which *is* you & after that the beauty
> that is in Death too—It is as if Ive just realised this, dear, I've
> known your loveliness for a long time but it is as if the revelation
> of it has burst on me & it is so wonderful that I can hardly bear
> it, & it makes me want to weep. But such joyful tears, darling.
> It has been such a happy time, everything beautiful every little
> commonplace act & even acts some think not clean made divine
> because done by you & for you. It gives one quite a new view-
> point. One is taught to do good deeds & become good Now I
> see that any & every deed of good is good if done 'goodly.'
>   Oh, Havelock. How happy I am to believe in life again and
> in myself Give Françoise dear my love when you see her and so
> much love to you darling darling from
>
>   Winifred[54]

A few days later she wrote, "The time with you was lovely altogether. It seems lonely & strange to be making golden streams all
alone & not in a lovely garden with the great god Pan in loving
attendance."[55] It was on this visit that Winifred met one of Ellis's

neighbours, A. E. Coppard, author of *Adam and Eve and Pinch Me,* whom she later married.

In August, Ellis was to form an intimate friendship with yet another young American woman—Josephine Walther, the curator of the Detroit Institute of Arts. A gentle, frail creature, she had lost all her note-books on her first visit to Brixton that summer. Ellis later discovered that she was constantly losing things, but he was so charmed with her that on this first visit he impulsively invited her to stay with him at Little Frieth following Winifred de Kok's visit. (Winifred had cut short her visit in order to allow Josephine to come, and wrote magnanimously: "I'm so glad you decided to have Josephine. You know I once said to you I wished every woman in the world could know you—even if only for an hour or two."[56]) Josephine's visit turned out to be a great success and on her departure for America, Ellis wrote: "I knew as soon as I saw you that we are naturally friends, though it has never before happened to me—who am so very slow—to make friendship . . . so speedily. So your visit has been a wonderful experience for me as well as for you. I am grieved that you are so far away, but we can be close in heart; I was charmed at your discovery that you can feel my presence near in absence; I too have the very closest realisation of you, & if sometimes you feel my arms around you it may not be an empty illusion, for it is possible that at the same moment I shall be holding you close. . . ."[57] He begged "Josie" for a photograph in the nude—a request he made of many others; she visited him at Little Frieth the following summer and they maintained an affectionate correspondence until her premature death in 1937.

This summer, too, another woman, Winifred Henderson, appeared in his life. Like so many other women, she wrote to tell him how much she admired his work. Women seem to have formed an image of him as a great lover and would tell him the most intimate details of their lives. She, too, was invited to stay at Little Frieth after only one meeting. Before her visit Ellis described to her his idea of friendship with a woman: "For myself, in personal relationships, my ideal is an affectionate intimacy, with something of the body in it, & something of the spirit harmoniously blended, & leaving the mind free from any too devastating desire, although lifting one up to a plane one could not reach alone."[58] She, too, had her affectionate nickname—"Amigita"—and they kept in close touch and frequently attended art exhibitions together. There is a note of reserve in his letters to her, and he once told Margaret Sanger that early in the friendship he had discovered that she was "dangerous"—although he did not elaborate on what he meant by this.

It is clear that Ellis was unconsciously—or deliberately—seeking his own "Soleil de Joie."

HIS OWN SOLEIL DE JOIE

THE GHOST OF SÉLINCOURT WAS EXORCISED FROM CADGWITH, AND
Ellis returned for a profitable and contented winter. As usual
Françoise joined him after Christmas 1925, the most peaceful
holiday they had had for years. After she left he had a very tender
dream of her with her hand at his waist and the other caressing his
head while she murmured "My darling." "Nothing more happened
but it was quite lovely."[1] There was no doubt that they had reached
a new stage of understanding where Ellis was now prepared to act
as the loved confidant of Françoise's frustrated passion for Sélincourt;
they both agreed that Sélincourt managed in his self-indulgent way
to protect himself from suffering. Ellis told her that any pain he had
experienced over his rival was "long, long over" and he only wished
that she and Sélincourt could somehow straighten things out between themselves. Ellis realized that with him Françoise found peace,
while Soleil de Joie's inability to love her with consistent passion
left her miserable and frustrated. "But you know," Ellis tried to
explain to her, "it is part of the everlasting problem between men
& women. It is the man's business to hunt the woman & chase her
with all his most ardent energy & set a fascinating trap for her, baited
with all sorts of nice things. As soon as she walks into the trap there
is nothing more for her to do; he can repose in peace. He feels: What
more can I do?—except to assure the victim that she has been very
lucky to be caught—I am not like that, but then, as you know, I am

not at all a proper sort of man. So women have to love me with their souls!"[2]

Ellis was working more industriously than he had been able to do for years. By the time he returned to Brixton in March he had written a preface to the fourth edition of *The New Spirit* (Houghton Mifflin), a preface to the sixth edition of *Man and Woman* (London: Black), and was well advanced with the supplementary seventh volume of the *Studies* which he had promised F. A. Davis since 1923. He rather welcomed the General Strike in May as it kept visitors away and he was able to finish the book without interruption. During the strike Françoise was in a nursing home in Hampstead, where she had a hysterectomy. Someone drove Ellis to see her and she seemed to be recovering so well that he left her in good conscience, thankful that she was able to have a prolonged rest.

That spring Isaac Goldberg's biography was published, completed remarkably quickly by means of Ellis's help and co-operation. Ellis was very pleased with the result. "Wonderful how Jews are sometimes capable of intelligence, receptivity & enthusiastic appreciation!" he told Margaret Sanger.[3] (Ellis's anti-Semitism, expressed here with characteristic obliqueness, was a source of distress to Margaret, who remarked on it in a letter to Hugh de Sélincourt.) Few of his friends liked the book, and he had to admit that it was excessively adulatory. In June another American, Houston Peterson, a graduate student in philosophy at Columbia, paid him a visit to announce that he also planned to write a book on him. Peterson didn't like Goldberg's biography and intended to write a work which concentrated more on Ellis's ideas and spiritual development. Ellis found him very agreeable and was relieved by his assurances that this study would be in no way biographical. Peterson told him that he believed such a book should really be written by a woman, a view with which Ellis concurred.

Ellis and Françoise had talked of making a trip to Corsica, but it seemed too arduous an undertaking and he decided to rent Little Frieth again for the summer months. At the end of term Françoise went to France, where she made inquiries about getting a divorce but was speedily discouraged when she learned that she would have to have her husband's consent, for she had lost all track of Serge. In her absence Josephine Walther came again for a short visit.

In late June Ellis received a letter which had the familiar ring of many other enthusiastic letters from women readers. Faith Oliver was twenty-nine years old, a teacher, who had found herself lost among conflicting ideas and philosophies. Seven years before, she had read *Affirmations* and since then "the sense of hopeless futility and fear has never returned."[4] (She had not read the Sex *Studies*, as she did not think she was "ready" for them yet.) Ellis found her letter interesting and encouraged her to write again. "I have not the least wish to have disciples," he told her, "but I am always glad to think that I have been of help in enabling others *to be themselves*."[5] After she returned from a holiday in France—during which they continued the correspondence—he asked her to come to tea in Brixton. The very tall, auburn-haired woman he found charming in her simplicity and openness and inexperience. On October 3rd, just after her first visit, he wrote asking her to come soon again. "I am fortunate in having many dear & loving & devoted friends, but they are mostly very scattered & it would be nice to feel that there is somebody who could easily & informally come across in half an hour, if inclined—"[6] He reassured her about her nervousness: "I understand all you say about nervousness, know it all by heart, being so highly nervous myself as (naturally of course!) I think all the best people are. I am not by any means drawn to the self-confident people who are so sure of themselves."[7]

By their second meeting it was apparent that this was an encounter of kindred souls. Ellis told her that she would never grow unless she came close to another person, and that it might well be that he had been "sent" to be that person. Faith realized that her whole life before this had been a preparation for him, and that what he gave her was so unique that jealousy of another woman was impossible. Ellis also told her that they were probably "too near" to become actual lovers, and in her rapturous exaltation she agreed. "When I remember," he mused after this second meeting, "what a very slow deliberate person I am, & take years to think over things beforehand, it seems marvellous to me that I can feel so near to someone I have only seen twice! But I am a faithful person & never lose a friend once found."[8]

Ellis gave Françoise an account of the visit: "Quite beautiful time with Faith Oliver yesterday; she came at 6 and stayed till near 11. She is my height, I find, which I hadn't realised, & has, she says green eyes. It is a fine honest open character but still undeveloped (or, as she says, irregularly developed); evidently a little afraid of sex, but we did not talk very closely of sex things; she mentioned that she has never before felt so *at home* with another person & looks upon me as a 'miracle.' She asks about you & wants to meet you & I feel sure you will like her."[9]

And so began this relationship with its three-way correspondence. It was a measure of the new understanding between Havelock and Françoise that he could speak to her more openly about a friendship with another woman than he had ever been able to do before. Nevertheless, in his letters to Françoise he stresses Faith's feelings and reactions, and does not divulge how deeply his own had been stirred up. On October 10th he told Faith that he would be happy and content "if I could think that in later days you would be able to look back on me as a stepping-stone to a greater love, a help & not a hindrance & I should be glad also if you were able to tell him of what I had been to you, & that he would be able to understand, as he would, if he is the right man for you. I am longing to see you & you are constantly in my thoughts, & I am very often talking to you silently. Directly, I shall put some Franck & Bach on the gramophone, & that will bring your presence still nearer."[10] Later in the day he wrote to her again to tell her of his sense of wonderment at her sensitivity to the mystery of love. "For it is a mystery (& a miracle as well), & not what those poor people think who say it is just a matter of the flesh, with a little sentiment thrown in, or those others who say it is a matter of the soul with the flesh as a mere accident. For it is body-soul in one—soul becoming body and body becoming soul, & that is why it is ecstasy—of Joy & also sometimes of Pain, but that also good, for without the possibility of it there cannot be joy."[11] "It was so puzzling to me," he told Françoise, "that a virginal English woman should have such an instinctive feeling for the delicacies & subtleties of love. It is the solid roast beef & plum pudding of love which English women possess."[12] Faith was concerned that she had little to give him, and he replied: "I feel as though we knew each other in another life & now we have to tell each other all the things that have happened since. I never forgive myself for not having seen you in June when you first wrote."[13]

At the same time he was telling Françoise that Faith "after a phase of pain & disturbance, is now rapturously in love, and most beautifully so without any selfish or jealous feelings." And he continues: "I can't a bit imagine why charming & delightful women of 29 & 33 like Josephine & Faith (to say nothing of Naiads!) wait all that time before falling in love & then choose this silly decrepit old

Faun. Can you?"[14] And the next day he tells her that Faith is "full of quiet virginal ecstasy, & likes to be simply near me, & to enjoy the new sense of perfect rest &, she says, the sense that 'perfect love casteth out fear': and nothing whatever happens and is wanted to happen. But it is all so gay and fresh that I find it quite a little intimidating!"[15]

The same day he was writing with great speed to Faith: "The first moment I saw you I felt—more instantaneously than I have ever felt with anyone before—the sense of nearness & every moment I have been with you since, whether actually or in spirit, I have been realising how right my intuition was."[16] But the essence of their relationship was freedom to be themselves and "I do *not* propose or desire that you should make that complete & final surrender of your-self which you feel should be reserved for marriage. We both agreed that marriage is very unsatisfactory, but, as the world is today, there is nothing possible to replace it, & anyhow, in or out of marriage, it would be presumptuous for me to ask for the supreme place in your life. I am more than twice your age & in the ordinary course shall die long before you: I cannot offer you the exuberant passion you are entitled to receive (even though it is bound to pass & often leaves nothing behind); I cannot even offer an undivided love, even though it may be in its way unique & different from anything I feel for anyone else."[17]

And so it went on—Faith rushing over from Chelsea whenever she was free, both writing if she wasn't, pouring out love to each other in the middle of the night after an evening spent together. Ellis had found his "Soleil de Joie," the first woman, he told her, who had ever come to him not wanting something. Françoise had been a miracle to him; now Faith was "a ravishing miracle." His delight in her was based primarily on her virginal emptiness into which he could pour wisdom and experience. "She is always grow-ing: I teach her nothing, I only supply the atmosphere. But, as you know, it is rather a magic atmosphere."[18] Ellis soon realized with what delicacy he must approach her virginal sensibilities: "She is like a shy friendly bird that you know will fly away *if you put out your hand*. So I have never put out my hand! All the same, she says she has gone through more ordeals these few days, more pain & joy, than in all her life before. But in all her virginal ardour & reticence, she is far from being silly, is highly intelligent, & even analytic; so that she is alternately intense & quite a new experience for me—&

an excellent training!"[19] But by December 9th it was apparent that Faith was beginning to become a little bit tedious: "It is just the *virginal* attitude which is so troublesome to deal with. I do not make the smallest demands on her, & leave her absolutely free to be herself & follow her own impulses in everything—but even then there is still a shock to the virginal spiritual equilibrium and mental intactness."[20]

Before he left for his usual winter sojourn in Cornwall, where he wanted to work on Volume VII of the *Studies*, he arranged that the two women should meet alone in his flat. Françoise reported: "Je l'aime. She is adorable." Faith also expressed her complete satisfaction with Françoise, but to me in old age she was much franker. She found a coarse strain in Françoise—"a peasant," she described her, lacking in sensitivity. Clearly, Faith regarded herself as Ellis's real soul-mate, even though she has admitted that they had spent only one intense period together.

Margaret Sanger was back in England for a brief visit in early December, but took time to travel down to Cornwall for two days of long walks and conversation. Her departure was followed as usual by an enormous hamper of delicacies from Fortnum & Mason, which he was able to share with Françoise and Faith on their successive visits after Christmas. Two devoted women were too much of a good thing, and by the time Faith arrived he was too tired to play the rapturous lover. On January 17th Françoise left and Faith arrived. A note of querulousness creeps into his letter to Françoise: "I fear I am rather an *exclusive* person, & the presence of another F. does not by any means make up for the absence of one F. Is it that one needs the 'tightened strings' to play on? But she is always nice & we get on easily."[21] She tried to be gracious to the landlady, but Mrs. Pollard missed the Naiad's Gallic charm. Ellis was busy working on the conclusion of his book and Faith spent her time reading or going for walks. The novelty of her wide-eyed ingenuousness and lack of experience—which had first attracted him—was beginning to wear a bit thin. By January 30th it was evident that the fine, careless rapture of October had burned itself out: "I don't think I regret asking Faith to come here, she has evidently enjoyed the visit; but I trust she won't take for granted that I'll ask her again some other time. . . . I am so tired of people. The older one gets the more one is content with the society of one's own soul. I realise how possible it is to love a person at a distance. It is true, as you say, that one can always call up a person one loves. There is no such thing as absence—& I never feel that my Naiad is absent."[22] Ellis was clearly trying to persuade Faith that there would always be a sweet friendship between them but that she must go on to larger experiences. "I love you so tenderly that I think of a large life ahead for you, & picture myself as a step in your development, & an influence on the flowering of your loving nature that you will always look back at with sweet memories because, you see, you will have to look *back* at me. I am more than twice your age. All my active life is in the past, & what little is left is taken up in all sorts of ways, so that I cannot possibly fill your life. I can only be an influence—& a spirit more than a person! Do not let me take too much of you, Dear!"[23]

Nevertheless, in a letter of February 3rd, 1927, just before his return to London, it is apparent that he was still very much enthralled with her:

"I wrote to you this morning, Dear, but you feel so close this evening, Darling One, that I have to write to you again. I am longing for you to be here this moment, so that I could feel your kisses, & kiss you all over & know that your lovely body was thrilling through & through, & your soul feeling close to mine. You said I was 'deliciously near' on Tuesday night when you wrote that beautiful birthday letter, which I have now read many times, & it is so that you have come to me this evening, in spirit & almost in body so that I feel my arms around you & inhale your fragrance. You almost thrill me too much. It is wonderful to know you are 'a thousand times more alive' since we have known each other, & it is a great & sacred privilege for me to be able to know that life in you, & to feel it in every exquisite touch of your lips & hands on your lover.

"Good-night, my darling. Shall we meet on Tuesday of next week?"[24]

They continued to meet regularly—and tenderly—all during 1927; but in November Faith met an architect, with whom she fell speedily in love. He was unhappily married and it was some time before he was able to be free. In Ellis's letters to Françoise it is apparent that he rather resented the diversion of Faith's affections, although they were still very close. Ellis naturally became the recipient of all her anguished confidences about the course of the affair. Between her and Françoise, he was moved to imagine what his tombstone would be:

> Here lie the Remains of
> *Havelock Ellis*
> He had many Faults
> *But his Breast was Useful*
> For Women to come and Weep on
> Now only the Skies Weep there.[25]

The Sélincourt affair dragged on interminably. In *Friendship's Odyssey*, the book Françoise wrote about her relationship with Ellis, she gives a misleading view of the length of the affair. In her exaggerated way, she describes their relationship in terms that might be applied to Abélard and Héloïse. The times when they could see each other were few, and Hugh did not hesitate to find consolation in many other women. One of these was Juliet Rublee, Margaret's co-worker, who lavished money on him. "I say," Hugh asked Margaret teasingly, "ought she to do it? I'm not *deserving* you know; I'm not *in need*. But how much difference it'll make—more freedom, more fun. Heavens! I'm all in such an utter excitement. I think I shall burst. Why are you all so adorable to me?" Françoise says that after she and Sélincourt had ceased to be lovers she did everything possible to effect a reconciliation between the two men. A final break between Françoise and Sélincourt did not take place until 1931, although it is probable that sexual intimacy had ceased by then; but this continued well into the twenties, and during these years she was constantly pouring her troubles into Ellis's ears and trying to push him into friendship with Sélincourt. "You can't alter him," Ellis tried to tell her, "you can't make a child into a man or a weak one into a strong one, you can only help a person to develop *what is already there within them* (as I do with Faith, who is turning from a child into a woman)."[26] Her desire for the two men to be friends was genuine enough, for an improved situation would both ease her conscience and allow her to handle the delicate situation of having a relationship with two men at the same time. Sélincourt resented the emotional demands Françoise made upon him and in a letter shortly after his first visit to Little Frieth he tells her: "I often think when sunbathing by the pool that it was my few inches of penis wrought the mischief, & I eye him sadly, wondering at his terrible importance, wondering too whether he will ever function again as he has done, & not much minding whether he does or whether he doesn't, as long as my friends are happy & kind & pleased to see me. Anyhow he has behaved himself as well as any ever has. I am enfeebled and long for utter isolation from *all* women seeming to be *not* inspirers, *not* helpers, but monsters longing merely to suck your life's blood."[27]

Françoise was a very determined woman, and it is a measure of the power she exerted over Ellis that she persuaded him to write twice to Sélincourt in the summer of 1927 to ask if he and Françoise could settle their differences—and, in addition, she actually induced Ellis to stay at Sand Pit in September of that year. Ellis's letters were written with great care and pain. In May, Sélincourt confided to Ellis that he and Françoise had a "distressing effect" upon each other. The central passage of Ellis's reply reads:

"That 'distressing effect' which she often has on you, & you on her, is most sad, & greatly depresses her. I always assure her that it will come right in time; that (exactly as you say) she must learn to know you & accept you as you are; & that, on the other hand, there is no occasion for her to feel any 'inferiority complex' on her own part. She seems to feel you will not allow her to talk & explain herself & so attain the harmony she regards as essential. Her irritable hyper-sensitiveness is, of course, due to the fact that she loves you so much, & that in all relations between people of different sex that are more than merely superficial such sensitiveness exists—symbolized by the fairy princess who suffered much from the hard peas beneath her nine (was it?) mattresses. This cannot fail to be your experience as it has all through life been mine. But sensitiveness to pain is only another aspect of sensitiveness to joy, & I have always found it was worth while.

"With regard to my coming into it (which certainly rather complicates matters), I always say to her that a relationship between two people, must always *primarily* be between those two people, however much it may secondarily concern a third. (And I tell her you must be sick of hearing my name!) But as I know this hurts her, since she says I am the foundation of everything, I never more than touch on it lightly."[28]

More letters were exchanged during this summer of 1927, a particularly busy summer in which Ellis was the victim of an American invasion of visitors—"invited and uninvited." With Sélincourt Ellis kept the tone light and did not refer to Françoise again until August 16th. This was an extraordinary letter—written after a visit by Sélincourt to Little Frieth. Sélincourt had been pressing him to come to Sand Pit; and what Ellis said in effect was that he would do so on the condition that the differences between him and Françoise were resolved. "There is nothing I want more than her happiness," Ellis assured him, "& it grieves me that her fine spirit should be overclouded. I trust that any misunderstandings between you & her—due no doubt to her own over-sensitiveness at present—may be cleared up in course of time, & should be pleased if I could contribute to that end. She is full of intelligent affection, & believes that she now possesses (ever since your visit) a greater power of understanding you sympathetically than ever before." The letter was phrased with extreme delicacy, and he found the conclusion particularly hard to write: "I am, as you know, much of a snail living in my shell, & very unsociable. But if the misunderstanding between you & Françoise begins happily to melt away, & an old invitation should be renewed, I would like some day to forget my devil, & accompany Françoise for a brief glimpse of your Sand Pit, & perhaps to hear better music than I can offer you at Frieth."[29] It was the first time he had signed himself "Affectionately" since before September 1923.

Sélincourt replied excitedly, suggesting dates for a visit, but made no mention of the difficulties with Françoise. Ellis was moved to anger. "Just at the present," he told Françoise, "I cannot, day & night, shake off the thought of Soleil, & am constantly brooding on his silly sloppy response to the definite & serious letter, which it cost me such a tremendous effort to write—almost more than any letter I have ever written, (because it is hateful to me to make advances when they are not invited). The letter in which I wrote '*if the mis-understandings between you & Françoise are happily cleared up then I shall be pleased if an old invitation, etc.*' And he replies with mere tosh, & says not a word of the central point which for me is *every-thing*. And what for me is so sad is that *you* actually enjoy this giggling imbecility which makes me so sick & ill."[30] But he had now committed himself to going to Sand Pit; and in the brief letters written before his visit in early September he says that he will leave all arrangements to Sélincourt. He signed himself "Yours, Havelock."

To Sélincourt it was an evening of unadulterated joy. Janet

played for them after dinner and Havelock seemed the image of benevolent contentment, but both he and Françoise were miserable. That night Françoise crept into his room and cried herself to sleep in his arms. The day he returned to London—September 11th—he wrote a *very* brief note to Sélincourt telling him that he had "lovely memories of the Sand Pit which will remain—of the delightful visits in the garden, of late Beethoven sonatas, & other dear things which I will not enumerate."[31] But his nervous irritability breaks out in a letter to Françoise written the same day: "To go to other peoples' houses always makes me nervous & irritable, so in the train yesterday I was trying to forget that there ever had been such a place as Sand Pit, & it was a shock to find that Naiad, who it seemed to me ought under the circumstances, to be nicer to me than any other person in the world, should, instead, have tried to do all she could do to upset me still more."[32] For the next fortnight he continued to complain about the strain on his nervous system. "The one thing I need after society is complete rest—to be away from everything & even you."[33]

While all this emotional turbulence was taking place, Houston Peterson was busily going about with his index cards interviewing Ellis's friends. Ellis was extremely apprehensive about the result and warned everyone not to talk about anything personal or current. He over-reacted when he heard that his sister Louie had told Peterson a good deal about their childhood. When she retorted that she had done so only to give him an idea of the atmosphere of their home, never dreaming that he would print such details, Ellis replied that she didn't take into account that Peterson was an American. He was indignant that Peterson could receive a £300 advance from Houghton Mifflin for a book about himself when he had never received more than a £25 advance. Then a Dr. Herbert, a psycho-analyst in Manchester, appeared. He didn't like Goldberg's book either, because it had paid scant attention to Ellis's scientific work, and he wanted to write a book that would redress the balance. His wife, too, wanted to compile an anthology of Ellisian nuggets.* The final edge to Ellis's worries was Sélincourt's insensitive proposal that *he* write the definitive biography. Faith declared that Sélincourt was too "dangerously sentimental." Ellis agreed with her, adding that

---

* *The Art of Life: Gleanings from the Works of Havelock Ellis*, selected and arranged by Mrs. S. Herbert (London: Constable; Boston and New York: Houghton Mifflin, 1929).

there would be too much "King" and not enough "black beetle" in any book written by him. "My only hope is that *you* will exert your most severe restraining influence on Soleil," he pleaded with Françoise. "After the exuberance of Goldberg a fresh dose of exuberance would be a tragedy, & I am already feeling very worried. Do write & tell me if you will be able to control Soleil. There ought to be a law passed that no one is to write anything more about me till I'm dead."[34] Françoise's answer was pages and pages of defence of Sélincourt. Ellis tried to make her see reason: *"It is what the public that it is written for thinks that will matter.* That is why Faith's opinion is significant. If she, who admires him is troubled, what will be the effect on the public that doesn't admire him?"[35] The idea was dropped; and the fact that it could not be pursued seemed to recharge Françoise's fury against Sélincourt, who complained to Margaret: "Whatever I do seems to hurt her. Oh, it is *so stupid!* I merely pray for guidance: & don't know what else to do. I do wish people wouldn't get cross with me, & upset me."[36]

Early in 1929 Margaret Sanger wrote to Françoise that she wanted to give Havelock a very special birthday present that year. What she suggested was that Françoise give up her job and Margaret would give her the equivalent of her salary so that she could act as Havelock's secretary and they could finally live together.

Françoise was overjoyed.

Ellis was beginning to feel that other people were trying to take over his life.

PROFESSIONAL CONTACTS

IN MAY 1928 THE SEVENTH VOLUME OF *Studies in the Psychology of Sex—Eonism and Other Supplementary Studies*—was published. It was the first major work on sex Ellis had produced since 1910, when he had completed the sixth and what he then considered the final volume of the *Studies*. These books he regarded as his major life's work; and after their completion his writing was largely confined to essays, most frequently on literary subjects. When Ellis published the first volume in Germany in 1897, Freud was still largely unknown; even by 1910 Ellis was much more widely known in the English-speaking world. But in the succeeding years, partly as a result of the more general outspokenness following the war, innumerable books on sex poured from the world's presses. Aspects of intimate behaviour became the subject of general discussion, of jokes, of official censorship, of private speculation, of professional advice. The world was a far different place from the Victorian environment of prudery and reticence which Ellis had had to break through. Ellis was no longer a pioneer, a trail-blazer. He had amassed data about actual sexual behaviour, he had helped to dissipate the anxieties and guilt experienced by countless people, but he had long since surrendered pride of place to Freud. Ellis was a contributor to the sexual revolution, but Freud was its arch-priest.

Ellis felt justifiably proud of his own methodical, painstaking collection of data. He saw his work as a monument standing sufficient unto itself. He wanted peace, he could not stand altercation; he often referred to the disputes within the Freudian camp as the inevitable outcome of a situation in which one man assumed authoritarian leadership. He admired Freud, but he viewed with distaste what he considered Freud's arrogant assumption of supreme power, presenting himself as the arbiter of unchallengeable doctrine. In his time he made copious references to Freud's writings, and while he tended to over-emphasize the differences between them, he never ceased to recognize Freud's genius, particularly his flexibility in proliferating daring new hypotheses. Ellis was a magnanimous man; he also knew that he was temperamentally incapable of being a public leader or of paying the price for such leadership. But he had a strong streak of vanity and cherished every expression of appreciation of his work. As the years went by, his reservations about Freud's theories increased, and while his attitude was motivated by genuine scepticism, envy also played its part. He knew Freud owed little to Ellis's investigations,* and he lacked Freud's energy, initiative, and, above all, the imaginative insight to pursue his studies into deeper and more hazardous depths. Ellis I have already described as an anthropologist of sex. It is possible to imagine another man—or team of men—ultimately producing the same kind of results as Ellis did. While he contributed to a changing world, he did not become an eponym of that world. As a pioneer he ploughed the fields in the valley, but the great conquistador Freud surveyed the shattered detritus of the nineteenth century from a summit only he could ascend. Although Ellis was nearly an exact contemporary of Freud, Dr. Norman Haire was right in describing him *after* his death as "a pre-Freudian."

Why did Ellis add this new volume after all these years? For the first time since the publication of the first volume he restored the acknowledgement to Edith of his "indebtedness, for the assistance and sympathy which, here and always, I have received from my wife." He had removed this tribute from all subsequent volumes because of the pain Edith had suffered from the publicity of the Bedborough trial. The essays he describes in Schopenhauer's terminology as "paralipomena and parerga"—leftovers that had not been sufficiently investigated, by-products lying on the borderland

---

* In *Three Essays on the Theory of Sexuality* (1920 edition) Freud includes many footnotes acknowledging his indebtedness to Ellis, particularly for the term "narcissism," although the Freudians used it in another sense.

of sex. The first six volumes had been produced in little over a decade; this final collection of pieces had taken nearly twenty years to assemble. Why had it taken him so long?

It is my own belief that Ellis added a seventh volume principally because it gave him an opportunity to defend an inclination of his own which he had not discussed in the earlier volumes. But a word first about the structure of the book. It is composed of essays previously published in journals—on cross-dressing, erogenous zones, the menstrual curve of sexual instinct, the synthesis of dreams, narcissism.* It could plausibly be argued that the justification for reprinting these pieces was that they would now reach a wider public than the scientific journals in which they had first appeared. Three of these essays deserve particular consideration. The first of these is "The History of Florrie and the Mechanism of Sexual Deviation," which had originally appeared in *The Psychoanalytic Review* in 1919. It is very long—over one hundred pages—and is intended in part as an attack on psychoanalytic methods, and is clearly intended to parallel Freud's case of Dora. The story Ellis tells is based on that of a woman who had written to him seeking help. Ellis was in touch with her over a period of three years "during which numerous interviews took place, and over sixty written communications, some of considerable length, reached me." In this case he feels that his approach as a patient listener, occasionally injecting a sympathetic suggestion, was far more successful than if he had followed the Freudian procedure of analysis in which it is deemed necessary for the patient to develop a transference experience towards the analyst. Unfortunately, he tells us nothing more specific about the nature of

---

* F. A. Davis nervously rejected "Memories of a South Russian," which is included in the French edition. A wave of puritanical repression was sweeping the States, and it was the first time anything in the *Studies* had been altered or omitted. On August 13th, 1927, the F. A. Davis people wrote to him: "We are glad to see by your letter of July 26, that you are in full accord with us as to the necessity of watching our step on anything that might offend the censorship.

"We shall probably send you the first instalment of galleys of the 7th volume some time next week, and also the doubtful section, the appendix, which comes last, at the same time. The criticism of this is, that while it would probably pass in Germany and other European countries where freedom of speech is so customary, all the details which that Russian gives could not be rendered into English. They say anything, write anything, and do anything they like in Russia, but we cannot do it here. Our suggestion is that you tone it down, so that it accords with the other volumes of the work and return it to us at your early convenience. Then it can be set up to follow the rest of the book" (Lafitte Collection). But it was decided to omit it entirely.

his help beyond his being a patient listener and at periodic intervals offering a sympathetic suggestion. Florrie came to him because she suffered from a whipping fixation which was connected with intense pleasure in the act of urination. Ellis begins with an account of the "audacious joy" she experienced while urinating in unconventional and dangerous situations. He then goes on at length to describe her tormented longing to be whipped, the origin of which he traces to childhood beatings and to the large development of her buttocks(!). Her visits and letters ceased when Florrie ultimately reached the point in her sexual odyssey when she could face squarely the impulses which at one time had been beyond her control. The obsessions which gripped her she now understood, and she was able at this point to develop into a sexually mature woman. The manifestations of the obsessional phase Ellis refuses to term "perversions"; rather he calls them "manifestations of a normal and necessary play instinct in her development." They were the outcome of a complex of factors— hereditary, physical, and environmental—which in time she was able to control—mainly because she found someone as understanding as Ellis to help her with her difficulties. This puzzling case-history raises all sorts of unanswered questions. In Ellis's view, it is instructive to study such a case. But how is our understanding of human behaviour enriched by this story? While Florrie, he assures us, has gained confidence in herself, in what way has she reached a greater level of maturity? Any conclusions we draw—or Ellis draws— are implicit. Presumably, Florrie's behaviour is immature because she is fixated on a private fantasy which can only be enacted with an unsuitable partner. Flagellation is presented as degrading her sense of dignity; urethral eroticism, on the other hand, is described tenderly. There are many urethral eroticists who have no inclination for flagellation, Ellis tells us. It would appear, then, a strong pos-sibility that Florrie discarded one anomaly while retaining the other. Ellis retreats into ambiguity, particularly in his response to Wilhelm Stekel's quasi-psychoanalytic analysis* of the case (made after the publication of the original article).† Stekel found traces of homo-sexuality in the fact that Florrie urinated in an upright position. Ellis will not deny that such a tendency exists in *other* cases, but he

---

* It should be noted that orthodox Freudians have refused to view Stekel as a genuine psychoanalyst ever since his break with Freud in 1912, despite the Master's considerable influence on his erstwhile and erratic disciple.

† First published in *The Psychoanalytic Review*, May 1919.

insists it is not present here; and besides, many women actually prefer this posture, he asserts (one which Ellis encouraged with his intimate women friends). Stekel also believed that Florrie had a great deal of repressed infantile sexual material in her unconscious which Ellis never uncovered because he did not analyze her dreams. Stekel finds substantiation for his view, but, Ellis protests, Florrie's reaction on being shown Stekel's interpretations was that they were "fantastic"; and Ellis seems to regard this as sufficiently positive proof that Stekel was wrong. Moreover, he adds,

> I would like to say that it is very hazardous for a psychoanalyst, however skillful and experienced, to put forth speculations concerning a subject he has never seen which over-ride the conclusions of the reporter, who, however inferior he may be in skill and experience, has had opportunities of minutely studying the peculiarities of that subject[1]

Similarly, he deliberately eschewed dream interpretation; yet he might have rejected it because he would find it difficult to construct a whole new vocabulary of dreams after Freud published *Die Traumdeutung* in 1899. His own *The World of Dreams* (1911) seems utterly pedestrian in comparison with Freud's daring speculations. Ellis discusses physiological discomfort and external noise as evoking certain dreams, but has little to say about the significance of the content of the dream. On June 23rd, 1911, Jung wrote to Freud: "Have you seen Havelock Ellis's book on dreams? Won't you do a critical review for the *Jahrbuch*? What a watery brew Ellis has concocted! Just what is needed to make everything unclear."[2] Freud agreed, but the review never appeared. Perhaps he was as anxious as Ellis to avoid an open rift between them.

The long essay "The Synthesis of Dreams" (which had appeared four years earlier in *The Psychoanalytic Review*) is sufficient reason for the low esteem in which the Freudians held him. He records a hundred dreams by a method of "dream-synthesis," a method carried out in "a really conscientious and relentlessly scientific spirit" —as compared to what? The dream-analyst he likens to a geologist who works from below upward; his own method is similar to that of a geographer who travels over the surface of the earth in all directions and is able to present "a comprehensive balanced picture," so that his results are "usually less disputable than the geologist's and may often serve to check the geologist's more revolutionary speculations."[3] The dreams were collected from Mrs. N, "a lady of French birth on both sides, born and bred in France, but for many years resident in London. She was thirty-two years of age at the period in question, married and the mother of children." "F"—a gentleman with a white beard—is not difficult to identify in Dream CV: "I know that F. is pretending that he feels it to be quite natural that I should take a lover of my own age, but his dejected air contradicts that assurance."[4] This was one of the letters Ellis had turned to during the crisis over Sélincourt to prove to Françoise that in the early stages of their relationship she, too, had believed in sexual fidelity.

After recording these dreams Ellis then divides them up into classifications—erotic, parental, eating, vesical, filial, vocational, intestinal—in descending order of recurrence. Believing as he did that Freud over-estimated the importance of wish-fulfilment in dreams, Ellis for instance claimed that several of the dreams involving copious eating occurred while the subject had a full stomach. If she had a large proportion of erotic dreams, it was because she was leading a somewhat deprived sexual life. He contends that her dreams registered accurately the emotions of the dreamer in waking life, and as for the exercise of a censor who suppresses or distorts wish-fulfilments, "That may be prominently true in the case of many abnormal or neurotic dreamers, but such censorship is not pronounced in the case of normal, healthy dreamers. . . ."[5] This view is highly questionable. Beyond telling us that the subject of the dreams is a charming French lady, what evidence have we that she is so altogether "normal" as Ellis claims? How does he differentiate between "normal" and the "abnormal"? Unless he had at hand the comparable data of a large number of other people—particularly those who are emotionally disturbed—he has no justification in asserting that there is a qualitative difference between the dreams of the normal and the abnormal. Ellis concludes by saying:

> The object of the present study has not been to investigate a particular person, and still less to analyze a particular case. The object has been to illustrate a method.[6]

This method—dream-synthesis—he believes will furnish an important complementary guide to the narrow confines of Freudian dream analysis. How? Is he actually setting up Françoise's dreams as a norm against which to measure the dreams of abnormal people?

In addition to his lack of a conceptual framework, Ellis's great weakness was his over-reliance on his old-fashioned method—on collecting and classifying like a nineteenth-century botanist—and he always hesitates before making a judgement, drawing a conclusion, or formulating a general law. When Karl Pearson attacked him for his mild assertion that there was greater variability in men than in women, Ellis responded that Pearson had been confining himself too exclusively to the study of crabs—in other words, that his method lacked sophisticated judgement. Nevertheless, the statistical methods which Pearson initiated were precisely the sort of tool that Ellis needed if he relied, as he intrinsically did, on quantitative analysis.

The section on "Undinism" Ellis considered the most important in the book. He was particularly satisfied with the long introductory historical account of the importance man has always attached to water. He told Françoise that it was "the first treatise on the important subject of Peeing ever written, & perhaps the most learned & scholarly study I have ever written."[7] It was in fact an apologia for his own proclivities. He substituted the term "undinism" for "urolagnia," probably because it seemed more romantic than the latter term, with its clinical connotation. The whole essay is highly eccentric. He gives cases where the love of peeing is abnormal, as with a woman who is not able to merge it with her sexual life, but the general impression is that it is a highly pleasurable experience. Freud had made a distinction between the psychic character of the anal and the vesical temperaments—on the one hand, orderliness, cleanliness, economy, and, on the other, burning ambition. Ellis refuses to commit himself to the validity of the description of the anal personality; but he denies categorically that aggressiveness forms a part of the urethral temperament.

> This seems, according to my observations, to be almost the opposite of the truth. Reversely, moreover, I have sometimes noted that in the women who are unsympathetically described as "aggressive" whether or not inclined to homosexuality, there is a complete absence of urethral eroticism. It would almost have been more plausible to argue that urethral eroticism is a substituted activity for the absence of aggressiveness.[8]

Although one hundred pages are devoted to undinism, Ellis records only one female case known to him, an American correspondent long since dead. As for men, there is only one correspondent

who wrote that the sight of his wife peeing was a delightful con-
comitant to sex. Yet the evidence about Ellis himself is plentiful. He
discussed his own proclivity fairly frankly in *My Life*, where he calls
it "the germ of a perversion."* There are many references to it in
his letters to Françoise and to other women, always discussed in a
playful fashion. On one occasion he chides Margaret Sanger for
leaving her purse behind and adds in the margin: "I've no objection
to your leaving *liquid* gold behind."[9] To Josephine Walther, his
friend at the Detroit Art Institute, before the publication of this
essay he wrote that even though peeing has been a subject of interest
since Adam and Eve there had never before been an essay written
on it. "So that this essay is an event in the history of Man! ought
alone to secure to immortality its author! It will certainly interest
you, but before I show it you, I shall expect *you* to send me some
interesting notes of your own on the subject."[10] Some women proved
recalcitrant. Jane Burr considered it a perversion. Another was the
American dancer Marguerite Agniel, to whom he wrote after a visit:

---

* I fear it was becoming more than a germ of a perversion. There is an extant
letter from a rare-book dealer in Blackheath, written in 1926: "As to your inquiry, all
I know is comprised in the fact that long ago—many years back—I saw at times
photographs—certainly some represented the 'famous pisseuses'—in the act—the
receptacles, I believe were the inverted high hats of their two cavaliers—at the time
I thought it a strange scene to depict" (Lafitte Collection). In a late note added to
My Life Ellis says: "I may be regarded as a pioneer in the recognition of the beauty
of the natural act in women when carried out in the erect attitude, and it is
described in the passage of my *Impressions and Comments* which some critics consider my best piece of prose, as well as in an early sonnet entitled 'Madonna,' while
for the more scientific side my study 'Undinism' is the first serious discussion of the
whole subject. But Rembrandt preceded me. There is a fine and admired picture of
his in the National Gallery (No. 54) of a woman standing in a pool and holding
up her smock, with parted legs, in an attitude which has always seemed to me undoubtedly to represent the act of urination. In recent years I have learnt on good
authority that so it really came from the artist's hands, but that at some later date
(whether or not before it reached the National Gallery in 1836) the falling stream
was painted out. The picture is dated 1654, and experts now consider that it probably represents Hendrickje Stoffels, the charming and beloved figure whom, about
that time, Rembrandt painted in various intimate situations. I should like to think
that the indignation I feel at his sacrilegious distortion of a supreme artist's work will
some day be generally shared."

I am indebted to Dr. John Tanner for pointing out his doubts about Ellis's surmise. I then turned to the Director of the National Gallery, Michael Levey, who
kindly replied: "With regard to the Rembrandt here, there is no justification at all
for what Ellis wrote. The picture was cleaned in 1946 and the only areas repainted, as
far as I can learn, were the woman's right hand and wrist. The over-paint was removed
in 1946."

One can only conclude that it is a form of obsessionalism to see what is not
there.

"With regard to the 'divine stream,' I never quite knew why you were so shy about that. Most women (if not quite all) are prepared to be natural about it, & I should have thought that *you* especially would, in view of your attitude towards natural functions of the body."[11] One woman told him that she could not enter into what he described as "perfect intimacy" with him because she found what he also called "the Sacrament" "unaesthetic." He replied: "Indeed while that intimacy is to me really a joy, it can only be so when I feel that my presence is *also* really delicious to you—It is an intimacy which has existed with all my most dear friends & they have all loved it, though naturally some more than others. I should be genuinely grieved, & feel that there was a barrier between us, if I thought that you would desire that reserve to go on indefinitely. But for the moment I am sure your feeling is natural & reasonable & it is only I that am at fault (though I am glad I was!!) in hastening your growth, when I ought not to do so even by the lightest touch. . . . I will not feel grieved though when you *do* spontaneously invite my presence—I am sure it will be an exquisite moment!—But let me say in regard to the 'aesthetic' reason you gave that I of course understand your feeling, although it is a feeling that will not last. These little troubles are annoying, but they are not troubles that *love* feels, for love welcomes them as giving an opportunity for proof that it *is* love & eager to show its tenderness."[12]

There was another section of the book to which he attached great importance, an essay on marriage, which he added to a review of Edward Westermarck's *The History of Human Marriage.** This final section he called "The Tail," and he derived enormous satisfaction from writing it.† It quite clearly grew out of the crisis over Sélincourt, and could have been written only after he had achieved a state of acceptance of the situation. Here he turns to a consideration of the future of marriage, if, indeed, it has a future at all in view of the emancipation of women. Eternal fidelity can never be expected in marriage, or in erotic comradeship; jealousy is inevitable and

---

* Reviewed in *The Nation*, 28 Jan. 1922, pp. 92–3; 11 Feb. 1922, pp. 26–7.

† To Françoise he wrote on December 18th, 1926: "—it's a fiery tail, with sparks that fly out at every swish, but I'm very pleased to know you will like some of the wags. I've grinned over it immensely (though—or because—it's very serious); no wonder I've got such a broad mouth when I spend so much of my time in grinning over what I write. Fauns shouldn't write books!" (Mugar Library).

must be conquered. The following passage came directly from his heart:

> To deal with it [jealousy] is part of the discipline of love. It is a very necessary part, for though the jealousy may at first seem to its object an agreeable mark of devotion it quickly becomes fatal to the love it thus seeks to hold. The victim of jealousy falls to the level of the victims of passion generally, the level of the dipsomaniac or the drug-addict, an object of pity perhaps, no longer fitted to be a master of love, which is the epitome of life. The conquest of jealousy must sometimes be hard, but without it there is no entering the kingdom of marriage.[13]

On February 3rd, 1927, while in the midst of writing "The Tail," he broke off to write to Françoise: "Got as far as erotic comradeship, & what an exquisite relationship it is, when two people who love each other are so near in heart that they can tell each other everything & how rare & intimate & precious that is."[14] Then, shortly before the publication of the book, he wrote to her again to reassure her that he was not losing interest in her, especially for a younger woman: "As to loving her dear sweet body all over, there is not, & never has been, the least doubt about that. All that is wrong is not my love, but my vital energy, which is not what it was a few years ago. It is the same loss of energy which has taken away the old eagerness to wander around France with my beloved Naiad, though I am always hoping it will come back, & I haven't even the faintest wish to go with anyone else. The love is still the same, the only difference being that it is deeper, & my Naiad's body is just as sweet all over as her spirit."[15]

Volume VII was not to be Ellis's last word on sex. Until his death he continued to write popular articles for American publications. He answered innumerable letters requesting personal help. "If I answered all the questions sent me about negroes, Tagore, & Jews I should have no time for anything else," he complained to Françoise.[16] A seventeen-year-old American, Henry Miller,* wrote in

---

* Not *the* Henry Miller. The renowned Henry Miller himself first began writing Ellis in 1936 and sending him copies of his books which were banned in England (Ellis never particularly cared for them). Miller told him that "I have read a number of your works and have found in them a source of great inspiration. In an unfinished work on D. H. Lawrence, which I have been engaged on intermittently for several years now, I am making reference to your 'Dance of Life,' a book which treats of the creative powers of man in a way which I think is unequalled" (16 Nov. 1936, Lafitte Collection). In 1937 Lawrence Durrell wrote to Henry Miller: "Listen, I went down and bearded Havelock. I should say rather that he bearded me. He is covered with hair like a wild boar. Likes your work and promises to write you in detail

1931 to tell him of the emotional mess he was in. He found himself caught between

> "two poles, that could never merge, and one exacerbated the other: I gazed with greater longing at the veiled body of woman (making myself disregard the knowledge that they would eagerly unveil themselves to me); but when my eyes came to the naked face, insipid and ogling, disgust was my reaction, no matter how beautiful or intelligent the woman was commonly reckoned. Soon I began to hate women entirely. I do now. And still livid with desire! What is one to do, that hates and desires with equal intensity? I have tried everything I know of from yoga to writing a normal youth's romance. There is a story of a man who desecrated dead women, recently interred! Tell me what I am to do, I beg of you."[17]

In 1928 a butler in Burlingame, California, wrote that he found "coitus repugnant and impossible without carressing [sic] shoe. Am very fortunate and thankful that for many years high heels have not been in vogue. If they ever return—despite earnest prayer—their attraction and power to disturb would be greater than ever and life would be almost unbearable." Ellis replied:

Dear Sir,

In reply to yours, it is clear that you have had the best medical advice possible in regard to the fetichism, & I do not know of any doctor in America to whom it would be worth your while to go for further advice.

My own opinion is that the best course would be to find an attractive woman friend in whom you could confide and who would assist you to gratify your desire in association with her. To an intelligent woman it is possible to explain that there are people with peculiarities of this kind, but who are none the worse on that account. I have known some (I have described

---

about the books. Hasn't finished them yet. Disagrees with you about urination!! Lovely old man" (*Lawrence Durrell and Henry Miller: A Private Correspondence,* edited by George Wickes, London: Faber & Faber, 1963, p. 117). One of the books Miller sent Ellis was *Black Spring,* and the reference appears to be Miller's boast, "I am a man who pisses largely and frequently, which they say is a sign of great mental activity." Incidentally, Miller wrote six essays on Lawrence, but never finished the book, which was to be called *The World of Lawrence.*

one in one of my books) who were of fine character, high ability and who lived active and useful lives.

It may be very difficult to destroy the attraction of the object, but it is quite possible to combine the fascination of the object with an attractive woman to whom it belongs.

> Yours very truly
> Havelock Ellis[18]

One correspondent told him that he would be happy to send him notes on homosexuality in the Royal Navy. Another, in 1938, said, "I suffer under a peculiar sense of being responsible for events in Europe since just before Herr Hitler came to power."[19] And so it continued for eleven pages. From India he received the following:

> Honoured Master,
>
> Having heard of your Almighty mercy and loving kindness to us worms I tell you my circumstances.
>
> By the Grace of God and your Lordship I have seven children, all babes and sucklings. Besides this abominable litter I have many male and female relations. What have I done that I should be blessed with cares and trials? As your Lordship is my Father and my Mother I write to request that you will take this Worm and Wife and Sucklers and relations both the Male and Female and provide from your Bounty at a remuneration of five rupees twenty a month. By the Grace of Almighty Lordship I look forward to years of prosperity and happiness.
>
> All in Delhi sing of your praises, your justice and mercy. Therefore call us all that we may fatten on your love and gentleness. Call quickly.
>
> Your faithful Worm and Beast
> Munni Lel
> Despicable Brute and unwilling Father of Babies[20]

His unknown correspondents addressed him as everything from "Dear Whiskers" to "Dear Benefactor of Mankind." Women sent nude photographs of themselves. One woman in California wrote to him as often as five times a week for years. Eventually, in 1930, she travelled to England to meet him, and when she was invited to Little Frieth, the prospect was so overwhelming that she turned around and returned to California. Ellis tried to answer every letter he received, but he refused to write prefaces, sit on committees, or attend congresses.* When Edward Carpenter and some like-minded friends in 1914 founded the British Society for the Study of Sex Psychology (later the British Sexological Society),† Ellis became an *ex officio* member, but never attended a meeting. He contributed three papers which were read for him at meetings.‡ He was particularly careful not to become embroiled in the feuding that was an unpleasant aspect of the early days of the birth-control movement. One fairly close friendship with an English supporter of Margaret Sanger, Stella Browne, was threatened when the latter turned violently against Margaret Sanger for persuading the English group that a British magazine (on which Stella Browne had been promised a post) was redundant on the grounds that her own *Birth Control Review* was all that the movement needed. Ellis chided Margaret gently, for he believed that a British journal on birth control was necessary; but he was never able to establish a truce between the two strong-minded women, especially as Stella Browne believed that Margaret Sanger, with her love of power, expensive clothes, and luxury hotels, had sold out to capitalism.

It was inevitable that he should come into contact with the egregious Marie Stopes, Margaret Sanger's counterpart as the leader of the birth-control movement in Britain. Margaret Sanger's account in *My Fight for Birth Control* of her meeting with Marie Stopes on her first visit to England in 1915 seems accurate. Ellis had met her the year before Edith's death, and seems to have been unenthusiastic about her from the outset. At this date Marie Stopes, who was three years older than Margaret Sanger, was a lecturer in paleobotany at University College. According to Margaret Sanger, she knew nothing about birth control, but, emerging from a disastrous first marriage, she listened eagerly to Margaret Sanger's teaching; and the women seemed on the way to becoming fast friends. When Mrs. Sanger returned to the States and was indicted for her birth-control activities, Marie Stopes organized a petition on her behalf to President Woodrow Wilson, enclosing the signatures of a dis-

---

* Henri Barbusse pleaded ineffectually with him to attend Le Congrès contre la Guerre in Amsterdam in August 1932.

† Its purpose was to provide a forum for "the consideration of problems and questions connected with sexual psychology from their medical, juridical, and sociological aspects." It hoped to create an informed public that would accept and support reforms in law and in time to modify general prevailing prejudices about sex.

‡ "The Objects of Marriage," "The Love Rights of Women," and "The Play Function of Sex."

tinguished group of people, including H. G. Wells and Arnold Bennett. The suit against her was dropped, and Margaret Sanger seemed to have every reason to be grateful to her English adherent. After her thirty days' imprisonment for running a birth-control clinic in Brooklyn, Margaret Sanger's position as the heroine of the movement seemed assured, but an unknown contender was determined to wrest the title from her. In 1918 Marie Stopes published what was to be a *cause de scandale, Married Love*. Ellis was intrigued by her formulation of the Law of the Periodicity of Recurrence of Natural Desire in Healthy Women. For all his espousal of the erotic rights of women, such an idea had never occurred to him, although in the first volume of the *Studies* he had utilized F. H. Perry-Coste's periodic pulse rate for men.* On November 9th, 1918, he wrote to Marie Stopes that he found the Fundamental Pulse section in her book of special interest and had "at once" begun to test it. Aware of Margaret Sanger's sensibilities, he referred to the essay which he subsequently wrote as "a little paper" based on Marie Stopes's theory of periodicity, "which, I am inclined to think, has something in it, as it happened to be supported by the one case I have since completely investigated."[21] His method of testing was by charting the erotic dreams of "Mrs. F." and by keeping a record of the acts of masturbation by "Mrs. A.," a lady with whom he had been in correspondence only.† The results, in which he pays qualified tribute to Marie Stopes, eventually appeared as "The Menstrual Curve of Sexual Impulse" in Volume VII of the *Studies*.‡ He told Marie Stopes that he was "probably on the way to become an enthusiastic adherent of your doctrine";[22] but to Margaret Sanger he confessed that he did not find her theory "quite convincing." He also detected in her "a sort of concealed hostile feeling to me."[23] Although Margaret Sanger had found an American publisher for *Married Love*, the book marked the beginning of the stridently demarcated zones staked out in the feuding world of birth control. Havelock Ellis had been first in the field of sexology, his friendship

---

* Although in "The Phenomena of Sexual Periodicity" in Volume I he had approached the subject of female rhythm in his discussion of the intensity of desire during menstruation.
    † I believe this was also "Mrs. F."
    ‡ The original article, which he sent to her on November 9th, 1918, was far more flattering than the essay he eventually published (British Library). In his correspondence with Marie Stopes, "Mrs. F." is described as "a professor."

with Margaret Sanger was well known; Marie Stopes was on her way to becoming a humourless megalomaniac, and she found it necessary to diminish or destroy anyone who had been there before her. In a letter of February 9th, 1923, to Margaret Sanger, Ellis refers to some "unpleasant & insulting" behaviour of Marie Stopes, adding, "I am afraid the advocates of B.C. *are* rather objectionable people, what with Marie Stopes, & Norman Haire. . . ."[24]

Ellis loathed controversy. He adored Margaret Sanger, but he often thought she was wrong. Marie Stopes he found distasteful and, although he had no desire to quarrel with her, there were times when she drove him to heavy irony. Marie Stopes was ruthless in her self-aggrandizement; after Ellis's death she was to recall that reading the *Studies* was "like breathing a bag of soot; it made me feel choked & dirty for three months,"[25] yet she never hesitated to exploit him through flattery, wheedling self-pity, offers of financial help, and invitations to dinner. When he declined these with the assurance that he was "not a social person but very much of a hermit," she pleaded with him, "Don't live *too* much out of the world!"[26] The woman's vulgar insensitivity was unbelievable; and Ellis managed to remain firm without losing dignity in the difficult course of their correspondence. He told Hugh de Sélincourt that she was a brilliant and accomplished woman, yet "There is something quite childlike, simple, ingenuous, about her even in her self-conceit, but beneath the sentiment there is a vulgar sexual platitude that is quite American in quality—& a something ineffable that is lacking."[27]

Marie Stopes was paranoid about any form of criticism and from time to time Ellis felt compelled to adopt an avuncular tone towards her. When she complained about an adverse review of *Wise Parenthood* in *The Eugenics Review*, he advised her, "I nearly always think it more dignified to be silent when I am the object of attack or misstatement. If Truth cannot conquer by virtue of her own simple beauty—then she does not deserve to conquer!"[28] He was under no illusions that her principal aim was self-glorification when he pointed out to her that surely she should not object to other people stealing her ideas since it was an opportunity for those ideas to gain an even wider audience. As for critics or plagiarizers, his view was that "I feel that I can be much better employed than in worrying over the sins of other people. I expect that when you have had as much experience of this sort of thing as I have you will accept it as cheerfully as I do. In any case to me, at all events, there seems more dignity in remaining silent and leaving the world to judge for itself."[29]

By 1922 they were in a state of covert warfare. He refused to write prefaces for her books or to be a counsellor for the birth-control clinic which she opened in 1921—"but as you have so many good friends at hand that cannot matter," he opined smoothly.[30] All he would ever agree to do was to circulate pamphlets privately among friends.

He reported to Margaret Sanger that the gynaecologist Norman Haire had told him that the birth-control movement in Britain needed a beautiful personality like Margaret Sanger. "I am sure," he commented, "Marie Stopes would say, 'What more can you want than ME.' "[31] The indefatigable lady had called on him "on some mysteriously urgent business"[32] when he was, fortunately, at the British Museum, but she left a note threatening to come again—"It will be nice to be in Cornwall!" However, she managed to track him down in the British Museum the following day and bullied him into writing a letter—but not a preface or introduction—endorsing *Married Love* for a new American edition of the book.

Then, in 1922, overt hostility erupted. He had tried manfully not to be implicated in the feud between the two M.S.'s, but when the Stopes house organ, *Birth Control News* (of which Marie's husband, H. V. Roe, was editor), included "a factual error" in a nasty review of Margaret Sanger's book *The New Motherhood*, for which Ellis *had* written an introduction, he felt he must intervene out of loyalty to Margaret Sanger. What the factual error was he does not specify in his letter of protest to Marie Stopes. Could it have been the charge that Margaret Sanger had completely revised her views on methods of birth control after reading Marie Stopes's *Wise Parenthood*, as the review alleged? In any event, Ellis asked to have his name removed from the list of sponsors of *Birth Control News* and suggested that a public apology to Margaret Sanger be printed— an impossible demand on Marie Stopes. She replied—reasonably enough—that she couldn't correct the error unless he told her what it was. She warned him also that she feared he would be cross when he read her new book "for I *don't* ALWAYS agree with you! But when you see my disagreements remember we have had nearly 1600 actual *cases* at the clinic to say nothing of my correspondents."[33] He did not reply.

It was no longer necessary even to preserve the guise of politeness. In *Contraception: Its Theory, History and Practice* (1923) Marie Stopes made it clear that Ellis's ideas were *passé*, that he had contributed nothing to sexology since 1910. Ellis was willing enough to concede this point, but he took issue with her description of his interpretation of *coitus reservatus* as *coitus interruptus*.* "Many women," he told her, "have occasion to complain of *coitus interruptus*, but I have never heard of any woman who found anything but complete satisfaction in *coitus reservatus*; & I never expect to."†[34] Marie Stopes replied arrogantly that as usual he had based his judgement on a rapid and cursory reading of the text. And that was that. Her final word was that she sincerely hoped and trusted that "in speaking to others or writing about my work, you will not criticise so hastily."[35] As Ellis complained to Margaret Sanger, "it is impossible to make her admit she ever makes any wrong statements!"[36] When Margaret Sanger objected to being referred to as "the American woman" or "the American nurse," Ellis told her consolingly that Marie Stopes was "altogether too ridiculous in her childlike self-glorification not to be easily seen through."[37]

From this date he and Marie Stopes exchanged letters only when she sent him a copy of her latest book, which he politely acknowledged, although making it clear that he had not missed "the many little digs" she made at him in *Change of Life in Men and Women* in 1930. But, undeterred, in 1934 she wrote to ask him for a preface to *Birth Control Today*: "If you would do a thing which I should look upon not only as an act of very charming kindness, but as a crowning reward for all the toils, tribulations & torments I have endured on behalf of my work for women you would write me just three or four sentences of introduction for publication to encourage people to view the book with favour."[38] And this very curious creature, hearing that he was ill and in financial distress in 1938, wrote—after many years of silence—to ask if there was any way in which she could help him. He replied that he did not anticipate any real financial difficulty and went on to speak glowingly of her collection

---

* The disputed passage occurs on p. 75: "Freud also lists coitus reservatus as one of the causes of anxiety neuroses in men, and Fürbringer speaks against it. Nevertheless, Havelock Ellis who recognizes that it may injure the woman, mistakenly says: 'The injurious effect on the man, who obtains ejaculation, is little or none.' " There are evidently here two disputes—one concerning the definition of terms and the other, the respective effects—and the confusion is certainly, therefore, understandable.

† Was he thinking of Hugh de Sélincourt?

of atrocious poems, *We Burn*. Was he becoming a little dotty? Repeatedly through the years in a perfunctory way he praised her fine
work in "the great cause," but seemed as indifferent to her efforts
as he was to Margaret Sanger's. His own *Studies* were strictly
descriptive and the closest he came to practical advice was his
espousal of the vaguely phrased "love rights" of women. For all her
conceit and limitations, perhaps Marie Stopes helped people in a
more substantially real way. Her motive might have been self-
aggrandizement, but her lawsuits, her embarrassingly public private
life, and her platform performances possibly achieved more than
Ellis's deliberately chosen withdrawal from the fray.

Another controversial figure who, in turn, tangled with Marie
Stopes and who sought out Ellis for his own purposes was the
gynaecologist Dr. Norman Haire. Haire was an Australian Jew who
had changed his name from Zions when he moved to England in
1919. The friendship between two such disparate men is puzzling.
Haire first wrote to Ellis requesting him to help him join the BSSSP
(British Society for the Study of Sex Psychology). Since Ellis was not
an actual member of the Society, he could only put him in touch
with someone else—in this case, Stella Browne—but this was the
beginning of a long correspondence, and Ellis, who during the
twenties had become a semi-recluse, found time to see Haire while
he pleaded indisposition to many others who sought to take up his
time. In record time Haire established a lucrative practice in Harley
Street and was to become one of the most controversial and colourful figures at international congresses. There seems to have been
something repellent about his large, fleshy body, and the invariable
reaction I have elicited when asking about him has been a horrified shudder—"a slug" was the term most people used about him.
The only person who actually seems to have liked him was Françoise.* Ellis was aware of the reaction provoked by Haire's aggressive
manner, but he was judicious enough to overlook his personality
because of the genuine interest he took in Haire's work. Ellis, in
turn, was of immense help to Haire in sending him patients, as well
as providing him with valuable contacts and lending him books, although, as usual, he refused to write a preface for any of Haire's
works. He persistently refused the chauffeur-driven car Haire offered

---

* Yet she turned against him in 1948 when he contributed a cool review of
Friendship's Odyssey to *Marriage Hygiene*, to which she wrote a characteristically
long, impassioned reply.

to send for him as well as invitations to his home, although he made an exception once in order to see a special film. They did meet fairly frequently for a meal in a Soho restaurant, and Ellis was often so eager to discuss some topic with him that he would make the long trip from Brixton to Haire's Harley Street office. Haire commissioned the painter Tennyson Cole to paint a portrait of Ellis, but was very disappointed because it didn't catch his "faun" aspect.

Ellis's interest was initially aroused by Haire's radical practice of performing vasectomies, not simply on the Steinachian basis of rejuvenation, but as a means of birth control—and of course because of his preoccupation with selective breeding. That Ellis should approve of so drastic a method is a measure of his distrust of the then unperfected methods of contraception. Characteristically, he warned Haire to obtain the signatures of both husband and wife, and sent him to obtain advice from a lawyer, an acquaintance of long standing, E. S. P. Haynes. In November 1921 the Malthusian League opened a clinic at Walworth, a slum in south-east London, under Haire's direction. Only a month earlier, Marie Stopes had opened a clinic of her own where she prescribed the pessary, while Haire favoured the Dutch cap (the diaphragm). Marie Stopes was never to abandon her total faith in the efficacy of the pessary, while Haire, ever ready to experiment, was one of the first in England to insert Grafenberg rings, or what are now known as intra-uterine devices.

While Ellis had retreated from the embattled world of sexology, he continued to watch developments, and for Haire, who was obviously destined to be an energetic luminary, he was ever ready with fatherly advice. When from time to time Haire endeavoured to draw him into taking a more active part in various polemical issues, he would protest that he was no longer needed, that the cause was virtually won, and that he had no medical standing, particularly in England, where he was scarcely known. "My influence is confined to America." When Haire began to shake up the moribund BSSSP, Ellis warned him about his over-zealousness on behalf of homosexuals: "The usefulness of the Society will be largely destroyed if it comes to be regarded as simply a homo-club."[39] Ellis must have known that Haire was a homosexual.* Ellis approved of Haire's success in the sterilization of some mentally defective patients, a

---

* Many people were not certain. I asked Anatole James, who once worked for him, if Haire was homosexual, to which he replied: "Heavens, yes! But he was an old humbug."

policy he had advocated for years. "But," he cautioned him, "it is just as well that advance should not be *too* rapid, & that it should be unobtrusive—otherwise there may be an outcry & a reaction & a demand for legislation, which at this stage would be disastrous—Let things be *quietly* established, & then they will not be easy to overthrow."[40] (Ellis's premonition was right and he reacted in horror in 1931 when there was a move in Parliament to "legalize" voluntary sterilization.)

Haire had reason to be grateful to Ellis. In the spring of 1925, on Ellis's recommendation, he was invited to address a number of American medical societies, and while in Philadelphia called upon Ellis's editor at the F. A. Davis Company, to whom Ellis had written on his behalf, to discuss a possible book. But Haire's hot-headedness spilled over into his work, and when Kegan Paul rejected the first draft of his manuscript on marriage, Ellis read it to see what helpful advice he could extract from it. A lifetime's experience lay behind his summation: "To persuade people you need to soothe, not stimulate, their prejudices. Also you frequently appeal to *reason*, as though that were the creative force in life, & not, at the most, a very slowly & imperfectly modifying influence in life. Nature develops by growth not by reasoned construction, & the sense-organs, for instance, are unreasonably & absurdly developed out of structures which developed for quite a different end."[41] Ellis told Winifred Henderson that he hoped his letter would not mortally offend Haire, who "seems to go out of his way to stir up all the antagonisms he can."[42] But a grateful Haire replied: "You are one of my spiritual parents, & your word carries far more weight with me than my physical father's ever did."[43] He even told Ellis that his aggressiveness was part of his Jewishness and said that he would try to tone it down. In the summer of 1933 he motored down to Ellis's cottage in Sussex, Haslemere, where he took films of Ellis in the garden. After describing the afternoon, Ellis told Margaret Sanger that Haire was "engagingly simple & childlike, in spite of the qualities which make so many people detest him."[44]

Another personality whom Ellis found difficult but admired greatly was Magnus Hirschfeld, a neurologist who founded in Berlin in 1919 the Institute of Sexual Science, the first of its kind in the world for teaching all branches of sex science. When Margaret Sanger visited Germany the following year he urged her to pay a visit to the Institute and wrote to Hirschfeld asking him to provide her with an English interpreter. Hirschfeld, Ellis told her, "though he looks rather a coarse type, is a man of vast knowledge & an enormous enthusiasm & power for work."[45] (She included a very colourful account of the Institute in her autobiography, which gives a far more graphic and plausible account of the work of the Institute than an article written in 1920 for the *Medical Review of Reviews* by Ellis, who never actually visited it.) Three years later he also directed Haire to the Institute. Ellis's attention had been drawn first to Hirschfeld in 1904 when he published *Die Transvestiten*, which placed what Ellis was later to term "Eonism" (Volume VII of the *Studies*) on a solid basis as an anomaly distinguishable from homosexuality (unlike Krafft-Ebing, who had related it to insanity). He was even more impressed by *Homosexualität* (1914), which he recognized as a much more comprehensive study of the subject than he had been able to make in *Sexual Inversion*. In the third edition of *Sexual Inversion* (1915) he paid tribute to Hirschfeld for his scholarly history of the antiquated laws against homosexuality in Germany, as the first authority to deal adequately with lesbianism, for his rejection of inversion as degeneracy, and for his hypothesis that the study of internal secretions might be a path to an understanding of the deepest foundations of inversion.* For a time he considered translating the work into English. Later he realized that Hirschfeld was using the Institute for his own particular interests, as he informed Lonsdale Deighton of the BSSSP in a letter dated January 3rd, 1932: "It has been unfortunate for the Berlin Sexual Institute, established with so fine a programme, that it has been so largely homosexualised."[46] In view of the fact that both the Institute and the BSSSP were founded by homosexuals, Ellis's caveats seem rather naïve. Ellis found it difficult to carry on a conversation with Hirschfeld in German and his personality tended to be tiresome, so that when he visited England in 1926, Ellis asked Haire to tell him that he was prevented by ill-health from seeing him. It was an excuse he used to avoid innumerable conferences, and for years there was a widespread belief that he was a permanent invalid. Curiously enough, in 1929, at the Congress of the World League for Sexual Reform in London, Hirschfeld himself had to support the fiction and announced from the chair that Ellis was too ill to be present. But he still had to

---

* In 1933 in *The Psychology of Sex,* pp. 194–6, Ellis speculates on the genetic factors—i.e., XX and XY chromosomes—affecting inversion.

retreat to the country to escape the well-wishers who turned up at his door. "I am very wild over that infernal Congress," he told Françoise. "I think of withdrawing my name from the League. When people come there is nothing to do but to say I am away, my whereabouts uncertain, & that it is not known when I shall, if ever return, & that I may have committed suicide. Meanwhile they can be invited to write their damndest in the Visitors Book. I don't mean to see *any* of them."[47] And when the Congress was actually over, expecting another wave of invaders, he warned Françoise to be "ready with pokers & shovels to beat them back."[48]

II

Two figures for whom Ellis had unqualified respect, and whose ideas cross-fertilized each other's work, were Bronislaw Malinowski and Edward Westermarck. Malinowski, a Pole, had been inspired by Sir James Frazer, and in 1910 went to the London School of Economics,* where a department of anthropology had just been established. Between 1915 and 1918 he made an extensive visit to the Trobriand Islands, where he developed his functional theory which attributed to every custom, belief, and norm a function vital to that particular society. Ellis, who had wanted as a young man to visit a Pacific island, was interested from the beginning in Malinowski's work, and through the years a warm intellectual comradeship developed between the two men. In 1923 and 1924 Malinowski sent him some articles he had published in *Psyche*, in one of which he discussed how Freud's sexual theories might apply to the Western nuclear family but were not applicable to a matriarchal society such as the Trobriand Islanders.† While he pointed out a limitation in Freud's view, he was not actually attacking Freud's basic theories, which he does not seem to question within their special context. Ellis, however, ascribed more emphasis than Malinowski seems to have intended:‡ "With regard to Freud's indefiniteness & bad formulation, what you say is quite true, & I have often found it

---

* Where he became professor of anthropology in 1927.
† It is generally believed among Freudians that Malinowski's view was discredited by Géza Róheim in "Australian Totemism" (1921), in which he confirmed the universality of the Oedipus Complex.
‡ For Malinowski's view on Freud's contribution to psychology, see *Sex, Culture, and Myth* (Rupert Hart-Davis, 1963), pp. 114–16.

extremely confusing & annoying. But it has to be recognised as inevitable in the exploration of an entirely new field. Definition & formulation, in investigating living things, can only come *at the end*. At the beginning, things are constantly changing their shape & developing as they grow clearer, & Freud was very wise to avoid so carefully a precision which he would have had to change at every step. With what you say of his treatment of sex I entirely agree. Jung (whom I put decidedly below Freud) has just given a lecture of which I chanced this morning to have read the report; it is throughout a most admirable criticism of Freud."[49]

Ellis's eye lit on the importance of sea-water in the Trobriand belief in reincarnation: "You refer to the importance of water, & especially salt water, but nothing about urine, & I suppose this means they do not attach importance to urine. (This interests me as I have been collecting notes on urine & the psychology of urination, for a supplementary study of my Sex Studies.)"[50] Ellis believed that aggressiveness was not instinctive to man but that war had been introduced at some point in pre-history. (It was an argument that was to antedate Ashley Montagu's quarrel with Lorenz, Ardrey, and Morris, although Ellis never brought any supporting evidence to his suggestion.) "There is no warfare among the animals below Man, so the problem is: At what period in this history of Man (and of the Paleolithic Age? beginning of the Neolithic Age?) can evidence of warfare first be discovered? That is what I have long wanted to know."[51] In referring to the work Malinowski was then engaged upon, Ellis's comment indicates that it was probably best that he did not have an opportunity to visit a South Sea island: "It is of course the sex book that specially interests me. The kinship question always seems to me a sort of mathematical problem which requires too great an effort for my non-mathematical mind."[52]

Ellis broke his rule about refusing to write introductions when, through the instrumentality of Westermarck, he was asked if he would write one for Malinowski's *The Sexual Life of Savages* (1929). Malinowski replied delightedly: "I have learnt with great joy from Dr. E. Westermarck that you have kindly consented to write a Preface to a book on the sexual life of the Trobriand Indians which I am now preparing. It will be both a great advantage and an honour for the book to be introduced by you and to me it will be a great pleasure, for I am a great admirer of your sincere & courageous attitude and of your pioneer work. Forgive my putting this so crudely—

but I feel it so."[53] Some fascinating material about the influence of Ellis on Malinowski's book has emerged from unpublished Malinowski papers at the British Library of Political and Economic Science. On December 26th, 1923, Ellis wrote commiserating with Malinowski on a bout of depression from which he had been suffering. "I can sympathise as I have throughout life been from time to time subjected to the cruel buffetings of Fate, whether from without or from within. Fortunately one seems to survive them & even be, in some ways, though not in all, the better for them." This was written, it must be remembered, at the time when he was suffering most cruelly from the revelation of Françoise's affair with Sélincourt. Ellis then turns from personal problems to intellectual standards—and he tells his young disciple that he is "really alarmed & shocked" by Malinowski's admission that he had to tone down certain details—particularly the subject of unpleasant smells—because of the sensibilities of his readers. "From your previous work," Ellis admonished him, "I had assumed—quite as a matter of course—that you were adopting a strictly scientific attitude in ethnographic work & would not dream of being influenced by any extra-scientific considerations. Otherwise, why should you choose to write about sexual relationships, for unless sex relationships are treated in relentlessly scientific spirit they are altogether unprofitable for science, the whole thing would become merely a piece of pseudo-scientific charlatanism. During recent years it has, for the first time, become possible to deal with sex matters scientifically. But it has been a very slow & painful & difficult process to lift the subjects of sex investigation into the pure air & the sunshine, & if you, who are so prominent a leader in anthropological science, propose to allow science to slide back into the swamp of superstition & prudery, out of an abject desire to cringe to the obscene mob, what hope can there be for the world?" He goes on to tell him that readers' sensibilities have changed and cites instances in e. e. cummings's novel *The Enormous Room* (lent to him by Bryher), which had very explicit descriptions of smell. If there was to be a "holocaust"—as Malinowski feared—it was not for him to produce it, but for him to stand firm.

"With regard to the special subject of olfaction, it may be accepted that only 'nice' smells are to be discussed in the drawing-room, & magazines (even *Psyche*) are commonly regarded as drawing-room literature, & amenable to the same standard. I would myself not only accept but welcome this limitation of 'polite' conversation to 'nice' subjects, & the avoidance of the discussion of sexual details in general conversation. *But what on earth has that to do with science?* It might just as well be said that surgical operations should not be performed in the drawing-room nor on the dining-room table between courses. It seems very true. But what bearing has it on the matter in hand??? The part played by olfaction in the higher animals below man is so large, & Man has inherited a brain which is so largely olfactory that it is of the highest importance to ascertain what part it (smell) plays among seemingly primitive people in so vital a function as that of sex. You cannot possibly deal with this too fully or too minutely. (The same may be said of every other aspect of sex, & they are all far removed from the sphere of the conventionally 'nice.') Smell in relation to sex is discussed at length, as a matter of course, in the fourth volume of my *Studies* & nobody wrote to tell me it wasn't 'nice,' but many to express their interest in the investigation or to furnish new facts."[54]

Malinowski's reply reassured Ellis, who answered on January 10th, 1924:

"That you would agree with my point of view I had no doubt. But I know so many people, scholarly, unprejudiced, amiable people—too amiable!—who seem to think nothing of suppressing their own personal feelings & attitudes if they think them perhaps contrary to those of the prudish & superstitious crowd. They never pause to consider how disastrous it is when those who should be the leaders of the herd stoop to become its slaves. It is one of the few things by which I am infuriated!—Quite necessary, as you say, to avoid any temptation to shock, épater le bourgeois, because, although it may be good for *him*, it prevents oneself being taken seriously. But to me it seems not so very difficult to hold this tendency in check. As you refer to my attitude in the matter, I may say that I do not think that I *want* to shock my reader. I know that I sometimes *will* shock him, but that is not my motive. My aim is either (in impersonal & scientific writings) to express the subject before me, or (in more personal writings) to express myself. I would prefer *not* to shock. So in my more scientific work, while seeking to say everything necessary to be said in simple bald uncoloured words (avoiding the use of any Latin, which I regard as a most offensive practice), I have always omitted any crude & repellent details which do not seem to me necessary for the comprehension of the matter in hand, while in my personal writings I seek to express the shocking things in a quiet, suave, matter-of-course way, sugar-coating the pill. (Some of my shocking things have never been discovered!) I do not mean that I regard the sugar-coating as indispensable, but merely that I prefer to use it so far as possible. Only, when used, it must not be visible! It seems to me a serious error to show even the *slightest* consciousness that one is shocking. Any excuse or apology is fatal."[55]

Never had Ellis spelled out his ideological approach more clearly or more candidly. Malinowski took the advice to heart and from then on they were in complete accord. After picking up one of the chapters at Malinowski's home, Ellis wrote: "It is not only an instructive & admirable exposition, but of incidental interest in showing how your islanders, both in the method of treating children & in the attitudes towards sex, present a stage of development towards which we seem to be moving. I shall begin to suspect that you are a moralist in disguise & that you aim to follow up Diderot with a 'Deuxième Supplément au Voyage de Bougainville.' "[56] He read the typescript at Broadstairs, where he was wintering in 1928, and found it wholly admirable apart from some "small matters of detail, especially terminology, which often seems to be lacking in scientific precision. In an ordinary traveller's record of impressions words can be used in a random way which is out of place in ethnography."[57]

Edward Westermarck, the other focus of Ellis's interest at this time, was professor of sociology at the University of London. Ellis's first contact with him was in 1902 through the painter Henry Bishop, who was then living in Tangier. Ellis knew of Westermarck as a young Finn who had published *The History of Human Marriage* in 1891. Aware that his knowledge was limited only to European cultures, Westermarck spent six years in Morocco, where he lived in close contact with the natives, the result of which was *Marriage Ceremonies in Morocco* (1914). It was during this period that Ellis wrote to him suggesting that they exchange books, a proposal to which Westermarck enthusiastically agreed. He already owned *The Criminal* and was anxious to obtain a copy of *Sexual Inversion*. Ellis was also profoundly impressed by *The Origin and Development of the Moral Ideas* (1906–8), a series of monographs on the various human virtues and vices. Westermarck's thesis that what from one point of view was a virtue was from another point of view a vice was a stance of moral relativity which appealed to Ellis, whose first published essay, "What Is Pureness?," had questioned the rigidity of accepted norms. Westermarck's book was quoted extensively throughout the *Studies*. Reviewing the fifth edition of *The History of Human Marriage* in *The Nation and the Athenaeum* in February 1922, Ellis described it as "the nearest approximation to a completely adequate history of marriage that has ever appeared, or that we are ever likely to see."[58] Ellis approved of the principles which guided Westermarck—a biological basis and an inductive collection of comparative facts—and he regarded his method as less hazardous than the "pure" sociology of Durkheim and Rivers, the first of whom did not hesitate to draw general conclusions from a study of totemic Australian tribes while Rivers was "profuse in conjectures." Ellis himself had suggested a revision which Westermarck incorporated into this edition. Westermarck had originally regarded the horror of incest as instinctive, but Ellis persuaded him to modify this view. Here Westermarck takes a stand against both Frazer and Freud and quotes Ellis:

> Between those who have been brought up together from childhood all the sensory stimuli of vision, hearing, and touch have been dulled by use, trained to the calm level of affection, and deprived of their potency to arouse erethistic excitement which produces sexual tumescence.[59]

In his review Ellis dwelt at length on this point, which he felt required further elaboration.

> Dr. Westermarck might have pointed out that, in our civilization, the occasional examples of truly passionate attraction which arise are nearly always between those persons who have been separated during the pubertal period, so that the dulling effect of familiarity on the development of sexual stimuli has been suspended.[60]

Ellis, it will be remembered, says frankly in *My Life* that his understanding of this phenomenon was gained from the intimate friendship which developed between himself and his sister Louie on his return from his long sojourn in Australia.

From Finland Westermarck wrote gratefully:

"I have received your reviews of my book and they have made me both grateful and proud. It was indeed very good of you to devote so much time to the book, and I can frankly say that there is nobody whose opinion I appreciate so highly as yours. In a way you have yourself provided this new edition. Some years ago, when we met at the Reading Room, you asked me if I was going to revise the book, and you added, somewhat reproachfully, that it would be a pity to leave it as it was. I took it to heart, and shortly afterwards I rather unexpectedly found an opportunity to stay in England so long that I could undertake the work."[61]

In 1935 Westermarck, again in Morocco, wrote to tell Ellis that his *Studies*, particularly Volume VI, had been extremely useful to him in his recent work and that he would consider it "a great favour" if Ellis would allow him to dedicate *The Future of Marriage in Western Civilization* (1936) to him.

Ellis was often asked to give his comments on marriage. With the emancipation of women and the growing acceptance of birth control, he foresaw that there would be inevitable changes in marriage, but was convinced that biologically it must remain basically the same, since its main object would continue to be reproduction. He was fond of telling the story of how Barker Smith, while experimenting with mescal, found himself confronted with the Almighty, to whom he addressed the question: What is the meaning of the universe? "Reproduction" came the booming answer. It might seem a curious stand for a man whose own marriage was childless, yet the marriage relationship was one upon which he wrote extensively. One of his most thoughtful pieces on the subject was written for Count Hermann Keyserling's *Book of Marriage* (1925). George Bernard Shaw refused to contribute to it on the grounds that "No man dare write the truth about marriage while his wife lives. Unless, that is, he hates her, like Strindberg, and I don't. I shall read the volume with interest, knowing that it will consist chiefly of evasions; but I will not contribute to it."[62] Ellis's contribution, "The Art of Love," was an evasion to the point that he concentrated on woman and the development of "the erotic personality" to the almost complete exclusion of men. He was fascinated by the psychology of women, but he never came to terms with "normal" male reactions. This omission is so glaring that it is curious that it has never been commented on.

Ellis approved so strongly of Malinowski and Westermarck because from empirical evidence they were able to refute Freud. He himself spoke tactfully of Freud in print, apart from the essay in *The Philosophy of Conflict* where he had irritated Freud so much by referring to him as an "artist," a back-handed compliment in a field where precision of terminology was all-important. Freud always asserted that he had a basic need to have an enemy, but it was clear that he was not going to find one in Ellis. Ellis had made it abundantly explicit that he did not want to quarrel, but so long as he wrote critically of Freud, Freud was bound to respond irritably. Their relationship fell into a customary pattern: Ellis would write an article critical of Freud—or, more precisely, of "Freudians"; Freud would write to him in protest; Ellis would reply placatingly, attempting to soothe the ruffled feathers, protesting that he had not meant to speak as baldly as he had appeared to have done. Then a long interval of silence until a further outburst.

The occasion for the next altercation was Ellis's review of William McDougall's *An Outline of Abnormal Psychology*, which appeared in the July 1926 issue of *The Forum* under the title "A Tribute to Freud." It is understandable that McDougall reacted indignantly to a review of his six-hundred-page book which referred to his work almost in passing. A large part of McDougall's book is devoted to Freud, but in a highly critical way, as McDougall was the leading exponent of what he called "hormic" psychology, centred on goal-motivated man who is driven entirely by his instincts. Ellis's review is thin and evasive and one can only wonder what *his* motivation was in writing it. (In a private letter to Dr. Joseph Wortis on October 2nd, 1936, he is far more frank: "Indeed I am a little inclined to agree with McDougall about 'the greatest figure in psychology since Aristotle'—who is nearly always wrong! I do *not* agree with McDougall that he himself anticipated F. That is absurd. F. is an extravagant genius. McDougall is merely pedestrian.") Aware by now of Freud's sensitivities, Ellis uses more modified language to make the same points which he had expressed more directly in 1919. If McDougall sees himself as a mediator between Freud and a largely hostile world, Ellis reminds him that he had written about Freud ten years before McDougall had shown any interest in him. He then goes into his usual diatribe about Freud's followers, but is never explicit about what their offences are. More serious, he praises Freud to the skies—but for what? He does not give a single concrete example of Freud's contribution to psychology. It is as though the total achievement amounted to vapour: "He is in perpetual vital movement. His standpoint to-day is not where it was yesterday, and tomorrow it will not be where it is to-day."[63] If Freud is praised, it is for his "childlike quality." The highly sophisticated Freud, with the great body of a profoundly thought-out *Weltanschauung* behind him, expressed what he called "petty annoyance." Ellis again hastened to mollify him by his customary tactic of an account of his own failing powers; his enfeebled body, he told Freud, was confined to the garden of Little Frieth. But what pleasure it gave him to remember that he had been "almost the first person"* in England to recognize the genius of Freud. "It is true," he confesses, "I do consider that there is a sect of 'Freudians.' But that is not your fault. It is inevitable. It is what has happened for thousands of years. Whenever a giant appears, a number of small men group around him, & tie him down to the ground with their own small threads, as the Lilliputians tried to tie down Gulliver, so that he shall not move. But I am quite able to distinguish Gulliver from the Lilliputians around him." As for his "little review," it was "so rapidly written, and I was allowed so small a space, that my meaning could easily be misunderstood." McDougall had also been moved to protest that "I have not paid sufficient attention to all his criticisms of you. But I can only repeat that they are no matter!" Since McDougall had gone very thoroughly into all the major subjects to which Freud had addressed himself—dream-analysis, the origin of homosexuality, the Oedipus Complex, libido, phobias, repression, resistance, etc., one would have thought that Ellis would have considered this a God-given opportunity to spell out precisely his areas of agreement and disagreement with Freud. But this was not the way Ellis operated: what he seems to be saying is that all these petty differences will pass

---

* Ellis often claimed that he was the first to bring Freud to the attention of the English-speaking world, e.g.: "While I share your admiration for Freud," he told Dr. Grace Pailthorpe on November 11th, 1932 (Author's Collection),"(Having indeed come first in expounding his work in an English book in 1898) I do not feel that his results can be converted into dogmas. . . . "In actual fact, Ellis was antedated by J. W. H. Myers in "Hysteria and Genius," *Journal of the Society for Psychical Research*, VIII, No. 138 (April 1897), 50–9; and Mitchell Clark's long review of *Studien über Hysterie* in *Brain*, XL (1896), 401–14. In Ellis's article "Hysteria in Relation to the Sexual Emotions," *Alienist and Neurologist*, XIX, 599–615, Ellis does not get around to discussing Freud's and Breuer's theories until p. 609.

away and meanwhile he stands serenely above them. Did he really think that Freud would be taken in by this? There is always the possibility that he would have had to acknowledge Freud's greatness in concrete terms—and then he would have been a Freudian! And if he disagreed as strongly as McDougall did, then he would have had to have thought out an epistemological system of his own. His final consolatory note must have been particularly galling to Freud: "I can quite understand that you find all these misunderstandings painful. But I can assure you that they *always* occur! Every man of original genius has had to experience them. They must be accepted with calmness. You remember the complaint of Hegel, as reported by Heine: 'No-one has ever understood me, except one man—and even he did not understand me.' The remark may have not been authentic, but it ought to have been!"[64] As surety of his good will, he sent along a copy of Goldberg's biography. Freud's reply is ingenious. The biography, he says, is of interest to him because he had always wanted to know more personal details about Ellis. He had not been able to create so harmonious a life for himself, nor been able to achieve the same "kindness" because he had been forced far more than Ellis to make decisions. The underlying insinuation is that his work was so fearlessly controversial that it was necessarily polemical and that to take a stand on certain convictions precluded a wishy-washy general benevolence. Did they share anything? Goldberg mentioned that Ellis had a picture of St. Hieronymus hanging on his wall. Then, Freud concludes, if they share an admiration for St. Hieronymus they must share some ideals, whatever they were. Freud could be as politely banal as Ellis. Were they both enjoying the cat-and-mouse game?

And so it went on. Ernest Jones many years before had been in friendly correspondence with Ellis about a projected book he was to write for the Contemporary Science Series, but as he became totally devoted to Freud, his initial friendliness to Ellis was replaced by condescension. In 1928 he wrote a long review of Volume VII of the *Studies* in *The International Journal of Psychoanalysis* in what Ellis considered "his most superior and supercilious tone."[65] Ellis claimed that he never bothered to read more than a few paragraphs of it. Why? Did it reveal unpleasant truths? Did he read far enough to find that Ernest Jones did not consider that he had contributed anything of substance to the science of sex and that, jealous of Freud's success, on every occasion he sought to denigrate him?* It is understandable that Ellis would have been distressed before he finished reading the first paragraph, which deserves to be quoted:

> It is doubtful if this volume, the seventh in the famous series, will enhance the high reputation of the author, whom we all gladly honour as the doyen of "sexual psychologists." Not that it does not exhibit in a high degree many of the qualities for which he is so justly renowned: the beautifully limpid and gracious prose, the recondite learning, and the wealth of material on which he draws. But into the dignity and serenity which have always distinguished his writings there has of late crept a note of a different kind, a somewhat personal querulousness which a little mars a character so many have come to love. To put the matter plainly, contact with psycho-analysis has revealed limitations that were previously imperceptible. It would have been better if Dr. Ellis's career had either preceded the advent of psycho-analysis or else come after this had been assimilated by the general body of thought. An unhappy clash which has no other result than causing distress would then have been avoided, to the benefit of both the author and his audience.[66]

Jones then goes on to make an extremely important point: that throughout the seventh volume Ellis, in an attempt to refute Freud, again and again denies that this or that phenomenon is sexual in origin—indeed, his final attitude becomes *anti-sexual!* Jones further regrets Ellis's increasing preoccupation with nomenclature—which, he tacitly suggests, is an attempt to assert his priority in retaliation for the lack of recognition accorded him for the coining of several terms such as "auto-erotism." As for the opening section on "Eonism"—or cross-dressing, he cannot find any evidence within Ellis's essay for his "astonishing conclusion" that transvestism is not related to homosexuality; indeed, in his own experience—of dealing with actual patients—he has found the contrary to be decisively the case. He wastes no time on the Florrie story, devoting to it a single dismissive comment: "Dr. Ellis lays great stress on the extreme sympathy with which he investigated and treated the case." The section on the

---

* In Ernest Jones's autobiography, *Free Associations* (London: Hogarth, 1959), he speaks of a number of medical psychologists such as Morton Prince and Ellis "who felt that their achievements, substantial enough in themselves, were threatened by the new discoveries Freud was making, and who could not rise above the jealousy they, rather naturally, felt" (p. 241).

menstrual curve is simply an endorsement of Marie Stopes's findings. As for Ellis's "Synthesis of Dreams"—in which Ellis maintains that dreams of flying are not sexual in origin but derive from disturbed breathing—Jones makes no comment on this, which is comment enough. As for Ellis's imperfect grasp of wish-fulfilment dreams, Jones fears that Ellis can understand dreams only in their manifest content. The chapter on narcissism and auto-erotism apparently does not deserve discussion because, as Jones says, it is a literal and historical study.* As for the chapter on "Undinism," Jones finds it staggering that Ellis sees an interest in urine as subordinate to a still more primary interest in water itself. He is clearly thankful that the final chapter, on marriage, lends itself to a gracious conclusion. Here, according to Jones, Ellis exhibits his best qualities: suavity, breadth of mind, gentle wisdom. He quotes Ellis's final words: "For my own part, notwithstanding various archaeological interests, I find it tedious to be among those who are several centuries behind their own time; it has amused me more to share the disdain bestowed upon those who are a little in front. I may be permitted, as I depart, to make this one personal observation."[67] What and whom did he mean by this ambiguous remark? The Freudians? Apparently Jones thought so, because he allows the statement to speak for itself. He ends with a gracefully veiled remark: "In its wealth of knowledge and thought, as well as in its charm of exposition, it can rank as a

---

* Yet the previous year he had written a friendly letter after Ellis had sent him a reprint of his article on narcissism, which is essentially the same essay.

81 Harley Street
10th June 1927

Dear Dr. Havelock Ellis.

Many thanks for sending me your reprint on "Narcissism." I greatly enjoyed the remarkably interesting historical account, especially as many of the points were new to me, and I fully agree with your main conclusions. I was puzzled by one reference to myself (p. 145) where I am supposed to regard the absence of narcissism as "deplorable." As I cannot conceive its ever being absent, I have never speculated on whether its absence could be advantageous or otherwise, but possibly you are referring to repression of narcissistic libido.

I wonder if our use of the word autoerotism really differs so much from yours. You say "For the psychoanalyist 'autoerotism' generally means sexual activity directed towards the self as its object." I should have said that directing of the activity of the self towards an object is just what distinguishes narcissism from autoerotism and that autoerotism is essentially objectless. To me autoerotism is about identical with what Lawrence in his novels calls sensationalism.

Yours very sincerely,
Ernest Jones
(Lafitte Collection)

worthy member of the famous series to which it belongs."[68] In sum, he denies the possibility that Ellis has contributed anything of profundity to our understanding of man's most basic instinctual drive.

Françoise was furious and, with Ellis's knowledge, in her impetuous way sent a letter to Freud objecting to Jones's interpretation of Ellis's attitude towards Freud. She gave no indication that she was in any way connected with Ellis; and in his reply Freud addressed her as "Herr." She gave the letter to Ellis to translate for her: "I can never read German writing," he told her, "and Freud's is specially bad. But in the first sentence he seems to say that he can assure you that you are entirely right in your conception of his relationship with H. Ellis.* I *think* that in the second paragraph he tries to explain & defend Jones—as he would be bound to do—since Jones is his chief disciple."[69] Four years later Freud told Dr. Joseph Wortis that Ellis had written to protest about a hostile review; this is how he had interpreted it, and had not been taken in by Françoise's apparent noninvolvement with Ellis.

In 1930 Freud sent Ellis a copy of *Civilization and Its Discontents*. Ellis was utterly repelled by what he considered its bleak view of mankind, and for once he did state precisely what his objections were. In the opening pages Freud had discussed why he rejected the validity of Romain Rolland's "oceanic" feeling towards the universe; as far as Freud was concerned, psychoanalysis had revealed that it was an illusion that the ego was autonomous and unitary. Ellis immediately sat up and took notice because the description of Rolland's sense of eternity, an assurance which at the same time precluded any belief in personal immortality, was so close to his own experience. (The following year, in his Introduction to Hinton's *Life in Nature*, he described this as "a sort of home-feeling in the universe.") "For myself," he told Freud, "I can only sympathise with the friend you mention in the early pages. I do not claim any 'oceanic' feelings but (as described in my 'Dance of Life') a very similar emotionally religious attitude towards the universe, which first appeared at the age of nineteen, when I was living, quite alone, in Australian solitudes. It may possibly be constituted in part by sublimated libido. It is allied to mysticism, but not to any of the pseudo-intellectual religious creeds."[70]

Most disturbing of all was Freud's belief that "aggression is an

---

* I.e., "mutual appreciation which has grown into feelings of sincere friendship."

original, self-subsisting instinctual disposition in man." Ellis's response could have been taken from the pages of Kropotkin's *Mutual Aid*, a book which Ellis never seems to have read. "As regards the primary impulse of aggression," he went on, "I would not object to this if you insist equally on a primary impulse of mutual help. If the primary aggressive impulse was predominant,—we should not be here! A species can only survive by the predominance of the impulse of mutual help. You quote the saying of Hobbes, 'Homo homini lupus.' But, as Shaftesbury pointed out, two centuries ago, the saying is not valid, since we cannot compare the attitude of an animal to its *own* species with that to *another* species. If man is like the wolf, then, said Shaftesbury, we have to remember that 'wolves are to wolves very kind and loving creatures.' The impulse of aggression is, fundamentally, a manifestation of the impulse of mutual help. We are aggressive towards those whom, we think, threaten those we love. If we view aggression *biologically*, this seems to me its only explanation." Lest Freud be in any doubt that his objections might encompass personal animosity, Ellis concluded with an expression of "affectionate greetings."

CHAPTER 24

A SHARED LIFE

1928 AND 1929 WERE YEARS OF DISTURBING CHANGE IN HAVELOCK Ellis's life. He tried to arrange his routine to give himself the quiet and privacy he so much needed, but other people seemed to be taking decisions out of his hands, and since it was done with good intentions, it was difficult for him to raise much protest.

Houston Peterson's book was published in May 1928 and, although Peterson meekly agreed to the changes Ellis wanted him to make in the manuscript, Ellis always resented its prying into his private life, particularly since Peterson had assured him that the book would not be a biography but an assessment of his ideas. There is a note of querulous irritability in a letter to Margaret Sanger: "What he does here, & at a number of other points, is to plunge into intimate things of which he knows nothing & naturally commits all sorts of blunders. While he was quite right to conclude I was much in love with Olive, he goes on to quote a number of passages from Olive's letters which don't refer to me at all! And his attitude towards Olive, & nearly all the women associated with me, is unpleasant & superior. I tell him he has an academic anti-woman complex."[1] Ellis seemed particularly to detest the title of the book—*The Philosopher of Love*—a rather curious reaction, since it seems extremely appropriate. Ellis had other objections. On another occasion he told Margaret that Peterson "seems to have no very definite opinions or standpoints of his own, & I've no idea why he ever decided to write about me at all."[2]

Ellis never more than dipped into the completed book and, while there were sections such as the account of the Bedborough trial which he found excellent, the book as a whole was always a sore point with him.*

Much as he cherished Margaret Sanger, it was she who was primarily responsible for disturbing the quiet routine of his life. On January 22nd, 1928, she wrote to Françoise from Switzerland—where she was organizing the first World Population conference—asking her help in implementing Havelock's birthday gift that year, which she mistakenly—and characteristically—thought was his seventieth birthday.

"When I see Harold Cox† & all the men in the world who write, having the details done for them by a capable secretary, in order to save the energy & strength of the writer, I froath [sic] at the mouth to think that our dear Havelock toils over details of proof reading, indexes, etc etc which could easily be done for him. I want terribly to give him a Secretary for his 70th birthday & for the rest of his blessed life—& I would love it if you would be that Secretary. I do not know how to ask him to accept this, & so I come to you Françoise dear to ask your help. I have £300 a year that is doing nothing nothing. It is not much I know, but perhaps for half time you would be able to make that do, & then be free for translations or what ever else you may wish to take on. Oh dear Françoise, I do so want you to be near that blessed man, as much as ever you can. Is this possible at all? Do you think you can persuade him to accept this—(I shall die if he refuses). I

---

* When Ellis protested to Ferris Greenslet of Houghton Mifflin about the manuscript, Greenslet replied on November 21st, 1927:

Dear Mr Havelock Ellis
    Thank you for yours of Armistice Day. *What you say about the Peterson book is very much what I expected.* We are signing him up and hope to publish the volume early next spring. I think it is pretty sure to have a large sale and be very helpful in the sale of your other books and generally spreading the gospel according to H.E.
                                                            Faithfully yours,
                                                            Ferris Greenslet.

(Ellis wrote angrily across the letter: "I like the coolness of this remark in reply to what I had written to him of Peterson's offensiveness and inaccuracy in personal matters!")

† Harold Cox (1859–1936), an economist, author of *Economic Liberty* (1920), *The Problem of Population* (1923).

have three secretaries & know what a good one means to my living. Why we would spare him for creative work for twenty-five years if you will do this. I am breathless to dare suggest it, but all is fair in love & war. This both—love for him & war against the ravages of time & the waste of energy.

"I am going to leave this in your dear hands Françoise dear. Write me what to do, I shall sit trembling to get your reply—bless you—lovingly Margaret."[3]

Françoise had frequently complained about the burden of her life. She had difficulty keeping discipline in class, so that she was worn out by the end of the day, but had to take on night school as well in order to maintain her children in their miserable East End home. Hugh de Sélincourt had on a number of occasions told Margaret that some such arrangement as she ultimately proposed would be Françoise's salvation. Margaret pounced on the hint. Françoise was overjoyed by the letter and rushed down to Broadstairs to confront a bewildered Havelock with the proposal. His ambivalent feelings are expressed in a letter written shortly after her flying visit. The offer, he told her, was "so entirely in accordance with all my desires, & all your desires, that I do not see how it would be possible for me to say No. The only thing to insist on is *not to be in a hurry*. Margaret must have full time to think it over—as she is very impulsive—& to be quite sure that she sees her way to be as generous as she desires to be. And you have noticed that she says *70th* birthday, which is next year, not this. You must not be in a hurry to give up school. *On no account until everything is absolutely settled*."[4] He added that his work was different in kind from Margaret Sanger's or Harold Cox's in that he would always have to do his own secretarial work but, fearing lest she might be hurt, he assured her, "Your presence & help & love would be, as you know, an everlasting joy, & real practical assistance as well."

On February 23rd Margaret reached London and he had no strength to resist the will of two determined women. Margaret wrote delightedy to Françoise: "Yes it is unique this giving a woman as a present! We have heard of women presenting babies, twins, triplets & even themselves to husbands, but to give another woman to an adored man is unusual—& all goes to prove how noble I am!!"[5] Everything seemed to be conspiring to make him change the habits of a lifetime. Mneme, who had always lived close enough to forward his letters when he was away and to attend to little details of his household, gave up her Brixton flat and moved permanently to the coast with her husband. On February 22nd her father, his dear friend Barker Smith, died at eighty-two years of age. A day or so before, Ellis had sat by his bed for a long time while Smith held his hand affectionately. A cherished part of his life was over. For years they had made annual excursions to Suffolk, exploring old graveyards and records in search of ancestors. A tie with his past was broken and the sadness he experienced made it more difficult to cope with immediate situations.*

He took Little Frieth again but on the understanding that the owners had put it up for sale, which left him feeling very unsettled. The determined Françoise had tendered her resignation at the school, and was urging Ellis to do something about finding a house to be shared with her and her two sons, who still remained total strangers to him. He moved to Little Frieth in April in order to complete the Introduction to Volume VII of the *Studies*, and no sooner had he plunged into it than the owners of the cottage told him that he had to vacate it by the beginning of June. He felt old and tired and dispirited, but had enough obstinacy to resist Françoise's understandable demands that they should at least begin to look for a house in the Herne Hill area, since he didn't wish to move far afield. He recognized that Françoise needed this freedom, but he hated the thought of surrendering his own freedom, and he assured various correspondents that he was in no hurry to move out of his flat in Dover Mansions, where he had lived for twenty years. If Françoise gave up her job to become his secretary, she and her boys would have to set up housekeeping with Havelock. This meant buying a house, for which he would have to borrow money. It was all very upsetting. There is a querulous, if not slightly desperate, note in a letter he wrote to her from Little Frieth on April 28th: "I seem to feel that my Naiad does not realise that I cannot be *forced* to do things, whether to stay in other people's houses† or to buy a house for myself. It has

---

* On March 5th he wrote to Françoise: "For many years I have had in my head the idea of some day writing a life of Smith, & *may* do it. He is the only person I have ever known whose life I *could* write because I would be able to do it *not* too seriously, but quite faunishly" (Mugar Library).

† He is referring to the pressure she had put on him to stay at Sand Pit in 1927.

the very worst effect, & not only makes things hateful to me, but makes me think that there is a possibility that I may have to keep at a distance from Naiad, & I love her so much that I cannot bear to feel that there is a possibility I may have to be content to love her only at a distance. I love to know what you want, & I love to do it when I can, but it cannot be forced, it has to come spontaneously. . . ."[6] Again on May 21st he writes: "I am glad to be alone for I need to be alone to work, much as I love the presence of my Naiad & helpful as she is."[7]

But even a dwelling in the heart of the country was not sufficient to bar determined visitors. In the spring he was suddenly confronted by two formidable lesbians, Lady Troubridge and Marguerite Radclyffe Hall—"terribly modern & shingled & monocled & not at all Faun's style."[8] These women had been much in the news in 1920 when Radclyffe Hall brought a slander action against St. George Fox-Pitt. It was alleged that he had described her as "a grossly immoral woman" and accused her of coming between Admiral Sir Ernest Troubridge and his wife, wrecking their marriage. The Lord Justice decided in favour of Radclyffe Hall, who wore male attire in court, and awarded her £550 damages. The two women had already persuaded Ellis to read the typescript of her novel, *The Well of Loneliness*; and they now extracted from him a promise to write "a notice" for the book. There followed a complete—and I believe innocent—misunderstanding about this notice and where it should appear. On April 21st Ellis wrote to Radclyffe Hall:

> "As you know, I would not be able to see my way to writing any Preface for the novel, but I am deeply interested in the subject, having had many near friends, both men & women, who were, as they sometimes say, 'so,' & if the book appeals to me I would be glad to express an opinion that might be used."[9]

The publishers, Jonathan Cape, asked him to leave out the words "sexual inversion" from whatever he submitted. Ellis wrote a brief note in which he endorsed the novel, which, so far as he knew, was the first faithful depiction of lesbianism and possessed "a notable psychological and sociological significance." When the novel appeared in July, including Ellis's "Commentary," Ellis fired off an angry letter of expostulation to the publisher. He probably reacted as he did because of the tense state he was in over the projected change in his life; and Radclyffe Hall's apologetic letters do not seem

to suggest that she acted in bad faith.* A storm soon broke over the novel. "I would rather give a healthy boy or girl a phial of prussic acid than this book," wrote James Douglass in the *Sunday Express*.†
A copy was sent to the Director of Public Prosecutions and on August 23rd the Home Secretary ordered the novel banned. Ellis wrote to Radclyffe Hall sympathetically, suggesting that a public subscription be taken up for her appeal in December, but even though she had sold her house and car, she did not want to become involved in anything where she would have to ask for money; and, in any case, it was the publishers, not herself, who were made responsible. Ellis made it clear that he could only cheer from the sidelines:

> "I hope you will not misunderstand if I say at once that I should *not* be willing to be a witness. I *never* have been in the witness box. There are two good reasons against it. The first is that I do not possess the personal qualities that make a good witness, & would probably make a bad impression, & certainly not a good impression. The second is that, being the author of a book, on this very same subject, that has been judicially condemned, I am 'tarred with the same brush,' & even if I were a personally effective witness, my testimony could be of no assistance. You may say that it would carry weight with some people. True,—*but not in Police Court circles!* You may be quite sure that in those circles the Bedborough case is remembered, & would be dragged forward again. So the less said about me, the better for you."‡[10]

Incredibly enough, in early September Cape suggested that they bring out an English edition of the *Studies*, but Ellis replied that he "did not feel sufficient confidence in the courage of English publishers."[11] Before the appeal, Ellis assured Una Troubridge that

> "an adverse decision may be even better than a favourable decision, for in the latter case the matter will be settled & quickly

---

* On July 19th he wrote to Marguerite Agniel: "Radclyffe Hall is today very apologetic, says she understands (though I had clearly said what I was willing to do) that I did not want to write a *long* Preface, & did not mind how my little note was used. I quite believe her" (Morris Library, Southern Illinois University).

† On September 6th Ellis told Radclyffe Hall, "I hear that the 'Sunday Express' man [Douglass] is, or has been, insane, which is ample excuse for his foolishness—though not for Cape's!" (Lovat Dickson Papers, Public Archives of Canada).

‡ But he did give some practical help by arranging for his German translator, Dr. Eva Schumann, to translate *The Well of Loneliness* into German.

forgotten; while an unjust decision would be a perpetual flame to light up the principle involved & stir enthusiasm."[12]

The appeal did fail, and in March 1929 Radclyffe Hall wrote to thank him for all his moral support, and added: "Many is the time in these last anxious months that I have thought of and spoken of your wife. I have said: 'She would have sympathised with me in my will to fight and not be beaten, because she was a mighty fighter!' "[13] Moved to indignation by this case, Ellis wrote an essay, "The Revaluation of Obscenity,"[14] which he sent to the Public Prosecutor, Edward Atkinson, who replied:

> "May I respectfully suggest that you are in advance of the times in holding that education would now sufficiently protect the young from the dangers of really pornographic literature and pictures? Quite apart from the problems of literary works—I instance some of D.H. Lawrence's by way of contrast—such practical experience as I have had leads me to think that really pornographic wares still in these imperfect days need that attention of what you possibly regard as a clumsy weapon viz: the criminal law."[15]

But to return to the summer of 1928. The owners of Little Frieth allowed him to stay on until the middle of June, and he found it very difficult to tear himself away from the flowers and vegetables he had been looking after, particularly for tiresome details with estate agents and lawyers in London. There was some attempt to get Barker Smith's house, but it was too expensive, and Françoise finally found an assertively middle-class house on the same street, 24 Holmdene Avenue in Herne Hill. Françoise was ecstatic and immediately christened it The Fairy Tale House. Ellis had another opinion, especially after the visit of an American admirer: "I've got to be friendly to Americans! Where should I be without Americans? And where would the Naiad's new house be if the Americans hadn't bought the 'Dance of Life'? It ought to be named The House of the Dance of Life!"[16] Françoise was aware of his reluctance and, in a mood of anxiety, attributed it to his greater affection for Faith Oliver. Ellis hastened to assure her that nobody could take her place. Her jealousy over Faith was "absurd," he told her. "I should be mad if I wanted her to take your place. She is a dear & I am fond of her, & always get on with her nicely, but would be entirely unsuitable for

me to live with & work with—too young and inexperienced, too unsettled & absorbed in her own problems.

"You are just perfect, & while you offer all sorts of 'difficulties,'
it is the difficulties that make you perfect! I've never been able to
love a woman, or be in love with her, unless she was difficult—the
more difficult the more suitable for me. It is your vices that are your
great asset! All your independence & self-will & self-interest—terrible
vices that I cannot possibly do without."[17] Besides, he had become
terribly dependent on Françoise. Faith was totally absorbed by now
in her lover, and all Ellis's other friends were far away, involved in
their own affairs, some invalids, others dead. Without Françoise,
he admitted frankly, he would be completely alone.

On July 22nd Françoise planned a celebratory dinner in the new
house. When Ellis failed to arrive she sent one of her sons in search
of him. He had suddenly, it appeared, been incapacitated by an
attack of lumbago similar to the one which had assailed him a year
before immediately following Hugh de Sélincourt's overnight visit to
Little Frieth. There was absolutely no question, he assured himself
and everyone else, but that he desperately needed sunshine. He began
to think he was going to end up like "poor dear Edward Carpenter,"
who was so frail that he had two nurses in constant attendance. In
every way Suffolk would revive him and as soon as the pain subsided
he set off for the coast near Lowestoft, where he was joined by Faith
—and later by Françoise—in a secluded spot where they were able
to take nude sun-baths—and the lumbago miraculously disappeared.
When he returned to London in September he found himself "over-
whelmed" with work on a revised fifth edition of Man and Woman.
Françoise was left happily on her own to complete the living arrangements at Holmdene Avenue while he could quietly go about sorting
the mountain of papers he had accumulated over the years. He also
took an absorbed interest in a book of tributes the American anarchist printer Joseph Ishill was preparing.* After the unfortunate
Peterson biography, he took more than a proprietary interest in what
went into the book. Some of the writers, he suggested, might "now
wish to correct or modify statements. Would it not be desirable for
them to have a chance of doing this?"[18] He was particularly con-

---

* Ishill had already endeared himself to Ellis by lovingly printing essays and
short stories of Edith's, helping Ellis to exorcise his guilt over her by producing the
most beautiful memorial possible to her unrecognized worth.

cerned with Percival Chubb's allusion to his "aloof Epicureanism." After all, he protested, "He knew me fairly well forty years ago, but has not been in touch during my chief periods of activity." When Ishill seemed disinclined to tamper with any of the statements, Ellis felt that he had perhaps pushed him too far: "As regards Chubb, though I (& some others) do not agree about the Epicureanism, I have no wish that he should alter the statement. I am very far from being an advocate for unity of opinion (even about myself!)"[19] But he continued to make as many suggestions about what should be included as he had with the Goldberg book, although eventually he couldn't fail to notice that all the pieces he had considered important might give a one-sided view: "I fear this stream of extravagant eulogy becomes rather a worry to me, the more so since it is bound to lead to a reaction to the opposite extreme. I wish you could continue to get hold of a few thoroughly damnatory estimates of my work, where-with to spice your 'tributes,' & to qualify the monotonous lauda-tions!"[20] But he also wanted to get the picture straight. For instance, he did not want to be described as "a man of the study."* "My study is the open air!" he protested. "Nearly all my work has been done out of doors. . . . Although I had rooms at Brixton for so many years, I cannot recall that any book of mine is specially associated with Brix-ton. I do not regard London as a place to work in. The only place I can think of as a 'study' is the studio shed at Hawkes Point. . . . I do not feel really alive indoors, mentally or physically."[21] In reply to Ishill's inquiry as to whether an element of anti-Semitism entered into his feelings about Goldberg's book, he replied firmly: "As re-gards Jews, I am myself an admirer of Jews, with a high personal regard for many, & I have long collected material for an essay on the Genius of the Jews (though I may never find time to write it). There is no anti-Semitic feeling in England (except among a few individuals who in other respects also are recognized as cranks) & what many of my friends feel about Goldberg's book is that it is too cheap, too effusive, exuberant & journalistic."[22] When Ishill's volume appeared in July 1929—*Havelock Ellis—In Appreciation* with tributes from forty-two contributors including Malinowski, Mencken, Margaret Sanger, and Clarence Darrow—he expressed himself well pleased: "It is a book which will appeal to me much

---

* This was a term Olive Schreiner applied to him because of his lack of interest in social issues.

more than the would-be biographic volumes already published—whatever good points these possessed—for I find here so many affectionate testimonials from friends who are dear to me."[23]

On Ellis's return to Brixton from Norfolk in September he again set about the tedious task of sorting out his papers. It was apparent that a great quantity of valuable manuscripts and letters must be thrown out because there would clearly be no room for them in the cramped little house in Holmdene Avenue. (During these months his letters to Margaret Sanger are unusually repetitive and distraught, an index of his preoccupied state of mind.) But the unwelcome task had to be abandoned early in November when he decamped for Worthing to escape the foul winter air of London and to be able to work without distractions. Grubby Worthing—"the Nice of England"!—was chosen, as it was close enough for Françoise to continue her "secretarial" duties but, as far as Françoise was concerned, advantageous because it was within easy reach of Sand Pit. She was still plunged into gloom if she did not receive satisfactory letters from Sélincourt, and Ellis continued to lecture her like a Dutch uncle: "The love that Soleil offers you is beautiful, & you risk losing it by being discontented. In love you must either accept or refuse; you can't ask for *something different*. The wild part of his love he put into the beginning of it, & you are far too wise not to know that the end of love cannot be like the beginning."[24] Before Ellis left for Worthing the three of them had a meeting in the new house. On receiving Françoise's account of the occasion, Margaret Sanger wrote ecstatically: "It was heavenly to have you write about Hugh's visit. I know how supremely happy you must have been to see the two beloved boys in the Fairy Tale House. Hugh wrote me about it too and insists that the King never looked so rugged and strong and happy."[25] She went on to beg Françoise to try to find him a cottage in the country, to which she could immediately contribute up to $2,000.

In the middle of December Ellis spent one night in the new house—in a new bed Françoise had persuaded him to buy from Heal's, the first really comfortable bed he had ever had. Actually, his stay in Worthing was interrupted by a sad mission—Louie, his favourite sister, who had been in a nursing home in Sussex for years with rheumatoid arthritis, died suddenly from acute bronchitis.

He could not move into the new house until a self-contained section, containing a small room in which he could cook for himself, was ready. Repeatedly in his letters he told people that this was going to be only "a foothold" in London. He had thrown out a mountain of notes, but the small rooms in the new house could not possibly accommodate essential books. Again Margaret Sanger came to the rescue. Knowing how much he longed to have a cottage in the country, she suggested buying one for him and letting him live in it as a tenant. In her charming way she told him that it would give her a sense of possession. Early in March 1929 the ideal place was found in Wivelsfield Green in Sussex, completely secluded, with over an acre of grounds, orchard, and woods. Ellis was overjoyed. With this retreat he no longer felt that his freedom was being curtailed. The house, Haslemere, could be taken on a long lease. His bedroom would have windows on three sides so his beloved sunshine could flood in. Margaret sent a generous cheque which helped to lay out a garden and to buy a revolving shelter (such as Shaw had) in which to write and have sun-baths. He also had small trees planted around it to ensure complete privacy from the house. (He reluctantly agreed to the inclusion of a radio and telephone in the house at Françoise's insistence.) An assertively cheerful note enters his letters, which are now completely filled with details about his country cottage. Few people were given his Wivelsfield Green address—"except for a few special friends." He told people that he didn't mind at all moving from Brixton. It had become noisy and crowded, and the traffic was so bad that he felt nervous about crossing the road. By early May he was ready to leave the flat, although, even with the cottage, he was compelled to abandon masses of valuable papers, including material for projected books.

The move didn't prove to be as traumatic as he had feared. Françoise's boys, whom he had felt very shy about meeting, were interesting and clever. The plan of having his meals apart from them was abandoned, but he took no real interest in the house and left its details completely to Françoise. He moved to Haslemere as soon as it was habitable, and before the end of May the new cottage had a festive christening by the American dancer Marguerite Agniel, performing on the lawn to the music of the gramophone. Margaret Sanger—"the acknowledged Patron Saint"—arrived early in August to inspect it, accompanied by Hugh de Sélincourt, who of course worked himself up into a state of ecstatic jubilation over such an occasion. "It was simply perfect," he later gushed to her, "for me to be able, so to speak, to deliver you at Wivelsfield Green. A postman with such a parcel. You sitting in the dining room is a picture stamped for ever on my memory, with Havelock one large and shy beam of happiness opposite: neither looking at the other: me brazenly staring at each in turn. I wholly, openly, unblushingly, exulted: and didn't care a toss who minded. It was one of the happiest moments of my life, & will remain so."[26]

But Sélincourt was growing more distant from Françoise and the affair was slowly coming to an end. "I cannot tell you how much I wish I could cure myself of loving him," Françoise cried to Havelock.

> "I ache for him for months & months & we seem no nearer & closer never seeing one another. I have never in my life known a poorer lover. Yet I love him. Perhaps it is even because he is such a poor lover, so lacking in vitality that keeps me attached to him. While other men have been great males without sensitiveness, they have repelled me. But he with his sensitiveness & his lack of vitality, his weakness to carry through anything appeals to me as I always long & hope to give him strength. But I so often doubt I can ever do so. He wastes his days & time, scatters his energy, meets crowds of people (the Sand Pit has always people at the week-end) & achieves but little. Yet he says I am the last person he wishes to see & when he could see me this work he has neglected is always my foe. I get pushed in a corner. Faun I wish I were with you . . . I need you & wish that I could ache less with the longing for Soleil. Why can't he & I feel alike if I am to love him? And to love him I must for if I owe him much unrest & longing & hard fighting with myself, I also owe him much else! Fairy Tale House & Havelock. Hard paradigms!"*[27]

Ellis wasn't quite as open about his own intimate experiences. In Haslemere he hoped to have another visit from his tender American friend Josephine Walther. In September he told her of dreaming of her the previous night: "My thoughts became more and more full of my darling Jozia until I seemed to feel her in my arms & to be kissing her—kissing her all over & I lived over again that heavenly rapture—there is really nothing like it—which sometimes seems to lift her spirits into a higher world of ecstasy and music when she is pressed close against my breast."[28]

Haslemere he regarded from the beginning as his real home, and

---

* With her imperfect English, she probably meant "paradoxes."

a routine was established whereby he spent only a third of the year in London. Here, in the house in Holmdene Avenue, Dr. Helena Wright, the distinguished gynaecologist, first met him in September 1929. She had recently returned from China, where she worked for some years as a medical missionary. She had completed a book, *The Sex Factor in Marriage*, which she sent to Ellis for his comments. He told her that he had long felt that such a book should be written by a woman, but was critical of the fact that she had *assumed* birth control but had refrained from discussing it, a common approach in current books on the subject. It was not an approach he approved of, he told her: "It would have meant saying nothing at all at the time I began to write! It seems to me that one has to say everything that one thinks *ought* to be said, but *to say it so persuasively that it can give no offence*. To me it seems that, at the present day, a book on marriage in general cannot postpone for future discussion the subject of birth control, and that, moreover, there are far more people, even religious people, who would object to its omission than would object to its inclusion."[29]

Ellis invited Dr. Wright to tea, and her memories of him, of Françoise, and of the house in Holmdene Avenue are remarkably interesting. Her first over-riding impression was: What a horrible house! It might have been a lodging-house in a back street in Worthing. The sunless sitting-room smelled of cabbage and poverty. She was stunned by the incongruity of Ellis's intellectual and physical stature in that mean little room. "It was as though," she recalled, "he was *sojourning* in that room like an Arab in a tent and like an Arab, had arrived yesterday and would be gone tomorrow. His personality seemed to have kept itself separate from his surroundings, and I felt he had *resigned* himself to living there."

They sat down together on either side of the table. He talked with great facility, was generous and courteous in listening to her views, but she was made uneasy by the coldness of his eyes. At first she thought the air of coldness, of obliqueness, might be the result of shyness, but she sensed that the eyes were taking no part in what the brain was saying. "I had the queer feeling that here was someone who was two people but I wasn't certain he knew he was two people." A woman entered the room. He introduced her as Madame Cyon without any explanation as to who she was. Françoise sat down at the table and silently listened to what was being said, but with her appearance the whole mood of the discussion changed. Dr. Wright sensed that between these two there was a relationship both very complicated and very simple. "It was very, very subtle. I could feel two notes going." Although Ellis's manner to Françoise was perfectly polite, she felt that he did not respect her opinions or consider her mind to have any weight. The silent woman was obviously essential to him, but in a conversational duet she knew she had no place and accepted this with absolutely no resentment. The relationship had "the feeling of an old established fur coat." Again Dr. Wright reverted to Ellis's eyes. She shuddered. "They were so repellent. I didn't want to touch him. I began to feel that the coldness in his eyes was a real angle of his personality." A woman of great intuitive perception, Dr. Wright saw him as a man who had spent years contemplating emotions, but did not himself know how to express sexual emotion; and that at some time or other he had offered something of himself and had been repulsed (Olive? Edith? Françoise?). "He was just in his judgement, scholarly, sympathetic, possessed a great wide-mindedness, but was blocked by the intrinsic sadness of sexuality in itself."

LATE YEARS

THE LAST DECADE OF ELLIS'S LIFE WAS NOT A TRANQUIL PRELUDE TO death. New friendships were formed. Unexpected anxieties emerged. Fresh work was undertaken. Old friends died—both Edward Carpenter and F. H. Perry-Coste in 1929. As for his own health, his old duodenal pain sometimes troubled him, but, as he told Margaret Sanger, "One must end *somehow!* And I have outlived so many of my old friends that I have not the slightest right to complain."[1] Life went on. Faith Oliver married A. R. Powys and Ellis stood as godparent to her twins in 1931. In April 1930 a young American admirer, Joseph Wortis, asked him if he would like to be young again, and Ellis replied: "I should certainly say, No. It seems to me that the younger one is the more difficult it is to look around & beyond one's troubles. I certainly find that in recent years my life is happier, less apt to be crowded with anxieties, than ever before. And when one is old, & one's work is done, & one has extracted the most delicious essences out of the world, it is easy to treat lightly what is left."[2] It was a moment of rare optimism for a basically pessimistic man. The tulips were in bloom in the garden at Haslemere, the mortgage on the Holmdene Avenue house was almost paid off, and Françoise was radiantly happy in her new life. Why should he not accept the serenity due to old age? Because life had taught him that a moment of tranquillity is a rare hiatus, that circumstances are constantly changing, and that life is more apt than not to be painful but at least it is always interesting.

Ellis had habitually avoided controversy, but within a couple of months of writing this letter to Wortis he engaged more actively in polemical dispute than he had ever done in his life.* The basic premise behind all his writings on sex was an undeviating faith in congenital inheritance. In a number of letters Ellis argued with Dr. Joseph Wortis, who disagreed with what he considered Ellis's extreme views on heredity. "It cannot be controversial," Ellis replied to one objection, "that physical traits are inherited. Nor can it be controversial that psychic traits are inherited. Nor that no two individuals who come into the world are alike. What is in doubt are some of the natural laws ruling their genetic process, & that I leave open, admitting the infinite individualism of the phenomena."[3] Characteristics which seemed acquired, he was convinced, were really constitutional.† Ellis's reasoning went thus: Edith was an invert and had come from a line of unbalanced ancestors. It was not difficult for an understanding doctor to persuade an intelligent woman that she should not have children. (It was not her inversion but her neuroticism which was in question, although Ellis believed that one accompanied the other.) In a more serious case of inheritance, such as insanity, doctors should persuade those afflicted that they owed it to society to allow themselves to be sterilized. He was always vague about the mode of persuasion, and sometimes spoke about patients coming forward voluntarily. This seems both naïve and wilfully blind about the dangers inherent in such a situation. Ellis's adherence to

---

* The dispute with Karl Pearson over the variability in men and women (in the years immediately following 1897) was conducted in public print, whereas Ellis's part in this dispute was confined mainly to private letters.

† Dr. Marie Jahoda has pointed out to me the inconsistency of Ellis's position. "Ellis called himself a Darwinian," she writes, "but was also an unwavering hereditarian, not taking note of the fact that Darwin recognised the enormous power of the environment in selecting successful species. I believe that most of the social Darwinians in the 19th and the beginning of the 20th century made the same mistake of ignoring Darwin's interactionist position between heredity and environment." In another letter, in discussing the attitudes of Ellis and Symonds towards homosexuality, she writes: "Had those chaps been real Darwinians they would have argued that homosexuality transmitted by genes has little chance of surviving as healthily as it does, because homosexuals have many fewer children than heteros. My own guess is that it has another survival value to the extent that it creates a bond between same sex people who otherwise might murder each other even more frequently than they do. (Survival value for the species, not for the individual). We are really all bisexual. What is culturally produced is the exclusive emphasis on hetero. sex and the repression of homosex. It really hinges on an appropriate definition of sexuality. If you take Freud's—a peculiarly pleasurable sensitivity of the skin to the self—or other manipulation—any apparent reason for requiring a partner of the other sex drops away. But that's my own view. Freud deserted his bisexuality idea too quickly."

eugenics was in a strange sense an offshoot of nineteenth-century optimism and the related belief in progress through the instrumentality of science: that is, that man had it in his control to create a better race. Nowadays—with the horrors of mass exterminations behind us—such racial views are very much in discredit. But in 1906 it seemed to him a matter of social duty to support Francis Galton's notion that those desiring them should be supplied with "eugenics certificates" of fitness, especially before marriage. Ellis suggested refinements on Galton's rather vague scheme, such as a thorough medical examination, a determination of inherited physical "anomalies," and a psychological test covering "the integrity of the various senses, perception, discrimination, attention, etc. etc."[4] In an important sentence of a letter to Galton written on June 13th, 1907, Ellis said: "In the concluding volume of my Sex 'Studies'* I shall do what I can to insinuate the eugenic attitude. Public opinion is the only lever at present, and legislative action must be impossible—& futile— for a very long time to come."[5] Ellis remembered the occasion on June 23rd, 1880, when he watched from the Visitors' Gallery as Bradlaugh was dragged from the House for having sought to make the Oath illegal. Ellis did not admire dramatic gestures such as Bradlaugh's, which he considered ineffectual. Time and persuasion were the wise course in changing public opinion. (Similarly, he showed no sympathy or interest in Margaret Sanger's incarceration in 1917.) In a pamphlet which he wrote in 1911 for the National Council of Public Morals, *The Problem of Race Regeneration*,† he advocated the betterment of the race by "persuading" the unfit to be sterilized. It is curious that vasectomy was the only method he was enthusiastic about. He found birth control "quite dull & commonplace & best left to dull & commonplace people."[6] But he approved of Margaret Sanger's motto for *The Birth Control Review*: "To Breed a Race of Thoroughbreds."

Numerous letters on eugenics‡ were exchanged between Galton and Ellis, but it was Ellis's adversary to whom Galton looked as the man best equipped to formulate his ideas—Karl Pearson. In 1884

---

* *Sex in Relation to Society* (1910).

† On November 3rd, 1930, he wrote to Margaret Sanger: "That 'Race Regeneration' booklet, which you like (as I do also) deals with the *future*. I am no good for writing about the past. I was meant to be a pioneering person" (Library of Congress). This letter was in answer to her plea that he write a book on birth control.

‡ The term was coined by Sir Francis Galton.

Pearson was appointed to the Goldsmid Professorship of Applied Mathematics and Mechanics at University College, London, and in his laboratory set about to "prove" the Darwinian theory correct by the application of mathematics.[7] During the last decade of Galton's life the two men worked closely together. In 1904 Galton offered the University of London £1,500 for a three-year study of National Eugenics, "the study of the agencies under social control that may improve or impair the racial qualities of future generations either physically or mentally." After Galton's death in 1911, by the terms of his will a Galton Professorship of Eugenics was founded at University College and Pearson, by Galton's express wish, became the first occupant of the chair, which he held until 1933.

Pearson was a Social Darwinist who developed into an imperialist, a nationalist, and a racist; he believed, for instance, that war was a necessary means of eliminating inferior stock. In the midst of the Boer War he upheld the validity of the conflict in an extraordinary speech. A nation, he said was "an organized whole," which was "kept up to a high pitch of external efficiency by contest, chiefly by way of war with inferior races, and with equal races by the struggle for trade-routes and for the sources of raw material and of food supply."[8] Ellis did not believe that war was necessary to regulate the birth-rate, rather that it would decrease naturally with each successive rise in culture; but he and Pearson were in agreement in their rejection of legislative action as a means of improving the race. "No degenerate and feeble stock," said Pearson, "will ever be converted into healthy and sound stock by the accumulated effects of education, good laws, and sanitary surroundings."[9]

The leading Fabians were deeply interested in the ideas expounded by Galton and Pearson. H. G. Wells advocated "the sterilization of failures." Sidney Webb, a firm supporter of Pearson, warned that "Twenty-five per cent of our parents, as Professor Karl Pearson keeps warning us, is producing fifty per cent of the next generation. This can hardly result in anything but national deterioration; or, as an alternative, in this country gradually falling to the Irish and the Jews."[10] Webb and Pearson believed in the "endowment of motherhood," that is, family allowances, which Ellis opposed. Bernard Shaw agreed with Galton and Pearson that "nothing but a eugenic religion can save our civilization from the fate that has overtaken all previous civilizations." Shaw lectured for a time to the Eugenics Education Society, and Pearson suggested to him that he was going further than Galton would have approved, and warned him to be a Fabian in his eugenics, cautioning that "he who would practically reform mankind must not begin by alarming it."[11]

These ideas, then, were current among Ellis's contemporaries, and while his own ideas were not forged in the heat of controversy, he cannot be regarded as an isolated crank. He was a member of the Eugenics Society from the outset,* but in 1930, provoked to rare anger, he threatened to resign when the society, under the leadership of its secretary, Dr. C. P. Blacker, set up a committee for seeking means to legalize sterilization and issued a widely circulated pamphlet entitled *Eugenic Sterilization*; while at the same time they drafted a bill to be introduced into Parliament to legalize voluntary sterilization, under certain conditions, among both the general public and mental defectives. Ellis saw this as prejudicial to the very cause it was intended to further. In a strongly worded protest, he wrote to Blacker:

"The Society admits that the legal objection to voluntary sterilization is 'ambiguous.' It ought not to be ambiguous. The real meaning of a 'maim' was long ago clearly stated by Blackstone: 'the loss of limbs useful to a man in fighting,' he said, 'alone amounts to mayhem.' It is fantastic, even fatuous, to apply to the modern operation of vasectomy the prohibition of a violent maim which was proper and necessary in Anglo-Saxon times. It is the more so since no attempt seems anywhere yet to have been made to interfere with voluntary sterilization. If the attempt ever *is* made—that will be the time to deal with it.

"I have been publicly in favour of voluntary (not compulsory) sterilization for over twenty years, and it is carried out (sometimes simply as a contraceptive measure when the family is sufficiently large) not only in Great Britain, but in states of the U.S.A. (like New York) where there are no sterilization

---

* On November 15th, 1907, a meeting was held in the Caxton Hall, Westminster, at which certain members of the Committee of the Moral Education League and a number of people interested in eugenics attended. After discussion, a Provisional Council was elected to draw up a constitution for a new society to be called The Eugenics Education Society. On February 14th, 1908, the first general meeting was held. In May Sir Francis Galton agreed to be Honorary President (*The Eugenics Review*, Vol. I).

In October 1909 Ellis contributed a rather disturbing article, "The Sterilisation of the Unfit," to *The Eugenics Review*, pp. 203–6. This same year Karl Pearson published *Groundwork of Eugenics*, which he had worked out in his biometric laboratory in University College.

laws, & elsewhere. To propose a law to authorise a voluntary act which is already being practised is a retrograde & stupid notion. Sterilization is becoming recognised as simple, harmless, in many ways beneficial. It will certainly continue to grow in favour. To invite ignorant and prejudiced legislators to meddle with an open medical question of this kind is a proceeding we ought not to encourage and are entitled to resent."*12

Norman Haire acted as his bulldog, eagerly cornering M.P.s and members of the Eugenics Society. For months the issue became an *idée fixe* for Ellis. When Joseph Ishill pointed out to him an article by Vincent Starrett in the leftist periodical *Road to Freedom*, Ellis sent the author an impassioned statement about his beliefs:

"Many of the remarks about my work show a happy insight, as for instance that I do not tear the veil of mystery from sex, but render it transparent. I would only protest against the remark that I approve of 'breeding human beings like race horses.' I am completely opposed to anything of the kind. Sterilization (*when voluntary*) I strongly advocate, & a sound race (that is, eugenics, in other words) is essential; but these have nothing to do with breeding human beings like race horses. Until the stock which produces men like —— and —— and —— and (you can easily fill in the names) are sterilised, *voluntarily if possible* [italics mine] there can be no anarchism, no liberty unrestricted by man-made laws, for they are the kind of men who make those laws. At present there are not enough people who have inherited such finely constituted natures that they can safely be entrusted with 'unrestricted liberty.' The unrestricted liberty of even so great a genius as Lenin has meant much restricted liberty for other people."13

Blacker seemed gradually to be persuaded by Ellis's arguments, even by the ingenious suggestion that the society would morally, legally, and financially(?) support any doctor who performed a vasectomy. The proposed bill was toned down to the voluntary sterilization of mental defectives under control—a limitation which seemed to Ellis to render the bill less mischievous but still undesirable. The bill was duly introduced into the House of Commons

---

* He published a criticism of the Bill in *The Eugenics Review* in January 1931.

and at once turned down by a large majority, as Ellis had anticipated. The Eugenics Society then had nothing left to do to keep itself busy except to try to bring the cost of vasectomies within reach of those who could not afford to pay for them.

Unfortunately, this was not the end of Ellis's concern with eugenics. In 1937 Heinemann published a revised version of *Sex in Relation to Society*. In a section on eugenics Ellis turns to the subject of the sterilization laws in Nazi Germany, particularly the law of 1934 which came into effect to promote the "biological health" of the German people.

> This law has not usually been understood on account of a natural reaction to the intolerant and violent Nazi policy in general. It has been confounded with the "Nordic" and Anti-Semitic efforts of the German Government. It is, however, on a quite independent foundation, and, if properly administered, it has no relation to "Aryan" aspirations.[14]

Ellis then goes on to say that Hitler's ideas on this subject had been inspired while in prison by reading "a standard work of genuine scientific character," *Human Heredity* by Baur, Fischer, and Lenz. In *Mein Kampf* Hitler emphasized the importance of procreation by people of sound mind and body, and the suffering that would be eliminated by the initiation of a sound policy of careful breeding which would take a thousand years to implement. Ellis describes the resulting legislation as a "carefully framed law" in which people apply voluntarily for sterilization. "In some cases, however, the procedure may be carried out without the subject's consent. (This feature of the law has been condemned by the leading German eugenic authority, Professor Muckermann in his *Eugenik*.)"*[15] Whatever Ellis thinks of the dangers of such a procedure, he characteristically refuses to speculate; and, characteristically, quotes another authority. It is as if he feared that if he expressed any indignation, he might weaken the case for eugenics. This is the most gross and blinkered example of obstinacy in his whole career. It is crypto-naïve: he is

---

* One wonders what happened to Professor Muckermann.

As early as 1911 Ellis was writing to the German eugenist Dr. Henry Bergen: "Quite true what you say as to the English and Americans only playing with eugenics, compared to the Germans—who are, of course, more thorough in all respects. But the amateurish and playing manner leads to a certain amount of good results, in spite of its obvious defects. It is especially useful in pioneering" (University of California at Los Angeles).

purporting to pierce the propaganda line and arrive at the underlying truth of the matter. When Norman Haire repeatedly told him of the suicides and tragedies of Jews in Germany he showed absolutely no interest. It is true that he seldom read a newspaper, but he cannot be excused for cutting himself off from reality to this extent.

While Ellis grew in moral stature with the passing years, he was not the god that some of his most ardent admirers seemed to regard him as being. He was a human being who in some ways was now a rather silly old man. Life had taught him a great deal of wisdom, but his vanity, his need for praise and the adulation of women, was part of the complex whole. His life showed a recurring pattern of refusals to offend, reluctance to stand up and be counted (except in the eugenics incident), and a deep need for admiration and love. Thus he could say that he never lost a friend. Karl Pearson he saw as an enemy because Pearson disagreed with him. In a competition held by the American magazine *Vanity Fair* in 1928 for the most distinguished people who had ever lived, one of the judges, the philosopher Santayana, allotted him only one point; and thereafter Ellis always referred to him as "my enemy."

In *Friendship's Odyssey* Françoise Lafitte relates that in the same year that he was incensed over the Sterilization Bill—1931—he began to lose his "body fire" for her. A hint of a reason may be detected in a sentence of a letter to Margaret Sanger: "I am—as usual!— busier than ever, not to mention numerous new women friends with souls to be patched up—sometimes a troublesome task and sometimes cosy."[16] To the "cosy" group belonged Gloria Neville, probably the last erotic relationship of his life. Françoise detected that there was something wrong from his increasingly repeated assertions that he wanted to be alone. On October 24th, 1930, he wrote: "Much as I love to have my Naiad near, I am never happier than when alone & have been used to it all my life."[17] Again, on January 29th, 1931: "I can't imagine why you think I mind being alone! I *love* it. It isn't the *loneliness* I mind, it's the *other people!!* It isn't because of any fear of loneliness that I love *you* being here. It's because your presence is so lovely that it reconciles me to not being alone."[18]

Gloria Neville was one of those brief, intense interludes in his life. She had been brought up in Canada of British parents, and was apparently in her early twenties, if not younger, when Ellis met her. Her letter of admiration for his work elicited the usual invitation to tea. On January 5th, 1931, she told him that she was looking forward to the visit as "the most glorious adventure that has ever come to me —I do not know how to express my thoughts."[19] Apparently it was one of those immediate and unexpected meetings of souls that had happened to him so often in the past. In February Gloria told him that "Not only do I adore you and admire you mentally and spiritually but physically also—and ask nothing better than to feel your kiss on my neck again."[20] She was moved to write an "Impression" of him:

"There is an air of remote strangeness about him—he is Apollo—Dionysius—a shy Pan—

"He is absolutely pure in spirit, with a delicate and profound feeling of Lao-Tse.

"His vast erudition, his tremendously wide range of knowledge sits lightly on him. One does not feel awed by him—he is so sweet and genuine, so sincere, human and absolutely charming —with a realization of almost perfect understanding which to one who senses it—produces an emotion of poignant tenderness.

"He is the perfect combination of artist, scientist and philosopher. He seems more than any modern personality of note, to enact the new spirit in the world, that invisible circular wave which is weaving the thought and work of all peoples into one.

"For a while his mind is subtle, as delicate, as aesthetic as any of the Chinese seers—so he has that Greek élan—that vital physical love of life—accepting all things realistically and such patient humour. He is as natural and simple as a child, with an almost feminine concern and compassion—robbing him not in the slightest of that virile courage and strength which is the dominant note of his radiant personality."[21]

What man could help being charmed by this?—particularly when she also told him that she had

"the desire to throw myself at a man's feet and confess. I don't know what exactly—but just an overpowering desire to fall down in abnegation and to pour out midst tears and lamentations all the anguish and overwhelming feelings that lie in one's innermost depths. And the confessor must necessarily be a man—considerably older in years—spiritually sympathetic, mentally one's equal or superior—sexually attractive—(though not necessarily physically—although preferably so.)"[22]

Unfortunately, Gloria had to leave for Italy shortly after their meeting, but the adulatory letters continued to flow in. "You are so marvellously developed and balanced on every side," she told him, "and I love your sensuous side—as I love the human 'realistic' one. Your nearness in things of the body—as your aloofness and air of spirituality—Personality—most glamorous of things—you are to me—the complete Personality—so that I can understand and adore you on every side."[23] When she returned in the spring she was very much disturbed to hear that there was another permanent lady in his life. A meeting, as usual, was arranged between the two women—and Gloria seems to have disappeared from the scene.

Many other strands of Ellis's lifelong convictions and reflections were drawn together in an extraordinary pair of experiments in which he was involved in this late period of his life. The story can never be reconstructed fully, but by piecing together a large number of letters and through conversations with some of the people involved, I believe a fairly faithful account can be given. On June 27th, 1927, a twenty-year-old American medical student, Joseph Wortis, called on Ellis at his Brixton flat. He greatly admired Ellis's writings and told him that he wanted to follow in his footsteps and devote his life to a study of sex. Ellis received him kindly and courteously, and Wortis's admiration increased to what he has described as "hero worship." A regular correspondence ensued, covering a wide variety of subjects—painting, films, nationalism, landscape—and these are among the most interesting letters Ellis ever wrote, since Wortis was eager to probe Ellis's mind at so many points. After studying in Vienna, Wortis returned to the Bellevue Psychiatric Hospital in New York as an intern; and one day in October 1933 he received an extraordinary letter from Ellis:

"There is a very large sum of money in the good hands of an American friend of mine (and Françoise's) which is, in some as yet undetermined way, to be devoted to the scientific study of homosexuality, with the full study and following up of cases, etc. with the view of illuminating the subject and of promoting a rational and humane attitude towards it. (The holder of the money, I should add, is not personally a sexual invert.) The idea in mind so far has been of a legacy to found a chair at some university or medical school. I am more in favour of selecting a suitable person for the post and enabling him to go ahead as soon as possible (as my friend Mrs. D—— of Chicago has done with such fine results) and my recommendations are likely to be influential in making a decision. It seems to me that you would be peculiarly suitable for this work, and while it would take up a large part of your time, perhaps for life, you would be able to make conditions leaving you free for other neurological etc. work. I hope that you are willing to consider the matter. I will give you more precise details. So far as I can see, there would be nothing of an undesirable character about the scheme."[24]

After careful consideration—which Wortis describes in his book, *Fragments of an Analysis with Freud*—Wortis agreed to take advantage of the providential offer; and he set off for Europe to gain background training in physiology, biochemical endocrinology, and related subjects. Ellis often met him at the British Museum Reading Room, where he made suggestions about his reading and put him in touch with a number of people who he felt would be helpful.

What Wortis did not feel free to reveal in his book was the identity of the unknown benefactor. Here was a very strange story indeed. In the summer of 1932 Kingsley Porter, a professor of art history at Harvard, and his wife paid Ellis a visit. Porter was a homosexual and was suffering from deep depression, as he was in danger of losing his job because of scandal. His wife was very sympathetic. What advice had Ellis to proffer? There is no way of knowing exactly what Ellis actually said, but in a letter of July 31st, 1932, Porter told Ellis: "I feel a deep sense of gratitude to you, deeper that I know how to express, for having put me in touch with Alan."[25] Alan Campbell was a young aspiring American novelist, a homosexual also, who moved into the Porters' beautiful home in Cambridge, Massachusetts, a few months later, and there apparently a *ménage à trois* was established. With Ellis's views on the impossibility of "curing" homosexuality and with his own experience of accepting Edith's lovers (the Porters were among the few people in whom he ever confided the truth about his own marriage), one can only assume that this was the solution Ellis proposed for their difficulties. In October Porter wrote to him: "You have made over my life. You know it. I do not need to tell you. And I know that that knowledge combined with infinite similar knowledges, makes your happiness."[26] However, during the following months Porter's letters indicate that Campbell was restless and did not settle easily into the Cambridge scene. Campbell wanted to become a male nurse, and Ellis said that he must feel free to follow his own bent. Eventually Campbell left for a trip to California. On January 3rd, 1933, Porter wrote: "We are sailing on the 14th, not without misgivings on my part, for depression has been gaining again since Alan went to California."[27] Again on the 12th he wrote: "I fear I am hardly turning out to be the prize exhibit of the results of your kindness & sympathy, as I had so confidently hoped."[28] He and Mrs. Porter then crossed the Atlantic to their castle in County Donegal, Ireland, and in June they paid Ellis a visit in London. On July 11th Alan Campbell wrote that Porter had thrown himself off a cliff near his home. Mrs. Porter reacted with amazing composure. She was an extremely wealthy woman, and she told Ellis that she wanted to do something positive in memory of her late husband, to endow a chair, perhaps, for the "scientific" study of homosexuality. Ellis suggested that the money would be better spent in training an individual, but not under the auspices of any large institution or organization. It was then that the idea of Joseph Wortis struck him suddenly one morning on waking. And thus this unique opportunity was given to Wortis.

After some months in Europe in 1933 Wortis suggested to Ellis that it might be beneficial for his training to experience a didactic analysis under Freud; Ellis, predictably, opposed the idea because, "If you are psychoanalysed you either become a Freudian or you don't. If you don't you remain pretty much where you are now; if you do—you are done for!—unless you break away, like Jung or Adler or Rank (& he has done it too late)."[29]

Wortis was both persistent and persuasive in getting both Mrs. Porter and Ellis to agree to the scheme; and Freud, after assuring himself that he would be paid, consented to take him on for a four months' trial analysis. Wortis told Freud from the outset that he was acting against Ellis's advice. A photograph of Ellis (which Ellis had sent him) hung on the wall of Freud's office; and Freud seemed extremely interested in anything Wortis could tell him about Ellis. Wortis read Freud a passage from Ellis's letter in which he urged him to follow Freud's *example* rather than his *precept* and go his own way, to which Freud replied, "Ellis, in a fundamental sense, has rejected psychoanalysis."[30] In his fascinating book Wortis has recorded his memories of the day-to-day sessions which he wrote down in his diary in a coffeehouse directly upon leaving Freud. From the outset he seems to have been as sceptical about the value of psycho-

analysis as Ellis was, and at the end of the four months he and Freud
parted, mutually agreeing that the experience had been inconclusive.
During this period Wortis made clear his veneration of Ellis and
frequently seemed to raise his name in order to provoke a reaction
from Freud. Freud was particularly annoyed by Ellis's advice that
Wortis might do better by consulting Stekel, and this led him into
a long diatribe against Stekel. Freud told him that Ellis did not know
what he was talking about when he attacked psychoanalysis, that he
was, indeed, doing great harm. He also suggested that Ellis's interest
in Wortis was part of his general benevolence. "It is true that it is
helpful to be liked by Ellis," said Freud, "but that is all superficial—
it just gives you a kind of pleasant social standing. Ellis goes about
and picks people, as one might pick out a good-looking woman at a
ball."[31] Freud described Ellis as a "type of the man of culture—not
really the scientific man" in response to Wortis's admission that he
believed Freud was capable of pursuing a subject far more ruthlessly
than Ellis, but that Ellis had a profound wisdom—"He was a perfect
type of *man*."[32] When Wortis said that he thought that Ellis would
write an autobiography, Freud replied: "Not even he could be altogether honest."[33] Wortis's intransigence to analysis Freud attributed
to the fact that Ellis had "spoiled" him, implying that because of
Ellis's interest in him Wortis had developed such inordinate self-
confidence that he could question Freud's basic tenets.

Human beings are very complex, and I should prefer the reader
to draw his own conclusions from a reading of Dr. Wortis's book.*
Why he regarded Ellis with such excessive veneration belongs to
Wortis's story rather than to Ellis's;† but it would seem impossible
for any analysis to be more than an exercise in futility unless Wortis

---

* Dr. Wortis received Mrs. Porter's stipend for seven years before his interest was
diverted to insulin treatment for disturbed patients. At one point Ellis wrote to Anatole
James to ask if he would care to contribute to the Wortis fund. Mr. James tells me
that he is very thankful that he refused.

† Ellis was delighted by Wortis's impertinence to Freud, but when Wortis
eventually published his notes, few found the young American's attitude particularly
endearing. Wladimir Granoff was reminded of lines from Pushkin:

> A l'Académie des sciences
> Siège le prince Outrance.
> Pourquoi a-t-il ce siège?
> Pourquoi ce grand honneur?
> C'est très simple, il a ce siège
> Parce qu'il a un postérieur.

(*Filiations*, Paris: Les Editions de Minuit, 1975, p. 255.)

reached the point where he recognized that, partially at any rate, his hostility to Freud stemmed from what appears to me to be anxiety that Freud would disturb his image of Ellis. In one dream related to Freud he is distressed because Ellis's beard is too straggly—and one's facetious interpretation of this is that Ellis didn't look sufficiently like Jehovah to suit Wortis! He clearly resented Freud for not holding Ellis in sufficient esteem. One conversation alone will suffice to illustrate this:

> In the fourth dream, I was slipping into my high school classroom late and with feelings of guilt, and hid myself in a corner seat out of the teacher's gaze. All I could say about this dream was that it suggested the discomfort I felt when Freud spoke as he did about Ellis.
>
> "It was just a supposition," said Freud. "It is not the sort of thing I would write an essay on."
>
> I said that was the sort of lay opinion that made Ellis's life so difficult* and cheapened his accomplishment. Freud then gave the reasons: I had said his wife was homosexual; besides, he had no children, and a man who makes so few judgments is suspect of being impotent. I insisted I never said his wife was homosexual; so far as I knew she wasn't. He had no children because his wife was diabetic—besides, he was too poor; and as for the last argument, it was weak. Shakespeare made few judgments too—he saw too many sides to an argument.
>
> Freud was angrier than I had ever seen him. He sputtered: "Do you know Shakespeare, then, as well as you know Ellis? Anyway, he was a poet, not a scientist." Besides, what did I mean by denying that his wife was homosexual?
>
> I could not say what I meant for I did not remember—I could only suggest that a certain friend of his, who was heterosexual, once had a brief experimental homosexual period. If Freud had read the Ishill book in his waiting room, he could himself have seen from Ellis's little prose poem, "A Revelation," that he was not impotent. Freud had me go into the waiting room for proof, which I produced, but which did not satisfy him, for there was no clear evidence of a sexual act. "I would advise you to be more cautious (*gewissenhaft*) hereafter in your statements."
>
> "One can never be too cautious," I said.[34]

In a footnote Wortis added, regarding Edith's homosexuality, "Freud must have acquired this information from another source, for

---

* In what way had Ellis's life been made so difficult?

with the later publication of Ellis's *Autobiography* there appeared to be some [sic] justification for this characterization of Edith Ellis."[35] (It might have come from H.D., who was at that time being psycho-analyzed by Freud.) A year later when Wortis submitted his notes on the sessions to Ellis to read, Ellis corrected him about his inter-pretation of "The Revelation": "There is no coitus, real or assumed, in the narrative."[36] Ellis made no comment on Freud's suggestion that Edith was a lesbian; rather disingenuously he admitted that she was "neurotic" and that her doctor had advised her not to have children, and added in parenthesis: "My own spermatozoa looked quite healthy under the microscope!"[37] It was exactly the same com-ment he was to make in *My Life*, where he said that he had no difficulty obtaining spermatozoa for Olive Schreiner to examine under the microscope. I find these statements—and, indeed, the whole long letter to Wortis—disturbingly suspect. For all its seem-ing candour—and from the linkage or ideas—Ellis's comments are evasive. Speaking of "The Revelation," Ellis says: "H.D. had told me that at that period I was an immense help to her—I have never known why."[38] Ellis knew precisely why; and there is an extant letter in which H.D. explicitly says that it was because he had helped her during her lesbian attachment to Bryher. Then he goes on to comment on Freud's surmise that he was impotent:

> "With regard to impotence, F's notion that it is associated with a lack of decision in intellectual judgments is new to me. The notion seems based on a false analogy. In most of the cases that come to me, the impotence is not due to any hesitation or lack of decision, but is a hyperaesthetic over-rapidity of nervous re-action, reaching its climax before entrance is effected."[39]

Ellis had told Margaret Sanger that this was his own sexual problem; and it is to be noted that here Ellis gives his own explanation of im-potence, but never explicitly (only implicitly) denies the charge that *he* is impotent. It is my own conviction that Freud's surmise was close to the truth.

DEPRESSION YEARS

THE DEPRESSION YEARS WERE AS DIFFICULT FOR ELLIS AS THEY WERE for most people. In September 1931 Margaret Sanger wrote that she would have to reduce "the Secretary's" salary because her husband's business had been hit seriously by the crash. Ellis immediately wrote to tell her that she was not to worry because for him things were looking a little brighter than they had done in the past year. "We shall be able to manage. Françoise is already considering economies. And I have always *enjoyed* difficulties."[1] Besides, he thought there were hopeful signs that the economic situation was improving.

In the past few years his popularity in the United States had reached its peak and he had been earning between $500 and $1,000 for articles; but with changing times he was ready to accept $100 from the Sunday Magazine of the *Herald Tribune* for a piece, "Changing Spain."* He was delighted by an offer in November to write a series of weekly articles for Hearst's *New York American* at $100 each. Either he didn't know or he didn't much care what Hearst's politics were; besides, he was instructed that he wasn't to discuss politics in his column. What was important was that if the wolf came to the door of Fairy Tale House, he would find, Ellis told Margaret, a large notice: "No Admittance. By Order Hearst." At first

---

* He was offered $1,000 for the manuscript of the *Studies*, but apparently it no longer "existed." Where it had disappeared is never explained. Perhaps in the destruction of the papers when he moved from Dover Mansions?

the agreement was for a year, but after Ellis conceived the idea of "My Mail Bag" the articles became so popular that they were extended for another four years, appearing as well in the *Los Angeles Examiner*. He seldom knew in advance what he was going to write, but it wasn't an onerous task, as he could simply comment upon subjects such as love, marriage, birth control, euthanasia, subjects he had reflected upon for years. The column usually grew out of comments in letters from his correspondents. When someone wrote, addressing him as "dear comrade and teacher," he remarked: "Comrade? Yes! Teacher? No!" Thinking of the influence Thomas Davidson had tried to exert on him in 1883, he recalled, "But I proved an unprofitable pupil. Not only did my whole nature rise up in revolt against such a manifestation of spiritual authority, but from that period I date my disbelief in all metaphysical doctrines, save as the personal conviction of those who maintain them."[2] As always, he insisted that the impulse must come from within. The closest he got to politics was a discussion in 1933 of the prevalent faith in authority. "We live again in a world of certitudes," he declared. "I stand aside and gaze."[3] These columns may have kept the wolf from the door, but to develop into a Popular Sage did nothing for his professional reputation.

The attitude of calm detachment was not so easy to maintain in face of the involved complications that arose over the *Studies* as a result of the Depression. In 1933 he published *Psychology of Sex: A Manual for Students* with an American publisher, Long and Smith.* The *Studies* had been issued since 1901 by publishers of medical books, F. A. Davis of Philadelphia, who raised objections to the publication of the *Manual* as they claimed it was cutting into the sales of the *Studies*. They also claimed that publication of the new book was a breach of contract and demanded compensation. Moreover, they were justified in their objections since Long and Smith had advertised the *Manual*—without consulting Ellis—as superseding the *Studies*. To add to his difficulties, Long and Smith were now on the verge of bankruptcy. Ellis maintained that he could not believe that the *Manual* was cutting into the sales of the original works, as it was intended for a more general audience than the professional readers at whom the *Studies* were aimed—a very unrealistic argument, par-

---

* The publishers repeatedly tried to persuade him to change the title to *Sex Without Prudery*.

ticularly in the existing economic situation. For twenty-five years
Ellis had been receiving a small but steady income from the *Studies*
—five per cent of the published price on the first six volumes and
ten per cent on the seventh. After the publication of the *Manual*
F. A. Davis ceased paying him royalties, either in retaliation or because they were headed for bankruptcy. Early in 1934 Ellis turned to
an American acquaintance, Dr. Louise Bryant, director of the National Committee for Maternal Health,* for advice as to where he
could transfer the *Studies*, emphasizing that he did not want to put
them into the hands of a general publisher.

Dr. Bryant turned out to be another guardian angel. She replied
that she would consider it an honour to do anything she could to
help. Within weeks it proved necessary to give her power of attorney.
Ellis followed the negotiations with close attention and retained a
thoroughly business-like attitude to the proceedings. "Thirty years
ago I was not so careful as I am now over agreements," he admitted
ruefully.[4] To Dr. Bryant's suggestion that Houghton Mifflin (publishers of his literary works) take over the sex books, Ellis insisted
that he didn't want to combine his literary and scientific works. None
of the *Studies* had been revised since 1915, which troubled some
publishers. Ellis, who had no energy or inclination to tackle them
afresh, maintained that revisions might be desirable but were not
imperative for any of them, except perhaps Volume VI. Nor could
Ellis provide any royalty statements, as Davis had not sent them to
him for the past two years. All that could be ascertained at first was
that the *Manual* had sold over 600 copies during March of 1934.
Dr. Bryant did manage, however, to extract some figures from Davis,
who by now were willing to transfer the *Studies*. Between 1926
and 1931 the total sale on the series was 34,792, on which Ellis
had earned seventeen cents a book. During the Depression years
sales had dwindled to a trickle, and in the summer of 1934 the publishers had only 2,693 copies in stock. Dr. Bryant also discovered that
Davis had sold about $650,000 worth of the books in the thirty-five
years since the first volume was published, of which $600,000 must
have been clear profit, as they sold directly to individual purchasers.
As to foreign translations, they had always given the vaguest replies

---

* The committee had published a series of books on medical aspects of fertility,
of which *A Thousand Marriages: A Medical Study in Sex Adjustment* had a Foreword
by Ellis and another, *Human Sex Anatomy: A Topographical Atlas*, was dedicated
to him.

to Ellis's request for facts and figures. The first four volumes sold for $4, the last two for $5. Volume VII had a very small sale and a large number (3,497) had to remaindered. Davis now owed him $1,300 in unpaid royalties and Dr. Bryant advised him that it would be impossible to collect this sum.

Despite the poor sale of Volume VII, in a letter of July 28th, 1934, Ellis told her: "I have in mind an entirely new edition of the most important volume, 'Sex in Relation to Society,' which I would certainly bring out here as well as with the American publisher of the 'Studies.' "[5] (But until the negotiations with an American publisher were settled, Ellis's hands were tied as to securing an English publisher for the *Studies*.) Ferris Greenslet, Ellis's editor at Houghton Mifflin, suggested that Dr. Bryant contact Bennett Cerf, the head of Random House and editor of the Modern Library series, who had long been eager to publish the *Studies* in a two- or three-volume edition. Ellis's immediate reaction was that the Modern Library "does not to me seem at all the right quarter for anything like my 'Studies.' "[6] A weary Dr. Bryant assured him that Random House published Eugene O'Neill, Proust, Robinson Jeffers, etc. "Nothing remotely resembling a scientific book, but all of the ultra-modern radical literature,"[7] to which Ellis replied: "I am *entirely* against the 'Modern Library' idea. I am quite able to admire Joyce & Jeffers, & the rest, but the *Studies* belong to a totally different class & could only be injured by appearing amongst them."[8] As discussions seemed to be dragging on interminably, he agreed that she should at least talk the matter over with Cerf. "I begin to think that almost any decent publisher may now be better than the Davis Co!"[9] Nevertheless, Random House was not cautious enough for his liking and he continued to feel "nervous" about being associated with them. But by the summer of 1935 negotiations were on their way to being finalized when the *Psychology of Sex* manual was transferred to Emerson Books, and he finally agreed that Random House was probably the best alternative that could be found for the *Studies*.

But he continued to have problems with the *Studies* until his death. Bennett Cerf put the books into the Modern Library series as he had planned, but Ellis was extremely disturbed by the flamboyant way in which the books were advertised. There were disagreements as to who held world rights. Bodley Head acted as agent for the *Studies* in Britain, and when Penguin made a suggestion that they bring out the series in twelve cheap volumes, Random House (through Bodley Head) vetoed the idea. Ellis did go ahead with a revised version of Volume VI—*Sex in Relation to Society*—which was published by Heinemann in 1937.* Ellis repeatedly tried to persuade Random House to publish it in the United States, but he was alway refused on the grounds that it would interfere with the sale of the *Studies* and that it was not in any way a radically different book from the original edition. Besides, they argued, the original volume had had a very poor sale in America. His hard-headed American publishers seem to have been absolutely right, for it had a disappointing reception in England, no important reviews and a very small sale.

At first, all went well with the *Studies*. When they were issued in their new format in the spring of 1936,† the first printing of 4,000 sets at $15 was sold out in a fortnight. In April Ellis told Françoise: "I am so pleased to think that with the sale of the 'Studies' there is now no need for money worries. Not so much for myself, since with three feet in the grave I can look at things from the standpoint of the moon, but I am so glad to save Naiad from worries."[10] This letter was addressed to Aix-les-Bains, where Françoise was staying on the advice of Lord Horder that she go away for at least six weeks in order to avoid a complete nervous breakdown. Since her affair with Hugh de Sélincourt had come to an end in 1931, she had been devoting all her energies to Ellis. High-strung and emotional, she had worried herself into a state of anxiety over the management of the two households. She set about translating books which Ellis suggested (under the name "Delisle," an anagram of "de Ellis"),‡ and from which she made about £75 a year, but this was petering out. Havelock now lacked what she called "body fire" and she was suffering from intense sexual deprivation. Ellis by 1932 was beginning to show signs of the throat problem which eventually killed him. At Christmas 1935 he had such a serious attack of influenza that it seemed a miracle that he recovered, and by the late winter Françoise was thoroughly worn out. Ellis told Margaret Sanger that Françoise was "much too easily depressed, nervous, worried & fatigued."[11] Their ever-generous angel then suggested that Françoise consult Lord Horder at Margaret's expense; and the physician was in full accord with Ellis's proposal

---

* They had already brought out *Psychology of Sex* in 1933.
† At first in four volumes; later compressed into two.
‡ *Le Grand Meaulnes* by Alain-Fournier (1928), *La Grange à trois belles* by Robert Francis (1935), and *Memoirs of the Count de Tilly* (1933). Ellis helped her with these translations and wrote Introductions for all of them.

that she go to Aix-les-Bains, where he had taken Edith in a similar state in 1902 when she was suffering from the effects of the Bedborough trial. It had been selected then because it was off-season, and Ellis always looked back on it as one of the most pleasant interludes in his life and the perfect rest for Edith. Although Françoise, too, went off-season—for a time she was the only guest—six weeks in a hotel was an additional money worry, and Ellis did his best to keep up her spirits: "On *no* account worry over money. Money is expensive, but health in the end is even more expensive."[12] "I am always thinking of you," he told her in another letter, "and when you are away I realise more than ever how much more dear to me you are than anyone else in the world,"[13] to which Françoise replied: "You really are so strong, dear, this is perhaps why it was hard for you to see that I was ill & worn out."[14] He was particularly jubilant when the royalties of the *Studies* seemed to promise further security.

The previous year Constable had been forced to remainder *More Essays of Love and Virtue*, and then in March, as Françoise was about to leave for Aix, Ellis received a grave blow. Hearst dropped him after five years, without even a month's notice. (The only straw in the wind had been their recent refusal to print an innocuous article on revolutions.) It was a blessing that Françoise had to leave so abruptly for a change of scene, and he told her, "I don't want to worry you by being too greedy for news, & I want you to rest, & not try hard to do anything; rest even to get well! Just rest & let everything come to you."[15] He loved to think of her there, and pictured her receiving letters delivered to her bedroom by the postman, as he used to do with Edith. Ellis was delighted to hear of her excursion to Les Charmettes—"since my visit there was one of the most memorable days in my life, besides being the beginning of my interest in Rousseau."[16] He had never been parted from her for so long before; and he began, despite his efforts to cheer her, to be aware of his own mortality after reading of the death of Karl Pearson late in April—"my early friend and later enemy"—whom *The Times* described as "one of the last great Victorian figures."

"Honour, love, obedience, troops of friends" he still could look to have. Shortly after Françoise's return in May he received an honour which delighted him more than he would admit. He was made an honorary Fellow of the Royal College of Physicians—at the same time as Sir Frederick Banting, the discoverer of insulin, which would probably have saved Edith's life if it had been available in 1916.* Ellis had always been sensitive about not having a proper medical degree and believed that the medical profession in England regarded him with a certain amount of condescension. The move to elect him was initiated by Lord Horder and was at first met with opposition by some of the Fellows, but when he appeared at the ceremony people came up from all over the room to shake hands with him. At the dinner following the ceremony he was placed at the right of the President, Lord Dawson, who in his speech referred chummily to "my friend Dr. Havelock Ellis"—although he had never met him before that evening. To Margaret Sanger, Ellis wrote: "One would never expect an 'obscene' rebel like me to be treated by everyone with so much respect at such a place!"[17] Other honours followed, but to these he paid little attention. He was selected by the Council of the Royal Anthropological Institute as Huxley Memorial Lecturer for 1937 (naturally declined) and the following year he was asked to become a member of the Committee of the Royal Society of Literature.

There was other good news to tell Françoise. C. E. M. Joad had praised his "wisdom and charm" in a review of *Questions of Our Day* in *The New Statesman*. "He doesn't think I have added to my 'teaching,' & am now in danger of 'canonisation.' But 'there is, I fancy, no living writer who, in the strict sense of the word, is so preeminently "readable." Like most of the great stylists, he gives the impression that to write is the easiest thing in the world.' "[18] Ellis was always very sensitive about his British public, which was never large. After Constable dropped him, the various collections of essays were brought out by different publishers—*Views and Reviews* (Desmond Harmsworth, 1932), *My Confessional* (John Lane, 1934), and *Morals, Manners, and Men* (Watts, 1939). The collection of essays *From Rousseau to Proust*, which was published by Houghton Mifflin in the United States in 1935, could not find an English publisher. The great flaw in these collections is the extreme brevity of the essays, almost random impressions which might have been appropriate for the passing experiences and reflections of *Impressions and Comments* but are thin and insubstantial when applied to subjects requiring some depth.

---

* Insulin was discovered by two Canadian doctors, Banting and Best, in 1921.

He could perhaps have earned a good deal of money if he had let his American editor, Ferris Greenslet, persuade him to publish his autobiography in 1936. To his pleas, Ellis replied:

"I began it nearly forty years ago, though it is not yet all in final shape. But its publication in my lifetime is *absolutely impossible*. Not because of any scandal about my contemporaries or any crude adventures of the Frank Harris type, but because it is far too intimate & personal. I have not the faintest wish to compete with the so-called 'autobiographies,' which are appearing every day. I am very well aware of the arguments for speedy publication & not by any means indifferent to them. I believe that, in every way, the book will be valuable, it is the only book of mine I expect to be remembered. But it could only appear when I am no longer here, so that I must dispense with the accruing benefits."[19]

With his diminished earning power and the cessation of Françoise's allowance from Margaret Sanger, combined with his failing health and Françoise's uncertain condition, a radical change in their life-style was imperative. For some years they had realized that they could not maintain two homes indefinitely. If it was a choice between the country and London, there was no question in Ellis's mind. "So far as I am concerned," he told Françoise, "I less & less want to be in London, or to see even nice people. I am quite happy nowadays to be in the country & have my own society, with as much of the Naiad as she can give me."[20] Charming as Haslemere was, it was damp and rather primitive, so another place had to be found. This time Françoise concentrated on looking for something in East Anglia and after two months she settled on a house, Cherry Ground, near Ipswich. The cottage at Wivelsfield Green was given up and Françoise's younger son, François, and his wife moved into the Herne Hill house.

In his beloved Suffolk Ellis hoped to find a peaceful atmosphere in which to die. But troubles pursued him. In 1938 Dr. Alex Forbath, an Hungarian, published an anthology, *Love and Marriage*, with a twenty-four-page extract from Ellis's *Psychology of Sex*. Emerson Books protested vigorously to Forbath's publisher, the Liveright Publishing Corporation. Cables flashed back and forth between New York and Ellis's quiet Suffolk home. Forbath claimed that Ellis had in 1936 given him *carte blanche* to quote from the book and produced a smudged photostat to prove it. Ellis denied that he had given more than permission to quote a few passages, but I am inclined to believe that his memory was failing him on this point because Ellis's commitment read: "Our arrangement is for a certain number of pages, & you can take them from any part of my book, not only the marriage chapter."[21] However, both Forbath and Liveright were exploiting Ellis's name in their advertisements for the book. Eventually Liveright made a cash settlement for the first 1,000 copies—agreeing to omit the quoted section in later copies—but it was all very disturbing to an old man who was by now gravely ill. For years his friends had been begging him to get an American agent, and by 1938 he agreed to let Jacques Chambrun handle his business and in the last months of his life Chambrun placed a number of articles in popular magazines. In October 1938 Ellis had a brief visit from Bennett Cerf, the head of Random House. The cocky Cerf's reminiscences are not to be trusted, since he makes himself the hero of every event. He visited Ellis, he recalled, "up toward Oxford" (actually, in the opposite direction, near Ipswich).

> Ellis was a very nice, charming man, rather shy, with a possessive housekeeper. He left no impression on me except that of a quiet, dignified gentleman. Actually, he was a slight disappointment to me; he was getting old—he didn't live much longer—and he didn't want to talk with a young publisher about sex.[22]

Cerf's recollection of the acquisition of the *Studies* was that *he* had gone to Philadelphia to see the Davis people, "and talked them into letting us do an edition for the general public." It was a publishing coup and "exceeded our fondest expectations."[23] This might have been so for a year or two, but by 1939 Ellis was complaining that sales had dropped to such a low that he was earning less from the *Studies* than he had ever done from the Davis Company. Until only a few weeks before his death he continued to press unsuccessfully for an American edition of *Sex in Relation to Society*.

Other problems persisted. In December 1937 Paul Palmer, who had succeeded Ellis's old admirer H. L. Mencken as editor of *The American Mercury*, suggested that Ellis write two articles, on Sexual Impotency in the Male and Sexual Frigidity in Women, for which he would pay him $450 each if submitted on approval. Ellis, with his recently acquired business sense, agreed to the fee but would not submit them unless the fee were guaranteed. Palmer suggested a compromise—$125 for each even if not used. Ellis agreed, sure that they would be accepted. Palmer liked both immensely and the first appeared in the issue of May 1938. He planned to print the piece—which now seems innocuous—on female frigidity in July, but one of the country's periodic waves of censorship was then sweeping through the United States and Palmer had to tell Ellis that the magazine would be banned from the newsstands if the putatively offensive article were included.* As for another article on the approximation of the sexes, Palmer felt obliged to reject it as he found it "rather slight." Ellis replied that this was because "the subject is complicated, so that it is impossible to give to the question a single decisive answer which could be elaborated and emphasised. I am familiar with the subject, & I believe the article is at all events quite sound."[24] But he was not asked to write for *The American Mercury* again.

As the Depression continued to hold life in its oppressive grip, Ellis no longer talked about seeing signs of improvement ahead. "The 'depression' continues to be depressing," he wrote to Margaret Sanger. "I am always reading financial etc articles in the papers, vainly trying to make something out of it. Unfortunately hardly anyone agrees with anyone else. It is the lack of agreement which is fatal to any concerted action which might improve the situation."[25] Never, he repeatedly said, had he seen so many friends in difficulties, financial and emotional. After the final rupture with Françoise, Hugh de Sélincourt's behaviour became increasingly erratic. Even his dearly loved Margaret Sanger was criticized for her treatment of Marie Stopes and her own evasiveness about her marriage in her autobiography, which was published in 1931. "Hugh sent me into the depths of blues for a week," she complained to Havelock. "He said I was egotistical in regard to Dennett & Stopes, & cheap & false in regard to my marriage—(which marriage he did not say). Oh it was a dreadful letter he wrote me, heart breaking because he failed to know the ME who wrote the book.

"Perhaps my treatment of Stopes was not as finished & noble as some one else would have done it, but what I said was true & *considering* the facts as you & I know them, she was not treated too badly." "Very strange about Hugh de Sélincourt." Ellis replied. "And the points he criticises are just those where I thought you had shown so much discretion! But there is something very queer about him.

---

* It was eventually published as "The Supposed Frigidity of Women" in *Sex and Marriage*, ed. John Gawsworth (New York: Random House, 1952).

He goes out of his way to shock & alienate his friends, & he has done it so often to so many of his friends."[26] Letters between the two men had by now almost ceased. What news they had of him was conveyed by Margaret. They were intrigued by a long affair he had begun with Ellis's German translator, Eva Schumann. Sélincourt had always had difficulty in securing a publisher for his books and during the thirties he was faced with such a severe financial crisis that he almost lost Sand Pit. He disappears now from the story until his furious reaction to Françoise's account of the triangle in *Friendship's Odyssey*. He was so disturbed by her romanticized version that Margaret Sanger believed that it hastened his death.*

The ebullient Jane Burr continued to write articles about companionate marriage, unorthodox dress, birth control, and divorce reform. In 1929 she had to have a mastectomy and was constantly worried about her health. She became embroiled in a fierce lawsuit with the rest of her family which left her poor and embittered. At one point she asked Ellis if he would write a testimonial to her sanity, which he readily agreed to do if she really needed it. In one of her last letters to him, addressed from French Lick Springs, Indiana, she wrote:

Dear Prospero

In my house there is nothing but heart break and sorrow. I have not written for fear it might creep into the words of my letter.

There is never a day in my life that is not filled with tender and affectionate thought of you.

Rosalind[27]

Faith Oliver's marriage was wonderfully happy; then, suddenly, her husband died in 1936. Ellis's heart ached for Faith and he tried to give her what comfort he could: "Nothing can rob us of the beautiful past, & it becomes a perpetual comfort & strength in the present."[28]

Arthur Symons he still saw occasionally. Ellis was extremely upset by an article which appeared in *The Psychological Review* in 1933 in which the author, assuming Symons to be dead,† described his life as one of frightful perversions. To the editor Ellis wrote protesting about this portrait of "an impossible person—certainly a

---

* He died January 20th, 1957.
† Symons died in 1945.

person with whom I, with my quiet and respectable ways of living, could not have associated, or found so delightful a companion as in old days I always found A.S. to be."[29]

Suffering seemed to surround him, tempered for a brief time by the wonderful radiance of a sixteen-year-old Spanish girl, Hildegart Rodriguez, who began to write to him in November 1931. Ellis had always greatly admired Spanish women, whom he celebrated in a chapter in *The Soul of Spain*. Here he prophesied:

> As her political and social development enters a more vital stage, no doubt the women of Spain will naturally and inevitably take their part in the national life which they are so well fitted to take.[30]

He had no first-hand experience of republican Spain, but his pen-friend excelled anything he could visualize. To Margaret Sanger he wrote: "My Spanish lawyer girl seems quite one of the wonders of the world! She was born within a few days of your first visit to Brixton; could read at 2; went to the University at 13; knows five languages, and has published *nine* books. The most recent one, on 'Contraception and Voluntary Parentage' sold 2,000 copies in the first week in Madrid, & there is a separate edition in Barcelona. In her portrait she looks very mature, solid & healthy & sweet & she writes me in a very simple & natural way,—and calls me her 'dear master.' "[31] Ellis attributed her wonderful qualities to her mother, one of his "New Mothers," and both women he celebrated in an article, "The Red Virgin," in *The Adelphi* in June 1933. The article had no sooner appeared than he saw in a newspaper that Hildegart had been killed by her mother, who shot her, it was said, for fear of being separated from her. He was stunned; it seemed the most tragic death he had ever heard of. Norman Haire had just returned from Spain, where he had filmed both mother and daughter, and Ellis was so anxious to see the film that for the first time he accepted Haire's invitation to his home for an evening to view it. As he learned more about the tragedy, it appeared that Hildegart's mother, far from being one of Ellis's idealized "New Mothers," had been unbalanced, and that the girl's life with her had been a martyrdom. Hildegart was an illegitimate child and her mother was fearful of her having any contact with men. When she learned that Hildegart was having an affair, she shot her while she was sleeping. In court she said that "a prominent Englishman, whose name is a household word, offered to take the girl to England, but she would not let her go alone"

(*Daily Herald*, May 28th, 1934). In May 1934 she was sentenced to twenty-six years' imprisonment.

The rise of the Nazis was also turning the world upside down. In 1933 Ellis heard that both his and Margaret Sanger's books had been burned, a speech recounting their infamies prefacing the destruction of their works. Hirschfeld's institute was looted, many of his assistants committed suicide, and his library was destroyed. Hirschfeld himself escaped and died in Nice in 1935. Bryher was deeply involved in smuggling intellectuals out of Germany into Switzerland. Dr. Helene Stocker, an acquaintance of many years, who had long been active in advanced sexual work in Berlin, escaped to England, where she was in a pitiful condition. In his straitened circumstances Ellis could contribute only £3 to a fund organized to help her. But actually he had elected to withdraw from the world long years before.

CHAPTER 2 7

LAST DAYS

THE MOVE FROM DOVER MANSIONS TO HOLMDENE AVENUE IN 1929 had seemed momentous enough, but now in 1938 two final moves when he was very old and obviously very ill were depressing and exhausting. He knew he had not long to live and there were so many details still to be attended to. On that last Christmas in the cottage at Wivelsfield Green he wrote to Faith: "I just sit in front of the fire, not inclined to do anything, except reproach myself for not being able to answer all the dear & loving letters I receive at this season. And as one gets old one hasn't the reserve of strength to recover properly from the blows which even a slight illness gives. . . . I don't feel equal to the strain of giving up the houses."[1] But somehow his books were sorted out, and the majority sold to the dealer Bertram Rota.

His strength was gone; and in the spring, after leaving Wivelsfield Green, he was in bed with pleurisy for six weeks. The first effort he made after being allowed to get up was to walk slowly to the postbox with a short letter to Margaret Sanger. By then Françoise had found the small house at Hintlesham in Ellis's beloved East Anglia. Cherry Ground was in the parish of Washbrook, where one of Ellis's ancestors had been vicar two centuries before. In the middle of June he was installed in rooms in Felixstowe while Françoise made the house comfortable for him. It was the house she had always dreamed of. "If ever you love this place as much as I do," she told him joyfully, "then we shall live very happily here. It is just a dream to me; I can't believe I am going to live here for ever & ever. No matter out of what window one looks one has such a glorious view. . . ."[2] Ellis still had enough spirit to instruct her: "I hope you will do as little as possible to *my* room until I am there as I shall have to have things *my* way,"[3] to which she replied, "Your bedroom is now ready, the curtains are up & look very nice indeed. It certainly looks a nice room, & *of course* you will arrange it *your* way."[4] It almost seemed too good to be true. To Margaret Sanger he wrote: "There are two acres of ground with all sorts of things in it—I am always discovering something new—including a small meadow where we keep a few fowls. My sun-hut is of course set in the garden & I am lying there now. I have always wanted to live in Suffolk & the air suits me better than anywhere else. I say it is because it is the home of my ancestors!"[5]

On his eightieth birthday he received a telegram from America signed by many of his admirers. To Margaret he wrote: "All these tributes in my old age are very wonderful to me—almost impossible to believe!"[6] Margaret and Bronislaw Malinowski had dinner together on the eve of his birthday—"in honour of you . . . and drank to your health and our devotion to you." Then came a letter from Malinowski, as chairman of a committee (organized by Margaret), enclosing a cheque for $1,000; Malinowski told him that Margaret "really is a wonderful person & she loves & admires you truly. And so do millions of others."[7] He and Françoise decided to spend the money on a car. By now the other old man, Freud, had been driven out of Austria and was living in exile in Hampstead. Through H.D. he expressed a wish to see Ellis, but each was too weak to travel to the other. Despite the cancer in his jaw, Freud was still to write *The Splitting of the Ego* and *An Outline of Psychoanalysis* in this last year of his life, but the only work Ellis was able to do was to add bits to his autobiography, and he unfortunately succeeded in muddling the chronology by these insertions. While living much in his memory, the past seemed to complete a symbolic circular route. From Australia he received a letter from the last survivor of his pupils in 1877, a man of seventy-four. C. E. Attwater recalled how some of the older boys, nearly Ellis's own age, resenting so young a schoolmaster, called him "English Johnnie" and buried his cane and hat. From Missouri he heard from Percival Chubb, now President of the American Ethical Union: "The ranks of the Veterans are getting thin. 'Simple-lifers' seem to last best."*[8]

---

* Another link with the past occurred in 1935 when he saw the name of an Australian, Howard Hinton, in the New Year's Honours list. The following (in the

Ellis's throat was now so bad that life was becoming a misery. Seven years earlier he had begun to notice that he was having difficulty in swallowing. He told Françoise that he thought he had cancer. She begged him to have an X-ray, but he refused. Four years went by and there was no marked deterioration in his health. After one bad bout of influenza in the spring of 1936 he went to recuperate in Brighton, where a street photographer caught him looking amazingly spry for his years. When visitors came he ate sparingly—usually a junket—but often had to leave the room to regurgitate. Within a year his strong constitution was broken and he had become very frail. He couldn't sleep unless he was propped up with pillows. Doctors told Françoise confidentially that they could find nothing organically wrong, that it was all in his head. A doctor in Felixstowe who examined him in June 1938 believed it was cancer and suggested that he take belladonna three times a day to relieve the discomfort. By the time Lord Horder was called in, a correct diagnosis was finally established—a pouch in his throat (dysphagia) was catching all the food he swallowed; but by then it was too late to operate. Françoise and Ellis had both long been supporters of euthanasia. The end would now be only a few months at most, but how long could he stand the discomfort? The question now was: By what means would he end his life?

Lafitte Collection) is a draft of a letter Ellis wrote to a man he believed to be the grandson of the man responsible for his conversion at Sparkes Creek:

13 March /35

Dear Sir,
    At the beginning of this year, glancing through the New Year's Honours in the London "Times," I came with a shock of surprise on the name of my early friend, Howard Hinton. I wrote, with discretion, to friends in Sydney for a little information, & I will address you on the supposition that you may be my old friend's son. If so I knew your mother around about the time of your birth & was acquainted with all the circumstances.
    I have reason to be interested in the whole Hinton family. Four generations have stood out as exceptional persons & it would be a real satisfaction to me to be able to add a further generation. Your deep interest in art would bring you well into this tradition as it was a subject in which James Hinton took an almost passionate interest. I may mention that I used to possess a David Cox water colour which had formerly belonged to him. [Miss Caroline Haddon's wedding present to him?]
    I do not give my name at present, not knowing how you will view my letter. But I should be pleased to write in more detail if you care to hear. If so, please address to X under cover to
                    F. Lafitte-Cyon,
                    Haslemere, Wivelsfield Green, Sussex, England.
    Regretfully, I have been unable to discover whether Ellis ever received a reply.

Françoise was worn out by worry and crippling neuritis. Gas masks had been issued in October 1938, and, deeply committed as she was to pacifism, she had gone into a deep depression over the state of the world. She was persuaded in June to go away for two weeks on a walking holiday near Matlock in Derbyshire, where Ellis had stayed with Olive Schreiner so many years before. In her absence Laura and Edie came from Tunbridge Wells to look after their brother.

The previous summer Margaret Sanger, while visiting them, told Françoise that she had heard that Havelock had married her secretly. Françoise replied that she was still married to her Russian husband, Serge, and, besides, she didn't believe in marriage. They were sitting in the garden, and Ellis, in his study, overheard the conversation. The next day, as Françoise put the coffee tray on his table, he reached towards her, assuring her that he would marry her if she were free. Françoise, deeply touched, told him that she didn't believe in marriage, and they clung to each other, in silent acknowledgement of the durability of their relationship.

By the following summer it was clear that he was slowly dying. Françoise later recalled for Arthur Calder-Marshall that she had gone away, knowing that Ellis would secure the means for his death in her absence. Her memory of it was of a rather dramatic death-pact. There are differing versions of what actually took place in Calder-Marshall's biography, in *Friendship's Odyssey*, and in the unpublished letters on which I shall primarily rely. It is true that in the spring Françoise had gone to see Winifred de Kok, the South African doctor who was devoted to Havelock, to ask her advice about an operation for him. After Françoise had left for Derbyshire, on June 26th Ellis wrote to Winifred thanking her for taking so much interest in "treatment" for him, but "I am sorry you have, for I am no longer interested in treatment." He then turned to the main question he wanted to put to her,

> "which the ordinary conventional doctor will not usually talk about freely. I am one of the founders of the Voluntary Euthanasia Society & want your advice on some points. At my age, of course, there are always new troubles developing (many out of the throat trouble) which do not admit of any treatment & become at last intolerable, so that life is no longer worth living. I am in no hurry for the moment; I still have much I could do, &

want to enjoy my garden & am even meditating just now the purchase of an expensive gramophone record. And in any case, of course, what help you give will be entirely confidential. In one sense the matter is far from urgent, but as regards *my feelings* it is *very* urgent. I need to feel that when the worst comes to the worst I have already in my hands a safe & easy method of escaping. It is not quite easy, for solids (tablets, etc) are uncertain with my throat, may not go down, & be returned. I want something more or less liquid. We thought your advice would be helpful & that you would help to put into my hands—for possible use *some time*—the adequate & reliable opiate or other remedy. Then the matter could be put out of mind. If you would do this, & if possible almost at once, I would be most *deeply grateful*. This was really the *main point* we had in mind in turning to you, though you don't seem quite to have realised."[9]

Two days later he again wrote:

"You won't expect to hear from me so soon again. But ever since that letter went developments in my condition are arising which make what I said then even more urgent for me & cause me to worry you again. My doctor yesterday found that my heart is beginning to grow weak & though that, as he pointed out, does not mean any speedy fatal result, it makes it necessary to be *prepared*, & also it obviously puts any further manipulation of the throat out of the question, for that might be immediately fatal. Also it anyhow adds to discomfort—shortness of breath—even when lying quietly in bed, & difficulty of getting sleep. Also other troubles are appearing & death may come quite naturally. Still I am now even more anxious to have in my hands the consolation of a last resort, even though meanwhile I go on enjoying life as long as I can. I cannot say how deeply grateful I shall be if you will do what you can to arrange this at once. Françoise will be pleased & it will be much the best before she returns from Matlock so that we can treat it as a matter settled without further discussion."[10]

The following day he sent off a more urgent letter:

It is so sweet of you to write as you do & be so willing to help when help means so much to me, even if only as a mental relief. And I am anxious to settle it at once before Françoise returns.

The idea is hers, quite as much hers as mine (indeed she wants it for herself also eventually) but the details would worry her.

I like the insulin idea, but I have no experience at all with injections, so I should feel nervous over something going wrong, &, however privately & secretly, it would not be easy to ask someone else to do it & indeed impossible.

This leaves what you say is second best—the morphia suppositories. They seem possible, & should offer, I suppose, no difficulties. You seem to put opiate suppositories by preference before liquid opiates by mouth.

No doubt I can obtain the drugs (by instalments best as you say) from the wholesale dealers like B. Davis or P. Davis. But as I never go to them I am a little shy of asking for such things as these.

I write to you at once so that you can again speak to R. Greene* who is very kind in the matter.

I remain in bed & cheerful & comfortable on the whole, though with trying times.

You must not think there is anything sad in leaving the world after a long & successful life. I don't. Nor am I yet in a hurry. But I want to be prepared. I am now expecting my doctor.

Affectionately & gratefully,
Havelock

Of course I will destroy all documents & never (there would be no occasions) any names.[11]

On July 4th he sent his last note to her:

Thank you so very much, very dear Winifred, for all you are doing. In my present slight muddled mental state it means a great deal that you are thus helping me. In my old marriage days I knew omnopon & would give a small sedative dose occasionally to Edith or myself. I suppose the solution in water would be quite satisfactory & with care I could probably keep it down. But it might be as well to take a few suppositories as well. If you do all this I shall certainly feel easy in my mind. As you know, I have no immediate wish to go. But my difficulties increase, & there seems little or no immediate relief. My voice is becoming reduced

---

* I have been unable to identify R. Greene.

to a whisper. I enjoy the beautiful flowers from the garden, but I hardly stir out of bed & reading & writing are reduced very low. My sisters are very good, & I have a nurse every morning. I expect Françoise back about Monday. She goes to London first (leaving Matlock Friday).

> With much love & gratitude
> Havelock[12]

These letters are quoted from copies made by Françoise from the originals which Winifred lent her after his death. The letters Winifred wrote to him were returned to her. After all, she had to be very careful, particularly as a doctor, in aiding and abetting him in what was a legal crime.

For Françoise, too, it would be a crime to help him. She walked the Derbyshire hills, which she found dull and lifeless. Her letters to Havelock express the conflict she felt between her longing for rest and her longing to be with him. She was in such agony of spirit that she began to think she was going insane. None of the letters written by either of them even hint at what they were planning to do. By now Ellis's handwriting was very shaky, but in the last letter he wrote to his "beloved Naiad"—on July 2nd—he gives an extraordinarily coherent account of how the doctor had found him downstairs and had ordered him to stay in bed as the effort to climb the stairs was too debilitating. A district nurse was coming in to relieve his sisters and he liked her very much. He ended:

> I am happy & comfortable, & occupied in my room & mostly bed. Too cold, anyhow, to be outside. Eat fairly good meals though so often tasteless. Dinner today: melon (I always start on melon) special brand of bottled chicken, Laura and Edie covered the raspberries with the net yesterday. Clark not having done it as told. I wish I could go round garden but no escalator! Lovely roses & other flowers in my bedroom.
>
> Very long letter from me but it brings you all sorts of loving thoughts
>
> F[13]

Françoise wrote back impatiently that she didn't want him to trouble her with what he was eating. "Provided you are fairly fit this is all I want to know at present concerning your physical self which I cannot help at this distance."[14] She was dreading the week-end, when there would be no letter from him: "So I hope there will be one tomorrow, & that it will be close & intimate, my real Faun, my inner Faun, of whom I am so found [sic]. I long to be back near him. And if I am stronger in body & in mind, all will be well. To have a rest from one another is needed at times. Also to have a total change of occupations & surroundings. We shall be more able to get on with our problem after this." But the prospect of the lonely week-end was too miserable, and on the 7th she left for London, first sending a telegram to Hintlesham to let the sisters know where she could be reached. The following morning—Saturday, the 8th—she was summoned from the breakfast table at her hotel by a telephone message from Edie with the news that Havelock seemed to be sinking and was urgently insistent that he see her. By eleven o'clock she was at his bedside. It was immediately apparent how much his condition had deteriorated in her absence. She later told Arthur Calder-Marshall that her first startled discovery was that Edie had by mistake substituted for his vitamin pills some prescription pills which in the past Françoise had administered to him on two occasions when he was suffering from oedema in his legs. Her instant reaction was that his weakness had resulted from these pills taken when he was already dehydrated. All day she sat by his bed holding his hands in hers, which he pressed from time to time. His voice was now so faint that she could no longer hear him and she gave him a pad on which he occasionally scrawled a few notes. In one he wrote: "I liked the nurse much from the first, very prompt & businesslike & not a bit prudish." In another, almost indecipherable scrawl: "You see I can't go on long like this—It must be brought to an end."[15]

Françoise's account in a letter of 1958 to Calder-Marshall seems to indicate that he already had obtained what she describes in her melodramatic way as "the poison"— that is, the tablets—"the nature of which I refuse to state, for I need caution after all."[16] (She claimed she still possessed them.) She also found a box containing anal suppositories wrapped in a slip of paper with directions on it in Ellis's handwriting. But there doesn't seem to be any indication that they were used that afternoon. It is all a little puzzling because Winifred did not visit Ellis at Cherry Ground during Françoise's absence. In 1947 she wrote to Françoise: "I did not know how near he was to death and looking back, I wonder if I failed him in being slow to realise how urgent his need was. I cannot even now remember whether I eventually solved the problem for him."[17] A strange lapse of memory! Winifred did not show Ellis's letters to Françoise until 1947; and my own belief is that Françoise, who became extremely eccentric as she grew older, wove these elements into a fantasy in which the imagined death, in which she would have played a major role, became far more real to her than what actually happened. It is significant that she never suggests that Havelock told her where the pills were, even though he was writing perfectly coherent messages to her. But the very fact that he urged his sisters to summon her home indicates that he realized he was dying.

That evening about nine o'clock he seemed to be having a heart attack. Françoise rushed to telephone the doctor, but he implied that she was over-reacting; he had given Dr. Ellis an injection that morning, he said, and would look in again early the next morning. Françoise, certain that he was dying, called his sisters to go in and say good-bye to him. At about eleven he seemed to be having another attack, but he would not allow her to call the doctor. "There is nothing anyone can do now," he said. He urged her to go to bed because she looked so weary, promising that he would pull the bell if he needed her. He complained that the light bothered him. She turned it off and went downstairs to put the kettle on. When she returned, the light was on under his door. Thinking that he could not sleep, she went in. The massive white head lay utterly still.

* * *

Ellis's last published article appeared in the *London News Chronicle* on his eightieth birthday. He had written it in his sun-hut. It was entitled "World Peace Is Our Next Upward Movement." "Can we suppose," he asked, "that, at this crucial point man will for the first time fail?" George Bernard Shaw, asked to comment on Ellis's death, replied: "Havelock's work was done. We mustn't grudge him his rest. The new generation must carry on."

Two days after his death Françoise read the letter which he had written to her during the last summer at Wivelsfield Green.

My darling Naiad

This is the last letter you will ever receive from me, so I want to say over again—though I have said it so often before—with what deep love in my heart I shall leave you. I want to say again, too, that you must not feel I am dead. Those whom we love go on living in our hearts so long as we live. I have felt that now for a long time. (And I read only yesterday that Anatole France said just the same thing in the same words after the death of the woman he really loved). I like to feel that I shall still be alive in your heart and not really dead until you die, which I hope will not be just yet.

Do not think me selfish if I want you still to live. There are things to be done for me that no one can do as well as you. And I have tried, so far as I can, by my Will to provide in part for you, as well as for my sisters, so that you may not be in danger of real hardship & be kept on your feet, perhaps for some time. Largely this depends on my future reputation.

The chief thing I leave behind is my Autobiography which I want you to get published two years after my death. To do this you have to begin seeing about it at once. I mean as soon as all the immediate things are settled. It is complete to 1916 (as far as I feel able to carry it at present) and I am slowly getting it all typed. The still untyped part is at Haslemere, either in the old chest in my bedroom or in the locked cupboard in the study there. There are three sets of the typed part,—two at Haslemere and one at Holmdene Avenue in the locked drawer at left of my study table. I want the typed part published exactly as it stands. If publishers insist on omissions of any words, asterisks *** are to be attributed for every letter omitted. The untyped part may need a little correction of mistakes.

This autobiography is certain to bring in money. It is quite likely to bring in much money, which is to be divided in accordance with my Will. Take the advice of the Society of Authors regarding agreement.

It is a joy to me to think that perhaps for the years after 1916, which have been lived with you, *you* will perhaps write a little separate book—the Later Life of H.E.—after the autobiography is published. When I first met you I thought my life was over. But the happiest years of my life have been with you. I had never dreamed such happiness possible for me. Those years still seem a miracle. And even the troubles in our life have still left love untouched. That love has never been disturbed for a moment. The chief love of my life was naturally for Edith because its most active period was passed by her side, as the Autobiography shows. But my life with her was often stormy, & our love was ruined with pain & trouble, even though that may have made it deeper. It could not clash with my love for you with whom I have known such heavenly peace & joy.

It is likely that two or three volumes could still be made of my work at present uncollected in volumes. It is mostly in the old chest in Haslemere bed-room.

Some manuscripts of *published* work, perhaps of value, are in my father's chest in Haslemere bed-room.

Do not easily give permission for publication of my letters. It isn't that I fear intimate things being published. On the contrary I think it is *only* the real & intimate letters (if not injurious to living persons) that ought to be published & none of the manufactured & banal letters of which I have had to write thousands.

But there are some letters of mine, even to strangers, probably worth publishing. It might be worthwhile, some day for you to collect them for publication—But there is no hurry about that.

> My everlasting love to my darling Naiad
> Faun[18]

At the cremation ceremony at Golders Green the only friend present besides Françoise and her sons was Winifred de Kok. As with Edith, the ashes were scattered through the garden. Two months later Freud's ashes were placed in a Grecian vase, also at Golders Green. It seems particularly fitting that these two men who did so much to change the world, each in his distinctive way, should come at last to the same final resting-place.

The executors were Françoise, Ellis's sister Edie, and Mneme Kirkland. The beneficiaries were Françoise, who was to receive one-half of future royalties, and his three sisters, among whom the other half was to be divided. Trouble started immediately. The sisters seized the little car that had been bought with the birthday cheque from America. Mneme swept in and stalked out with the letters Havelock had written to her. There was one locked chest which, in a codicil to his will, Ellis instructed was to be destroyed after his death. It contained many personal letters; and Françoise told Margaret Sanger that "I meant to look at them nevertheless in case the trunk contained other things which had been placed there by mistake."[19] However, one day when she was out shopping the sisters took

it to the garden and burned its contents. It must have contained all
Edith's letters and other letters as well; we can only regret their loss,
as they might have completed the story more fully for us.

As for the publication of *My Life*, it was a great disappointment
in terms of sales or critical reception. In 1940 people's minds were
too preoccupied with the war to pay much attention to it and the
reviews tended to be either patronizing or outraged by the accounts
of Edith's lesbianism and Ellis's urolagnia. In my view, it is a book
that deserves reappraisal. For all its faults—the *longueurs* of the extended account of his Suffolk ancestors, the absence of any real discussion about the writing of the *Studies*, and the disproportionate
length at which he dwells on Edith's problems—it is a book that
still ranks with the great autobiographies in its candour and revealing
self-depiction.

Françoise did not die until 1974—after more than thirty years in
which she dedicated herself to honouring Ellis's memory. She—like
Edith—turned to spiritualism and wrote a book about how Ellis
appeared to her from time to time. She became paranoid at detecting
any slight against Ellis or herself. She even quarrelled with Margaret
Sanger because she felt she wasn't treated adequately in a book
written about Margaret Sanger. As for her own book, *Friendship's
Odyssey*, Margaret told her rather gently that the public would prefer
more about Ellis and less about herself. Sélincourt was outraged by
her book, which led up to "that nauseating climax of *My Man*." He
also saw it as "a distorted lying account of what was perhaps the loveliest thing in my life."[20]

In his last letter to Françoise, Ellis told her that he believed that
those we love don't die because they live on in our hearts. The people
still living who knew him continue to speak of him as a radiance who
touched their lives in a way they will never forget. Soon they will all
be gone.

APPENDIX A

Onward, brothers, march still onward,
  Side by side and hand in hand,
Ye are bound for man's true kingdom,
  You are an increasing band.

Though the way seem often doubtful,
  Hard the toil which ye endure,
Though at times your courage falter,
  Yet the Promised Land is sure.

Older sages saw it dimly,
  And their joy to madness wrought;
Living men have gazed upon it,
  Standing on the hills of thought.

All the past has done and suffered,
  All the daring and the strife,
All has helped to mould the future,
  Make Man master of his life.

Still brave deeds and kind are needed,
  Noble thoughts and feelings fair;
Ye too must be strong and suffer,
  Ye too have to do and dare.

Onward, brothers, march still onward,
  March still onward hand in hand;
Till ye see at last Man's Kingdom,
  Till ye reach the Promised Land.

APPENDIX B

AU MAÎTRE

Françoise Delisle

Quand maître,—maître de la mort,
Quand par folie, éperdument,
On a de l'angoisse à plein coeur,
Quand de douleurs et de tourment
On vous arrive tout en pleurs,
Vous vous dressez contre le sort.
Oh! vous le plus humain des hommes,
Le moins faible par leurs faiblesses,
C'est votre bonté qui nous somme
Aux beaux espoirs, grandes prouesses,
Cher grand dieu!—Maître de la mort!

Grand maître,—maître de la vie,—
Nous avons appris qu'on la danse
Avec du sang plein les souliers,
Mais qu'elle est noble et douce trance,
Riante pour le coeur altier,
Mystérieuse et folle amie;
Dès lors, assis à ses banquets
Que les sanglots et les chansons
Sont belles fleurs et ses bouquets
Nous vous bénissons pour ses dons
Vous, grand dieu!—maître de la vie!

(*Birth Control Review,* February 1926)

APPENDIX C

To V. C. Calverton, 25 April 1930 (Manuscripts and Archives Division, New York Public Library, Astor, Lenox and Tilden Foundations)

I have yours of 10 April in which you tell me of your idea of writing a *History of Women* in five to ten volumes. I trust you will not feel offended if I tell you that my opinion (which you ask for) is decidedly *against* such a scheme. It does not seem to me a good idea *in itself*, nor, assuming it to be a good idea, does it seem to me a specially suitable task for *you* to undertake.

As regards the first objection, it is a superficial view to regard the history of *woman* as something apart from the history of *man*. The female of every species is in perpetual relationship to the male, & the more thorough & searching your study of woman the closer it will bring you to man. All those "short histories" of woman (Langdon-Davies & the rest) are insignificant—slight & superficial & secondhand (often without acknowledgment of their source), the reason being that no serious writer would even think of writing such a book, while the serious writer, realising the only kind of book that is possible on the subject, hesitates a very, very long time, & has not yet undertaken it. He realises that it means a history of mankind in a more intimate sense than anything yet attempted. It would require an enormously long period of preliminary preparation, a knowledge of many sciences, and a familiarity with many languages. Even my Sex "Studies," a related but smaller task, involved nearly twenty years of preliminary preparation & work before the actual writing was even begun. How vastly longer a period a history such as this would require! The chief work on women at present is Ploss's *Das Weib*, quite correctly limited to women because it is strictly ethnographical & limited to the bald facts. But its three large volumes have taken fifty years and three generations of editors to produce. Frazer has spent a long life over the perhaps rather similar, but still much more limited, task of his Golden Bough & its related works, but to do so he has lived the life of a recluse & sacrificed nearly all other interests.

NOTES AND REFERENCES

CHAPTER 1–*CHILDHOOD*

1. Havelock Ellis, *My Life* (London: Heinemann, 1940), p. 1.
2. Mitchell Library, State Library of New South Wales.
3. Ernest Jones, *The Life and Work of Sigmund Freud*, eds. Lionel Trilling and Steven Marcus (London: Penguin, 1964), p. 34.
4. 17 Dec. 1928 (Margaret Sanger Papers, Library of Congress).
5. Mitchell Library.
6. *My Life*, p. 49.
7. Havelock Ellis, *The Soul of Spain* (London: Constable, 4th impression, 1911), p. v.
8. *My Life*, p. 49.
9. *Ibid*.
10. *Ibid*., p. 50.
11. *Ibid*., p. 51.
12. *Ibid*., p. 53.
13. *Ibid*., p. 61.
14. British Library.
15. *My Life*, p. 79.
16. Lafitte Collection.
17. *My Life*, p. 79.
18. Lafitte Collection.
19. Houston Peterson, *Havelock Ellis: Philosopher of Love* (Boston: Houghton Mifflin, 1928), p. 55.
20. *My Life*, p. 66.
21. *Ibid*., p. 67.
22. *Ibid*.
23. *Ibid*.
24. *Ibid*., p. 68.
25. *Ibid*.
26. *Ibid*., p. 69.
27. *Ibid*., p. 72.
28. Lafitte Collection.
29. 20 May 1916 (Library of Congress).

CHAPTER 2–*AUSTRALIA*

1. Mitchell Library, State Library of New South Wales.
2. *Ibid*.
3. Havelock Ellis, *My Life* (London: Heinemann, 1940), p. 97.
4. Mitchell Library.

5. *Ibid.*
6. *Ibid.*
7. *Ibid.*
8. *Ibid.*
9. *Ibid.*
10. *Ibid.*
11. *Ibid.*
12. *Ibid.*
13. *Ibid.*

14. *Ibid.*
15. *Ibid.*
16. *Ibid.*
17. *Ibid.*
18. 1892 Preface to Havelock Ellis, *The New Spirit* (London: Bell).
19. *My Life*, p. 106.
20. Mitchell Library.
21. *Ibid.*

CHAPTER 3–*SPARKES CREEK*

1. Mitchell Library, State Library of New South Wales.
2. Havelock Ellis, *Kanga Creek* (Waltham St. Lawrence: Golden Cockerel Press, 1922), p. 23.
3. *Ibid.*
4. Havelock Ellis, *My Life*, (London: Heinemann, 1940), p. 123.
5. Mitchell Library.
6. *My Life*, p. 125.
7. Havelock Ellis, *Studies in the Psychology of Sex*, Vol. III (New York: Random House, 1936), Part Two, p. 424.
8. Mitchell Library.

9. *Kanga Creek*, p. 37.
10. Humanities Research Center, University of Texas.
11. *My Life*, p. 131.
12. *Ibid.*
13. Mitchell Library.
14. *Ibid.*
15. *Ibid.*
16. *Ibid.*
17. *Ibid.*
18. *Ibid.*
19. *Ibid.*
20. *My Life*, p. 139.
21. Mitchell Library.

CHAPTER 4–*THE LONDON IDEALISTS*

1. Mitchell Library, State Library of New South Wales.
2. Havelock Ellis, *An Open Letter to Biographers* (Berkeley Heights, N.J.: Oriole Press, 1931), p. 11.
3. British Library.
4. Havelock Ellis, *My Life* (London: Heinemann, 1940), p. 1.
5. Mitchell Library.
6. *Ibid.*
7. *My Life*, p. 142.
8. Lafitte Collection.
9. *Ibid.*
10. James Hinton, *Others' Needs* (Lafitte Collection).
11. Havelock Ellis, "What Is

Pureness?", *Modern Thought*, III (April 1881), 98.
12. *Ibid.*
13. *Ibid.*
14. Havelock Ellis, "Thomas Hardy's Novels," *The Westminster Review*, CXIX (April 1883), 334.
15. John Bayley, *An Essay on Hardy* (Cambridge, 1978), p. 211.
16. *The Collected Letters of Thomas Hardy*, eds. R. L. Purdy and Michael Millgate (Oxford, 1978), p. 117.
17. 16 April 1884 (British Library).
18. Lafitte Collection.
19. Havelock Ellis, "The Two

Worlds," *Modern Thought*, April 1882, p. 129.

20. *My Life*, p. 159.
21. Lafitte Collection.
22. *Ibid.*
23. Yale University Library.
24. *Ibid.*
25. 4 Oct. 1885 (Yale University Library).
26. *Ibid.*
27. 17 Oct. 1885 (Yale University Library).
28. *Ibid.*

29. Lafitte Collection.
30. 21 Oct. 1885 (Yale University Library).
31. Lafitte Collection.
32. *Ibid.*
33. *Fabian Tract*, no. 41.
34. Humanities Research Center, University of Texas.
35. Lafitte Collection.
36. 6 Jan. 1884 (Yale University Library).
37. Yale University Library.

CHAPTER 5—*OLIVE SCHREINER*

1. February 1884 (Humanities Research Center, University of Texas).
2. *The Letters of Olive Schreiner*, ed. S. C. Cronwright-Schreiner (London: T. Fisher Unwin, 1924), p. 12.
3. *Ibid.*, p. 14.
4. *Ibid.*, p. 13.
5. University of Texas. The precise dating of these letters is difficult to establish. Many of them bear no date; others have been mutilated. Consequently, it has been impossible to footnote every quotation.
6. 14 March 1884 (University of Texas).
7. *The Letters of Olive Schreiner*, p. 14.
8. *Ibid.*
9. *Ibid.*, p. 18.
10. University of Texas.
11. *The Letters of Olive Schreiner*, p. 15.
12. Havelock Ellis, *My Life* (London: Heinemann, 1940), p. 183.
13. University of Texas.
14. *Ibid.*
15. *The Letters of Olive Schreiner*, p. 21.

16. *Ibid.*
17. University of Texas.
18. *The Letters of Olive Schreiner*, p. 24.
19. *Ibid.*, p. 21.
20. University of Texas.
21. *Ibid.*
22. *Ibid.*
23. *My Life*, p. 184.
24. University of Texas.
25. *Ibid.*
26. *Ibid.*
27. *Ibid.*
28. *Ibid.*
29. I am indebted to Dr. Michael Gormley for this information.
30. University of Texas.
31. *The Letters of Olive Schreiner*, p. 27.
32. University of Texas.
33. *The Letters of Olive Schreiner*, p. 34.
34. *Ibid.*, p. 36.
35. Mitchell Library, State Library of New South Wales.
36. Havelock Ellis, "Eleanor Marx," *The Modern Monthly*, Sept. 1935, p. 286.
37. Mitchell Library.
38. *My Life*, p. 185.
39. *Ibid.*, p. 180.

40. University of Texas.
41. *Ibid.*
42. *Ibid.*
43. *Ibid.*
44. *Ibid.*

45. *Ibid.*
46. *Ibid.*
47. *Ibid.*
48. Mitchell Library.
49. *My Life*, p. 186.

CHAPTER 6–*THE HINTON IMBROGLIO*

1. Mitchell Library, State Library of New South Wales.
2. Betty Fredkin, "Olive Schreiner and Karl Pearson," *Quarterly Bulletin of South African Library*, XXXI (June 1977), 86.
3. *Little Essays of Love and Virtue* (London: A. and C. Black, 1922), p. 69.
4. *The Letters of Olive Schreiner*, ed. S. C. Cronwright-Schreiner (London: T. Fisher Unwin, 1924), p. 56.
5. *Ibid.*, p. 55.
6. Humanities Research Center, University of Texas.
7. *Ibid.*
8. *The Letters of Olive Schreiner*, p. 8.
9. Pearson Papers, University College.
10. *Ibid.*
11. *The Letters of Olive Schreiner*, p. 20.
12. 19 Dec. 1885 (Pearson Papers).
13. *Ibid.*
14. *Ibid.*
15. 17 Dec. 1885 (*Ibid*).
16. *Ibid.*

17. Havelock Ellis, *Studies in the Psychology of Sex* (New York: Random House, 1936), IV, 116.
18. *The Letters of Olive Schreiner*, p. 93.
19. Pearson Papers.
20. University of Texas.
21. *The Letters of Olive Schreiner*, p. 96.
22. *Ibid.*, p. 98.
23. University of Texas.
24. 19 Oct. 1886 (Pearson Papers).
25. University of Texas.
26. Pearson Papers.
27. *Ibid.*
28. *Ibid.*
29. *Ibid.*
30. *Ibid.*
31. University of Texas.
32. *Ibid.*
33. Carpenter Collection, Sheffield Public Libraries.
34. *Ibid.*
35. *Ibid.*
36. University of Texas.
37. Mitchell Library.
38. University of Texas.
39. Mitchell Library.

CHAPTER 7–*EARLY PROFESSIONAL YEARS*

1. Havelock Ellis, *My Life* (London: Heinemann, 1940), p. 163.
2. 12 March 1885 (Carpenter Collection, Sheffield Public Libraries).

3. 30 Oct. 1885 (*Ibid.*).
4. 2 Dec. 1887 (*Ibid.*).
5. 6 March 1885 (Humanities Research Center, University of Texas).

6. Havelock Ellis, "Eleanor Marx," *The Modern Monthly*, Sept. 1935, p. 288.
7. *Ibid.*, p. 290.
8. *Ibid.*
9. *Ibid.*, p. 291.
10. *Ibid.*
11. 6 Aug. 1888 (Yale University Library).
12. University of Texas.
13. "The Present Position of English Criticism," *Time*, Dec. 1885, p. 37.
14. *The Letters of John Addington Symonds*, eds. H. M. Schueller and R. L. Peters (Detroit: Wayne State University Press, 1969), III, 98
15. *My Life*, p. 165.
16. "Eleanor Marx," p. 292.
17. *Ibid.*, p. 294.
18. *My Life*, p. 167.
19. 11 Dec. 1889 (British Library).
20. *Bernard Shaw—Collected Letters 1898–1910*, ed. Dan H. Laurence (Max Reinhardt, 1972), p. 201.
21. 16 Oct. 1888 (British Library).
22. *My Life*, p. 167.
23. 1 July 1892 (Copy, University of Bristol).
24. *The Criminal* (London: Walter Scott, 2nd ed., 1895), p. 187.
25. University of Texas.
26. Mitchell Library, State Library of New South Wales.
27. *Ibid.*
28. N.d. (University of Texas).
29. 2 Dec. 1887 (Sheffield Public Libraries).
30. 2 May 1888 (University of Texas).
31. "Eleanor Marx," p. 292.
32. Mitchell Library.
33. 11 June 1889 (British Library).
34. Mitchell Library.

CHAPTER 8–*THE YOUNG HERETIC*

1. 11 Dec. 1889 (British Library).
2. Arthur Calder-Marshall, *Havelock Ellis* (London: Rupert Hart-Davis, 1959), p. 111.
3. 23 May 1890 (Yale University Library).
4. *The Spectator*, LXIV (29 March 1890).
5. 27 March 1890 (Humanities Research Center, University of Texas).
6. 6 May 1890, *The Letters of John Addington Symonds*, eds. H. M. Schueller and R. L. Peters (Detroit: Wayne State University Press, 1969), III, p. 458.
7. *The Spectator*, LXIV (29 March 1890).
8. *The Athenaeum*, No. 3255 (15 March 1890), p. 339.
9. *The Academy*, XXXVII (5 April 1890), 232.
10. *The Echo*, No. 6766 (9 Sept. 1890).
11. Ernest Rhys, *Everyman Remembers* (London: J. M. Dent, 1931), p. 81.
12. I am indebted for this idea and others in this chapter to an unpublished dissertation, "Havelock Ellis: Literary Critic of the Nineties" (University of Chicago, 1968) by Leslie B. Mittleman.
13. 14 May 1890 (Copy, Lafitte Collection).
14. *The Bookman*, LXXIV (March 1932), 621.

CHAPTER 9–MARRIAGE

1. Ernest Rhys, *Everyman Remembers* (London: J. M. Dent, 1931), p. 47.
2. Havelock Ellis, *My Life* (London: Heinemann, 1940), p. 47.
3. *Ibid.*, p. 212.
4. *Ibid.*, p. 217.
5. *Ibid.*
6. *The Letters of Olive Schreiner*, ed. S. C. Cronwright-Schreiner (London: T. Fisher Unwin, 1924), p. 197.
7. *My Life*, p. 200.
8. *Ibid.*, p. 234.
9. *Ibid.*, pp. 238–40.
10. *Ibid.*, p. 243.
11. *Ibid.*, p. 218.
12. *Ibid.*
13. *Ibid.*, p. 233.
14. Edith Lees Ellis, "Sincerity in Marriage," *Seed-Time*, July 1892, p. 12.
15. *My Life*, p. 263.
16. *Ibid.*, p. 260.
17. 25 Nov. 1891 (Pearson Papers, University College).
18. *My Life*, p. 247.
19. *Ibid.*, p. 256.
20. British Library.
21. *My Life*, p. 252.

CHAPTER 10–MARRIED LIFE

1. Havelock Ellis, *My Life* (London: Heinemann, 1940), p. 259.
2. *Ibid.*, p. 257.
3. 4 Nov. 1934 (Dr. Joseph Wortis).
4. Humanities Research Center, University of Texas.
5. 8 June 1897 (Lafitte Collection).
6. Havelock Ellis, *Man and Woman* (London: Walter Scott, 1894), p. 395.
7. Bernard De Voto, "Widower's House," *The Saturday Review of Literature*, 4 Nov. 1939, p. 12.
8. *My Life*, p. 262.
9. *Ibid.*
10. *Ibid.*, p. 263.
11. *Ibid.*
12. *Ibid.*, p. 265.
13. *Ibid.*, p. 264.
14. *Ibid.*, p. 265.
15. *Ibid.*, p. 267.
16. Edward Carpenter, *My Days and Dreams* (London: Allen & Unwin, 1916), p. 226.
17. *My Life*, p. 264.
18. *Ibid.*, p. 269.
19. *Ibid.*, p. 272.
20. 6 May 1932 (Dr. Joseph Wortis).
21. 20 April 1896 (Carpenter Collection, Sheffield Public Libraries).
22. *My Life*, p. 288.
23. *Ibid.*, p. 289.
24. *Ibid.*, p. 287.
25. *Ibid.*, p. 286.
26. *Ibid.*, p. 291.
27. *Ibid.*, p. 292.

CHAPTER 11–CONTROVERSIAL MATTER

1. I am indebted for this suggestion to Leslie B. Mittleman's unpublished dissertation, "Havelock Ellis: Literary Critic of the Nineties" (University of Chicago, 1960), although I have

been unable to find any evidence to substantiate it.

2. Havelock Ellis, "Mescal: A Study of a Divine Plant," *Popular Science Monthly*, May 1902, p. 58. See also "A Note on the Phenomena of Mescal Intoxication," *The Lancet*, 5 June 1897, pp. 1540–2; "Mescal—A New Artificial Paradise," *Contemporary Review*, Jan. 1898, pp. 130–1.
3. 9 Oct. 1899 (Galton Papers, University College).
4. *Popular Science Monthly*, May 1902, p. 71.
5. Havelock Ellis, "Concerning Jude the Obscure," *The Savoy*, Oct. 1896, pp. 35–49.
6. August 1897 (Carpenter Collection, Sheffield City Libraries).
7. 25 Oct. 1897 (*Ibid.*).
8. 25 Oct. 1897 (Pearson Papers, University College).
9. 27 March 1903 (Humanities Research Center, University of Texas).
10. 29 Sept. 1901 (Lafitte Collection).
11. 25 Aug. 1901 (University of Texas).
12. Havelock Ellis, *My Life* (London: Heinemann, 1940), p. 295.
13. *Ibid.*
14. 18 June 1892 (Copy, University of Bristol).
15. 1 July 1892 (*Ibid.*).
16. 7 July 1892, *The Letters of John*

Addington Symonds, eds. H. M. Schueller and R. L. Peters (Detroit: Wayne State University, 1969), III, 708.
17. 29 Dec. 1892 (*Ibid.*).
18. 21 Sept. 1892 (*Ibid.*).
19. 21 Dec. 1892 (Copy, University of Bristol).
20. *The Letters of John Addington Symonds,* III, 808.
21. 19 Feb. 1893 (Copy, University of Bristol).
22. *The Letters of John Addington Symonds,* III, 755.
23. 21 Dec. 1892 (Copy, University of Bristol).
24. 17 Dec. 1892 (Carpenter Collection, Sheffield Public Libraries).
25. 1 July 1892 (Copy, University of Bristol).
26. 22 Jan. 1894 (Carpenter Collection, Sheffield Public Libraries).
27. 24 April 1896 (*Ibid.*).
28. *My Life*, p. 293.
29. 12 Dec. 1897 (Lafitte Collection).
30. University of Texas.
31. *Ibid.*
32. August 1897 (Carpenter Collection, Sheffield Public Libraries).
33. 21 Nov. 1897 (*Ibid.*).
34. August 1897 (*Ibid.*).
35. 28 Nov. 1895 (University of Texas).
36. 11 Jan. 1898 (Lafitte Collection).

CHAPTER 12–*SEXUAL INVERSION*

1. 25 Nov. 1895 (Humanities Research Center, University of Texas).
2. Obituary notice, *The Literary Guide*, Sept. 1939, p. 171.
3. Havelock Ellis, *Studies in the*

Psychology of Sex (New York: Random House, 1936), Vol. II, Part Two, p. 226.
4. *Ibid.*, p. 308.
5. *Ibid.*, p. 338.

CHAPTER 13–*THE BEDBOROUGH TRIAL*

1. Lafitte Collection.
2. John Sweeney, *At Scotland Yard* (London: Alexander Moring, 1905), p. 184.
3. *Ibid.*, p. 185.
4. Havelock Ellis, *My Life* (London: Heinemann, 1940), p. 305.
5. *Ibid.*, p. 307.
6. *Bernard Shaw—Collected Letters 1898–1910*, ed. Dan H. Laurence (London: Max Reinhardt, 1972), pp. 57–8.
7. *A Note on the Bedborough Trial* (privately printed), p. 23.
8. 15 Jan. 1898 (Lafitte Collection).
9. 9 June 1898 (*Ibid.*).
10. 11 Oct. 1898 (*Ibid.*).
11. Lafitte Collection.
12. *My Life*, p. 311.
13. Lafitte Collection.
14. *My Life*, p. 308.
15. Lafitte Collection.
16. *My Life*, p. 299.
17. Lafitte Collection.
18. *Ibid.*
19. *Sayings of George Bedborough* (Letchworth Garden City Press, 1917), not paginated.
20. Harvard University Library.

CHAPTER 14–*NORMAL LIFE AGAIN*

1. 19 March 1899 (Carpenter Collection, Sheffield Public Libraries).
2. Houston Peterson, *Havelock Ellis, Philosopher of Love* (Boston: Houghton Mifflin, 1928), p. 236.
3. See "Pagan and Mediaeval Sentiment," *Essays in Criticism* (1865).
4. "Nietzsche" (1909), *Encyclopaedia of Religion and Ethics*, ed. James Hastings (New York and Edinburgh, 1908–1928), p. 368. In a letter to Grant Watson, dated 17 Sept. 1917, he writes: "With regard to Nietzsche, I have always felt that I might be tempted to over-estimate his importance. If I have not done so, the reason probably is that I was not too young when I first fell in with him. I give him a very high place. But I have to recognize that he lacks the complete sanity, balance, and comprehensiveness of his master Goethe" (Pennsylvania State University).
5. *My Life*, p. 325.
6. *Ibid.*, p. 328.
7. *Ibid.*
8. *Ibid.*, p. 338.
9. 7 Nov. 1895 (Carpenter Collection, Sheffield Public Libraries).
10. *My Life*, p. 358.
11. *Ibid.*
12. *Ibid.*, p. 363.

CHAPTER 15–*STUDIES IN THE PSYCHOLOGY OF SEX*

1. Yale University Library.
2. But a great many books were being written about Spain in addition to Baedeker: e.g., W. H. James, *A Tandem Trip in Spain* (1905); B. Kennedy, *A Tramp in*

Spain (1904); and C. B. Luffman, *A Vagabond in Spain* (1895).

3. Humanities Research Center, University of Texas.

4. Paul Robinson, *The Modernization of Sex* (London: Paul Elek, 1976), p. 3.

5. *The Autobiography of Bertrand Russell* (London, 1968), II, 60. The novelist Naomi Mitchison wrote to him about her reactions to *The Psychology of Sex*: "It is a curiously reassuring book; most of us deviate to some extent from sexual normality—if that exists!—and it is a comfort to realise that one's deviations are after all so usual and harmless" (Butler Library, Columbia University).

6. Havelock Ellis, *Studies in the Psychology of Sex* (New York: Random House, 1936), Vol. I, Part One, p. 103.

7. *Ibid.*, p. 161.

8. *Ibid.*, p. 263.

9. *The Lancet*, 12 Jan. 1901, p. 108.

10. *Ibid.*

11. Steven Marcus, *The Other*

Victorians (London: Weidenfeld & Nicolson, 1966), p. 25.

12. *Studies*, Vol. I, Part Two, p. 17.

13. *Ibid.*, p. 127.

14. *Ibid.*, p. 160.

15. *Ibid.*, Part One, p. 206.

16. *Ibid.*, p. 209.

17. *Ibid.*, Vol. III, Part One, p. 59.

18. *Ibid.*, p. 113.

19. *Ibid.*, IV, vii.

20. *Ibid.*, p. 427.

21. *The Lancet*, 30 April 1910, p. 1207.

22. *Studies*, Vol. III, Part One, p. 123.

23. *Ibid.*, Vol. I, Part Two, p. 253.

24. Lewis Mumford, *The Condition of Man* (London: Secker & Warburg, 1944), pp. 361–2.

25. See Michel Foucault's *The Birth of the Clinic* (London: Tavistock Publications, 1973).

26. *Studies*, Vol. I, Part One, p. 210.

27. *Ibid.*, Vol. II, Part Two, p. 304.

28. *Ibid.*, Vol. III, Part Two, p. 191.

29. *Ibid.*, p. 196.

30. *Ibid.*, p. 204.

31. *Ibid.*, p. 239.

CHAPTER 16—COMPLICATED RELATIONSHIPS

1. Mrs. Havelock Ellis, *The New Horizon in Love and Life* (London: A. & C. Black, 1921), p. 67.

2. Havelock Ellis, *My Life* (London: Heinemann, 1940), p. 376.

3. *Ibid.*, p. 389.

4. *The Letters of Olive Schreiner*, ed. S. C. Cronwright-Schreiner (London: T. Fisher Unwin, 1924), p. 332.

5. *My Life*, p. 394.

6. *Ibid.*, p. 411.

7. *Ibid.*, p. 417.

8. 6 Jan. 1915 (Humanities Research

Center, University of Texas).

9. 15 Dec. 1914 (Margaret Sanger Papers, Library of Congress).

10. Margaret Sanger, *An Autobiography* (London: Victor Gollancz, 1939), p. 131.

11. *Ibid.*, p. 132.

12. 26 Dec. 1914 (Margaret Sanger Papers, Library of Congress).

13. 30 Dec. 1914 (*Ibid.*).

14. Havelock Ellis, *Fountain of Life* (Boston: Houghton Mifflin, 1930), p. 205.

15. 5 Jan. 1915 (Margaret Sanger Papers, Library of Congress).

16. 13 Jan. 1915 (*Ibid.*).
17. 2 Feb. 1915 (*Ibid.*).
18. *My Life*, p. 430.
19. *Ibid.*
20. *Ibid.*, p. 433.
21. *Ibid.*, p. 434.
22. Margaret Sanger Papers, Library of Congress.
23. *Ibid.*
24. *My Life*, p. 435.
25. *Ibid.*
26. *Ibid.*, p. 437.
27. 13 March 1915 (Margaret Sanger Papers, Library of Congress).
28. 18 March 1915 (*Ibid.*).

29. 30 March 1915 (*Ibid.*).
30. 13 April 1915 (*Ibid.*).
31. *My Life*, p. 437.
32. *The New Horizon in Love and Life*, p. 24.
33. *My Life*, p. 438.
34. *Ibid.*, p. 452.
35. 21 April 1921 (Margaret Sanger Papers, Library of Congress).
36. *Ibid.*
37. 8 May 1915 (*Ibid.*).
38. *My Life*, p. 453.
39. *Ibid.*, p. 456.
40. *Ibid.*, p. 430.
41. *Ibid.*, p. 454.

CHAPTER 17–*EDITH'S DEATH*

1. Havelock Ellis, *My Life* (London: Heinemann, 1940), p. 460.
2. Margaret Sanger Papers, Library of Congress.
3. *Ibid.*
4. 22 July 1915 (*Ibid.*).
5. 1 Sept. 1915 (*Ibid.*).
6. *My Life*, p. 463.
7. 28 Sept. 1915 (Margaret Sanger Papers, Library of Congress).
8. 21 Oct. 1915 (*Ibid.*).
9. Havelock Ellis, *Fountain of Life* (Boston: Houghton Mifflin, 1930), p. 198.
10. 22 Oct. 1915 (Margaret Sanger Papers, Library of Congress).
11. 1 Feb. 1906 (Humanities Research Center, University of Texas).
12. *My Life*, p. 473.
13. Margaret Sanger Papers, Library of Congress.
14. *My Life*, p. 473.
15. 25 Nov. 1915 (Sophia Smith Collection, Smith College).
16. 25 Nov. 1915 (*Ibid.*).
17. Margaret Sanger Papers, Library of Congress.
18. *Ibid.*
19. 24 March 1916 (Humanities

Research Center, University of Texas).
20. 27 March 1916 (Carpenter Collection, Sheffield Public Libraries).
21. *Ibid.*
22. 2 April 1916 (Margaret Sanger Papers, Library of Congress).
23. *Fountain of Life*, p. 221. Ellis reviewed Durkheim's book in *Mind*, April 1898.
24. 10 June 1916 (Margaret Sanger Papers, Library of Congress).
25. 14 June 1916 (*Ibid.*).
26. 26 May 1916 (*Ibid.*).
27. 25 June 1916 (*Ibid.*).
28. *Ibid.*
29. 18 June 1916 (*Ibid.*).
30. Lafitte Collection.
31. *My Life*, p. 506.
32. *Ibid.*
33. 19 Sept. 1916 (Margaret Sanger Papers, Library of Congress).
34. 14 Sept. 1916 (University of Texas).
35. 19 Sept. 1916 (*Ibid.*).
36. 30 Sept. 1916 (*Ibid.*).
37. 19 Sept. 1916 (Margaret Sanger Papers, Library of Congress).

CHAPTER 18–RENEWAL

1. 26 Sept. 1916 (Margaret Sanger Papers, Library of Congress).
2. 24 Dec. 1916 (*Ibid.*).
3. *The Birth Control Review*, Feb. 1917, p. 7.
4. *The Birth Control Review*, June 1917, p. 4.
5. 13 May 1917 (Margaret Sanger Papers, Library of Congress).
6. 26 May 1917 (*Ibid.*).
7. 13 Oct. 1917 (*Ibid.*).
8. 5 Nov. 1917 (*Ibid.*).
9. *Ibid.*
10. Françoise Delisle, *Friendship's Odyssey* (London: Delisle, 1964), p. 29.
11. *Ibid.*
12. *Ibid.*, p. 31.
13. 21 Sept. 1917 (Mugar Library, Boston University).
14. 28 May 1917 (Sophia Smith Collection, Smith College).
15. 14 March 1918 (Mugar Library).
16. *Friendship's Odyssey*, p. 121.
17. 26 Sept. 1918 (Mugar Library).
18. 3 April 1918 (*Ibid.*).
19. Mugar Library.
20. 6 April 1918 (*Ibid.*).
21. 7 April 1918 (*Ibid.*).
22. 6 Sept. 1918 (*Ibid.*).
23. 7 Sept. 1918 (*Ibid.*).
24. *Friendship's Odyssey*, p. 57.
25. *Ibid.*, p. 58.
26. 21 July 1947 (Lafitte Collection).
27. *Friendship's Odyssey*, p. 61.
28. Lafitte Collection.
29. 11 Jan. 1921 (Margaret Sanger Papers, Library of Congress).
30. Mugar Library.
31. 19 May 1918 (Margaret Sanger Papers, Library of Congress).
32. Havelock Ellis, *Fountain of Life* (Boston: Houghton Mifflin, 1930), p. 267.
33. N.d., Lafitte Collection.
34. 19 Nov. 1918 (Margaret Sanger Papers, Library of Congress).

CHAPTER 19–THE POST-WAR WORLD

1. 21 Feb. 1919 (Margaret Sanger Papers, Library of Congress).
2. Graham Greene, *The Lost Childhood and Other Essays* (London: Eyre & Spottiswoode, 1951), p. 136.
3. Sigmund Freud, *The Origins of Psychoanalysis*, eds. M. Bonaparte, A. Freud, E. Kris (London: Imago Publishing Co., 1954), pp. 271–2.
4. Havelock Ellis, *The Philosophy of Conflict* (London: Constable, 1919), p. 493.
5. *Ibid.*, p. 206.
6. Ernest Jones, *The Life and Work of Sigmund Freud* (Penguin, 1961), p. 493.
7. 15 April 1920 (Humanities Research Center, University of Texas).
8. *Ibid.*
9. Lafitte Collection.
10. 24 Oct. 1919 (Mugar Library, Boston University).
11. Amy Lowell, *Tendencies in Modern American Poetry* (New York: Macmillan, 1917), p. 251.
12. 6 Dec. 1920 (Mugar Library).
13. 16 Oct. 1920 (*Ibid.*).
14. 22 June 1949 (Letter to Margaret Grierson, Sophia Smith Collection, Smith College).
15. 3 Jan. 1922 (Smith College).
16. 11 May 1919 (Mugar Library).

17. 24 Feb. 1920 (*Ibid.*).
18. Havelock Ellis, *Fountain of Life* (Boston: Houghton Mifflin, 1930), p. 305.
19. 28 Feb. 1920 (Mugar Library).
20. July 1920 (*Ibid.*).
21. 13 Aug. 1920 (Margaret Sanger Papers, Library of Congress).
22. 14 Oct. 1920 (*Ibid.*).
23. 16 Dec. 1920 (Mugar Library).

24. *Little Essays of Love and Virtue* (London: A. & C. Black, 1922), p. 128.
25. *Ibid.*, p. 129.
26. *Fountain of Life*, p. 354.
27. *Ibid.*, p. 371.
28. 23 June 1920 (Mugar Library).
29. 5 June 1921 (Humanities Research Center, University of Texas).
30. 13 July 1921 (Mugar Library).

CHAPTER 20–*SOLEIL DE JOIE*

1. 23 Jan. 1915 (Library of Congress).
2. 2 Feb. 1915 (*Ibid.*).
3. 3 Feb. 1915 (*Ibid.*).
4. 11 July 1915 (*Ibid.*).
5. 27 March 1915 (*Ibid.*).
6. 30 July 1915 (*Ibid.*).
7. 20 May 1916 (*Ibid.*).
8. 23 Nov. 1917 (*Ibid.*).
9. 9 June 1920 (*Ibid.*).
10. 30 July 1920 (*Ibid.*).
11. 4 Sept. 1920 (Margaret Sanger Papers, Library of Congress).
12. 14 March 1922 (Library of Congress).
13. 7 May 1922 (Mugar Library, Boston University).
14. 24 May 1922 (*Ibid.*).
15. 29 May 1922 (*Ibid.*).
16. 8 Sept. 1922 (*Ibid.*).
17. 9 Sept. 1922 (*Ibid.*).
18. 1 Nov. 1922 (To Hugh de Sélincourt, Library of Congress).
19. 31 Oct. 1922 (Mugar Library).
20. 25 Nov. 1922 (*Ibid.*).
21. 30 Nov. 1922 (Margaret Sanger Papers, Library of Congress).
22. 15 Nov. 1922 (Mugar Library).
23. 28 Nov. 1922 (*Ibid.*).
24. 1 Dec. 1922 (Library of Congress).
25. 29 Nov. 1922 (Mugar Library).
26. 10 Dec. 1922 (*Ibid.*).

27. 22 Dec. 1922 (Sophia Smith Collection, Smith College).
28. 11 Dec. 1922 (Mugar Library).
29. Christmas Day 1922 (*Ibid.*).
30. 31 Dec. 1922 (Margaret Sanger Papers, Library of Congress).
31. 13 Feb. 1923 (Mugar Library).
32. 8 Jan. 1923 (*Ibid.*).
33. 29 Jan. 1923 (Margaret Sanger Papers, Library of Congress).
34. 13 Jan. 1923 (Mugar Library).
35. 24 Jan. 1923 (*Ibid.*).
36. 2 June 1923 (*Ibid.*).
37. 24 Sept. 1923 (*Ibid.*).
38. 25 Sept. 1923 (*Ibid.*).
39. 26 Oct. 1923 (*Ibid.*).
40. 7 Feb. 1923 (*Ibid.*).
41. 12 March 1923 (*Ibid.*).
42. 14 May 1923 (*Ibid.*).
43. *Ibid.*
44. 17 June 1929 (Houghton Library, Harvard University).
45. 25 July 1923 (Mugar Library).
46. 20 May 1923 (*Ibid.*).
47. 2 Oct. 1923 (Sophia Smith Collection, Smith College).
48. 5 Oct. 1923 (Mugar Library).
49. Havelock Ellis, *The Dance of Life* (Boston: Houghton Mifflin, 1923), p. 66.
50. *Ibid.*, p. 111.
51. *Ibid.*, p. 129.
52. *Ibid.*, p. 283.

53. 12 Dec. 1930 (Sophia Smith Collection, Smith College).
54. *The Dance of Life*, p. viii.
55. 31 Aug. 1923 (Mugar Library).
56. 3 Oct. 1923 (*Ibid.*).
57. 25 Sept. 1923 (*Ibid.*).
58. 3 Oct. 1923 (*Ibid.*).
59. 26 Sept. 1923 (*Ibid.*)
60. 29 Sept. 1923 (*Ibid.*).
61. 8 Oct. 1923 (*Ibid.*).
62. 3 Oct. 1923 (*Ibid.*).
63. 11 Oct. 1923 (*Ibid.*).
64. 3 Oct. 1923 (*Ibid.*).
65. 17 Oct. 1923 (*Ibid.*).
66. 16 Oct. 1923 (*Ibid.*).
67. Lafitte Collection.
68. 24 Oct. 1923 (Mugar Library).
69. 24 Sept. 1923 (*Ibid.*).
70. 24 Sept 1923 (*Ibid.*).
71. 18 Oct. 1923 (*Ibid.*).
72. 7 Oct. 1923 (*Ibid.*).
73. 15 Oct. 1923 (*Ibid.*).
74. *Ibid.*
75. 9 Dec. 1923 (*Ibid.*).
76. 27 Sept. 1923 (*Ibid.*).
77. 14 Nov. 1923 (*Ibid.*).
78. 1 Oct. 1923 (*Ibid.*).
79. 29 Nov. 1923 (*Ibid.*).
80. 4 Dec. 1923 (*Ibid.*).
81. 6 Dec. 1923 (*Ibid.*).
82. 10 Oct. 1923 (*Ibid.*).
83. 6 Dec. 1923 (*Ibid.*).
84. 10 Oct. 1923 (*Ibid.*).
85. 7 Dec. 1923 (*Ibid.*).
86. 13 Dec. 1923 (*Ibid.*).
87. 9 Dec. 1923 (*Ibid.*).
88. 17 Dec. 1923 (*Ibid.*).
89. 26 Sept. 1923 (*Ibid.*).

CHAPTER 21–*HEALING*

1. 26 Jan. 1924 (Mugar Library, Boston University).
2. 16 Feb. 1924 (*Ibid.*).
3. Havelock Ellis, *Fountain of Life* (Boston: Houghton Mifflin, 1930), p. 355.
4. *Ibid.*, pp. 359–60.
5. 9 May 1923 (Sophia Smith Collection, Smith College).
6. 25 Feb. 1924 (Mugar Library).
7. N.d. (Lafitte Collection).
8. N.d. (*Ibid.*).
9. Mugar Library.
10. 3 April 1924 (*Ibid.*).
11. 11 April 1924 (*Ibid.*).
12. 11 May 1924 (Smith College).
13. 5 June 1924 (*Ibid.*).
14. 25 July 1924 (Margaret Sanger Papers, Library of Congress).
15. 1 Oct. 1924 (Lafitte Collection).
16. 14 Dec. 1924 (*Ibid.*).
17. 2 July 1924 (Library of Congress).
18. 2 July 1924 (Mugar Library).
19. 2 July 1924 (Library of Congress).
20. Sylvia Beach, *Shakespeare & Company* (London: Faber & Faber, 1956), pp. 181–2.
21. *Ibid.*
22. 25 July 1924 (Margaret Sanger Papers, Library of Congress).
23. 30 Sept. 1924 (Mugar Library).
24. 5 Oct. 1924 (*Ibid.*).
25. 6 Oct. 1924 (*Ibid.*).
26. 16 Oct. 1924 (*Ibid.*).
27. *Ibid.*
28. 24 Nov. 1924 (*Ibid.*).
29. Mugar Library.
30. 11 Jan. 1925 (*Ibid.*).
31. 5 Feb. 1925 (*Ibid.*).
32. *Ibid.*
33. *Ibid.*
34. *Ibid.*
35. 8 Feb. 1925 (*Ibid.*).
36. 24 Feb. 1924 (Manuscripts and Archives Division, New York Public Library, Astor, Lenox and Tilden Foundations).
37. 16 Sept. 1924 (*Ibid.*).

38. 7 June 1925 (*Ibid.*).

39. 2 Dec. 1925 (*Ibid.*).

40. 4 Jan. 1925 (International Instituut voor Sociale Geschiedenis).

41. 10 Dec. 1922 (Lafitte Collection).

42. 30 June 1925 (Mugar Library).

43. 2 Sept. 1925 (Library of Congress).

44. 1 April 1925 (Mugar Library).

45. 23 July 1925 (Lafitte Collection).

46. 24 March 1925 (Mugar Library).

47. 13 Feb. 1925 (Library of Congress).

48. 5 May 1925 (Smith College).

49. Mugar Library.

50. 19 June 1925 (Smith College).

51. *Ibid.*

52. 5 June 1925 (Mugar Library).

53. 13 Nov. 1925 (*Ibid.*).

54. 7 July 1925 (Lafitte Collection).

55. N.d. (*Ibid.*).

56. *Ibid.*

57. 3 Sept. 1925 (Lilly Library, Indiana University).

58. 19 Aug. 1925 (Humanities Research Center, University of Texas).

CHAPTER 22—HIS OWN SOLEIL DE JOIE

1. 27 Jan. 1926 (Mugar Library, Boston University).

2. 21 July 1926 (*Ibid.*).

3. 23 April 1926 (Margaret Sanger Papers, Library of Congress).

4. 20 June 1926 (Lafitte Collection).

5. 27 June 1926 (Oliver Collection).

6. *Ibid.*

7. 5 Oct. 1926 (*Ibid.*).

8. 9 Oct. 1926 (Lafitte Collection).

9. 8 Oct. 1926 (Mugar Library).

10. Oliver Collection.

11. *Ibid.*

12. 12 Oct. 1926 (Mugar Library).

13. 10 Oct. 1926 (Oliver Collection).

14. 11 Oct. 1926 (Mugar Library).

15. 12 Oct. 1926 (*Ibid.*).

16. 11 Oct. 1926 (Oliver Collection).

17. *Ibid.*

18. 25 Oct. 1926 (Mugar Library).

19. 14 Oct. 1926 (*Ibid.*).

20. *Ibid.*

21. 17 Jan. 1927 (Mugar Library).

22. *Ibid.*

23. 26 Jan. 1927 (Oliver Collection).

24. *Ibid.*

25. 14 Nov. 1928 (Mugar Library).

26. 22 Oct. 1926 (*Ibid.*).

27. 9 June 1925 (*Ibid.*).

28. 19 May 1927 (Library of Congress).

29. 16 Aug. 1927 (*Ibid.*).

30. 26 Aug. 1927 (Mugar Library).

31. Library of Congress.

32. 11 Sept. 1927 (Mugar Library).

33. 14 Sept. 1927 (*Ibid.*).

34. 13 Jan. 1928 (*Ibid.*).

35. 16 Jan. 1928 (*Ibid.*).

36. 1 July 1928 (Sophia Smith Collection, Smith College).

CHAPTER 23—PROFESSIONAL CONTACTS

1. Havelock Ellis, *Studies in the Psychology of Sex* (New York: Random House, 1936), Vol. III, Part Two, p. 212.

2. *The Freud/Jung Letters*, ed. William McGuire (London: Hogarth Press, 1974), p. 430.

3. *Studies*, Vol. III, Part Two, p. 239.

4. *Ibid.*, p. 311.

5. *Ibid.*, p. 316.

6. *Ibid.*, p. 346.

7. 5 Dec. 1926 (Mugar Library, Boston University).

8. *Studies*, Vol. III, Part Two, p. 432.
9. 1915 (Margaret Sanger Papers, Library of Congress).
10. 27 Dec. 1926 (Lilly Library, Indiana University).
11. 11 April 1930 (Morris Library, Southern Illinois University).
12. Private collection.
13. *Studies*, Vol. III, Part Two, p. 527.
14. 3 Feb. 1927 (Mugar Library).
15. 7 May 1927 (*Ibid.*).
16. 18 Nov. 1928 (*Ibid.*).
17. Lafitte Collection.
18. *Ibid.*
19. *Ibid.*
20. *Ibid.*
21. 26 July 1918 (Library of Congress).
22. 9 Nov. 1918 (British Library).
23. 19 May 1918 (Library of Congress).
24. Margaret Sanger Papers, Library of Congress.
25. *The Literary Guide*, Sept. 1939, p. 171.
26. 25 March 1922 (British Library).
27. 12 April 1921 (Library of Congress).
28. 8 Sept. 1919 (British Library).
29. 22 Nov. 1921 (*Ibid.*).
30. 9 April 1921 (*Ibid.*).
31. 6 Oct. 1922 (Library of Congress).
32. 4 Oct. 1922 (Mugar Library).
33. 1 Feb. 1923 (Yale University Library).
34. 12 July 1923 (British Library).
35. 27 July 1923 (Lafitte Collection).
36. 15 Sept. 1923 (Library of Congress).
37. 26 Feb. 1924 (*Ibid.*).
38. 27 June 1934 (Butler Library, Columbia University).
39. 16 April 1924 (Fisher Library, University of Sydney).
40. 12 Feb. 1924 (*Ibid.*).
41. 15 Feb. 1927 (*Ibid.*).
42. 12 Feb. 1927 (University of Texas).
43. 16 Feb. 1927 (Fisher Library).
44. 3 Sept. 1933 (Library of Congress).
45. 19 Aug. 1920 (*Ibid.*).
46. Humanities Research Center, University of Texas.
47. 18 Aug. 1929 (Lafitte Collection).
48. 16 Sept. 1929 (*Ibid.*).
49. 17 May 1924 (Yale University Library).
50. 9 Dec. 1923 (*Ibid.*).
51. 17 May 1924 (*Ibid.*).
52. 22 Jan. 1925 (*Ibid.*).
53. 12 July 1923 (Lafitte Collection).
54. 26 Dec. 1923 (British Library of Political and Economic Science).
55. *Ibid.*
56. 18 March 1927 (Yale University Library).
57. N.d. (Lafitte Collection).
58. *The Nation and the Athenaeum*, Feb. 1922, p. 727.
59. Edward Westermarck, A *Short History of Marriage* (New York: Humanities Press, 1968), p. 80.
60. *The Nation and the Athenaeum*, Feb. 1922, p. 727.
61. N.d. (Lafitte Collection).
62. *The Book of Marriage*, ed. Count Hermann Keyserling (New York: Harcourt, Brace, 1926), p. iii.
63. "A Tribute to Freud," *The Forum*, LXXVI (July 1926), 151.
64. 31 Aug. 1926 (University of Texas).
65. 1 Feb. 1936 (Dr. Joseph Wortis Collection).
66. *International Journal of Psychoanalysis*, IX (1928), 480.
67. *Ibid.*, p. 489.
68. *Ibid.*
69. 6 Feb. 1929 (Mugar Library).
70. 24 March 1930 (University of Texas).

CHAPTER 24–A *SHARED LIFE*

1. 6 Jan. 1928 (Margaret Sanger Papers, Library of Congress).
2. 15 June 1928 (*Ibid.*).
3. 22 Jan. 1928 (Lafitte Collection).
4. 28 Jan. 1928 (Mugar Library, Boston University).
5. Feb. 1928 (Lafitte Collection).
6. Mugar Library.
7. *Ibid.*
8. 18 March 1928 (*Ibid.*).
9. 21 April 1928 (Lovat Dickson Papers, Public Archives of Canada).
10. 14 May 1928 (*Ibid.*).
11. 6 Sept. 1928 (*Ibid.*).
12. 3 Nov. 1928 (*Ibid.*).
13. 11 March 1929 (Humanities Research Center, University of Texas).
14. First printed by The Hours Press in Paris, 1931; reprinted in *More Essays of Love and Virtue*

(London: Constable, 1931).
15. 21 Aug. 1931 (Butler Library, Columbia University).
16. 6 July 1928 (Mugar Library).
17. 21 June 1928 (*Ibid.*).
18. 4 Sept. 1928 (Harvard University Library).
19. 8 Feb. 1929 (*Ibid.*).
20. 12 Feb. 1929 (*Ibid.*).
21. 19 May 1929 (*Ibid.*).
22. 17 June 1929 (*Ibid.*).
23. 16 July 1929 (*Ibid.*).
24. 31 Dec. 1929 (Mugar Library).
25. 4 Nov. 1928 (Lafitte Collection).
26. N.d. (Sophia Smith Collection, Smith College).
27. June, 1929 (Mugar Library).
28. 23 Sept. 1929 (Lilly Library, Indiana University).
29. 15 Aug. 1929 (Dr. Helena Wright).

CHAPTER 25–*LATE YEARS*

1. 14 April 1930 (Margaret Sanger Papers, Library of Congress).
2. 24 April 1930 (Dr. Joseph Wortis).
3. 11 July 1934 (*Ibid.*).
4. 18 June 1906 (Galton Papers, University College).
5. *Ibid.*
6. 3 Nov. 1930 (Margaret Sanger Papers, Smith College).
7. I am indebted for the information on Pearson to an excellent article by Bernard Semmel, "Karl Pearson: Socialist and Darwinist" in *British Journal of Sociology*, Vol. IX, No. 2 (June 1958), pp. 111–25.
8. *Ibid.*, p. 115.
9. *Ibid.*, p. 120.

10. *Ibid.*, p. 122.
11. *Ibid.*, p. 125.
12. Draft copy (Lafitte Collection).
13. Fales Library, New York University.
14. Havelock Ellis, *Sex in Relation to Society* (London: Heinemann, 1937), p. 488.
15. *Ibid.*, p. 489.
16. 28 Dec. 1932 (Sophia Smith Collection, Smith College).
17. Lafitte Collection.
18. *Ibid.*
19. *Ibid.*
20. 25 Feb. 1931 (Lafitte Collection).
21. 1 Jan. 1931 (*Ibid.*).
22. 1 July 1931 (*Ibid.*).
23. 3 May 1931 (*Ibid.*).
24. Joseph Wortis, *Fragments of an*

Analysis with Freud (New York: McGraw-Hill, 1954), p. 2.
25. Lafitte Collection.
26. 2 Oct. 1932 (*Ibid.*).
27. 3 Jan. 1933 (*Ibid.*).
28. 13 Jan. 1933 (*Ibid.*).
29. Wortis, p. 11.
30. *Ibid.*, p. 16.
31. *Ibid.*, p. 64.

32. *Ibid.*, p. 120.
33. *Ibid.*, p. 122.
34. *Ibid.*, pp. 166–7.
35. *Ibid.*, p. 156.
36. *Ibid.*, p. 177.
37. *Ibid.*
38. *Ibid.*, p. 178.
39. *Ibid.*

CHAPTER 26–*DEPRESSION* YEARS

1. 13 Sept. 1931 (Margaret Sanger Papers, Library of Congress).
2. 6 Dec. 1933, *Los Angeles Examiner*.
3. 6 Sept. 1933, *Los Angeles Examiner*.
4. To Françoise, 31 July 1930 (Lafitte Collection).
5. Sophia Smith Collection, Smith College.
6. 8 Sept. 1934 (*Ibid.*).
7. 24 Sept. 1934 (*Ibid.*).
8. 30 Sept. 1934 (*Ibid.*).
9. 6 Oct. 1934 (*Ibid.*).
10. Mugar Library, Boston University.
11. 24 Feb. 1936 (Margaret Sanger Papers, Library of Congress).
12. Mugar Library.
13. 25 March 1936 (Lafitte Collection).
14. 3 April 1936 (Mugar Library).
15. 28 March 1936 (Lafitte Collection).
16. 2 April 1936 (Mugar Library).

17. 19 May 1936 (Margaret Sanger Papers, Library of Congress).
18. 16 March 1936 (Mugar Library).
19. 8 Nov. 1936 (Lafitte Collection).
20. 17 April 1936 (*Ibid.*).
21. 14 Oct. 1936 (Mugar Library).
22. Bennett Cerf, *At Random* (New York: Random House, 1977), pp. 112–13.
23. *Ibid.*, p. 112.
24. 29 Sept. 1938 (Yale University Library).
25. 29 Jan. 1932 (Margaret Sanger Papers, Library of Congress).
26. 11 Dec. 1931 (*Ibid.*).
27. 4 Nov. [?] 1933 (Lafitte Collection).
28. 14 June 1936 (Faith Oliver Powys).
29. To Dr. John Rickman, draft copy, 13 Aug. 1933 (Lafitte Collection).
30. Havelock Ellis, *The Soul of Spain* (London: Constable, 1911), p. 87.
31. 11 Dec. 1931 (Margaret Sanger Papers, Library of Congress).

CHAPTER 27–*LAST* DAYS

1. 26 Dec. 1937 (Faith Oliver Powys).
2. 26 June 1938 (Mugar Library, Boston University).
3. N.d. (Mugar Library).
4. 26 June 1938 (*Ibid.*).

5. 10 July 1938 (Margaret Sanger Papers, Library of Congress).
6. 16 Feb. 1939 (*Ibid.*).
7. 12 Feb. 1938 (Lafitte Collection).
8. 17 Dec. 1938 (*Ibid.*).
9. Copy, 28 June 1938 (*Ibid.*).

10. Copy, 30 June 1938 (*Ibid.*).
11. Copy, 31 June 1938 (*Ibid.*).
12. Copy, 4 July 1938 (*Ibid.*).
13. Mugar Library.
14. 2 July 1939 (*Ibid.*). There seems to be some confusion in the dating here.
15. Mugar Library.
16. 16 July 1958 (Copy, Lafitte Collection).
17. 1 June 1947 (Lafitte Collection).
18. Mugar Library.
19. 14 Dec. 1939 (Sophia Smith Collection, Smith College).
20. 27 Feb. 1947 (*Ibid.*).

BIBLIOGRAPHY

WORKS BY HAVELOCK ELLIS LISTED
IN ORDER OF PUBLICATION

1890   *The Criminal.* New York: Schribner and Welford.

       The New Spirit. London: Bell.

1892   *The Nationalization of Health.* London: T. Fisher Unwin.

1894   *Man and Woman: A Study of Human Secondary Sexual Characters.* London: Walter Scott.

1897   *Sexual Inversion* by Havelock Ellis and John Addington Symonds. London: Wilson and Macmillan (withdrawn before publication). A German translation of this work by Hans Kurella, entitled *Das Konträre Geschlechtsgefühl,* was published at Leipzig by George H. Wigands Verlag in 1896.

       Sexual Inversion (Studies in the Psychology of Sex, Vol. I). Watford: University Press; 2nd ed. (revised and renumbered as *Studies,* Vol. II), Philadelphia: F. A. Davis, 1901; 3rd ed. revised and enlarged, 1915.

1898   *Affirmations.* London: Walter Scott.

       A Note on the Bedborough Trial. Watford: University Press (privately printed).

1899   *The Evolution of Modesty, The Phenomena of Sexual Periodicity, Auto-Erotism (Studies in the Psychology of Sex,* Vol. II). Leipzig: University Press (actually published at Watford). 2nd ed. (revised and renumbered as *Studies,* Vol. I), Philadelphia: F. A. Davis, 1900; 3rd ed. 1910.

1900   *The Nineteenth Century: A Dialogue in Utopia.* London: Grant Richards.

1903   *The Analysis of the Sexual Impulse, Love and Pain, The Sexual Impulse in Women* (Studies in the Psychology of Sex, Vol. III). Philadelphia: F. A. Davis.

1904   *A Study of British Genius.* London: Hurst and Blackett.

1905   *Sexual Selection in Man* (Studies in the Psychology of Sex, Vol. IV). Philadelphia: F. A. Davis.

1906   *Erotic Symbolism, The Mechanism of Detumescence, The Psychic State in Pregnancy* (Studies in the Psychology of Sex, Vol. V). Philadelphia: F. A. Davis.

1908   *The Soul of Spain.* London: Constable.

1910   *Sex in Relation to Society* (Studies in the Psychology of Sex, Vol. VI). Philadelphia: F. A. Davis.

1911   *The Problem of Race Regeneration.* London: Cassell.

       The World of Dreams. Boston: Houghton Mifflin; London: Constable.

1912   *The Task of Social Hygiene.* Boston: Houghton Mifflin; London: Constable.

1913   *The Forces Warring Against War.* Boston: World Peace Foundation Pamphlet.

1914   *Impressions and Comments,* First Series. London: Constable; Boston: Houghton Mifflin.

1917   *Essays in War-Time.* London: Constable.

1918   *The Erotic Rights of Women* and *The Objects of Marriage.* London: British Society for the Study of Sex Psychology.

1919   *The Philosophy of Conflict and Other Essays in War-Time.* London: Constable; Boston: Houghton Mifflin.

1921   *Impressions and Comments,* Second Series, 1914–1920. London: Constable; Boston: Houghton Mifflin.

       The Play-Function of Sex. London: British Society for the Study of Sex Psychology.

1922   *Kanga Creek: An Australian Idyll.* Waltham St. Lawrence: Golden Cockerel Press.

       Little Essays of Love and Virtue. London: Black.

1923   *The Dance of Life.* London: Constable; Boston: Houghton Mifflin.

1924   *Impressions and Comments,* Third Series, 1920–1923. London: Constable; Boston: Houghton Mifflin.

1925   *Sonnets, with Folk Songs from the Spanish.* Waltham St. Lawrence: Golden Cockerel Press.

1928   *Eonism and Other Supplementary Studies* (Studies in the Psychology of Sex, Vol. VII). Philadelphia: F. A. Davis.

1929   *The Art of Life: Gleanings from the Works of Havelock Ellis,* selected by Mrs. S. Herbert. London: Constable; Boston and New York: Houghton Mifflin.

1930 *Fountain of Life* (the three series of *Impressions and Comments* brought together in one volume). Boston and New York: Houghton Mifflin.

1931 *The Color-Sense in Literature*. London: Ulysses Book Shop.

Concerning Jude the Obscure. London: Ulysses Book Shop.

An Open Letter to Biographers. Berkeley Heights, N.J.: Oriole Press.

The Revaluation of Obscenity. Paris: Hours Press.

More Essays of Love and Virtue. London: Constable.

1932 *Views and Reviews: A Selection of Uncollected Articles, 1884–1932*. 2 vols. London: Desmond Harmsworth; Boston: Houghton Mifflin.

1933 *Psychology of Sex: A Manual for Students*. New York: Long and Smith; London: Heinemann.

1934 *My Confessional: Questions of Our Day*. Boston and New York: Houghton Mifflin; London: John Lane.

1935 *From Rousseau to Proust*. Boston and New York: Houghton Mifflin.

1936 *Questions of Our Day*. New York: Vanguard Press; London: John Lane.

Selected Essays (Everyman). London: Dent; New York: Dutton.

Studies in the Psychology of Sex (rearranged, with a new Foreword). 4 vols. New York: Random House.

1937 *Poems*. Selected by John Gawsworth, with Preface by Havelock Ellis. London: Richards Press.

1939 *Morals, Manners, and Men*. London: Watts.

My Life: Autobiography of Havelock Ellis. Boston: Houghton Mifflin; London: Heinemann.

1950 *From Marlowe to Shaw: The Studies, 1876–1936, in English Literature of Havelock Ellis*, ed. John Gawsworth. London: Williams and Norgate.

1951 *Sex and Marriage: Eros in Contemporary Life*, ed. John Gawsworth. New York: Random House; London: Ernest Benn.

The Genius of Europe. London: Williams and Norgate, 1950; New York: Rinehart, 1951 (actually written in 1939).

In addition Ellis wrote over two hundred articles and reviews, about thirty-five introductions and editions, and a dozen translations.

BIBLIOGRAPHY OF MRS. HAVELOCK ELLIS
(EDITH MARY OLDHAM LEES)

Attainment. London: Alston Rivers, 1909.

Democracy in the Kitchen ... A Lecture [Haslemere, 1894].

The Imperishable Wing. London: Stanley Paul, 1911.

James Hinton: A Sketch. London: Stanley Paul, 1918.

Kit's Woman: A Cornish Idyll. London: Alston Rivers, 1907.

Love-Acre: An Idyll in Two Worlds. New York: Mitchell Kennerley, 1914; London: Grant Richards, 1915.

Love in Danger: Three Plays. Boston and New York: Houghton Mifflin, 1915.

The Lover's Calendar, compiled and ed. by Mrs. Havelock Ellis. London: Kegan Paul, 1912.

The Masses and the Classes: A Plea [Manchester, 1893].

The Mine of Dreams: Selected Short Stories. London: A. & C. Black, 1925.

My Cornish Neighbours. London: Alston Rivers, 1906.

The New Horizon in Love and Life, with a Preface by Edward Carpenter. London: A. & C. Black, 1921.

A Noviciate for Marriage [Haslemere, 1894].

Personal Impressions of Edward Carpenter. Berkeley Heights, N.J.: Free Spirit Press, 1922.

Seaweed: A Cornish Idyll. Watford: University Press, 1898.

Stories, with a Preface by Charles Marriott. Privately printed. Berkeley Heights, N.J.: Free Spirit Press, 1924.

The Subjection of Kezia: A Play in One Act. Stratford-on-Avon: Shakespeare Head Press, 1908.

Three Modern Seers (James Hinton, Friedrich Nietzsche, Edward Carpenter). London: Stanley Paul, 1910.

GENERAL BIBLIOGRAPHY

Allen, Gay Wilson. *Walt Whitman as Man, Poet, and Legend.* Carbondale: Southern Illinois University Press, 1961.

Armytage, W. H. G. *Heavens Below: Utopian Experiments in England, 1560–1960.* Carbondale: Southern Illinois University Press, 1961.

Barzun, Jacques. *Race: A Study in Modern Superstition.* London: Methuen, 1938.

——. *Romanticism and the Modern Ego.* Boston: Little, Brown, 1947.

Batho, Edith C., and Bonamy Dobree. *The Victorians and After, 1830–1914.* London: Cresset Press, 1938.

Beach, Sylvia. *Shakespeare & Company.* London: Faber & Faber, 1956.

Sayings of George Bedborough. Letchworth Garden City Press, 1917.

Bennett, Charles A. *A Philosophical Study of Mysticism.* New Haven: Yale University Press, 1923.

Besant, Annie. *An Autobiography.* London: T. Fisher Unwin, 1893.

Bloch, Iwan. *The Sexual Life of Our Time in Its Relation to Modern Civilization.* London: Rebman, 1909.

Brecher, E. H. *The Sex Researchers*. London: Deutsch, 1971.

Briggs, Asa. *Victorian People: A Reassessment of Persons and Themes, 1851–1867*. University of Chicago Press, 1954.

Brinton, Crane. *Nietzsche*. Cambridge, Mass.: Harvard University Press, 1941.

Brome, Vincent. *Havelock Ellis: Philosopher of Love*. London: Routledge & Kegan Paul, 1979.

Bryher. *The Heart of Artemis*. London: Collins, 1963.

Buckley, Jerome. *The Victorian Temper: A Study in Literary Culture*. London: George Allen & Unwin, 1952.

Calder-Marshall, Arthur. *Havelock Ellis: A Biography*. London: Rupert Hart-Davis, 1959.

Calverton, V. F. *Sex Experience in Literature*. New York: Boni and Liveright, 1926.

Cargill, Oscar. *Intellectual America: Ideas on the March*. New York: Macmillan, 1948.

Carpenter, Edward. *My Days and Dreams*. London: Allen & Unwin, 1916.

——. *Towards Democracy*. First published anonymously, Manchester and London: John Heywood, 1883. Complete edition in four parts, London and Manchester: Sonnenschein, 1905.

Carter, Angela. *The Sadeian Woman*. London: Virago, 1979.

Cerf, Bennett. *At Random*. New York: Random House, 1977.

Collis, John Stewart. *Havelock Ellis, Artist of Life: A Study of His Life and Work*. New York: William Sloane Associates, 1959.

Craig, Alex. *The Banned Books of England*. London: Allen & Unwin, 1937.

Cronwright-Schreiner, S. C. *The Life of Olive Schreiner*. London: T. Fisher Unwin, 1924.

Memorials of Thomas Davidson, the Wandering Scholar, collected and edited by William A. Knight. Boston and London: Ginn, 1917.

Davidson, Thomas. *The Philosophical System of Antonio Rosmini-Serbati*. London: Kegan Paul, 1882.

Decker, Clarence. *The Victorian Conscience*. New York: Twayne, 1952.

Delisle, Françoise. *Francoise, In Love with Love*. London: Delisle, 1962.

——. *Friendship's Odyssey*. London: Delisle, 1964.

——. *The Return of Havelock Ellis, or Limbo or the Dove*. London: Regency Press, 1968.

Dickson, R. Lovat. *Radclyffe Hall at the Well of Loneliness*. London: Collins, 1975.

Douglas, Emily Taft. *Margaret Sanger: Pioneer of the Future*. Garrett Park, Md.: Garrett Park Press, 1975.

Eissler, K. R. *Leonardo da Vinci*. New York: International Universities Press, 1961.

Ellenberger, Henri F. *The Discovery of the Unconscious*. London: Allen Lane, 1970.

Field, Michael. *Works and Days*. London: John Murray, 1933.

Flugel, J. C. *A Hundred Years of Psychology*. London: Duckworth, 1933.

Foucault, Michel. *The Birth of the Clinic*. London: Tavistock Publications, 1973.

——. *The History of Sexuality*, Vol. I: *An Introduction*. London: Allen Lane, 1979.

Franc, Miriam Alice. *Ibsen in England*. Boston: Four Seas Company, 1919.

Frazer, J. G. *The Golden Bough: A Study in Comparative Religion*. 2 vols. London: Macmillan, 1890.

Fremantle, Anne. *This Little Band of Prophets: The Story of the Gentle Fabians*. London: Allen & Unwin, 1960.

Friedmann, Marion V. *Olive Schreiner: A Study in Latent Meanings*. Johannesburg: Witwatersrand University Press, 1954.

The Freud/Jung Letters, ed. William McGuire. London: Hogarth, 1974.

Freud, Sigmund. *The Origins of Psychoanalysis: Letters to Wilhelm Fliess*, eds. M. Bonaparte, A. Freud, E. Kris. London: Imago Publishing Co., 1954.

——. *The Standard Edition of the Complete Psychological Works of Sigmund Freud*, ed. James Strachey. 24 vols. London: Hogarth, 1953–1964.

Fryer, Peter. *The Birth Controllers*. London: Secker & Warburg, 1965.

Goldberg, Isaac. *Havelock Ellis: A Biographical and Critical Survey*. London: Constable, 1926.

Goldman, Emma. *Living My Life*. 2 vols. New York: Knopf, 1931.

Gould, Vera Buchanan. *Not Without Honour: The Life and Writings of Olive Schreiner*. London: Hutchison, 1949.

Grant, Douglas. *Walt Whitman and His English Admirers*. Leeds University Press, 1962.

Gray, Madeline. *Margaret Sanger*. New York: Richard Marek, 1979.

Green, Julien. *Diary, 1928–1955*. New York: Harcourt, Brace, 1964.

Greene, Graham. *The Lost Childhood and Other Essays*. London: Eyre and Spottiswoode, 1951.

Greenslet, Ferris. *Under the Bridge*. Boston: Houghton Mifflin, 1943.

Gregg, Lyndall. *Memories of Olive Schreiner*. London and Edinburgh: W. & R. Chambers, 1957.

Grosskurth, Phyllis. *John Addington Symonds: A Biography*. London: Longmans, 1964.

Haddon, Caroline. *The Larger Life: Studies in Hinton's Ethics*. London: Kegan Paul, 1886.

Hall, Radclyffe. *The Well of Loneliness*. New York: Covici-Friede, 1928.

Hall, Ruth. *Marie Stopes*. London: Andre Deutsch, 1977.

The Collected Letters of Thomas Hardy, eds. R. L. Purdy and Michael Millgate. Oxford, 1978.

Harmel, Michael. *Olive Schreiner, 1855–1955*. Cape Town: Real Publishing Co., 1955.

Havelock Ellis: In Appreciation by Elie Faure, Bertrand Russell, H. L. Mencken, etc. Berkeley Heights, N.J.: Oriole Press, 1929.

Hemmings, F. W. J. *Emile Zola*. Oxford: Clarendon Press, 1953.

Hirschfeld, Magnus. *Men and Women: The World Journey of a Sexologist*. New York: Putnam, 1935.

Hobman, D. L. *Olive Schreiner: Her Friends and Times*. London: Watts, 1955.

Huxley, Aldous. *Doors of Perception*. London: Chatto & Windus, 1954.

Hynes, Edward. *The Edwardian Frame of Mind*. Princeton University Press, 1968.

Jackson, Holbrook. *The Eighteen Nineties*. London: Grant Richards, 1913.

Jones, Ernest. *Free Associations*. London: Hogarth, 1959.

——. *The Life and Work of Sigmund Freud*, eds. Lionel Trilling and Steven Marcus. London: Penguin, 1961.

Kapp, Yvonne. *Eleanor Marx*, Vol. I.: *Family Life*. London: Lawrence & Wishart, 1972.

——. *Eleanor Marx*, Vol. II.: *The Crowded Years*. London: Lawrence & Wishart, 1976.

Kennedy, David. *Birth Control in America*. Yale Publications in American Studies, 1970.

Keyserling, Count Herman, ed. *The Book of Marriage*. New York: Harcourt, Brace, 1926.

Kinsey, Alfred C., Wardell B. Pomeroy, Clyde E. Martin. *Sexual Behaviour in the Human Male*. Philadelphia and London: W. B. Saunders, 1948.

Krafft-Ebing, Richard von. *Psychopathia Sexualis*. New York: Bell, 1965.

Krutch, Joseph Wood. *The Modern Temper: A Study and a Confession*. New York: Harcourt, Brace, 1929.

Lawrence Durrell and Henry Miller: A Private Correspondence, ed. George Wickes. London: Faber & Faber, 1963.

Lhombreaud, Roger. *Arthur Symons: A Critical Biography*. London: Unicorn Press, 1963.

Lippmann, Walter. *Preface to Morals*. London: Allen & Unwin, 1929.

Longaker, Mark. *Ernest Dowson*. University of Pennsylvania Press, 1945.

Lowell, Amy. *Tendencies in Modern American Poetry*. New York: Macmillan, 1917.

Lynd, Helen M. *England in the 1880's*. London: Frank Cass, 1968.

Malinowski, Bronislaw. *Sex and Repression in Savage Society*. London: Routledge & Kegan Paul, 1927.

——. *Sex Culture and Myth*. London: Rupert Hart-Davis, 1963.

Marcus, Steven. *The Other Victorians*. London: Weidenfeld & Nicolson, 1966.

Marquand, David. *Ramsay MacDonald*. London: Jonathan Cape, 1977.

Masters, William H., and Virginia E. Johnson. *Human Sexual Response*. Boston: Little, Brown, 1966.

McDougall, William. *An Outline of Abnormal Psychology*. London: Methuen, 1926.

Meintjis, Johannes. *Olive Schreiner: Portrait of a South African Woman*. Johannesburg: Hugh Keartland, 1965.

Mencken, H. L. *The Bathtub Hoax and Other Blasts and Bravos from the Chicago Tribune*. New York: Knopf, 1958.

——. *Prejudices*. Second and Third Series. New York: Knopf, 1922.

Mitchell, Juliet. *Psycho-Analysis and Feminism*. New York: Vintage Books, 1975.

Mittleman, Leslie B. "Havelock Ellis: Literary Critic of the Nineties." Unpublished dissertation, University of Chicago, 1968.

Montagu, Ashley. *The Natural Superiority of Women*. New York: Macmillan, 1953.

Montgomery Hyde, H. *The Cleveland Street Scandal*. London: W. H. Allen, 1976; New York: Coward, McCann and Geoghagan, 1976.

Mordell, Albert. *The Literature of Ecstasy*. New York: Boni & Liveright, 1921.

Mumford, Lewis. *The Condition of Man*. London: Secker & Warburg, 1944.

Nichols, T. L. *Human Physiology: The Basis of Sanitary and Social Science*. London: Nichols & Co., 1872.

Pascal, Roy. *Design and Truth in Autobiography*. Cambridge, Mass.: Harvard University Press, 1960.

Pearson, Karl. *The Life, Letters, and Labours of Francis Galton*. Cambridge, 1930.

Pease, Edward R. *The History of the Fabian Society*. London: A. C. Fifield, 1916.

Peterson, Houston. *Havelock Ellis: Philosopher of Love*. Boston: Houghton Mifflin, 1928.

Plarr, Victor. *Ernest Dowson*. London: Elkin Mathews, 1914.

Read, Donald. *Edwardian England, 1905–15: Society and Politics.* London: Harrap, 1972.

Rhys, Ernest. *Everyman Remembers.* London: J. M. Dent, 1931.

Robinson, Paul. *The Modernization of Sex.* London: Paul Elek, 1976.

Rowbotham, Sheila. *A New World for Women: Stella Browne—Socialist Feminist.* London: Pluto Press, 1977.

——. and Jeffrey Weeks. *Socialism and the New Life: The Personal and Sexual Politics of Edward Carpenter and Havelock Ellis.* London: Pluto Press, 1977.

Salt, Henry. *Company I Have Kept.* London: Allen & Unwin, 1930.

Sanger, Margaret. *An Autobiography.* New York: Norton, 1938.

——. *Married Happiness.* London: Cromwell Press, 1926.

——. *My Fight for Birth Control.* New York: Farrar and Rinehart, 1931.

The Letters of Olive Schreiner 1876–1920, ed. S. C. Cronwright-Schreiner. London: T. Fisher Unwin, 1924.

Bernard Shaw—Collected Letters 1898–1910, ed. Dan H. Laurence. London: Max Reinhardt, 1972.

Singer, J. Astor. *Judicial Scandals and Errors.* Paris: University Press, 1898.

Smith, Warren Sylvester. *The London Heretics.* London: Constable, 1967.

Sprich, Charles Robert. "Energetic Movement and Well-balanced Grace: The Literary Criticism of Havelock Ellis." Unpublished dissertation, Tufts University, 1971.

Stopes, Marie. *Contraception: Its Theory, History and Practice.* London: Bale, Sons & Danielson, 1923.

——. *Early Days of Birth Control.* London: Putnam, 1922.

——. *Married Love.* London: A. C. Fifield, 1918.

Sulloway, Frank W. *Freud, Biologist of the Mind.* New York: Basic Books, 1979.

The Letters of John Addington Symonds, Vol. III, eds. H. M. Schueller and R. L. Peters. Detroit: Wayne State University Press, 1969.

Symons, Arthur. *London Nights.* London: L. C. Smithers, 1895.

——. *Mes Souvenirs.* Chapelle-Réanville, 1931.

——. *The Symbolist Movement in Literature.* London: Heinemann, 1899.

Van de Velde, Theodore H. *Ideal Marriage: Its Physiology and Technique.* London: William Heinemann, 1928.

"Walter." *My Secret Life.* Panther Books, 1972.

Westermarck, Edward. *Memories of My Life.* London: Allen & Unwin, 1929.

——. *A Short History of Marriage.* New York: Humanities Press, 1968.

Whyte, Frederic. *The Life of W. T. Stead*. 2 vols. London: Jonathan Cape, 1925.

Winster, Stephen. *Salt and His Circle*. London: Hutchison, 1951.

Woodcock, George. *Anarchism*. Pelican, 1963.

Wortis, Joseph. *Fragments of an Analysis of Freud*. New York: Simon & Schuster, 1954.

Wright, Helena. *Sex and Society*. London: George Allen and Unwin, 1968.

INDEX

A NOTE ON THE TYPE

THE TEXT OF THIS BOOK WAS SET IN ELECTRA, A TYPE FACE designed by William Addison Dwiggins for the Mergenthaler Linotype Company and first made available in 1935. Electra cannot be classified as either "modern" or "old-style." It is not based on any historical model, and hence does not echo any particular period or style of type design. It avoids the extreme contrast between thick and thin elements that marks most modern faces, and is without eccentricities that catch the eye and interfere with reading. In general, Electra is a simple, readable typeface that attempts to give a feeling of fluidity, power, and speed.

W. A. Dwiggins (1880–1956) began an association with the Mergenthaler Linotype Company in 1929 and over the next twenty-seven years designed a number of book types, including the Metro, Electra, Caledonia, Eldorado, and Falcon.

This book was composed by The Maryland Linotype Composition Company, Inc., Baltimore, Maryland. Printed and bound by The Haddon Craftsmen, Inc., Scranton, Pennsylvania.